Accounting for Managers

Fourth Edition

Accounting for Managers

Interpreting Accounting Information for Decision Making

Fourth Edition

Paul M. Collier

Professor of Accounting, Monash University, Melbourne, Australia
Previously at Aston Business School, UK

WILEY

A John Wiley and Sons, Ltd., Publication

This edition first published 2012
Copyright © 2012 John Wiley & Sons Ltd

Registered office

John Wiley & Sons Ltd, The Atrium, Southern Gate, Chichester, West Sussex, PO19 8SQ, United Kingdom

For details of our global editorial offices, for customer services and for information about how to apply for permission to reuse the copyright material in this book please see our website at www.wiley.com.

The right of Paul M. Collier to be identified as the author of this work has been asserted in accordance with the Copyright, Designs and Patents Act 1988.

Wiley also publishes its books in a variety of electronic formats and by print-on-demand. Some content that appears in standard print versions of this book may not be available in other formats. For more information about Wiley products, visit us at www.wiley.com.

Designations used by companies to distinguish their products are often claimed as trademarks. All brand names and product names used in this book are trade names, service marks, trademarks or registered trademarks of their respective owners. The publisher is not associated with any product or vendor mentioned in this book. This publication is designed to provide accurate and authoritative information in regard to the subject matter covered. It is sold on the understanding that the publisher is not engaged in rendering professional services. If professional advice or other expert assistance is required, the services of a competent professional should be sought.

Library of Congress Cataloging-in-Publication Data

Collier, Paul M.
    Accounting for managers : interpreting accounting information for decision-making / Paul M. Collier.—4th ed.
      p.   cm.
    Includes bibliographical references and index.
    ISBN 978-1-119-97967-8 (pbk.)
      1. Managerial accounting.   I. Title.
  HF5657.4.C647   2012
  658.15′11—dc23

                                                                              2011041449

British Library Cataloguing in Publication Data

A catalogue record for this book is available from the British Library

Typeset in 9/13pt Kuenstler by MPS Limited, a Macmillan Company, Chennai, India
Printed in Great Britain by TJ International Ltd, Padstow, Cornwall

This book is printed on acid-free paper responsibly manufactured from sustainable forestry in which at least two trees are planted for each one used for paper production.

For Loredana and Alexis

Contents

Preface to the Fourth Edition

Rationale for the book

My own education as an accountant many years ago was aimed at achieving professional recognition and emphasized an uncritical acceptance of the tools and techniques that I was taught. Teaching accounting hasn't changed much since then. However, it was only after moving from financial to general management positions in industry that I began to see the limitations and questionable assumptions that underlay accounting tools and techniques. When I returned to study later in my career, I was exposed for the first time to alternative perspectives on accounting that helped me to understand the assumptions and limitations of accounting that I had seen in practice. This book is therefore as much a result of my practical experience as a producer and user of accounting information as it is a result of my teaching and training experience.

The title of the book, *Accounting for Managers: Interpreting accounting information for decision making*, emphasizes the focus on accounting to meet the needs of managers. As accounting increasingly becomes decentred from the accounting department in organizations, line managers in all functional areas of business are expected to be able to prepare budgets, develop business cases for capital investment, calculate prices and exercise cost control to ensure that profit targets are achieved. Managers are also expected to be able to analyse and interpret accounting information so that marketing, operations and human resource decisions are made in the light of an understanding of the financial consequences of those decisions.

The material contained in the book stresses the interpretation of accounting information as well as a critical (rather than unthinking) acceptance of the underlying assumptions behind accounting. This book has been continually motivated by my experience in teaching accounting at postgraduate level (MBA and MSc) at Aston Business School in Birmingham (UK) and subsequently in the MBA and MPA at Monash University in Melbourne (Australia). It has also been used to support customized training programmes for non-financial managers in the use of financial tools and techniques in their own organizations. Hence the emphasis in this book is on *using* accounting, not *doing* accounting. Most accounting texts are a 'cut down' version of a text used to train accountants, but this book takes a *user*, not a *preparer*, focus. It has been written specifically focused on the needs of non-financial managers who need a solid grounding in accounting.

There is a focus in most accounting texts on manufacturing organizations, perhaps because many of those books have been issued as revised editions for many years and have not adequately reflected the changing nature of the economies in the developed world. The growth of service businesses and the knowledge economy is not sufficiently explored in most accounting texts. This book uses examples, case studies and questions that are more equally balanced between the needs of organizations in manufacturing, retail and services. It also uses corporate examples, rather than small business examples that lack realism to practising managers. Most of the examples and illustrations in this book are simplified versions of real-life business problems, drawn from my experiences with various companies.

In most accounting books there is insufficient attention to theory, particularly for postgraduate students who should have a *wider theoretical underpinning* of the assumptions and limitations of accounting information. Theory should encourage the reader to enquire more deeply into the alternative theoretical positions underlying accounting as well as its social and behavioural consequences, both within their own organizations and in the wider society. This book introduces the reader to some of the journal literature that is either fundamental to the role of accounting or is 'ground breaking'. This book provides, through the ample references in each chapter, an accessible route for those who want to reach into the wider literature.

Accounting books are often inaccessible to those from non-English-speaking backgrounds, because of the complexity of the language used. Many of the examples and questions in accounting books rely on a strong knowledge of the nuances of the English language to interpret what the question is asking, before students can make any attempt to answer them. This book adopts a more plain English style that addresses the needs of European and Asian students.

Finally, the examples in most accounting books focus on the calculations that accountants perform, rather than on the *interpretive needs* of managers who use those reports. While some calculation questions are needed to ensure that readers understand how information is produced, the emphasis for the non-financial manager should be on *critical understanding and questioning* of the accounting numbers and of the underlying assumptions behind those numbers, and on the need to supplement accounting reports with non-financial performance measures and broader perspectives than satisfying shareholder wealth alone.

This fourth edition takes into account the author's experience in teaching accounting to non-financial managers. While it has not been possible to incorporate every suggestion made, this edition has benefited from feedback from many students and from a number of reviewers and academics who use the text in their teaching. There has been considerable updating of every chapter, and new and revised questions have been added. An important change has been to include illustrations, questions and solutions using multiple currency symbols: the £, € and $. This should help the book to be seen as more relevant across national boundaries and reflects the internationalization of accounting tools and techniques.

Outline of the book

The book is arranged in four parts. The first part describes the context and role of accounting in business. The first two chapters are provided for those students who are coming to business studies for the first time, although even the experienced reader will find value in reading them. Chapter 3 provides a basic introduction to accounting, without the confusion that usually accompanies 'debits' and 'credits'.

Some theoretical frameworks are provided in Chapters 4 and 5. It is hoped that this will provide a foundation for readers' understanding that accounting is more than a technical subject but is grounded in competing theories and values. These theories and values are themselves rooted in historical, political, economic and social causes. The theoretical framework should help to make the subject more meaningful to students and practitioners alike.

In Part II, Chapters 6 and 7 provide a comprehensive review of financial statements and ratio analysis from the perspective of a user of financial statements and reflect the latest practice under International Financial Reporting Standards (IFRS). Chapter 8, which looks at inventory valuation, provides an important link between Parts II and III of the book.

The third part of the book shows the reader how accounting information is used in decision making, planning and control. In this third part the accounting tools and techniques are explained and illustrated. Beginning with an introduction to accounting and information systems in Chapter 9, subsequent chapters review how accounting is integral to decisions about marketing (Chapter 10), operations (Chapter 11), and human resources (Chapter 12). The problem of overhead allocation is covered in Chapter 13, followed by capital expenditure decisions (Chapter 14), the evaluation of business unit performance (Chapter 15), budgeting (Chapter 16) and budgetary control (Chapter 17). Chapter 18 introduces a range of the more recent, strategic accounting approaches.

Theory is integrated with tools and techniques, and case studies, drawn mainly from real business examples, help draw out the concepts in each chapter. A critical approach to the assumptions underlying financial information is presented, building on the theoretical framework provided in Chapters 4 and 5. The questions at the end of each chapter rely on knowledge gained from reading that and preceding chapters. Consequently, there is a greater level of detail involved in questions in the later chapters. Attempting these questions will help the reader to understand how accountants produce information needed by non-accounting managers. The end-of-chapter case studies provide the reader with the opportunity to interpret and analyse financial information produced by an accountant for use by non-accounting managers in decision making.

Part IV provides a wealth of supporting material, including an extensive glossary of accounting terms. Four readings from the accounting literature cover a broad spectrum and support the most important theoretical concepts in the book. They present four different yet complementary perspectives on accounting in organizations. Each reading has several questions that the reader should think about and try to answer in order to help understand the concepts. The fourth part of the book also contains solutions to the end-of-chapter questions and case studies. The case study answers are indicative answers only, as different approaches to the same problem can highlight different aspects of the case and, as in real life, there is a range of possible approaches.

About the Author

Dr Paul M. Collier PhD (Warwick), BBus (NSWIT), MComm (NSW), Grad Dip Ed (UTS), CPA (Aust) is Professor of Accounting at Monash University in Melbourne, Australia. He was until 2006 a senior lecturer at Aston Business School in Aston University, Birmingham, UK. Paul has worked in senior financial and general management roles in the UK and Australia. He was chief financial officer and company secretary and subsequently general manager (operations) for a public listed company in Sydney before moving to the UK in 1993. He also worked in the public sector before completing his PhD and moving to academia.

Paul has been a board member and chair of the audit committee of a non-profit distributing housing association in the UK with assets of £200 million; and a board member, chair of the finance and resources committee and member of the audit committee of a health service in Australia with a budget of over $350 million. He has been an examiner for the Chartered Institute of Management Accountants (CIMA) in the UK, and has written study material for both CIMA and CPA Australia.

This book uses material developed by the author based on his experience as a practitioner, in his teaching at Aston and Monash, and in delivering financial training to non-financial managers in diverse industries over many years. Paul's research interests are in the use of management accounting and non-financial performance information in decision making and the behavioural aspects of management accounting and management control systems. He has published many case studies of accounting in academic journals and as book chapters. He is also the author of *Fundamentals of Risk Management for Accountants and Managers*, published in 2009.

Acknowledgements

I acknowledge the indirect contribution of staff at Aston Business School and Monash University who have provided valuable comments on each edition of the text, and to the reviewers of each edition who have provided valuable feedback and suggestions. Thanks also to the many students who have invariably identified errors or ambiguities which have been corrected despite careful proofreading.

I am also grateful to the staff at John Wiley, particularly Steve Hardman for his support for each new edition and to Anneli Mockett and Jenni Edgecombe, for their support and helpful advice throughout the writing and updating of each edition of this book.

Context of Accounting

Part I describes the context and role of accounting in business and provides some theoretical frameworks. It is hoped that this will offer a foundation for readers' understanding that accounting is more than a technical subject. Accounting presents a particular view of the world, but by no means the only view of the world. As such it has strengths, but also weaknesses. Accounting itself is grounded in competing theories, and these theories are derived from various historical, political, economic and social roots. The theoretical framework presented in Part I should help to make the subject more meaningful to students and practitioners alike.

Chapter 1 provides an introduction to accounting, and an overview of accounting history as well as describing how the role of accounting has changed, including the influence that this changed role has had on non-financial managers. Chapter 2 describes the context in which management accounting operates: the capital market emphasis on shareholder value, as well as the business context of corporate governance and company regulation.

Chapter 3 describes how transactions are recorded by accounting systems and the principles that underlie the preparation and presentation of financial statements.

Chapter 4 covers the traditional theoretical approach to management control, which encompasses management accounting and performance measurement.

Chapter 5 offers alternative perspectives on the role of accounting. The theoretical framework in Chapters 4 and 5 is important to support the interpretive analysis and critical perspective taken by this book.

Introduction to Accounting

This chapter introduces accounting and its functions and provides a short history of accounting, highlighting the roles of both financial and management accounting, and the interaction between both. It also describes the recent developments that have changed the roles of accountants and non-financial managers in relation to the use of financial information. The chapter concludes with a brief critical perspective on accounting.

Accounting, accountability and the account

Businesses exist to provide goods or services to customers in exchange for a financial reward. Public-sector and not-for-profit organizations also provide services, although their funding may be a mix of income from service provision, government funding and charitable donations. While this book is primarily concerned with profit-oriented businesses, most of the principles are equally applicable to the public and not-for-profit sectors. Business is not about accounting. It is about markets, people and operations (the delivery of products or services), although accounting is implicated in all of these decisions because it is the financial representation of business activity.

Although it is quite a dated definition, the American Accounting Association defined accounting in 1966 as:

> The process of identifying, measuring, and communicating economic information to permit informed judgements and decisions by users of the information.

This is an important definition because:

- it recognizes that accounting is a process: that process is concerned with capturing business events, recording their financial effect, summarizing and reporting the result of those effects, and interpreting those results (we cover this in Chapter 3);
- it is concerned with economic information: while this is predominantly financial, it also allows for non-financial information (which is explained in Chapter 4);
- its purpose is to support 'informed judgements and decisions' by users: this emphasizes the decision usefulness of accounting information and the broad spectrum of 'users' of that information. While the primary concern of this book is the use of accounting information for decision making, the book takes a broad stakeholder perspective that users of accounting information include all those who may have an interest in the survival, profitability and growth of a business: shareholders, employees, customers, suppliers, financiers, government and society as a whole.

The notion of accounting for a narrow (shareholders and financiers) or a broad (societal) group of users is an important philosophical debate to which we will return throughout this book. This debate derives from questions of accountability: to whom is the business accountable? For what is the business accountable? And what is the role of accounting in that accountability?

Boland and Schultze (1996) defined accountability as:

> The capacity and willingness to give explanations for conduct, stating how one has discharged one's responsibilities, an explaining of conduct with a credible story of what happened, and a calculation and balancing of competing obligations, including moral ones (p. 62).

Hoskin (1996) suggested that accountability is:

> more total and insistent . . . [it] ranges more freely over space and time, focusing as much on future potential as past accomplishment (p. 265).

Boland and Schultze argued that accountability entails both a narration of what transpired and a reckoning of money, while Hoskin focused on the future as well as the past. There are many definitions of accountability, but they all derive from the original meanings of the word *account*.

Accounting is a collection of systems and processes used to record, report and interpret business transactions. Accounting provides an account – *an explanation or report in financial terms* – about the transactions of an organization. Exhibit 1.1 provides a number of different definitions for the word 'account'.

An account enables managers to satisfy the *stakeholders* in the organization that they have acted in the best interests of stakeholders rather than themselves. This is the notion of accountability to others, a result of the *stewardship* function of managers by which accounting provides the ability for managers to show that they have been responsible in their use of resources provided by various stakeholders. Stewardship is an important concept because in all but very small businesses, the owners of businesses are not the same as the managers. This separation of ownership from control makes accounting particularly influential due to ac · count (-kount) *n*.

- A narrative or record of events.
- A reason given for a particular action or event.
- A report relating to one's conduct.
- To furnish a reckoning (*to* someone) of money received and paid out.
- To make satisfactory amends.
- To give satisfactory reasons or an explanation for actions.

Exhibit 1.1 Definitions of 'account'

the emphasis given to increasing shareholder wealth (or shareholder value) as well as the broader stakeholder perspective that organizations need to contribute to the sustainability of natural resources and the environment (we cover corporate social responsibility in Chapter 7).

Introducing the functions of accounting

Accounting is traditionally seen as fulfilling three functions:

- *Scorekeeping*: capturing, recording, summarizing and reporting financial performance.
- *Attention-directing*: drawing attention to, and assisting in the interpretation of, business performance, particularly in terms of the trend over time, and the comparison between actual and planned, or a benchmark measure of performance.
- *Problem-solving*: identifying the best choice from a range of alternative actions.

In this book, we acknowledge the role of the scorekeeping function in Chapters 6 through 8. We are not concerned with how investors make decisions about their investments in companies, so we emphasize attention directing and problem solving as taking place through three inter-related functions, all part of the role of non-financial (marketing, operations, human resources, etc.) as well as financial managers:

- *Planning*: establishing goals and strategies to achieve those goals.
- *Decision making*: using financial (and non-financial performance) information to make decisions consistent with those goals and strategies.
- *Control*: using financial (and non-financial) information to improve performance over time, relative to what was planned, or using the information to modify the plan itself.

Planning, decision making and control are particularly relevant as increasingly businesses have been decentralized into many business units, where much of the planning, decision making and control is focused.

Accountability results in the production of financial statements, primarily for those interested parties who are external to the business. This function is called financial accounting. Managers need financial and non-financial information to develop and implement strategy by planning for the future (budgeting); making decisions about products, services, prices and what costs to incur (decision making using cost information) and ensuring that plans are put into action and are achieved (control). This function is called management accounting.

A short history of accounting

The history of accounting is intertwined with the development of trade between tribes and there are records of commercial transactions on stone tablets dating back to 3600 BC (Stone, 1969). The early accountants were 'scribes' who also practised law. Stone (1969) noted:

> In ancient Egypt in the pharaoh's central finance department . . . scribes prepared records of receipts and disbursements of silver, corn and other commodities. One recorded on papyrus the amount brought to the warehouse and another checked the emptying of the containers on the roof as it was poured into the storage building. Audit was performed by a third scribe who compared these two records (p. 284).

However, accounting as we know it today began in the fourteenth century in the Italian city-states of Florence, Genoa and Venice as a result of the growth of maritime trade and banking institutions. Ship-owners used some form of accounting to hold the ships' captains accountable for the profits derived from trading the products they exported and imported. The importance of maritime trade led to the first bank with customer facilities opening in Venice in 1149. Trade enabled the movement of ideas between countries and the Lombards, Italian merchants, established themselves as moneylenders in England at the end of the twelfth century.

Balance sheets were evident from around 1400 and the Medici family (who were Lombards) had accounting records of 'cloth manufactured and sold'. The first treatise on accounting (although it was contained within a book on mathematics) was the work of a monk, Luca Pacioli, in 1494. The first professional accounting body was formed in Venice in 1581.

Much of the language of accounting is derived from Latin roots. 'Debtor' comes from the Latin *debitum*, something that is owed; 'assets' from the Latin *ad + satis*, to enough, i.e. to pay obligations; 'liability' from *ligare*, to bind; 'capital' from *caput*, a head (of wealth). Even 'account' derives initially from the Latin *computare*, to count, while 'profit' comes from *profectus*, advance or progress. 'Sterling' and 'shilling' came from the Italian *sterlino* and *scellino*, while the pre-decimal currency abbreviation 'LSD' (pounds, shillings and pence) stood for *lire, soldi, denarii*.

Little changed in terms of accounting until the Industrial Revolution. Chandler (1990) traced the development of the modern industrial enterprise from its agricultural and commercial roots in the last half of the nineteenth century. By 1870, the leading industrial nations – the USA, Great Britain and Germany – accounted for two-thirds of the world's industrial output. One of the consequences of growth was the shift from home-based work to factory-based work and the separation of ownership from management. Although the corporation, as distinct from its owners, had been in existence in Britain since 1650, the separation of ownership and control was enabled by the first British Companies Act, which formalized the law in relation to 'joint stock companies' and introduced the limited liability of shareholders during the 1850s. The London Stock Exchange had been formed earlier in 1773. These changes raised the importance of accounting and accountability.

The era of mass production began in the early twentieth century with Henry Ford's assembly line. Organizations grew larger and this led to the creation of new organizational forms. Based on an extensive historical analysis, Chandler (1962) found that in large firms strategic growth and diversification led to the creation of decentralized, multidivisional corporations. Chandler's work thus emphasized structure following strategy. Chandler studied examples like General Motors, where remotely located managers made decisions on behalf of absent owners and central head office functions.

Ansoff (1988) emphasized that success in the first 30 years of the mass-production era went to firms that had the lowest prices. However, in the 1930s General Motors 'triggered a shift from production to a market focus' (p. 11).

In large firms such as General Motors, budgets were developed to coordinate diverse activities. In the first decades of the twentieth century, the DuPont chemicals company developed a model to measure the return on investment (ROI). ROI (see Chapters 7, 14 and 15) was used to make capital investment decisions and to evaluate the performance of business units, including the accountability of managers to use capital efficiently.

The role of financial accounting

Financial accounting is the recording of financial transactions, aimed principally at reporting performance to those outside the organization, with a primary focus on shareholders. In countries like the UK, USA, Canada and Australia, companies legislation usually dictates that directors of companies are required to report the financial performance of the companies they run to shareholders. They do so through an Annual Report to shareholders, which comprises four financial statements: the Statement of Comprehensive Income (or Income Statement, and in old terminology the Profit and Loss Account); the Statement of Financial Position (or Balance Sheet); the Statement of Changes in Equity; and the Statement of Cash Flows (these are the topics of Chapters 6 and 7).

These financial statements are regulated by legislation and by accounting standards, and subject to independent audit in order to provide comparisons between different companies (Chapter 6 explains this in detail). However, the information they provide is of limited decision usefulness for managers because the financial information is produced only once per year, is highly aggregated and provides no comparison to target (although the financial statements do provide a prior year comparison).

While financial accounting is extremely important for investors, it is also important for managers for two reasons. First, many managerial decisions, whether they relate to planning, decision making or control involve decisions that will ultimately be reported in financial statements and affect shareholder reaction in stock markets. Hence the decisions of managers are influenced by how those decisions will be presented to (and interpreted by) users of financial statements. Second, the accounting system that produces financial reports is the same system that managers use for planning, decision making and control. This financial accounting information is supplemented by non-financial performance measures and by more detail and analysis derived from outside the financial accounting system. However, financial accounting still provides the foundation on which managers plan, make decisions and exercise managerial control. As a result of these two reasons, managers need to understand financial accounting in order to take full advantage of the range of management accounting techniques that are available. We explore this in far more detail in Chapters 2, 3, 6 and 7.

The role of management accounting

The advent of automated production following the Industrial Revolution increased the size and complexity of production processes, which employed more people and required larger sums of capital to finance machinery. Accounting historians suggest that the increase in the number of limited companies that led to the separation of ownership from control caused an increase in attention to what was called 'cost accounting' (the forerunner of 'management accounting') in order to determine the cost of products and exercise control by absent owners over their managers. Reflecting this emergence, the earlier title of management accountants was cost or works accountants. Typically situated in factories, cost or works accountants tended to understand the business at a technical level and were able to advise non-financial managers in relation to operational decisions. Cost accounting was concerned with determining the cost of an object, whether a product, an activity, a division of the organization or market segment. The first book on cost accounting is believed to be Garcke and Fell's *Factory Accounts*, which was published in 1897.

Historians, such as Chandler (1990), have argued that the new corporate structures that were developed in the twentieth century – multidivisional organizations, conglomerates and multinationals – placed increased demands on accounting. These demands included divisional performance evaluation and budgeting. It has also been suggested that developments in cost accounting were driven by government demands for cost information during both world wars. It appears that 'management accounting' became a term used only after World War II.

In their acclaimed book *Relevance Lost*, Johnson and Kaplan (1987) traced the development of management accounting from its origins in the Industrial Revolution supporting process-type industries such as textile and steel conversion, transportation and distribution. These systems were concerned with evaluating the efficiency of internal processes, rather than measuring organizational profitability. Financial reports were produced using a separate transactions-based system that reported financial performance. Johnson and Kaplan (1987) argued that 'virtually all management accounting practices used today had been developed by 1925' (p. 12).

Calculating the cost of different products was unnecessary because the product range was homogeneous, but Johnson and Kaplan (1987) described how the early manufacturing firms attempted to improve performance through *economies of scale* by increasing the volume of output in order to lower unit costs. This led to a concern with measuring the efficiency of the production process. Over time, the product range of businesses expanded to meet the demands of the market and so businesses sought *economies of scope* through producing two or more products in a single facility. This led to the need for better information about how the mix of products could improve total profits.

Johnson and Kaplan (1987) described how

> a management accounting system must provide timely and accurate information to facilitate efforts to control costs,
> to measure and improve productivity, and to devise improved production processes. The management accounting

system must also report accurate product costs so that pricing decisions, introduction of new products, abandonment of obsolete products, and response to rival products can be made (p. 4).

The Chartered Institute of Management Accountants' definition of the core activities of management accounting includes:

- participation in the planning process at both strategic and operational levels, involving the establishment of policies and the formulation of budgets;
- the initiation and provision of guidance for management decisions, involving the generation, analysis, presentation and interpretation of relevant information;
- contributing to the monitoring and control of performance through the provision of reports including comparisons of actual with budgeted performance, and their analysis and interpretation.

One of the earliest writers on management accounting described 'different costs for different purposes' (Clark, 1923). This theme was developed by one of the earliest texts on management accounting (Vatter, 1950). Vatter distinguished the information needs of managers from those of external shareholders and emphasized that it was preferable to get less precise data to managers quickly than complete information too late to influence decision making. Johnson and Kaplan (1987) commented that organizations

> with access to far more computational power . . . rarely distinguish between information needed promptly for managerial control and information provided periodically for summary financial statements (p. 161).

They argued that the developments in accounting theory in the first decades of the twentieth century came about by academics who

> emphasized simple decision-making models in highly simplified firms — those producing one or only a few products, usually in a one stage production process. The academics developed their ideas by logic and deductive reasoning. They did not attempt to study the problems actually faced by managers of organizations producing hundreds or thousands of products in complex production processes (p. 175).

They concluded:

> Not surprisingly, in this situation actual management accounting systems provided few benefits to organizations. In some instances, the information reported by existing management accounting systems not only inhibited good decision-making by managers, it might actually have encouraged bad decisions (p. 177).

Johnson and Kaplan (1987) described how the global competition that has taken place since the 1980s has left management accounting behind in terms of its decision usefulness. Developments such as total quality management, just-in-time inventory, computer-integrated manufacturing, shorter product life cycles (see Chapters 11 and 18) and the decline of manufacturing and rise of service industries have led to the need for 'accurate knowledge of product costs, excellent cost control, and coherent performance measurement'

(p. 220). And 'the challenge for today's competitive environment is to develop new and more flexible approaches to the design of effective cost accounting, management control, and performance measurement systems' (p. 224).

There have been many changes since *Relevance Lost* was published in 1987. However, most of those changes have been in financial accounting. The next section describes relatively recent developments in accounting practice.

Recent developments in accounting

Compared to 20 years ago, financial accounting has gained in importance relative to management accounting. This is due to two reasons. First, the globalization of financial markets and the ability of investors to invest in stock markets around the world increased the need for financial statements that were comparable across different countries, rather than being based on local legislation and standards. The development of the UK-led International Financial Reporting Standards (IFRS) has resulted in almost all significant economies adopting a single set of reporting standards that enables investors to compare company performance across national boundaries. The only significant economy not to have yet adopted IFRS is the USA which still relies on Generally Accepted Accounting Principles (GAAP). The topic of financial reporting standards is discussed in detail in Chapter 6.

The second reason has been the large corporate failures that have raised questions about why financial statements have not provided early warning signals about the risk of failure. The size of some of these failures, with Enron and WorldCom as notable examples, and the increasing complexity of business transactions (some of which have been designed to improve the perception of reported performance, rather than the underlying reality) have led to a continual change in accounting standards in trying to improve their usefulness to investors.

The advent of IFRS, corporate failures and transactional complexity has led to an emphasis (and this author would argue an undue overemphasis) on reporting past – and typically short-term – performance designed to satisfy stock market investors, rather than improving the value-added capability of organizations to be successful in the longer term. While there have been significant management accounting developments in the last 20 years, these have tended to be overshadowed by financial reporting. We will return to these issues throughout this book. Of particular importance is recognizing that financial accounting is essential in *reporting* business performance and demonstrating accountability to investors, but management accounting comprises the set of tools and techniques that will help to *improve and sustain* business performance.

Partly as a result of the stimulus of *Relevance Lost* (Johnson and Kaplan, 1987) but also as a consequence of rapidly changing business conditions, management accounting has moved beyond its traditional concern with a narrow range of numbers to incorporate wider issues of performance measurement and management. Management accounting is now concerned, to greater or lesser degrees in different organizations, with:

- value-based management;
- non-financial performance measurement;
- a focus on horizontal business processes or activities, rather than hierarchical reporting based on individual managerial responsibilities;

- quality management and environmental management;
- strategic issues beyond the boundaries of the organization and the annual reporting cycle; and
- lean methods of producing goods and services.

Value-based management is more fully described in Chapter 2, but it is in brief a concern with improving the value of the business to its shareholders. A fundamental role of non-financial managers is to make marketing, operational, human resource and investment decisions that contribute to increasing the value of the business. Accounting provides the information base to assist in planning, decision making and control.

The limitations of accounting information, particularly as a lagging indicator of performance, have led to an increasing emphasis on non-financial performance measures, which are described more fully in Chapter 4. Non-financial measures are a major concern of both accountants and non-financial managers, as they tend to be leading indicators of the financial performance that will be reported at some future time.

Activity-based management is an approach that emphasizes the underlying business processes that cut across the traditional organizational structure but are essential to produce goods and services. This approach reflects the need to identify the drivers or causes of those activities in order to be able to plan and control costs more effectively. Activity-based approaches are introduced throughout Part III.

Improving the quality of products and services is also a major concern, since advances in production technology and the need to improve performance by reducing waste have led to management tools such as total quality management (TQM), and continuous improvement processes such as Six Sigma and the Business Excellence model. Greater attention to environmental issues as a result of climate change has also led companies to better understand the short-term and long-term consequences of inefficient energy usage and environmental pollution. Managers can no longer ignore these issues and accounting has a role to play in measuring and reporting quality and environmental costs (see Chapter 11).

Strategic management accounting, which is described more fully in Chapter 18, is an attempt to shift the perceptions of accountants and non-financial managers from inward-looking to outward-looking, recognizing the need to look beyond the business to the whole supply chain with suppliers and customers, and beyond the current accounting period to product life cycles, and to seek ways of achieving and maintaining competitive advantage.

Lean accounting is a consequence of lean manufacturing, itself a development of the just in time philosophy which focuses on the elimination of inventory. Lean approaches emphasize reducing all waste, and its application to accounting is to identify and eliminate wasteful accounting practices which contribute little to management decision making.

In addition to these changes has been the rapid improvement in information and communications technologies. Computerization has eliminated many routine accounting processes (which were more correctly book-keeping processes) and has expanded information systems beyond accounting to enterprise resource planning systems (ERPS, see Chapter 9) which integrate marketing, purchasing, production, distribution and human resources with accounting. The ready availability of information systems has also enabled detailed financial reports to be available for non-financial managers soon after the end of each accounting period.

These changes have had two impacts: (i) to change the role of accountants and (ii) to change the role of non-financial managers. Computerization has taken (especially management) accountants away from their 'bean counter' image to a role where they are more active participants in formulating and implementing business strategy, and act more as business consultants and advisers to management, providing information and advice that support improving business performance. These changes have also increased the responsibility of non-financial managers from their technical areas of expertise. Most non-financial managers now have responsibility in setting budgets and meeting financial targets. This means that non-financial managers need an increased understanding of accounting to fulfil their accountability to higher levels of management.

The relationship between financial accounting and management accounting

Financial accounting is focused on the needs of external users and demonstrates accountability to shareholders under the stewardship principle. Financial statements have to comply with accounting standards (see Chapter 6) and are subject to audit. They are produced annually, are highly aggregated using historical figures, and provide only a comparison to the prior year. There is a common form of presentation of the Income Statement, Statement of Financial Position and Statement of Cash Flows that applies to all companies.

Management accounting meets the needs of internal users (directors and managers) for planning, decision making and control purposes. They are not subject to audit or accounting standards so organizations can present the information that is relevant to the needs of their business. Management accounting reports typically are produced more frequently (e.g. monthly) and are disaggregated to business unit level with more detail, often supplemented by non-financial information (see Chapter 4) with comparison to budget targets.

Both forms of accounting are important and useful for managers. Figure 1.1 shows the relationship between the accounting system from which is derived both financial statements and management accounting information. However, the inter-relationship goes further than in the use of a common

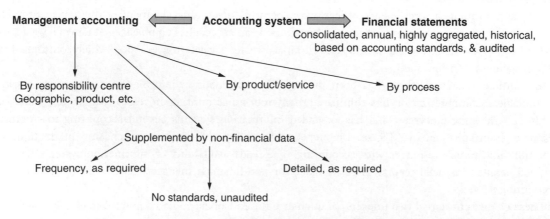

Figure 1.1   The accounting system, financial statements and management accounting.

accounting system. The needs of shareholders drive many decisions about using management accounting information, and consequently the planning, decision-making and control activities carried out by managers has an unavoidable impact on reported financial information. Therefore, the decisions that are made by managers in organizations need to integrate the day-to-day operational choices from the result of those choices as they impact on financial statements.

Finally, financial accounting is largely the domain of qualified accountants, as it is a specialist activity requiring a great deal of knowledge and skill. By contrast, management accounting information is far more routinely in the domain of line managers with various functional roles, who cannot avoid budgetary pressures and the need to control the costs and profitability of the products and services for which they are responsible.

In the USA virtually no-one now calls him or herself a 'management accountant'. Management accounting knowledge is now incorporated into a variety of financial and increasingly non-financial positions. The title 'management accountant' is far more prevalent in the UK where it has been institutionalized by the Chartered Institute of Management Accountants (CIMA). In Continental Europe the specific terminology of management accountant has never existed and 'controller' is a more common title (Hopwood, 2008).

Many non-financial roles now incorporate much of the roles carried out by management accountants. This is particularly so for managers with engineering or technical backgrounds who as line managers have considerable financial autonomy, including responsibility for budgets, cost control, pricing and proposing new capital expenditure. This has been a considerable change in the role of non-financial managers and is why such managers increasingly need a strong financial understanding to complement their technical or operational skills:

> Forms of economic calculation now extend into marketing, operations, strategy, and even human resource management, increasingly being prevalent throughout the entire organization as economic considerations have become ever more important. Reflecting increasing pressures from the capital markets, the international intensification of competition and a more general cultural shift toward concerns with economic and monetary considerations, economic calculation now is relevant for most of the organization and its knowledge base is accordingly one that is associated with a much wider variety of occupational positions. Indeed we are now seeing much more of a mixing of economic and non-economic forms of information and control (Hopwood, 2008, p. 10).

A critical perspective

Although the concepts and assumptions underlying accounting are yet to be introduced, having begun this book with an introduction to accounting history, it is worthwhile introducing here a contrasting viewpoint. While this viewpoint is one that may not be accepted by many practising managers, it is worth being aware of the role that accounting plays in the capitalist economic system in which we live and work.

The Marxist historian Hobsbawm (1962) argued that the cotton industry once dominated the UK economy, and this resulted in a shift from domestic production to factory production. Sales increased but profits shrank, so labour (which was three times the cost of materials) was replaced by mechanization during the Industrial Revolution.

Entrepreneurs purchased small items of machinery and growth was largely financed by borrowings. The Industrial Revolution produced 'such vast quantities and at such rapidly diminishing cost, as to be no longer dependent on existing demand, but to create its own market' (Hobsbawm, 1962, p. 32).

Advances in mass production followed the development of the assembly line, and were supported by the ease of transportation by rail and sea, and communications through the electric telegraph. At the same time, agriculture diminished in importance. Due to the appetite of the railways for iron and steel, coal, heavy machinery, labour and capital investment, 'the comfortable and rich classes accumulated income so fast and in such vast quantities as to exceed all available possibilities of spending and investment' (Hobsbawm, 1962, p. 45).

While the rich accumulated profits, labour was exploited with wages at subsistence levels. Labour had to learn how to work, unlike agriculture or craft industries, in a manner suited to industry, and the result was a draconian master–servant relationship. In the 1840s a depression led to unemployment and high food prices, and 1848 saw the rise of the labouring poor in European cities, who threatened both the weak and obsolete regimes and the rich.

This resulted in a clash between the political (French) and industrial (British) revolutions, the 'triumph of bourgeois-liberal capitalism' and the domination of the globe by a few Western regimes, especially the British in the mid-nineteenth century, which became a 'world hegemony' (Hobsbawm, 1962). These concepts of industrial production and exploitation of labour were exported to developing countries in the centuries before the twentieth, through the process of British colonialism, and hence the 'British' capitalist system was exported throughout the world, not least with the support of a colonial expansionist Empire that lent large sums of money in return for countries' adoption of the British system. Similar approaches were taken by other European countries as they colonized countries in the African continent and in South-East Asia.

This 'global triumph' of capitalism in the 1850s (Hobsbawm, 1975) was a consequence of the combination of cheap capital and rising prices. Stability and prosperity overtook political questions about the legitimacy of existing dynasties and technology cheapened manufactured products. There was high demand but the cost of living did not fall, so labour became dominated by the interests of the new owners of the means of production. 'Economic liberalism' became the recipe for economic growth as the market ruled labour and helped national (and especially British) economic expansion. Industrialization made wealth and industrial capacity decisive in international power, especially in the USA, Japan and Germany. National colonialism, it can be argued, has been superseded by a system of colonialism by multinational corporations, largely based in the USA, and to a lesser extent by British and European companies.

Armstrong (1987) traced the historical factors behind the comparative pre-eminence of accountants in British management hierarchies (in relation to other professions) and the emphasis on financial control. He concluded that accounting controls were installed by accountants as a result of their power base in global capital markets, which was achieved through their role in the allocation of the profit surplus to shareholders. Armstrong argued that mergers led to control problems that were tackled by

> American management consultants who tended to recommend the multidivisional form of organization . . . [which] entirely divorce headquarters management from operations. Functional departments and their managers are subjected to a battery of financial indicators and budgetary controls . . . [and] a subordination of operational to financial decision-making and a major influx of accountants into senior management positions (p. 433).

A different reading of history is designed to do more than raise readers' awareness that accounting is not a neutral tool, objectively reporting performance. Accounting is intimately bound up with reinforcing a capitalist system, and privileging shareholders over other stakeholders. This raises a significant question: whether accounting should only be concerned with maximizing short-term profits for current shareholders, or whether it should be more concerned with longer term performance to satisfy a broader range of stakeholders. This implies notions of corporate social responsibility, sustainability for future generations and a consideration of ethics. Roberts (1996) suggested that organizational accounting embodies the separation of instrumental and moral consequences, which is questionable. He argued:

> The mystification of accounting information helps to fix, elevate and then impose upon others its own particular instrumental interests, without regard to the wider social and environmental consequences of the pursuit of such interests. Accounting thus serves as a vehicle whereby others are called to account, while the interests it embodies escape such accountability (p. 59).

This is a more critical perspective than that associated with the traditional notion of accounting as a report to shareholders and managers. We will revisit the critical perspective throughout this book.

Conclusion

This chapter introduces the notion of accountability and the function of accounting. It identifies the different roles played by financial accounting and management accounting, and the interaction between those roles. A short history of accounting and a summary of recent developments in accounting are supplemented by a critical perspective on the historically derived position of accounting in Western economies. This chapter provides a broad introduction to many concepts that will be developed further throughout this book.

While this book is designed to help non-financial managers understand the tools and techniques of accounting, it is also intended to make readers think critically about the role and limitations of accounting. One intention is to reinforce to readers that:

> accounting information provides a window through which the real activities of the organization may be monitored, but it should be noted also that other windows are used that do not rely upon accounting information (Otley and Berry, 1994, p. 46).

References

American Accounting Association (1996). *A Statement of Basic Accounting Theory*. Sarasota, FL: American Accounting Association.

Ansoff, H. I. (1988). *The New Corporate Strategy*. New York: John Wiley & Sons.

Armstrong, P. (1987). The rise of accounting controls in British capitalist enterprises. *Accounting, Organizations and Society*, 12(5), 415–36.

Boland, R. J. and Schultze, U. (1996). Narrating accountability: cognition and the production of the accountable self. In R. Munro and J. Mouritsen (Eds), *Accountability: Power, Ethos and the Technologies of Managing*, London: International Thomson Business Press.

Chandler, A. D. J. (1962). *Strategy and Structure: Chapters in the History of the American Industrial Enterprise*. Cambridge, MA: Harvard University Press.

Chandler, A. D. J. (1990). *Scale and Scope: The Dynamics of Industrial Capitalism*. Cambridge, MA: Harvard University Press.

Clark, J. M. (1923). *Studies in the Economics of Overhead Costs*. Chicago: University of Chicago Press.

Hobsbawm, E. (1962). *The Age of Revolution: Europe* 1789–1848. London: Phoenix Press.

Hobsbawm, E. (1975). *The Age of Capital*:1848–1875. London: Phoenix Press.

Hopwood, A. G. (2008). Management accounting research in a changing world. *Journal of Management Accounting Research*, 20, 3–13.

Hoskin, K. (Ed.) (1996). The 'awful idea of accountability': inscribing people into the measurement of objects. In R. Munro and J. Mouritsen (Eds), *Accountability: Power, Ethos and the Technologies of Managing*, London: International Thomson Business Press.

Johnson, H. T. and Kaplan, R. S. (1987). *Relevance Lost: The Rise and Fall of Management Accounting*. Boston, MA: Harvard Business School Press.

Otley, D. T. and Berry, A. J. (1994). Case study research in management accounting and control. *Management Accounting Research*, 5, 45–65.

Roberts, J. (1996). From discipline to dialogue: individualizing and socializing forms of accountability. In R. Munro and J. Mouritsen (Eds), *Accountability: Power, Ethos and the Technologies of Managing*. London: International Thomson Business Press.

Stone, W. E. (1969). Antecedents of the accounting profession. *The Accounting Review*, April, 284–91.

Vatter, W. J. (1950). *Managerial Accounting*. New York: Prentice Hall.

Questions

1.1 Explain the difference between accounting, an account and accountability.

1.2 Summarize the main activities of (i) financial accountants and (ii) management accountants.

2

Accounting and its Relationship to Shareholder Value and Corporate Governance

This chapter relates the role of accounting in terms of shareholder value and strategy. The reader is introduced to the difference between capital and product markets and the importance of shareholder value. This is then developed through the relationship between shareholder value, strategy and accounting. The regulation of companies and corporate governance is explained as the context in which accounting operates, including the role of directors, audit, the audit committee and Stock Exchange listing rules. A brief coverage of risk, internal control and accounting is followed by a critical perspective, introducing a concern with stakeholder compared to shareholder value, and highlighting potential weaknesses in the dominance of strategy.

Capital and product markets

Since the seventeenth century, companies have been formed by shareholders in order to consolidate resources and invest in opportunities. Shareholders had *limited liability* through which their personal liability in the event of business failure was limited to their investment in the company's share capital. Shareholders appointed directors to direct and control the business, and the directors in turn employed managers. Shareholders have few direct rights in relation to the conduct of the business. Their main powers are to elect the directors, approve the directors' recommendation of a dividend and appoint the auditors in an annual general meeting of shareholders. They are also entitled to an annual report containing details of the company's financial performance (see Chapter 7).

The market in which investors buy and sell the shares of companies (the term commonly used in the USA is 'stock', but we retain the Anglo term 'shares' throughout this book) is called the capital market, which is normally associated with a Stock Exchange. Companies obtain funds raised from shareholders (capital, or equity) and borrowings from financiers (debt). Both of these constitute the capital employed in the business.

The cost of capital represents the cost incurred by the organization to fund all its investments, comprising the cost of equity and the cost of debt weighted by the mix of debt and equity. The cost of debt is **interest**, which is the price charged by the lender. The cost of equity is partly dividend and partly capital growth, because most shareholders expect both regular income from profits (the dividend) and an increase in the value of their shares over time in the capital market. Thus the different costs of each form of capital, weighted by the proportions of different forms of debt and equity, constitute the weighted average cost of capital (WACC). The management of the business relationship with capital markets is called financial management or corporate finance. The calculation of the WACC is beyond the scope of this book and is covered by texts on corporate finance. It will be assumed as given when required in this book.

Companies use their capital to invest in technologies, people and materials in order to make, buy and sell products or services to customers. This is called the product market. The focus of shareholder wealth, according to Rappaport (1998), is to obtain funds at competitive rates from capital markets and invest those funds to exploit imperfections in product markets. Where this takes place, shareholder wealth is increased through dividends and increases in the share price. The relationship between capital markets and product markets is shown in Figure 2.1.

Shareholder value-based management

Since the mid-1980s, there has been more and more emphasis on increasing the value of the business to its shareholders. Traditionally, business performance has been measured through accounting ratios such as return on capital employed (ROCE), return on investment (ROI), earnings per share and so on (which are described in Chapter 7). However, it has been argued that these are historical rather than current measures, and they vary between companies as a result of different accounting treatments.

Rappaport (1998) described how companies with strong cash flows diversified in the mid-twentieth century, often into uneconomic businesses, which led to the 'value gap' – the difference between the market value of the shares and the value of the business if it had been managed to maximize shareholder value. The consequence was the takeover movement and subsequent asset stripping of the 1980s, which provided a powerful incentive for managers to focus on creating value for shareholders. The takeover movement itself led to problems as high acquisition premiums (the excess paid over and above the calculated value of the business, i.e. the goodwill) were paid to the owners and financed by high levels of debt. During the 1990s institutional investors (pension/superannuation funds, insurance companies, investment trusts etc.),

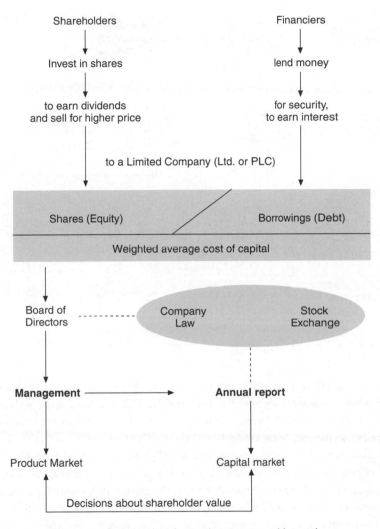

Figure 2.1   Capital and product market structure and interaction.

through their dominance of share ownership, increased their pressure on management to improve the financial performance of companies.

Value-based management (VBM) emphasizes shareholder value, on the assumption that this is the primary goal of every business. Research into the use of value-based management approaches by UK companies was described by Cooper *et al.* (2001). VBM approaches include:

- total shareholder return;
- market value added;
- shareholder value added; and
- economic value added.

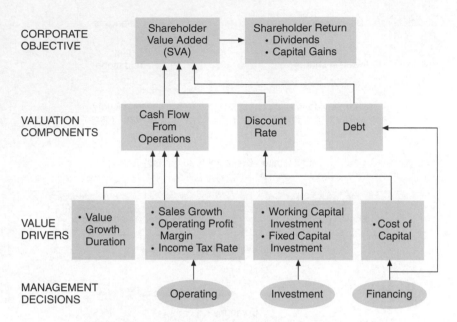

Total shareholder return (TSR) compares the dividends received by shareholders and the increase in the share price with the original shareholder investment, expressing the TSR as a percentage of the initial investment.

Market value added (MVA) is the difference between total market capitalization (number of shares issued times share price plus the market value of debt) and the total capital invested in the business by debt and equity providers. This is a measure of the value generated by managers for shareholders.

Rappaport (1998) coined *shareholder value added (SVA)* to refer to the increase in shareholder value over time. He defined shareholder value as the economic value of an investment, which can be calculated by using the cost of capital to discount estimated future cash flows (which he called *free cash flows*) into present values (discounted cash flow techniques are described in detail in Chapter 14). The business must generate profits in product markets that exceed the cost of capital in the capital market for value to be created (if not, shareholder value is eroded).

Rappaport developed a shareholder value network (see Figure 2.2) which identifies seven drivers of shareholder value: sales growth rate; operating profit margin; income tax rate; working capital investment; fixed capital investment; cost of capital; and forecast duration. Managers make three types of decisions that influence these value drivers and lead to shareholder value:

- Operating decisions – product mix, pricing, promotion, customer service etc., which are then reflected in the sales growth rate, operating profit margin and income tax rate.
- Investment decisions – in both inventory and capacity, which are then reflected in both working capital and fixed capital investment.

- Financing decisions – the mix of debt and equity and the choice of financial instrument determine the cost of capital, which is assessed by capital markets in terms of business risk.

The value growth duration is the estimated number of years over which the return from investments is expected to exceed the cost of capital.

The seven value drivers determine the cash flow from operations, the level of debt and the cost of capital, all of which determine shareholder value. However, a detrimental consequence of the emphasis on shareholder value is that it has led to a focus on short-term financial performance, sometimes at the expense of longer-term investment and sustainable performance.

Economic Value Added^{TM}*(EVA)* is a financial performance measure developed by consultants Stern Stewart & Co. It claims to capture the economic profit of a business that leads to shareholder value creation. In simple terms, EVA is net operating profit after deducting a charge to cover the opportunity cost of the capital invested in the business (when by taking one course of action you lose the opportunity to undertake an alternative course). EVA's 'economic profit' is the amount by which earnings exceed (or fall short of) the minimum rate of return that shareholders and financiers could get by investing in other securities with a comparable risk (see Stern Stewart's website at http://www.sternstewart.com/?content=proprietary&p=eva).

EVA accepts the assumption that the primary financial objective of any business is to maximize the wealth of its shareholders. The value of the business depends on the extent to which investors expect future profits to be greater or less than the weighted average cost of capital. Returns over and above the cost of capital increase shareholder wealth, while returns below the cost of capital erode shareholder wealth. Stern Stewart argues that managers understand this measure because it is based on operating profits. By introducing a notional charge based on assets held by the business, managers (whether at a corporate or divisional level) manage those assets as well as the profit generated.

EVA has its critics. For example, the calculation of EVA allows a large number of adjustments to reported accounting profits in order to remove distortions caused by arbitrary accounting rules, although Stern Stewart argues that most organizations need only about a dozen of these. EVA also estimates the risk-adjusted cost of capital, which can be argued as subjective. The increase in shareholder value is reflected in compensation strategies for managers whose goals, argues Stern Stewart, are aligned to increasing shareholder wealth through bonus and share option schemes that are paid over a period of time to ensure consistent future performance.

The pursuit of shareholder value (or economic value added) can be achieved through new or redesigned products and services, expansion to new markets, introduction of new technologies, the management of costs, the development of performance measurement systems and improved decision making. Value-based management aims to improve shareholder wealth, however it may be measured. Improving shareholder value is inextricably linked with both strategy and accounting.

Shareholder value, strategy and accounting

This book treats accounting as integral to the formulation and implementation of strategy, through decisions about the functional areas of marketing, operations and human resources. The purpose of strategy 'is to pursue profit over the long term' (Grant, 1998, p. 34). Strategy is concerned with long-term direction, achieving and maintaining competitive advantage, identifying the scope and boundaries of the organization and matching the activities of the organization to its environment. Strategy is also about building on resources and competences to create new opportunities and take advantage of those opportunities by managing change within the organization. There is also a link between strategy and operational decisions in order to turn strategy formulation into strategy implementation. Implementation is about converting strategy into action by setting performance targets (both financial and non-financial) for the business as a whole and for individual business units and then measuring and controlling performance against those targets (this is the subject of Chapter 4).

The strategic focus of accounting in business organizations is shareholder value – increasing the value of the business to its shareholders – through dividends from profits and/or through capital growth. Strategy both influences, and is influenced by, shareholder value. Strategy therefore also influences accounting: what performance is measured; how it is measured; and how it is reported. The organization's accounting system (which we introduce in Chapter 3) is about providing useful information to two distinct groups: external parties and managers.

Financial accounting relates to the stewardship function (Chapter 1), that managers are accountable to those with a financial interest in the business. Accounting results in producing financial statements to satisfy that accountability (Chapters 6 and 7) and measures, to some extent, the creation of shareholder value. Management accounting provides the information for managers to assist in planning, decision making and control (Chapters 9 through 18). Management accounting is more concerned with strategy and supplements the accounting system data with additional non-financial information and analysis and provides more detail, as managers have quite different requirements than those outside the business. Figure 2.3 (which is a copy of Figure 1.1) shows the relationship between financial and management accounting (which were introduced in Chapter 1). The principal focus of this book is on how accounting provides information to assist non-financial managers.

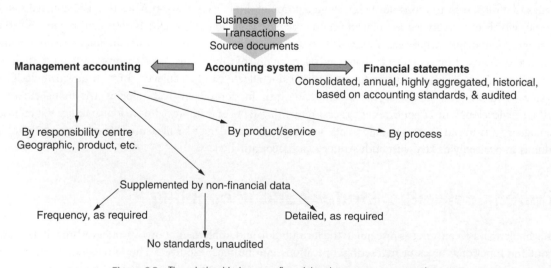

Figure 2.3   The relationship between financial and management accounting.

The importance of strategy for accounting and the information it provides is that strategy involves taking a longer term view about the sustainable performance of the business. Financial accounting reports are essential in reporting and enabling decisions by investors and lenders, however, it focuses on short-term, highly aggregated financial performance. Management accounting comprises a set of tools and techniques to support planning, decision making and control by managers in business organizations. So management accounting is about creating shareholder value, while financial accounting is more concerned with reporting it to investors.

Accounting is a requirement of legislation, and the analysis of financial statements and reporting to shareholders is a fundamental role of boards of directors. The next section provides the context of accounting in terms of the regulation of companies and corporate governance.

Company regulation and corporate governance

The regulation of companies

The Companies Act of 2006 is the primary UK legislation governing companies. Similar legislation operates throughout most Commonwealth countries. The Act sets out the need for companies to have a constitution, formally known as the *Memorandum of Association* and *Articles of Association*. Each company has a share capital, enabling ownership to be divided over many 'share holders' or 'members' of the company. The Act sets out the effects of incorporation, i.e. the 'limited liability' of shareholders for any unpaid portion of the shares they own. In most cases, issued shares are fully paid and therefore shareholders have no liability beyond this in the event of a company's failure.

Shareholders appoint directors to manage the company on their behalf. Those directors have various duties. Directors may authorize the company to borrow money. The directors must keep accounting records and produce financial statements in a specified format. If the company makes a profit, the directors may recommend that a dividend be paid out of profits. An auditor must be appointed to report annually to shareholders. Shareholders have no management rights. However, shareholders receive an Annual Report (see Chapter 7) containing the financial statements and an annual general meeting of shareholders must be held which elects directors, ratifies the dividend and appoints auditors, etc.

Corporate governance

Corporate governance is the system by which companies are directed and controlled. Boards of directors are responsible for the governance of their companies. The responsibilities of the board include setting the company's strategic goals, providing leadership to senior management, monitoring business performance and reporting to shareholders.

Corporate governance in the UK dates back to a report by Sir Adrian Cadbury in 1992 and followed several major corporate collapses. The high-profile failures of companies, and the press coverage given to Enron and WorldCom, brought corporate governance to worldwide attention. Large-scale failures have become a feature of business history throughout the world, with the most recent spate of collapses attributed to the global financial crisis. The increased attention to corporate governance has also been global, with many Commonwealth countries following the Cadbury principles which have evolved into codes of corporate governance.

The UK Corporate Governance Code (Financial Reporting Council, 2010) is the most recent code of practice. The Code adopts a principles-based approach that provides best practice guidelines for corporate governance in companies. The Code is aimed at Stock Exchange-listed companies which are required to either comply with the Code or explain reasons for any departure from it. The Code is also regarded as best practice for unlisted companies.

Even before the advent of corporate governance codes, a growing number of institutional investors were encouraging greater disclosure of governance processes, emphasizing the quality and sustainability of earnings, rather than short-term profits alone. Research has shown that an overwhelming majority of institutional investors are prepared to pay a significant premium for companies exhibiting high standards of corporate governance.

The introduction of the *Sarbanes–Oxley Act* in 2002 (often referred to as SOX) was the legislative response in the USA to the financial and accounting scandals of Enron and WorldCom and the misconduct at the accounting firm Arthur Andersen. Although not a corporate governance code as such, Sarbanes–Oxley focused on financial reporting and introduced the requirement to disclose all material off-balance sheet transactions. The Act requires the certification of annual and quarterly financial statements by the chief executive and chief financial officer of all companies with US securities registrations, with criminal penalties for knowingly making false certifications.

Principles of corporate governance

The role of a company's board of directors is to provide entrepreneurial leadership of the company within a framework of prudent and effective controls which enables risk to be assessed and managed. The board should set the company's strategic aims, and ensure that the necessary financial and human resources are in place for the company to meet its objectives and review management performance. The board should set the company's values and standards and ensure that its obligations to its shareholders and others are understood and met.

The five main principles of corporate governance found in the *UK Corporate Governance Code* are in relation to: leadership by the board; the effectiveness of the board; accountability; remuneration of board directors; and relations with shareholders.

Responsibility of directors

Under Companies legislation, the financial statements of a company are the responsibility of directors, not managers. Directors are responsible for keeping proper accounting records which disclose with reasonable accuracy the financial position of the company at any time and to ensure that financial statements comply with the Companies Act. They are also responsible for safeguarding the company's assets and for taking reasonable steps to prevent and detect fraud.

The financial statements must show a true and fair view (see Chapter 6) of the state of affairs of the company and of the profit or loss for that year. In preparing the financial statements, directors must select suitable accounting policies and apply those policies consistently, make judgements and estimates that are reasonable and prudent and prepare financial statements on a going concern basis unless it is inappropriate to presume that the company will continue in business (see Chapter 3 for a discussion of these principles).

Although in practice these functions will be delegated to a company's managers, the responsibility for financial records and financial statements cannot be delegated by the board of directors. Both are, however, subject to audit.

Audit

Audit is a periodic examination of the accounting records of a company carried out by an independent accountant to ensure that those records have been properly maintained and that the financial statements which are drawn up from those records present a true and fair view. An audit includes examination, on a test basis, of evidence relevant to the amounts and disclosures in financial statements. It also includes an assessment of significant estimates and judgements made by directors in the preparation of financial statements, and whether the company's accounting policies are appropriate, consistent and adequately disclosed. Auditors carry out their audit in accordance with UK Auditing Standards, issued by the Auditing Standards Board.

Each year the auditors present a report to shareholders, giving their opinion as to whether the financial statements present a true and fair view and are properly prepared in accordance with the Companies Act and applicable accounting standards (see Chapter 7).

Audit committees

The audit committee is a committee of the board of directors. The *UK Corporate Governance Code* states that the board should establish an audit committee of at least three, or in the case of smaller companies (below FTSE 350) two, members, who should all be independent non-executive directors. The board should satisfy itself that at least one member of the audit committee has recent and relevant financial experience.

The main role and responsibilities of the audit committee include:

- Monitoring the integrity of the company's financial statements; significant judgements made in relation to the financial statements; and formal announcements made by the company to the Stock Exchange.
- Reviewing the company's internal control and risk management systems.
- Monitoring and reviewing the effectiveness of the internal audit function.
- Making recommendations to the board for the board to place a resolution before shareholders in an annual general meeting for the appointment, reappointment and removal of the external auditor, and to approve the terms of engagement and remuneration of the external auditor.
- Reviewing and monitoring the external auditor's independence and objectivity and the effectiveness of the audit process.
- Developing and implementing policy on the engagement of the external auditor to supply non-audit services in order to maintain auditor objectivity and independence.

Stock Exchange Listing Rules

The primary aim of a Stock Exchange is to provide issuers, intermediaries and investors with attractive, efficient and well-regulated markets in which to raise capital and fulfil investment and trading requirements. Stock exchanges in the UK are subject to oversight by the UK Listing Authority, currently part of the Financial Services Authority. All companies are subject to the Companies Act, but publicly listed (i.e. listed on a Stock Exchange) companies have to abide by additional regulations called the 'Listing Rules'. The Listing Rules set out mandatory standards for any company wishing to list its shares or securities for sale to the public, and are aimed at protecting investors and maintaining standards of transparency, conduct, shareholder rights and due diligence. The Listing Rules dictate such matters as the contents of the prospectus on an initial public offering (IPO) of shares, and ongoing obligations such as the disclosure of price-sensitive information, and communications on new share offers, rights issues, and potential or actual takeover bids for the company.

The Listing Rules require listed companies to disclose how they have applied the principles in the *UK Corporate Governance Code*; and to confirm either that the company complies with the Code's provisions or, if it does not comply, to provide an explanation. This approach is known as 'comply or explain'.

Risk management, internal control and accounting

The benefits of applying good corporate governance are to reduce risk, stimulate performance, improve access to capital markets, enhance the marketability of product/services by creating confidence among stakeholders and demonstrate transparency and accountability.

The *UK Corporate Governance Code* takes a strong position in relation to risk. Risk is defined as 'uncertain future events which could influence the achievement of the organization's strategic, operational and financial objectives' (International Federation of Accountants, 1999). Risk may be business or operational, arising from the normal course of business (loss of customers, failure of computer systems, poor quality products, etc.); financial (arising from changes in interest rates, foreign currency exposure, poor credit control, etc.); environmental (arising from changes in political, economic, social or technological factors); or reputational. Risk may be considered in relation to downside factors ('bad things may happen') or upside factors ('good things may not happen'). This recognizes that taking risks is a necessary part of conducting business, with returns being the compensation for taking risks. The *UK Corporate Governance Code* requires that boards of directors institute a system of internal control based on the organization's risk appetite and the identification and assessment of risks facing the organization. A comprehensive approach to risk management ensures appropriate risk responses, monitoring and reporting processes and the development of appropriate internal controls to help manage risk.

Internal control is the whole system of internal controls, financial and otherwise, established in order to provide reasonable assurance of effective and efficient operation, internal financial control and compliance with laws and regulations. The *UK Corporate Governance Code* provides that the board should maintain a sound system of internal control to safeguard shareholders' investment and the company's assets. The board should, at least annually, conduct a review of the effectiveness of the group's system of internal controls and should report to shareholders that they have done so. The review should cover all material controls, including financial, operational and compliance controls and risk management systems.

Although there are forms of control other than financial ones (see Chapter 4), internal financial controls are established to provide reasonable assurance of the safeguarding of assets against unauthorized use or disposition, the maintenance of proper accounting records and the reliability of financial information used within the business or for publication.

Accounting controls are important in all organizations. They include control over cash, receivables, inventory, payables, the business infrastructure (non-current assets, see Chapter 7), as well as borrowings, income and expenses. Financial controls also exist over the costing of products and services (Chapters 10–13), capital investment decisions (Chapter 14), divisional performance evaluation (Chapter 15), budgets and budgetary control (Chapters 16 and 17). Accounting is fundamental to a system of internal control, and is the subject of Part III of this book, although the theoretical foundations are laid in Chapters 4 and 5.

A critical perspective

Shareholders' interests dominate business and accountants occupy a privileged position as those who establish the rules and report business performance. This can be seen as a historical development (see Chapter 1). However, the dominant concern with shareholder value has subsumed much consideration of the wider accountability of business to other stakeholders.

Stakeholder theory looks beyond shareholders to those groups who influence, or are influenced by, the organization. The theory argues that shareholders are not representative of society and stakes are held in the organization by employees, customers, suppliers, government and the wider community. Stakeholder theory is concerned with how the power of stakeholders, with their competing interests, is managed by the organization in terms of its broader accountabilities. Although this chapter has been concerned with share-holder value and corporate governance, a critical approach questions this emphasis on the privilege accorded to shareholder value. The stakeholder model takes a broader view, for example that found in South Africa, where the King Committee on Corporate Governance (2002) provides an integrated approach to corporate governance in the interest of all stakeholders, embracing the social, environmental and economic aspects of organizational activities.

Corporate governance is founded on the shareholder value principle, reflecting the political-historical position which was described in Chapter 1. The broader stakeholder approach to accountability suggests a broader responsibility to provide an explanation – an account – of the actions for which an organization is responsible (as we saw in Chapter 1), implying a right to information by various stakeholder groups in a democracy, i.e. a *corporate social responsibility* (discussed in Chapter 7). The shareholder and stakeholder models represent different means by which the functioning of boards of directors and top management can be understood. However, in company law, there is no doubt that shareholders are in a privileged position compared with other stakeholders. A critical perspective merely asks why this is so, and whether such a position ought to be taken for granted.

The idea of strategy oriented towards achieving goals is also open to criticism. Mintzberg (1994) was critical of the theory of strategic planning, particularly focused on financial projections, branding it a 'calculating style of management' which results in strategies that are extrapolated from the past or copied from others. Mintzberg saw some strategy as deliberate, but other strategy as an emergent process, which should lead to continual learning. He argued:

> Strategic planning often spoils strategic thinking, causing managers to confuse real vision with the manipulation of numbers (p. 107).

The pursuit of shareholder value implies a particular goal-oriented, economic and rational theory of management behaviour and organizational action. We will consider the theoretical assumptions behind this perspective in Chapters 4 and 5.

Conclusion

While Chapter 1 provided an introduction to accounting, its history and the changing role of the accountant, this chapter has provided the context for accounting. First, we considered the importance of capital markets and how they dictate the drive for shareholder value-based management through strategic planning. We then introduced the notions of company regulation and corporate governance that underlie the functioning of business organizations. The roles of boards of directors, auditors, stock exchanges and their regulators are intimately bound up with the practice of accounting, risk management and internal control. Finally, we concluded with a critical perspective that challenges the dominant (and narrow) view of shareholder value and contrasts it with a broader stakeholder view.

References

Cooper, S., Crowther, D., Davies, M. and Davis, E. W. (2001). *Shareholder or Stakeholder Value: The Development of Indicators for the Control and Measurement of Performance*. London: Chartered Institute of Management Accountants.

Financial Reporting Council (2010). *The UK Corporate Governance Code*. http://www.frc.org.uk/documents/pagemanager/Corporate_Governance/UK%20Corp%20Gov%20Code%20June%202010.pdf.

Grant, R. M. (1998). *Contemporary Strategy Analysis: Concepts, Techniques, Applications*. Oxford: Blackwell.

International Federation of Accountants (1999). *Enhancing Shareholder Wealth by Better Managing Business Risk*.

King Committee on Corporate Governance (2002). *King Report on Corporate Governance for South Africa – 2002 (King II Report)*. Institute of Directors, South Africa.

Mintzberg, H. (1994). The fall and rise of strategic planning. *Harvard Business Review*, Jan–Feb, 107–14.

Rappaport, A. (1998). *Creating Shareholder Value: A Guide for Managers and Investors*. New York: Free Press.

Websites

Stock Exchange listing rules are produced by the Financial Services Authority, whose website is http://www.fsa.gov.uk/Pages/index.shtml. The website of the London Stock Exchange is http://www.londonstockexchange.com/en-gb/.

Questions

2.1   Explain the idea of value-based management and how shareholder value relates to the interaction between product and capital markets.

2.2   Explain the key issues in corporate governance as they relate to accounting.

CHAPTER 3

Recording Financial Transactions and the Principles of Accounting

In order to understand the accounting process, we need to understand how accounting captures information that is subsequently used for producing financial statements and for managerial planning, decision making and control purposes. This chapter describes how business events are recorded as transactions into an accounting system using the double-entry method that is the foundation of accounting. The elements of the accounting system are introduced: assets; liabilities; income; expenses and equity. We introduce a simple form of the Income Statement and Statement of Financial Position (Balance Sheet) and explain the basic principles of accounting that underlie how financial statements are produced. Finally, the chapter introduces one of the first limitations of accounting systems – the calculation of 'cost' for decision making, and how cost may be interpreted in multiple ways.

Business events, transactions and the accounting system

Businesses exist to make a profit. They do this by producing goods and services and selling those goods and services at a price that covers their cost. Conducting business involves a number of *business events* such as buying equipment, purchasing goods and services, paying expenses, making sales, distributing goods and services etc. In accounting terms, each of these business events is a transaction. A transaction is the financial description of each business event.

It is important to recognize that transactions are a financial representation of the business event, measured in monetary terms. This is only one perspective on business events, albeit the one considered most important for accounting purposes. A broader view is that business events can also be recorded in non-financial terms, such as measures of product/service quality, speed of delivery, customer satisfaction etc. These non-financial performance measures (which are described in detail in Chapter 4) are important aspects of business events that are not captured by financial transactions. This is a limitation of accounting as a tool of business decision making that the reader must always bear in mind.

Each transaction is recorded on a source document that forms the basis of recording in a business's accounting system. Examples of source documents are invoices and cheques, although increasingly source documents are records of electronic transactions, such as electronic funds transfer. The accounting system, typically computer based (except for very small businesses), comprises a set of accounts that summarize the transactions that have been recorded on source documents and entered into the accounting system. Accounts can be considered as 'buckets' within the accounting system containing similar transactions (e.g. sales income, salary payments, inventory).

There are five types of accounts:

- Assets: things the business *owns*.
- Liabilities: debts the business *owes*.
- Income: the *revenue* generated from the *sale* of goods or services.
- Expenses: the *costs* incurred in *producing* the goods and services
- Equity (or capital): the investment made by shareholders into the business.

The main difference between these categories is that business profit is calculated as:

$$\text{profit} = \text{income} - \text{expenses}$$

while the equity or capital of the business (the owner's investment) is calculated as

$$\text{equity} = \text{assets} - \text{liabilities}$$

Financial statements comprise the Income Statement (which used to be called the Profit and Loss account and which now forms part of the Statement of Comprehensive Income) and the Statement of Financial Position (previously termed Balance Sheet). Both are produced from the information in the accounting system (see Chapter 6).

The double entry: recording transactions

Businesses use a system of accounting called double entry, which derives from the late fifteenth-century Italian city-states (see Chapter 1). The double entry means that every business transaction affects two accounts. Those

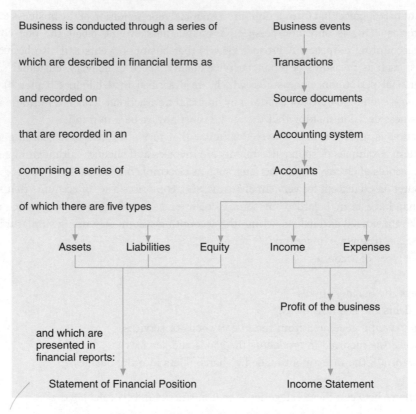

Figure 3.1   Business events, transactions and the accounting system.

accounts may *increase* or *decrease*. Accountants record the increases or decreases as debits or credits, but it is not necessary for non-accountants to understand this distinction. It is sufficient for our purposes to:

1. identify what type of account is affected (assets, liability, income, expense or equity); and
2. determine whether the transaction increases or decreases that account.

Transactions may take place in one of two forms:

- *Cash*: If the business sells goods/services for cash, the double entry is an increase in income and an increase in the bank account (an asset). If the business buys goods/services for cash, either an asset or an expense will increase (depending on what is bought) and the bank account will decrease.
- *Credit*: If the business sells goods/services on credit, the double entry is an increase in debts owed *to* the business (called Receivables in financial statements but commonly referred to as Debtors, an asset) and an increase in income. If the business buys goods/services on credit, either an asset or an expense will increase (depending on what is bought) and the debts owed *by* the business will increase (called Payables in financial statements, but commonly referred to as Creditors, a liability).

When goods are bought for resale, they become an asset called Inventory (commonly referred to as Stock). When the same goods are sold, there are two transactions:

1. the sale, either by cash or credit, as described above; and
2. the transfer of the cost of those goods, now sold, from inventory to an expense, called either cost of sales, or cost of goods sold.

In this way, the profit is the difference between the *price* at which the goods were sold (1 above) and the purchase *cost* of the same goods (2 above). Importantly, the purchase of goods into inventory does not affect profit until the goods are sold.

Some examples of business transactions and how the double entry affects the accounting system are shown in Table 3.1.

Table 3.1   Business transactions and the double entry.

Business event	Transaction	Source document	Accounts affected	Type of account	Increase or decrease
Install new equipment for production	Buy equipment for cash £25,000	Cheque	Equipment	Asset	Increase £25,000
			Bank	Asset	Decrease £25,000
Receive stock of goods for resale	Purchase stock on credit £15,000	Invoice from supplier	Inventory	Asset	Increase £15,000
			Payables	Liability	Increase £15,000
Pay weekly wages	Pay wages £3,000	Cheque	Wages	Expense	Increase £3,000
			Bank	Asset	Decrease £3,000
Sell goods to customer from stock	Sell stock on credit £9,000	Invoice to customer	Receivables	Asset	Increase £9,000
			Sales	Income	Increase £9,000
Deliver goods from stock	The goods that were sold for £9,000 cost £4,000 to buy	Goods delivery note	Cost of sales	Expense	Increase £4,000
			Inventory	Asset	Decrease £4,000
Advertising	Pay £1,000 for advertising	Cheque	Advertising	Expense	Increase £1,000
			Bank	Asset	Decrease £1,000
Receive payment from customer for earlier sale on credit	Receive £4,000 from customer	Bank deposit	Bank	Asset	Increase £4,000
			Receivables	Asset	Decrease £4,000
Pay supplier for goods previously bought on credit	Pay £9,000 to supplier	Cheque	Bank	Asset	Decrease £9,000
			Payables	Liability	Decrease £9,000

The accounts are all contained within a ledger, which is simply a collection of all the different accounts for the business. The ledger would summarize the transactions for each account, as shown in Table 3.2.

In the example in Table 3.2 there would be a separate account for each type of expense (wages, cost of sales, advertising), but for ease of presentation in this text these accounts have been placed in a single column. The ledger is the source of the financial statements that present the performance of the business. However, the ledger would also contain the balance of each account brought forward from the previous

Table 3.2 Summarizing business transactions in a ledger.

Account transaction	Asset equipment	Asset inventory	Asset receivables	Asset bank	Liability: payables	Income: sales	Expenses
Buy equipment for cash £25,000	+25,000			−25,000			
Purchase stock on credit £15,000		+15,000			+15,000		
Pay wages £3,000				−3,000			+3,000
Sell stock on credit £9,000			+9,000			+9,000	
The goods that were sold for £9,000 cost £4,000 to buy		−4,000					+4,000
Pay advertising £1,000				−1,000			+1,000
Receive £4,000 from customer			−4,000	+4,000			
Pay £9,000 to supplier				−9,000	−9,000		
Total of transactions for this period	+25,000	+11,000	+5,000	−34,000	+6,000	+9,000	+8,000

Table 3.3 Summarizing business transactions with opening balances in a ledger.

Account	Capital	Asset equipment	Asset inventory	Asset receivables	Asset bank	Liability: payables	Income: sales	Expenses
Investment by owner	+50,000				+50,000			
Total of transactions for this period		+25,000	+11,000	+5,000	−34,000	+6,000	+9,000	+8,000
Totals of each account at end of period	+50,000	+25,000	+11,000	+5,000	+16,000	+6,000	+9,000	+8,000

period. In our simple example, assume that the business commenced with £50,000 in the bank account that had been contributed by the owner (the owner's *capital*). Table 3.3 shows the effect of the opening balances.

Extracting financial information from the accounting system

To produce financial statements we need to separate the accounts for income and expenses from those for assets and liabilities. In this example, we would produce an Income Statement (see Table 3.4) based on the income and expenses:

Table 3.4 Income Statement.

Income		9,000
Less expenses:		
Cost of sales	4,000	
Wages	3,000	
Advertising	1,000	8,000
Profit		1,000

The Statement of Financial Position lists the assets and liabilities of the business, as shown in Table 3.5. The double-entry system records the profit earned by the business as an addition to the owner's investment in the business.

Table 3.5 Statement of Financial Position (simple version).

Assets		Liabilities	
Equipment	25,000	Payables	6,000
Inventory	11,000	**Equity**	
Receivables	5,000	Owner's original investment	50,000
Bank	16,000	Plus profit for period	1,000
		Total equity	51,000
Total assets	57,000	Total liabilities plus equity	57,000

The Balance Sheet must *balance*, i.e. assets are equal to liabilities plus equity.

assets (£57,000) = liabilities (£6,000) + equity (£51,000)

This is called the accounting equation and reflects that all the assets of the business must be financed either by liabilities or by equity (as we saw in Chapter 1). Although shown separately, equity (or capital) is a kind of liability as it is owed by the business to its owners, although there must be special circumstances for it ever to be repaid.

The accounting equation can also be restated as:

$$\textbf{equity (£51,000) = assets (£57,000) − liabilities (£6,000)}$$

Table 3.5 is a format no longer used for the Statement of Financial Position, but it is shown here as an example because it more clearly shows the accounting equation. The Statement of Financial Position has for many years been shown in a vertical format as shown in Table 3.6.

Table 3.6   Statement of Financial Position.

Assets:	
Equipment	25,000
Inventory	11,000
Receivables	5,000
Bank	16,000
Total assets	57,000
Liabilities:	
Payables	6,000
Net assets	51,000
Equity:	
Owner's original investment	50,000
Plus profit for period	1,000
Owner's equity	51,000

There are some important points to note about Table 3.6:

1. The purchase of equipment of £25,000 has not affected profit (although we will consider depreciation in Chapter 6).
2. Profit is not the same as cash flow. Although there has been a profit of £1,000, the bank balance has reduced by £34,000 (from £50,000 to £16,000).
3. Most of the cash has gone into the new equipment (£25,000), but some has gone into working capital (this is covered in Chapter 7).

Working capital (see Chapter 7) is the investment in assets (less liabilities) that continually revolve in and out of the bank, comprising receivables, inventory, payables and the bank balance itself (in this case £32,000 less £6,000 = £26,000). Note that Equipment (£25,000) is not part of working capital as it forms part of the business infrastructure. The purchase of infrastructure is commonly called capital expenditure (often abbreviated as cap ex), and is also referred to as capitalizing an amount of money paid out, which does not affect profit. Whether a payment is treated as an expense (which affects profit) or as an asset (which appears in the Statement of Financial Position) is important, as it can have a significant impact on profit, which is one of the main measures of business performance.

Both the Income Statement and the Statement of Financial Position are described in detail in Chapter 6. In financial reporting, as this chapter and Chapters 6 and 7 will show, there are strict requirements for the content and presentation of financial statements. One of these requirements is that the reports (produced from the ledger accounts) are based on line items. Line items are the generic types of assets, liabilities, income, expenses and equity that are common to all businesses. This is an important requirement as all businesses are required to report their expenses using much the same line items, to ensure comparability between companies.

Basic principles of accounting

Basic principles or conventions have been developed over many years and form the basis upon which financial information is reported. These principles include:

- accounting entity;
- accounting period;
- matching principle;
- monetary measurement;
- historic cost;
- going concern;
- conservatism;
- consistency.

Each is dealt with in turn below.

Accounting entity

Financial statements are produced for the business, independent of the owners – the business and its owners are separate entities. This is particularly important for owner-managed businesses where the personal finances of the owner must be separated from the business finances. The problem caused by the entity principle is that complex organizational structures are not always clearly identifiable as an 'entity' (see the Enron case study in Chapter 5).

Accounting period

Financial information is produced for a financial year. The period is arbitrary and has no relationship with business cycles. Businesses typically end their financial year at the end of a calendar or national fiscal year. The business cycle is more important than the financial year, which after all is nothing more than the time taken for the Earth to revolve around the Sun. If we consider the early history of accounting, merchant ships did not produce monthly accounting reports. They reported to the ships' owners at the end of the business cycle, when the goods they had traded were all sold and profits could be calculated meaningfully. However, companies are required to report to shareholders on an annual basis.

Matching principle

Closely related to the accounting period is the matching (or accruals) principle, in which income is recognized when it is *earned* and expenses when they are *incurred*, rather than on a cash basis. The accruals method of accounting provides a more meaningful picture of the financial performance of a business from year to year. However, the preparation of accounting reports requires certain assumptions to be made about the recognition of income and expenses. One of the criticisms made of many companies is that they attempt to 'smooth' their reported performance to satisfy the expectations of stock market analysts in order to maintain shareholder value. This practice has become known as 'earnings management'. A significant cause of the difficulties faced by WorldCom was that expenditure had been treated as an asset in order to improve reported profits (see the case study in Chapter 5).

Monetary measurement

Despite the importance of market, product/service quality, human, technological and environmental factors, accounting records transactions and reports information in purely financial terms. This provides an important but limited perspective on business performance. The criticism of accounting numbers is that they are *lagging* indicators of performance. Chapter 4 considers non-financial measures of performance that are more likely to present *leading* indicators of performance. An emphasis on financial numbers tends to overlook important issues of customer satisfaction, quality, innovation and employee morale, which have a major impact on business performance. It also means that these essential ingredients to a successful business may not be given the same weighting as that given to financial information.

Historic cost

Accounting reports record transactions at their original cost less depreciation (see Chapter 6), not at market (realizable) value or at current (replacement) cost. The historic cost may be unrelated to market or replacement value. Under this principle, the Statement of Financial Position does not attempt to represent the value of the business and the owner's equity is merely a calculated figure rather than a valuation of the business. The Statement of Financial Position excludes assets that have not been purchased by a business but have been built up over time, such as customer goodwill, brand names etc. The *market-to-book ratio (MBR)* is the market value of the business divided by the original capital invested. Major service-based and high technology companies such as Apple and Microsoft, which have enormous goodwill and intellectual property but a low asset base, have high MBRs because the stock market values shares by taking account of information that is not reflected in accounting reports, in particular the company's expected future earnings.

Going concern

The financial statements are prepared on the basis that the business will continue in operation. Many businesses have failed soon after their financial statements have been prepared on a going concern basis, making the asset values in the Statement of Financial Position impossible to realize. As asset values after the liquidation of a business are unlikely to equal historic cost, the continued operation of a business is an important assumption. The going concern principle is a significant limitation of financial statements as the case study on Carrington Printers in Chapter 7 reveals.

Conservatism

Accounting is a prudent practice, in which the sometimes over-optimistic opinions of non-financial managers are discounted. A conservative approach tends to recognize the downside of events rather than the upside. However, as mentioned above, the pressure on listed companies from analysts to meet stock market expectations of profitability has resulted from time to time in earnings management practices, such as those that led to problems at Enron and WorldCom.

Consistency

The application of accounting principles should be consistent from one year to the next. Where those principles vary, the effect on profits must be separately disclosed. However, some businesses have tended to change their rules, even with disclosure, in order to improve their reported performance, explaining the change as a once-only event.

These basic principles have been elaborated by International Financial Reporting Standards (IFRS) and the *Framework for the Preparation and Presentation of Financial Statements*, both of which are described in Chapter 6.

One of the most important pieces of financial information for managers concerns cost, which forms the basis for most of the chapters in Part III. The calculation of cost is influenced in large part by accounting principles and the requirements of financial reporting. However, the cost that is calculated for financial reporting purposes may have limited decision usefulness for managers.

Cost terms and concepts: the limitations of financial accounting

Cost can be defined as 'a resource sacrificed or foregone to achieve a specific objective' (Horngren *et al.*, 1999, p. 31).

Accountants define costs in monetary terms, and while this book focuses on monetary costs, readers should recognize that there are not only financial costs but non-financial (or at the very least difficult to measure) human, social and environmental costs, and these latter costs are not reported in the financial statements of companies. For example, making employees redundant causes family problems (a human cost) and transfers to society the obligation to pay social security benefits (a social cost). Pollution causes long-term environmental costs that are also transferred to society. These are as important as (and perhaps more important than) financial costs, but they are not recorded by accounting systems (see Chapter 7 for a discussion of corporate social responsibility). The exclusion of human, social and environmental costs is a significant limitation of accounting.

For planning, decision-making and control purposes, cost is typically defined in relation to a cost object, which is anything for which a measurement of costs is required. While the cost object is often an *output* – a product or service – it may also be a resource (an *input* to the production process), a *process* of converting resources into outputs, or an *area of responsibility* (a department or cost centre) within the organization. Examples of inputs are materials, labour, rent, advertising, etc. These are line items (see above). Examples of processes are purchasing, customer order processing, order fulfilment, dispatch, etc. Departments or cost centres may include Purchasing, Production, Marketing, Accounting, etc. Other cost objects are possible when we want to consider profitability, e.g. the cost of dealing with specific customers is important for customer profitability analysis, or the costs of a distribution channel when we compare the profitability of different methods of distribution.

Businesses typically report in relation to line items (the resource inputs) and responsibility centres (departments or cost centres). This means that decisions requiring cost information on business processes and product/service outputs are difficult, because most accounting systems (except activity-based systems, as will be described in Chapter 13) do not provide adequate information about these other cost objects. Reports on the profitability of each product, each customer or distribution channel are rarely able to be produced from the traditional financial accounting system and must be determined through management accounting processes that use, but are not incorporated within, traditional accounting systems (however, the more sophisticated enterprise resource planning systems, see Chapter 9, can provide much of this more comprehensive information).

Businesses may adopt a system of management accounting to provide this kind of information for management purposes, but rarely will this second system reconcile with the external financial statements because the management information system may not follow the same accounting principles described in this chapter and in Chapter 6. Therefore, the requirement to produce financial statements based on line items and responsibility centres, rather than more meaningful cost objects (customers, processes, etc.), is a second limitation of accounting as a tool of decision making.

The notion of cost is also problematic because we need to decide how cost is to be defined. If, as Horngren *et al.* defined it, cost is a resource sacrificed or forgone, then one of the questions we must ask is whether that definition implies a cash cost or an opportunity cost. A cash cost is the amount of cash expended (a valuable resource), whereas an opportunity cost is the lost opportunity of not doing something, which may be the loss of time or the loss of a customer, or the diminution in the value of an asset (e.g. machinery), all equally valuable resources. If it is the cash cost, is it the *historical* (past) cost or the *future* cost with which we should be concerned?

For example, is the cost of an employee:

- the historical cash cost of salaries and benefits, training, recruitment etc. paid?
- the future cash cost of salaries and benefits to be paid?
- the lost opportunity cost of what we could have done with the money had we not employed that person, e.g. the benefits that could have resulted from expenditure of the same amount of money on advertising, computer equipment, external consulting services etc.?

Wilson and Chua (1988) quoted the economist Jevons, writing in 1871, that past costs were irrelevant to decisions about the future because they are 'gone and lost forever'. We call these past costs sunk costs. The problematic nature of calculating costs may have been the source of the comment by Clark (1923) that there were 'different costs for different purposes'.

This, then, is our third limitation of accounting: what do we mean by cost and how do we calculate it? We return to many of these issues throughout Part III of this book. The point to remember here is that, while financial statements are important and do report many costs, they are not necessarily the costs that should be used by managers for decision making.

Conclusion

This chapter has described how an accounting system captures, records, summarizes and reports financial information using the double-entry system of recording financial transactions in accounts. It has introduced the Income Statement and Statement of Financial Position. The simple examples of financial statements introduced in this chapter (which are dealt with in more detail in Chapters 6 and 7) rely on the separation between assets, liabilities, income, expenses and equity. This chapter has also identified the basic principles underlying the accounting process. One of the limitations of financial accounting for managerial decision making is highlighted through a brief introduction to 'cost'.

References

Clark, J. M. (1923). *Studies in the Economics of Overhead Costs*. Chicago: University of Chicago Press.
Horngren, C. T., Bhimani, A., Foster, G. and Datar, S. M. (1999). *Management and Cost Accounting*. London: Prentice Hall.
Wilson, R. M. S. and Chua, W. F. (1988). *Managerial Accounting: Method and Meaning*. London: VNR International.

Questions

3.1   An accounting system comprises accounts that can be grouped into:

a. income, expenses, assets, liabilities and profit
b. financial position, profit and cash flow
c. assets, liabilities, income, expenses and equity
d. profit, capital, financial position and cash flow

3.2   A transaction to record the sale of goods on credit would involve a double entry for the sales value to the following accounts:

a. increase sales and reduce inventory
b. increase sales and increase inventory
c. increase payables and increase sales
d. increase receivables and increase sales

3.3   A retail business has cash sales of £100,000, the cost of sales for which was £35,000. Salaries of £15,000, rental of £4,000 and advertising of £8,000 have been paid in cash. The owners have contributed equity of £25,000. In addition, the business paid cash of £40,000 for stock and purchased equipment on credit for £20,000. The financial statements of the business would show:

a. Profit of £38,000 cash of £13,000 and equity of £25,000
b. Profit of £38,000 cash of £58,000 and equity of £63,000
c. Profit of £65,000 cash of £33,000 and equity of £38,000
d. Profit of £63,000 cash of £33,000 and equity of £25,000

3.4   A Statement of Financial Position (Balance Sheet) shows liabilities of £125,000 and assets of £240,000. The Income Statement shows income of £80,000 and expenses of £35,000. Equity is:

a. £45,000
b. £115,000
c. £160,000
d. £365,000

3.5   A transaction to record the purchase of asset equipment on credit would involve:

a. increasing asset equipment and reducing payables
b. reducing asset equipment and reducing payables
c. increasing payables and increasing asset equipment
d. increasing payables and reducing asset equipment

3.6 For each of the following transactions, identify whether there is an increase or decrease in profit, cash flow, assets or liabilities.

Transaction	Profit Income – Expenses	Cash flow	Assets (excluding cash)	Liabilities
Issues shares to public				
Borrows money over 5 years				
Pays cash for equipment				
Buys inventory on credit				
Sells goods on credit				
Pays cash for salaries, rent, etc.				
Pays cash to suppliers				
Receives cash from customers				

3.7 The following balances are shown in alphabetical order in a professional service firm's accounting system at the end of a financial year:

	£
Advertising	15,000
Bank	5,000
Equity	71,000
Income	135,000
Equipment	100,000
Payables	11,000
Receivables	12,000
Rent	10,000
Salaries	75,000

Calculate:

a. the profit for the year
b. the equity at the end of the year

Management Control, Accounting and its Rational-Economic Assumptions

Accounting needs to be understood in its broader context as part of a management control system. In this chapter, we describe management control systems and their relationship with accounting; and planning and control systems including the role of feedback and feedforward, with particular reference to cybernetic forms of control. This chapter also explains the importance of non-financial performance measurement and introduces the Balanced Scorecard and strategy mapping processes. We conclude with a brief introduction to a theoretical framework for accounting.

Management control systems

In his seminal work on the subject, Anthony (1965) defined management control as:

> The process by which managers assure that resources are obtained and used effectively and efficiently in the accomplishment of the organization's objectives.

Management control encompasses both financial and non-financial performance measurement. Anthony developed a model that differentiated three planning and control functions:

- Strategy formulation was concerned with goals, strategies and policies. This fed into
- Management control, which was concerned with the implementation of strategies and in turn led to
- Task control, which comprised the efficient and effective performance of individual tasks.

Anthony was primarily concerned with the middle function. Otley (1994) argued that such a separation was unrealistic and that management control was 'intimately bound up with both strategic decisions about positioning and operating decisions that ensure the effective implementation of such strategies' (p. 298). Building on Anthony's earlier definition, Anthony and Govindarajan (2000) defined management control as a 'process by which managers at all levels ensure that the people they supervise implement their intended strategies' (p. 4).

Berry *et al.* (1995) defined management control as:

> the process of guiding organizations into viable patterns of activity in a changing environment . . . managers are concerned to influence the behaviour of other organizational participants so that some overall organizational goals are achieved (p. 4).

These organizational goals, as we have seen in previous chapters, are generally financial goals. Companies need to produce profits and generate increases in their share price in order to achieve wealth for their shareholders. Managers must plan, make decisions and exercise control to ensure that these goals are achieved. We introduced the distinction between financial and management accounting in Chapter 1. Management control is concerned with both generating shareholder wealth (management accounting) and reporting shareholder wealth (financial accounting).

The accounting system is often at the centre of the information system used by top management and boards of directors to ensure that the organization is on track to meeting its objectives. However, management control is a broader function that incorporates a wide range of controls: accounting systems; non-financial performance information (described in detail later in this chapter); strategic plans; organizational policies and procedures; human resource recruitment, training and socialization processes into the organizational culture (Chapter 5 describes this kind of control in more detail).

Management controls have been described in various ways over time:

- Through the market in which prices convey the information necessary for decisions; through bureaucracy, characterized by rules and supervision; and as an informal social mechanism – clan – which operates through socialization processes that may result in the formation of an organizational culture (Ouchi, 1979).
- Strategic plans; long-range plans; annual operating budgets; periodic statistical reports; performance appraisal; and policies and procedures (Daft & Macintosh, 1984).
- Formal, informal and crisis modes of control: 'Individual measures are used to direct short-term attention, cultural norms are the basis for guiding long-term behaviour, and a crisis mode of operation is

adopted whenever performance of a unit falls outside of acceptable parameters' (Euske *et al.*, 1993, p. 294).

- Personnel, action and results controls (Merchant, 1998).
- Objectives, strategies and plans, target-setting, incentive and reward structures, and information feedback loops (Otley, 1999).

In this chapter we are concerned with management control as a *system* (a collection of inter-related mechanisms) of rules which include, but are not limited to, accounting. However, controls may not be inter-related if they are developed organically over time rather than systematically (Machin, 1983). The problem for many organizations is that elements of the control system such as strategic plans, budgets, non-financial performance measures and human resource policies may give different signals to employees as to what is expected of them. Hence the idea of a management control system may be inappropriate where controls are piecemeal and not integrated – the result of them having emerged over time rather than being the subject of a deliberate design.

The term 'control package' may better reflect the idea of a set of controls that operate towards common goals, but not necessarily as an integrated management control 'system'. One recent typology of the management control package includes planning, cybernetic, reward and compensation, administrative, and cultural elements (Malmi and Brown, 2008). Cybernetic controls include the more formal budgets, financial and non-financial measurement systems. Administrative controls include the governance and organization structure, policies and procedures. Culture includes clans, values and symbols. The concept of a package 'points to the fact that different systems are often introduced by different interest groups at different times, so the controls in their entirety should not be defined holistically as a single system' (Malmi and Brown, 2008, p. 291).

While in many organizations, one type of control may be dominant (often accounting-based controls), Alvesson and Karreman (2004) have argued for understanding various forms of control as simultaneously active. As controls may be linked to and supporting of each other, they argue that it might be counterproductive to assume the existence of a dominating form of control. Building on Otley's (1999) argument that performance management provided a better integrating framework for management control systems, Ferreira and Otley (2009) developed a framework for performance management systems (PMS) which contains eight core elements: vision and mission; key success factors; organization structure; strategies and plans; key performance measures; target setting; performance evaluation; and reward systems. These are influenced by four other factors: PMS change; PMS use; strength and coherence of the core elements; and information flows, systems and networks. The PMS exists within a set of broader contextual and cultural influences.

Simons (1994, 1995) identified how top managers can simultaneously operate with four types of control systems: boundary; belief; diagnostic; and interactive. Boundary systems establish explicit limits and rules. Belief systems are concerned with values, purpose and direction. Diagnostic control systems provide formal feedback to enable corrections from preset standards. Interactive control systems are used by managers to regularly and personally involve themselves in the decisions of subordinates. Simons described the actions taken by newly appointed top managers attempting revolutionary and evolutionary strategic change, all of whom used control systems to: overcome inertia; communicate the substance of their agenda; structure implementation timetables; ensure continuing attention through incentives; and focus organizational learning on strategic uncertainties.

Research by Simons (1990) found that the choice by top managers to make certain control systems interactive provided signals to organizational participants about what should be monitored and where new ideas should be proposed and tested. This signal activated organizational learning. Simons developed a model of the relationship between strategy, control systems and organizational learning in order to reduce strategic uncertainty. The model is reproduced in Figure 4.1.

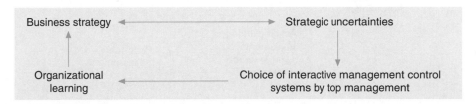

Figure 4.1 Process model of relationship between business strategy and management control systems.
Source: Reprinted from *Accounting, Organizations and Society*, Vol. 15, No. 1/2, R. Simons, The role of management control systems in creating competitive advantage, pp. 127–43. Copyright 1990, with permission from Elsevier Science.

Irrespective of which approach is taken to management control, it is clear that the definition of management control systems has evolved from formal, financially quantifiable information to include external information relating to markets, customers and competitors; non-financial information about production processes; predictive information; and a broad array of decision support mechanisms and informal personal and social controls (Chenhall, 2003).

Planning and control in organizations

We can distinguish systems for planning from systems for control. *Planning systems* interpret environmental demands and constraints and use a set of numbers to provide a 'common language which can be used to compare and contrast the results obtained by each activity' (Otley, 1987, p. 64). These numbers may be financial or non-financial performance expectations, represented in accounting and in non-financial performance measurement reports. Otley *et al.* (1995) noted that:

> accounting is still seen as a pre-eminent technology by which to integrate diverse activities from strategy to operations and with which to render accountability (p. S39).

Control systems are concerned with *feedback* control, in which 'the observed error is fed back into the process to instigate action to cause its reduction' (Otley, 1987, p. 21). By contrast, planning systems are also concerned with *feedforward* control, 'because it is only an expected error that is used to stimulate the control process' (p. 21).

We can consider the management planning and control system as a single system in which both feedback and feedforward are concerned with reducing the performance gap (Downs, 1966). Downs defined this as 'the difference in utility [an individual] perceives between the actual and the satisfactory level of performance' (p. 169). According to Downs, the larger the gap, the greater is the motivation to undertake more intensive search for ways of bridging that gap. We can show this diagrammatically in Figure 4.2.

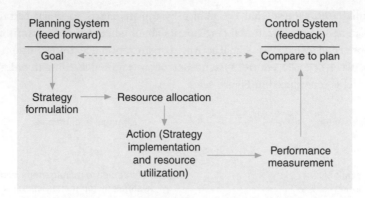

Figure 4.2   Model of planning and control system.

Feedforward is the process of determining, prospectively, whether strategies are likely to achieve the target results that are consistent with organizational goals. **Feedback** is the retrospective process of measuring performance, comparing it with the plan and taking corrective action. These two approaches need to be integrated in the management control system as they share common targets, the need for corrective action to be reflected either in goal adjustment or in changed behaviour, and the allocation or utilization of resources (i.e. budgeting and budgetary control, which are covered in Chapters 16 and 17).

According to Anthony and Govindarajan (2000), every control system has at least four elements:

1. A detector or sensor that measures what is happening.
2. An assessor that determines the significance of what is happening by comparing it with a standard or expectation.
3. An effector (feedback) that alters behaviour if the assessor indicates the need to do so.
4. A communication network that transmits information between the other elements.

This can be represented in the diagram in Figure 4.3.

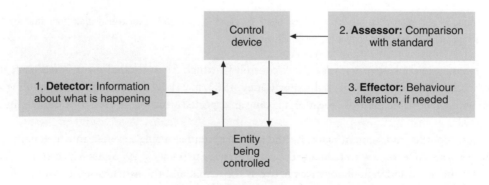

Figure 4.3   Elements of a control system.
Source: Reprinted from Anthony, R. N. and Govindarajan, V. (2000). *Management Control Systems* (10th edn), McGraw-Hill Irwin.

There are five major standards against which performance can be compared (Emmanuel *et al.*, 1990):

1. Previous time periods.
2. Similar organizations.
3. Estimates of future organizational performance *ex ante*.
4. Estimates of what might have been achieved *ex post*.
5. The performance necessary to achieve defined goals.

Hofstede (1981) provided a typology for management control: routine, expert, trial-and-error, intuitive, judgemental or political. The first three are cybernetic and are described in this chapter. Non-cybernetic controls are described in Chapter 5. A *cybernetic control* process involves four conditions (Berry *et al.*, 1995, originally published in Otley and Berry, 1980):

1. The existence of an objective that is desired.
2. A means of measuring process outputs in terms of this objective.
3. The ability to predict the effect of potential control actions.
4. The ability to take actions to reduce deviations from the objective.

The simplest example of a cybernetic control system is a thermostat. A desired room temperature is set (1); a thermometer measures the room temperature (2); knowledge is available to enable heating and cooling in response to deviations from the desired room temperature (3); and the heating/cooling system is automatically engaged in response to the measured deviation (4).

However, Otley and Berry (1980) recognized that in organizations, cybernetic control was more difficult than in this simple example, because:

> organizational objectives are often vague, ambiguous and change with time . . . measures of achievement are possible only in correspondingly vague and often subjective terms . . . predictive models of organizational behaviour are partial and unreliable, and . . . different models may be held by different participants . . . the ability to act is highly constrained for most groups of participants, including the so-called 'controllers' (p. 241).

Based on work by Berry *et al.* (1995), Emmanuel *et al.* (1990) presented a simplified diagram of the control process as a regulator. This is contained in Figure 4.4.

This model emphasizes the importance for control of a predictive model, which is necessary for both feedback (reactive) and feedforward (anticipatory) modes of control. The predictive model is essential in organizational control because it defines the explicit or implicit cause–effect or action–outcome relationships, i.e. the expectation that if something is done, there will be a likely result, e.g. that advertising will lead to increased sales orders; or that increasing price may cause the volume of sales to fall. The predictive model has to be defined by each organization to suit its particular strategy and its competitive environment. The difficulty with any form of control is the reliability of the predictive model. It is also critical that the organization's management control system reflects the predictive model adopted by the business. A management control or accounting system that fails to reflect the nature of the business and its strategy is likely to impede, rather than

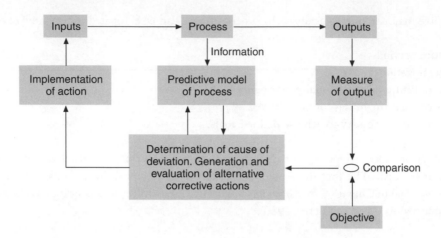

Figure 4.4   Necessary conditions for control.
Source: Reprinted from Emmanuel, C., Otley, D. and Merchant, K. (1990). *Accounting for Management Control* (2nd edn). London: Chapman & Hall.

assist, the organization in achieving its goals: 'Attempting to design control systems without having a detailed knowledge of how the business works is likely to prove a recipe for disaster' (Otley, 1999, p. 381).

Understanding the predictive model means that managers can try to influence behaviour and measure results. Ouchi (1977) argued that there were 'only two phenomena which can be observed, monitored, and counted: behavior and the outputs which result from behavior' (p. 97). To apply behaviour control, organizations need agreement or knowledge about means–ends relationships. To apply output control, a valid and reliable measure of the desired outputs must be available. Ouchi argued that as organizations grow larger and hierarchy increases, there is a shift from behaviour to output control.

Otley and Berry (1980) defined four types of control in response to deviations from desired performance:

1. First-order control adjusts system inputs (e.g. resources) and causes behaviour to alter.
2. Second-order control alters system objectives (e.g. goals) or the standards to be attained.
3. Internal learning amends the predictive model on the basis of past experience and the measurement and communication processes associated with it.
4. Systemic learning or adaptation changes the nature of the system itself – inputs, outputs and predictive models.

Accounting should be understood in this broader context of management control. Emmanuel *et al.* (1990) believed that accounting was important because it represents 'one of the few integrative mechanisms capable of summarizing the effect of an organization's actions in quantitative terms' (p. 4). Because management information can be expressed in monetary terms, it can be aggregated across time and across diverse organizational units and provides a means of integrating activities. Otley and Berry (1994) described how in management control:

> accounting information provides a window through which the real activities of the organization may be monitored, but it should be noted also that other windows are used that do not rely upon accounting information (p. 46).

Otley (1994) called for a wider view of management control, with less emphasis on accounting-based controls. Criticizing Anthony's model of planning and control (see earlier in this chapter), Otley argued that '[t]he split between strategic planning, management control and operational control, which was always tendentious, now becomes untenable' (p. 292). Otley claimed that there was widespread agreement that undue emphasis was given to financial controls rather than to a more 'balanced scorecard' approach, hence the increasing importance given to non-financial (or multidimensional) performance management in the study of management control systems. Otley *et al.* (1995) argued for expanding management control beyond accounting, distinguishing financial control from management control, the latter as:

> a general management function concerned with the achievement of overall organizational aims and objectives . . . management control is concerned with looking after the overall business with money being used as a convenient measure of a variety of other more complex dimensions, not as an end in itself (p. S33).

The next section introduces the importance of non-financial performance measures to supplement financial ones.

Non-financial performance measurement

The limitations of financial measures were identified most clearly by Johnson and Kaplan (1987), who argued that there was an excessive focus on short-term financial performance. They commented:

> Managers discovered that profits could be 'earned' not just by selling more or producing for less, but also by engaging in a variety of non-productive activities: exploiting accounting conventions, engaging in financial entre-preneurship, and reducing discretionary expenditures (p. 197).

Examples of exploiting accounting conventions have been seen in corporate collapses such as Enron and WorldCom, while financial entrepreneurship can be seen as one of the causes of the Global Financial Crisis. The discretionary costs that could be 'eliminated' in pursuit of short-term profit include:

> R&D, promotion, distribution, quality improvement, applications engineering, human resources, and customer relations — all of which, of course, are vital to a company's long-term performance. The immediate effect of such reductions is to boost reported profitability, but at the expense of sacrificing the company's long-term competitive position (p. 201).

Johnson and Kaplan (1987) emphasized the importance of non-financial indicators, arguing:

> Short-term financial measures will have to be replaced by a variety of non-financial indicators that provide better targets and predictors for the firm's long-term profitability goals (p. 259).

There have many attempts at non-financial performance measurement. Eccles (1991) argued that 'income-based financial figures are better at measuring the consequences of yesterday's decisions than they are at indicating tomorrow's performance'. Meyer (1994) proposed a 'dashboard', arguing that traditional performance measurement systems don't work as they track what happens within not across functions. Innes (1996) described the *tableaux de bord* that had been developed by 'sub-departments' in French factories. These comprise non-financial measures that managers identified as critical to success and that were developed and monitored locally, rather than being part of the formal reporting process.

The development of the Balanced Scorecard (Kaplan and Norton, 1992, 1993, 1996, 2001) has received extensive coverage in the business press and is perhaps the best-known example of a more balanced approach to performance measurement than was available from financial performance alone. The Balanced Scorecard took as a starting point the goal to generate long-term economic value, which required other than financial measures as drivers of long-term performance and growth. Kaplan and Norton (1996) argued that the Scorecard provided the ability to link a company's long-term strategy with its short-term actions, emphasizing that:

> meeting short-term financial targets should not constitute satisfactory performance when other measures indicate that the long-term strategy is either not working or not being implemented well (p. 80).

The Balanced Scorecard (BSC) presents four different perspectives and complements traditional financial indicators with measures of performance for customers, internal processes and learning and growth, and 'translates a company's strategic objectives into a coherent set of performance measures' (Kaplan and Norton, 1993, p. 134) with the customer, business process and learning and growth perspectives being leading indicators of performance (measures of what is happening now) and the financial indicators being the lagging indicators of performance (what has happened in the past) as a consequence of performance against the other three perspectives.

Kaplan and Norton did not prescribe the specific performance measures that should be used for each perspective, but suggested that organizations developed performance measures linked to their strategy and competitive position.

Examples of performance measures in the customer perspective may include market share, customer satisfaction, customer retention and brand reputation. Performance measures in the business process perspective may include quality, on-time delivery, cycle time (from order to delivery) and productivity. In the learning and growth perspective, performance measures may include employee retention and satisfaction, investment in training, research and development expenditure and new patent registrations.

Kaplan and Norton argued that three or four performance measures for each perspective should be sufficient (12 to 16 in total) as any more than that becomes difficult to monitor and issues can subsequently arise about the relative importance of some performance measures over others. The relative importance of performance measures is addressed to some extent in the BSC by the assumption of a hierarchical relationship between the four perspectives, and hence between the four sets of performance measures. Improving learning and growth will transform business processes, which will in turn lead to more satisfied customers and finally to financial performance. Kaplan and Norton also showed that the organizational-level performance measurement approach needed to cascade down through each layer of the organization to business units and ultimately to each employee, so that everyone's goals were linked hierarchically to achieving the organizational goals.

One of the distinguishing features of the BSC is the notion of 'balance', that organizations cannot maximize performance on all four perspectives simultaneously. Rather, optimum overall performance is the likely result of finding the right balance between performance as measured by all four perspectives.

The Balanced Scorecard is shown in Figure 4.5.

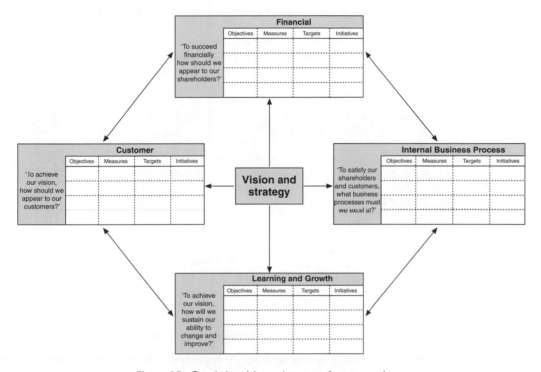

Figure 4.5   Translating vision and strategy: four perspectives.
Source: Reprinted by permission of *Harvard Business Review*. From 'Using the Balanced Scorecard as a strategic management system' by R. S. Kaplan and D. P. Norton, Jan–Feb 1996. Copyright 1996, Harvard Business School Publishing Corporation; all rights reserved.

Strategy mapping (Kaplan and Norton, 2001) is a development of the Balanced Scorecard approach (see Figure 4.6), and reflects the assumptions of the organization's predictive model. A strategy map identifies the assumed cause–effect relationships. Performance targets are developed for each of the elements in the strategy map, and financial resources are allocated (through the budget process) to support the achievement of those targets. Regular monitoring and review of performance takes place through comparing actual performance against targets. Where performance needs to be improved, the strategy mapping process involves making resource reallocations through changing budgets. This approach is challenging to the traditional accounting view of fixed resource allocations for the year. In few organizations are budgets revised in mid-year due to performance shortfalls. However, reallocating budgets mid-year is a logical extension of managing performance more flexibly and this lies at the heart of the strategy mapping process. Strategy mapping is a continual process through which performance measures are used as a method of learning (see Figure 4.1 earlier in this chapter) what works and what doesn't work. Learning results in changes to the assumed cause–effect relationships, and to performance measures and targets.

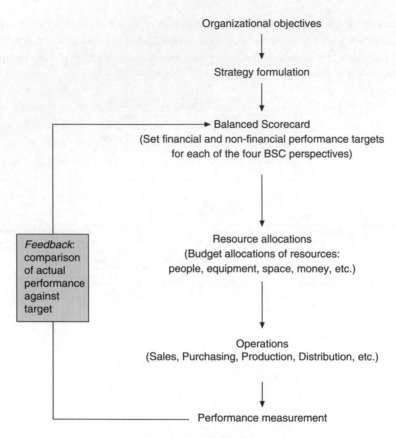

Figure 4.6   Strategy mapping process.

The difficulty with performance measurement systems is that there are multiple stakeholders inside and outside the organization, and their expectations may need to be reconciled. The *Performance Prism* was developed at Cranfield University by Neely *et al.* (2002). It differs from other non-financial performance measurement systems in that it takes a stakeholder approach (see Chapter 2) to the organization, considering for example regulatory agencies, community interest groups and suppliers. This ensures that the performance measurement system presents a balanced picture of business performance. It also differs from Balanced Scorecard-type systems in that the performance measures are not developed from strategy, as Kaplan and Norton (2001) suggest, but they inform management whether the business is going in the intended strategic direction.

Research suggests that the management control paradigm may still be dominated by accounting and that non-financial performance measurement is isolated from, rather than integrated with, financial performance. Despite the proliferation of non-financial measures, many remain rooted in short-term financial quantification. Otley (1999, see earlier in this chapter) concluded that performance *management* (which he contrasted with performance *measurement*) goes beyond the boundaries of traditional management accounting. It is achievable by accountants having a better understanding of the operational activities of the business and building this understanding into control systems design; connecting control systems with business strategy, which has to some extent been addressed by strategic management accounting (see Chapter 18); and focusing on the external environment within which the business operates.

One avenue that may address the need for a more holistic approach to performance management is provided by *enterprise resource planning systems* (see Chapter 9). This is an information system that supports the strategic management process, and aims to overcome the difficulties of integrating information from diverse systems. It is based on the concept of a data warehouse holding large amounts of data that can be accessed by a range of analytical tools such as Balanced Scorecard-type measures, and shareholder value measures. The end result is argued to be faster and better managerial decision making throughout the organization using information captured both from inside and outside the organization.

A theoretical framework for accounting

In this chapter we have identified accounting as part of a broader management control system that is driven by goals and strategy. We have also expanded the notion of management control to incorporate non-financial performance measurement. This description of management control systems implies a cybernetic system of control, with feedforward and feedback processes that influence behaviour and resource allocation decisions.

There are certain assumptions underlying the cybernetic model that are based on what is called a rational or economic *paradigm*, or view of the world. *Rational* means following reasoning as opposed to experience or observation (which is called *empiricism*). The traditional approach to decision making for management control and accounting has been from an *economically rational* perspective. Under this perspective, alternatives can be evaluated and decisions computed as a result of economic preferences.

March and Simon (1958) laid the basis for economic theories of the firm in distinguishing the neoclassical assumption that economic decisions were made by perfectly rational actors possessing relatively complete information aimed at *maximizing* from *satisficing* behaviour. Satisficing is based on *bounded rationality*: actors with general goals searching for whatever solution more or less attained those goals. March and Simon used the example of searching a haystack for the sharpest needle (maximizing) versus searching for a needle sharp enough to sew with (satisficing). March and Simon's notion of bounded rationality recognized that decision-makers have limited information and limited ability to process that information in an uncertain and complex environment.

Scott (1998) described three perspectives on organizations: as rational systems; natural systems; and open systems. We consider natural and open systems in Chapter 5. The *rational perspective* sees organizations as 'purposeful collectivities', i.e. in which the actions of participants are coordinated to achieve defined goals. Organizations are highly formalized with rules governing behaviour and roles which are determined independent of the attributes of the people occupying those roles. Scott argued that Taylor's scientific management, Fayol's administrative theory, Weber's bureaucracy and Simon's theory of administrative behaviour were all examples of rational systems. Rational systems are predicated on the division of labour and specialization of tasks, reducing transaction costs, efficiently processing information and monitoring the work of agents.

Within the rational perspective, accounting has been dominated by the notion of contract, which is reflected in two theories: agency and transaction cost economics. *Agency theory* (see Chapter 6) focuses on the contractual relationship between owners and managers and on the cost of the information needed by owners to monitor contractual performance. The cost of information is also an important aspect of *transaction cost economics* (see Chapter 15), which considers whether transactions should take place in the marketplace (outsourcing) or within the organizational hierarchy (in house).

The rational perspective and the notion of contract determine how the accounting and control systems used by organizations are viewed. However, different perspectives to the rational one will suggest different interpretations of events, grounded in the different ways in which the preparers and users of accounting information may see the world. We return to the theoretical framework of accounting, its assumptions and limitations, throughout this book. We begin with a contrast to the economically rational approach in Chapter 5.

Conclusion

This chapter has shown that in delivering shareholder value, accounting cannot be seen as separate from the organizational control system. Accounting is integral to management control, but many elements of management control do not rely on accounting information. The importance of non-financial performance measurement has been emphasized, particularly the important role played by Kaplan and Norton in developing the Balanced Scorecard and subsequently the strategy mapping approach. Both reflect accounting numbers as lagging measures, with strategy implementation more a question of getting the balance right with performance on customer, business process and learning and growth perspectives.

Accounting and the Balanced Scorecard are, however, rooted in the rational, economics-based paradigm, which emphasizes a goal orientation and a cybernetic control system based on feedback and feedforward. The next chapter provides alternative perspectives on the inter-relationship between accounting and organizations.

References

Alvesson, M. and Karreman, D. (2004). Interfaces of control. Technocratic and socio-ideological control in a global management consultancy firm. *Accounting, Organizations and Society*, 29, 423–44.

Anthony, R. N. (1965). *Planning and Control Systems: A Framework for Analysis*. Boston, MA: Harvard Business School Press.

Anthony, R. N. and Govindarajan, V. (2000). *Management Control Systems* (10th edn). New York: McGraw-Hill Irwin.

Berry, A. J., Broadbent, J. and Otley, D. (1995). The domain of organizational control. In A. J. Berry, J. Broadbent and D. Otley (Eds), *Management Control: Theories, Issues and Practices*. London: Macmillan.

Chenhall, R. H. (2003). Management control systems design within its organizational context: findings from contingency-based research and directions for the future. *Accounting, Organizations and Society*, 28(2–3), 127–68.

Daft, R. L. and Macintosh, N. B. (1984). The nature and use of formal control systems for management control and strategy implementation. *Journal of Management*, 10(1), 43–66.

Downs, A. (1966). *Inside Bureaucracy*. Boston, MA: Little, Brown.

Eccles, R. G. (1991). *The Performance Measurement Manifesto, Getting Numbers You Can Trust: The New Accounting*. Boston, MA: Harvard Business Review Paperbacks.

Emmanuel, C., Otley, D. and Merchant, K. (1990). *Accounting for Management Control* (2nd edn). London: Chapman & Hall.

Euske, K. J., Lebas, M. J., *et al.* (1993). Performance management in an international setting. *Management Accounting Research*,4, 275–99.

Ferreira, A. and Otley, D. (2009). The design and use of performance management systems: an extended framework for analysis. *Management Accounting Research*, 20(4), 263–82.

Hofstede, G. (1981). Management control of public and not-for-profit activities. *Accounting, Organizations and Society*, 6 (3), 193–211.

Innes, J. (1996). Activity performance measures and tableaux de bord. In I. Lapsley and F. Mitchell (Eds), *Accounting and Performance Measurement: Issues in the Private and Public Sectors*. London: Paul Chapman.

Johnson, H. T. and Kaplan, R. S. (1987). *Relevance Lost: The Rise and Fall of Management Accounting*. Boston, MA: Harvard Business School Press.

Kaplan, R. S. and Norton, D. P. (1992). The Balanced Scorecard – Measures that drive performance. *Harvard Business Review, Jan–Feb*, 71–9.

Kaplan, R. S. and Norton, D. P. (1993). Putting the Balanced Scorecard to work. *Harvard Business Review, Sept–Oct*, 134–47.

Kaplan, R. S. and Norton, D. P. (1996). Using the Balanced Scorecard as a strategic management system. *Harvard Business Review, Jan–Feb*, 75–85.

Kaplan, R. S. and Norton, D. P. (2001). *The Strategy-Focused Organization: How Balanced Scorecard Companies Thrive in the New Business Environment*. Boston, MA: Harvard Business School Press.

Machin, J. L. J. (1983). Management control systems: whence and whither? In E. A. Lowe and J. L. J. Machin (Eds), *New Perspectives in Management Control* (pp. 22–42). London: Macmillan.

Malmi, T. and Brown, D. A. (2008). Management control systems as a package – opportunities, challenges and research directions. *Management Accounting Research*, 19, 287–300.

March, J. G. and Simon, H. A. (1958). *Organizations*. Chichester: John Wiley & Sons.

Merchant, K. A. (1998). *Modern Management Control Systems: Text and Cases*. Upper Saddle River, NJ: Prentice Hall.

Meyer, C. (1994). How the right measures help teams excel. *Harvard Business Review, May–June*, 95–103.

Neely, A., Adams, C. and Kennerly, M. (2002). *The Performance Prism: The Scorecard for Measuring and Managing Business Success*. London: Prentice Hall.

Otley, D. (1987). *Accounting Control and Organizational Behaviour*. London: Heinemann.

Otley, D. (1994). Management control in contemporary organizations: towards a wider framework. *Management Accounting Research*, 5, 289–99.

Otley, D. (1999). Performance management: a framework for management control systems research. *Management Accounting Research*, 10, 363–82.

Otley, D. T. and Berry, A. J. (1980). Control, organization and accounting. *Accounting, Organizations and Society*, 5(2), 231–44.

Otley, D. T. and Berry, A. J. (1994). Case study research in management accounting and control. *Management Accounting Research*, 5, 45–65.

Otley, D. T., Berry, A. J. and Broadbent, J. (1995). Research in management control: an overview of its development. *British Journal of Management*, 6, Special Issue, S31–S44.

Ouchi, W. G. (1977). The relationship between organizational structure and organizational control. *Administrative Science Quarterly*, 22, 95–113.

Ouchi, W. G. (1979). A conceptual framework for the design of organizational control mechanisms. *Management Science*, 25(9), 833–48.

Scott, W. R. (1998). *Organizations: Rational, Natural, and Open Systems* (4th edn). Upper Saddle River, NJ: Prentice Hall.

Simons, R. (1990). The role of management control systems in creating competitive advantage: new perspectives. *Accounting, Organizations and Society*, 15(1/2), 127–43.

Simons, R. (1994). How new top managers use control systems as levers of strategic renewal. *Strategic Management Journal*, 15, 169–89.

Simons, R. (1995). *Levers of Control: How Managers Use Innovative Control Systems to Drive Strategic Renewal*. Boston, MA: Harvard Business School Press.

Websites

A useful website on performance measurement and management is provided by the Performance Measurement Association at www.performanceportal.org.

The Management Control Association promotes the study of management control and management accounting. Its website is www.managementcontrolassociation.ac.uk.

Interpretive and Critical Perspectives on Accounting and Decision Making

In Chapter 4 we described the rational-economic paradigm that underpins management control systems in general and accounting reports in particular. There are, however, alternative paradigms. For example, Otley and Berry (1980) questioned the usefulness of cybernetic controls (goal-oriented, with targets and using feedback to take corrective action) given the limitations of accounting systems as a result of organizational complexity and rapid environmental change. Accounting systems provide an important, but limited, perspective on organizations which is enhanced by non-financial performance measurement (as we saw in Chapter 4). However, organizations are typified by more informal, and often more subtle, forms of control than formal systems like accounting and the Balanced Scorecard.

While Chapter 4 assumed a rational paradigm (a paradigm is a way of viewing the world), this chapter explores alternative ways to understand the role played by accounting and management control in organizations. We look at the role of research and review the interpretive paradigm and the social constructionist perspective and how organizational culture is implicated in accounting. We then consider the radical paradigm and how power is a major concern of critical accounting theory. These alternative paradigms to the rational-economic one described in Chapter 4 are an important focus of this book to which we return in subsequent chapters. This chapter concludes with an introduction to ethics as it affects the accountant and manager. We commence with a review of the role of research and theory in management control and accounting.

Research and theory in management control and accounting

Theory is an explanation of what is observed in practice. This is not the 'ivory tower' for which academics are often criticized, but the use of 'real-world' evidence to inform and explain. The development of theory from practice is the result of a process of research. Practice informs theory, which in turn, via various forms of publication and education, can influence the spread of practice between organizations and countries. Otley (2001) argued that management accounting research 'has, in a number of respects, lost touch with management accounting practices' (p. 255), having concentrated too much on accounting and not enough on management. Otley reinforced earlier arguments that management accounting had become 'irrelevant to contemporary organizations, but worse that it was often actually counter-productive to good management decision making' (p. 243) and that we need to 'put the management back into management accounting' (p. 259). Hopper *et al.* (2001) argued that there have been few British scholars who have achieved innovation in practice, either because of 'the anti-intellectualism of British managers and accountants . . . or the marginal role of academics in British policy making' (p. 285), a criticism that could equally be applied to most other English-speaking countries.

An understanding of accounting tools and techniques without an understanding of theory has the same problems as theories divorced from business practice. An understanding of the underlying assumptions of accounting and the limitations of the tools and techniques of accounting is essential. If we ignore those assumptions and limitations, we are likely to make decisions on the basis of numbers alone that do not adequately reflect the complexity of the business environment and the predictive model which underlies the way organizations carry on business (the predictive model was discussed in Chapter 4).

Theory typically takes one of two forms:

- Quantitative studies of a large number of business organizations through surveys or analysis of publicly available data that can be analysed statistically in order to produce generalizations about accounting practice.
- Qualitative studies of a single organization or a small number of organizations through case studies comprising interviews, observation and documentary research that aims to explain accounting practice in the context in which it is situated.

Both methods are valuable in helping to understand accounting practice. The reader is encouraged to look at some of the academic research literature referred to in the chapters throughout this book in order to understand the context of accounting in organizations. The Readings in Part IV of this book are intended to provide readers with an exposure to some key academic accounting literature.

Hopper *et al.* (2001) traced the development of accounting research through four approaches:

- conventional teaching emphasizing the needs of the professional accounting bodies;
- the application of economics and management science;
- history and public-sector accounting;
- behavioural and organizational approaches.

The first approach is that traditionally taken by students of accounting. The second approach relies heavily on econometric and mathematical models, which are outside the scope of this book. This book has taken the view that managers and accountants should take a more interpretive and critical perspective. This implies a concern with organizations that is situated in their historical context, and a behavioural and organizational approach, rooted in the unique circumstance of each organization.

Research in accounting tends to fall into two distinct categories:

- The normative view – *what ought to happen* – that there is one best way of doing accounting, that accounting information is economically rational and serves an instrumental purpose in making decisions in the pursuit of shareholder value. The normative view was reflected in Chapter 4 and is evident through the presentation of accounting tools and techniques in each chapter in Part III.
- The interpretive and critical view – *what does happen* – the explanation of how accounting systems develop and are used in particular organizational settings. This is the subject of this chapter. This view recognizes that people do not necessarily make decisions based on economically rational reasons but have limited information, limited cognitive ability and are influenced by organizational structures and systems (including, but not limited to, accounting systems) and by organizational power and culture. We contrast the normative view with interpretive and critical perspectives in each chapter.

While the normative view is most commonly associated with quantitative studies which examine, for example, the variables that are most likely to be related to organizational performance, the interpretive and critical view tends to be more descriptive or qualitative rather than statistical. This is a necessary approach to explain the practice of accounting in both its organizational setting and the wider social, political and historical context in which it exists.

The study of organizations is important because what happens may be contrary to what management control theory suggests. Kaplan (1986) argued for empirical studies of accounting systems in their organizational contexts, by 'observing skilled practitioners in actual organizations' (p. 441). Kaplan described empirical research methods, especially case or field studies that communicate the 'deep, rich slices of organizational life' (p. 445) and are 'the only mechanism by which management accounting can become a scientific field of inquiry' (p. 448).

The interpretive or critical view has tended to be developed through case study research. The quantitative approach is important in making broad generalizations based on statistical analysis, while the qualitative approach is more situation-specific, and while both research approaches contribute to the development of theory, quantitative studies lead to statistical generalizations while qualitative studies lead to analytic or theoretical generalizations. Spicer (1992) argued that case study research is appropriate when 'why?' or 'how?' questions are asked about contemporary events. He classified two types of case study research: descriptive and/or exploratory; and informing and/or explanatory, arguing that:

> the case method, when used for explanatory purposes, relies on analytical not statistical generalization. The objective of explanatory case research is not to draw inferences to some larger population based on sample evidence, but rather to generalize back to theory (p. 12).

Birnberg (2009) described three periods of accounting research in the USA. In the pre-World War II period, the dominant market for accounting research was practice. The post-war period was a transitional period and can be characterized as one reflecting the professionalization of management education. The modern period reflects a product that is predominantly interested in using tools to contribute to the theoretical literature, i.e. research for research's own sake, and to a far lesser degree with the concerns of practice. Birnberg argued that researchers not only needed to concern themselves with the academic rigour of research, but to make it relevant to practice as well.

Hopper *et al.* (2001) emphasized the rise of behavioural and organizational accounting research since 1975. In the UK, a paradigm shift occurred that did not happen in the USA (where shareholder value using agency theory – see Chapter 6 — remains the dominant research approach), as more sociological and political approaches drew from European social theory and were influenced by Scandinavian case-based research. Under the 'new public management' reforms of the Thatcher and Reagan governments, private-sector approaches were adopted in the public sector, where:

> accounting data and the consulting arms of accounting firms had been central to economic and policy debates, involving privatization, industrial restructuring, reform of the public sector, and worries about de-industrialization . . . it appeared apparent that accounting had to be studied in its broader social, political and institutional context (Hopper *et al.*, 2001, p. 276).

The adoption of efficiency-based practices, often termed 'managerialism' in the public-sector context, is important in the private sector in terms of delivering profitability, but is more questionable in the public sector where there is a far greater focus by professionals on the quality of service delivery, whether that be improved education, health, or justice outcomes, etc.

Hence the need to closely study how management control and accounting are actually used in organizations, and affect organizational decision making. Humphrey and Scapens (1996) argued for the capacity of explanatory case studies 'to move away from managerialist notions of accounting and to provide more challenging reflections on the nature of accounting knowledge and practice' (p. 87) and to its 'intricacies, complexities and inconsistencies' (p. 90).

Theory is integrated with practical examples in this book to reflect the importance of taking not only the rational or economics-based paradigm which is most commonly associated with management control and accounting in particular, but also applies an interpretive and critical perspective on management control and financial statements.

Alternative paradigms

One non-rational approach to decision making is the 'garbage can', which March and Olsen (1976) described as a 'fortuitous confluence' whereby problems, solutions, participants and choice opportunities somehow come together. Cooper *et al.* (1981) detailed the rational model of financial and management accounting systems as planning and control devices that measure, report and evaluate individuals and business units. In the bounded rationality model (see Chapter 4), accounting systems are stabilizers, emphasizing consistency.

By contrast, the garbage-can view recognizes that systems provide an appearance of rationality and create an organizational history, but that 'the sequence whereby actions precede goals may well be a more accurate portrayal of organizational functioning than the more traditional goal–action paradigm' (p. 181) whilst 'accounting systems represent an ex post rationalization of actions, rather than an ex ante statement of organizational goals' (p. 188).

A non-rational (as opposed to irrational) paradigm has also been taken in relation to non-financial performance measurement. For example, Waggoner *et al.* (1999) took a multidisciplinary approach to the drivers of performance measurement systems and identified four categories of force that can influence the evolution of those systems: internal influences such as power relations and dominant coalitions within the firm; external influences such as legislation and technology; process issues such as the implementation of innovation and the management of political processes; and transformational issues including the level of top-down support for, and risks from, change.

Bourne *et al.* (2000) developed a framework for analysing the implementation of a performance measurement system and interpreted three case studies of manufacturing companies against that framework. They identified problems in each company with IT infrastructure, resistance to measurement and management commitment that arose in designing, implementing, using and updating performance measurement systems.

These perspectives can be linked to Scott's (1998) conceptualization of organizations as rational, natural and open systems. Figure 5.1 shows the different perspectives in diagrammatic form. The *rational perspective* is of the organization as a goal-oriented collective that acts purposefully to achieve those goals through a formal structure governing behaviour and the roles of organizational members (see Chapter 4). The *natural perspective* is based on the human relations school and argues that rules and roles do not significantly influence the actions of people in organizations. In this natural perspective people are motivated by self-interest and the informal relations between them are more important than the formal organizational structure in understanding organizational behaviour. These informal relations emphasize the social aspect of organizations, which may operate in *consensus* where common goals are shared or are in *conflict*. Conflictual approaches stress organizational structures as systems of power where the weaker groups are dominated by the more powerful ones.

Both rational and natural perspectives view the organization as a *closed system*, separate from its environment. By contrast, the *open systems perspective* emphasizes the impact of the environment on organizations. In the open perspective, organizations are seen as shifting coalitions of participants and a collection of interdependent activities that are tightly or loosely coupled. Thompson (1967) contrasted the technical core of the organization with its goal achievement and control-oriented rationality, implying a closed system and the elimination of uncertainty, with the organization's dependency and lack of control at an institutional level where the greatest uncertainty existed, implying an open system. Thompson argued that at a managerial level there was mediation between the two, provided by a range of manoeuvring devices and organizational structures (which include management control and accounting systems).

Studies result in competing theories being developed to explain practice. Rational theories are often based on the one 'best way' of doing things, which was developed through the work study methods of Frederick Taylor (1911) and termed 'scientific management'. It is also founded on the work of philosophers like Max Weber (1922/1947) on bureaucracy. Shareholder value (see Chapter 2) lies at the heart of rational theories.

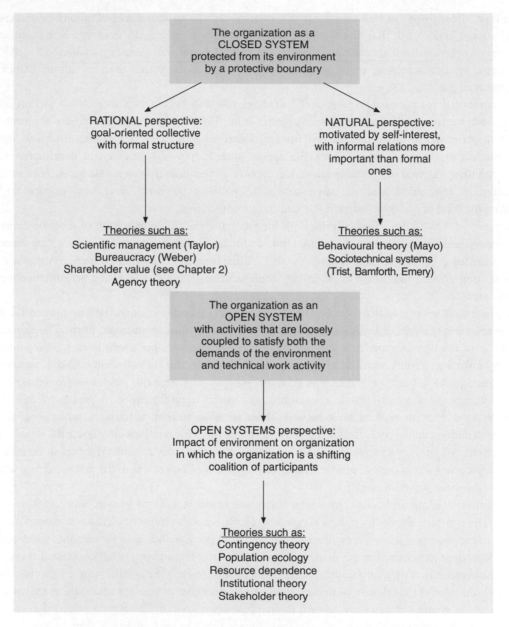

Figure 5.1   Organizations as closed or open systems: Rational, natural and open systems perspectives.
Source: Based on Scott (1998).

Agency theory (see Chapter 6) is the basis of much accounting, with boards of directors and managers acting as the agents of their principals, the shareholders. The natural perspective is based on *behavioural theory* and what is often called the 'Human Relations School' which developed from the work of management researchers such as Elton Mayo (1945) and his experiments at the Hawthorne plant of General Electric, and the socio-technical systems theory of Trist and Bamforth (1951).

Within the open systems perspective, *contingency theory* (see Chapter 13) suggests that there is no one best way of exercising management control or of accounting. The appropriate systems emerge from the influence of the environment (which may be turbulent or static), technology, organizational size, and the need to fit controls and accounting to the organizational strategy, structure and culture. *Population ecology theory* is based on the biological analogy of natural selection and holds that environments select organizations for survival on the basis of the fit between the organizational form and the characteristics of the environment. *Resource dependence theory* emphasizes adaptation as organizations act to improve their opportunity to survive, particularly through the relationships of power that impact the organization. *Institutional theory* (see Chapter 7) stresses the rules that are imposed by external parties, especially by government; the values and norms that are internalized in roles as part of socialization processes; and the cultural controls that underpin the belief systems that are supported by the professions. *Stakeholder theory* (Chapter 2) recognizes that organizations should be accountable to a variety of stakeholders (and not just shareholders as in agency theory).

One problem that has arisen in academic research is the variety of theories used to explain practice, which Humphrey and Scapens (1996) believe excessively dominate the analysis of case study evidence. Similarly, Hopper *et al.* (2001) argued that 'the research thrust may lie in attempting to integrate and consolidate the variety of theories and methodologies which have emerged in recent years, rather than seeking to add yet more' (p. 283).

In their categorization of the nature of knowledge, Burrell and Morgan (1979) proposed four paradigms – functionalist (or rational), interpretive, radical humanist and radical structuralist – based on two dimensions: subjective–objective and regulation–radical change. Figure 5.2 shows a representation of rational, interpretive and radical (or critical) paradigms.

In his classification of the types of management control, Hofstede (1981) separated cybernetic (rational) models from non-cybernetic ones, which were dependent on values and rituals. The cybernetic model of control systems is located in the rational paradigm. Non-cybernetic systems are located in interpretive or critical paradigms. The rational paradigm relies on an 'objectively knowable, empirically verifiable reality' (Boland and Pondy, 1983, p. 223), which has been described in Chapter 4. We turn first to the interpretive paradigm and then to the critical paradigm. Each paradigm is a different way of seeing the world – think of it as taking off one pair of glasses and replacing it with another pair which sees the same things but from a different perspective.

The interpretive paradigm and the social construction perspective

The interpretive view reflects a subjectively created, emergent social reality, which Chua (1986) links to an understanding of 'accounting in action'. The interpretive approach offers 'accounts of what happens as opposed to what should happen' (Chua, 1988, p. 73).

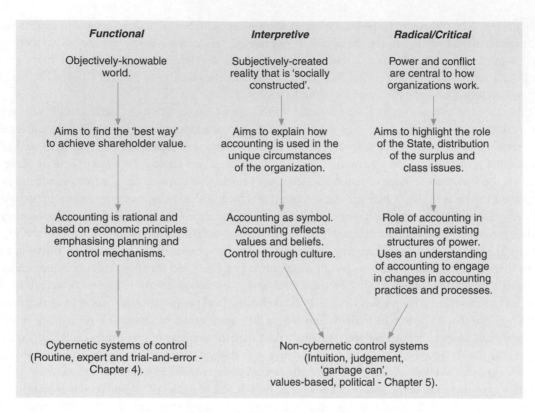

Figure 5.2   Paradigms of understanding.

Hopwood (1983) coined the term *accounting in action* to describe the 'ways in which accounting reflects, reinforces or even constrains the strategic postures adopted by particular organizations' (p. 302). Hopwood (1987) contrasted the constitutive as well as reflective roles of accounting. By separating these, Hopwood recognized that accounting does not merely report (the reflective role) but actually creates the organizational reality (the constitutive role).

The aim of the interpretive perspective is:

> to produce rich and deep understandings of how managers and employees in organizations understand, think about, interact with, and use management accounting and control systems (Macintosh, 1994, p. 4).

Individuals perceive things differently, as a result of their education, past experiences, values, etc. But how individuals perceive is affected significantly by the social groups to which individuals belong (family groups, national cultures, sporting or work groups, etc.). So reality, which in the interpretive paradigm is subjective rather than objective, is not just the result of individual perceptions, but is influenced by social groups – we call this 'socially constructed' reality such that members of particular social groups tend to see the world in a similar way.

Preston (1995) described the social constructionist model of behaviour not as a rational process but a product of the 'creative individual'. Individuals act towards things on the basis of the *meaning* that things have for them. Preston described the critical process that takes place between encountering a situation or event and interpreting it, in which the individual constructs a meaning of the situation or event and acts in accordance with that meaning. Meaning is not inherent, it is brought to the situation by the individual. These meanings are derived through social interaction, the ways in which people meet, talk, work and play together and in doing so construct and share meanings. These meanings are socially constructed, internalized and shared between individuals.

Preston (1995) added that the social constructionist perspective does not preclude the existence of organizational structures and processes, but suggests that these are symbolic representations of a particular view of organizational reality. These meanings are also expressed symbolically through language. In this context accounting information is a symbolic representation of reality. Individual behaviour is guided by the meanings, values and beliefs that are constructed and shared by organizational members. These symbols are then subject to interpretation by individuals, who act towards them on the basis of the meaning they have for them. However, Preston recognized that these structures and processes may influence the development of an organizational culture – the shared values, beliefs and meanings that are collectively held by organizational participants.

Whilst what Alvesson and Karreman (2004) call 'technocratic control' emphasizes plans, arrangements and systems which focus on behaviour and measurable outputs; socio-ideological control comprises efforts to persuade people to adapt to certain values, norms and ideas about what is good, important and praiseworthy in terms of work and organizational life. It comprises methods of controlling worker mindsets through social relations, identity formation and ideology. This distinction between formal and informal elements of control is important because of the role that culture plays in management control and accounting.

Culture, control and accounting

Allaire and Firsirotu (1984) contrasted a *sociostructural* system based on formal structures, strategies, policies and management processes with a *cultural* system based on myths, ideology, values and artefacts and shaped by society, the history of the organization and the contingency factors affecting it. They argued that sociostructural and cultural systems were in a complex relationship, with potential for stress when an organization is subject to sudden pressures for change.

The review of research on organizational culture undertaken by Smircich (1983) reflected a convergence of views around culture as 'shared key values and beliefs' (p. 345). These values and beliefs convey a sense of identity, generate commitment, enhance social system stability and serve as a sense-making device to guide and shape behaviour. Smircich also identified the existence of multiple organization subcultures – a multiplicity of cultures within an organization, rather than one pervading culture.

There are many different ways of describing culture. Handy (1978) described four different organizational cultures: club, based on informal relationships; role, based on tightly defined jobs; task, a focus on solving problems; and existential, an orientation to individual purpose. Deal and Kennedy (1982) identified: tough guy/macho (individualists who take high risks); work hard/play hard (fun and action with low risk); bet-your-company (big stakes decisions); and process (bureaucratic emphasis).

Schein (1988/1968) described the process that brings about change in the values and attitudes of different groups of people throughout their career as 'organizational socialization'. It occurs whenever an individual enters an organization, changes departments or is promoted. Socialization determines employee loyalty, commitment, productivity and turnover. It is the process whereby a new member of a group learns the values, norms and behaviour patterns – the 'price of membership' (p. 54). These norms, values and behaviours are learned from organizational publications, from training, line managers, peers and role models, and from the rewards and punishments that exist. Where the values of the immediate group that the individual joins are out of line with the value system of the organization as a whole, the individual learns the values of the immediate group more quickly than those of the organization. The essence of management, according to Schein, is that managers must understand organizations as social systems that socialize their members, and then gain control over those forces.

Some of the control system frameworks introduced in Chapter 4 included culture. Ouchi (1979) identified three mechanisms for control: market (based on prices); bureaucracy (based on rules); and clan (based on tradition). Clan mechanisms are represented in professions, where different organizations have the same values. Ouchi used the example of a hospital, where a highly formalized and lengthy period of socialization leads to both skill and value training. Simons (1994, 1995) referred to belief systems, and Ferreira and Otley (2009) and Malmi and Brown (2008) both recognized cultural elements to control.

Accounting can be one such element of control. Scott (1998) described accounting systems as 'one of the most important conventions connecting institutionally defined belief systems with technical activities' (p. 137). Scott argued that some organizations rely less on formal controls and more on developing a set of beliefs and norms to guide behaviour.

Langfield-Smith (1995) contrasted culture as the setting for control; as a control mechanism itself; and as a filter for perceiving the environment. Langfield-Smith described a model in which culture facilitates control when the control system is consistent with the social norms of the organization, or inhibits control when it is at variance with those norms. Langfield-Smith also described research in which culture influences the effectiveness of a control system by influencing individual perceptions and value judgements about those perceptions.

Hofstede (1981) argued that control systems must be sensitive to organizational cultures and that those running counter to culture are unlikely to be successfully imposed. Markus and Pfeffer (1983) suggested that resistance to and failure of accounting control systems was common, arguing that control systems will be implemented when they are consistent with the dominant organizational culture and paradigm in their implications for values and beliefs. The idea of resistance brings us to the radical paradigm and a consideration of the role of power in management control and accounting.

The radical paradigm and critical accounting

Radical approaches (Burrell and Morgan, 1979) emphasize broader structural issues such as the role of the State, distribution of the surplus of production and class difference (Hopper *et al.*, 1987). Hopper and Powell (1985) claimed that the rational approach does not address issues of power and conflict and argued that interpretive approaches 'indicate how accounting systems may promote change, albeit within a managerial conception of the term, rather than being stabilizers' (p. 449).

Those writers who sought a more radical interpretation than the interpretive one drew on the work of Karl Marx. In Chapter 1, we saw through the perspective of the Marxist historian Eric Hobsbawm that much of what we take for granted in capitalist society and the role of accounting is a result of the history of industrial revolution and British colonialism, and subsequently American industrial power.

There are three approaches within the radical perspective: political economy, labour process and critical theory (Roslender, 1995). All are concerned with promoting change in the status quo. The *political economy* approach recognizes power and conflict in society and the effect that accounting has on the distribution of income, power and wealth. *Labour process theory* focuses on the corruption of human creativity in the pursuit of wealth, especially deskilling and management control as a reproducer of capitalism, a point taken up effectively by Braverman (1974) who wrote of the degradation of work as a result of industrialization. Labour process theorists argue that:

> the driving force for social change in capitalist society is the development and displacement (i.e. of impediments to capital accumulation and their resolutions) . . . [that] are inherent in the structural instabilities that characterize capitalism's unequal and antagonistic social relations (Neimark and Tinker, 1986, p. 378).

Neimark and Tinker emphasized the 'on-going conflict among and between social classes over the disposition and division of the social surplus' (p. 379) and how '[s]ocial and organizational control systems are not neutral mechanisms in these struggles but are attached to and legitimate concrete power interests' (p. 380).

The third radical perspective, *critical theory*, emphasizes a critique of the status quo and emancipation towards a better life. Hopper and Powell (1985) argued that critical studies show how 'accounting measures alienate through subordinating behaviour to perceived imperatives which are in fact socially created' (p. 454). The role of accounting, according to critical theorists, is to challenge the status quo.

Laughlin (1999) defined *critical accounting* as providing:

> a critical understanding of the role of accounting processes and practices and the accounting profession in the functioning of society and organizations with an intention to use that understanding to engage (where appropriate) in changing these processes, practices and the profession (p. 73).

A critique of accounting training, for example, was provided by Michael Power (1991), who described his own experience of a professional accounting education and argued that 'the lived reality of accounting education shows that it does not serve the functional ends that are claimed for it' (p. 347). He described:

> the institutionalization of a form of discourse in which critical and reflective practices are regarded as 'waffle' . . . of a cynicism and irony among students towards the entire examination process . . . and the public game that they are required to play (p. 350).

Power (1991) concluded that this 'may be dysfunctional for the profession itself and for the goal of producing flexible and critical experts' (p. 351).

Critical theory does not necessarily imply a Marxist view of the world and a desire to overthrow capitalism, but it does imply a questioning and critical approach to the role of accounting in organizations and society. An example of the application of critical theory is provided by Perrow (1991), who argued:

> If one raised profits by externalizing many costs to the community, exploiting the workforce, evading government controls by corrupting officials, manipulating stock values, and controlling the market by forming quasi-cartels or other predatory practices — all common practices in the nineteenth and twentieth century — then profits will not reflect the efficient use of labor, capital, and natural resources (p. 746).

Of course, writing in 1991, Perrow did not realize that these same practices exist in the twenty-first century, and hence critique remains important if society is to improve. Much of critical theory is concerned with opening up the discourse from a narrow economic-rational application of accounting to question its underlying assumptions and its (often dysfunctional) consequences. *Discourse* is a conversation, albeit an informed one, through which arguments and counter-arguments are considered. Accounting is implicated in discourse because in its written form, it presents ostensibly objective 'facts' that contain implicit assumptions. An accounting discourse of profit and return on investment is dominated by an economic-rational logic. Thus, accounting 'serves to construct a particular field of visibility' (Miller and O'Leary, 1987, p. 239), i.e. financial numbers, but which makes some things invisible, or at least less visible.

In promoting critical theory, Broadbent and Laughlin (1997) emphasized 'recognition of the choice between seeking to develop change through meaningful debate [rather than] through the application of power or coercion' (p. 645). However, power is evident in how organizations actually work, and we must consider the role of power in relation to accounting.

Power and accounting

We have seen how control systems and accounting are aimed at influencing behaviour to achieve goals. This is inextricably bound up with a consideration of power. Pfeffer (1992) defined power as

> the potential ability to influence behavior, to change the course of events, to overcome resistance, and to get people to do things that they would not otherwise do (p. 30).

Morgan (1986) identified power as either a resource or a social relation, defining it as 'the medium through which conflicts of interest are ultimately resolved' (p. 158). As a resource, power is concerned with the dependency of one party on particular allocations, and the control over the distribution of that resource by another party. As a social relation, power is concerned with domination of one person (or group) over another. By contrast, Giddens (1976) argued that power does not of itself imply conflict. Because power is linked to the pursuit of interest, it is only when interests do not coincide that power and conflict are related.

Power is implicit in organizational functioning and in the definition of what is important. Child (1972) concluded:

> When incorporating strategic choice in a theory of organization, one is recognizing the operation of an essentially political process in which constraints and opportunities are functions of the power exercised by decision-makers in the light of ideological values (p. 16).

Cooper *et al.* (1981) saw accounting systems having:

> [an] impact on sustaining and influencing an organization's culture and language and in terms of their ideological and legitimizing influence in maintaining systems of power and control in organizations (p. 175).

Markus and Pfeffer (1983) argued that accounting and control systems are related to intra-organizational power:

> because they collect and manipulate information used in decision making . . . [and] because they are used to change the performance of individuals and the outcomes of organizational processes (pp. 206–7).

One only has to observe the budget process in organizations, when accountants exert considerable power over resource allocations to particular business units or functions, and approval over bids for capital expenditure (we explore these issues more in Chapters 14 and 16). In Chapter 4 we described the strategy mapping process (see Figure 4.6) whereby strategy should drive performance targets and in turn budget allocations. However, in most organizations, different power structures are often in place to establish budget strategy, control the budget and set non-financial targets. Different power bases can result in a lack of systematic management control, with each dominant coalition wishing to retain its own power base (i.e. the strategic plan, the budget, or the Balanced Scorecard).

Case study 5.1: easyJet

easyJet provides an interesting and well-known example to illustrate many of the aspects of management control described in Chapter 4 and this chapter as it illustrates rational-economic, interpretive and critical perspectives.

Background

easyJet, the low-cost airline, was founded by Sir Stelios Haji-Ioannou in 1995 and floated on the London Stock Exchange in late 2000, which then valued the company at £777 million. It has subsequently taken over smaller airlines including Go in 2002 from British Airways. It is part of the FTSE 250 index. In its 2010 Annual Report, easyJet reported that it had 196 aircraft flying 540 routes across 30 countries. In financial year 2010, the company carried 50 million passengers, earning revenue of almost £3.6 billion and a net profit before tax of £154 million. The airline is well known internationally through the popular

TV series 'Airline', first aired in 1999, although discontinued in 2007. The company's market capitalization in June 2011 was about £1.5 billion, however, it has never paid a dividend, but plans to do so in 2012. At the time of writing, easyJet's 2010 Annual Report was downloadable from http://corporate.easyjet.com/~/media/Files/E/easyJet/pdf/investors/result-center/easyJet_AR10_18_1_2011.pdf.

Cost advantages

The company's low cost strategy is based on various cost advantages:

- lower administration, e.g. no ticketing costs, no seat allocations;
- direct sales, avoiding travel agent commissions and third-party reservation system costs;
- no free catering or in-flight amenities, which provides opportunity for on-board sales;
- cost reductions by avoidance of exceptions that incur overheads e.g. no unaccompanied children, no pets, no flexibility with late airport check-ins;
- cheaper aircraft (easyJet pitched Boeing against Airbus in the aircraft manufacturers' battle to win orders in 2002);
- lower crew costs through fast airport turnaround, hence higher productivity;
- lower airport costs through use of secondary airports (although the company now has a large base at Gatwick);
- higher seat density – more seats per aircraft;
- use of marginal pricing formula and yield management to maximize capacity utilization and revenue – the average load factor on their aircraft in 2010 was 87%.

Performance measurement

As well as cost control and revenue maximization, the key non-financial performance measures reported in the company's 2010 Annual Report were:

- million seats flown;
- number of passengers;
- load factor (i.e. % of seat capacity utilized);
- available seat kilometres (ASK) – the total number of seats available for passengers multiplied by the number of kilometres flown;
- revenue passenger kilometres (RPK) – the total number of paying passengers carried multiplied by the number of kilometres flown;
- number of sectors (point-to-point destinations);
- average sector length (kilometres).

In addition, it is likely that the company reports internally other performance measures that it does not make public.

Importantly, many of these performance measures are common across the airline industry, including load factor, ASK and RPK. Costs and revenues may be monitored for each route, so that only profitable and strategically important routes are retained.

A rational-economic perspective

easyJet is clearly focused on shareholder value through its focus on revenue growth and profitability. The company's approach to shareholder value is that it has never declared or paid any cash dividends on Ordinary Shares as it preferred to retain the funds for use in the business. However, it does anticipate paying a dividend out of profits for the year ended September 2011.

An interpretive perspective

The interpretive perspective reveals aspects of socially constructed reality and different aspects of interpreting easyJet's performance. easyJet promotes its culture as informal with a very flat management structure and informal dress code in an open plan office environment. However, there have been criticisms of its industrial relations practices, with the CEO admitting in 2011 to a continued deterioration in relationships between the company and its pilots and the pilots union over several years. From the passenger perspective, the low-cost focus of easyJet means that it can be criticized and the 'Airline' TV documentary series has often revealed passenger complaints about easyJet's inflexibility, especially over late airport check-ins. In 2004, easyJet was criticized for failing to observe European Union rules on compensation to passengers who had been denied boarding, or who experienced delays or cancellations. In 2008, the Advertising Standards Authority criticized easyJet's misleading environmental claim in its corporate publicity that its aircraft had lower carbon emissions than its competitors.

A critical perspective

Power is also an important element in understanding easyJet. The company was founded by Stelios Haji-Ioannou who was forced to stand down as chairman of the board when easyJet listed on the Stock Exchange in 2000. However, Stelios remained a director of the company until he resigned in 2010. The Haji-Ioannou family held about 37% of easyJet's shares (as reported in its 2010 Annual Report), and in addition held (through a separate company) a restrictive agreement that controlled the 'easy' brand name and gave Stelios the power to appoint himself as chairman. These rights have been reduced following litigation and agreement between the company and its founder. However, these issues demonstrate the power of an important and influential shareholder set against the expectations of the Stock Exchange for good governance by the board of directors.

Finally in this chapter, we turn to the issue of ethics and how ethical issues affect accounting information and the roles of financial and non-financial managers.

Ethics and accounting

Accounting choices are moral choices:

> Accounting is important precisely to the extent the accountant can transform the world, can influence the lived experience of others in ways which cause that experience to differ from what it would be in the absence of accounting, or in the presence of an alternative kind of accounting (Francis, quoted in Gowthorpe and Blake, 1998, p. 3).

However, many accountants and non-financial managers have not adopted particularly ethical approaches to the preparation, reporting and use of financial information. 'Creative accounting' is a process of artificially manipulating accounting figures by taking advantage of loopholes in accounting rules or making estimates or judgements that are unrealistic, the purpose of which is to present financial statements in a way that shareholders or other stakeholders may prefer. Creative accounting practices have been justified by managers for reasons of income smoothing, to bring profits closer to forecasts or stock market expectations; changing accounting policies to distract attention from poor performance; or maintaining or boosting share prices (Gowthorpe and Blake, 1998).

Despite the role of accounting standards (see Chapter 6) and other regulations, creative accounting has always played a part in the efforts made by a few companies to present their performance in a better light. However, although accounting standards continually improve, there are always loopholes that accountants seem to find as quickly as standards are produced. Griffiths (1986) commented on the power of financial analysts and investment advisers in the City (of London) and the aim of company directors to present the business as having steady growth in income and profits. Smith (1992) was one of the first analysts to describe the techniques adopted by companies and claimed that

> much of the apparent growth in profits which had occurred in the 1980s was the result of accounting sleight of hand rather than genuine economic growth (p. 4).

This desire for a smoothing effect can be achieved by practices such as accruals, stock valuation, creating or reducing provisions, capitalizing or expensing costs (WorldCom fraudulently capitalized expenses as assets) and off-Balance Sheet financing (creating special-purpose entities that hid liabilities from shareholders, which was the main factor in Enron's downfall in the USA). The term 'creative accounting' has tended to be replaced with 'earnings management' in practice. Earnings management is aimed at avoiding the criticism of being creative with financial information, however, whatever the practice is called, directors still aim to satisfy stock market expectations influenced by stock analysts.

Ethics is important for accountants and non-accountants alike. The members of any of the professional accounting bodies are governed by their ethical rules. These rules also provide useful guidance for non-accountants, not only in their dealings with professional accountants, but also in terms of their own behaviour.

A new *Code of Ethics for Professional Accountants* was first introduced in 2006 by the International Federation of Accountants (IFAC) and has been subsequently updated. The latest version of the Code (IFAC, 2010) is in three parts. Part A establishes the fundamental principles of professional ethics for professional accountants and provides a conceptual framework which provides guidance on fundamental ethical principles. Part B applies to professional accountants in public practice. Part C applies to professional accountants in business. The Code states that a distinguishing mark of the accountancy profession is its responsibility to act in the public interest, and not exclusively to satisfy the needs of an individual client or employer. This is an important point and one often overlooked by accountants who seek to serve their clients or employers without regard to their wider effects.

The conceptual framework states that a professional accountant is required to comply with the following fundamental principles:

- *Integrity*: A professional accountant should be straightforward and honest in all professional and business relationships.
- *Objectivity*: A professional accountant should not allow bias, conflict of interest or undue influence of others to override professional or business judgements.
- *Professional competence and due care*: A professional accountant has a continuing duty to maintain professional knowledge and skill at the level required to ensure that a client or employer receives competent professional service based on current developments in practice, legislation and techniques. A professional accountant should act diligently and in accordance with applicable technical and professional standards when providing professional services.
- *Confidentiality*: A professional accountant should respect the confidentiality of information acquired as a result of professional and business relationships and should not disclose any such information to third parties without proper and specific authority unless there is a legal or professional right or duty to disclose.
- *Professional behaviour*: A professional accountant should comply with relevant laws and regulations and should avoid any action that discredits the profession.

The conceptual framework underlying the fundamental principles requires a professional accountant to identify, evaluate and address threats to compliance with the fundamental principles, rather than merely comply with a set of specific rules. Compliance with the fundamental principles may potentially be threatened by a broad range of circumstances. Threats may fall into the following categories:

- Self-interest threats, which may occur as a result of the financial or other interests of a professional accountant or of an immediate or close family member.
- Self-review threats, which may occur when a previous judgement needs to be re-evaluated by the professional accountant responsible for that judgement.
- Advocacy threats, which may occur when a professional accountant promotes a position or opinion to the point that the accountant's objectivity may be compromised.
- Familiarity threats, which may occur when, because of a close personal relationship, a professional accountant becomes too sympathetic to the interests of others.
- Intimidation threats, which may occur when a professional accountant may be deterred from acting objectively by threats, whether actual or perceived.

In attempting to resolve potential ethical problems, a professional accountant should determine the appropriate course of action that is consistent with the fundamental principles. The professional accountant should also weigh the consequences of each possible course of action. It may be in the best interests of the professional accountant to document the substance of the issue and details of any discussions held or decisions taken, concerning that issue. Where a matter involves a conflict with, or within, an organization, a professional accountant should also consider consulting with those charged with governance of the organization, such as the board of directors or the audit committee. If a significant conflict cannot be resolved, a professional accountant may wish to obtain professional advice from the relevant professional body or legal advisors, and thereby obtain guidance on ethical issues without breaching confidentiality. The professional accountant should consider obtaining legal advice to determine whether there is a legal requirement to report. If, after exhausting all relevant possibilities, the ethical conflict remains unresolved, a professional accountant should, where possible, refuse to remain associated with the matter creating the conflict. The professional accountant may determine that, in the circumstances, it is appropriate to withdraw from the specific assignment, or to resign altogether from the engagement, the firm or the employing organization.

While non-financial managers are not bound by any accounting Code of Ethics, different professions may have their own codes that do apply. Nevertheless, the basic principles of integrity, objectivity, competence and due care, confidentiality and standards of behaviour are societal expectations of most people and are difficult to ignore. Therefore, all managers, when faced with ethical issues, need to consider and weigh the consequences of alternative courses of action. One simple test is whether you would be happy to see your name and your actions reported on the front page of the daily newspaper. If you would find such a report embarrassing and necessitating your accountability for those actions, this may be an indication that the actions may be unethical. Such a standard was clearly not applied by the staff of Enron and WorldCom.

Case study 5.2: Enron

In December 2001, US energy trader Enron collapsed. Enron was the largest bankruptcy in US history. Even though the USA was believed by many to be the most regulated financial market in the world, it was evident from Enron's collapse that investors were not properly informed about the significance of off-Balance Sheet transactions. Enron had taken out large loans that were created through special-purpose entities such that they were not treated as liabilities in Enron's financial reports. US accounting rules may have contributed to this, in that they are concerned with the strict legal ownership of investment vehicles rather than with their control. There were some indications that Enron may have actively lobbied against changing the treatment in US financial reporting of special-purpose entities used in off-balance sheet financing. As a consequence of the failure of Enron and WorldCom, the USA introduced Sarbanes–Oxley legislation to address many of the criticisms of reporting and auditing practice.

Former chief executive Kenneth Lay died in 2006 before he could stand trial. Enron's former chief financial officer Andrew Fastow was sentenced to prison in 2006 for stealing from Enron and devising schemes to deceive investors about the energy company's true financial condition. Lawyers have to date won settlements totalling US$7.3 billion from banks including JPMorgan Chase, Bank of America, and Citigroup.

Case study 5.3: WorldCom

WorldCom filed for bankruptcy protection in June 2002. The company had used accounting tricks to conceal a deteriorating financial condition and to inflate profits. It was the biggest corporate fraud in history, largely a result of treating operating expenses as capital expenditure. WorldCom (now renamed MCI) admitted in March 2004 that the total amount by which it had misled investors over the previous 10 years was almost US$75 billion (£42 billion) and reduced its stated pre-tax profits for 2001 and 2002 by that amount. The Securities and Exchange Commission (SEC) said WorldCom had committed 'accounting improprieties of unprecedented magnitude' – proof, it said, of the need for reform in the regulation of corporate accounting.

Former WorldCom chief executive Bernie Ebbers resigned in April 2002 amid questions about US $366 million in personal loans from the company and a federal probe of its accounting practices. Ebbers was subsequently charged with conspiracy to commit securities fraud and filing misleading data with the SEC and is currently serving a 25-year prison term. Scott Sullivan, former chief financial officer, pleaded guilty to three criminal charges and was sentenced to five years in prison as part of a plea agreement in which he testified against Ebbers.

Conclusion

This chapter has balanced the rational, economics-based paradigm of management control in Chapter 4 with a more interpretive and critical approach. We began with an overview of how research has developed different insights into accounting and broader management control practices and introduced a number of theories that are aimed at explaining how organizations actually work. We then considered alternative paradigms through open/closed systems, and rational/natural approaches. We looked at the interpretive paradigm and how reality can be socially constructed, and the relationship between culture, control and accounting. We then looked at the radical or critical paradigm and the relationship between power and accounting. While much of accounting relies on the rational-economic paradigm, we will return to make comparisons with interpretive and critical perspectives throughout this book. So for example, Chapter 7 applies these different perspectives to financial statements, Chapter 13 applies them to costs and Chapter 17 addresses budgets. However, a practical difficulty in adopting a perspective other than the rational-economic one is that organizational discourse suggests that the rational-economic perspective of shareholder value is the only valid one, while individuals often act in the pursuit of power and self-interest.

Otley *et al.* (1995) suggested that while the definition of management control was 'managerialist in focus . . . this should not preclude a critical stance and thus a broader choice of theoretical approaches' (p. S42).

The aim of interpretive and critical accounting is to promote a greater level of self-awareness in management accountants and so develop an improved use of accounting information by managers that is more insightful as to its consequences (Roslender, 1995). An advantage in understanding interpretive and critical alternatives to the rational-economic one is what Covaleski *et al.* (1996) called 'paradigmatic pluralism . . . alternative ways of understanding the multiple roles played by management accounting in organizations and society' (p. 24). The full text of the Covaleski *et al.* paper is included as one of the readings in Part IV of this book.

Now and again, it is worthwhile removing our rational-economic glasses and looking at the world through the lens of interpretive and critical theory. After you have read Chapters 4 and 5, you should now read and think about Reading B, which describes the development of approaches to management control and the role of accounting in terms of open/closed and rational/natural system perspectives. You should also read and think about Reading C which contrasts contingency theory (a rational theory) with interpretive and critical perspectives. The Readings are in Part IV of this book.

References

Allaire, Y. and Firsirotu, M. E. (1984). Theories of organizational culture. *Organization Studies, 5*(3), 193–226.

Alvesson, M. and Karreman, D. (2004). Interfaces of control. Technocratic and socio-ideological control in a global management consultancy firm. *Accounting, Organizations and Society, 29*, 423–44.

Birnberg, J. G. (2009). The case for post-modern management accounting: thinking outside the box. *Journal of Management Accounting Research, 21*, 3–18.

Boland, J. R. J. and Pondy, L. R. (1983). Accounting in organizations: a union of natural and rational perspectives. *Accounting, Organizations and Society, 8*(2/3), 223–34.

Bourne, M., Mills, J., Wilcox, M., Neely, A. and Platts, K. (2000). Designing, implementing and updating performance measurement systems. *International Journal of Operations and Production Management, 20*(7), 754–71.

Braverman, H. (1974). *Labor and Monopoly Capital: The Degradation of Work in the Twentieth Century.* New York: Monthly Review Press.

Broadbent, J. and Laughlin, R. (1997). Developing empirical research: an example informed by a Habermasian approach. *Accounting, Auditing and Accountability Journal, 10*(5), 622–48.

Burrell, G. and Morgan, G. (1979). *Sociological Paradigms and Organizational Analysis.* London: Heinemann.

Child, J. (1972). Organizational structure, environment and performance: the role of strategic choice. *Sociology, 6*, 1–22.

Chua, W. F. (1986). Radical developments in accounting thought. *Accounting Review, LXI*(4), 601–32.

Chua, W. F. (1988). Interpretive sociology and management accounting research – a critical review. *Accounting, Auditing and Accountability Journal, 1*(2), 59–79.

Cooper, D. J., Hayes, D. and Wolf, F. (1981). Accounting in organized anarchies: understanding and designing accounting systems in ambiguous situations. *Accounting, Organizations and Society, 6*(3), 175–91.

Covaleski, M. A., Dirsmith, M. W. and Samuel, S. (1996). Managerial accounting research: the contributions of organizational and sociological theories. *Journal of Management Accounting Research, 8*, 1–35.

Deal, T. E. and Kennedy, A. A. (1982). *Corporate Cultures.* Reading, MA: Addison-Wesley.

Ferreira, A. and Otley, D. (2009). The design and use of performance management systems: an extended framework for analysis. *Management Accounting Research, 20*(4), 263–82.

Giddens, A. (1976). *New Rules of Sociological Method: A Positive Critique of Interpretative Sociologies.* London: Hutchinson.

Gowthorpe, C. and Blake, J. (Eds) (1998). *Ethical Issues in Accounting.* London: Routledge.

Griffiths, I. (1986). *Creative Accounting: How to Make Your Profits What You Want Them to Be.* London: Waterstone.

Handy, C. (1978). *Understanding Organizations.* Harmondsworth: Penguin.

Hofstede, G. (1981). Management control of public and not-for-profit activities. *Accounting, Organizations and Society, 6*(3), 193–211.

Hopper, T. and Powell, A. (1985). Making sense of research into the organizational and social aspects of management accounting: a review of its underlying assumptions. *Journal of Management Studies*, *22*(5), 429–65.

Hopper, T., Otley, D. and Scapens, B. (2001). British management accounting research: whence and whither: opinions and recollections. *British Accounting Review*, *33*, 263–91.

Hopper, T., Storey, J. and Willmott, H. (1987). Accounting for accounting: towards the development of a dialectical view. *Accounting, Organizations and Society*, *12*(5), 437–56.

Hopwood, A. G. (1983). On trying to study accounting in the contexts in which it operates. *Accounting, Organizations and Society*, *8*(2/3), 287–305.

Hopwood, A. G. (1987). The archaeology of accounting systems. *Accounting, Organizations and Society*, *12*(3), 207–34.

Humphrey, C. and Scapens, R. W. (1996). Theories and case studies of organizational and accounting practices: limitation or liberation? *Accounting, Auditing and Accountability Journal*, *9*(4), 86–106.

International Federation of Accountants (IFAC, 2010). *Handbook of the Code of Ethics for Professional Accountants*.

Kaplan, R. S. (1986). The role for empirical research in management accounting. *Accounting, Organizations and Society*, *11*(4/5), 429–52.

Langfield-Smith, K. (1995). *Organizational culture and control*. In A. J. Berry, J. Broadbent and D. Otley (Eds), *Management Control: Theories, Issues and Practices*. London: Macmillan.

Laughlin, R. (1999). Critical accounting: nature, progress and prognosis. *Accounting, Auditing and Accountability Journal*, *12*(1), 73–8.

Macintosh, N. B. (1994). *Management Accounting and Control Systems: An Organizational and Behavioral Approach*. Chichester: John Wiley & Sons.

Malmi, T. and Brown, D. A. (2008). Management control systems as a package – opportunities, challenges and research directions. *Management Accounting Research*, *19*, 287–300.

March, J. G. and Olsen, J. P. (1976). *Ambiguity and Choice in Organizations*. Bergen: Universitetsforiagen.

Markus, M. L. and Pfeffer, J. (1983). Power and the design and implementation of accounting and control systems. *Accounting, Organizations and Society*, *8*(2/3), 205–18.

Mayo, E. (1945). *The Social Problems of an Industrial Civilization*. Boston, MA: Harvard Business School Press.

Miller, P. and O'Leary, T. (1987).Accounting and the construction of the governable person. *Accounting, Organizations and Society*, *12*(3), 235–65.

Morgan, G. (1986). *Images of Organization*. Newbury Park, CA: Sage.

Neimark, M. and Tinker, T. (1986). The social construction of management control systems. *Accounting, Organizations and Society*, *11*(4/5), 369–95.

Otley, D. (2001). Extending the boundaries of management accounting research: developing systems for performance management. *British Accounting Review*, *33*, 243–61.

Otley, D. T. and Berry, A. J. (1980). Control, organization and accounting. *Accounting, Organizations and Society*, *5*(2), 231–44.

Otley, D. T., Berry, A. J. and Broadbent, J. (1995). Research in management control: an overview of its development. *British Journal of Management*, *6*, Special Issue, S31–S44.

Ouchi, W. G. (1979). A conceptual framework for the design of organizational control mechanisms. *Management Science*, *25*(9), 833–48.

Perrow, C. (1991). A society of organizations. *Theory and Society*, *20*(6), 725–62.

Pfeffer, J. (1992). *Managing with Power: Politics and Influence in Organizations*. Boston, MA: Harvard Business School Press.

Power, M. K. (1991). Educating accountants: towards a critical ethnography. *Accounting, Organizations and Society*, *16*(4), 333–53.

Preston, A. (1995). *Budgeting, creativity and culture*. In D. Ashton, T. Hopper and R. W. Scapens (Eds), *Issues in Management Accounting* (2nd edn). London: Prentice Hall.

Roslender, R. (1995). *Critical management accounting*. In D. Ashton, T. Hopper and R. W. Scapens (Eds), *Issues in Management Accounting* (2nd edn). London: Prentice Hall.

Schein, E. H. (1988/1968). Organizational socialization and the profession of management. *Sloan Management Review*, Fall, 53–65.

Scott, W. R. (1998). *Organizations: Rational, Natural, and Open Systems* (4th edn). Upper Saddle River, NJ: Prentice Hall.

Simons, R. (1994). How new top managers use control systems as levers of strategic renewal. *Strategic Management Journal*, 15, 169–89.

Simons, R. (1995). *Levers of Control: How Managers Use Innovative Control Systems to Drive Strategic Renewal*. Boston, MA: Harvard Business School Press.

Smircich, L. (1983). Concepts of culture and organizational analysis. *Administrative Science Quarterly*, 28, 339–58.

Smith, T. (1992). *Accounting for Growth: Stripping the Camouflage from Company Accounts*. London: Century Business.

Spicer, B. H. (1992). The resurgence of cost and management accounting: a review of some recent developments in practice, theories and case research methods. *Management Accounting Research*, 3, 1–37.

Taylor, F. W. (1911). *Scientific Management: Comprising Shop Management; the Principles of Scientific Management; Testimony before the Special House Committee*. New York: Harper & Brothers.

Thompson, J. (1967). *Organizations in Action: Social Science Bases of Administrative Theory*. New York: McGraw-Hill.

Trist, E. L. and Bamforth, K. W. (1951). Social and psychological consequences of the Longwall method of coal-getting. *Human Relations*, 4, 3–28.

Weber, M. (1922/1947). *The Theory of Social and Economic Organization*. Oxford: Oxford University Press.

Waggoner, D. B., Neely, A. D. and Kennerley, M. P. (1999). The forces that shape organizational performance measurement systems: an interdisciplinary review. *International Journal of Production Economics*, 60, 53–60.

The Use of Financial Statements for Decision Making

The major concern of this book is with accounting information for decision making, so financial statements provide a crucial ingredient to decision making due to the importance of shareholder value (as we saw in Chapter 2). Therefore, the concept of 'decision usefulness', i.e. the value of information for making decisions, while largely based on notions of cost (the recurrent theme in Part III), is also intertwined with the value of the business as perceived by shareholders and capital markets. Thus the focus of Part II is on understanding and interpreting financial statements. Our focus here is not so much on how investors use financial information to make investment decisions, but on how managers can interpret and use the expectations of shareholders and the financial information they have at hand to make decisions that contribute to improving shareholder value.

Chapter 6 describes the main financial statements and the accruals basis and accounting standards that underpin them. Chapter 7 helps the reader to interpret the main financial statements using the tool of ratio analysis. Chapter 8 is concerned with accounting for inventory, which is a crucial link between financial accounting and management accounting. The introduction to financial accounting in these chapters is an important building block for an understanding of management accounting in Part III.

Constructing Financial Statements: IFRS and the Framework of Accounting

The chapter begins with International Financial Reporting Standards (IFRS) and the *Framework for the Preparation and Presentation of Financial Statements* which sets out the concepts underlying the preparation and presentation of financial statements for external users. The chapter then introduces each of the principal financial statements: Statement of Comprehensive Income; Statement of Financial Position; and Statement of Cash Flow. It describes examples of the accruals or matching principle, which emphasizes prepayments, accruals and provisions such as depreciation. The chapter then describes four important accounting treatments: sales taxes; goodwill; research and development; and leases. The chapter concludes with an introduction to agency theory and a critical perspective on financial statements and accounting standards.

As we saw in Chapter 1, accounting provides an account – an explanation or report in financial terms – about the transactions of an organization. Accounting enables managers to satisfy the *stakeholders* in the organization (owners, government, financiers, suppliers, customers, employees etc.) that they have acted in the best interests of stakeholders rather than themselves. We referred to this in Chapter 1 as *accountability*.

These explanations are provided to stakeholders through financial statements, often referred to as the company's 'accounts'. The main financial statements are: the Income Statement (previously called the Profit and Loss account); the Statement of Comprehensive Income (which is an extended Income Statement); the Statement of Financial Position (previously, and still more commonly called the Balance Sheet); and Statement of Cash Flows. The first two of these were introduced briefly in Chapter 3.

International Financial Reporting Standards (IFRS)

Accounting standards reflect the basic accounting principles that are generally accepted by the accounting profession (see Chapter 3) and which are an essential requirement under the Companies Act for reporting financial information. Historically, each country had its own set of accounting standards. The move towards the harmonization of accounting standards between countries through the work of the International Accounting Standards Board (IASB) has been a consequence of the globalization of capital markets, with the consequent need for accounting rules that can be understood by international investors. The dominance of multinational corporations and the desire of companies to be listed on multiple stock exchanges have led to the need to rationalize different reporting practices in different countries to enable comparisons between the financial statements of companies irrespective of national jurisdiction.

The IASB has sole responsibility for setting accounting standards. It comprises 14 individuals. Of those, at least five are practising auditors, at least three are preparers of financial statements, at least three are users of financial statements and at least one is an academic. The objectives of the IASB are:

- to develop a single set of high quality, understandable, enforceable and globally accepted international financial reporting standards;
- to promote the use and rigorous application of those standards;
- to take account of the financial reporting needs of emerging economies and small and medium-sized entities; and
- to bring about convergence of national accounting standards and IFRSs to high quality solutions (Source: http://www.ifrs.org/The+organisation/IASCF+and+IASB.htm).

International Financial Reporting Standards (IFRS) are published by the IASB. The predecessor of the IASB was the Board of the International Accounting Standards Committee (IASC) which published International Accounting Standards (IAS). The term International Financial Reporting Standards (IFRS) includes both the newer IFRS and the older IAS, together with Interpretations issued under these standards. The European Union mandated that all companies must adopt IFRS by 2005. Australia adopted IFRS from 2005 and adoption of IFRS is mandated in Canada from 2011. China has also effectively converged with IFRS. All major economies have established time lines to converge with or adopt IFRS. The international convergence efforts are supported by the Group of 20 Leaders (G20) who, at their September 2009 meeting in the USA, called on international accounting bodies to redouble their efforts to achieve this objective. In the USA, the equivalent of IFRS is Generally Accepted Accounting Principles (GAAP). In the UK, accounting standards are said to be 'principles-based' rather than the 'rules-based' approach in the USA. The rules-based approach has been criticized following the failures of Enron and WorldCom.

The IASB and the US Financial Accounting Standards Board (FASB) is involved in a convergence project which is expected to report in late 2011.

In the UK, the Financial Reporting Council (FRC) is the independent regulator responsible for promoting high-quality corporate governance and reporting to foster investment. The FRC promotes high standards of corporate governance through the UK Corporate Governance Code (see Chapter 2), sets standards for corporate reporting, and monitors and enforces accounting and auditing standards. The FRC also oversees the regulatory activities of the professional accountancy bodies and operates independent disciplinary arrangements for public interest cases involving accountants. The FRC comprises the Accounting Standards Board and the Financial Reporting Review Panel.

The Accounting Standards Board issues accounting standards for the UK but is increasingly focused on influencing the setting of IFRS by the IASB. The Financial Reporting Review Panel reviews company accounts for compliance with the law and accounting standards. The Panel reviews the annual accounts of some 300 public and large private companies a year. It is the role of the Panel to enquire into cases where, in the words of the Companies Act, it appears to the Panel that there is, or may be, a question of whether accounts comply with the requirements of the Act.

IFRS set out recognition, measurement, presentation and disclosure requirements dealing with transactions and events that are important in general-purpose financial statements, although some standards refer to specific industries. General-purpose financial statements are directed towards the common information needs of a wide range of users. A full list of IFRS is contained in the Appendix to this chapter. While IFRS are designed for profit-oriented entities, many organizations in the not-for-profit or public sector may find them appropriate, and many such entities will use IFRS in the preparation of their financial statements. Australia has already adopted IFRS for its public-sector entities.

The IASB has produced a *Framework for the Preparation and Presentation of Financial Statements*. While this is not part of IFRS, the *Framework* is used when an accounting policy is needed and there is no appropriate Standard to choose. All IFRS are based on the *Framework*.

Framework for the Preparation and Presentation of Financial Statements

A complete set of financial statements includes a:

- Statement of Financial Position (previously Balance Sheet);
- Income Statement and/or Statement of Comprehensive Income;
- Statement of Changes in Equity (i.e. changes in shareholders' funds);
- Statement of Cash Flows (previously Cash Flow Statement);
- Explanatory Policies and Explanatory Notes.

Information about financial position is primarily provided in the Statement of Financial Position. Information about performance is primarily provided in the Statement of Comprehensive Income. Information about changes in financial position is provided by way of a separate financial statement, although the Statement of Cash Flows is largely concerned with this.

Users of financial statements are defined as:

- investors;
- employees;
- lenders;

- suppliers and trade creditors;
- customers;
- government and their agencies;
- the public.

Importantly, management is not defined as a user in terms of financial statements. This is because management has the ability to determine the form and content of additional information to meet its needs. The reporting of information to meet such needs is beyond the scope of the *Framework*. Part III of this book is concerned with the information needs of managers, although, as we will see in Chapter 7, the analysis and interpretation of financial performance trends and benchmarks through ratio analysis is important for managers in improving shareholder value.

The *Framework* sets out the concepts underlying the preparation and presentation of financial statements for external users. Where there is conflict between the requirements of a Standard and the *Framework*, the Standard prevails. The *Framework* is concerned with:

1. the objectives of financial statements;
2. the qualitative characteristics that determine decision usefulness;
3. the definition, recognition and measurement of the elements from which financial statements are constructed;
4. concepts of capital maintenance.

Each of these is considered in turn.

Objectives of financial statements

The objective of financial statements is to provide information about the financial position, performance and changes in financial position (i.e. cash flow) of an entity that is useful to a wide range of users in making economic decisions (i.e. 'decision usefulness'). The financial statements show the results of the stewardship or accountability of management for the resources entrusted to them by shareholders.

Qualitative characteristics of financial statements

The underlying assumptions of financial statements are that they are prepared on an accruals basis and as a going concern (see Chapter 3, note that accruals accounting is covered later in this chapter). The following qualitative characteristics make the information useful to users. These are:

1. *Understandability*: users are assumed to have a reasonable knowledge of business and economic activities and accounting.
2. *Relevance*: information must be relevant to the decision-making needs of users. The relevance of information is affected by its nature and *materiality*. Information is material if its omission or misstatement could influence the economic decisions of users taken on the basis of financial statements.

3. *Reliability*: information is reliable when it is free from material error and bias and can be depended upon by users to *represent faithfully* that which it purports to represent. To be represented faithfully, it is necessary that transactions are accounted for and presented in accordance with their substance and economic reality and not merely their legal form, which may be contrived (this is called *'substance over form'* – see the case studies of Enron and WorldCom in Chapter 5). Information may lose its relevance and reliability if there is undue delay in reporting.

4. *Comparability*: users must be able to compare the financial statements of an entity through time and compare the financial statements of different entities in order to evaluate their relative financial position, performance and changes in financial position. Measurement and presentation must therefore be consistent throughout an entity and over time (see Elements of financial statements below). Importantly, users must be informed of the accounting policies employed in the preparation of financial statements, any changes in those policies and the effects of those changes (the principle of consistency, introduced in Chapter 3). However, it is not appropriate for an entity to leave its accounting policies un-changed when more relevant and reliable alternatives exist. The corresponding information for the preceding period is essential for comparability.

Elements of financial statements

Financial reports portray the financial effects of transactions by grouping them into broad classes according to their economic characteristics. These broad classes are the elements of financial statements. The elements related to the measurement of financial position in the Statement of Financial Position are assets, liabilities and equity. The elements related to the measurement of performance in the Statement of Comprehensive Income are income and expenses.

Recognition is the process of incorporating in the Statement of Financial Position or Statement of Comprehensive Income an item that meets the definition of an element. Recognition depicts an item in words and a monetary amount and the inclusion of that figure in the Statement of Financial Position or Statement of Comprehensive Income totals. An item that meets the definition of an element should be recognized if:

- it is probable that any future economic benefit associated with the item will flow to or from the entity; and
- the item has a cost or value that can be measured with reliability.

An item that has the characteristics of an element but does not meet these criteria for recognition may warrant disclosure in a Note to the financial statements (see Chapter 7).

An asset is not recognized in the Statement of Financial Position when expenditure has been incurred for which it is considered improbable that economic benefits will flow to the entity beyond the current accounting period. This should be treated as an expense (see the WorldCom case study in Chapter 5).

A liability is recognized in the Statement of Financial Position when it is probable that an outflow of resources which have economic benefit will result from the settlement of a present obligation.

Measurement is the process of determining the monetary amounts at which the elements of the financial statements are to be recognized and carried in the Statement of Financial Position and Statement of Comprehensive Income. There are four bases of measurement:

- *Historical cost*: assets are recorded at the cash or fair value consideration given at the time of their acquisition.
- *Current cost*: assets are carried at the cash amount that would have to be paid if the same or equivalent asset was acquired currently.
- *Realizable value*: assets are carried at the cash amount that could currently be obtained by selling the asset.
- *Present value*: assets are carried at the present discounted value of the future net cash inflows that the item is expected to generate (see Chapter 14 for a full explanation of present discounted value).

The most common measurement basis is historical cost. However:

- inventories are usually carried at the lower of cost or net realizable value (see Chapter 8);
- marketable investments are carried at market value;
- pension liabilities are carried at present value.

Concepts of capital maintenance

The *financial* concept of capital comprises invested money, being equal to net assets or the equity of a company. The *physical* concept of capital refers to the productive capacity of the business. The concept chosen indicates the goal to be attained in determining profit.

Capital maintenance provides the linkage between concepts of capital and profit because it provides the point of reference as to how profit is measured. Under *financial capital maintenance*, a profit is earned only if the financial amount of net assets at the end of a period exceeds the financial amount of net assets at the beginning of a period, excluding distributions to (i.e. dividends) and contributions from (i.e. share issues) shareholders. Under *physical capital maintenance*, a profit is earned only if the physical productive capacity of the business at the end of a period exceeds the physical productive capacity at the beginning of a period, after excluding distributions to and contributions from shareholders.

The physical capital maintenance concept requires the adoption of the current cost basis of measurement, which is not a requirement of financial capital maintenance. The principal difference between the two concepts is the treatment of changes in the prices of assets and liabilities. For the purposes of this book, we will assume that the concept of financial capital maintenance applies.

True and fair view

In addition to the need to comply with IFRS, the presentation of financial statements must comply with Chapter 4 of the Companies Act, 2006, which requires the financial statements to represent a *'true and fair* view' of the state of affairs of the company and its profits. The Companies Act requires directors to state whether the accounts have been prepared in accordance with international accounting standards and to explain any significant departures from those standards. For companies listed on the Stock Exchange, there are 'Listing Rules' that require the disclosure of additional information (see Chapter 2). Although the *Framework* does not deal directly with the need for a 'true and fair view', the application of the qualitative characteristics and the appropriate accounting standards normally results in financial statements that convey what is generally understood as a true and fair view.

The requirement for a true and fair view has never been tested at law, but it takes precedence over accounting standards. The notion of 'true and fair' is somewhat subjective and it can be argued that it encourages flexibility and can provide the potential to ignore accounting standards because of the 'true and fair view' override. The Financial Reporting Review Panel has the power to seek revision of a company's accounts where those accounts do not comply with accounting standards and if necessary to seek a court order to ensure compliance. The US equivalent under GAAP to the 'true and fair view' is that financial statements be 'presented fairly and in accordance with generally accepted accounting principles'.

We now turn to the first financial statement: the Statement of Comprehensive Income.

Reporting profitability: the Statement of Comprehensive Income

Businesses exist to make a profit. Thus, as we saw in Chapter 3, the basic accounting concept is that:

$$\textbf{profit} = \textbf{income} - \textbf{expenses}$$

If expenses exceed income, the result is a loss.

Profits are determined by the matching principle – *matching income earned with the expenses incurred in earning that income*. Income is the value of sales of goods or services produced by the business. The IFRS definition is that income is increases in economic benefits during the accounting period. Expenses are all the costs incurred in buying, making or providing those goods or services and all the marketing and selling, production, logistics, human resource, IT, financing, administration and management costs involved in operating the business. Expenses are decreases in economic benefits during the accounting period.

The definition of income includes both revenue and gains. Revenue arises in the ordinary course of business (e.g. sales, fees, interest, dividends, royalties and rent). Gains represent other items such as income from the disposal of non-current assets or revaluations of investments. Gains are usually disclosed separately in the financial statements.

The definition of expenses includes those expenses that arise in the ordinary course of business (e.g. salaries, advertising, etc.) as well as losses. Losses represent other items such as those resulting from disasters such as fire and flood and following the disposal of non-current assets or losses following from changes in foreign exchange rates. Losses are usually disclosed separately in the financial statements.

In the past, some items were shown in financial statements as 'extraordinary' but this is no longer possible under IFRS. However, the results (revenue, expenses, profit or loss and income tax) of any discontinued operations (e.g. where a part of the business is disposed of) are shown separately in the Income Statement.

In both financial accounting and management accounting, we distinguish gross profit and operating (or net) profit.

Gross profit is the difference between the selling *price* and the purchase (or production) *cost* of the goods or services sold. Using a simple example, a retailer selling baked beans may buy each tin for 5p and sell it for 9p. The gross profit is 4p per tin.

$$\text{gross profit} = \text{sales} - \text{cost of sales}$$

Gross margin is gross profit expressed as a percentage of sales. So in our baked beans example the gross margin is 44.4% (4p/9p).

The cost of sales is either:

- the cost of providing a service; or
- the cost of buying goods sold by a retailer; or
- the cost of raw materials and production costs for a product manufacturer.

However, not all the goods bought by a retailer or used in production will have been sold in the same period as the sales are made. The matching principle requires that the business adjusts for increases or decreases in *inventory* – the stock of goods bought or produced for resale but not yet sold (this is described in detail in Chapter 8). Therefore, the cost of sales in the financial statements is more properly described as the cost of goods *sold*, not the cost of goods *produced*. Because the production and sale of services are simultaneous, the cost of services produced always equals the cost of services sold (there is no such thing as an inventory of services).

Expenses deducted from gross profit will include all the other (selling, administration, finance etc.) costs of the business (in the USA, the term commonly used is General and Administrative expenses, or G&A), that is those not directly concerned with buying, making or providing goods or services, but supporting that activity. The same retailer may treat the rent of the store, salaries of employees, distribution and computer costs and so on as expenses in order to determine the operating profit.

$$\text{operating profit} = \text{gross profit} - \text{expenses}$$

The operating profit is one of the most significant figures because it represents the profit generated from the ordinary operations of the business. It is also called net profit, profit before interest and taxes (PBIT) or earnings before interest and taxes (EBIT).

The distinction between cost of sales and expenses can vary between industries and organizations. A single retail store may treat only the product cost as the cost of sales, and salaries and rent as expenses. A large retail chain may include the salaries of staff and the store rental as cost of sales with expenses covering the head office corporate costs. Many service businesses do not disclose cost of sales or gross profit figures. It is only in manufacturing where accounting standards dictate what costs should be included in the cost of production. For any particular business, it is important to determine the demarcation between cost of sales and expenses.

From operating profit, a company must pay *interest* to its lenders, and *income tax* to the government. The profit (or loss) of a business for a financial period (after income tax is deducted) is reported in a Statement of Comprehensive Income (known previously as an Income Statement, and even earlier as a Profit and Loss Account, although Profit and Loss Account (or P&L) is still a term in common usage).

Companies have two options in reporting comprehensive income:

- a single Statement of Comprehensive Income; or
- two statements, one an Income Statement, and the second a statement beginning with profit or loss and also showing the components of other comprehensive income.

The Income Statement (with which we are predominantly concerned) will typically appear as in Table 6.1.

Table 6.1   Income Statement.

Revenue	2,000,000
Less: cost of sales	1,500,000
Gross profit	500,000
Less: selling, administration and finance expenses	400,000
Operating profit	100,000
Less: finance expenses	16,000
Profit before income tax	**84,000**
Less: income tax	14,000
Profit for the year	**70,000**

'Other comprehensive income' can best be explained by way of example. It includes: foreign currency translation adjustments on investments in overseas subsidiaries; actuarial gains and losses arising from a defined benefit pension plan for employees; revaluations of property, plant and equipment; and changes in the fair value of financial assets. (IFRS defines fair value as the amount for which an asset or liability could be exchanged between knowledgeable, willing parties in an arm's length transaction.) Many of the examples of other comprehensive income refer to movements in the price or valuation of something resulting in a change in measurement (measurement is one of the *Framework* elements) although some changes in price or valuation are included in the main Income Statement. This is quite a difficult concept, and is outside the scope of this book as it is not necessary for non-financial managers to understand this level of detail.

Chapter 3 explained that profit is transferred to shareholders' funds in the Statement of Financial Position. From the company's after-tax profits, a *dividend* is usually paid to shareholders (for their share of the profits as they – unlike lenders – do not receive an interest rate for their investment). The *Statement of Changes in Equity* shows the profit from the Income Statement, other comprehensive income and the payment of dividends out of profits. It also shows various other movements in shareholders' funds, including the issue of new shares, the purchase of a company's own shares and so on. In other words, it shows the change between the shareholders' funds from one year to the next. The Statement of Changes in Equity is shown in Table 6.2.

Table 6.2   Statement of Changes in Equity.

At beginning of year	**960,000**
Profit for the year	70,000
Other comprehensive income	–
Total comprehensive income	**70,000**
Less: dividend	30,000
At end of year	**1,000,000**

Reporting financial position: the Statement of Financial Position

Not all business transactions appear in the Statement of Comprehensive Income. The Statement of Financial Position (previously and still commonly referred to as the Balance Sheet) shows the financial position of the business – its assets, liabilities and equity – at the *end* of a financial period.

Some business payments are to acquire assets. The IFRS definition of an asset is a resource controlled by an entity as a result of past events and from which future economic benefits are expected to flow to the entity. An entity acquires assets to produce goods or services capable of satisfying customer needs. Physical form is not essential. Non-current assets (which used to be called fixed assets) are things that the business *owns* and uses as part of its infrastructure. There are two types of non-current assets: tangible and intangible. *Tangible assets* comprise those physical assets that can be seen and touched, such as buildings, machinery, vehicles, computers etc. *Intangible assets* comprise non-physical assets such as the goodwill of a business (described later in this chapter) or its intellectual property, e.g. its ownership of patents and trademarks.

Current assets include money in the bank, receivables (also called debtors: the sales to customers on credit, but unpaid) and inventory (the stock of goods bought or manufactured, but unsold). The word *current* in accounting means 12 months, so current assets are those that will change their form during the next year (see working capital in Chapter 7). By contrast, non-current assets (see above) do not normally change their form in the ordinary course of business; as part of the business infrastructure they have a longer term role.

Sometimes assets are acquired or expenses incurred without paying for them immediately. In doing so, the business incurs liabilities. Liabilities are debts that the business *owes*. The IFRS definition of a liability is a present obligation of the entity arising from past events, the settlement of which is expected to result in an outflow from the entity of resources embodying economic benefits. Current liabilities include payables (also called creditors: purchases from suppliers on credit, but unpaid), loans due to be repaid and amounts due for taxes etc. As for assets, the word current means that the liabilities will be repaid within 12 months. Current liabilities also form part of working capital.

Non-current liabilities include loans to finance the business that are repayable after 12 months, other amounts owing that are not current and certain kinds of provisions (see later in this chapter). Equity (or shareholders funds, commonly referred to as capital) is a particular kind of liability, as it is the money invested by the owners in the business. As mentioned above, equity is increased by the retained profits of the business (the profit after paying interest and income tax) and reduced by payment of dividends, as was described above for the Statement of Changes in Equity. Equity is defined by IFRS as the residual interest in the assets of the entity after deducting all its liabilities.

The Statement of Financial Position will typically appear as in Table 6.3. In the Statement of Financial Position, net assets is the difference between total assets and total liabilities, which must 'balance' with the total of equity. This is called the accounting equation which can be shown in a number of different ways:

net assets = total assets – total liabilities (as shown in a Statement of Financial Position, equal to equity)

total assets = liabilities + equity (reflecting the total capital employed in a business, see Chapter 7)

or

assets – liabilities = equity (reflecting the shareholder's investment in the business)

Importantly, the equity of the business does not represent the value of the business. It represents the funds initially invested by owners (or the shareholders in a company) plus the retained profits (after payment of taxes and dividends). In Table 6.3, equity represents the initial investment and retained earnings and comes from the Statement of Changes in Equity in Table 6.2.

Table 6.3   Statement of Financial Position.

Assets	
Non-current assets	
Property, plant & equipment	1,150,000
Current assets	
Receivables	300,000
Inventory	200,000
	500,000
Total assets	1,650,000
Liabilities	
Non-current liabilities	
Long-term loans	300,000
Current liabilities	
Payables	300,000
Bank overdraft	50,000
	350,000
Total liabilities	650,000

Table 6.3. Continued

Net assets	1,000,000
Equity	
Share capital	900,000
Retained earnings	100,000
Total equity	1,000,000

IAS1 is the standard concerned with the Presentation of Financial Statements. However, IAS1 does not prescribe either the order or format in which items are presented in the Statement of Financial Position. The size, nature or function of an item or the degree to which items are aggregated and the actual terminology used in the Statement of Financial Position therefore varies between companies. The key requirement under IFRS is that the presentation must be relevant to understanding a company's financial position.

Accruals accounting

An important principle that is particularly relevant to the interpretation of accounting reports is the matching principle. The matching (or accruals) principle recognizes income when it is *earned* and recognizes expenses when they are *incurred* (this is called accrual accounting), not when money is received or paid out (a method called cash accounting). While cash is very important in business (as we will see later in this chapter), the accruals method provides a more meaningful picture of the financial performance of a business from year to year.

Accrual accounting takes account of the timing differences between receipts and payments and when those cash flows are treated as income earned and expenses incurred for the calculation of profit.

Accruals accounting recognizes Receivables (a current asset, sales not yet paid for by customers), Inventory (a current asset, stock purchased or made but not yet sold) and Payables (a current liability, payments due to suppliers for goods and services purchased) and also makes adjustments for other timing differences:

- prepayments;
- accruals; and
- provisions.

The matching principle requires that certain cash payments made in advance are treated as prepayments, i.e. made in advance of when they are treated as an expense for profit purposes. Other expenses are accrued, i.e. treated as expenses for profit purposes even though no cash payment has yet been made.

A good example of a prepayment is insurance, which is paid 12 months in advance. Assume that a business which has a financial year ending 31 March pays its 12-month insurance premium of €12,000 in advance on 1 January. At its year end, the business will only treat €3,000 (3/12 of €12,000) as an expense and will treat the remaining €9,000 as a prepayment (a current asset in the Statement of Financial Position).

A good example of an accrual is electricity, which like most utilities is paid (often quarterly) in arrears. If the same business usually receives its electricity bill in May (covering the period March to May) it will need to accrue an expense for the month of March, even if the bill has not yet been received. If the prior year's bill was €2,400 for the same quarter (allowing for seasonal fluctuations in usage) then the business will accrue €800 (1/3 of €2,400).

The effect of prepayments and accruals on profit, the Statement of Financial Position and cash flow is shown in Table 6.4.

Table 6.4   Prepayments and accruals.

	Effect on profit in Income Statement	Effect on Statement of Financial Position	Effect on Cash flow
Prepayment	Expense of €3,000	Prepayment (current asset) of €9,000	Cash outflow of €12,000
Accrual	Expense of €800	Accrual (current liability) of €800	No cash flow until quarterly bill received and paid

A further example of the matching principle is in the creation of provisions. Provisions are estimates of possible liabilities that may arise, but where there is uncertainty as to timing or the amount of money. Some provisions are shown as a liability in the Statement of Financial Position. An example of a possible future liability is a provision for warranty claims that may be payable on sales of products. The estimate will be based on the likely costs to be incurred in the future.

Other types of provisions cover reductions in asset values such that only the net asset value is shown on the face of the Statement of Financial Position, with the provision only being shown in the Notes to Financial Statements. The main examples are:

- *Doubtful debts*: customers may experience difficulty in paying their accounts and a provision may be made based on experience that a proportion of those customers will never pay. This provision is deducted from the current asset Receivables.
- *Inventory*: some stock may be obsolete but still held in the store. A provision reduces the value of the obsolete stock to its sale or scrap value (if any). This provision is deducted from the current asset Inventory.
- *Depreciation*: this is a charge against profits, intended to write off the value of each fixed asset over its useful life. This provision is deducted from each type of non-current asset.

The most important provision, because it typically involves a large amount of money, is for depreciation.

Depreciation

Non-current assets are capitalized in the Statement of Financial Position so that the purchase of non-current assets does not affect profit. Depreciation is an expense that spreads the cost of the asset over its useful life. The following example illustrates the matching principle in relation to depreciation.

A non-current asset costs €100,000. It is expected to have a life of four years and have a resale (e.g. trade-in) value of €20,000 at the end of that time. The depreciation charge is:

$$\frac{\text{asset cost} - \text{resale value}}{\text{expected life}} = \frac{100,000 - 20,000}{4} = 20,000\text{p.a.}$$

It is important to recognize that the cash outflow of €100,000 occurs when the asset is bought. The depreciation charge of €20,000 per annum is a non-cash expense each year. However, the value of the asset in the Statement of Financial Position reduces each year as a result of the depreciation charge, as Table 6.5 shows. The asset can be depreciated to a nil value in the Statement of Financial Position even though it is still in use. If the asset is sold, any profit or loss on sale is treated as a separate item in the Statement of Comprehensive Income. While buildings are depreciated, land is never depreciated.

Table 6.5   Effect of depreciation charges on Statement of Financial Position.

	Original asset cost €	Provision for Depreciation €	Net value in Statement of Financial Position €
End of year 1	100,000	20,000	80,000
End of year 2	100,000	40,000	60,000
End of year 3	100,000	60,000	40,000
End of year 4	100,000	80,000	20,000
End of year 5	100,000	100,000	Nil

Non-current assets may be measured at their historical cost or revalued. Historical cost results in a potentially misleading picture as to the true value of non-current assets. Revaluation provides more relevant information to the user of the accounts than the asset's historical cost. However, the usefulness of this information diminishes over time as the valuation ceases to reflect the current value of the asset. Under accounting standards, revaluing tangible non-current assets remains optional. However, the standards require that where a policy of revaluation is adopted, it must be applied to a whole class of assets (not individual assets) and the valuations must be kept up to date through regular independent valuations. This ensures consistency in the treatment of similar assets from year to year.

A type of depreciation used for intangible assets, such as goodwill (see later in this chapter) or leasehold property improvements, is called amortization, which has the same meaning and is calculated in the same way as depreciation. However, intangible assets and securities may be valued at fair value. *Fair value* is a measure of market value, defined as the value which is determined by knowledgeable and willing buyers and sellers in arm's-length transactions (however, the dramatic falls in asset values following the global financial crisis have called fair value into question).

In reporting profits, some companies show the profit before depreciation (or amortization) is deducted, because it can be a substantial cost, but one that does not result in any cash flow. A variation of EBIT (see earlier in this chapter) is EBITDA: earnings before interest, taxes, depreciation and amortization.

Specific IFRS accounting treatments

The full list of IFRS and their predecessor IAS is contained in the Appendix to this chapter. Many relate to specific accounting treatments or specific industries that are beyond the scope of this book. However, some important standards are:

- IAS1 *Presentation of Financial Statements* requires that an entity whose financial statements comply with IFRS must make an explicit and unreserved statement of compliance in the Notes to the financial statements. The impact of changed accounting policies must also be shown in the financial statements.
- IFRS2 *Share Based Payment*: companies have increasingly used grants of shares through share options, and share ownership plans to employees. Previously, these were not reflected in financial statements until such time as the option was exercised. There has been much criticism of this accounting treatment by shareholders. The Standard now requires an entity to reflect in its Statement of Comprehensive Income the effects of share-based payment transactions based on the fair value of the equity instruments granted, measured at the date of the grant. Some companies changed their employee share schemes as a result of this standard.
- IAS2 *Inventory*: stock is valued at the lower of cost and net realizable (i.e. sales proceeds less costs of sale). The cost of inventory includes all costs of purchase, costs of conversion and other costs incurred in bringing the inventory to its present location and condition. Costs of purchase include import duties and transport, less any discounts or rebates. Accounting for Inventory is covered in detail in Chapter 8. Costs of conversion include direct labour and a systematic allocation of fixed and variable production overheads (this is covered in detail in Chapters 11 through 13).
- IAS11 *Construction Contracts*: how profits generated over long-term constructions is covered in Chapter 8.
- IAS16 *Property, Plant & Equipment*: assets are valued at either cost less accumulated depreciation or are regularly revalued independently (explained above).
- IAS17 *Leases*: requires accounting for most non-rental leases as though they were owned and depreciated by the lessee. Lease accounting is covered later in this chapter.
- IAS19 *Employee Benefits*: over time, stock market losses have resulted in defined pension fund liabilities (to pay pensions for retired employees) exceeding their assets. This requires companies to recognize the liability for a deficit in their pension funds in their financial statements. A result of this Standard has been to close many defined benefit pension schemes and replace them with accumulation schemes.
- IAS36 *Impairment of Assets*: impairment refers to the reduction in value of an intangible asset such as goodwill (see later in this chapter for an example of goodwill and impairment).
- IAS37 *Provisions, Contingent Liabilities and Contingent Assets*: a provision is a liability of uncertain timing or amount. Examples include warranty obligations and retail policies for refunds. The amount recognized as a provision is the best estimate of the expenditure required to settle the obligation.
- IAS38 *Intangible Assets*: internally generated goodwill, brands, customer lists etc. are not recognized as assets. Intangible assets can only arise when they are purchased (see later in this chapter for examples of goodwill and research and development).

There are also standards relating to accounting for hedging and changes in foreign exchange (IAS21) and financial instruments (IAS39) but these are outside the scope of this book.

Four accounting treatments are important for managers to understand and each is treated in turn:

- accounting for sales taxes;
- accounting for goodwill and impairment testing;
- accounting for research and development expenditure;
- accounting for leases.

Accounting for sales taxes

Sales taxes are taxes added to the invoiced price of goods and services and which are then remitted to taxation authorities, after deducting sales taxes on purchased goods and services. In the UK Value Added Tax (or VAT) is not shown in most financial statements (although an exception is in some retail businesses). VAT is added to sales by businesses selling goods and services. When businesses purchase goods and services, they have to pay VAT. The business must remit the difference between the VAT it recovers from customers and the VAT it pays its suppliers to the tax authorities. As a transaction, the receipts (from sales) equal the payments (to suppliers and to the tax authorities) and hence these are not shown in the Statement of Comprehensive Income although the unremitted liability to the taxation authorities appears in the Statement of Financial Position as a current liability. In retail businesses, where VAT is more complex (as some retail transactions are exempt from VAT) the VAT-inclusive and VAT-exclusive turnover may both be shown in the Statement of Comprehensive Income.

Accounting for goodwill and impairment testing

Goodwill is an intangible asset. It arises where a company buys a business and pays more than the fair value of the tangible assets. Goodwill represents the value of brands, customer lists, location, reputation, etc. and is reflected in an expectation of future profits. Goodwill cannot be created on a Statement of Financial Position from internally generated sources, but only arises on the acquisition of another business. Goodwill is amortized (amortization is the same principle as depreciation, but the term is used in relation to intangible assets) over a maximum of 20 years.

IAS36 requires intangibles like goodwill to be subject to an impairment test. Impairment involves the annual assessment of the recoverable amount of an asset. The *recoverable amount* is the higher of its fair value less costs to sell; and the value in use, i.e. the present value of future cash flows (see Chapter 14 for the calculation of present value of cash flows). An increase in the amortization provision would need to be made (reducing the goodwill carried in the Statement of Financial Position) if future cash flows were unable to justify the existing carrying value.

Example of goodwill

Negotiations are completed for the acquisition of a business for €1 million. The fair value of tangible assets purchased is €700,000. The goodwill is therefore €300,000 and the acquiring business decides to amortize the goodwill over 10 years. The annual amortization cost is therefore €30,000. At year end, the Statement of Financial Position will show:

Intangible asset − goodwill	€300,000
Less provision for amortization	30,000
	€270,000

The €30,000 annual charge will need to be reassessed annually to determine if the goodwill has been impaired. This is called an annual impairment test. As most businesses are bought on a price/earnings multiple (or P/E ratio, covered in Chapter 7) based on discounted future cash flows, the annual impairment test essentially repeats the exercise each year to determine whether the goodwill carried is excessive. Although the detailed method of calculating impairment is beyond the scope of this book, a simple example would be a case where at year end, the impairment test results in a maximum goodwill figure of €250,000, in which case the company would need to increase its provision for amortization to €50,000, and the net goodwill in its Statement of Financial Position would reduce to €250,000.

Accounting for research and development expenditure

In companies that invest heavily in research and development (e.g. pharmaceuticals), expenditure on research is recognized as an expense although expenditure on development may be recognized as an asset provided specific criteria can be satisfied. Examples of research include activities aimed at gaining new knowledge and the search for, evaluation and selection of alternative materials, products, processes, services and so on. Examples of development include design, construction and testing of prototypes; design of tooling, moulds and dies; design, construction and operation of a pilot plant; and the design, construction and testing of a selected alternative for improved materials, products, processes and services. Whilst research is expensed as it is incurred, development may be capitalized and amortized over a number of years. However, as for goodwill, an annual impairment test needs to be carried out.

Accounting for leases

Leasing arose as a method of finance for equipment used by business organizations, in which a business needing equipment (the lessee) 'rented' that equipment from a financial institution (the lessor) which in turn paid the supplier for the equipment. The lessee pays a fixed monthly sum over a number of years to the lessor in payment of the debt. Many businesses finance at least some of their tangible non-current assets through leasing facilities.

There are two types of leases: operating and finance. Under an operating lease, all the risks and rewards are with the lessor, so lease payments are no more than rental payments. In the case of finance leases, the substance and economic reality are that the lessee acquires the economic benefits of the use of the leased asset for the major part of its useful life in return for entering into an obligation to pay an amount, usually in instalments, approximating the fair value of the asset and the interest cost.

Accounting standards require lessees to capitalize material finance leases because the transaction is considered to be the economic equivalent of borrowing to acquire an asset; accordingly, the lessee records the asset and the liability to pay lease rentals in its Statement of Financial Position. This is not the case with an operating lease.

The lessee capitalizes the fair value of the asset, or the present value of the minimum lease payments (described in Chapter 14), as the cost of the non-current asset and this same amount (the total of the future lease payments) is recorded as the liability (some of which will be current and some non-current). The leased asset has to be depreciated over the shorter of the period of the lease and the useful life of the asset, as though it was owned. Depreciation expense appears in the Statement of Comprehensive Income and reduces the Statement of Financial Position asset value as though the leased asset was owned. As for other assets, there needs to be an annual impairment test.

Lease payments owing are shown as a (current and/or non-current) liability in the Statement of Financial Position. The periodic (usual monthly) lease payment is not simply a revenue expense but represents both the repayment of the capital element of the loan and also the interest charge on the loan. The interest on the lease is treated as an expense to give a constant periodic return on the balance of the outstanding loan.

Operating lease payments, where risk and rewards are maintained by the lessor (the most common example is the company motor vehicle) are treated as an expense and are not capitalized in the Statement of Financial Position, although a disclosure of the lease liability must be made in the Notes to the financial statements.

Apart from the Income Statement and Statement of Financial Position, the third very important financial statement is the Statement of Cash Flows.

Reporting cash flow: the Statement of Cash Flows

The Statement of Cash Flows shows the movement in cash for the business during a financial period. It includes:

- cash flows from operations (profit adjusted by non-cash expenses and movements in working capital);
- cash flows from investing (purchase and sale of non-current assets);
- cash flow from financing (borrowings and repayment of debt; new share issues and purchase of a company's own shares);

The cash flow from operations differs from the operating profit because of:

- depreciation, which as a non-cash expense is added back to profit (since operating profit is the result *after* depreciation is deducted);
- increases (or decreases) in working capital (e.g. changes in Receivables, Inventory, Prepayments, Payables and Accruals), which reduce (or increase) available cash.

IFRS allow two different presentation formats for showing cash flow from operations in the Statement of Cash Flows:

- the direct method, disclosing major classes of gross cash flows receipts and payments; and
- the indirect method, whereby profit or loss is adjusted for the effect of non-cash transactions.

In this book, we will only show the indirect method as it more clearly shows the link between the profit or loss in the Statement of Comprehensive Income and the Statement of Cash Flows.

An example of a Statement of Cash Flows using the indirect method is shown in Table 6.6.

Table 6.6   Statement of Cash Flows.

Cash flows from operating activities	
Profit before tax	100,000
Depreciation	20,000
	120,000
Movement in inventories	(10,000)
Movement in receivables	(15,000)
Movement in payables	20,000
Cash generated from operations	**115,000**
Income tax paid	−12,000
Net cash flows from operating activities	**103,000**
Cash flows from investing activities	
Purchase of plant & equipment	−100,000
Cash flows from financing activities	
Additional borrowing	50,000
Interest paid	−16,000
Dividends paid	−25,000
Net cash flows from financing activities	9,000
Net increase in cash and cash equivalents	12,000
Opening cash and cash equivalents	−62,000
Closing cash and cash equivalents	−50,000

In the Statement of Cash Flows, cash equivalents are short-term, highly liquid investments that are readily convertible to known amounts of cash and which are subject to an insignificant risk of changes in value. Cash equivalents are held for the purpose of meeting short-term cash commitments rather than for investment or other purposes and include bank overdrafts that are an integral part of an authority's cash management.

IFRS does not specify where cash flows from interest or dividends received or paid should be shown in the Statement of Cash Flows, and so each company must decide whether to classify interest and dividends paid as either operating or financing activities; and interest and dividends received as either operating or investing activities. In reading the Statement of Cash Flows, it is important to note that the amounts shown for taxation, interest and dividend payments are not the same as the amounts shown in the Income Statement because of timing differences between when those items are treated as expenses and when the cash payment is made, which is normally after the end of the financial year.

Differences between the financial statements

The Income Statement shows the profit (or loss) of a business for a financial year, using the accruals method by which income earned is matched with expenses incurred in earning that income, irrespective of the timing of receipts from sales and payment of expenses.

The Statement of Cash Flows shows the movements in and out of the company's bank account (or cash equivalents) during a financial year. This is split into three sections: cash flows from operations; cash flows from investing activities; and cash flows from financing activities.

Cash flows from operations in the Statement of Cash Flows is not the same as profit. First, non-cash items such as depreciation are added back to profit. Second, working capital changes increase or decrease the cash flows from operations (increases in Receivables or Inventory reduce cash flows, while increases in Payables increase cash flows).

Other items in the Statement of Cash Flows do not appear in the Income Statement. The major items are: capital expenditure or the disposal of non-current assets (cash flows from investing); borrowings and repayments of debt; and changes in shareholders' equity (cash flows from financing) all of which affect cash flow, but not profit.

The Statement of Financial Position shows the assets, liabilities and equity on the last day of the financial year. The Statement of Cash Flows reflects the movements between the Statement of Financial Position at the beginning and end of the financial year, while the Income Statement and the Statement of Comprehensive Income and the Statement of Changes in Equity show the movement in equity between the beginning and end of the financial year.

Illustration

The following illustration shows how several typical transactions influence the three main financial statements.

ABC Ltd buys a new computer system for $150,000 on the first day of the financial year and on the same day borrows $100,000 to do so. XYZ depreciates its computers at the rate of 20% per annum. During the year $10,000 of the loan was repaid together with $1,000 interest.

Prepare a simple Income Statement, Statement of Financial Position and Statement of Cash Flows to show how each of these transactions would appear.

The double entry (see Chapter 3) is carried out using Table 6.7, which is then used to construct the financial statements which are shown in Table 6.8.

Table 6.7   Double entry for transactions.

	Non-current asset	Non-current liability	Bank account	Expense
Purchase of computer system	+150,000		−150,000	
Borrowing		+100,000	+100,000	
Depreciation 20% of $150,000	−30,000			+30,000
Repayment of loan		−10,000	−10,000	
Interest on loan			−1,000	+1,000
Total	120,000	90,000	−61,000	31,000

Table 6.8   Effect of transactions on financial statements.

Income Statement:

Depreciation expense	$30,000
Interest cost	$1,000
Loss (total expense)	$31,000

Statement of Financial Position:

Non-current asset $150,000 less depreciation $30,000 Net	$120,000
Liability $100,000 less repayment $10,000 balance	−$90,000
Bank overdraft balance (see below)	−$61,000
Net assets	−$31,000
Equity (loss, see above)	−$31,000

Statement of Cash Flows:

Loss	−$31,000
Add back depreciation	$30,000
Cash flow from operations	−$1,000
Cash flow from investing activities	
Cash paid for purchase of asset	−$150,000
Cash flow from financing activities	
Borrowing	+$100,000
Repayment	−$10,000
Reduction in bank balance	−$61,000

A theoretical perspective on financial statements

A necessary ingredient for shareholder value (see Chapter 2), given the separation of ownership from control in most large business organizations, is the control of what managers actually do. Control is considered in the rational-economic paradigm (see Chapter 4) through the notion of *contract*, in which the role of control is to measure and reward performance such that there will be greater *goal congruence*, i.e. that individuals pursuing their own self-interest will also pursue the collective interest.

There are two main versions of contractual theory: agency theory and transaction cost economics. Agency theory sees the economy as a network of interlocking contracts. The transaction cost approach sees the economy as a mixture of markets, hierarchies and networks (transaction cost economics is discussed further in Chapter 15).

Agency theory

Agency theory is concerned with contractual relationships within the firm, between a principal (shareholders) and an agent (directors and managers), whose rights and duties are specified by a real or notional contract of employment. This theory recognizes the behaviour of an agent, whose actions the management control and accounting system seeks to influence and control. Both principals and agents are assumed to be rational-economic persons motivated solely by self-interest, although they may differ with respect to their preferences, beliefs and information.

The principal wishes to influence what the agent does, but delegates tasks to the agent in an uncertain environment. The agent expends effort in the performance of these tasks. The outcome of the agent's efforts depends on both environmental factors and the effort expended by the agent. Under the *sharing rule*, the agent usually receives a reward, being a share of the outcome (typically a bonus, share options, and so on). The reward will depend on the information system used to measure the outcome. Consequently, financial statements play an important role in regulating the actions of agents. The assumption of agency theory is that the agent obtains utility (a benefit) from the reward but disutility from expending effort. Both principal and agent are assumed to be risk averse and utility maximizers.

The agency model involves seeking an employment contract that specifies the sharing rule and the information system. An accounting system can provide output measures from which an agent's efforts can be inferred, but the measures may not accurately reflect the effort expended. This leads to uncertainty about the relationship between the accounting measure and the agent's effort. If the principal cannot observe the agent's effort, or infer it from measured output, the agent may have an incentive to act in a manner different from the employment contract – this is called *moral hazard*. A principal who can observe the agent's effort but does not have access to all the information held by the agent does not know whether the effort expended has been based on the agent's information or whether the agent has 'shirked'. This is called *adverse selection*.

Moral hazard and adverse selection are both a consequence of *information asymmetry*. This happens because principal and agent have different amounts of information. Although both principals and agents will have access to financial statements, only managers will have access to the vastly more comprehensive management accounting information available within the organization. A function of accounting under agency theory is to improve efficiency by minimizing the losses caused through moral hazard and adverse selection.

We see simple examples of agency transactions, for example in buying or renting real estate, in booking travel through a travel agent, or using an insurance broker. When we apply the same principle to organizations, agency theory becomes more complex because there are multiple principals (rather than a single shareholder) and multiple agents (the board may be unified but is composed of individuals, including the chief executive officer). Agency theory ignores the effect of capital markets by assuming a single owner rather than a group of owners. The model also focuses on single-period behaviour rather than the longer term. Many individuals violate the assumptions of rational self-interested behaviour and the agency perspective is narrow because there is no regard given to power, trust, ethical issues or equity, all of which may affect behaviour (see Chapter 5). We consider some alternative theories to agency in the next chapter.

A critical perspective on financial statements and accounting standards

There have been various criticisms of accounting standards including:

- The almost continual introduction of new and amended standards, making comparisons over longer time periods difficult.
- Standards that fail to consider practical implementation issues, e.g. the impact of pension fund accounting (IAS19) and accounting for stock options (IFRS2).
- 'International' standards that do not yet incorporate the USA.
- Lobbying which may influence the development of standards (there is evidence from the USA of lobbyists for Enron attempting to influence standard setters).
- The absence of any explicit statement in IFRS about the relationship between the legal requirement for a true and fair view and compliance with accounting standards.
- The potential for standards to lead to more creative accounting through a focus on presentation rather than the underlying business reality.
- Standards having a narrow accounting focus rather than being inclusive of non-financial performance and broader accountability issues such as social and environmental reporting (see Chapter 7 for a discussion of these issues).

Perhaps the biggest criticism of financial statements is that the ever-increasing complexity of accounting standards has made financial statements so much more difficult to understand, even for accountants themselves, who increasingly rely on the expertise of auditors to advise them in terms of detailed presentational aspects of IFRS compliance. Stock market analysts often discount financial statements and use supplementary sources of data to make judgements about company performance and prospects. The absence of comparisons to plan (even though financial statements make comparison to prior years) also limits the usability of financial statements, which are rarely available less than two months after the end of each financial year. Perhaps most importantly, financial statements reinforce the dominant stock market focus on short-term profits rather than with longer term sustainability of performance.

Conclusion

This chapter has covered the three main financial statements: Income Statement, Statement of Financial Position and Statement of Cash Flows. It has introduced International Financial Reporting Standards (IFRS) and the *Framework for the Preparation and Presentation of Financial Statements*. The principles of accrual accounting (including prepayments, accruals and depreciation) as well as accounting for sales tax, goodwill, research and development and leases have all been covered. The chapter concluded with an introduction to what has been historically one of the main theories underlying the construction of financial statements, agency theory, and has provided a critique of financial statements and accounting standards. In the next chapter, we introduce the tools and techniques that are used to interpret financial statements and consider some alternative theoretical perspectives.

Reference

International Accounting Standards Board (2011). *International Financial Reporting Standards IFRSs* 2011 version. Bound Volume. London: IASB.

Websites

The website of the International Accounting Standards Board is http://www.ifrs.org/Home.htm.
The website of the Financial Reporting Council in the UK is http://www.frc.org.uk/.

Appendix: IFRS as at 1 January 2011

IFRS:

- IFRS 1 First-time Adoption of International Financial Reporting Standards
- IFRS 2 Share-based Payment
- IFRS 3 Business Combinations
- IFRS 4 Insurance Contracts
- IFRS 5 Non-current Assets Held for Sale and Discontinued Operations
- IFRS 6 Exploration for and evaluation of Mineral Resources
- IFRS 7 Financial Instruments: Disclosures
- IFRS 8 Operating Segments

IAS:

- IAS 1 Presentation of Financial Statements
- IAS 2 Inventories
- IAS 7 Statement of Cash Flows
- IAS 8 Accounting Policies, Changes in Accounting Estimates and Errors
- IAS 10 Events After the Balance Sheet Date
- IAS 11 Construction Contracts
- IAS 12 Income Taxes
- IAS 16 Property, Plant and Equipment
- IAS 17 Leases
- IAS 18 Revenue
- IAS 19 Employee Benefits

- IAS 20 Accounting for Government Grants and Disclosure of Government Assistance
- IAS 21 The Effects of Changes in Foreign Exchange Rates
- IAS 23 Borrowing Costs
- IAS 24 Related Party Disclosures
- IAS 26 Accounting and Reporting by Retirement Benefit Plans
- IAS 27 Consolidated and Separate Financial Statements
- IAS 28 Investments in Associates
- IAS 29 Financial Reporting in Hyperinflationary Economies
- IAS 31 Interests in Joint Ventures
- IAS 32 Financial Instruments: Presentation
- IAS 33 Earnings per Share
- IAS 34 Interim Financial Reporting
- IAS 36 Impairment of Assets
- IAS 37 Provisions, Contingent Liabilities and Contingent Assets
- IAS 38 Intangible Assets
- IAS 39 Financial Instruments: Recognition and Measurement
- IAS 40 Investment Property
- IAS 41 Agriculture

The current list of standards can be seen at http://www.ifrs.org/IFRSs/IFRS+technical+summaries/Summaries+Eng+11.htm.

Questions

6.1 Kazam Services begins the month with capital of £200,000 and the following assets and liabilities:

Assets	**Liabilities**
Non-current assets £500,000	Bank overdraft £35,000
Receivables £125,000	Payables £90,000
	Long-term loan £300,000

The following transactions took place in the accounting records of the business during the last month:

Take out long-term loan for new building £150,000.

Receivables reduce by £45,000 as customers pay their accounts.

Payables reduce by £30,000 as suppliers are paid.

Invoice customers for £70,000 for services carried out.

Pay salaries £15,000.

Pay various office expenses £5,000.

In addition, depreciation of £20,000 is to be provided for the period.

- Produce a schedule of transactions under appropriate headings for each account.
- Total each account and produce an Income Statement and Statement of Financial Position.

6.2   Vibro plc has non-current assets of £250,000, current assets of £125,000, long-term debt of £125,000 and payables of £75,000.

- What is the working capital?
- What is the capital employed in the company?
- What is the shareholders' capital?

6.3   XYZ Ltd's Income Statement shows the following:

	2011	2010
	€	€
Sales	1,250,000	1,175,000
Cost of sales	787,000	715,000
Selling and admin expenses	324,000	323,000

Based on these figures, which of the following statements is true?

a. Sales, cost of sales and expenses have all increased, therefore profit, gross margin and operating margin have all increased.
b. The operating profit has increased due to sales growth, higher gross margins and similar expenses.
c. Although the operating profit has decreased, the operating margin has increased as a result of sales growth and an increase in gross profit.
d. The operating profit has decreased due to lower gross margins and higher expenses, despite sales growth.
e. Although the operating profit has increased, the operating margin has decreased as a result of a reduction in the gross margin and higher expenses, despite sales growth.

6.4   What is the impact of the following prepayment, accrual and provision transactions on profit, the Statement of Financial Position and cash flow?

a. A business has 24 motor vehicles that it leases in return for a monthly payment, excluding insurance. The company's financial year is 1 April/31 March, but the annual insurance premium of $400 per vehicle for the calendar year January–December is due for payment on 31 December.

b. A business budgets for energy costs of $6,000 per annum over its financial year 1 January/31 December. Bills for usage are sent each quarter on the last days of each of February, May, August and November. Historically, 70% of the annual energy cost is spent during the autumn and winter (September–February).

c. A business with a financial year of 1 April/31 March purchases a new computer network server for $12,000 on 30 June. The business depreciates computer hardware at the rate of 20% of cost per annum, beginning the month following purchase.

6.5 NOP plc has recently acquired a business, for which it paid £12 million. The assets of the business comprise:

Plant & Equipment	£7,000,000
Receivables	£1,500,000
Inventory	£2,300,000
Payables	£ 500,000

The directors decide to amortize any goodwill over a period of 10 years. Calculate the goodwill in the Statement of Financial Position (ignoring any impairment) at the end of the first year after the business was purchased.

6.6 PUH Ltd leases all of its assets. In its Statement of Financial Position, PUH shows a current liability of £750,000 and a long-term debt of £1,640,000 for lease commitments. What type of expenses will a user of PUH's financial statements expect to see in the Income Statement?

6.7 A business sells a non-current asset for less than its Statement of Financial Position value. Under IFRS, how will the difference between the asset value in the Statement of Financial Position and the amount received on the sale of the asset be disclosed in the Income Statement?

6.8 A business sells a non-current asset for more than its Statement of Financial Position value. Under IFRS, how will the difference between the asset value in the Statement of Financial Position and the amount received on the sale of the asset be disclosed in the Income Statement?

6.9 A manufacturing business has invoiced customers $5,875,000 including sales taxes of 17.5%. What sales value will be shown in the Income Statement?

6.10   MNJ Ltd borrows €200,000 from a finance company. The next day, the company uses those funds to purchase new plant and equipment for €150,000. MNJ depreciates its plant and equipment at the rate of 20% per annum. During the year MNJ also incurs advertising expenditure of €5,000. Present an extract from each of the Income Statement, Statement of Financial Position and Statement of Cash Flows to show how these transactions would be presented.

Interpreting Financial Statements

This chapter begins with an overview of a company's Annual Report and shows how ratio analysis can be used to interpret financial statements. This interpretation covers profitability, liquidity (cash flow), gearing (borrowings), activity/efficiency and shareholder return. We also look at working capital management in detail. Two case studies demonstrate how ratios can be used to look 'behind the numbers' contained in financial statements. The chapter concludes with several alternative theoretical perspectives on financial reporting including corporate social and environmental reporting.

Annual Reports

For all companies, the Companies Act requires the preparation of financial statements. Financial statements are an important part of a company's Annual Report, which must be available to all shareholders for all companies listed on the Stock Exchange.

The Annual Report for a listed company typically contains:

- A financial summary – the key financial information.
- A list of the main advisers to the company: legal advisers, bankers, auditors and so on.
- The chairman's, directors' and/or chief financial officer's report(s). These reports provide a useful summary of the key factors affecting the company's performance over the past year and its prospects for the future. It is important to read this information as it provides a background to the financial statements, and the company's products and major market segments (much of this information may be

contained in an Operating and Financial Review, see the next section). The user must 'read between the lines' in this report, since an intention of the Annual Report is to paint a realistic yet often 'glossy' picture of the business. However, as competitors will also read the Annual Report, the company takes care not to disclose more than is necessary.

- The statutory reports (i.e. those required by the Companies Act) by the directors and auditors. These will contain a summary of financial performance, major policies, strategies and activities, details about the board of directors, and statements about corporate governance and internal control and the responsibility of the board for the financial statements.
- The audit report which will define the auditors' responsibilities, an opinion as to whether the financial statements give a true and fair view and are compliant with the Companies Act and IFRS (see Chapter 6) and the basis upon which that opinion has been formed.
- The financial statements: Income Statement and/or Statement of Comprehensive Income, Statement of Changes in Equity, Statement of Financial Position and Statement of Cash Flows (see Chapter 6). Where consolidated figures are provided, these should be used, as they are the total figures for the group of companies that comprise the whole business. Prior year figures must be shown for comparative purposes.
- Notes to the financial statements, which provide detailed explanations to the figures in the financial statements, and usually run to many pages. As well as a breakdown of many of the figures contained in the Income Statement, Statement of Financial Position and Statement of Cash Flows, the Notes will include details such as: the major accounting policies adopted; staff numbers and staff costs; directors' remuneration; depreciation of assets; investments; taxation; share capital; capital expenditure contracted for; pension liabilities; lease liabilities; subsidiaries; events occurring after the end of the financial year.
- A five-year summary of key financial information (a Stock Exchange listing requirement, see Chapter 3).
- Operating and Financial Review (OFR).

The Accounting Standards Board published a *Reporting Statement: Operating and Financial Review* (OFR) in 2006. The statutory requirement for all companies to produce an OFR was subsequently removed and the reporting statement is now a voluntary statement according with 'best practice' principles for listed companies. The OFR (different companies may use different terminology) is intended to be forward-looking, providing details of strategy for shareholders and a broader group of stakeholders, to complement and supplement financial statements, including key performance indicators (KPIs: see the Balanced Scorecard in Chapter 4).

The OFR should provide information to enable shareholders 'to assess the strategies adopted by the entity and the potential for those strategies to succeed' (Accounting Standards Board, 2006, p. 13), including:

- The nature of the business, description of the market, the competitive and regulatory environment and the organization's objectives and strategies.
- The development and performance of the business in the last year and in the future.
- The resources, principal risks, uncertainties and relationships that may affect long-term value.
- Description of the capital structure, treasury policies and objectives and liquidity of the business in the last year and in the future.

The context of financial statements

Before we commence analysing the financial statements themselves, it is particularly important to understand the context in which the business operates. While much information can be obtained from the Annual Report and the company's website, it must be remembered that these are at least in part produced for public relations purposes, hence it is important to seek out broader information about the company which will then provide the context in which the financial statements can be interpreted and understood.

Access to past newspaper articles using library databases (Factiva is one example) can provide a more rounded picture of a company, including criticisms of its operations. A good example is the press coverage given to BP's *Deepwater Horizons* drilling rig explosion and oil spill in the Gulf of Mexico in 2010, where press reports (and government enquiries) provided a much different picture of the company than that found in BP's Annual Report. However, it is important to remember that press reports themselves can be inaccurate and biased. Nevertheless, making enquiries into a company through newspaper articles can help to understand the 'bigger picture'.

This bigger picture can also be obtained from industry publications, trade associations and exhibitions, where information extends not just to individual companies but to a whole industry. Market research and consulting firms also produce detailed analyses of industries but can be expensive, while credit rating agencies provide independent information about companies' financial position including litigation and credit reputations. Stock market analysts undertake their own analysis and use that to support the buy or sell recommendations they give to their investment clients.

Personal experience is also important. If you are looking at the financial statements of a large supermarket chain such as Sainsbury's or Tesco in the UK, personal experience of shopping can help to understand the business operations. So for example, if you notice that food prices are lower, it may be that supermarkets are carrying out a price war to win market share, and this may affect their profits in the short term.

The key issue in interpreting financial statements is to understand the context: What is happening in the company's market? Is customer demand changing? What technological and regulatory changes are affecting it? Who are the major competitors? Only with this contextual awareness can we begin to understand financial statements.

Ratio analysis

Ratio analysis is perhaps the most important tool used to analyse financial statements: the Income Statement, Statement of Financial Position and Statement of Cash Flows. *Ratios* are typically two numbers, with one being expressed as a percentage of the other. Ratio analysis can be used to help interpret *trends* in performance year on year; by *benchmarking* to industry averages or to the performance of individual competitors; or comparison against a predetermined *target*. As companies are required to show a comparison with their prior year financial statements, ratios should be applied, at the very least, to current and past years. However, trends can really only be interpreted properly over a longer period, ideally five years. Trade association, market research and consultancy reports often benchmark companies in an industry and some government statistical data is published (e.g. on retail sales and automobile registrations). Annual Reports do not provide comparisons against target, so this kind of ratio analysis is only possible for managers within the company. Most financial statements provide consolidated (or group) data and data for the parent (or holding) company. We are usually only concerned with the consolidated or group figures. However, companies show some detailed segmental analysis of major parts of their business, which is often very important in understanding business performance.

Ratio analysis can be used to interpret performance against five criteria:

- the rate of profitability;
- liquidity, i.e. cash flow;
- gearing, i.e. the proportion of borrowings to shareholders' equity;
- how efficiently assets are utilized; and
- the returns to shareholders.

There are different definitions that can be used for each ratio. Different text books, credit rating agencies and stock market analysts use varying definitions. However, it is important that whatever ratios are used, they are meaningful to the business and applied consistently. The most common ratios follow. The calculations refer to the example Income Statement and Statement of Financial Position in Chapter 6 which are repeated below in Tables 7.1, 7.2 and 7.3. Ratios may be calculated on the end of year Statement of Financial Position figures (as has been done in the examples that follow) or on the basis of the average of Statement of Financial Position figures over two years.

Table 7.1   Income Statement.

Revenue	2,000,000
Less: cost of sales	1,500,000
Gross profit	500,000
Less: selling, administration and finance expenses	400,000
Operating profit	100,000
Less: finance expenses	16,000
Profit before income tax	**84,000**
Less: income tax	14,000
Profit for the year	**70,000**

Table 7.2   Statement of Changes in Equity.

At beginning of year	960,000
Profit for the year	70,000
Other comprehensive income	–
Total comprehensive income	**70,000**
Less: dividend	30,000
At end of year	**1,000,000**

Table 7.3 Statement of Financial Position.

Assets	
Non-current assets	
Property, plant & equipment	1,150,000
Current assets	
Receivables	300,000
Inventory	200,000
	500,000
Total assets	1,650,000
Liabilities	
Non-current liabilities	
Long-term loans	300,000
Current liabilities	
Payables	300,000
Bank overdraft	50,000
	350,000
Total liabilities	650,000
Net assets	1,000,000
Equity	
Share capital	900,000
Retained earnings	100,000
Total equity	1,000,000

Ratios are nearly always expressed as a percentage (by multiplying the answer by 100). In the following examples, only £'000 (thousands of pounds) are shown.

Profitability

Return on (shareholders') investment (ROI)

$$\frac{\text{net profit after tax}}{\text{shareholders' funds}} = \frac{70}{1000} = 7\%$$

Return on capital employed (ROCE)

$$\frac{\text{operating profit before interest and tax}}{\text{shareholders funds} + \text{long-term debt}} = \frac{100}{1,000 + 300} = 7.7\%$$

Operating margin (or operating profit/sales)

$$\frac{\text{operating profit before interest and tax}}{\text{sales}} = \frac{100}{2{,}000} = 5\%$$

Gross margin (or gross profit/sales)

$$\frac{\text{gross profit}}{\text{sales}} = \frac{500}{2{,}000} = 25\%$$

Overheads/sales

$$\frac{\text{overheads}}{\text{sales}} = \frac{400}{2{,}000} = 20\%$$

Each of the profitability ratios provides a different method of interpreting profitability. Satisfactory business performance requires an adequate return on shareholders' funds and total capital employed in the business (the total of the investment by shareholders and lenders). ROI will often be higher when shareholders' funds are low, but this involves higher risk (see gearing, below). Profit must also be achieved as a percentage of sales. The operating profit and gross profit margins emphasize different elements of business performance. It is important to maximize gross margin (the difference between selling price and the cost of sales for the volume of goods or services sold) and to control the proportion of overhead in relation to sales.

Sales growth

A further method of interpreting performance is sales growth, which is simply

$$\frac{\text{sales in year 2} - \text{sales in year 1}}{\text{sales in year 1}}$$

Hence, had the sales in the previous year been £1,800,000 (not shown in the example in Table 7.1), the sales growth would be

$$\frac{2000 - 1800}{1800} = \frac{200}{1800} = 11.1\%$$

Businesses and the stock market not only like to see increasing profitability but also increasing sales, which is an important measure of the long-term sustainability of profits.

Liquidity

Working capital

$$\frac{\text{current assets}}{\text{current liabilities}} = \frac{500}{350} = 143\%$$

Acid test (or quick ratio)

$$\frac{\text{current assets} - \text{inventory}}{\text{current liabilities}} = \frac{500 - 200}{350} = 86\%$$

Working capital is explained in more detail later in this chapter, but is essentially the liquid funds that circulate in and out of the bank account, comprising, in the main, receivables, inventory, payables and bank account (or overdraft). Many businesses will aim for a working capital ratio of around 150% and an acid test of around 100%. A business that has an acid test of less than 100% may experience difficulty in paying its debts as they fall due. On the other hand, a company with too high a working capital ratio may not be utilizing its assets effectively. However, there are substantial variations between industries. In retail for example, a lot of inventory is held and this is reflected in payables to suppliers, but there are no receivables from customers. Customers pay cash as they buy goods and hence the working capital and acid test ratios will often be less than 100.

Gearing

Gearing ratio

$$\frac{\text{long-term debt}}{\text{shareholders funds} + \text{long-term debt}} = \frac{300}{1,000 + 300} = 23.1\%$$

Interest cover

$$\frac{\text{profit before interest and tax}}{\text{interest payable}} = \frac{100}{16} = 6.25 \text{ times}$$

Gearing is the amount of borrowings relative to shareholders' equity. The higher the gearing, the higher the risk of repaying debt and interest. In the short term, repaying interest is more important, so the lower the interest cover, the more pressure there is on profits to fund interest charges. However, because borrowings are being used, the *rate of profit* earned by shareholders is higher where there are higher borrowings. The relationship between risk and return is an important feature of interpreting business performance. Consider the example in Table 7.4 of risk and return for a business under different assumptions of the mix between debt and equity (which was covered in Chapter 2) in financing the total assets of the company.

Table 7.4 Risk and return – effect of different debt/equity mix.

	100% equity	50% equity 50% debt	10% equity 90% debt
Capital employed	100,000	100,000	100,000
Equity	100,000	50,000	10,000
Debt	0	50,000	90,000
Operating profit before interest and tax	20,000	20,000	20,000
Interest at 10% on debt	0	5,000	9,000
Profit after interest	20,000	15,000	11,000
Tax at 30%	6,000	4,500	3,300
Profit after tax	14,000	10,500	7,700
Return on investment	14%	21%	77%

While in the example in Table 7.4 the return on capital employed is a constant 20% (an operating profit of £20,000 on capital employed of £100,000), the return on shareholders' funds increases as debt replaces equity. This improvement to the return to shareholders shows the value of leveraging other people's money, but it carries a risk, which increases as the proportion of profits taken by the interest charge increases (and is reflected in the interest cover ratio). If profits turn down, there are substantially more risks carried by the highly geared business in repaying both interest and the loan principal.

Many businesses aim for a gearing in the range of 40–60%, but there are wide variations between industries and in the risk attitude of companies within industries.

Activity/efficiency

Asset turnover

$$\frac{\text{sales}}{\text{total assets}} = \frac{2,000}{1,150 + 500} = 121\%$$

Investment in assets has as its principal purpose the generation of sales. Asset turnover is a measure of how efficiently assets are utilized to generate sales, with the goal being to work the assets as hard as possible to generate sales.

Working capital

The management of working capital is a crucial element of cash flow management. Working capital is the difference between current assets and current liabilities. In practical terms, we are primarily concerned with inventory and receivables (debtors), although prepayments are a further element of current assets. Current liabilities comprise trade payables (creditors) and accruals. The other element of working capital is bank, representing either surplus cash (a current asset) or short-term borrowing through a bank overdraft facility (a current liability).

The working capital cycle is shown in Figure 7.1. Money tied up in receivables and inventory puts pressure on the firm, which often results in late payments to suppliers (and potentially a higher cost of sales). Managing working capital is essential for success, as the ability to avoid a cash crisis and pay debts as they fall due depends on:

- managing receivables through effective credit approval, invoicing and collection activity;
- managing inventory through effective ordering, storage and identification of stock;
- managing payables by negotiation of trade terms and through taking advantage of settlement discounts; and
- managing cash by effective forecasting, short-term borrowing and/or investment of surplus cash where possible.

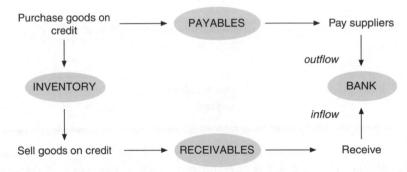

Figure 7.1 The working capital cycle.

Ratios to determine the efficiency of the management of working capital and methods for managing and monitoring receivables, inventory and payables are described below.

Managing receivables

The main measure of how effectively receivables (debtors) are managed is the number of days' sales outstanding. Days' sales outstanding (DSO) is:

$$\frac{\text{receivables}}{\text{average daily sales}}$$

The business has sales of £2,000,000 and receivables of £300,000. Average daily sales are £5,479 (£2,000,000/365). There are therefore 54.75 average days' sales outstanding (£300,000/£5,479). Management of receivables will aim to reduce days' sales outstanding over time and minimize bad debts. The target number of days' sales outstanding will be a function of the industry, the credit terms offered by the firm and its efficiency in both credit approval and collection activity. In practice, a firm with 30-day trading terms will typically aim to have its days' sales outstanding at around 45–50.

Acceptance policies will aim to determine the creditworthiness of new customers before sales are made. This can be achieved by checking trade and bank references, searching company accounts and consulting a credit bureau for any adverse reports. Credit limits can be set for each customer. Collection policies should ensure that invoices are issued quickly and accurately, that any queries are investigated as soon as they are identified and that continual follow-up of late-paying customers should take place. Discounts may be offered for settlement within credit terms.

Bad debts may occur because a customer's business fails. For this reason, firms establish a provision (see Chapter 6) to cover the likelihood of customers not being able to pay their debts.

Managing inventory

The main measure of how effectively inventory (stock) is managed is the inventory turnover (or stock turn). Inventory turnover is:

$$\frac{\text{cost of sales}}{\text{stock}}$$

In the example, cost of sales is £1,500,000 and inventory is £200,000. The inventory turnover is therefore 7.5 (£1,500,000/£200,000). This means that inventory turns over (is bought or manufactured and sold) 7.5 times per year, or on average every 49 days (365/7.5). Sound management of inventory requires an accurate and up-to-date inventory control system.

Often in inventory control the *Pareto principle* (also called the 80/20 rule) applies. This recognizes that a small proportion (often about 20%) of the number of inventory items accounts for a relatively large proportion (say 80%) of the total value. In inventory control, ABC analysis takes the approach that, rather than attempt to manage all stock items equally, efforts should be made to prioritize the 'A' items that account for most value, then 'B' items and only if time permits the many smaller value 'C' items. Increasingly manufacturing businesses adopt *just-in-time* (*JIT*) methods to minimize investment in inventory, treating any inventory as a wasted resource. JIT requires sophisticated production planning, inventory control and supply chain management so that inventory is only received as it is required for production or sale. Stock may be written off because of stock losses, obsolescence or damage. For this reason, firms establish a provision to cover the likelihood of writing off part of the value of stock. Accounting for Inventory is the subject of Chapter 8.

Managing payables

Just as it is important to collect debts from customers, it is also essential to ensure that suppliers are paid within their credit terms. As for receivables, the main measure of how effectively payables (creditors) are managed is the number of days' purchases outstanding. Days' purchases outstanding (DPO) are:

$$\frac{\text{payables}}{\text{average daily purchases}}$$

The business has cost of sales (usually its main credit purchases, as many expenses, e.g. salaries, rent, are not on credit) of £1,500,000 and creditors of £300,000. Average daily purchases are £4,110 (£1,500,000/365). There are therefore 73 average days' purchases outstanding (£300,000/£4,110).

The number of days' purchases outstanding will reflect credit terms offered by the supplier, any discounts that may be obtained for prompt payment and the collection action taken by the supplier. Failure to pay trade payables will likely result in a higher cost of sales, and may result in the loss or stoppage of supply, which can then affect the ability of a business to satisfy its customers' orders. The average payment time for trade payables has to be disclosed in a company's Annual Report to shareholders.

Managing working capital

Importantly, improving days' sales outstanding or inventory turnover will not improve the working capital ratio as there is only a shift from one type of current asset to another. Table 7.5 shows the effect of changes in working capital. In the first column our working capital ratio is 150% and acid test 100%. In the second column, faster collection of receivables and faster inventory turnover converts those current assets into

Table 7.5   Effects of changes in working capital.

	1. Original working capital	2. Improved DSO and Inventory turnover	3. Improved DPO	4. Repayment of long term loan
Bank	10,000	15,000	9,000	6,000
Receivables	10,000	7,000	7,000	7,000
Inventory	10,000	8,000	8,000	8,000
Total current assets	30,000	30,000	24,000	21,000
Payables	20,000	20,000	14,000	14,000
Total current liabilities	20,000	20,000	14,000	14,000
Working capital ratio	150%	150%	171%	150%
Acid test ratio	100%	110%	114%	93%

money in the bank. While this will show improved days' sales outstanding and inventory turnover, there is no change in the working capital ratio, although there is an improvement in the acid test (as inventory has fallen). In the third column, the cash funds are used to reduce payables. This improves our days' purchases outstanding ratio and increases our working capital ratio as there are now more current assets relative to current liabilities. In the final column, some of the cash funds are used to repay long-term debt (a non-current liability). This will improve the gearing ratio but results in a fall (still to an acceptable level) in the working capital and acid test ratios, as there are now less current assets available to meet current liabilities.

One of the issues in calculating the receivables, inventory and payables ratios is the number of days to be used in calculating average daily sales, inventory or purchases. Provided you are consistent, it doesn't matter too much, but in practice it is best to try to approximate the number of days a business is open. So a retail business operating 365 days per year could use that number while a professional service firm operating 5 days per week for 52 weeks may use only 260 days.

The final group of ratios comprises measures used by shareholders as measures of investment performance.

Shareholder return

For these ratios we need some additional information:

$$
\begin{array}{ll}
\text{number of shares issued} & 100{,}000 \\
\text{market value of shares} & £2.50
\end{array}
$$

Dividend per share

$$
\frac{\text{dividends paid}}{\text{number of shares}} = \frac{30{,}000}{100{,}000} = £0.30 \text{ per share}
$$

Dividend payout ratio

$$
\frac{\text{dividends paid}}{\text{profit after tax}} = \frac{30{,}000}{70{,}000} = 43\%
$$

Dividend yield

$$
\frac{\text{dividends paid per share}}{\text{market value per share}} = \frac{0.30}{2.50} = 12\%
$$

Earnings per share (EPS)

$$\frac{\text{profit after tax}}{\text{number of shares}} = \frac{70,000}{100,000} = £0.70 \text{ per share}$$

Price/earnings (P/E) ratio

$$\frac{\text{market value per share}}{\text{earnings per share}} = \frac{2.50}{0.70} = 3.57 \text{ times}$$

The shareholder ratios are measures of returns to shareholders on their investment in the business. The dividend and earnings ratios reflect the annual return to shareholders. Stock market investors have an expectation for stable or increasing dividends per share, hence the dividend payout ratio may have to increase to maintain a stable dividend. It is quite common for companies to pay out around half their after-tax profits as dividend, retaining the balance for reinvestment in the business, however, there are substantial variations between companies. The P/E ratio measures the number of years over which the investment in shares will be recovered through earnings. The long-term average P/E ratio for Stock Exchange listed companies in the UK, USA and Australia is around 15. Earnings per share represent the 'return' to shareholders through profits (even though part of the profits is paid as dividend and part reinvested in the company as retained earnings). Because share issues can take place during the year, the number of shares needs to be weighted. Companies are required to calculate this weighting in a particular way and show their earnings per share as part of the Income Statement.

The relationship between financial ratios

As can be seen from the ratios, some are drawn from only the Income Statement, some from only the Statement of Financial Position and some are drawn from both. While ratios can provide useful information individually, it is important to understand the relationships between the ratios. Figure 7.2 shows the relationships between the 'elements' (see the *Framework* in Chapter 6) in the Income Statement and Statement of Financial Position and the financial ratios. Although this is rather a complex diagram, it can help to see how different ratios affect each other. So, for example, total assets (capital employed) in the Statement of Financial Position affect both ROCE, a profitability measure (because capital employed is the denominator in that ratio) and asset turnover, an efficiency measure (where capital employed is also the denominator). These relationships between ratios will help you to interpret financial information.

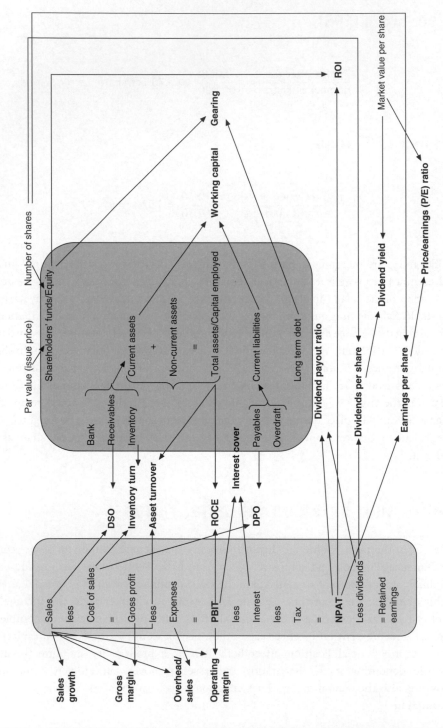

Figure 7.2   Structure of financial statement elements (Income Statement and Statement of Financial Position) and financial ratios.

Interpreting financial statements using ratios

The interpretation of any ratio depends on the industry. In particular, the ratio needs to be interpreted as a trend over time, or by comparison to industry averages or to competitor ratios or to predetermined targets. These comparisons help determine whether performance is improving and where further improvement may be necessary. Based on the understanding of the business context and competitive conditions, and the information provided by ratio analysis, users of financial statements can make judgements about the pattern of past performance, financial strength and future prospects. Our focus is not on how investors use financial ratios to make investment decisions (a topic that falls more easily into corporate finance) but on how ratios are used by boards of directors and managers in their own organization. There will be two particular emphases: how to improve performance as measured by ratios over time; and how the company appears to its investors when they look at the company's financial ratios. In addition, managers will also be concerned with the financial statements of competitors, customers and suppliers.

Broadly speaking, businesses seek:

- increasing rates of profit on shareholders' funds, capital employed and sales, and sales growth;
- adequate liquidity (a ratio of current assets to liabilities of not less than 100%) to ensure that debts can be paid as they fall due, but not an excessive rate to suggest that funds are inefficiently used;
- a level of debt commensurate with the business risk taken;
- high efficiency as a result of maximizing sales from the business's investments in assets; and
- a satisfactory return on the investment made by shareholders.

When considering the movement in a ratio over two or more years, it is important to look at possible causes for the movement. This understanding can be gained by understanding that either the numerator (top number in the ratio) or denominator (bottom number in the ratio) or both can influence the change. Some of the possible explanations behind changes in ratios are described below.

Profitability

Improvements in operating profitability as a proportion of sales (PBIT or EBIT) are the result of profitability growing at a faster rate than sales growth, a result either of a higher gross margin or lower overheads. Note that sales growth may result in a higher profit but not necessarily in a higher rate of profit as a percentage of sales.

Improvement in the rate of gross profit may be the result of higher selling prices, lower cost of sales or changes in the mix of product/services sold or different market segments in which they are sold, which may reflect differential profitability. Naturally, the opposite explanations hold true for deterioration in profitability.

Improvements in the returns on shareholders' funds (ROI) and capital employed (ROCE) may either be because profits have increased and/or because the capital used to generate those profits has altered. When businesses are taken over by others, one way of improving ROI or ROCE is to increase profits by reducing costs (often as a result of economies of scale), but another is to maintain profits while reducing assets and repaying debt. By shifting from debt to equity for example, the ROCE may not alter (because capital employed is a combination of debt and equity) but the ROI will decrease (assuming constant profits) as there is more equity.

Liquidity

Improvements in the working capital and acid test ratios are the result of changing the balance between current assets and current liabilities. As the working capital cycle in Figure 7.1 showed, and as illustrated in Table 7.5, money changes form between receivables, inventory, bank and payables and results in changes to liquidity ratios. Borrowing over the long term in order to fund current assets will improve this ratio, as will profits that generate cash flow. By contrast, using liquid funds to repay long-term loans or incurring losses will reduce the working capital used to repay creditors.

Gearing

The gearing ratio reflects the balance between long-term debt and shareholders' equity. It changes as a result of changes in either shareholders' funds (more shares may be issued, or there may be a buyback of shares), raising new borrowings or repayments of debt. As debt increases in proportion to shareholders' funds, the gearing ratio will increase.

Interest cover may increase as a result of higher profits or lower borrowings (and reduce as a result of lower profits or higher borrowings), but even with constant borrowings changes in the interest rate paid will also influence this ratio.

Activity/efficiency

Asset turnover improves either because sales increase or the total assets used reduce, but the goal is to make the business assets work hard to generate sales, and to sell off assets that are no longer productive.

Shareholder return

Decisions made by directors about the dividend to be paid influence the dividend payout ratio. Dividends are a decision made by directors on the basis of the proportion of profits they want to distribute and the capital needed to be retained in the business to fund growth. Often, shareholder value considerations will dictate the level of dividends, which businesses do not like to reduce on a per share basis. This is sometimes at the cost of retaining fewer profits and then having to borrow additional funds to support growth strategies. However, the number of shares issued also affects this ratio, as share issues will result in a lower dividend *per share* unless the total dividend is increased.

As companies have little influence over their share price, which is a result of market expectations of future performance as much as past performance, dividend yield, while influenced by the dividend paid per share, is more readily influenced by changes in the market price of the shares.

Earnings per share are influenced, as for profitability, by the profit but also (like dividends) by the number of shares issued. As for the dividend yield, the price/earnings (P/E) ratio is often more a result of changes in the share price based on future expectations of stock market investors than in the profits reflected in the earnings per share.

One way of improving shareholder value is through a share buyback. A buyback occurs when a company purchases its own shares and then either cancels them or holds them as treasury shares for re-issue in the future. A company can buy its shares in the open market as for any other investor, or it may make a proportional offer to all shareholders (in much the same way that a rights issue offers new shares to shareholders in proportion to their existing shareholding). Companies normally buy back their shares from their retained earnings. Large-scale share buybacks are a way by which companies can distribute surplus cash by carrying out a return of equity to shareholders. One advantage of a buyback is that by reducing the number of issued shares, the share price increases, resulting in a capital gain to shareholders. An alternative to increasing dividends is to carry out a small buyback of shares each year. This results in a capital gain to shareholders rather than income, and does not commit the company to any future dividend payment, given the desire to maintain constant dividends per share.

Using the Statement of Cash Flows

While financial ratios do not use information from the Statement of Cash Flows, cash flow information does provide valuable information that helps in interpreting ratios. You will recall that the Statement of Cash Flows separates cash flows into their operating, investing and financing components. Changes in profitability, affected by changes in working capital, are revealed in the operating cash flows. So increasing or decreasing profits and/or improved or worsening working capital management will be reflected here. Where capital employed has increased, you would expect to see the purchase of new non-current assets or business acquisitions (including goodwill) under investing activities, where you would also see proceeds of sale of any surplus non-current assets. This kind of investment is also likely to influence the asset turnover ratio. Financing decisions will appear under the cash flow from financing section. Here you would expect to see proceeds from borrowings or repayments of debt, equity raised from shareholders or payments for share buybacks, as well as the payment of dividends. In interpreting the financial ratios, check your interpretation with the Statement of Cash Flows as this will reinforce (or challenge) your interpretation.

The following case study provides an example of how to interpret financial ratios.

Case study 7.1: HMV Group – interpreting financial statements

HMV Group has 417 retail stores in four countries, supplying DVDs, music and games. HMV operates Waterstone's, the largest bookseller in the UK. Waterstone's has 314 stores and generates 25% of HMV's annual sales. The information in Tables 7.6 and 7.7 has been extracted from the company's Annual Report for the year ended 28 April 2010. The full Annual Report including financial statements and notes to the accounts is available from http://www.hmvgroup.com//media/Files/H/HMV-Group/Annual%20Reports/hmv_annual-report-2010.pdf.

Table 7.6   Income Statement for HMV Group plc (modified from the original).

	2010 £m	2009 £m
Revenue	2,017	1,957
Cost of sales	−1,856	−1,804
Gross profit	161	153
Administrative expenses	−86	−84
Operating profit	75	69
Finance costs	−6	−8
Profit before taxation	69	61
Taxation	−20	−17
Profit	49	44

The Statement of Changes in Equity discloses that the company paid a dividend of £31m in financial year 2010 and £30m in financial year 2009.

Earnings per share	11.6p	10.8p

Accounting standards require companies to disclose the earnings per share in their annual reports.

Dividend per share	7.4p	7.4p

Equity

The company had 423,587,057 shares on issue at the end of financial years 2009 and 2010.

In April 2010, the share price was 79p. In April 2009, the share price was £1.50

Table 7.7   Balance Sheet* for HMV Group plc (modified from the original).

	2010 £m	2009 £m
Assets		
Non-current assets		
Property, plant & equipment	167	162
Intangible assets	122	73
Other assets	43	41
Trade receivables	13	1
	345	277
Current assets		
Inventories	248	214
Trade & other receivables	80	72
Other assets	2	1
Cash and short-term deposits	30	53
	360	340
Total assets	705	617
Liabilities		
Non-current liabilities		
Retirement benefit & other liabilities	39	21

Table 7.7   Continued

	2010 £m	2009 £m
Interest bearing loans	12	5
Other liabilities	2	
Provisions	1	-
	54	26
Current liabilities		
Trade & other payables	442	416
Income tax payable	21	17
Interest-bearing loans and borrowings	84	53
Provisions	4	5
	551	491
Total liabilities	**605**	**517**
Net assets	**100**	**100**
Equity		
Share capital	347	347
Reserves	13	12
Retained earnings	(260)	(259)
Total equity	**100**	**100**

Notes: * HMV used the term 'Balance Sheet' in its 2010 Annual Report.

The number of shares issued in both 2010 and 2009 was 423.6 million. HMV's share price has varied dramatically, from a high of £2.82 in February 2005 to a low of 7.75p in May 2011, impacting shareholder ratios significantly. At the end of financial year in April 2010, the share price was 79p. In April 2009, the share price was £1.50. At the time of writing, HMV's share price was 10.5p, valuing the company at £44.5 million.

Current prices of UK-listed shares are available from the London Stock Exchange at http://www .londonstockexchange.com/prices-and-markets/stocks/stocks-and-prices.htm and similar data is available from US, Australian and other stock markets.

A reading of HMV's Annual Report for 2010 reveals the context in which the financial statements should be read and the ratios calculated. In particular:

- A very competitive market environment, with online competitors prepared to offer many of the same products to their customers at loss-leading prices, and competition from the free, illegal download market.
- The disappointing financial performance of Waterstone's.
- The acquisition of MAMA, which owns and operates live music venues.
- HMV's strategy has three pillars: the turnaround of Waterstone's; evolution of the product mix building on the HMV brand; and growing the business in live and digital music.

Although ratios can be calculated without reference to the Notes, the following comments show that more meaningful ratios can often be calculated using the additional information in the Notes. The Notes, together with other information in the Annual Report, are essential in interpreting the ratios for HMV. Ratios for profitability are shown in Table 7.8.

Table 7.8   HMV's profitability ratios.

	2010	**2009**
Return on shareholders' investment (ROI)	$\dfrac{49}{100}$ $=49\%$	$\dfrac{44}{100}$ $=44\%$
Return on capital employed (ROCE)	$\dfrac{75}{100+12}$ $=66.9\%$	$\dfrac{69}{100+5}$ $=65.7\%$
Return on capital employed (ROCE) including current debt*	$\dfrac{75}{100+12+84}$ $=38.3\%$	$\dfrac{69}{100+5+53}$ $=43.7\%$
Operating profit/sales	$\dfrac{75}{2017}$ $=3.7\%$	$\dfrac{69}{1957}$ $=3.5\%$
Gross profit/sales	$\dfrac{161}{2017}$ $=8.0\%$	$\dfrac{153}{1957}$ $=7.8\%$
Overhead/sales	$\dfrac{86}{2017}$ $=4.3\%$	$\dfrac{84}{1957}$ $=4.3\%$
Sales growth	$\dfrac{2017-1957}{1957}$ $=3.1\%$	

Notes: * HMV's loans and borrowings (Note 22) include current liabilities because the loans are payable within 12 months. A more realistic ROCE may be calculated by using all loans, whether shown as current or non-current liabilities.

ROI is a high 49%, up from 44% in 2009, reflecting a high profit based on shareholders' funds. However, the Statement of Financial Position reveals that equity has been reduced substantially by past losses (reflected in the negative retained earnings figure). This means that the company's accumulated losses from prior years have eroded much of the original amount contributed as equity by shareholders. Return on capital employed increased marginally to 66.9%. In calculating ROCE, there is little long-term debt. However, there is an amount of £84 million (£53 million in 2009 shown as 'interest bearing loans and borrowings') in current liabilities. In this case, what in most companies would be long-term debt is shown as a current liability for HMV. This is because the debt is repayable within one year. This is an example of the care which needs to be taken in calculating ratios! A more accurate picture in HMV's case of gearing can be seen by including the current debt. This results in a

ROCE of 38.3%, a drop from the previous year. To explain this, we look at the Statement of Financial Position and see that total assets (i.e. the capital employed in the business) have increased from £617 million to £705 million, and as we will see below, this came from an increase in gearing.

Operating profit to sales has increased marginally, a result of slightly higher gross margins (from 7.8% to 8.0%) with overheads remaining as a constant proportion of sales, and a small 3.1% sales increase. The company needs to grow its sales more than this, maintain or improve its margin, and control overheads to increase its profitability.

Ratios for liquidity are shown in Table 7.9. The working capital ratio based on Statement of Financial Position figures has reduced from 69.2% to 65.3%. The acid ratio has fallen from 25.7% to 20.3%. In interpreting these ratios we must be careful to consider the business context. While there is a high level of inventory, there are few receivables in any retail business as virtually all sales are made on a cash basis (even if paid by credit card, the retailer receives payment almost immediately). So the 'standard' of having more current assets than current liabilities is less relevant. The ratios are also impacted by the inclusion of borrowings in current liabilities. If we recalculate the ratios by excluding the current debt, which we treated as long-term debt for ROCE purposes, the working capital ratio is a more acceptable 77.1% for 2010, little change to 2009. The acid test ratio without the current debt is 24.0%, down from 28.8%. This is largely because, for the acid test, current liabilities (excluding debt) have increased more than current assets (excluding inventory). Again, it is important to understand something of the industry for which ratios are being calculated. The fact that retail stores buy their inventory on credit, and tend to take long periods to pay their suppliers, but receive sales in cash means that their liquidity ratios are going to be affected! Of course, these ratios do highlight the necessity to monitor sales on a daily basis to ensure that sufficient cash funds are being generated to pay suppliers (we look at this below under activity/efficiency ratios).

Table 7.9 HMV's liquidity ratios.

	2010	2009
Working capital	$\dfrac{360}{551}$	$\dfrac{340}{491}$
	$= 65.3\%$	$= 69.2\%$
Working capital excluding current debt*	$\dfrac{360}{551-84}$	$\dfrac{340}{491-53}$
	$= 77.1\%$	$= 77.6\%$
Acid test	$\dfrac{360-248}{551}$	$\dfrac{340-214}{491}$
	$= 20.3\%$	$= 25.7\%$
Acid test excluding current debt	$\dfrac{360-248}{551-84}$	$\dfrac{340-214}{491-53}$
	$= 24.0\%$	$= 28.8\%$

Notes: * As for ROCE, as loans and borrowings are included in current liabilities, a variation of the working capital ratio is to eliminate current loans (Note 22).

Ratios for gearing are shown in Table 7.10. Again, without including the current debt there is a low gearing ratio of 10.7%. By including the current debt the gearing ratio shows an increase from 36.7% in 2009 to 49% in 2010. This is a more realistic level of debt and reflects the increase in capital employed. It is not shown here, but the Statement of Cash Flows in HMV's 2010 Annual Report reveals a £35 million borrowing in 2010 and a purchase of property, plant and equipment in the same year of almost £40 million, together with the cost of acquisition of MAMA for £47 million. This example shows that it is important to use the Statement of Cash Flows to help interpret the financial ratios. Returning to the gearing ratios, we can see that interest cover is a healthy 12.5 times, up from 8.6 times in 2009.

Table 7.10   HMV's gearing ratios.

	2010	2009
Gearing	$\dfrac{12}{100+12}$	$\dfrac{5}{100+5}$
	10.7%	4.8%
Gearing (including current debt)*	$\dfrac{12+84}{100+12+84}$	$\dfrac{5+53}{100+5+53}$
	49.0%	36.7%
Interest cover	$\dfrac{75}{6}$	$\dfrac{69}{8}$
	$= 12.5x$	$= 8.6x$

Notes: As for ROCE and working capital, a more comprehensive picture of gearing is available by looking at current as well as long-term loans and borrowings (Note 22).

The ratios for activity/efficiency are shown in Table 7.11. Asset turnover has fallen from 3.17 (or 317%) to 2.86 (or 286%), indicating a less efficient use of the company's asset base to generate sales. This is a consequence of the higher level of non-current assets and only a small sales increase. Inventory turnover has declined from 8.42 (equivalent to 43 days' holding of inventory) to 7.48 (or 49 days). However, Note 5 to the financial statements shows a 'cost of inventories recognized as expense'. Like many retailers, the 'cost of sales' figure is not just the cost of goods sold but includes the costs of retail stores (rental, staff costs, etc.) with 'administrative expenses' in the Income Statement generally including head office, distribution and other business-wide costs. Recalculating the inventory turn with the 'cost of inventories recognized as expense' figure rather than the cost of sales may show a more meaningful ratio, but still an increase in inventory holding from 61.2 days to 70 days. In either case, inventory is sitting in retail stores for longer between its purchase and its sale. While the second calculation is more accurate, the important thing to remember about calculating and interpreting ratios is to be consistent: choose a figure you think is most reliable in terms of the organization and apply the same calculation from year to year.

Days' purchases outstanding (DPO) have increased slightly from 84.2 to 87. While this is a high figure, it is not uncommon in retailing for retailers to have extended trading terms from suppliers.

Table 7.11   HMV's activity/efficiency ratio.

	2010	2009
Asset turnover	$\dfrac{2017}{705}$ $= 2.86 \times (286\%)$	$\dfrac{1957}{617}$ $= 3.17\times (317\%)$
Inventory turnover	$\dfrac{1856}{248}$ $= 7.48\text{x}$ $365/7.48 = 49 \text{ days}$	$\dfrac{1804}{214}$ $= 8.42\text{x}$ $365/8.42 = 43 \text{ days}$
Inventory turnover (using cost of inventories recognized as an expense)*	$\dfrac{1296}{248}$ $= 5.22\text{x}$ $365/5.22 = 70 \text{ days}$	$\dfrac{1276}{214}$ $= 5.96\text{x}$ $365/5.96 = 61.2 \text{ days}$
Days payables outstanding	$\dfrac{442}{(1856/365)}$ $= 87.0 \text{ days}$	$\dfrac{416}{(1804/365)}$ $= 84.2 \text{ days}$
Days sales outstanding	$\dfrac{80}{(2017/365)}$ $= 14.4 \text{ days}$	$\dfrac{72}{(1957/365)}$ $= 13.4 \text{ days}$

Notes: * Note 5 discloses this as a major item within cost of sales. This may be a more meaningful figure with which to calculate inventory turnover.

Days' sales outstanding (DSO) need to be interpreted with care as retail businesses do not have Receivables (debtors) in the way other businesses that sell on credit do. The ratio shows an increase from 13.4 to 14.4 days.

The shareholder return ratios are shown in Table 7.12. Both dividends per share and earnings per share are available from the Annual Report and are repeated at the bottom of Table 7.6. HMV's earnings per share have increased slightly from 10.8p to 11.6p due to the increase in profits (given that in this case we know that there has been no change in shareholder capital); the dividend paid has remained constant. It is a common strategy of listed companies to maintain their dividend payments at the same level rather than reduce (or increase) dividends dramatically in response to fluctuations in earnings. Dividends paid at this constant level have consumed a lower portion of the after-tax profits, as shown by the dividend payout ratio.

The dividend yield is an effective interest rate and therefore fluctuates in line with the share price. The yield has increased from 4.9% to 9.4%, but as dividends per share have remained constant, this improvement in yield is solely due to the dramatically falling share price (see earlier in this case study). The price/earnings ratio has dropped from 13.9 to 6.8 and this reflects depressed stock market conditions generally, and relatively low expectations by investors of future earnings by HMV.

Table 7.12   HMV's shareholder return ratios.

	2010	2009
Dividend per share (disclosed in Income Statement)	7.4p	7.4p
Dividend payout ratio	$\frac{31}{49}$	$\frac{30}{44}$
	63.3%	68.2%
Dividend yield (using April 2010 and April 2009 share prices)	$\frac{7.4p}{79p}$	$\frac{7.4p}{150p}$
	9.4%	4.9%
Earnings per share (disclosed in Income Statement)	11.6p	10.8p
Price/earnings ratio	$\frac{79p}{11.6p}$	$\frac{150p}{10.8p}$
	= 6.8x	= 13.9x

As was indicated earlier in this chapter, two years is too short a period to draw any really meaningful conclusions about company performance and we would need to look at the ratios over five years to identify any trends properly. Table 7.13 shows some of the information from the five-year summary of performance in HMV's Annual Report. This five-year summary is a Stock Exchange requirement under its Listing Rules. By calculating the ratios shown in Table 7.14 we can see the trend in these figures more clearly. These figures show the fairly flat sales (especially when taking inflationary pressures into account) over the last five years and the change in profits, with a substantial reduction between 2006–7 followed by a gradual improvement over 2008–10. In making comparisons with the ratios above, note that profits in Table 7.13 are profits before tax, whereas our operating margin ratio refers to profits before interest and tax. There has also been a stable dividend per share over the five-year period. The full set of ratios for the five-year period would of course provide far more informative data than our two-year comparison.

Table 7.13   HMV's five-year summary of performance.

In £m	2010	2009	2008	2007	2006
Turnover	2,017	1,957	1,936	1,895	1,826
Profit before tax	69	61	52	22	80
Earnings per share	11.6p	10.8p	22.1p	4p	14p
Dividend per share	7.4p	7.4p	7.4p	7.4p	7.4p

Table 7.14   HMV's ratios based on five-year summary of performance.

In £m	2010	2009	2008	2007	2006
Sales growth (year on year)	3.1%	1.1%	2.2%	3.8%	–3.2%
Profit before tax/sales	3.4%	3.1%	2.7%	1.2%	4.4%

Limitations of ratio analysis

The limitations of financial statements were discussed in Chapter 6. In particular for ratio analysis purposes, financial statements are historical records and backwards-looking. Inflation can impact on the values shown in financial statements, particularly where assets are held at historical cost in the Statement of Financial Position. The Statement of Financial Position, it should also be recognized, is merely a 'snapshot' of assets and liabilities on the last day of the financial year.

The calculation of profit in financial statements is arrived at after estimates which involve significant subjective judgement, as we saw in relation to estimates such as accruals, prepayments, depreciation, goodwill amortization and provisions (see Chapter 6). There is also some flexibility in how accounting standards are applied which involves issues of earnings management (see Chapters 3 and 5), i.e. reporting financial performance that the stock market expects, as well as ethical issues (see Chapter 5 for a discussion of ethics in accounting). These judgements all influence the numbers that are used in ratio analysis.

Ratios are of little value unless calculated over several years when a trend can be identified, or in comparison with similar organizations for benchmarking purposes. Ratios need to be interpreted in the context of economic, industry and competitive factors, and the organization's unique strategy. Ratios are only able to be calculated once per year on the basis of published financial statements but, of course, accountants within organizations will have access to much more detailed figures and will have those figures on a monthly basis, so the ratios calculated internally will be even more reliable in terms of identifying trends and opportunities for improvement. More detailed information is contained in the Notes to financial statements than in the financial statements themselves and judgements need to be made about whether to use data on the face of financial statements, or contained within the Notes (some of the examples in the HMV case study illustrated this).

Finally, there are different definitions of ratios used in different textbooks and by different financial statement analysts. However, the consistent use of a ratio definition is more important than the particular definition selected.

Consequently, care needs to be exercised in calculating and interpreting ratios and time needs to be spent understanding the economic and competitive context in which ratios are being interpreted (for example, thinking about the nature of the retail industry is necessary to properly interpret some of the ratios for HMV in this chapter). This broader contextual understanding can be gained for example by reading the company's Annual Report, financial and trade press, internet reports, market research, consultant and analyst reports that provide broader information about economic change, the industry, competitive conditions, supply chain issues, customer behaviour, regulatory change and so on.

The following case study highlights some of these limitations.

Case study 7.2: Carrington Printers – an accounting critique

Carrington Printers was a privately owned, 100-year-old printing company employing about 100 people and operating out of its own premises in a medium-sized town. Although the company was heavily indebted and had been operating with a small loss for the past three years, it had a fairly strong

Statement of Financial Position and a good customer base spread over a wide geographical area. Carrington's simplified Statement of Financial Position is shown in Table 7.15. Although the case study is several years old (the organization was real, but the name has been changed), the data has been presented in the format under current accounting standards.

Table 7.15   Carrington Printers' Statement of Financial Position.

	$
Non-current assets	
Land and buildings at cost less depreciation	1,000,000
Plant and equipment at cost less depreciation	450,000
	1,450,000
Current assets	
Receivables	500,000
Inventory	450,000
	950,000
Total assets	2,400,000
Non-current liabilities	
Borrowings	750,000
Current liabilities	
Payables	850,000
Bank overdraft	250,000
	1,100,000
Total liabilities	1,850,000
Net assets	550,000
Equity	
Issued capital	100,000
Retained earnings	450,000
Shareholders' funds	550,000

The nature of the printing industry at the time the financial statements were prepared was that there was excess production capacity and over the previous year a price war had been fought between competitors in order to retain existing customers and win new business. The effect of this had been that selling prices (and consequently profit margins) had fallen throughout the industry. Carrington's plant and equipment were, in the main, quite old and not suited to some of the work that it was winning. Consequently, some work was being produced inefficiently, with a detrimental impact on profit margins. Before the end of the year the sales director had left the company and had influenced many of Carrington's customers, with whom he had established a good relationship, to move to his new employer. Over several months, Carrington's sales began to drop significantly.

Lost sales and deteriorating margins on some of the business affected cash flow. Printing companies at that time typically carried a large stock of paper in a range of weights, sizes and colours, while customers often took up to 60 days to pay their accounts. Because payment of taxes and employees takes priority, suppliers are often the last group to be paid. The major suppliers of printers are paper merchants, who stop supply when their customers do not pay on time. The consequence of Carrington's cash flow difficulties was that suppliers limited the supply of paper that Carrington needed to satisfy customer orders.

None of these events was reflected in the financial statements and the auditors, largely unaware of changing market conditions, had little understanding of the gradual detrimental impact on Carrington that had taken place at the time of the audit. Although aware of the cash flow tightening experienced by the company, the auditors signed the accounts, being satisfied that the business could be treated as a going concern.

As a result of the problems identified above, Carrington approached its bankers for additional loans. However, the bankers declined, believing that existing loans had reached the maximum percentage of the asset values against which they were prepared to lend. The company attempted a sale and leaseback of its land and buildings (through which a purchaser pays a market price for the property, with Carrington becoming a tenant on a long-term lease). However, investors interested in the property were not satisfied that Carrington was a viable tenant and the property was unable to be sold on that basis.

Cash flow pressures continued and the shareholders were approached to contribute additional capital. They were unable to do so and six months after the Statement of Financial Position was produced the company collapsed, and was placed into receivership and subsequently liquidation by its bankers.

The liquidators found, as is common in failed companies, that the values in the Statement of Financial Position were substantially higher than what the assets could be sold for. In particular:

- Land and buildings were sold for far less than an independent valuation had suggested, as the property would now be vacant.
- Plant and machinery were almost worthless given their age and condition and the excess capacity in the industry.
- Receivables were collected with substantial amounts being written off as bad debts. Customers often refuse to pay accounts giving spurious reasons and it is often not worthwhile for the liquidator to pursue collection action through the courts.
- Inventory was discovered to be largely worthless. Substantial stocks of paper were found to have been held for long periods with little likelihood of ever being used and other printers were unwilling to pay more than a fraction of its cost.

As the bankers had security over most of Carrington's assets, there were virtually no funds remaining after repaying bank loans to pay the unsecured creditors.

This case raises some important issues about the value of audited financial statements:

1. The importance of understanding the context of the business, that is how its market conditions and its mix of products or services are changing over time, and how well (or in this case badly) the business is able to adapt to these changes.

2. The preparation of financial statements assumes a going concern, but the circumstances facing a business can change quickly and the Statement of Financial Position can become a meaningless document.

3. The auditors rely on information from the directors about significant risks affecting the company. The directors did not intentionally deceive the auditors, but genuinely believed that the business could be turned around and into profits through winning back customers. They also believed that the large inventory would satisfy future customer orders. The directors also genuinely believed that the property could be sold in order to eliminate debt. This was unquestioned by the auditors.

The company's failure was repeated over the next few years as Carrington's competitors also faced liquidation as technological change eroded much of the market that these companies sold into.

This case highlights the limitations of both financial statements (see Chapter 6) and the use of ratios based on those financial statements, without a thorough knowledge of the broader environment facing the business.

Alternative theoretical perspectives on financial statements

Chapter 6 described the traditional theoretical perspective that has informed financial statements, that is agency theory. The role of financial statements in agency theory is to hold directors and managers accountable to shareholders. One of the key roles of top management is to communicate with shareholders and 'signalling' occurs when a financial measure is used to communicate. The Annual Report provides information that is much more than financial, and acts as the primary focus of signalling between the company and its shareholders. Financial statements, for example, are signals prepared by directors for shareholders, about their performance in carrying out the operations of the organization (reported in the Income Statement) and in building the assets of the organization (reported in the Statement of Financial Position). Financial statements are therefore important signals to current and potential shareholders about the company.

However, signalling does not just occur between the organization and outside stakeholders. Management in large organizations often devote much time to competing for resources for their business unit, project or team. Performance measures can be used internally in organizations to support claims by managers for additional resources for their business units. Managers who can demonstrate success in achieving their performance goals are more likely to be given increased access to resources in the future.

In the remainder of this chapter, we consider some alternative perspectives to agency: intellectual capital and institutional theory. We also introduce corporate social and environmental reporting.

Intellectual capital

Edvinsson and Malone (1997) defined intellectual capital as 'the hidden dynamic factors that underlie the visible company' (p. 11). Stewart (1997) defined intellectual capital as 'formalized, captured and leveraged knowledge' (p. 68). Intellectual capital is of particular interest to accountants in increasingly knowledge-based economies in which the limitations of traditional financial statements erode their value as a tool supporting meaningful decision making (Guthrie, 2001). Three dimensions of intellectual capital have been identified in the literature: human (developing and leveraging individual knowledge and skills); organizational (internal structures, systems and procedures); and customer (loyalty, brand, image and so on).

The disclosure of information about intellectual capital as an extension to financial reporting has been proposed by various accounting academics through an *intellectual capital statement*. The most publicized example is the *Skandia Navigator* (see Edvinsson and Malone, 1997). Intellectual capital statements report on the activities that management initiates and supports. Bukh *et al.* (2001) argued that there are three dimensions of intellectual capital: (i) an identity story, a grand narrative of innovation, flexibility or knowledge; (ii) a management model specifying the management activities that give substance to the grand story in areas such as technology, structure or employee development; and (iii) a presentation model that identifies the objects that are committed to numbers in the intellectual capital statements. The intellectual capital statement 'is more than just a set of metrics . . . Together these metrics, sketches/visualisations and stories/narratives form a network, which constitutes the report . . . The sketches/visualisations construct a certain "wholeness" in the organisation of metrics or measurements, while the story/narrative suggests how the legitimacy of the intellectual capital statement is created' (Bukh *et al.*, 2001, p. 99).

Intellectual capital statements reveal the limitations of financial statements and how additional contextual knowledge is important, especially as Western companies move increasingly away from manufacturing into service and knowledge-based businesses.

While most businesses espouse a commitment to employees and the value of their knowledge, as well as to some form of social or environmental responsibility, this is often merely rhetoric, a facade to appease the interest groups of stakeholders. The *institutional* setting of organizations provides another perspective from which to view financial statements.

Institutional theory

Institutional theory is valuable because it locates the organization within its historical and contextual setting. It is predicated on the need for legitimation and on isomorphic processes. Scott (1995) describes *legitimation* as the result of organizations being dependent, to a greater or lesser extent, on support from the environment for their survival and continued operation. Organizations need the support of governmental institutions where their operations are regulated (and few organizations are not regulated in some form or other). Organizations are also dependent on the acquisition of resources (labour, finance, technology and so on) for their purposes. If an organization is not legitimated, it may incur sanctions of a legal, economic or social nature.

The second significant aspect of institutional power is the operation of *isomorphism*, the tendency for different organizations to adopt similar characteristics. DiMaggio and Powell (1983) identified three forms of isomorphism: coercive, as a result of political influence and the need to gain legitimacy; mimetic, following from standard responses to uncertainty; and normative, associated with professionalization. They held that isomorphic tendencies between organizations were a result of wider belief systems and cultural frames of reference. Processes of education, inter-organizational movement of personnel and professionalization emphasize these belief systems and cultural values at an institutional level, and facilitate the mimetic processes that result in organizations imitating each other. We can see the results of isomorphism in for example the similarity of banks to each other and retailers to each other.

Isomorphic tendencies exist because 'organizations compete not just for resources and customers, but for political power and institutional legitimacy, for social as well as economic fitness' (DiMaggio and Powell, 1983, p. 150).

These legitimating and isomorphic processes become taken for granted by organizations as they strive to satisfy the demands of external regulators, resource suppliers and professional groups. These taken-for-granted processes themselves become institutionalized in the systems and processes – including accounting and reporting – adopted by organizations. Meyer (1994) argued that accounting arises 'in response to the demands made by powerful elements in the environment on which organizations are dependent' (p. 122).

One significant institutional influence on organizations has been the emergence of investor concern with corporate social responsibility.

Corporate social responsibility

The concern with stakeholders rather than shareholders (introduced in Chapter 2) began in the 1970s and is generally associated with the publication in 1975 of *The Corporate Report*, a publication by the Accounting Standards Steering Committee. Accounting academics began to question profit as the sole measure of business performance and suggested a wider social responsibility for business and a more *socially responsible accounting*.

Stakeholder theory argues that managers should serve the interests of anyone with a 'stake' in (that is, anyone who is affected by) the organization. Stakeholders include shareholders, but also encompass employees, suppliers, customers, government and the communities in which the firm operates. Managers need to strike an appropriate balance between these interests when directing the firm's activities so that one stakeholder group is not satisfied to the detriment of others. Much of the argument behind stakeholder theory is that economic pressures to satisfy only shareholders is short-term thinking and organizations need to ensure their survival and success in the long term by satisfying other stakeholders as well – this is called *sustainability* (see below). A concern with stakeholders beyond shareholders has led to a wider view about the content of Annual Reports.

Concepts of *corporate social responsibility*, or corporate social and environmental reporting (CSR), attempt to highlight the impact of organizations on society, and to incorporate such reports into company Annual Reports to supplement the economic focus of financial statements.

Jones (1995) suggested three reasons for this:

- A moral imperative that business organizations were insufficiently aware of the social consequences of their activities.
- External pressure from government and pressure groups and the demand by some institutional investors for ethical investments.
- Internal change taking place within organizations as a result of education and professionalization, etc.

However, there has been little support for broader social accounting because accountants and managers have generally seen themselves as the agents of owners. CSR could be seen as undermining the power of shareholders and the foundation of the capitalist economic system. There are also technical difficulties associated with social reporting, and a dominant belief among business leaders that government and not business has the responsibility to determine what is reported.

During the 1980s and 1990s environmental accounting (see for example Gray *et al.*, 1996) focused on responsibility for the natural environment and in particular on sustainability as a result of concerns about ozone depletion, the greenhouse effect and climate change. These concerns were associated with the growth of pressure groups such as Greenpeace and Friends of the Earth. Part of the appeal of environmental accounting was that issues of energy efficiency, recycling and reductions in packaging had cost-saving potential for companies and therefore profits and social responsibility came to be seen as not necessarily mutually exclusive.

Zadek (1998) argued that social and ethical accounting, auditing and reporting together provide one of the few practical mechanisms for companies to integrate new patterns of civil accountability and governance with a business success model focused on stakeholders and core non-financial as well as financial values. Socially responsible businesses:

> find the spaces in the pipeline between investors and consumers where some choice in behaviour is possible . . . [and] a far more ambitious agenda of shifting the basic boundaries by raising public awareness towards social and environmental agendas, and supporting the emergence of new forms of investors that take non-financial criteria into account (p. 1439).

Sustainability and the 'triple bottom line'

The best-known definition of sustainability comes from *Our Common Future* (the so-called 'Brundtland Report') prepared under the auspices of the World Council on Environment and Development in 1987, which defines sustainable development as that which 'meets the needs of the present without compromising the ability of future generations to meet their own needs'. In other words, sustainability is a condition where the demands placed upon the environment by people and business organizations can be met without reducing the capacity of the environment to provide for future generations. Some of the major sustainability issues are population, climate change and energy use.

An example is climate change, which is a particular focus of politicians and businesses around the world, and generally accepted to be a consequence of poor use of technology and short-term management thinking. Reducing pollution and harmful carbon emissions through better technology will almost always lower cost or raise product value in the long term which will offset the cost of compliance with environmental standards, although doing so may require innovation. Some form of taxation or carbon pricing may be an advantage in forcing companies to address their level of emissions.

However, a broader understanding of sustainability is that economic sustainability and social and environmental sustainability are not mutually exclusive. Sustainability should not be seen as being just about 'green' issues but about the sustainability of economic performance to enable improvements in the environment and society. Equally, unless organizations pay attention to environmental and societal issues, they may not survive to generate sustainable profits for investors in the future. This is the triple bottom line: a concern with profits, with the environment, and with improving society.

The term 'triple bottom line' is credited to John Elkington and his consultancy firm *SustainAbility* to describe new types of markets and innovative business approaches that are needed to achieve success. The originators believe not only that profitable business must be socially and environmentally responsible, but further that social and environmental innovation is key to future market opportunities. In its broadest sense, the triple bottom line captures the spectrum of values that organizations must embrace – economic, environmental and social. In practical terms, triple bottom line accounting means expanding the traditional company reporting framework to take into account not just financial outcomes but also environmental and social performance. Such a framework is provided by the Global Reporting Initiative.

Global Reporting Initiative

The Global Reporting Initiative (GRI) is a multi-stakeholder and independent institution whose mission is to develop and disseminate globally applicable Sustainability Reporting Guidelines. These Guidelines are for voluntary use by organizations for reporting on the economic, environmental and social dimensions of their activities, products and services. The GRI incorporates the active participation of representatives from business, accountancy, investment, environmental, human rights, research and labour organizations from around the world. Started in 1997, GRI became independent in 2002, and is an official collaborating centre of the United Nations Environment Programme (UNEP).

In broad terms, the GRI Sustainability Reporting Guidelines (the third version of which was released in 2006) suggest that a sustainability report should include a description and performance indicators about the organization's economic, environmental and social impacts. It should identify the organization's stakeholders and their expectations, and report the organization's performance in the wider context of sustainability. The report should enable stakeholders to assess the organization's performance in relation to significant economic, environmental and social impacts.

A sustainability report is structured around a CEO statement, key environmental, social and economic indicators, a profile of the reporting entity, descriptions of relevant policies and management systems, stakeholder relationships, management performance, operational performance, product performance and a sustainability overview. The GRI has developed a set of core performance measures, or metrics, intended to be applicable to all business enterprises, sets of sector-specific metrics for specific types of enterprises and a uniform format for reporting information integral to a company's sustainability performance. The indicators cover six areas: economic, environment, human rights, labour, product responsibility and society.

Applying different perspectives to financial statements

In Chapters 4 and 5, we considered rational-economic, interpretive and critical perspectives that help to provide multiple views about the world in which we live. Chapters 6 and 7 have introduced many aspects of the construction and interpretation of financial statements.

Implicit in most of what is contained in the last three chapters is an acceptance of the rational-economic perspective described in Chapter 4. Financial statements support the agency model (see Chapter 6) by holding managers-as-agents accountable to shareholders-as-principals. The actions of managers, whose performance is represented in financial statements, are oriented to increasing shareholder value and financial statements are the most important device by which directors and managers provide signals to shareholders about the business.

How then can other perspectives inform the views we take about financial statements? The interpretive perspective (Chapter 5) relies on the notion of a reality that is socially constructed. This perspective accepts that shareholder value is a valid way of seeing the world, but it is not the only way of seeing the world. For example, a common phrase in many organizations is that 'people are our greatest asset' yet they do not appear in financial statements except in relation to salary expenses. Human resource managers may be critical of the focus on financial performance rather than issues of employee selection, retention, training and motivation as equally important for long-term business success. Similarly, marketing managers will value customer retention and satisfaction as necessary for achieving financial performance. Non-financial performance measures like the Balanced Scorecard (see Chapter 4) take a broader perspective, yet non-financial measures of performance on customer, process and learning and growth perspectives are not reflected in financial statements. The brief discussion of intellectual capital in this chapter reflected a broader approach to reporting on these kinds of issues.

The critical perspective (Chapter 5) questions the taken-for-granted assumptions behind financial statements and profit determination. At its extreme, this perspective questions why shareholders are in a privileged position and receive all the profits from business (in Chapter 3 we saw that the profit for a period is always transferred to shareholders' funds in the Statement of Financial Position). For example, Marxists ask why capital is more important than labour. A less extreme example is in relation to moral and ethical considerations. The discussion of creative accounting and ethics and the examples of WorldCom and Enron (see Chapter 5) reflect the unintended but often dysfunctional consequences of the shareholder value model. Power is a central issue in the critical perspective and institutional theory shows how power reinforces the status quo, through the way capital markets work and in the regulation of financial statements. This power is reinforced by top managers who use financial statements and rewards to reinforce their position. While this is to be expected under the rational-economic model, reinforcing the existing managerial hierarchy is not taken for granted in the critical perspective, which aims at questioning existing structures.

A good example of the interpretive and critical perspective is in relation to corporate social responsibility. This is a reflection of wider perspectives on a business (interpretive) and of power being exerted to require businesses to report in different ways, which by choice they are not likely to have done (critical).

Conclusion

This chapter has introduced the Annual Report and the importance of understanding the context of a business in order to interpret its financial performance. We have explained and illustrated the ratios for analysing financial statements in terms of profitability, liquidity, gearing, efficiency and shareholder return. We have looked in detail at interpreting these ratios using the case study of HMV and the chapter has identified some of the limitations of financial statement analysis, including a case study of privately owned Carrington Printers. It has also set financial statements in the context of alternative theoretical perspectives and corporate social responsibility that can provide different perspectives on financial statements and accounting information. These alternative perspectives continue throughout the third part of this book.

References

Accounting Standards Board (2006). *Reporting Statement: Operating and Financial Review*. London: ASB.

Bukh, P. N., Larsen, H. T. *et al.* (2001). Constructing intellectual capital statements. *Scandinavian Journal of Management*, *17*, 87–108.

DiMaggio, P. J. and Powell, W. W. (1983). The iron cage revisited: institutional isomorphism and collective rationality in organizational fields. *American Sociological Review*, *48*, 147–60.

Edvinsson, L. and Malone, M. S. (1997). *Intellectual Capital*. London: Piatkus.

Gray, R. H., Owen, D. L. and Adams, C. (1996). *Accounting and Accountability: Changes and Challenges in Corporate Social and Environmental Reporting*. London: Prentice Hall.

Guthrie, J. (2001). The management, measurement and the reporting of intellectual capital. *Journal of Intellectual Capital*, *2*(1), 27–41.

Jones, T. C. (1995). *Accounting and the Enterprise: A Social Analysis*. London: Routledge.

Meyer, J. W. (1994). Social environments and organizational accounting. In W. R. Scott and J. W. Meyer (Eds), *Institutional Environments and Organizations: Structural Complexity and Individuality*. Thousand Oaks, CA: Sage.

Scott, W. R. (1995). *Institutions and Organizations*. Thousand Oaks, CA: Sage.

Stewart, T. A. (1997). *Intellectual Capital: The New Wealth of Organizations*. London: Nicholas Brealey.

World Commission on Environment and Development (1987). Our Common Future (Bruntland Report). Annex to General Assembly document A/42/427. http://www.un-documents.net/wced-ocf.htm

Zadek, S. (1998). Balancing performance, ethics, and accountability. *Journal of Business Ethics*, *17*(13), 1421–41.

Website

The website of the Global Reporting Initiative (GRI) is at http://www.globalreporting.org/Home.

Questions

7.1   Following are the accounts for Drayton Ltd (Tables 7.16 and 7.17). Calculate the following ratios for Drayton for both 2010 and 2009:

- return on shareholders' investment (ROI);
- return on capital employed (ROCE);
- operating profit/sales;
- sales and expense growth;
- gearing;
- asset turnover;

Draw some conclusions from the change in the ratios over the two years.

Table 7.16   Drayton Ltd Income Statement for the year ended 31 December.

In £m	2010	2009
Turnover	141.1	138.4
Net operating costs	−113.9	−108.9
Operating profit	27.2	29.5
Non-operating income	1.4	1.3
Interest payable	−7.5	−8.8
Profit before tax	21.1	22.0
Income tax	−7.3	−5.7
Profit after tax	13.8	16.3
Dividends	−8.0	−8.0
Retained profit	5.8	8.3

Table 7.17   Balance Sheet as at 31 December.

In £m	2010	2009
Assets		
Non-current assets		
Tangible assets	266.7	265.3
Current assets		
Inventory	5.3	5.8
Trade receivables	15.7	20.9
Other receivables and prepayments	2.4	2.0
Bank	4.9	6.3
	28.3	35.0
Total assets	295.0	300.3
Liabilities		
Non-current liabilities		
Long-term loan	96.7	146.1
Current liabilities		
Trade payables	66.8	27.6
Total liabilities	163.5	173.7
Net assets	131.5	126.6
Equity		
Share capital	81.9	82.8
Retained earnings	49.6	43.8
Shareholders' funds	131.5	126.6

7.2   Jupiter Services has produced some financial ratios for the past two years. Use the ratios that have already been calculated to draw some conclusions about Jupiter's:

- profitability;
- liquidity;
- gearing;
- efficiency.

	Current year	Previous year
Return on (shareholders') investment (ROI)		
$\dfrac{\text{net profit after tax}}{\text{shareholders' funds}}$	$\dfrac{193.4}{2,610.1}$ 7.4%	$\dfrac{251.9}{2,547.0}$ 9.9%
Return on capital employed (ROCE)		
$\dfrac{\text{net profit before interest and tax}}{\text{shareholders' funds} + \text{long-term debt}}$	$\dfrac{367.3}{2,610.1 + 1,770}$ 8.4%	$\dfrac{394.7}{2,547 + 1,537.7}$ 9.7%
Net profit/sales		
$\dfrac{\text{net profit before interest and tax}}{\text{sales}}$	$\dfrac{367.3}{1,681.6}$ 21.8%	$\dfrac{394.7}{1,566.6}$ 25.2%
Working capital		
$\dfrac{\text{current assets}}{\text{current liabilities}}$	$\dfrac{613.3}{1,444}$ 42.5%	$\dfrac{475.3}{1,089.2}$ 43.6%
Gearing ratio		
$\dfrac{\text{long-term debt}}{\text{shareholders' funds} + \text{long-term debt}}$	$\dfrac{1,770}{2,610.1 + 1,770}$ 40.4%	$\dfrac{1,537.7}{2,547 + 1,537.7}$ 37.6%
Interest cover		
$\dfrac{\text{profit before interest and tax}}{\text{interest payable}}$	$\dfrac{367.3}{161.1}$ 2.28	$\dfrac{394.7}{120.7}$ 3.27
Days' sales outstanding		
$\dfrac{\text{receivables}}{\text{average daily sales}}$	$\dfrac{414.7}{1,681.6/365 = 4.607}$ 90	$\dfrac{353.8}{1,566.6/365 = 4.292}$ 82.4
Asset turnover		
$\dfrac{\text{sales}}{\text{total assets}}$	$\dfrac{1,681.6}{5,304.5 + 613.3}$ 28.4%	$\dfrac{1,566.6}{4,794.6 + 475.3}$ 29.7%

7.3 Jones and Brown Retail Stationery sells its products to other businesses. It has provided the following information:

Sales	€1,200,000
Cost of sales	€450,000
Inventory at end of year	€200,000
Receivables at end of year	€200,000
Payables at end of year	€100,000

Using 250 days as the number of days the business is open, calculate:

- the days' sales outstanding;
- the inventory turnover; and
- the days' purchases outstanding.

7.4 The five-year financial statements of RST plc show the following sales figures:

	2010	2009	2008	2007	2006
Sales (in €m)	155	144	132	130	120

Calculate the sales growth figures for each year.

7.5 RST's Income Statement for 2008 shows:

	€m
Sales	155
Cost of sales	45
Gross profit	110
Selling, administration expenses	65
Operating profit before interest and taxes	45
Interest	10
Profit before tax	35
Income tax	7
Profit after tax	28

Calculate the overhead to sales ratio.

Case study question: Paramount Services plc

Paramount Services provides a range of business consultancy services. Its financial statements for the last year with prior year comparison are reproduced in Table 7.18.

Table 7.18   Paramount Services plc.

Income Statement

In $'000	2010	2009
Income	34,000	29,000
Less expenses	16,500	13,000
Operating profit before interest	17,500	16,000
Less interest expense	4,000	2,700
Profit before tax	13,500	13,300
Income tax expense	5,400	5,320
Net profit after tax	8,100	7,980
The Statement of Changes in Equity shows the following:		
Dividends paid	4,000	3,750
Number of shares issued	10,000,000	10,000,000
Earnings per share	£0.81	£0.80
Dividend per share	£0.40	£0.38
Market price of shares	£8.55	£10.20

Statement of Financial Position

In $'000	2010	2009
Assets		
Non-current assets	21,933	17,990
Current assets		
Receivables	7,080	4,750
Bank	377	1,250
	7,457	6,000
Total assets	29,390	23,990
Liabilities		
Non-current liabilities		
Long-term loans	2,750	2,000
Current liabilities		
Payables	4,300	3,750
Total liabilities	7,050	5,750
Net assets	22,340	18,240
Equity		
Capital and reserves		
Shareholders' funds	10,000	10,000
Retained profits	12,340	8,240
	22,340	18,240

An analyst has produced the following ratio analysis (Table 7.19) and has asked you to comment on any aspects that you think are important.

Table 7.19   Paramount Services plc.

Ratio analysis

	2010	2009
Sales growth	17.2%	
Expense growth	26.9%	
Profit growth	9.4%	
Interest cover	4.4	5.9
PBIT/Sales	39.7%	45.9%
ROCE (PBIT/SHF + L/TD)	69.7%	79.1%
ROI (NPAT/SHF)	36.3%	43.8%
Dividend payout	49.4%	47.0%
Dividend yield	4.7%	3.7%
P/E ratio	10.56	12.78
Asset efficiency (Sales/TA)	1.2	1.2
Days sales outstanding	76.0	59.8
Working capital (CA/CL)	1.7	1.6
Gearing (LTD)/(SHF + LTD)	11.0%	9.9%

Case study question: General Machinery Ltd

General Machinery manufactures computer numerical control (CNC) equipment for its customers who use the equipment in the manufacture of electronic circuit boards. Ratios have been calculated from annual reports for the last five years and are shown in Table 7.20. The Statement of Cash Flows is shown in Table 7.21.

Table 7.20   Ratios.

	2010	2009	2008	2007	2006
ROI	5.0%	3.2%	3.6%	6.2%	5.8%
ROCE	9.2%	7.1%	6.2%	7.6%	6.4%
Operating margin	16.8%	13.9%	12.6%	15.7%	14.1%
Gross margin	70.0%	71.0%	72.0%	74.0%	75.0%
Overhead to sales	53.2%	57.1%	59.4%	58.3%	60.9%
Sales growth	11.4%	9.4%	6.7%	9.1%	
Working capital	198%	360%	340%	368%	326%
Acid test	135%	287%	270%	275%	243%
Gearing	42.0%	40.5%	38.6%	36.5%	37.4%
Interest cover	182%	162%	202%	376%	517%

Table 7.20   Continued

	2010	2009	2008	2007	2006
Asset turnover	48%	46%	44%	44%	41%
Days' sales outstanding	60	63	68	70	73
Inventory turn	3.3	3.1	2.8	2.2	2.3
Days' purchases outstanding	78	88	102	105	111
Dividend per share	$0.036	$0.027	$0.025	$0.036	$0.036
Dividend payout ratio	48.4%	57.9%	49.0%	41.4%	45.7%
Dividend yield	3.0%	2.5%	2.5%	4.5%	5.6%
EPS	$0.075	$0.047	$0.052	$0.088	$0.080
P/E ratio	16.0	23.4	19.3	9.1	8.2

General Machinery's Statement of Cash Flows is also shown for the last few years (Table 7.21).

Table 7.21   Statement of Cash Flows.

	2010	2009	2008	2007
Cash flow from operating activities				
Cash receipts	772,000	700,000	635,000	595,000
Cash payments	−628,000	−601,000	−537,200	−503,000
Interest paid	−72,000	−60,000	−40,000	−25,000
Income tax paid	−17,700	−11,100	−12,240	−20,700
Net cash from operating activities	54,300	27,900	45,560	46,300
Cash flow from investing activities				
Payments for property, plant & equipment	−200,000	−50,000	−50,000	−
Net cash used in investing activities	−200,000	−50,000	−50,000	−
Cash flow from financing activities				
Proceeds from borrowings	50,000	50,000	50,000	−
Dividends paid	−20,000	−15,000	−14,000	−20,000
Net cash from/used in financing activities	30,000	35,000	36,000	−20,000
Net increase/(decrease) in cash	−115,700	12,900	31,560	26,300
Cash at beginning of year	135,700	122,800	91,240	64,940
Cash at end of year	20,000	135,700	122,800	91,240

1. Discuss the major issues facing the company.
2. Recommend what actions the company should take to improve its overall performance, addressing each of profitability, liquidity, gearing, activity and shareholder return measures.
3. In what way does the Statement of Cash Flows help you to interpret the ratios and financial performance of the company?

Accounting for Inventory

Inventory is a crucial link between the Income Statement (as it affects the calculation of profit) and the Statement of Financial Position. However, it is also an important component of cost with which we are concerned throughout Part III of this book. Therefore, it is a useful bridging chapter on which to end our treatment of financial statements and lead into the use of accounting information for decision making, planning and control.

This chapter begins with an explanation of inventory as it relates to financial statements. It then looks at the alternative methods of inventory valuation (average cost and first in–first out) and then explains the two main costing systems used for inventory: job costing and process costing. The chapter also looks briefly at long-term contract costing for construction projects. The chapter also looks briefly at long-term contract costing for construction projects and concludes by looking at the management accounting statements for manufacturing businesses that are used by managers for internal decision making.

Introduction to inventory

Inventory (or stock) is the term used for goods bought or manufactured for resale but which are as yet unsold. Inventory enables the timing difference between purchasing or production and customer demand to be smoothed. The value of inventory according to IAS2 *Inventories* is the lower of cost and net realizable value.

The cost of inventory includes all costs of purchase, conversion (i.e. manufacture) and other costs incurred in bringing the inventory to its present location and condition. Costs of purchase therefore include import duties and transportation, less any rebates or discounts. Costs of conversion include production labour and an allocation of production overheads (overheads are covered in Chapter 13). Special methods of calculating inventory value apply to construction contracts, agriculture and commodities trading.

The matching principle (see Chapter 3) requires that business adjusts for changes in inventory in its Income Statement (the 'cost of sales', or 'cost of goods sold') and in its Statement of Financial Position (where inventory is a current asset).

Table 8.1   Cost of sales.

	£
Opening inventory (at beginning of period)	12,000
Plus purchases (or cost of manufacture)	32,000
= Stock available for sale	44,000
Less closing inventory (at end of period)	10,000
= Cost of sales	34,000

The cost of sales is calculated as shown in Table 8.1.

For a retailer or wholesaler, inventory is the cost of goods bought for resale. For a manufacturer, there are three different types of inventory:

- raw materials;
- work-in-progress;
- finished goods.

Manufacturing firms purchase raw materials (unprocessed goods) and undertake the *conversion process* through the application of labour, machinery and know-how to manufacture finished goods. The finished goods are then available to be sold to customers. Work-in-progress (or WIP) consists of goods that have begun but have not yet completed the conversion process.

Flow of costs

Figures 8.1 and 8.2 show in diagram form the flow of costs from purchasing to sales for a retail or wholesale business (Figure 8.1) and for a manufacturer (Figure 8.2).

Figure 8.1   The flow of costs in purchasing.

Cost formulas for inventory

Inventory valuation is important as the determination of the cost of inventory affects both:

- cost of sales in the Income Statement; and
- the inventory valuation in the Statement of Financial Position.

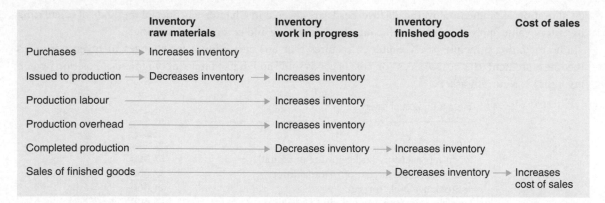

Figure 8.2   The flow of costs in manufacturing.

As inventory cost is an important element in management decision making, the valuation of inventory is an important link between financial accounting and management accounting.

The cost of inventory items that are distinct are assigned their individual costs. So, for example, a component purchased for a specific job with a cost of £600 but unused, would be valued at £600. A motor vehicle held for resale by a dealer would be valued at its purchase (or trade-in) cost. In each case, the inventory items would need to be readily identifiable from other similar items.

However, if inventory items are similar and cannot be differentiated (which would be the case for most goods bought in bulk for resale), costs are assigned by using either the weighted average cost or first in–first out (FIFO) methods. The last in–first out (LIFO) method, common in the USA, is not acceptable in the UK.

Inventory valuation under the weighted average method

Under the weighted average method, the cost of each item is determined from the weighted average of the cost of similar items at the beginning of a period and the cost of similar items purchased or produced during the period.

For example, a product is purchased on three separate occasions:

Units	Unit price	Total cost
5,000	£1.20	£6,000
2,000	£1.25	£2,500
3,000	£1.27	£3,810
10,000		£12,310

We need to calculate the cost of 6,000 units sold and the value of inventory using the weighted average method. The weighted average cost is £12,310/10,000 or £1.231 per unit. The cost of sales is 6,000 @ £1.231 = £7,386. The value of inventory is 4,000 @ £1.231 = £4,924.

Inventory valuation under FIFO

FIFO assumes that items of inventory purchased or produced first are sold first, so that those remaining in inventory are those most recently purchased or produced.

Using the same information as in the previous example:

Units	Unit price	Total cost
5,000	£1.20	£6,000
2,000	£1.25	£2,500
3,000	£1.27	£3,810
10,000		£12,310

We now need to calculate the cost of 6,000 units sold and the value of inventory using the FIFO method. Under FIFO, the 6,000 units sold come first from the original 5,000 purchased, and the balance of 1,000 from the second purchase of 2,000 units. The cost of sales is therefore:

$$5,000 @ £1.20 = £6,000$$
$$\text{and} \quad 1,000 @ £1.25 = \underline{£1,250}$$
$$\text{Total} \quad\quad\quad\quad £7,250$$

The remaining inventory is the last purchased, i.e. 1,000 from the second purchase of 2,000 and 3,000 from the third purchase. The value of inventory is therefore:

$$1,000 @ £1.25 = £1,250$$
$$\text{and} \quad 3,000 @ £1.27 = \underline{£3,810}$$
$$\text{Total} \quad\quad\quad\quad £5,060$$

Note that depending on the method used, the cost of sales (and therefore profit) differs. If the 6,000 units were sold at a price of £2.00:

- under weighted average the gross profit would be £4,614 (£12,000 − £7,386);
- under FIFO the gross profit would be £4,750 (£12,000 − £7,250).

Over time, these differences level out, but differences in gross profit are most common where the value of inventory is increasing or decreasing.

Retail method

The retail method is used for the measurement of inventory cost for retail organizations where there are large numbers of rapidly changing items with similar margins. The retail method of inventory valuation determines the cost of inventory by deducting an appropriate percentage profit margin from the sales value of inventory.

Net realizable value

Where the net realizable value is less than cost, this value should be used for inventory valuation. The net realizable value is the proceeds of sale, less any costs of disposal (e.g. transport, cleaning). The realizable value could be a discounted sales value, trade-in value or scrap value which is lower than the cost of purchase (or cost of production).

Methods of costing inventory in manufacturing

There are different types of manufacturing and it is important to differentiate alternative production methods to which different methods apply for the calculation of cost of sales and the valuation of inventory:

- *Custom*: where unique, custom products are produced singly, e.g. a building.
- *Batch*: where a quantity of the same goods are produced at the same time (often called a production run), e.g. textbooks.
- *Continuous*: where products are produced in a continuous production process, e.g. oil and chemicals, soft drinks.

For custom and batch manufacture, costs are collected through a job costing system that accumulates the cost of raw materials as they are issued to each job (either a custom product or a batch of products) and the cost of time spent by different categories of labour. To each of these costs overhead is allocated to cover the fixed and variable manufacturing costs that are a necessary part of production but that are not included in materials or labour (overhead will be explained in Chapter 13). When a custom product is completed, the accumulated cost of materials, labour and overhead is the cost of that custom product. For each batch, the total job cost is divided by the number of units produced (e.g. the number of copies of the textbook) to give a cost per unit (i.e. cost per textbook).

For continuous manufacture a process costing system is used, under which costs are collected over a period of time, together with a measure of the volume of production. At the end of the accounting period, the total costs are divided by the volume produced to give a cost per unit of volume. Under a process costing system, materials are issued to production, but as labour hours cannot be allocated to continuously produced products, conversion costs comprise the production labour and production overhead. In process costing, equivalent units measure the resources used in production relative to the resources necessary to complete all units.

We now present examples of job and process costing. In both cases, two important documents record the costs being incurred:

- Material issues: record the quantity of each type of raw material issued to production.
- Timesheets: record the number of hours worked by production labour to convert the raw material to finished goods.

Job costing illustration

Helo Europe manufactures components for helicopters. It does so in batches of 100 components. Each batch requires 500 kg of rolled and formed steel, which takes 15 hours of labour. During the course of a month, the following transactions take place:

Purchase of steel	1,000 kg @ €12/kg
Issue of steel to production	500 kg
Direct labour to roll and form	500 kg steel 15 hours @ €125/hour
Overhead allocated at completion of production of 100 components	€2,000
60 of the components manufactured in the batch were sold for	€130 each

At month end, 500 kg of steel has been issued to production and 7 hours have been worked. The job is incomplete. We need to calculate the value of work-in-progress at month end.

Using this information, work-in-progress will comprise:

Materials: steel 500 kg @ €12/kg	€6,000
Labour: 7 hours @ €125	875
Work-in-progress	€6,875

After completion of the job, it is necessary to calculate the:

- unit cost of production;
- gross profit;
- value of inventory.

The job cost for the production of a batch of 100 components is as follows:

Materials: steel 500 kg @ €12/kg	€6,000
Labour: 15 hours @ €125	1,875
Overhead	2,000
Total job cost	€9,875
Cost per component	€98.75 (€9,875/100)

The cost of sales of the 60 components sold is €5,925 (60 @ €98.75). The sales income is €7,800 (60 @ €130) and the gross profit is €1,875.

The stock of finished goods is €3,950 (40 @ €98.75). The stock of raw materials is the cost of 500 kg of steel that has been purchased but remains unused at its purchase cost of €12/kg, a value of €6,000.

Job costing and work-in-progress for services

Whilst inventory may be thought of as only relating to manufacturers and retailers, it also relates to professional service firms. Accountants and lawyers are examples of firms with large work-in-progress inventories covering work carried out on behalf of clients but not yet invoiced.

PLC Accountants have been conducting ABC's audit. At month end 15 partner hours and 60 audit hours have been allocated to ABC's work, which has not been invoiced. The hourly cost rates used by PLC are $200/hour for partners and $80/hour for managers.

The calculation of the work-in-progress for PLC at month end is:

15 partner hours @ $200	$3,000
60 audit hours @ $80	4,800
Total	$7,800

Process costing illustration

Voxic Co. manufactures lubricants. It does so in a continuous production process 24 hours per day, 7 days per week. During the course of a month, raw materials costing £140,000 were purchased and 100,000 litres of lubricant were produced. Materials issued to production cost £75,000 and conversion costs incurred were £55,000. 80,000 litres of lubricant were sold for £1.50/litre.

At the end of the month, calculations are necessary for the:

- unit cost of production;
- gross profit;
- value of inventory.

The cost of production for the month was £130,000 (materials £75,000 + conversion £55,000). As 100,000 litres were produced, the cost per litre is £1.30 (£130,000/100,000 litres).

The cost of sales for the 80,000 litres sold was £104,000 (80,000 @ £1.30). Sales proceeds were £120,000 (80,000 @ £1.50) and gross profit was £16,000.

Finished goods inventory is £26,000 (20,000 litres unsold @ £1.30). Raw materials inventory is valued at £65,000 (£140,000 purchased less £75,000 issued).

Process costing with partially completed units – weighted average method

Kazoo produced oils on a process basis during a month.

The opening work-in-progress was 7,000 units, consisting of materials €12,000 and conversion costs €30,000.

12,000 units commenced production during the month.

The closing work-in-progress was 4,000 units, 75% complete.

The cost of materials issued to production during the month was €140,000.

The conversion costs for production during the month were €80,000.

It is necessary to calculate:

- the number of units completed;
- the equivalent units in work-in-progress;

- the cost per unit, using the weighted average method;
- the cost of work-in-progress and finished goods at month end.

Note: in process costing examples, materials are usually assumed to be added at the beginning of the process (but in practice you would need to determine the stage at which they are added), and conversion costs are added uniformly throughout the process. Table 8.2 shows the calculations.

Table 8.2   Process costing example with partially completed units—Kazoo.

	Units
Opening WIP	7,000
Units commenced	12,000
	19,000
Closing WIP	4,000
Completed	15,000

Cost per unit:

	Opening WIP €	Cost for month €	Total €	Completed units	WIP equivalent units	Total equivalent units	Cost per equivalent unit* €
Material	12,000	140,000	152,000	15,000	4,000	19,000	€8.00
Conversion	30,000	80,000	110,000	15,000	3,000†	18,000	€6.11
Total	€42,000		€262,000				€14.11

Work-in-progress:

Materials 4,000 @ €8	€32,000
Conversion 3,000 @ €6.111	€18,333
	€50,333

Finished goods:

15,000 units @ €14.111	€211,666
Total costs	€262,000

*Total cost divided by total equivalent units.
†4,000 units, 75% complete at end of month = 3,000 equivalent units.

Note: if a FIFO method of costing and inventory valuation is used, a variation to this calculation is necessary. However, for most purposes the weighted average method is sufficient for process costing with partially completed units.

Long-term contract costing

Long-term contract costing is a method of job costing that applies to large units that are produced over a long period of time, e.g. construction projects. Because of the length of time the contract takes to complete, it is necessary to apportion the profit over several accounting periods. Although the goods that are the subject of the contract have not been delivered, IAS11 *Construction Contracts* requires that revenue and costs be allocated over the period in which the contract takes place (e.g. the construction period). The *stage of completion method* is the most common method to be applied to long-term contracts. Under this method, profit recognized is based on the proportion of work carried out, taking into account any known inequalities at the various stages of the contract. The costs incurred in reaching the relevant stage of completion are then matched with income. However, where the outcome of a contract is not known with reasonable certainty, no profit should be reflected, although losses should be recognized as soon as they are foreseen.

Long-term contracts will frequently allow for progress payments to be made by a customer at various stages of completion. For construction contracts, there will typically be an architect's certificate to support the stage of completion. Contracts may also include a retention value, a proportion of the total contract price that is retained by the customer and not paid until a specified period after the end of the contract.

Long-term contract costing illustration

Macro Builders has entered into a two-year contract to construct a building. The contract price is $1.2 million, with an expected cost of construction of $1 million. After one year, the following costs have been incurred:

Material delivered to site	$500,000
Salaries and wages paid	130,000
Overhead costs	170,000

The architect certifies the value of work completed to the contractual stage for a progress payment as $600,000. Macro estimates that it will cost $250,000 to complete the contract over and above the costs already incurred.

Table 8.3 shows the calculations for the:

- anticipated profit on the contract;
- amount of profit that can be considered to have been earned to date.

Table 8.3   Long-term contract costing example.

Costs of construction:	
Material delivered to site	$500,000
Salaries and wages paid	130,000
Overhead costs	170,000
	$800,000
Less work not certified	200,000
Cost of work certified	$600,000
Anticipated profit:	
Cost of work certified	$600,000
Work not certified	200,000
Estimated cost to complete	250,000
	1,050,000
Contract price	1,200,000
Anticipated profit	$150,000

Expected cost of construction $1,000,000 (or $1,050,000)
Percentage complete 60% ($600,000/$1,000,000)
Take up profit of 60% of $150,000 = $90,000

Management accounting statements

The collection and analysis of financial data on manufacturing activities, adjusted by the valuations of inventory for raw materials, work-in-progress and finished goods, results in a manufacturing statement and cost of sales statement produced for management accounting purposes. These statements are shown in Table 8.4.

Table 8.4   Management accounting statements.

Manufacturing statement

Direct material:

Raw material inventory at beginning of period	50,000	
Purchases of raw materials	150,000	
Raw material available for use	200,000	
Less raw material inventory at end of period	40,000	
Raw material usage in production		160,000
Direct labour		330,000
Manufacturing overhead:		
Factory rental	50,000	
Depreciation of plant & equipment	30,000	
Light & power	10,000	
Salaries & wages of indirect labour	60,000	150,000
Total manufacturing costs		640,000
Add work-in-progress inventory at beginning of period		100,000
		740,000
Less work-in-progress inventory at end of period		60,000
Cost of goods manufactured		680,000

Cost of sales statement

Finished goods inventory at beginning of period	160,000
Cost of goods manufactured	680,000
Goods available for sale .	840,000
Less finished goods inventory at end of period	120,000
Cost of sales	720,000

Income statement

Sales	1,000,000
Less cost of sales	720,000
Gross profit	280,000
Less selling and administrative expenses	150,000
Net profit	130,000

Included in the Notes to the Accounts would be a breakdown of the valuation of inventory in the current assets section of the Statement of Financial Position. This would show:

Inventory raw materials	40,000
Inventory work-in-progress	60,000
Inventory finished goods	120,000
Total	220,000

With the exception of the Income Statement, the information contained in Table 8.4 is presented only for management purposes. It is not published as part of the Annual Report and is not disclosed to shareholders or others outside the organization.

Conclusion

In this chapter we have looked at several methods of calculating the value of inventory and cost of sales, the main ones being weighted average and first in–first out (FIFO). We have also looked at the two main methods of costing for the production of goods and services: job costing and process costing and a method of long-term contract costing. We finished with the management accounting statements prepared for internal use by a manufacturing business that support the published Income Statement. This is a useful point at which to make the transition from Part II of this book and its concern with financial statements for external parties to the concern of Part III with the use of accounting information for decision making, planning and control.

Importantly for Part III, while it is essential to value inventory for financial statement purposes, inventory costs may not be suitable for decision-making purposes, as Chapters 10, 11 and 12 will show. In these chapters we demonstrate that the assumptions and limitations of costs based on accounting standards have to be understood and questioned in terms of their relevance for day-to-day decision making by managers.

Questions

8.1   Opening inventory for a month is €25,000 and closing inventory for the same month is €30,000. Cost of sales for that month is €35,000. Purchases for the month are:

a. €20,000
b. €30,000
c. €40,000
d. €50,000

8.2   Goods that complete production in a manufacturing business:

a. Increase work-in-progress inventory and decrease finished goods inventory
b. Decrease work-in-progress inventory and increase finished goods inventory
c. Decrease work-in-progress inventory and decrease finished goods inventory
d. Decrease finished goods inventory and increase cost of sales

8.3   An item of stock is purchased for £1,500. The sales price was £2,000 but as the item has now been superseded it can only be sold for a discounted price of £1,350. The scrap value of the item is £1,100. To sell or scrap the stock will involve transport costs of £100. The value of the stock for Statement of Financial Position purposes is:

a. £1,500
b. £1,350
c. £1,250
d. £1,000

8.4   The following purchases are made during a month:

Feb 10	6,000 @ $2
Feb 20	3,000 @ $2.20
Feb 28	2,000 @ $2.30

Calculate the cost of 8,000 units sold in the month and the value of inventory at month end, using the:

a. weighted average method
b. FIFO method.

8.5   Bluesky Ltd's Assembly Department had 20,000 units in WIP on 1 March 2011. Direct materials are added at the beginning of the assembly process. An additional 60,000 units were started during March, and 15,000 units were in WIP on 31 March 2011. The units in WIP on 31 March were 30% complete with respect to conversion.

Costs incurred in the Assembly Department for March 2011 were as follows:

	WIP 1 March	Costs incurred in March
	£	£
Direct material	62,000	192,000
Conversion	25,000	85,150

Using the weighted average method of process costing, calculate the cost of goods completed and transferred to finished goods inventory during March AND the cost of WIP at 31 March 2011.

8.6   Fisher Ltd manufactures custom furniture and uses a job costing system. On 1 January 2011, there were no balances in work-in-process or finished goods inventories.

The following events occurred in January 2011:

• The company began two jobs – A101 (comprising 40 tables) and B202 (comprising 60 chairs).
• 400 square metres of timber were purchased at a total cost of £5 800.
• 80 litres of glue were purchased at a cost of £6 per litre.

- The following raw materials were issued during the month:
  Issue #1: Job A101 – 200 square metres of timber
  Issue #2: Job B202 – 150 square metres of timber
  Issue #3: 20 litres of glue were used on each job.
- The following amount of direct labour hours were spent on the two jobs:
  A101: 200 direct labour hours
  B202: 100 direct labour hours.
  Actual direct labour cost per hour was £30.
- Overhead should be charged to each job on the basis of £25 per direct labour hour.
- Job A101 was completed, and 30 tables from the job were sold for a total price of £15,000. Job B202 was unfinished at month end.

  Calculate the inventory value at month end of:

- raw materials;
- work-in-progress; and
- finished goods.

  Calculate the cost of sales and gross profit for the month.

8.7   Jerry's Engineering has a three-year contract to construct a large piece of capital equipment for its client. The contract price is €4 million. At the end of the first financial year of the project, material, labour and overheads charged to the job totalled €850,000. Jerry estimates a further €2.65 million is still to be spent to complete the job. An independent valuer has certified the value of the work completed as €850,000 which the client has paid under the contract as a progress payment.

Calculate the amount of profit that Jerry can recognize as having been earned in the current year.

8.8   The following transactions relate to Mammoth Product Company for the year ended 31 December 2011.

	$
Sales revenue	900,000
Purchases of raw materials	250,000
Direct factory labour	450,000
Factory rental	75,000
Depreciation of plant and equipment	50,000
Factory light and power	25,000
Salaries and wages of factory labour	100,000
Selling and administrative expenses	75,000
Opening inventory 1 January 2011 –	
Finished goods	150,000
Work-in-progress	300,000
Raw materials	100,000

Closing inventory 31 December 2011 –	
Finished goods	250,000
Work-in-progress	400,000
Raw materials	150,000

Prepare a:

- Manufacturing Statement;
- Cost of Sales Statement; and
- Income Statement.

Calculate the value of inventory to be shown in the Statement of Financial Position.

Using Accounting Information for Decision Making, Planning and Control

Part II was concerned with the use of financial information, primarily for external reporting purposes. Part III shows the reader how accounting information is used by managers. While an analysis of financial statements is useful, particularly for external interested parties (e.g. shareholders, bankers and financiers, the government), the information is of limited use to the internal management of the business because:

- it is aggregated to the corporate level, whereas managers require information at the business unit level;
- it is aggregated to annual figures, whereas managers require timely information, usually at not less than monthly intervals (and for sales information, weekly or even daily);
- it is aggregated to headline figures (e.g. total sales), whereas managers require information in much greater detail (e.g. by customer, product/service, geographical area, business unit);
- it does not provide a comparison of plan to actual figures to provide a gauge on progress towards achieving business goals.

Consequently, the chapters in Part III are concerned with management accounting: the production of accounting information for use by managers. This information is disaggregated (to business unit level), more regular (typically monthly) and is more detailed for management decision making, planning and control. Management accounting is not regulated by accounting standards and is not subject to audit. This means that an organization's method of management accounting can be developed to meet its particular needs, which may be different from other companies, even in the same industry. However, the information used in management accounting comes from the same accounting system as produces financial accounting reports (although it is supplemented by other data) and the accounting system must still satisfy the requirement to produce financial statements for external parties. Hence, management accounting cannot be divorced completely from the practices of financial accounting.

In Part III, the accounting tools and techniques are explained and illustrated by straightforward examples. Case studies, drawn mainly from real business examples, help draw out the concepts. Theory is integrated with the tools and techniques, and the use of quotations from the original sources is intended to encourage readers to access the accounting academic literature that they may find of interest.

These chapters in Part III do not take an approach to accounting that is common to other accounting textbooks. The chapters in this Part are aimed particularly at non-financial managers in functional roles, for example, operations, marketing, purchasing, distribution, human resources and information technology. These managers are not accountants but their role often encompasses responsibility for budgets, pricing, cost control and capital investment proposals that require an understanding of how accounting is used in planning, decision making and control. The chapters in Part III therefore take a user-focused rather than a preparer-focused approach, demonstrating techniques that do not require any prior management accounting knowledge.

Chapter 9 provides a framework of accounting and information systems through which to understand the nature of business processes and how information systems are used in planning, decision making and control. Chapters 10, 11 and 12 consider the accounting techniques that are of value in marketing, operations and human resource decisions, respectively. The more traditional accounting focus is left to Chapter 13, by which time the reader should have little difficulty in understanding issues of overhead allocation. Chapter 14 focuses on strategic decisions such as capital investment and Chapter 15 on divisional performance measurement. Chapter 16 covers the subject of budgeting and Chapter 17 discusses budgetary control. Chapter 18 introduces the reader to the topic of strategic management accounting.

9

Accounting and Information Systems

This chapter considers the use of accounting information systems. We look at different methods of data collection and different types of information systems, with a particular focus on enterprise resource planning systems. The chapter also reviews the importance of a horizontal business process perspective on organizational functioning, rather than a vertical, hierarchical or functional business unit perspective. The chapter concludes with an overview of the importance of internal controls and systems development for information systems.

Introduction to accounting and information systems

An information system is a system that collects information and presents it, usually in summarized form, for management. Information is different from data because it has been made usable by some form of summarization and/or analysis. Whilst data is a set of raw facts, information is usable. For example, sales data can be summarized and analysed by customer and/or product/service in a monthly sales analysis report and thereby becomes meaningful management information which can then be used for decision making.

Organizations will typically have an information systems (IS) strategy which follows the organizational business strategy and determines the long-term information requirements of the business. The IS strategy provides an 'umbrella' for different information technologies to help ensure that appropriate information is acquired, retained, shared and available for use in strategy implementation. The IS strategy can be distinguished from the information technology (IT) strategy which defines the specific systems that are required to satisfy the information needs of the organization, including the hardware, software and operating systems. The third element is the information management (IM) strategy which is concerned with ensuring that the necessary information is being provided to users. This includes the type of database that is used, data warehousing and reporting systems.

Information is an essential tool of management, but it needs to be relevant, timely, accurate, complete, concise and understandable. The benefits of quality information that meets these criteria may include improved decision making, better customer service, product/service quality, productivity and reduced staffing. However, the collection, processing, analysis and reporting of information is an expensive process (e.g. the cost of hardware, software development, staff time), and organizations need to ensure that the value of the information obtained is greater than the cost of providing that information.

An accounting information system is one that uses technology to capture, store, process and report accounting information. However, in this chapter and from an accounting perspective, we consider accounting to be only one, albeit important, component of information systems.

Methods of data collection

Most data collection in organizations takes place as a by-product of transaction recording through computer systems, which have automated tasks that were carried out before computers by manual processing of documents and entries into journals and ledgers (Chapter 3 described the recording of financial transactions).

Computer systems have automated tasks substantially with multiple aspects of a transaction being carried out simultaneously. For example, credit sales typically incorporate the whole process of delivering goods (or services) by producing a delivery docket that accompanies goods, reducing inventory, producing an invoice, updating the accounts receivable (debtor) records to show the amount owed by customers, producing a sales analysis by customer/product and calculating the margin on the sale by deducting the cost of sales. This information is transferred into the general ledger, where along with all other similar transactions it is summarized and reported as sales and gross profit. Similar processes exist in relation to payments to suppliers and the collection of monies owed by customers.

Retailers make extensive use of electronic point of sale (EPOS) technology which uses bar code scanning to reduce inventory, price goods and calculate margins, and print a cash register listing for the customer. Over a time period (day, week or month) the outputs from such a system include a detailed analysis of business volume (e.g. number of customers, number of items sold, scanning time at the checkout), sales analysis by product, product profitability and inventory re-order requirements. Additional benefits of EPOS include information about peak sales times during each day, products that may need to be discounted and sales locations that may need to be expanded. The use of electronic funds transfer at point of sale (EFTPOS) means that customers do not have to pay cash (which is expensive for retailers to deal with due to security requirements) but can automatically transfer funds from their bank account (or credit card) to the retailer's bank account, thereby eliminating further transactions.

The increase in e-commerce for business-to-consumer (B2C) sales means that for many products and services, purchasing over the internet enables customers to carry out the data processing previously carried out by a retailer's own employees. Companies such as Amazon and iTunes save costs by not needing expensive retail premises or staff taking customer orders. Customers order and pay online. All the retailer has to do is ship the goods (and for iTunes, Apple doesn't even have to do that as the customer downloads the purchased product). For business-to-business (B2B), electronic data interchange (EDI) enables supplier and customer systems to be linked by a common data format so that purchase orders raised by the customer are automatically converted into sales orders on the supplier. For example, in the automotive industry, orders from the major vehicle assemblers are placed on suppliers using EDI. EDI transactions enable the supplier to confirm their ability to meet the order by online means. The use of EDI enables automatic generation of invoicing by the supplier, tracing of deliveries by the logistics supplier and receipt of goods by the vehicle assembler, ultimately leading to payment to the supplier (for a case study, see Berry and Collier, 2007).

An important part of data collection is collecting the financial details of a transaction. Also important is capturing as much information as is possible about the transaction from a non-financial perspective. An example of this is the information collected from customers through retail credit cards, store loyalty cards, frequent flyer and similar programs. These enable retailers to maintain a detailed knowledge of their customers' purchasing habits to enable targeted promotional campaigns aimed at specific customers.

Another source of data not used for financial reporting concerns the finances of suppliers. For example, in the automotive industry, the large vehicle assemblers collect vast quantities of information about their suppliers' costs: their cost of labour; the cost of manufacturing equipment and its capacity; the cost of raw materials such as steel. Much of this information is publically available but retaining it in an organization's information system supports subsequent negotiations between the automotive assembler's purchasing department and its suppliers. By using this information, buyers can check the reasonableness of supplier prices for component parts, as buyers can perform their own checks on what it should cost to produce the same components. This more strategic use of accounting information is described further in Chapter 18.

Of course, the more that is expected of an information system, the more data has to be collected, stored and reported. Accounting is one type rather than the only type of information that is collected. In Chapter 4, we saw that Balanced Scorecard-type performance measurement systems collate and report information about customers, business processes and innovation to supplement financial performance measures. Therefore, organizations need to capture information from their marketing, purchasing, production, distribution and human resource activities. Information about key factors such as customer satisfaction, cycle times (from order to delivery), quality, waste, and on-time delivery need to be part of an information system and integrated with and reported together with financial information.

Types of information system

There are various types of information system.

Transaction processing systems collect source data about each business transaction, for example, customer orders, sales, purchases, inventory movements, payments, receipts. Transaction processing reports are important for control and audit purposes but provide little usable management information. Data from transaction processing systems is predominantly financial in nature. The most common form of delivering management information to users has been the 'hard copy' report, a computer-generated report that may list transactions (a transaction report or audit trail), exceptions (an exception report, such as product sales below a predetermined price level), or a summarized report (e.g. a sales analysis) for a period.

Management information systems (MIS) may extend from financial to non-financial information and typically are more oriented to support management decisions. For example, displays of key performance data with graphical representation are becoming increasingly common. Traffic lights (red/amber/green) draw attention to those aspects of performance that are meeting target (green), those that are in need of urgent attention (red), and those that need to be considered as they are borderline (amber). However, these systems do not integrate accounting, manufacturing and distribution systems.

An *enterprise resource planning* (ERP) system helps to integrate data flow and access to information over the whole range of a company's activities. ERP systems typically capture transaction data for accounting purposes, together with operational, customer and supplier data which are then made available through data warehouses against which custom-designed reports can be produced. ERP systems take a whole-of-business approach. ERP system data can be used to update performance measures in a Balanced Scorecard system (Chapter 4) and can be used for activity-based costing (Chapter 13), shareholder value analysis (Chapter 2), strategic planning, customer relationship management and supply chain management. ERP systems are a development of earlier material requirements planning (MRP), distribution requirements planning (DRP) and manufacturing resource planning (MRP2) systems.

Information contained within ERP systems is in the form of a database. Many older systems and simple software packages contain many records (e.g. one for each customer) grouped into files (e.g. a customer file). Modern information systems and especially those for larger organizations rely on relational database technology. In this kind of database, data is recorded at a low level, separating unique pieces of information in a separate table, e.g. separating a customer name and address. Connections are made by links between tables using the key (an identifier). The advantage of this structure is that information (e.g. customer address) is held only once so there is no risk of different files containing different information (e.g. the address may be updated in a sales file, but not in an accounts receivable file). A further advantage is that reports can be produced for virtually any combination of data using the keys for each table. This is done by using a structured query language (usually referred to as SQL).

Strategic enterprise management systems (SEM) are a type of ERP system that provide support for the strategic management process. They are based on data stored in a data warehouse which is then used by a range of analytical tools. An SEM can be an important driver of organizational performance as it enables faster and better decision making at all organizational levels.

Decision support systems (DSS) go a step further and contain data analysis models that provide the ability for managers to simulate scenarios or ask 'What if?' questions so that different options can be considered to aid in decision making. DSS may be contained in a spreadsheet or in a complex software package.

Executive information systems (EIS) are systems used for decision support, which incorporate access to summarized data, often in graphical form, to enable senior managers to evaluate information about the organization and its environment. An EIS utilizes a 'drill-down' facility to move from aggregated data down to a more specific and detailed level (e.g. customer, product, business unit). Information is typically also available from external sources, for example, public databases. Ease of use is an important feature so that enquiries can be made without a detailed knowledge of the underlying data structures.

Expert systems store data relevant to a specialist area and are populated with knowledge gained from experts which is retained in a structured format or knowledge base. Expert systems provide solutions to problems that require discretionary judgement. Users access data through a graphical user interface (GUI) to ask questions of the system, which prompts the user for more information. Various rules are then applied by the expert system to make decisions. The best example of an expert system is that used for credit approval. Information is entered to the system in response to prompts, such as postcode, telephone number, age, employment history, which is compared with confidential data held by credit reference agencies on a large number of similar applicants to make an automated judgement about an applicant's credit worthiness and the allocation of a credit limit.

In this chapter, we will use the term 'enterprise resource planning' (ERP) systems to refer to information systems that are not limited to accounting but integrate different functional areas of the business and take a business process perspective. The best known examples of these systems include SAP and Oracle. These systems can be extended with tools such as Business Intelligence (or BI) or tools that enable SEM, DSS, EIS or expert applications. ERP systems avoid 'information silos' that provide limited and specialist information to narrow groups of managers. Often these silos (typical of older transaction processing or MIS systems) are based on different software packages, use different databases and do not always report timely, accurate or consistent data to users. Although different modules exist in an ERP (e.g. customer order entry, inventory, invoicing, accounts receivable, management reporting), these are all integrated so that each module provides consistent information to users. SAP, for example, has three versions of its software, one version for each of multinationals, large organizations and small and medium enterprises. It has also customized its system for about 20 different industries including banking, chemicals, automotive, retail and the public sector.

While an ERP system makes reporting easy in terms of the hierarchical or vertical structure of organizations, as reflected in the traditional organization chart, increasingly businesses are looking at the horizontal business processes that cut across departmental structures.

Business processes

We typically think of an organization in terms of its hierarchical structure: a head office with departments responsible for marketing, production, administration; or a business unit structure with autonomous units responsible for particular products/services or geographic territories. However, an organization can also be thought of as a collection of processes or activities that when combined form part of the value chain (see Chapter 11) that delivers value to customers. The hierarchical perspective is based on tasks carried out such as selling and accounting with specialists responsible for each. The business process perspective is a horizontal rather than a vertical perspective on the organization, where the focus is on how things are done to satisfy customer demand and expectation, with more emphasis on generalists rather than specialists. One business process is that which starts with accepting a customer's order and ends with delivering it to the customer, including the accounting transaction of invoicing the customer. Another business process is that of placing an order on a supplier through to receiving the goods or services and making payment to the supplier.

Flowcharting and process mapping are commonly used methods for representing business processes. Process maps are graphical representations of business processes showing the activities and flows of data between activities and the areas responsible for carrying out those activities. These can be simple or complex.

Figure 9.1 shows a simplified example of a process map for processing a customer order and its computer entry through the physical picking of goods from a warehouse to dispatch and invoicing. To satisfy the customer, this needs to be an effective, seamless and error-free process. However, in this example five separate departments are involved (Sales, Order Processing, Warehouse, Transport and Accounting). As we will see in Chapter 13, accounting systems generally capture costs for departments (i.e. at the hierarchical level) but what is more important in terms of cost, efficiency and quality is the cost of the business process itself, and the need to streamline that business process as much as possible.

Business process re-engineering (or BPR) is defined as 'the fundamental rethinking and radical design of business processes to achieve dramatic improvements in critical contemporary measures of performance, such as cost, quality, service, and speed' (Hammer & Champy, 1993).This approach can lead to improvements that eliminate duplication and waste and identify gaps where failures in quality, delivery or service can occur. A continual re-evaluation of business processes can lead to continuous improvement, increased competitiveness and profitability. ERP systems take a business process perspective and can help to re-engineer those processes to be more efficient and effective.

A business process perspective enables a different view of cost than the traditional approach to departments or product/services. Activity-based costing systems (see Chapter 13) provide a means by which costs can be accumulated for both hierarchical reporting purposes and on an activity basis. This means that, using Figure 9.1 as an example, we could produce total costs for customer order processing, and in an ERP system, link this to non-financial data such as the number of customer orders, number of picking slips, number of inventory items and number of deliveries to produce useful analytical data about the cost of these activities.

Internal controls for information systems

Internal control is broadly defined as a process, effected by an entity's board of directors, management and other personnel, designed to provide reasonable assurance regarding the achievement of objectives in the following categories: effectiveness and efficiency of operations; reliability of financial reporting; and compliance with applicable laws and regulations (Committee of Sponsoring Organizations, 2007).

As organizations increasingly rely on their ERP systems, information system controls are essential to ensure the security of data and the reliability of information. There are four main types of controls in relation to information systems:

1. Security controls: the prevention of unauthorized access, modification or destruction of stored data. Recruitment, training and supervision need to be in place to ensure the competency of those responsible for programming and data entry. Personnel controls include the separation of duties within departments and the separation of data processing between departments. Access controls provide security over

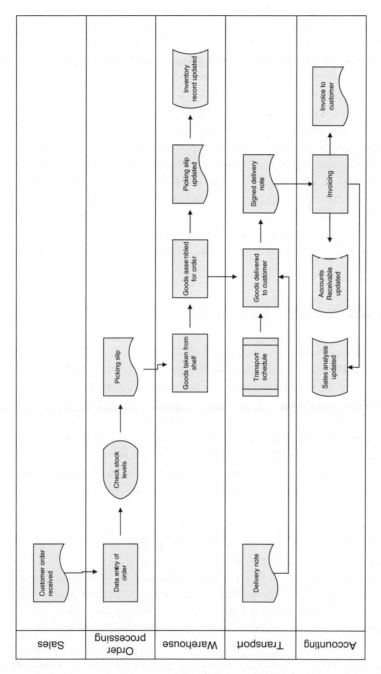

Figure 9.1   Customer order processing.

unauthorized access to data. The most common form of access security is through password authorization. Software controls also ensure that software used by the organization is authorized.
2. Application controls are designed for each individual application, such as payroll, accounting and inventory control. The aim of application controls is to prevent, detect and correct transaction processing errors. Input controls are designed to detect and prevent errors during transaction data entry to ensure that data entered are complete and accurate. Processing controls ensure that processing has occurred according to the organization's requirements and that no transactions have been omitted or processed incorrectly. Output controls ensure that input and processing activities have been carried out and that the information produced is reliable and distributed to users.
3. Network controls have arisen in response to the growth of distributed processing and e-commerce and the need for protection against hacking and viruses. A firewall comprises a combination of hardware and software located between the company's private network (intranet) and the public network. Data encryption can be used to convert data into a non-readable format before transmission and then re-converted after transmission.
4. Contingency controls are relied upon if security or integrity controls fail; there must be a back-up facility and a contingency plan to restore business operations as quickly as possible (e.g. a business continuity or disaster recovery plan).

Developing information systems

A particular risk and the need for tight control occur with the development of new information systems or changes to existing information system design. Organizations will frequently need to improve or change their ERP systems to meet changing customer demand or environmental constraints. However, there is a significant risk in the development of these systems that the system does not meet user needs, is late or costs more than was estimated. Therefore, it is important to have strong controls over information systems development. This is necessary even where proven ERP systems such as SAP and Oracle are introduced as these systems will usually require customization to meet an organization's specific needs.

A steering committee should monitor the system implementation and have overall responsibility to ensure that the system meets requirements in terms of quality, time and cost. Systems development projects should comprise four distinct stages:

- Feasibility study stage: there should be a clear understanding about the objectives of the new system, the deliverables, its cost and time to completion.
- System design stage: data security and levels of authorization need to be built into the system design. During this stage, the internal auditor should review system documentation, interfaces with other systems and acceptance of design by all in the project team, especially users.
- Testing stage: comprehensive testing by systems development staff, programmers, users and internal auditors.
- Implementation stage: a review of training and documentation, file conversion and operational issues, e.g. staffing and supervision.

The key elements of project management for information systems are:

- project planning and definition;
- obtaining top management support;
- project organization: defining the role and responsibilities of the steering committee and project manager;
- resource planning and allocation – both staff and money;
- quality control and progress monitoring;
- risk management;
- systems design and approval;
- system testing and implementation;
- user participation and involvement;
- communication and coordination;
- user education and training.

An implementation plan will cover parallel running, where the new system is operated in conjunction with the existing system until such time as the new system is proven to work by reconciling outputs from both systems; and ensuring that users are satisfied with the new system and are confident about discontinuing the existing system. If there is a changeover without parallel running, then testing prior to implementation becomes more important and additional monitoring may be needed during the early stages of implementation. A post-implementation review of the new system should also be carried out to establish whether the system is operating as intended and to confirm that user needs are being satisfied.

Conclusion

This chapter has shown the important role that information systems play in planning, decision making and control. We have not limited ourselves to purely accounting systems here but have focused on the role of enterprise resource planning systems (ERP, such as Oracle and SAP) which increasingly play a key role in providing financial and non-financial information for managers. In using ERP systems, organizations are able to refocus on business processes rather than the hierarchical organizational structures that are more allied with externally oriented financial reporting. We have also looked at the importance of internal controls and the development of information systems to ensure they can meet organizational needs.

References

Berry, A. J. and Collier, P. M. (2007). Risk management in supply chains: processes, organisation for uncertainty and culture. *International Journal of Risk Assessment and Management*, 7(8), 1005–26.

Committee of Sponsoring Organizations of the Treadway Commission (COSO) (2007). *Internal Control – Integrated Framework: Guidance on Monitoring Internal Control Systems.*

Hammer, M. and Champy, J. (1993). *Reengineering the Corporation: A Manifesto for Business Revolution.* London: Nicholas Brealey.

CHAPTER 10

Marketing Decisions

This chapter considers the use of accounting information in making marketing decisions. It begins with an overview of some of the key elements of marketing theory and introduces cost behaviour: the distinction between fixed and variable costs, average and marginal costs. Decisions involving the relationship between price and volume are covered through the technique of cost–volume–profit (CVP) analysis. Different approaches to pricing are covered: cost-plus pricing; target rate of return; the optimum selling price; special pricing decisions; and transfer pricing. The chapter concludes with an introduction to segmental profitability and customer profitability analysis.

Marketing strategy

Porter (1980) identified five forces that affect an industry: the threat of new entrants; the bargaining power of customers; the bargaining power of suppliers; the threat of substitute product/services; and the threat from competitors, each of which develops strategies for success. In a later book, Porter (1985) identified three generic strategies that businesses can adopt in order to achieve a sustainable competitive advantage. The alternative strategies were to be a low-cost producer, a higher-cost producer that can differentiate its product/services, or to focus on a market niche. The notion of cost is important in marketing decisions, but it will be more important for a low-cost strategy than for a differentiation or focus strategy, where the focus will be more on brand reputation, after-sales service and various non-financial performance measures (see the Balanced Scorecard in Chapter 4) rather than cost alone.

Marketing is the business function that aims to understand customer needs and satisfy those needs more effectively than competitors. Marketing can be achieved through a focus on selling products and services or through building lasting relationships with customers (customer relationship management). Marketing texts emphasize the importance of adding value through marketing activity. Adding value differentiates product/services from competitors, and enables a price to be charged that equates to the benefits obtained by the customer. However, for any business to achieve profitability, customers must be prepared to pay more for the product/service benefit than the benefit costs to provide.

Pricing of product/services is crucial to business success, in terms of increasing the perceived value so as to maximize the margin between price and cost and to increase volume and market share without eroding profits. Pricing strategies may be aimed at *penetration* – achieving long-term market share – or *skimming* – maximizing short-term profits from a limited market. Accounting can assist in understanding the profitability impact of high-volume/low-margin versus low-volume/high-margin strategies. A further element of marketing is the distribution channel to be used. This may range from the company's own salesforce to retail outlets, direct marketing and the number of intermediaries between the product/service provider and the ultimate customer.

The price customers are willing to pay depends on what Doyle (1998) calls the 'factors which drive up the utility of an offer', which he divides into four groups. Product drivers include performance, features, reliability, operating costs and serviceability. Services drivers include ease of credit availability, ordering, delivery, installation, training, after-sales service and guarantees. Personnel drivers include the professionalism, courtesy, reliability and responsiveness of staff. Image drivers reflect the confidence of customers in the company or brand name, which is built through the other three drivers and by advertising and promotional activity. Doyle (1998) recognized that each of these value drivers has cost drivers. Consequently, accounting needs to pay attention to these drivers so that their costs can be compared with the price able to be charged to customers.

The product mix or sales mix is the mix of product/services offered by the business, each of which may be aimed at satisfying different customer needs. Businesses develop marketing strategies to meet the needs of their customers in different *market segments*, each of which can be defined by its unique characteristics (e.g. different geographic areas or distribution channels). These segments may yield different prices and incur different costs as customers demand more or less of different product/services.

A focus on customer relationship management entails taking a longer term view than product/service profitability and emphasizes the profits that can be derived from a satisfied customer base. Doyle (1998) describes loyal customers as assets, quoting research that tried to measure the value of a loyal customer. Doyle says, 'If managers know the cost of losing a customer, they can evaluate the likely pay-off of investments designed to keep customers happy' (pp. 51–2). Doyle explained that the cost of winning new customers is high, loyal customers tend to buy more regularly, spend more and are often willing to pay premium prices. This is an element of the business goodwill that is shown in financial statements where a business is acquired (Chapter 6) and part of the 'intellectual capital' that is not reported in financial statements (see Chapter 7).

Marketing texts typically introduce marketing strategy as a combination of the 4 Ps of product, price, place and promotion. The marketing strategy for a business will encompass decisions about product/service mix, customer mix, market segmentation, value and cost drivers, pricing and distribution channel. Each element of marketing strategy implies an understanding of accounting, which can help to answer questions such as:

- How can accounting information support the marketing strategy?
- What is the volume of product/services that we need to sell to maintain profitability?
- What alternative approaches to pricing can we adopt?
- What is our customer, product/service and distribution channel profitability in each of our market segments?

This chapter is concerned with answering these questions. Although information on competitors, customers and suppliers is likely to be limited, strategic management accounting approaches (see Chapter 18) can apply the same tools and techniques in the pursuit of competitive advantage.

Cost behaviour

Marketing decisions cannot be made in isolation from knowledge of the costs of the business and the impact that marketing strategy has on operations and on business profitability. Profitability for marketing decisions is the difference between *revenue* – the income earned from the sale of product/services – and cost. As we saw in Chapter 3, it is the notion of cost that is problematic.

For many business decisions, it is helpful to distinguish between how costs behave, i.e. whether they are fixed or variable. Fixed costs are those that do not change with increases in business activity (such as rent). This is not to say that fixed costs never change (obviously rents do increase in accordance with the terms of a lease) but there is no connection (except sometimes in large retail shopping centres) between cost and the volume of activity. By contrast, variable costs do increase/decrease in proportion to an increase/decrease in business activity, so that as a business produces more units of a good or service, the business incurs proportionately more costs.

For example, advertising is a fixed cost because there is no relationship between spending on advertising and generating revenue (although we may wish there was). However, sales commission is a variable cost because the more a business sells, the more commission it pays out.

A simple example shows the impact of fixed and variable cost behaviour on total and average cost. XYZ Limited has the capacity to produce between 10,000 and 30,000 units of a product each period. Its fixed costs are £200,000. Variable costs are £10 per unit. The example is shown in Table 10.1.

In this example, even if the business produces no units, costs are still £200,000 because fixed costs are independent of volume. Total costs increase as the business incurs variable costs of £10 for each unit produced. However, the average cost declines with the increase in volume because the fixed cost is spread over more units.

Not all costs are quite so easy to separate between fixed and variable. Some costs are semi-fixed, while others are semi-variable. Semi-fixed costs (also called step fixed costs) are constant within a particular level of activity, but can increase when activity reaches a critical level. This can happen, for example, with changes

Table 10.1 Cost behaviour — fixed and variable costs.

Activity (number of units sold)	Fixed costs (£200,000)	Variable costs (£10 per unit)	Total cost (£)	Average cost (per unit)
10,000	200,000	100,000	300,000	£30.00
15,000	200,000	150,000	350,000	£23.33
20,000	200,000	200,000	400,000	£20.00
25,000	200,000	250,000	450,000	£18.00
30,000	200,000	300,000	500,000	£16.67

from a single-shift to a two-shift operation, which requires not only additional variable costs but also additional fixed costs (e.g. extra supervision). Semi-variable costs have both fixed and variable components. A simple example is a telephone bill, which will have a fixed component (rental) and a variable component (calls). Maintenance of motor vehicles can be both time based (the fixed component) and mileage based (the variable component).

This example introduces the notion of marginal cost. The marginal cost is the cost of producing one extra unit. In the above example, to increase volume from 10,000 to 15,000 units incurs a marginal cost of £50,000 (which in this case is 5,000 additional units at a variable cost of £10 each). However, in some circumstances marginal costs may include a fixed-cost element (in the case of semi-fixed costs).

The notion of cost is therefore quite difficult. Is the cost in Table 10.1 the average cost or the marginal cost? If it is the average cost, what level of activity is chosen to determine that average, given fluctuating volumes of sales from period to period? There are several possible answers: if our activity level last year was 10,000 units, we may say the cost is £30 per unit, but if we expect to have an activity level of 15,000 units this year, perhaps the cost is £23.33. Then again, if our marginal cost to produce one extra unit is only £10, isn't that our cost? As explained in Chapter 3, there are 'different costs for different purposes' (Clark, 1923) so we need to understand the purpose for which we want to use the cost before deciding what the appropriate measure of cost is.

Cost—volume—profit analysis

A method for understanding the relationship between profit, cost and sales revenue is cost—volume—profit analysis, or CVP. CVP is concerned with understanding the relationship between changes in activity (the number of units sold) and changes in selling prices and costs (both fixed and variable). Typical questions that CVP may help with are:

- What is the likely effect on profits of changes in selling price or the volume of activity?
- If we incur additional costs, what changes should we make to our selling price or to the volume that we need to sell?

CVP is used by accountants in a relatively simplistic manner. While most businesses will sell a wide range of product/services at many different prices (e.g. quantity discounts), accountants assume a constant sales mix and average selling prices per unit. The assumption is that these relationships are linear, rather than the curvilinear models preferred by economists that reflect economies and diseconomies of scale. The accountant limits this problem by recognizing the relevant range. The relevant range is the volume of activity within which the business expects to be operating over the short-term planning horizon, typically the current or next accounting period, and the business will usually have experience of operating at this level of output. Within the relevant range, the accountant's model and the economist's model are similar.

Profit can be shown as the difference between revenue and costs (both fixed and variable). This relationship can be shown in the following formula:

$$\textbf{net profit} = \textbf{revenue} - (\textbf{fixed costs} + \textbf{variable costs})$$

$$\textbf{net profit} = (\textbf{units sold} \times \textbf{selling price}) - [\textbf{fixed costs} + (\textbf{units sold} \times \textbf{unit variable cost})]$$

In mathematical terms, this is:

$$N = Pu - (F + Bu)$$

where:
  N = net profit
  u = number of units sold
  P = selling price per unit
  F = total fixed costs
  B = variable cost per unit

Using the example of XYZ Limited, a selling price of £25 for 20,000 units would yield a net profit of:

$N = (£25 \times 20,000) - [£200,000 + (£10 \times 20,000)]$
$N = £500,000 - £400,000$
$N = £100,000$

CVP permits sensitivity analysis. Sensitivity analysis is an approach to understanding how changes in one variable (e.g. price) affect other variables (e.g. volume). This is important, because revenues and costs cannot be predicted with certainty and there is always a range of possible outcomes, i.e. different mixes of price, volume and cost.

Using sensitivity analysis, a business may ask questions such as: What is the selling price (P) required for a profit (N) of £150,000 on sales of 25,000 units? To calculate this, we enter the data we know in the formula and solve for the missing figure (in this case price):

$$£150,000 = £P \times 25,000 - [£200,000 + (£10 \times 25,000)]$$
$$£150,000 = £25,000P - £450,000$$
$$P = \frac{£600,000}{25,000}$$

$$P = £24 \text{ per unit}$$

The **breakeven point** is the point at which total costs equal total revenue, that is where there is neither a profit nor a loss. How many units have to be sold for the business to break even? This question can be answered by using simple algebra to solve the above equation for u (the number of units), where N (net profit) is 0, as follows:

$$0 = Pu - (F + Bu)$$
$$0 = 20u - (200,000 + 10u)$$
$$u = \frac{200,000}{10}$$

$$u = 20,000$$

However, a simpler formula for breakeven is:

$$\text{breakeven sales (in units)} = \frac{\text{fixed costs}}{\text{selling price per unit} - \text{variable cost per unit}} = \frac{£200,000}{20 - 10}$$
$$= 20,000 \text{ units}$$

Note that £10 is the *unit contribution*, i.e. the difference between the selling price and the variable cost per unit. The unit contribution can also be expressed as a percentage of sales of 0.5 or 50% (£10/£20), which applies to any level of sales as the ratio of contribution (£10) to selling price (£20) remains constant within the relevant range.

$$\text{breakeven sales (in £s)} = \frac{\text{fixed costs}}{\text{unit contribution as a \% of sales}} = \frac{£200,000}{0.5} = £400,000$$

This is equivalent to the breakeven units of 20,000 at £20 selling price per unit.

Businesses establish profit targets, and a variation on the above calculations is to calculate the number of units that need to be sold to generate a target net profit.

$$\text{sales (in units) for profit of £150,000} = \frac{\text{fixed costs} + \text{target profit}}{\text{selling price per unit} - \text{variable cost per unit}}$$

$$= \frac{£200,000 + £150,000}{20 - 10}$$

$$= 35,000 \text{ units}$$

$$\text{sales (in £s) for profit of £150,000} = \frac{\text{fixed costs} + \text{target profit}}{\text{unit contribution as a \% of sales}}$$

$$= \frac{£200,000 + £150,000}{0.5}$$

$$= £700,000$$

This is equivalent to the sales in units of 35,000 at £20 selling price per unit. However, if the business has a maximum capacity of 25,000 units, the limit of its relevant range, this profitability may not be achievable and the cost structure of the business reflected in the CVP relationship would have to be revised.

CVP can be understood through a graphical representation. Using the same data, the CVP graph is shown in Figure 10.1. In this CVP diagram, the vertical axis represents money (both revenue and cost) and the horizontal axis represents volume (the number of units sold). Fixed costs are seen to be constant, as increases in volume do not influence total fixed cost within the relevant range. Variable costs are nil at zero level of activity and increase in proportion to that activity. Total costs are the sum of variable and fixed costs. They begin above zero because, even with zero level of activity, fixed costs are still incurred. Total revenue starts at nil and increases with the volume sold.

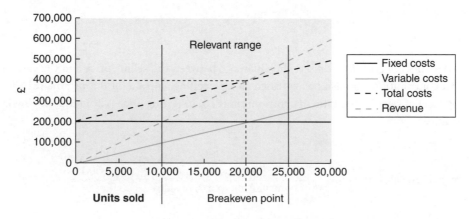

Figure 10.1   Breakeven chart for XYZ Ltd.

As fixed costs remain constant, profit per unit will vary at different levels of activity. The point at which the total cost line intersects the total revenue line is the breakeven point.

The breakeven point is shown by the dotted line and can be read as the revenue required (£400,000) to sell a given volume (20,000 units) at a selling price of £20 per unit. The area of profit is found to the right of the breakeven point, between total revenue and total cost. The area of loss is found to the left of the breakeven point, between total cost and total revenue. Note, however, that outside the relevant range (shown in the diagram as between 10,000 and 25,000 units) cost behaviour may be different and so the CVP diagram may have to be redrawn. The breakeven chart shows the margin of safety which becomes larger as volume moves to the right of the breakeven point. The *margin of safety* is a measure of the difference between the anticipated and breakeven levels of activity. It is expressed as a percentage:

$$\text{margin of safety (\%)} = \frac{\text{expected sales} - \text{breakeven sales} \times 100}{\text{expected sales}}$$

Using the same example, the margin of safety assuming anticipated sales of 25,000 units is:

$$\frac{25,000 - 20,000}{25,000} \times 100 = 20\%$$

The lower the margin of safety, the higher the risk, as sales do not have to fall much before reaching the breakeven point. Conversely, there is less risk where businesses operate with higher margins of safety.

Whereas the breakeven graph shows the breakeven point, the *profit–volume graph* shows the profit or loss at different levels of activity. For the same example, the profit–volume graph is shown in Figure 10.2.

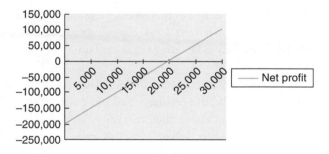

Figure 10.2 Profit–volume graph for XYZ Ltd.

At any level of output the net profit (or loss) can be seen. This example shows the breakeven point of 20,000 units and the small margin of safety to the anticipated sales level of 25,000 units, compared with the risk of substantial loss following from any level of activity below 20,000 units.

Breakeven with multiple products

Most businesses sell more than one product, but CVP can still be used in these instances, although the sales mix does need to be fairly constant. The same technique can be applied by weighting the sales and margins of each product.

In the following example, a company has fixed costs of €200,000 for a period. During the same period, Product A constitutes 60% of a company's sales and each unit is sold for €30 each, with variable costs of €12 each. Product B represents the other 40% of sales, with each unit selling for €15 and variable costs of €7.

The contribution per unit is calculated and weighted by the sales mix to give a breakeven number of units. Table 10.2 shows the calculation of the breakeven point.

Table 10.2   Breakeven with multiple products.

	Product A: 60% sales mix		Product B: 40% sales mix	
Selling price	€30		€15	
Variable costs	€12		€7	
Contribution per unit	€18	60% × €18 = €10.80	€8	40% × €8 = €3.20
Breakeven $\dfrac{€200,000}{€10.80 + €3.20}$	$\dfrac{€200,000}{€14} = 14{,}286$ units (both Products A & B)			
Units by product to breakeven	14,286 × 0.6 = 8,572		14,286 × 0.4 = 5,714	
Sales	8,572 @ €30 =	€257,160	5,714 @ €15	€85,710
Variable costs	@ €12	102,864	@ €7	39,998
Contribution		€154,296		€45,712
Total contribution			€200,008	

In this example, the breakeven is 14,286 units but this number represents combined sales of both products A and B. The sales mix (60/40) is applied again to derive the number of units for each of Products A and B. The accuracy of the result can be seen by calculating the contribution for the breakeven level of sales for each unit which is equal to fixed costs.

Importantly, if 14,286 units are sold but (compared to the calculation in Table 10.2) there are more units of Product A sold and less of Product B, the business will earn a higher total contribution because the contribution per unit from Product A is higher than that for Product B. The opposite is also true, that if the mix changes and more are sold of Product B than Product A, even though 14,286 units may be sold in total, breakeven will not be reached. Hence, whilst this method is useful, it does rely on a close monitoring of the sales mix itself.

Operating leverage

A similar situation arises where the mix of variable and fixed costs changes. Operating leverage refers to the mix of fixed and variable costs in a business and its ability to use its fixed costs to generate a contribution. A high operating leverage means that there are high fixed costs, low variable costs and a high contribution margin per unit sold. Assume that two companies sell the same number of products at the same price and make the same profit. However, the mix of fixed and variable costs is different between the two companies. Table 10.3 shows an example.

Table 10.3 Operating leverage: fixed and variable costs.

	Company A		Company B	
Sales	200,000 @ $1.50	$300,000	200,000 units @ $1.50	$300,000
Variable costs	90 cents per unit	180,000	30 cents per unit	60,000
Contribution	60 cents per unit	120,000	$1.20 per unit	240,000
Fixed costs		100,000		220,000
Profit		$20,000		$20,000
Breakeven point	$100,000/$0.60	166,667 units	$220,000/$1.20	183,333 units
		$250,000		$275,000
				Higher risk
Contribution from 50,000 units sold (after breakeven)	50,000 @ $0.60	$30,000	50,000 @ $1.20	$60,000 Higher return

Table 10.3 shows that Company B has a higher operating leverage. This leads to a higher breakeven point as more units must be sold to achieve breakeven. However, Company B also has a higher contribution margin per unit, which means that once it has passed the breakeven point and recovered its fixed costs, it will generate profits faster for each additional unit sold because its contribution margin per unit sold is higher than that for Company A. Company B can make a higher return but because of its higher fixed costs, also faces a higher risk if the breakeven point is not reached.

Limitations of CVP analysis

Despite the advantages presented by CVP analysis, there are some significant limitations arising from the assumptions made. The assumptions are:

- Volume is the only factor that causes prices and variable costs to alter (in practice, production efficiencies, product/service mix, price levels etc. all influence costs and revenues).
- There is a single product/service or a product/service mix that remains constant (in practice, product/service mix can vary significantly and different product/services may have different cost structures, prices and contributions).
- Costs can be accurately divided into fixed and variable elements (although in practice many costs are semi-variable and semi-fixed – we develop this idea further in Chapter 13).
- Fixed costs do not change (although in practice they vary with the range of items produced and with product complexity, as we will see in Chapter 13).
- Total costs and revenues are linear (while this is reasonably likely within the relevant range, increases in volume may still lead to lower unit prices or economies of scale and curvilinear costs and revenues may be more accurate).
- The CVP analysis applies only to the relevant range (although decisions may be made in the current period to move outside this range).
- The analysis applies only to the short term and cannot reliably be used in the longer term.

Despite its limitations, CVP analysis is a useful tool in making decisions about pricing and volume, based on an understanding of the cost structure of the business. The next section describes how businesses make decisions about what price to charge.

Alternative approaches to pricing

Accounting information can be used for pricing by a variety of approaches:

- cost-plus pricing;
- target rate of return pricing;
- optimum selling price;
- special pricing decisions;
- transfer pricing.

However, it is important to remember that in most cases (unless a business has a monopoly or is a *price-maker*/price leader in the marketplace), selling prices will be dictated by what customers are prepared to pay and the prices set by competitors. The company will then be a *price-taker*. Hence, accounting-based costs may not be a reliable guide to setting prices. In these cases, cost information will be used, not in price setting, but in calculating product/service profitability, and in decisions about product or market discontinuance, which we look at later in this chapter.

An understanding of the firm's marketing strategy is essential in using cost information for pricing decisions.

As well as being price-makers or price-takers, businesses also adopt *market-skimming* or *market-penetration* strategies at different phases of the product/service lifecycle (see Chapter 18). A common marketing strategy is *differential pricing*, where prices vary between each market segment. Where products/services are sold in different market segments at different prices, the price can be considered in different ways:

- A minimum short-term price taking into account only marginal, i.e. usually variable, costs.
- A minimum long-term price that covers the full product/service cost.
- A target long-term price that takes into account the return on investment necessary to increase shareholder value.

In each case, cost will be an important, but by no means the only, factor taken into account in pricing decisions.

Cost-plus pricing

Accounting information may be used in pricing decisions, particularly where the firm is a market leader or *price-maker*. In these cases, firms may adopt cost-plus pricing, in which a margin is added to the total product/service cost in order to determine the selling price. In CVP analysis, we differentiated variable costs from fixed costs and argued that in certain circumstances, a product/service could be sold where the con-tribution was positive, even though fixed costs were not covered. However, in the long term, the prices at which a business sells its goods/services must cover all of its costs. If it is unable to do so, it will make losses and may not survive. For every product/service the full cost must be calculated, to which the desired profit margin is added. Full cost includes an allocation to each product/service of all the costs of the business, including producing and delivering a good or service, and all its marketing, selling, finance and adminis-tration costs. The calculation of full cost is covered in Chapter 13, but it is taken as given for the purposes of this chapter.

Using the CVP example provided earlier, the average cost was £20 assuming a level of activity of 20,000 units. The cost-plus pricing formula may be applied as a *mark-up* on any element of cost. For example, a mark-up of 25% would result in a selling price of £25.

$$\textbf{cost} + \textbf{mark-up on cost} = \textbf{selling price}$$
$$£20 + (25\% \text{ of } £20) = £25$$

The profit margin is the profit as a percentage of the selling price. Using the same example, the profit *margin* of £5 is 20% of the selling price of £25. A mark-up is the percentage added to cost for profit, whereas the margin is the percentage of the selling price that is represented by profit.

Often the mark-up will be an arbitrary figure, based on past experience, but it may be based on a ratio (see Chapter 7) such as return on sales (as in the above example). When considering the gross and operating margin ratios in Chapter 7, it is important to remember that achieving a ratio for the business as a whole means that individual products/services must all contribute towards that ratio, even though in practice some product/services will achieve higher returns, and others lower.

Another way of looking at the price is in terms of a return on the investment.

Target rate of return pricing

Target rate of return pricing estimates the (fixed and working) capital investment required for the business and the need to generate an adequate return on that investment to satisfy shareholders.

For example, if the investment required to produce a product/service is €1,000,000 and the company wants a 12% return on investment, the desired profit is €120,000 (€1,000,000 @ 12%). Assuming a volume of 20,000 units, each unit would need to generate a profit of €6 (€120,000/20,000 units). If the total cost was €20, the selling price would be €26. This represents a 30% mark-up on cost and a 23.1% margin on selling price. Target rate of return pricing is likely to lead to pricing decisions that are more closely linked to shareholder value than adding an arbitrary margin to total cost.

Optimum selling price

While cost-plus and target rate of return pricing is useful, it ignores the relationship between price and demand in a competitive business environment. The sensitivity of demand to changes in price is reflected in the *price elasticity of demand*. *Elastic demand* exists when a price increase leads to a fall in demand as customers place little value in the product/service or switch to substitutes. *Inelastic demand* exists where small price increases/decreases cause only a small change in demand because customers value the product or because no substitute is available.

The optimum selling price is the point at which profit is maximized. To ascertain the optimum selling price, a business must understand cost behaviour in terms of variable or fixed costs and have some ability, via market research, to predict likely changes in volume as prices increase or decrease.

MNO Limited has used market research to estimate the likely increase in demand as the selling price falls. For each level of activity we can calculate the revenue, variable costs and total contribution. The figures are shown in Table 10.4.

Table 10.4   MNO Ltd — contribution at different activity levels.

Selling price per unit	Volume expected at given selling price (units)	Revenue (selling price × volume) ($)	Variable costs (@ $10 per unit)	Contribution (revenue − variable costs) ($)
40	10,000	400,000	100,000	300,000
35	15,000	525,000	150,000	375,000
30	20,000	600,000	200,000	400,000
25	25,000	625,000	250,000	375,000
20	30,000	600,000	300,000	300,000

An approach that seeks to maximize sales revenue will result in a strategy that seeks to sell 25,000 units at $25 each, with total revenue being $625,000. However, taking account of the price/volume relationship and costs (which were estimated at $10 variable cost per unit) shows that the business will *maximize its contribution* towards fixed costs and profit at $400,000 with an optimum selling price of $30. This is even though the number of units sold will be less at 20,000 with total revenue of $600,000.

The highest contribution will always be the highest profit as the fixed costs will be unchanged at each level of activity within the relevant range. Although businesses seek to *increase* sales revenue, they wish to *maximize* contribution and therefore profitability. This issue is often the cause of conflict between marketing and finance staff in business organizations.

Special pricing decisions

Special pricing decisions are usually one-time orders at a price below that usually sold in the market. In the long term, all the costs of the business must be covered by the selling price if the business is to be profitable. However, in the short term, spare capacity may lead to decisions to accept orders from customers at less than the full cost. As fixed costs remain the same irrespective of volume, provided that the selling price covers the variable costs it makes a positive contribution to recovering some of the fixed costs of the business and therefore to a greater profit (or lower loss).

A business may have adopted a marketing strategy to sell at a price of £30, but only 17,000 units have been sold. The business profitability will be:

		£'000
Revenue	17,000 @ £30	510
Variable costs	17,000 @ £10	170
Contribution		340
Fixed costs		200
Net profit		140

Accepting an order of 3,000 units at £12 will increase profits by £6,000 (3,000 at a selling price of £12 less variable costs of £10) because fixed costs will remain unchanged. The business profitability will then be:

		£'000
Revenue	17,000 @ £30	510
	3,000 @ £12	36
		546
Variable costs	20,000 @ £10	200
Contribution		346
Fixed costs		200
Net profit		146

Consequently, provided that the business can sell at a price that at least covers variable costs, in the short term the business will be better off. This argument does not follow through into the long term, over which the business must cover all its costs in order to be profitable. A business will also minimize its losses by selling at a price that covers variable costs but not full costs. If volume falls below the breakeven point:

		£'000
Revenue	8,000 @ £30	240
Variable costs	8,000 @ £10	80
Contribution		160
Fixed costs		200
Net loss		40

If an order of 3,000 units at £12 is accepted, the loss will be reduced by £6,000:

		£'000
Revenue	8,000 @ £30	240
	3,000 @ £12	36
		276
Variable costs	11,000 @ £10	110
Contribution		166
Fixed costs		200
Net loss		34

However, consideration needs to be given to the long-term marketing implications of accepting orders at less than normal selling price:

1. The future selling price may be affected by accepting a special order, if competitors adopt similar pricing tactics.
2. Customers who receive or become aware of a special selling price may expect a similar low price in the future.
3. Accepting this order may prevent the firm from accepting a more profitable order at a higher price if one subsequently comes along.
4. It is assumed that the business has spare capacity that has no alternative use.
5. It is assumed that fixed costs are unavoidable in the short term.

Transfer pricing

One special pricing decision is that concerned with the price at which goods or services are sold between business units in the same company, rather than the arm's-length price at which sales may be made to external customers. Transfer prices may be based on a variety of methods, but we leave discussing these in detail until Chapter 15.

One of the things that concerns managers about the transfer price is how the performance of their business unit will be perceived by the corporate head office who are concerned that each business unit is profitable.

Segmental profitability

Companies typically decentralize their operations to multiple business units, all of which are expected to be profitable. These business units (we discuss the evaluation of business unit profitability in more detail in Chapter 15) may be based on the function they carry out, or on the basis of some form of market segmentation. *Market segments* may be defined geographically, by customer or by customer groups, by product/service or by product/service groups, or by different distribution channels. In any of these cases, decisions may be made about expanding or contracting in different segments based on the relative profitability of those segments. These are important decisions, but the methods by which costs are allocated over each segment must be understood before informed decisions about the profitability, or even discontinuance of a market segment can be made.

As we will see in Chapter 13, major assumptions are involved in how costs are allocated within a business. However, for the purposes of the present chapter, we need to separate fixed costs into unavoidable business-wide costs and avoidable segment-specific costs. Unavoidable costs typically include the top management, finance and treasury, human resource specialists and the company's IT system. Companies often charge these costs out to different business units or market segments using an often arbitrary method (for example in proportion to sales volume). These costs are only able to be influenced at the corporate level and hence at the level of the individual business unit or market segment cannot be avoided. Avoidable costs are identifiable with and are able to be influenced by decisions made at the business unit level. Hence, if a decision is made to close a market segment, these costs would be avoidable. So for example in a retail chain, a poor performing shop could be closed down and this would avoid the fixed costs of shop rental and salaries of staff. However, the head office costs of the retail chain would be unaffected and so are unavoidable.

The idea of contribution (sales revenue less variable costs) introduced earlier in this chapter can be extended to the case of different market segments. This requires the separation of avoidable from unavoidable fixed costs.

An example is an accounting practice that prepares tax returns on behalf of clients. The clients are grouped into three market segments: business (where the practice also carries out accounting services); business (where the practice only completes the tax return); and personal returns. The practice thinks that personal returns may be unprofitable and a partner has produced the data in Table 10.5.

Table **10.5**   Profitability of business segments for an accounting practice.

	Business (accounting services)	Business (tax only)	Personal	Total
Revenue	120,000	50,000	30,000	200,000
Variable costs	50,000	22,000	18,000	90,000
Contribution	70,000	28,000	12,000	110,000
Avoidable fixed costs for administrative support	20,000	10,000	5,000	35,000
Contribution to overhead	50,000	18,000	7,000	75,000
Unavoidable fixed business expenses (rent, partner salaries etc.) allocated as a percentage of revenue	30,000	12,500	7,500	50,000
Profit	20,000	5,500	(500)	25,000
Note: unavoidable fixed costs have been allocated across the three market segments in proportion to sales	60%	25%	15%	

As the example in Table 10.5 shows, despite the loss made by the personal tax returns market segment, these clients contribute £7,000 in the period towards the unavoidable overhead. If this segment were discontinued, the profit of the practice would fall by £7,000 to £18,000. The same example, without the personal tax market segment, can be seen in Table 10.6.

This result is because, even though the fixed costs for administrative support of personal tax would be saved if the segment were discontinued, the whole of the unavoidable costs of £50,000 would continue. Table 10.6 shows that the reported profits of the two remaining segments would appear to fall as they would now carry a higher proportion of the unavoidable fixed costs.

Table 10.6   Profitability of business segments for an accounting practice – discontinuance of personal tax.

	Business (accounting services)	Business (tax only)	Personal	Total
Revenue	120,000	50,000		170,000
Variable costs	50,000	22,000		72,000
Contribution	70,000	28,000		98,000
Avoidable fixed costs for administrative support	20,000	10,000		30,000
Contribution to overhead	50,000	18,000		68,000
Unavoidable fixed business expenses (rent, partner salaries etc.) allocated as a percentage of revenue	35,300	14,700		50,000
Profit	14,700	3,300		18,000
Note: unavoidable fixed costs have been allocated across the three market segments in proportion to sales	70%	30%		

The following case study illustrates segmental profitability.

Case study 10.1: Retail Stores plc – the loss-making division

Retail Stores has three segments, producing the results in Table 10.7. The contribution as a percentage of sales, assuming a constant sales mix, is 70.6% (€600,000/€850,000).

Table 10.7   Retail Stores – analysis of trading results.

€	Clothing	Electrical	Toys	Total
Sales €	400,000	300,000	150,000	850,000
Variable costs %	25%	30%	40%	
Variable costs €	100,000	90,000	60,000	250,000
Contribution	300,000	210,000	90,000	600,000
Segment-specific fixed costs	120,000	100,000	60,000	280,000
Allocated business-wide costs (as a % of sales revenue)	120,000	90,000	45,000	255,000
Profit/(loss)	60,000	20,000	−15,000	65,000

The company's breakeven point in sales is calculated as:

$$\frac{\text{fixed costs}}{\text{unit contribution as a \% of sales}} \frac{280,000 + 255,000}{0.706} = \frac{535,000}{0.706}$$

or €758,000.

Current sales of €850,000 represent a margin of safety of:

$$\frac{\text{expected sales} - \text{breakeven sales}}{\text{expected sales}} \times 100 = \frac{£850,000 - £758,000}{£850,000}$$

or 10.8%.

Management is considering dropping the Toys segment due to its reported loss after deducting avoidable segment-specific fixed costs and unavoidable business-wide costs, which are allocated as a percentage of sales revenue.

However, an understanding of cost behaviour helps to identify that each segment is making a positive contribution to business-wide costs after deducting the segment-specific fixed costs, as the modification to the reported profits in Table 10.8 demonstrates.

Table 10.8   Retail Stores – contribution by business segment.

€	Clothing	Electrical	Toys	Total
Sales €	400,000	300,000	150,000	850,000
Variable costs %	25%	30%	40%	
Variable costs €	100,000	90,000	60,000	250,000
Contribution	300,000	210,000	90,000	600,000
Segment-specific fixed costs	120,000	100,000	60,000	280,000
Segment contribution to business-wide costs and profit	180,000	110,000	30,000	320,000
Allocated business-wide costs (as a % of sales revenue)	120,000	90,000	45,000	255,000
Profit/(loss)	60,000	20,000	−15,000	65,000

Based on the figures in Table 10.8, despite the Toys segment making a loss, it makes a positive contribution of €30,000 to allocated business-wide costs. If the Toys segment was discontinued, total profit would fall by €30,000, as Table 10.9 shows.

Table 10.9   Retail Stores – effect of closure of Toys business segment.

€	Clothing	Electrical	Toys	Total
Sales €	400,000	300,000		700,000
Variable costs %	25%	30%		
Variable costs €	100,000	90,000		190,000
Contribution	300,000	210,000		510,000
Segment-specific fixed costs	120,000	100,000		220,000
Segment contribution to business-wide costs and profit	180,000	110,000		290,000
Allocated business-wide costs (as a % of sales revenue)	146,000	109,000		255,000
Profit/(loss)	34,000	1,000		35,000

This is because the loss of the contribution by the Toys segment to business-wide costs and profits amounts to €30,000 (after deducting avoidable segment-specific fixed costs). The business-wide costs of €255,000 are reallocated over the two remaining business segments in proportion to sales revenue, which in turn makes the Electrical segment appear only marginally profitable.

If the Toys division were discontinued, the impact would be to reduce costs by €60,000 and a new, higher contribution as a percentage of sales results (€510,000/€700,000 = 72.9%, up from 70.6%). Consequently, Retail Stores' breakeven point in sales can be revised to:

$$\frac{\text{fixed costs}}{\text{unit contribution as a \% of sales}} \quad \frac{220,000 + 255,000}{0.729} = \frac{475,000}{0.729}$$

or €652,000.

Current sales of €700,000 represent a margin of safety of 6.8%, a fall of 4% from the three-division breakeven calculation. This is calculated by:

$$\frac{\text{expected sales} - \text{breakeven sales}}{\text{expected sales}} \times 100 = \frac{£700,000 - £652,000}{£700,000}$$

Segmental profitability is the result of avoidable variable costs and fixed costs that are segment-specific and an allocation of unavoidable business-wide fixed costs. It is important to differentiate these costs in decision making. We will return to the overhead cost allocation problem in Chapter 13.

Another example of segmental profitability is concerned with customer profitability analysis.

Customer profitability analysis

Just as some products/services are more profitable than others, so are particular customers, industry groups or geographic territories. Understanding customer profitability is essential to customer relationship management as the organization faces three alternatives:

- reducing the costs of servicing unprofitable customers;
- increasing prices to unprofitable customers to cover those costs;
- no longer doing business with unprofitable customers.

For example, some customers may make heavy demands on costs so as to make them unprofitable. An example is banking where corporate banking, mortgage lending, credit cards and so on are far more profitable for banks than 'mum and dad' banking. This is because many people have many bank accounts, often with small amounts of money, but banks provide a very expensive network of branches to support that particular customer type. Banks would most likely be more profitable if they eliminated this type of business, although there would be political and reputational consequences of doing so. However, technology has reduced the cost of processing large volumes of small-value customer transactions, e.g. automatic teller machines (ATMs) for cash withdrawals, and EFTPOS (electronic funds transfer at point of sale) and BACS (Bank Automated Clearing System) for making payments instead of using cheques which are costly for banks to process.

In the following example (see Table 10.10), Marquet Company has four geographic territories (it is simpler to show the example with four territories than with multiple customers, but the principle is the same). The North and West territories are fairly well established but lower prices are charged in South and East which have more price competition. While variable production costs are the same, selling and distribution costs are higher in South and West than in North and East. Each geographic territory has its own fixed costs to support a local office.

Table 10.10 shows that South and East are unprofitable. In the short term it would be better to close these down, but the business needs to consider whether it can either increase the selling price, increase the volume (which will contribute to the recovery of more of the territory's fixed costs) or reduce its variable selling and distribution costs in the loss-making territories. Using customer profitability analysis, like business segment contribution analysis, allows organizations to take a strategic view of multiple dimensions of profitability (products/services, customers, business units etc.) and make strategic decisions about which should be retained, which need further investment, which need price or cost adjustments and which should be abandoned.

Case study 10.2 shows how an understanding of financial information can assist more directly in carrying out the marketing function.

Table 10.10 Marquet Company.

	North	South	East	West	Total
Sales units	4,000	2,000	1,000	7,000	14,000
Average price per unit	£10	£7	£7	£11	
Sales revenue £	£40,000	£14,000	£7,000	£77,000	£138,000
Variable production costs (£3 per unit)	12,000	6,000	3,000	21,000	42,000
Variable selling and distribution costs (£2 per unit in North & East; £3 per unit in South & West)	8,000	6,000	2,000	21,000	37,000
Contribution	20,000	2,000	2,000	35,000	59,000
Fixed costs specific to territory	10,000	3,000	3,000	15,000	31,000
Contribution to corporate overhead	10,000	−1,000	−1,000	20,000	28,000
Corporate overhead					15,000
Net profit £					£13,000

Case study 10.2: SuperTech — using accounting information to win sales

One of Global Enterprises' target customers is SuperTech, a high-technology company involved in making semiconductors for advanced manufacturing capabilities. SuperTech has grown rapidly and its sales are $35 million per annum. Variable costs consume about 60% of sales and fixed selling, distribution and administrative expenses are about $10 million, leaving a profit of $4 million. The challenge facing SuperTech is to continue to grow while maintaining profitability. It plans to achieve this by continuing to re-engineer its production processes to reduce the lead time between order and delivery and improve the yield from its production by improving quality.

Global sees SuperTech as a major customer for its services. However, it operates in a highly price-competitive industry. Global is unwilling to reduce its pricing because it has a premium brand image and believes that it should be able to use its customer knowledge, including published financial information, to increase sales and justify the prices being charged. Global believes that its services can contribute to SuperTech's strategy of reducing lead time and improving yield.

Global has been able to ascertain the following information from the financial statements of SuperTech:

- Its cost of sales last year was $21.6 million and its inventory was $17.5 million. This is because the equipment made by SuperTech is highly technical and requires long production lead times.
- Employment-related costs for the 250 employees were $8 million, 25% of the total business costs of $31 million.
- The company has borrowings of $14.5 million, its gearing being 90%, and interest costs last year were $787,000.

We need to make a number of assumptions about the business, but these are acceptable in order to estimate the kind of savings that Global's services might obtain for SuperTech.

We can calculate that the company's cost of production, assuming 240 working days per year, as $90,000 per day ($21.6 million/240). Given the low number of employees and the knowledge that many of these are employed in non-production roles, the vast majority (over 80%) of production costs is believed to be material costs. Using the inventory days ratio (see Chapter 7), we can calculate that the year-end inventory holding is 194 days ($17.5 million/$90,000), equivalent to 81% of working days (194/240).

Global's services will increase the production costs because of its premium pricing, and it expects the price differential to be $250,000 per annum. However, Global's services will generate savings for SuperTech. First, the service will reduce the lead time in manufacture by 10 days. The company's interest cost of $787,000 is 5.4% of its borrowings of $14.5 million. This is a very rough estimate as borrowings increased during the year and the company most likely had different interest rates in operation. However, it is useful as a guide. If Global's services can reduce SuperTech's lead time by

10 days, that will reduce the level of inventory by $900,000 ($90,000 per day × 10), which can be used to reduce debt, resulting in an interest saving of $48,600 ($900,000 @ 5.4%).

Second, Global also believes that its services will increase the yield from existing production because of the higher quality achieved. Global estimates that this yield improvement will lower the cost of sales from 60% to 59%. This 1% saving on sales of $35 million is equivalent to $350,000 per annum.

Global's business proposal (which of course needs to demonstrate how these gains can be achieved from a technical perspective) can contain the following financial justification:

	per annum
Savings:	
Interest savings on reduced lead time	$48,600
Yield improvements	$350,000
Total savings	$398,600
Additional cost of Global's services	$250,000
Net saving per annum	$148,600

This is equivalent to an increase of 3.7% in the net profit (after interest) to SuperTech.

Conclusion

This chapter has shown how accounting information can contribute to marketing decisions. We have introduced the separation of costs into their fixed and variable components and the importance of understanding contribution. The use of CVP analysis has been shown to provide information about breakeven points and the sales required to achieve target profits given the different operating leverage of companies. Various approaches to pricing have also been introduced. We have also separated fixed costs into their avoidable and unavoidable components to consider the profitability of different market segments and also the analysis of customer profitability.

While marketing is critical to business success, so too is the fulfilment of the promises made by marketing, therefore the operations function is the subject of the next chapter.

References

Clark, J. M. (1923). *Studies in the Economics of Overhead Costs*. Chicago: University of Chicago Press.
Doyle, P. (1998). *Marketing Management and Strategy* (2nd edn). London: Prentice Hall.
Porter, M. E. (1980). *Competitive Strategy: Techniques for Analyzing Industries and Competitors*. New York: Free Press.
Porter, M. E. (1985). *Competitive Advantage: Creating and Sustaining Superior Performance*. New York: Free Press.

Questions

10.1   National Retail Stores has identified the following data from its accounting system for the year ended 31 December: sales £1,100,000; purchases £650,000; overhead expenses £275,000. It had an opening inventory of £150,000 and a closing inventory of £200,000.

Calculate the:

- gross profit; and
- operating profit.

10.2   Plastic Emoluments has a relevant range between 100,000 and 200,000 units, fixed costs are €645,000 and variable costs are €7 per unit. Calculate the average costs at a production volume of each of 100,000, 150,000 and 200,000 units.

10.3   Hilltop Solutions has a planned level of activity of 150,000 units, fixed costs are $300,000 and variable costs are $7 per unit. The actual production volume is 140,000 units.

Identify the:

- standard cost per unit;
- actual cost per unit;
- marginal cost per unit.

10.4   Corporate Document Service incurs variable costs of £7 every time a document is processed. The business providing the service has fixed costs of £100,000 per month. The selling price for each service is £25.

- By how much does the average cost change between processing 10,000 and 20,000 documents?
- Does the marginal cost change in the same way?
- Explain why the average cost changes.

10.5   The Cook Co. has two divisions, Eastern and Western. The divisions have the following revenue and expenses:

	Eastern €	Western €
Sales	550,000	500,000
Variable costs	275,000	200,000
Divisional fixed costs	180,000	150,000
Allocated corporate costs	170,000	135,000

The management of Cook is considering the closure of the Eastern division sales office. If the Eastern division were closed, the fixed costs associated with this division could be avoided but allocated corporate costs would continue.

Given this data:

- Calculate the effect on Cook Co.'s operating profit before and after the closure.
- Should the Eastern division be closed?

10.6   Jacobean Creek plc has provided the following data for last year:

Sales	5,000 units
Sales price	£80 per unit
Variable cost	£55 per unit
Fixed cost	£25,000

For the current year, Jacobean Creek believes that although sales volume will remain constant, the contribution margin per unit can be increased by 20% and total fixed cost can be reduced by 10%.

- Calculate the operating profit for last year and the current year.
- What is the increase in profit between the two years?

10.7   Relay Co. makes batons. It can make 300,000 batons a year at a variable cost of $750,000 and a fixed cost of $450,000. Relay predicts that next year it will sell 240,000 batons at the normal price of $5 per baton. In addition, a special order has been placed for 60,000 batons to be sold at a 40% discount. What will be Relay Co.'s total operating profit if the special order were accepted in addition to the planned sales at full price?

10.8   Yorkstar plans for a profit of £40,000 and expects to sell 20,000 units. Variable cost is £8 per unit and total fixed costs are £100,000. Calculate the selling price per unit if the target profit is to be achieved.

10.9   Jasper's IT consultancy has fixed costs of €450,000 per annum. There are 10,000 hours billed on average per annum. If variable costs are €35 per hour, calculate the breakeven charge rate per hour.

10.10   Hong Long Ltd has a product that is sold for $75, variable costs are $30 and fixed costs are $1,000 per month. Calculate how many products need to be sold to obtain a profit of $10,000 per annum.

10.11   John Richards plc has a cost per unit of £10 and an annual volume of sales of 18,000 units. If a £200,000 investment is required and the target rate of return is 12%, calculate the target mark-up per unit.

10.12 Victory Sales Co. predicts its selling price to be €20 per unit. Estimated costs are direct materials €8 per unit, direct labour €5 per unit and fixed overhead €7,000. Calculate the number of units to be sold to generate a profit of €5,000.

10.13 Luffer Enterprises estimates the following demand for its services at different selling prices. All demand is within Luffer's relevant range. Variable costs are £15 per unit and fixed costs are £10,000.

Price (£)	Quantity
26	1,075
27	1,000
28	925
29	850
30	775

Calculate the level of sales that will generate the highest profit.

10.14 Godfrey Consultancy adopts a cost-plus pricing system for its services and applies a target rate of return of 25% on an investment of $750,000. Its labour costs are $25 per hour and other variable costs are $4 per hour. The consultancy anticipates charging 20,000 hours per year to clients and has fixed overheads of $250,000.

Calculate Godfrey's target selling price per hour.

10.15 The marketing department of Giggo Hotels has estimated the number of hotel rooms (it has 120) that could be sold at different price levels. This information is shown below:

Number of rooms sold	Price per room per night (£)
120	90
100	105
80	135
60	155
50	175

Giggo Hotels has estimated its variable costs at £25 per room per night. Calculate the occupancy rate that Giggo will need in order to maximize its profits.

Operating Decisions

This chapter introduces the operations function: the fulfilment of a customer order following the marketing function. We consider operations through the value chain and contrast the different operating decisions faced by manufacturing and service businesses. Several operational decisions are considered, in particular capacity utilization, the cost of spare capacity and the product/service mix under capacity constraints. Relevant costs are considered in relation to the make versus buy decision, equipment replacement and the relevant cost of materials. The cost of quality and environmental costs are also introduced.

The operations function

Operations is the function that produces the goods or services to satisfy demand from customers. This function, interpreted broadly, includes all aspects of purchasing, manufacturing, distribution and logistics, whatever those activities may be called in particular industries. While purchasing and logistics may be common to all industries, manufacturing will only be relevant to a manufacturing business. There will also be different emphases such as distribution for a retail business and the separation of 'front office' (or customer-facing) functions from 'back office' (or support) functions for a service business or financial institution.

Irrespective of whether the business is in manufacturing, retailing or services, we can consider *operations* as the all-encompassing processes that *produce* the goods or services that satisfy customer demand. In simple terms, operations is concerned with the conversion process between resources (materials, facilities and equipment, people) and the products/services that are sold to customers. There are four aspects of the operations function: quality, speed, dependability and flexibility (Slack *et al.*, 1995). Each of these has cost implications and the lower the cost of producing goods and services, the lower can be the price to the customer, or the more profit may be retained by the business.

A useful analytical tool for understanding the conversion process is the *value chain* developed by Porter (1985) and shown in Figure 11.1. According to Porter every business is:

> a collection of activities that are performed to design, produce, market, deliver, and support its product . . . A firm's value chain and the way it performs individual activities are a reflection of its history, its strategy, its approach to implementing its strategy, and the underlying economics of the activities themselves (Porter, 1985, p. 36).

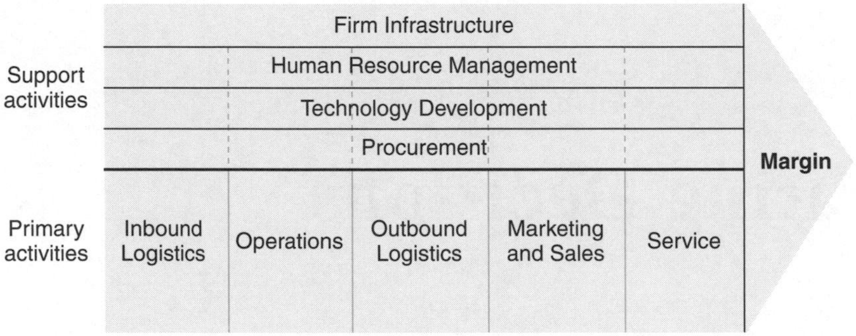

Figure 11.1   Porter's value chain.
Source: Reprinted from Porter, M. E. (1985). *Competitive Advantage: Creating and Sustaining Superior Performance.* New York: Free Press.

Porter separated the value chain into primary and secondary activities. Primary activities commence with the *upstream activities* of research and development, product design and sourcing (which Porter calls 'inbound logistics'), the production and distribution functions ('operations' and 'outbound logistics') and the *downstream activities* of marketing and after-sales customer service. This approach has similarities to the business process re-engineering approach of Hammer and Champy (1993, p. 32). Their emphasis on processes was on 'a collection of activities that takes one or more kinds of input and creates an output that is of value to the customer' (p. 35).

Accounting systems categorize costs through the hierarchical organization structure and line items (see Chapter 3) such as salaries and wages, rental and electricity. Porter argued that costs should be assigned to the value chain but that accounting systems can get in the way of analysing those costs. Traditional accounting systems 'may obscure the underlying activities a firm performs' (Porter, 1985). For many management decisions, far better information would be available from the categorization of costs in terms of value activities that are technologically and strategically distinct. This idea is part of the business process approach introduced in Chapter 9.

Porter developed the notion of cost drivers, which he defined as the structural factors that influence the cost of an activity and are 'more or less' under the control of the business. He proposed that the cost drivers of each value activity be analysed to enable comparisons with competitor value chains (we consider this further in Chapter 18). This would result in the relative cost position of the business being improved by better control of the cost drivers or by reconfiguring the value chain, while maintaining a differentiated product.

The value chain as a collection of inter-related business processes is a useful concept to understand businesses that produce either goods or services. Each element of the value chain contributes to the price a customer is willing to pay, but also attracts costs. As we saw with Porter's views on competitive strategy in Chapter 10, accounting systems should provide cost and profitability information that supports the businesses operations strategy. This strategy will vary considerably depending on the type of business.

We first consider the role of operations in manufacturing and service industries. In describing operations throughout this book, we will use the term *production* to refer to either goods or services and use *manufacturing* where we specifically refer to the conversion of raw materials into finished goods.

Managing operations — manufacturing

A distinguishing feature between the sale of goods and services is the need for inventory or stock in the sale of goods. This topic was covered in detail in Chapter 8. Inventory enables the timing difference between production capacity and customer demand to be smoothed. This is of course not possible in the supply of services.

Manufacturing firms purchase raw materials (unprocessed goods) and undertake the *conversion process* through the application of labour, machinery and know-how to manufacture finished goods. The finished goods are then available to be sold to customers. There are actually three types of inventory in this example: raw materials, finished goods and work-in-progress. Work-in-progress consists of goods that have begun but have not yet completed the conversion process.

There are different types of manufacturing and it is important to differentiate these production techniques as they lead to different costing methods:

- *Custom*: unique, custom products produced singly, e.g. a building.
- *Batch*: a quantity of the same goods produced at the same time (often called a production run), e.g. textbooks.
- *Continuous*: products produced in a continuous production process, e.g. oil and chemicals.

For continuous production processes, a process costing system is used. For custom and batch manufacture, costs are collected through a job costing system. In a manufacturing business the materials are identified by a bill of materials, a list of all the components that go to make up the completed project, and a routing, a list of the labour or machine-processing steps and times for the conversion process. To each of these costs overhead is allocated to cover the manufacturing costs that are not included in either the bill of materials or the routing (overhead will be covered in Chapter 13). This chapter will assume a job costing system is used, but readers interested in process costing are encouraged to read Chapter 8.

The bill of materials and routing contain standard quantities of raw material and labour time for a unit (or batch) of product. Standard quantities are the expected raw materials quantities, based on past and current experience and planned improvements in product design, purchasing and methods of production. Standard costs are the standard quantities of raw materials or labour times multiplied by the current and anticipated purchase prices for materials and the labour rates of pay. The standard cost is therefore a budget cost for a unit or batch of a product. As actual costs are not known for some time after the end of the accounting period, standard costs are generally used for decision making. Standard costs are usually expressed *per unit*.

The manufacturing process and its relationship to accounting can be seen in Figure 11.2. When a custom product is completed, the accumulated cost of materials, labour and overhead is the cost of that custom product. For a batch the total job cost is divided by the number of units produced. In process costing, at the end of the accounting period the total costs are divided by the volume produced to give a cost per unit of volume. The actual cost per unit can be compared to the budget or standard cost per unit. Any variation needs to be investigated and corrective action taken (we explain this in Chapter 17).

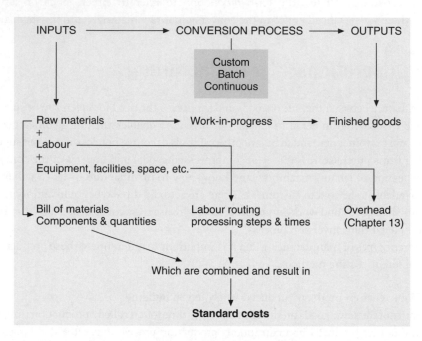

Figure 11.2   The manufacturing process and its relationship to standard costs.

The distinction between custom and batch is not always clear. Some products are produced on an assembly line as a batch of similar units but with some customization, because technology allows each unit to be unique. For example, motor vehicles are assembled as 'batches of one', since technology facilitates the sequencing of different specifications for each vehicle along a common production line. Within the same vehicle model, different colours, transmissions (manual or automatic), steering (right-hand or left-hand drive) and so on can all be accommodated.

Any manufacturing operation involves a number of sequential activities that need to be scheduled so that materials arrive at the appropriate time at the correct stage of production and labour is available to carry out the required process. Organizations that aim to have material arrive in production without holding buffer stocks are said to operate a just-in-time (JIT) manufacturing system. A case study of an automotive JIT can be found in Berry and Collier (2007).

Most manufacturing processes require an element of *set-up* or *make-ready* time, during which equipment settings are made to meet the specifications of the next production run (a custom product or batch). These settings may be made by manual labour or by computer through CNC (computer numerical control) technology. These investments involve substantial costs that need to be justified by an increased volume of production or by efficiencies that reduce production costs (we discuss investment decisions in Chapter 14). Set-up costs are built into the cost of production and are spread over the number of units in a batch.

The accumulated cost of materials, labour and overhead is the cost of a custom product or a batch of the same products. We can illustrate this with the example of a production run or batch of textbooks. The standard cost for the printing of 5,000 copies of a textbook is as follows:

Raw materials (paper, ink, etc.) from bill of materials	12,000
Machine set-up time (paper size, ink colours, etc.)	2,000
Labour time for printing (from labour routing)	18,000
Overhead allocated	10,000
Total job cost	€42,000

For a batch the total job cost is divided by the number of units produced (e.g. the number of copies of the textbook) to give a cost per unit (cost per textbook). In this illustration, the standard cost per textbook is €8.40 (€42,000/5,000 copies).

The most important difference between manufacturing goods and providing services is the absence of raw materials from the conversion process. Services are more concerned with the application of human knowledge, skill and experience, although often services can involve substantial investments in capital equipment, as the next section illustrates.

Managing operations — services

Service or knowledge-based industries have increasingly become the focus of Western economies. Fitzgerald *et al.* (1991) identified four key differences between products and services: intangibility, heterogeneity, simultaneity and perishability. Services are *intangible* rather than physical and are often delivered in a 'bundle' such that customers may value different aspects of the service. Services involving high labour content are *heterogeneous*, i.e. the consistency of the service may vary significantly. The production and consumption of services are *simultaneous* so that services cannot be inspected before they are delivered. Services are also *perishable*, so that unlike physical goods, there can be no inventory of services that have been provided but remain unsold.

Fitzgerald *et al.* also identified three different service types. *Professional services* are 'front office', people based, involving discretion and the customization of services to meet customer needs in which the process is more important than the service itself. Examples given by Fitzgerald *et al.* include professional firms such as solicitors, auditors and management consultants. *Mass services* involve limited contact time by staff and little customization, with services equipment based and product oriented with an emphasis on the 'back office' and little autonomy. Examples here are rail transport, airports and mass retailing. The third type of service is the *service shop*, a mixture of the other two extremes with emphasis on front and back office, people and equipment and product and process. Examples of service shops are banking and hotels.

Fitzgerald *et al.* emphasized how cost traceability differed between each of these service types. Their research found that many service companies did not try to cost individual services accurately either for price-setting or profitability analysis, except for the time-recording practices of professional service firms. In mass services and service shops there were:

> multiple, heterogeneous and joint, inseparable services, compounded by the fact that individual customers may consume different mixes of services and may take different routes through the service process (p. 24).

In these two categories of services, costs were controlled not by collecting the costs of each service but through responsibility centres (this topic is covered in more detail in Chapter 15). Following this argument, we can see that when you travel by rail, there is no calculation of the cost of your rail journey, or the cost of your hotel room. Nevertheless, these organizations must still understand their cost structures and ensure that the prices they charge, in the aggregate, cover all their costs and generate a profit.

Slack *et al.* (1995) contrasted types of service provision with types of manufacturing and used a matrix of low volume/high variety and high volume/low variety, comparing:

- professional service with customized or batch manufacturing (i.e. job costing);
- mass service with continuous manufacture (i.e. process costing); and
- service shop with a batch-type process (i.e. job costing).

Accounting information has an important part to play in operational decisions. Typical questions that may arise include:

- What is the cost of spare capacity?
- What product/service mix should be produced where there are capacity constraints?
- What are the costs that are relevant for particular operational decisions?

This chapter considers each of these in turn.

Accounting for the cost of spare capacity

Production resources (material, facilities/equipment and people) allocated to the process of supplying goods and services provide a capacity. The utilization of that capacity is a crucial performance driver for businesses, as the investment in capacity often involves substantial outlays of funds that need to be recovered by utilizing that capacity fully in the production of products/services. Capacity may also be a limitation for the production and distribution of goods and services where market demand exceeds capacity. So, for example, an airline will want to fully utilize all its seats on every flight. A factory will want to work its assets harder and maximize production volume. A professional services firm will want its professionals working all the time on behalf of clients.

A weakness of traditional accounting is that it equates the cost of *using* resources with the cost of *supplying* resources because financial statements reveal only the cost of resources supplied, not whether any of those resources were wasted through under-utilization. Activity-based costing (which is described further in Chapter 13) has as a central focus the identification and elimination of unused capacity. According to Kaplan and Cooper (1998), there are two ways in which unused capacity can be eliminated:

1. Reducing the supply of resources that perform an activity, i.e. spending reductions that reduce capacity.
2. Increasing the quantity of activities for the resources, i.e. revenue increases through greater utilization of existing capacity.

Identifying the difference between the cost of resources supplied and the cost of resources used as the cost of the unused capacity enables management to take appropriate corrective action.

cost of resources supplied – cost of resources used = cost of unused capacity

An example illustrates this.

Ten staff, each costing $30,000 per year, deliver banking services where the cost driver (the cause of the activity) is the number of banking transactions.

Assuming that each member of staff can process 2,000 transactions per annum, the cost of resources supplied is $300,000 (10 × $30,000) and the capacity number of transactions is 20,000 (10 × 2,000). The standard cost per transaction would be $15 ($300,000/20,000 transactions).

If in fact 18,000 transactions were carried out in the year, the cost of resources used would be $270,000 (18,000 @ $15) and the cost of unused capacity would be $30,000 (2,000 @ $15, or $300,000 resources supplied minus $270,000 resources used). If the cost of resources used is equated with the cost of resources supplied, the actual transaction cost becomes $16.67 ($300,000/18,000 transactions) and the cost of unused capacity is not identified separately. This is a weakness of traditional accounting systems.

Although there can be no carry forward of an 'inventory' of unused capacity in a service delivery function, management information is more meaningful if the standard cost is maintained at $15 and the cost of spare capacity is identified separately. Management action can then be taken to reduce the cost of spare capacity to zero, either by increasing the volume of business or reducing the capacity (i.e. the number of staff).

A different situation arises where there is insufficient capacity and management needs to make choices between alternative product/services.

Capacity utilization and product mix

Where demand exceeds the capacity of the business to produce goods or deliver services as a result of scarce resources (whether that is space, equipment, materials or staff), the scarce resource is the limiting factor. A business will want to maximize its profitability by selecting the optimum product/service mix. The product/service mix is the mix of products or services that will be sold by the business (we referred to this as the sales mix in Chapter 10 in relation to marketing, but we use product/service mix here to refer to the production process), each of which may have different selling prices and costs. It is therefore necessary, where

Table 11.1   Beaufort Accessories cost information.

	Part F	Part G	Part H
Selling price per unit	£150	£200	£225
Variable material cost per unit	£50	£80	£40
Variable labour cost per unit	£50	£60	£125
Contribution per unit	£50	£60	£60
Machine hours per unit	2	4	5
Estimated sales demand (units)	2,000	2,000	2,000
Required machine hours based on estimated demand	4,000	8,000	10,000

Table 11.2   Beaufort Accessories — product ranking based on contribution.

	Part F	Part G	Part H
Contribution per unit	£50	£60	£60
Machine hours per unit	2	4	5
Contribution per machine hour	£25	£15	£12
Ranking (preference)	1	2	3

demand exceeds capacity, to rank the products/services with the highest contributions, per unit of the limiting factor (i.e. the scarce resource).

For example, Beaufort Accessories makes three parts (F, G and H) for a motor vehicle, each with different selling prices and variable costs and requiring a different number of machining hours. These are shown in Table 11.1. However, Beaufort has an overall capacity limitation of 10,000 machine hours.

The first step is to identify the ranking of the products by calculating the contribution per unit of the limiting factor (machine hours in this case) for each product. This is shown in Table 11.2.

Although both Part G and Part H have higher contributions per unit, the contribution per machine hour (the unit of limited capacity) is higher for Part F. Profitability will be maximized by using the limited capacity to produce as many Part Fs as can be sold, followed by Part Gs. Based on this ranking, the available production capacity can be allocated as follows:

Production

2,000 of Part F @ 2 hours = 4,000 hours. 2,000 @ £50 per unit = £100,000

Based on the capacity limitation of 10,000 hours, there are 6,000 hours remaining, so Beaufort can produce 3/4 of the demand for Part G (6,000 hours available/8,000 hours to meet demand) equivalent to 1,500 units of part G (3/4 of 2,000 units).

1,500 of Part G @ 4 hours = 6,000 hours

Maximum contribution

There is no available capacity for Part H

Contribution

2,000 @ £50 per unit = £100,000

1,500 @ £60 per unit = £90,000

£190,000

This example shows that managers should not be swayed by simple measures of sales revenue (the highest price) or even the highest contribution per unit of product/service (as we saw in Chapter 10) but should focus on optimizing the use of limited production capacity by comparing the contribution earned from the use of the available production capacity. However, there is an alternative to this approach to capacity utilization.

Theory of Constraints

A different approach to limited capacity was developed by Goldratt and Cox (1986), who focused on the existence of bottlenecks in production and the need to maximize volume through the bottleneck (throughput) rather than through production capacity as a whole. This is because a bottleneck resource can limit the overall production volume of a business. Goldratt and Cox developed the Theory of Constraints (ToC), under which only three aspects of performance are important: throughput contribution, operating expense and inventory. Throughput contribution is defined as sales revenue less the cost of materials:

$$\text{throughput contribution} = \text{sales} - \text{cost of materials}$$

Goldratt and Cox considered all costs other than materials as fixed and independent of customers and products, so operating expenses included all costs except materials. Labour to them, at least in the short term, was a fixed cost. They emphasized the importance of maximizing throughput while holding constant or reducing operating expenses and inventory. Goldratt and Cox also recognized that there was little point in maximizing non-bottleneck resources if this leads to an inability to produce at the bottlenecks.

Applying the Theory of Constraints to the Beaufort Accessories example and assuming that machine hours are the bottleneck resource (in practice, the bottleneck resource may be a different measure), Table 11.3 shows the throughput ranking. Under the Theory of Constraints, Part F retains the highest ranking but Part H has a higher return per unit of the bottleneck resource than Part G after deducting only the variable cost of materials. This is a different ranking to the previous method, which used the contribution after deducting *all* variable costs. The difference is due to the treatment of variable costs other than materials.

Table 11.3 Beaufort Accessories — product ranking based on throughput.

	Part F	Part G	Part H
Selling price per unit	£150	£200	£225
Variable material cost per unit	£50	£80	£40
Throughput contribution per unit	£100	£120	£185
Machine hours per unit	2	4	5
Return per machine hour	£50	£30	£37
Ranking (preference)	1	3	2

Which is the preferred method? Both have value. As in many situations using management accounting information to make decisions, different assumptions can lead to different decisions. It is important to be explicit about your assumptions but to make assumptions that are most realistic in terms of the unique conditions that apply to each business. So a business with a lot of contract staff whose wage costs could readily be avoided might prefer the first approach treating labour costs as variable costs. A business which has long-term commitments to permanent staff will pay those staff irrespective, and so the throughput approach may lead to more meaningful information.

This leads us to think about the issue of when costs are relevant to a particular decision at a particular point in time.

Operating decisions: relevant costs

Operating decisions imply an understanding of costs, but not necessarily those costs that are defined by accountants and are recorded in the company's accounting system. We have already seen in Chapter 10 the distinction between avoidable and unavoidable costs. This brings us to the notion of relevant costs. Relevant costs are those costs that are relevant to a particular decision. Relevant costs are the *future, incremental cash flows* that result from a decision. Relevant costs specifically do not include sunk costs, i.e. costs that have been incurred in the past, as nothing we can do can change those earlier decisions. Relevant costs are avoidable costs because, by taking a particular decision, we can avoid the cost. Unavoidable costs are not relevant because, irrespective of what our decision is, we will still incur those costs. Relevant costs may, however, be opportunity costs. An opportunity cost is not a cost that is paid out in cash. It is the loss of a future cash flow that takes place as a result of making a particular decision.

Three examples illustrate how relevant costs can be applied:

- make versus buy decisions;
- equipment replacement decisions;
- pricing decisions using the cost of materials.

Make versus buy?

A concern with subcontracting or outsourcing has dominated Western business in recent years as the cost of producing goods and services in-house has been increasingly compared with the cost of purchasing goods on the open market, which has often entailed a shift to off-shore locations. The make versus buy decision should be based on which alternative is less costly on a *relevant cost* basis, that is, taking into account only future, incremental cash flows.

For example, the costs of in-house production of a computer processing service that averages 10,000 transactions per month are calculated as €25,000 per month. This comprises €0.50 per transaction for stationery and €2 per transaction for labour. In addition, there is a €10,000 charge from head office as the share of the depreciation charge for computer equipment. An independent computer bureau has tendered a fixed price of €20,000 per month.

Based on this information, we judge that stationery and labour costs are variable costs that are both avoidable if processing is outsourced. The depreciation charge will remain a cost to the business irrespective of the outsourcing decision. It is therefore unavoidable. The fixed outsourcing cost will only be incurred if outsourcing takes place.

The *total* costs for each alternative can be compared as shown in Table 11.4. The *relevant* costs for the alternatives are shown in Table 11.5. In Table 11.5 the €10,000 share of depreciation costs is not shown as it is not relevant to the decision because it is unavoidable.

Table 11.4   Total costs — make versus buy.

	Cost to make	Cost to buy
Stationery 10,000 @ €0.50	5,000	
Labour 10,000 @ €2	20,000	
Share of depreciation costs	10,000	10,000
Outsourcing cost	0	20,000
Total relevant cost	€35,000	€30,000

Table 11.5   Relevant costs — make versus buy.

	Relevant cost to make	Relevant cost to buy
Stationery 10,000 @ €0.50	5,000	
Labour 10,000 @ €2	20,000	
Outsourcing cost	0	20,000
Total relevant cost	€25,000	€20,000

Both Table 11.4 and 11.5 show the same information, but the presentation is different. In either case there would be a €5,000 per month saving by outsourcing the computer processing service (total costs of €30,000 compared to €35,000; or relevant costs of €20,000 compared to €25,000).

Equipment replacement

A further example of the use of relevant costs is the decision to replace plant and equipment. Once again, the concern is with future incremental cash flows, not with historical or sunk costs or with non-cash expenses such as depreciation. While the following illustration is unlikely to occur in practice, it does illustrate the different perspective that relevant costs brings to a decision.

Mammoth Hotel Company replaced its kitchen one year ago at a cost of $120,000. The kitchen was to be depreciated over five years, although it will still be operational after that time. The hotel manager wishes to expand the dining facility and needs a larger kitchen with additional capacity. A new kitchen will cost

$150,000, but the kitchen equipment supplier is prepared to offer $25,000 as a trade-in for the old kitchen. The new kitchen will ensure that the dining facility earns additional income of $25,000 for each of the next five years.

The existing kitchen incurs operating costs of $40,000 per year. Due to labour-saving technology, operating costs, even with additional dining, will fall to $30,000 per year if the new kitchen is bought. These figures are shown in Table 11.6. On a relevant cost basis, the difference between retaining the old kitchen and buying the new kitchen is a saving of $50,000 cash flow over five years. On this basis, it makes sense to buy the new kitchen.

Table 11.6   Relevant costs — equipment replacement.

	Retain old kitchen	Buy new kitchen
Purchase price of new kitchen		−$150,000
Trade-in value of old kitchen		+$25,000
Operating costs		
$40,000 p.a. × 5 years	−$200,000	
$30,000 p.a. × 5 years		−$150,000
Additional income from dining of		+$125,000
$25,000 p.a. × 5 years		
Total relevant cost	−$200,000	−$150,000

However, we cannot ignore the implications of this decision on the financial statements. The original kitchen cost has been written down to $96,000 (cost of $120,000 less one year's depreciation at 20% or $24,000). The original capital cost is a sunk cost and is therefore irrelevant to a future decision. The loss on sale of $71,000 ($96,000 written-down value − $25,000 trade-in) will affect the hotel's reported profit, but it is not a future incremental cash flow and is therefore irrelevant to the decision. But such a loss reported in the Statement of Comprehensive Income may not present the company in the best possible light to shareholders. There is a tension between a decision based on future incremental cash flows and how that decision (although positive for future profitability) will be seen in relation to past performance. A result of this tension could be that managers do not take advantage of this opportunity and so do not generate additional shareholder wealth because of the negative perceptions such a decision may leave in the year in which the old kitchen is written off. The political aspects of such a decision were discussed in Chapter 5. Other aspects of capital expenditure decisions are explained in Chapter 14.

Relevant cost of materials

As the definition of relevant cost is the future incremental cash flow, it follows that the relevant cost of materials is not the historical (or sunk) cost but the replacement cost of the materials. This is particularly important in pricing decisions for special orders (for an example see Chapter 10). It is irrelevant whether or not those materials are held in inventory, and they may well be used to fulfil a special order, but the relevant cost remains the future, incremental cash flow. In most cases this will be the replacement cost for the

Table 12.1   The cost of labour.

Cost	Time
Salaries and wages + oncosts (pensions, National Insurance etc.) + non-salary benefits (motor vehicles, expenses etc.) = total employment cost	Working days − annual leave, sick leave, public holidays, etc. = actual days at work × at work hours × productivity = actual hours worked

$$\frac{\text{total employment cost}}{\text{actual hours worked}} = \text{labour cost per hour}$$

In the longer term, a business may want to take a broader view of the total cost of employment. Many costs are incurred over and above the salary and wages paid to employees, who must be recruited and trained before they can be productive. A longer term approach to the total cost of employment may include recruitment and training costs as additional costs of employment. In relation to short term and long term, an important issue arises as to whether the cost of labour is a fixed or variable cost, following the distinction made in Chapter 10. It is clear that materials used in production are a variable cost, as no materials are consumed if there is no production, but the situation for labour is more complex. Accountants have historically considered labour that is consumed in producing goods or services, i.e. direct labour, as a variable cost. This is because it is usually expressed as a cost per unit of production, which, in total, increases or decreases in line with business activity (but often ignores the cost of spare capacity, which was explained in Chapter 11). Changing legislation, the influence of trade unions and business HR policies have meant that in the very short term, all labour takes on the appearance of a fixed cost. The consultation process for redundancy takes time, and legislation such as Transfer of Undertakings Protection of Employment (TUPE) in the UK or the European Union Acquired Rights Directive secures the employment rights of labour that is transferred between organizations, a fairly common occurrence as a consequence of outsourcing arrangements or business mergers and acquisitions. Consequently, reflecting the underlying practicality, many businesses now account for direct labour as a fixed cost.

Relevant cost of labour

The distinction between fixed and variable costs is not sufficient for the purpose of making decisions about labour in the very short term as, in that short term, labour will still be paid irrespective of whether employees are fully utilized or have spare capacity. Therefore, in the short term, a business bidding for a special order should only take into account the *relevant* costs associated with that decision. As we saw in Chapter 11, the relevant cost is the *future, incremental cash flow*, i.e. the cost that will be affected by a particular decision to do (or not to do) something. As decision making is not concerned with the past, historical (or *sunk*) costs are irrelevant. The relevant cost may be an additional cash payment or an *opportunity cost*, i.e. the loss from an opportunity forgone. For example, in the case of full capacity, the relevant cost could be the additional labour costs (e.g. overtime or casual labour) that may have to be incurred, or the opportunity cost following from the inability to sell products/services (e.g. both the loss of income from a particular order and the wider potential loss of customer goodwill).

Costs that are the same irrespective of the alternative chosen are irrelevant for the purposes of a particular decision, as there is no financial benefit or loss as a result of either choice. The costs that are relevant may change over time and with changing circumstances. This is particularly so with the cost of labour, where full capacity in one week or month may be followed by surplus capacity in the following week or month.

Where there is spare capacity, with surplus labour that will be paid irrespective of whether a particular decision is taken or not, the labour cost is irrelevant to the decision, because there is no future *incremental* cash flow. Where there is casual labour or use of overtime and the decision causes that cost to increase (or decrease), the labour cost is relevant. Where labour is scarce and there is full capacity, so that labour has to be diverted from alternative work involving an opportunity cost, the opportunity loss is the relevant cost.

For example, Brown & Co. is a small management consulting firm that has been offered a market research project for a client. The estimated workloads and labour costs for the project are:

	Hours	Hourly labour cost
Partners	120	€60
Managers	350	€45
Support staff	150	€20

There is at present a shortage of work for partners, but this is a temporary situation. Managers are fully utilized and if they are used on this project, other clients will have to be turned away, which will involve the loss of revenue of €100 per hour. Support staff are paid on a casual basis and are only hired when needed. Fixed costs are €100,000 per annum.

The relevant cost of labour to be used when considering this project can be calculated by considering the future, incremental cash flows:

Partners	120 hours – irrelevant as unavoidable surplus labour	Nil
Managers	350 hours @ €100 – this is the opportunity cost of the lost revenue from clients who are turned away	€35,000
Support staff	150 hours @ €20 cost	3,000
Relevant cost of labour		€38,000

However, the accounting system would have recorded the cost of labour (based on timesheets and hourly labour costs) as:

	Hours	Hourly labour cost	Total labour cost
Partners	120	€60	€7,200
Managers	350	€45	€15,750
Support staff	150	€20	€3,000
Total cost of labour			€25,950

While the accounting system records the historic cost, in this instance it does not take into account the opportunity cost of the lost revenue. Accounting costs are therefore a limited way in which to make management decisions. The relevant cost approach identifies the future, incremental cash flows associated with acceptance of the order. The relevant cost ignores the cost of partners as there is no future, incremental cash flow. The cost of managers is the opportunity cost – the lost revenue from the work to be turned away. The support staff cost is due to the need to employ more temporary staff. Fixed costs are irrelevant as they are unaffected by this project. In this case, Brown & Co. would be worse off by taking the market research project at a price less than €38,000. If it is unable to achieve a higher price, the existing clients should be retained at the €100 rate for managers.

Chapter 11 introduced outsourcing as a business strategy that has been in favour with many businesses to reduce the cost of labour. The following example illustrates the relevant costs of labour in an outsourcing decision.

Newgo Industries operates a telephone call centre as part of a larger company. The call centre employs 10 telephone operators at a total employment cost of $40,000 per annum each. Each operator is on a short-term employment contract which is cancellable with a month's notice. Management salaries cost $50,000 per annum and the call centre is charged a rental and utilities cost by head office of $20,000 per annum. An offshore company has offered to undertake the call centre function for $325,000 per annum. If the call centre is outsourced, management salaries will continue unchanged and the head office charge cannot be avoided. Table 12.2 shows the total cost under each alternative. Table 12.3 shows the relevant costs for each alternative, by eliminating those costs which are unavoidable under both alternatives. Both Tables 12.2 and 12.3 show that the cost differential is $75,000 per annum and therefore, from a financial perspective, the outsourcing should proceed.

Table 12.2   Total costs of call centre and outsourcing.

	Retain call centre	Outsourcing
Telephone operators, 10 @ $40,000	400,000	
Management	50,000	50,000
Office rental and utilities	20,000	20,000
Outsourcing cost	0	325,000
Total relevant cost	$470,000	$395,000

Table 12.3   Relevant costs of call centre and outsourcing.

	Retain call centre	Outsourcing
Telephone operators, 10 @ $40,000	400,000	
Outsourcing cost		325,000
Total relevant cost	$400,000	$325,000

Note in this example that the salaries of telephone operators are a relevant cost as these costs can be avoided by giving a month's notice. Management salaries are not a relevant cost as they are incurred irrespective of the decision to outsource. This example shows how it is important in any calculation of relevant costs to be sure about which costs involve future incremental cash flows, i.e. which costs are avoidable and which costs are unavoidable. However, it is also important to remember that financial information is only one element of a business decision such as outsourcing. Other factors that must be considered (but which are often difficult to quantify) include quality, customer service and reputation.

The following case studies illustrate how an understanding of labour costs and unused capacity can influence management decisions.

Case study 12.1: The Database Management Company – labour costs and unused capacity

The Database Management Company (DMC) is a call centre within a multinational company that has built a sophisticated database to hold consumer buying preferences. DMC contracts with large retail organizations to provide information on request and charges a fixed monthly fee plus a fee for each transaction (request for information). DMC estimates transaction volume based on past experience and recruits employees accordingly, to ensure that it is able to satisfy its customers' demands without delay.

Employees are on a mix of permanent and temporary contracts. Labour costs are separated into variable (transaction-processing costs, which can be directly attributable to specific contracts) and fixed elements (administration and supervision). DMC also incurs fixed costs, the main items being for building occupancy (a charge made by the parent company based on floor area occupied) and the lease of computer equipment. As these costs follow staffing levels that relate to specific contracts, they can be allocated with a reasonable degree of accuracy.

DMC's budget (based on anticipated activity levels and standard costs) is shown in Table 12.4. As a result of declining retail sales the demand for transactions has fallen, but because of uncertainty in DMC about how long this downturn will last, it has only been able to reduce its variable labour cost by ending the contracts of a small number of temporary staff. DMC's actual results for the same period are shown in Table 12.5.

Table 12.4 DMC budget.

(In £'000)	Contract 1	Contract 2	Contract 3	Total
Budgeted number of transactions	10,000	15,000	25,000	50,000
Fee per transaction	£1.00	£0.85	£0.70	
Budgeted transaction income	£10,000	£12,750	£17,500	£40,250
Fixed monthly fee	5,000	7,500	12,000	24,500
Total budgeted income	£15,000	£20,250	£29,500	£64,750
Variable labour costs	4,000	6,000	9,000	19,000
Contribution	£11,000	£14,250	£20,500	£45,750
Fixed labour costs	3,000	2,000	2,000	7,000
Occupancy costs	5,000	6,000	12,000	23,000
Computer costs	2,500	3,500	5,000	11,000
Budgeted net profit	£500	£2,750	£1,500	£4,750

Table 12.5   DMC actual results.

(In £'000)	Contract 1	Contract 2	Contract 3	Total
Actual number of transactions	9,000	10,500	22,000	41,500
Fee per transaction	£1.00	£0.85	£0.70	
Actual transaction income	£9,000	£8,925	£15,400	£33,325
Fixed monthly fee	5,000	7,500	12,000	24,500
Actual income	£14,000	£16,425	£27,400	£57,825
Variable labour costs	3,750	5,000	8,000	16,750
Contribution	£10,250	£11,425	£19,400	£41,075
Fixed labour costs	3,000	2,000	2,000	7,000
Occupancy costs	5,000	6,000	12,000	23,000
Computer costs	2,500	3,500	5,000	11,000
Actual net profit/(-loss)	£−250	£−75	£400	£75

How can the poor performance compared with budget be interpreted?

DMC's income has fallen across the board because of the reduced number of transactions on all its contracts. Because it has been unable to alter its variable labour cost significantly in the short term, the contribution towards fixed costs and profits has fallen. Therefore, although the business treats these costs as variable, in practice they are fixed costs, especially in the short term. The fixed salary and non-salary costs are constant despite the fall in transaction volume and so profitability has been eroded. DMC cannot alter its floor space allocation from the parent company or its computer lease costs despite having spare capacity.

What information can be provided to help in making a decision about cost reductions?

Calculating the variance (or difference) between the budget and actual income and variable costs shows how the difference between budget and actual profit of £4,675 (£4,750 − £75) is represented by a fall in income of £6,925 offset by a reduction in variable labour costs of £2,250 (all figures are in £'000). This is shown in Table 12.6.

Table 12.6   DMC loss of contribution.

	Contract 1	Contract 2	Contract 3	Total
Income reduction from budget	1,000	3,825	2,100	6,925
Variable labour costs reduction	250	1,000	1,000	2,250
Contribution reduction	£750	£2,825	£1,100	£4,675

Calculating the cost of unused capacity identifies the profit decline more clearly, as can be seen in Table 12.7.

Table 12.7   DMC cost of unused capacity.

	Contract 1	Contract 2	Contract 3	Total
Budgeted variable labour costs	£4,000	£6,000	£9,000	£19,000
Budgeted number of transactions	10,000	15,000	25,000	50,000
Budgeted cost per transaction	£0.40	£0.40	£0.36	
Actual number of transactions	9,000	10,500	22,000	41,500
Budgeted cost per transaction	£0.40	£0.40	£0.36	
Standard variable labour cost[1]	£3,600	£4,200	£7,920	£15,720
Cost of unused capacity (budget variable labour cost less standard variable labour cost)	£400	£1,800	£1,080	£3,280

Note: 1. The actual number of transactions multiplied by the budgeted variable labour cost per transaction.

Of the gap between budget and actual profit, £3,280 is accounted for by the cost of unused capacity in variable labour. This gap has been offset to some extent by the reduction in variable labour costs of £2,250. There remains the capability to reduce variable costs to meet the actual transaction volume, as Table 12.8 shows.

Table 12.8   DMC variable costs.

	Contract 1	Contract 2	Contract 3	Total
Actual variable labour costs	3,750	5,000	8,000	16,750
Standard variable labour costs	3,600	4,200	7,920	15,720
Difference	£150	£800	£80	£1,030

What conclusions can be drawn from this information?

It is clear that DMC has either to increase its income or reduce its costs in order to reach its profitability targets. The company has a significant cost of unused capacity. However, it can only reduce this unused capacity based on sound market evidence or else it may be constraining its ability to provide services to its customers in future, which may in turn result in a greater loss of income. DMC needs to renegotiate its prices and volumes with its customers.

Case study 12.2: Trojan Sales – the cost of losing a customer

Trojan Sales is a business employing a number of sales representatives, each costing the business €40,000 per annum, a figure that includes salary, oncosts and motor vehicle running costs. Sales representatives also earn a commission of 1% on the orders placed by their customers. On average, each sales representative looks after 100 customers (one driver of activity) and each year, customers place an average of five orders, with an average order size of €2,500. Therefore, each representative generates sales of:

$$100 \times 5 \times €2,500 = €1,250,000$$

and earns commission of 1%, amounting to €12,500.

However, Trojan suffers from a loss to competitors of about 10% of its customer base each year. Consequently, only about 70% of each sales representative's time is spent with existing customers, the other 30% being spent on winning replacement customers, with each representative needing to find 10 new customers each year (a second driver of activity). The business wants to undertake a campaign to prevent the loss of customers and has asked for a calculation of the cost of each lost customer.

A first step is to calculate the cost of the different functions carried out by each sales representative:

$$\frac{\text{employment cost of €40,000} \times 70\% \text{ of time}}{100 \text{ existing customers}} = £280 \text{ per customer (account maintenance)}$$

$$\frac{\text{employment cost of €40,000} \times 30\% \text{ of time}}{10 \text{ new customers}} = £1,200 \text{ per new customer}$$

The cash cost of winning a new customer is €1,200. However, the opportunity cost provides a more meaningful cost. If there were no lost business and sales representatives could spend all of their time with existing customers, each representative could look after 142 customers (100 × 100/70) in the same time.

If each of the 142 customers placed the average five orders with an average order size of €2,500, each representative could generate income of €1,775,000 and earn commission of €17,750. The opportunity cost is the loss of the opportunity by the company to generate the extra income of €525,000 (€1,775,000 − €1,250,000) and the opportunity cost to the representative personally of €5,250 (commission of €17,750 − €12,500).

Each customer lost costs Trojan €1,200 in time taken by sales representatives to find a replacement customer. However, on an opportunity cost basis, each lost customer potentially costs the company €52,500 in lost sales and the sales representative €525 in lost commission.

For this kind of reason, businesses sometimes adopt a strategy of splitting their salesforce into those representatives who are good at new account prospecting and those who are better at account maintenance.

Conclusion

This chapter has calculated the cost of labour and contrasted earnings from an employee's perspective with the total cost of employment to an employer. We have also developed the idea of relevant costs (introduced in Chapter 11) with examples of the relevant cost of labour.

Unfortunately, one of the first business responses to a downturn in profits is frequently to make staff redundant. Although the redundancy payments will be recognized as a cost in the Income Statement, there is a substantial social cost, not reflected in the financial reports of a business. These social effects will be borne by the redundant employee, while the financial burden of unemployment benefits may be borne by the taxpayer (see Chapter 5 for a discussion). This short-term concern with reducing labour cost often ignores the potential for cost improvement that can arise from a better understanding of business processes. It also ignores the investment in human capital: the knowledge, skills and experience of employees made redundant and the long-term costs associated with recruitment and training that will have to be incurred again if business activity returns to higher levels.

References

Armstrong, M. (1995a). *A Handbook of Personnel Management Practice* (5th edn). London: Kogan Page.
Armstrong, P. (1995b). Accountancy and HRM. In J. Storey (Ed.), *Human Resource Management: A Critical Text*, London: International Thomson Business Press.

Questions

12.1   Grant & McKenzie is a firm of financial advisers that needs to calculate an hourly rate to charge customers for its services.

The average salary cost for its advisers is £40,000. National Insurance is 11% and the firm pays a pension contribution of 6%. Each adviser has four weeks' annual holiday and there are 10 days per annum when the firm closes for bank holidays and Christmas. Each adviser is expected to do chargeable work for clients of 25 hours per week, the remainder of the time being administrative work. Calculate an hourly rate (to the nearest whole £) to cover the cost of each financial adviser.

12.2   Local Bank does not know how much of its cheque-processing costs are fixed and how much are variable. However, total costs have been estimated at €750,000 for processing of 1,000,000 transactions and €850,000 for processing of 1,200,000 transactions.

What are the variable costs per transaction?
What are the fixed costs?

12.3   Cardinal Co. needs 20,000 units of a certain part to use in one of its products. The following information is available in relation to the cost to Cardinal to make each part:

Raw materials	$4
Production labour	16
Variable manufacturing overhead	8
Fixed manufacturing overhead	10
Total	$38

The cost to buy the part from the Oriole Co. is $36. If Cardinal buys the part from Oriole instead of making it, Cardinal would have no use for the spare capacity. Additionally, 60% of the fixed manufacturing overheads would continue regardless of what decision is made. Cardinal decides that direct labour is an avoidable cost for the purposes of this decision.

Decide whether to make or buy the 20,000 parts, by comparing the relevant costs.

12.4   Cirrus Company has calculated that the cost to make a component is made up of raw materials £120, production labour £60, variable overhead £30 and fixed overhead of £25. Another company has offered to make the component for £140.

If the company has spare capacity and wishes to retain its skilled labour force, should it make or buy the component?

12.5   Bromide Partners provides three services: accounting, audit and tax. The total business overheads of €650,000 have been divided into two groups:

Partners	€200,000
Juniors	€450,000

Partner hours are a measure of complexity and junior hours define the duration of the work. The hours spent by each type of staff are:

	Accounting	Audit	Tax	Total
Partner hours	150	250	400	800
Junior hours	1,200	2,800	1,000	5,000

Calculate the total cost of providing audit services.

12.6   Bendix Ltd is considering the alternatives of either purchasing component VX-1 from an outside supplier or producing the component itself. Production costs to Bendix are estimated at:

Production labour	$200
Raw materials	600
Variable overheads	100
Fixed overheads	300
Total	$1,200

An outside supplier, Cosmo Ltd, has quoted a price of $1,000 for each VX-1 for an order of 100 of these components. However, if Bendix accepts the quote from Cosmo, the company will need to give three months' notice of redundancy to staff.

- Calculate the relevant costs of the alternative choices (show your workings) and make a recommendation to management as to which choice to accept.
- How would your recommendation differ if Bendix employees were on temporary contracts with no notice period?
- Explain the significance of a stock valuation of $1,300 for the VX-1 at the end of the last accounting period.

12.7   Victory Products Ltd manufactures high-technology products for the computer industry. Victory's accountant has produced a profit report showing the profitability of each of its three main customers for last year (Table 12.9).

Table 12.9   Victory Products profit report.

	Franklin Industries	Engineering Partners	Zeta PLC	Other customers	Total
Sales	1,000,000	1,500,000	2,000,000	1,500,000	6,000,000
Cost of materials	250,000	600,000	750,000	750,000	2,350,000
Cost of labour	300,000	200,000	300,000	75,000	875,000
Gross profit	450,000	700,000	950,000	675,000	2,775,000
Corporate overheads: allocated as 30% of sales	300,000	450,000	600,000	450,000	
Rental					250,000
Depreciation					350,000
Non-production salaries					600,000
Selling expenses					350,000
Administration					250,000
Operating profit	150,000	250,000	350,000	225,000	975,000

Victory is operating at almost full capacity, but wishes to improve its profitability further. The accountant has reported that, based on the above figures, Franklin Industries is the least profitable customer and has recommended that prices be increased. If this is not possible, the accountant has suggested that Victory discontinues selling to Franklin and seeks more profitable business from Engineering Partners and Zeta.

Labour is the most significant limitation on capacity. It is highly specialized and is difficult to replace. Consequently, Victory does all it can to keep its workforce even where there are seasonal downturns in business. The company charges £100 per hour for all labour, which is readily transferable between each of the customer products.

You have been asked to comment on the accountant's recommendations.

12.8   Seaford Group produces chocolate products including an exclusive range of chocolate Easter eggs, producing and selling a total of 100,000 eggs each year. The materials cost is $1.25 per egg and the labour cost is $0.70. Additional variable overhead costs are estimated at $0.20 per egg. Fixed overhead costs for Seaford Group total $150,000.

An international company has offered to produce the 100,000 Easter eggs to the same quality on behalf of Seaford for $2.50 per egg. If Seaford accepts this offer it can use its labour to produce other products and its fixed costs can be reduced by $50,000. However, there will be transportation costs that Seaford has to bear to bring the Easter eggs to its premises, amounting to $0.25 per egg.

Apply relevant cost principles to determine whether Seaford should continue to make the Easter eggs in-house or should subcontract to the international company.

Case study question: Call Centre Services plc

Call Centre Services (CCS) operates two divisions: a call centre that answers incoming customer service calls on behalf of its clients; and a telemarketing operation that makes outgoing sales calls to seek new business for its clients. In the call centre, each operator can handle on average about 6,000 calls per annum.

Although staff are allocated to one division or the other, when there is a high volume of incoming calls sales staff from the telemarketing division assist customer service staff in the call centre division. This is the result of a recruitment 'freeze' being in place.

The finance department has produced the information shown in Table 12.10.

Table 12.10   Call Centre Services.

	Call centre	Telemarketing	Total
Number of calls	70,000	25,000	
Fee per call	€5	€10	
Revenue	350,000	250,000	600,000
Less expenses			
Staff costs 10 @ €15,000 p.a. 5 @ €22,000 p.a.	150,000	110,000	260,000
Lease costs on telecoms and IT equipment (shared 50/50)	20,000	20,000	40,000
Rent (shared in proportion to staffing: 2/3, 1/3)	80,000	40,000	120,000
Telephone call charges		20,000	20,000
Total expenses	250,000	190,000	440,000
Operating profit	€100,000	€60,000	€160,000

What conclusions can you draw about the performance of the two divisions?

CHAPTER 13

Overhead Allocation Decisions

This chapter explains how accountants classify costs and determine the costs of products/services through differentiating product and period costs, and direct and indirect costs. The chapter emphasizes the overhead allocation problem: how indirect costs are allocated to determine products/service profitability and assist in pricing decisions. In doing so, it contrasts variable costing, absorption costing and activity-based costing. The chapter includes an overview of contingency theory, a comparison between Western and Japanese approaches to management accounting and a consideration of the behavioural consequences of accounting choices.

Cost classification

Product and period costs

The first categorization of costs made by accountants is between period and product. Period costs relate to the accounting period (year, month). Product costs relate to the cost of goods (or services) produced. This distinction is particularly important to the link between management accounting and financial accounting, because the calculation of profit is based on the separation of product and period costs. However, the value given to inventory is based only on product costs, a requirement of accounting standards. The IFRS accounting standard on Inventories (see Chapter 6), IAS2, requires that the cost of stock should:

> comprise that expenditure which has been incurred in the normal course of business in bringing the product or service to its present location and condition. Such costs will include all related production overheads.

Although Chapters 10, 11 and 12 introduced the concept of the contribution (sales less variable costs), as we saw in Chapter 6 there are two types of profit: gross profit and net profit:

$$\textbf{gross profit} = \textbf{sales} - \textbf{cost of sales}$$

The cost of sales is the product (or service) cost. It is either:

- the cost of providing a service; or
- the cost of buying goods sold by a retailer; or
- the cost of raw materials and production costs for a product manufacturer.

$$\textbf{net (or operating) profit} = \textbf{gross profit} - \textbf{expenses}$$

Expenses are the period costs, as they relate more to a period of time than to the production of products/ services. These will include all the other (marketing, selling, administration, IT, human resources, finance, etc.) costs of the business, i.e. those not directly concerned with buying, making or providing goods or services, but supporting that activity.

To calculate the cost of sales, we need to take into account the change in inventory, to ensure that we match the income from the sale of goods with the cost of the goods sold. As we saw in Chapter 6, *inventory* (*or stock*) is the value of goods purchased or manufactured that have not yet been sold. Therefore:

$$\textbf{cost of sales} = \textbf{opening stock} + \textbf{purchases} - \textbf{closing stock}$$

for a retailer, or:

$$\textbf{cost of sales} = \textbf{opening stock} + \textbf{cost of production} - \textbf{closing stock}$$

for a manufacturer. For a service provider, there can be no inventory of services provided but not sold, as the production and consumption of services take place simultaneously, so:

$$\textbf{cost of sales} = \textbf{cost of providing the services that are sold}$$

As we know, sales, cost of sales, gross profit, expenses and operating profit are all shown in the Income Statement.

Product costs are those that appear under cost of sales, while period costs are those that are deducted from gross profit to arrive at net or operating profit. While the valuation of inventory is prescribed by accounting standards, there are no such rules as to how gross profit is calculated and the distinction between product and period costs varies across different businesses. For example, in most large retail chains, the cost of sales include not only the cost of the goods sold but also all the costs of the supermarkets (store rental, staff costs, etc.) in which we shop. Period costs include the distribution centres that hold the bulk of inventory and the head office functions. One reason for this is to avoid competitors knowing what the mark-up or margin (see Chapter 10) is on the company's sales. In service businesses, there is no requirement to show gross profit and there is considerable variation in how service businesses report.

Therefore, when we speak of 'overheads' we are not sure what costs are included. Perhaps a more meaningful distinction is that between direct and indirect costs.

Direct and indirect costs

Accounting systems typically record costs in terms of line items. As we saw in Chapter 3, line items reflect the structure of an accounting system around accounts for each type of expense, such as raw materials, salaries, rent and advertising. Production costs (the cost of producing goods or services) may be classed as direct or indirect. Direct costs are readily traceable to particular products/services. Indirect costs are necessary to produce a product/service, but are not able to be readily traced to particular products/services. Any cost may be either direct or indirect, depending on its traceability to particular products/services. Because of their traceability, direct costs are nearly always variable costs because these costs increase or decrease with the volume of production. However, as we saw in Chapter 12, direct labour is sometimes treated as a fixed cost. Indirect costs may be variable (e.g. electricity) or fixed (e.g. rent). Indirect costs are often referred to as overheads.

Direct materials are traceable to particular products through *material issue* documents. For a manufacturer, direct material costs will include the materials bought and used in the manufacture of each unit of product. They will clearly be identifiable from a *bill of materials*: a detailed list of all the components used in production (see Chapter 11). There may be other materials of little value that are used in production, such as screws, adhesives and cleaning materials, which do not appear on the bill of materials because they have little value and the cost of recording their use would be higher than the value achieved. These are still costs of production, but because they are not traced to particular products they are *indirect material* costs.

While the cost of materials will usually only apply to a retail or manufacturing business, the cost of labour will apply across all business sectors. *Direct labour* is traceable to particular products or services via a *time-recording* system. It is the labour directly involved in the conversion process of raw materials to finished goods (direct labour was introduced in Chapter 12). Direct labour will be clearly identifiable from an instruction list or *routing*, a detailed list of all the steps required to produce a good or service. In a service business, direct labour will comprise those employees providing the service that is sold. In a call centre, for example, the cost of those employees making and receiving calls is a direct cost. Other labour costs will be incurred that do not appear on the routing, such as supervision, quality control, health and safety, cleaning and maintenance. These are still costs of production, but because they are not traced to particular products, they are *indirect labour* costs.

Other costs are incurred that may be direct or indirect. For example, in a manufacturing business, the depreciation of machines (a fixed cost) used to make products may be a direct cost if each machine is used for a single product (because the cost will be traceable) or an indirect cost if the machine is used to make many products (because it may be more difficult to trace the depreciation cost applicable to different products). The electricity used in production (a variable cost) may be a direct cost if it is metered to particular products or indirect if it applies to a range of products. A royalty paid per unit of a product/service produced or sold will be a direct cost. The cost of rental of premises, typically relating to the whole business, will be an indirect cost.

Prime cost is an umbrella term used to refer to the total of all direct costs. Production overhead is the total of all indirect material and labour costs and other indirect costs, i.e. all production costs other than direct costs. This distinction applies equally to the production of goods and services. However, not all costs in an organization are production costs. Some, as we have seen, relate to the period rather than the product. These other costs (such as marketing, sales, distribution, finance, IT, administration) are not included in production overhead. These other costs are classed generally as overheads, but in the case of period costs they are non-production overheads. A simple way to think about the distinction is to imagine a factory and office complex. These are generally separated by a large wall. The office on one side has nicely dressed people working at desks. On the other side of the wall, people work with machines and wear overalls. This is a bit simplistic, but it does help to understand the distinction. Production overheads relate to the factory side of the wall, and non-production overheads to the office side. Hence, a factory manager and his production clerks who sit in the factory will be classed as production overhead.

We do need to be careful when using the term 'overhead' to ensure that people we are talking to use the term in the same way, as its use may change from business to business and even from situation to situation. Here, we will define overheads as comprising indirect costs, i.e. those not readily traceable to products/ services, although those overheads may be limited to production overheads, or may comprise all the overheads of a business, both production and non-production.

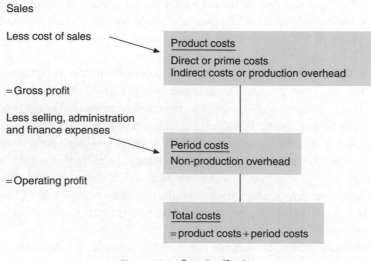

Figure 13.1   Cost classification.

Distinguishing between production and non-production costs and between materials, labour and overhead costs as direct or indirect is *contingent* on the type of product/service and the particular production process used in the organization. Contingency theory is described later in this chapter. There are no strict rules, as the classification of costs depends on the circumstances of each business and the decisions made by the accountants in that business. Consequently, unlike financial accounting, there is far greater variety between businesses – even in the same industry – in how costs are treated for management accounting purposes.

Figure 13.1 shows the relationship between these different types of costs.

The overhead allocation problem

We saw in Chapter 10 that there is an important distinction between fixed and variable costs, and the calculation of contribution (sales less variable costs) is important for short-term decision making. However, we also saw that in the longer term, all the costs of a business must be recovered if it is to be profitable. To assist with pricing, understanding profitability and other decisions, accountants calculate the *full* or *absorbed* cost of products/services.

As direct costs by definition are traceable, this element of product/service cost is usually quite accurate. However, indirect costs, which by their nature cannot be traced to products/services, must in some way be *allocated* over products/services in order to calculate the full cost. Overhead allocation is the process of spreading production overhead (i.e. those overheads that cannot be traced directly to products/services) equitably over the volume of production. The overhead allocation problem can be seen in Figure 13.2.

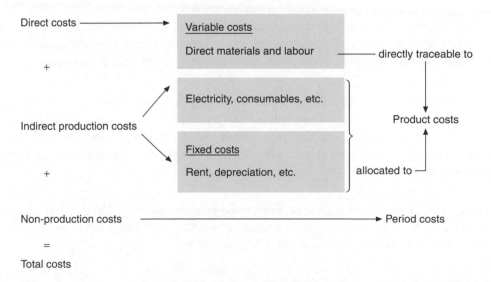

Figure 13.2 The overhead allocation problem.

The *overhead allocation problem* is a significant issue, as most businesses produce a range of products/ services using multiple production processes. The most common form of overhead allocation employed by accountants has been to allocate overhead costs to products/services in proportion to direct labour, i.e. the more direct labour involved in producing a product/service, the more overhead is attributed to it. While this is probably a realistic assumption in professional services, it rarely accurately reflects the resources consumed in the production of most goods and services. For example, some processes may be resource intensive in terms of space, automation, people or working capital. Some processes may be labour intensive while others use differing degrees of technology. The cost of labour, due to specialization and market forces, may also vary between different processes. Further, the extent to which these processes consume the (production and non-production) overheads of the business can be quite different. The allocation problem can lead to overheads being arbitrarily allocated across different products/services, which can lead to inappropriate pricing and misleading information about product/service profitability. As production overheads are a component of the valuation of inventory (because they are part of the cost of sales), an increase or decrease in inventory valuation will move profits between different accounting periods, so different methods of overhead allocation to products can influence reported profitability.

Shifts in management accounting thinking

In their book *Relevance Lost: The Rise and Fall of Management Accounting*, Johnson and Kaplan (1987) emphasized the limitations of traditional management accounting systems that have failed to provide accurate product costs:

> Costs are distributed to products by simplistic and arbitrary measures, usually direct-labor based, that do not represent the demands made by each product on the firm's resources . . . the methods systematically bias and distort costs of individual products . . . [and] usually lead to enormous cross subsidies across products (p. 2).

Management accounting, according to Johnson and Kaplan (1987), failed to keep pace with new technology and became subservient to the needs of external financial reporting, as costs were allocated by accountants between the valuation of inventory and the cost of goods sold. Johnson and Kaplan claimed that '[m]any accountants and managers have come to believe that inventory cost figures give an accurate guide to product costs, which they do not' (p. 145). They argued that:

> as product life cycles shorten and as more costs must be incurred before production begins . . . directly traceable product costs become a much lower fraction of total costs, traditional financial measures such as periodic earnings and accounting ROI become less useful measures of corporate performance (p. 16).

Johnson and Kaplan claimed that the goal of a good product cost system:

should be to make more obvious, more transparent, how costs currently considered to be fixed or sunk actually do vary with decisions made about product output, product mix and product diversity (p. 235).

The idea of cross subsidization is important to understand. If a business sells a number of products and overheads are inappropriately allocated, then some products will bear unrealistically high costs and others unrealistically low costs. This is particularly so when indirect costs are a high proportion of total costs. The market will tend to recognize a bargain and so the business will sell many products/services where the cost (and therefore price) is understated. Sales volume will increase but profits will fall, as the revenue will be insufficient to cover the true costs of production. The market will also tend to recognize something that is too expensive and sales volume will fall, so the over-costed (and over-priced) products/services will not earn enough revenue to compensate for the under-costed, under-priced products/services.

In *Relevance Lost*, Johnson and Kaplan also argued against the focus on short-term reported profits and instead argued for short-term non-financial performance measures that were consistent with the firm's strategy and technologies (these were described in Chapter 4). In a later book, Kaplan and Cooper (1998) described how activity-based cost (ABC) systems:

emerged in the mid-1980s to meet the need for accurate information about the cost of resource demands by individual products, services, customers and channels. ABC systems enabled indirect and support expenses to be driven, first to activities and processes, and then to products, services, and customers. The systems gave managers a clearer picture of the economics of their operations (p. 3).

ABC systems are a focus later in this chapter.

Kaplan and Cooper (1998) argued that cost systems perform three primary functions:

1. Valuation of inventory and measurement of the cost of goods sold for financial reporting.
2. Estimation of the costs of activities, products, services and customers.
3. Provision of feedback to managers about process efficiency.

Leading companies, according to Kaplan and Cooper (1998), use their enhanced cost systems to:

- design products and services that meet customer expectations and can be produced at a profit;
- identify where improvements in quality, efficiency and speed are needed;
- assist front-line employees in their learning and continuous improvement;
- guide product mix and investment decisions;
- choose among alternative suppliers;
- negotiate price, quality, delivery and service with customers;
- structure efficient and effective distribution and service processes to targeted market segments.

There are two methods of overhead allocation: absorption costing (the traditional method) and activity-based costing. These are compared in the next section, together with variable costing, a method that does not allocate overheads at all.

Table 13.1 shows a comparison between the three methods.

Table 13.1   Alternative methods of overhead allocation.

Variable costing	Absorption costing	Activity-based costing
Allocates only variable costs as product costs	Allocates all fixed and variable production costs as product costs	Allocates all costs to products/services that can be allocated by cost drivers
All fixed costs are treated as period costs	All non-production costs are treated as period costs	The distinction between production and non-production costs is less important
	Accumulates costs in cost centres and measures activity in each cost centre	Accumulates costs in cost pools based on business processes and measures the drivers of activities for each cost pool
	$\text{Budgeted overhead rate} = \dfrac{\text{cost centre costs}}{\text{unit of activity}}$ (e.g. labour hours)	$\text{Cost driver rate} = \dfrac{\text{activity cost pool}}{\text{activity volume}}$ (e.g. purchase orders)
	Calculate product/service cost for each cost centre as the unit of activity (e.g. labour hours) × budgeted overhead rate and adds this for all cost centres to give total product/service cost	Calculate product/service cost for each cost pool as activity volume × cost driver rate and adds this for all pools to give total product/service cost

Alternative methods of overhead allocation

Variable costing

We have already seen (in Chapters 10, 11 and 12) the separation of fixed from variable costs. A method of costing that does not allocate fixed production overheads to products/services is variable (or marginal) costing. Under variable costing, the product cost only includes variable production costs. The business focus is on contribution rather than gross profit. Fixed production costs are treated as period costs and charged to the Income Statement. This method avoids much of the overhead allocation problem, as most production overheads tend to be fixed rather than variable in nature. However, variable costing does not comply with accounting standard IAS2 which requires 'all related production overheads' to be included in the value of inventory. Variable costing cannot therefore be used in financial reporting. Although it can be, and is used, for internal management decision making, the effect of IAS2 is to require companies to account – for financial reporting purposes – on an absorption costing basis, as 'all related production overheads' include both fixed and variable production costs.

Absorption costing

Absorption costing is a system in which all (fixed and variable) production overhead costs are charged to products/services using an *allocation base* (a measure of activity or volume such as labour hours, machine hours or the number of units produced). The allocation base used in absorption costing is often regarded as arbitrary because there is usually no logical connection between the allocation base and overhead costs. Businesses using absorption costing will select an appropriate allocation base for their business. The allocation base tends to be selected because it is already measured (e.g. direct labour hours). Under absorption costing, a *budgeted overhead rate* can be calculated as either:

- a business-wide rate; or
- a cost centre overhead rate.

A *business-wide budgeted overhead rate* is calculated by dividing the production overheads for the total business by the selected measure of activity. Overhead rates can also be calculated for each cost centre separately. A *cost centre* is a location within the organization to which costs are assigned (it may be a department or a group of activities within a department, see Chapter 2). A *cost centre budgeted overhead rate* is a result of determining the overheads that are charged to each cost centre separately and an allocation base that measures the activity of that cost centre. Different cost centres may use different allocation bases in the same company, as the costs and activity levels for each cost centre may be quite different. Remember that these are budgeted rates, based on expected costs and levels of activity. Businesses cannot wait until after the end of an accounting period when financial statements are produced to calculate actual costs and prices (we discuss differences between budget and actual overhead expenses and activity levels later in this chapter).

The overhead charged to each cost centre must be recovered as a rate based on the principal unit of activity within that cost centre, typically direct labour hours, machine hours or the number of units produced. We therefore calculate a *direct labour hour rate* or a *machine hour rate* or a *rate per unit produced* for each production cost centre, or for the business as a whole, which allocates overheads.

Under both methods, the budgeted overhead rate is:

$$\frac{\text{estimated overhead expenditure for the period}}{\text{estimated activity for the period}}$$

For example, a business with budgeted overhead expenditure of £100,000 and an activity level of 4,000 direct labour hours would have a business-wide budgeted overhead rate of £25 per hour (£100,000/4,000). Most businesses are able to identify their overhead costs and activity to individual cost centre levels and determine cost centre overhead rates. This can be achieved using a three-stage process:

1. Identify indirect costs with particular cost centres. In many cases, although costs cannot be traced to products/services, they can be traced to particular cost centres. Accounting systems will separately record

costs incurred by each cost centre. For example, supervision costs may be traceable to each cost centre. Certain consumables may only be used in particular cost centres. Each cost centre may order goods and services and be charged for those goods and services separately.

2. Analyse each line item of expenditure that cannot be traced to particular cost centres and determine a suitable method of allocating each cost across the cost centres. There are no rules for the methods of allocation, which are contingent on the circumstances of the business and the choices made by accountants.

However, common methods of allocating indirect costs include:

Expense	*Allocation basis*
Management salaries	Number of employees in each cost centre
Premises cost	Floor area occupied by each cost centre
Electricity	Machine hours used in each cost centre
Depreciation on equipment	Asset value in each cost centre

3. Identify those cost centres that are part of the production process and those service cost centres that provide support to production cost centres. Allocate the total costs incurred by service cost centres to the production cost centres using a reasonable method of allocation. Common methods of allocating service cost centres include:

Service cost centre	*Allocation basis*
Maintenance	Timesheet allocation of hours spent in each production cost centre
Canteen	Number of employees in each cost centre
Scheduling	Number of production orders

An example of cost allocation between departments is shown in Table 13.2. Using the previous example and the same overhead costs of £100,000, suitable methods of allocation have been identified over five departments (stages 1 and 2) as follows:

Expense item	*Method of allocation*
Indirect wages	Allocated by payroll system
Factory rental	Floor area
Depreciation on equipment	Asset value
Electricity	Machine hours

Of the five departments, two are service departments. Their costs can be allocated as follows (stage 3):

Service cost centre	*Method of allocation*
Canteen	Number of employees
Scheduling	Number of production orders

Table 13.2 shows the figures produced to support the allocation process.

Table 13.2   Overhead allocations.

Expense	Total cost	Allocation calculation	Dept 1	Dept 2	Dept 3	Canteen	Scheduling
Indirect wages	£36,000	from payroll	£18,000	£9,000	£2,000	£2,000	£5,000
Factory rental	£23,000						
Area (sqm)	10,000	£2.30/sqm	5,000	2,500	1,500	500	500
Allocation £			£11,500	£5,750	£3,450	£1,150	£1,150
Depreciation	£14,000						
Asset value	£140,000		40,000	60,000	30,000	7,000	3,000
Allocation £		10% of asset value	£4,000	£6,000	£3,000	£700	£300
Electricity	£27,000						
Machine hours	9,000	£3 /machine hour	3,000	2,000	4,000		
Allocation £			£9,000	£6,000	£12,000		
Total	£100,000		£42,500	£26,750	£20,450	£3,850	£6,450
Reallocate service cost centres							
Canteen	£3,850						
Employees	60	£64.16/employee	20	25	15		
Allocation £			£1,283	£1,604	£963	-£3,850	
Scheduling	£6,450						
Prod. orders	250	£25.80/order	100	70	80		
Allocation £			£2,580	£1,806	£2,064		−£6,450
Total cost	£100,000		£46,363	£30,160	£23,477	£0	£0

Once the costs have been allocated, a reasonable measure of activity is determined for each cost centre. While this is often direct labour hours (the most common measure of capacity), the unit of activity can be different for each cost centre (e.g. machine hours, material volume, number of units produced). For non-manufacturing businesses the unit of activity may be hotel rooms, airline seats or consultancy hours. Using the above example and given the number of labour hours in each cost centre, we can now calculate a cost centre overhead rate, i.e. a budgeted overhead rate for each cost centre, as shown in Table 13.3.

Table 13.3   Cost centre budget overhead rate.

	Total cost	Dept 1	Dept 2	Dept 3
Total cost	£100,000	£46,363	£30,160	£23,477
Direct labour hours	4,000	2,000	750	1,250
Hourly rate	£25.00	£23.18	£40.21	£18.78

The most simplistic form of overhead allocation uses a single overhead rate for the whole business. As we previously calculated, the *business-wide budgeted overhead* rate is £25.00 *per direct labour hour* (£100,000/ 4,000). This rate would apply irrespective of whether the hours were worked in stages of production that had high or low machine utilization, different levels of skill, different pay rates or required different degrees of support.

Under the *cost centre budgeted overhead rate*, the rate per direct labour hour varies from a low of £18.78 for Dept 3 to a high of £40.21 for Dept 2. This reflects the different cost structure and activity level of each cost centre.

Consider an example of two products, each requiring 10 machine hours. The extent to which each product requires different labour hours in each of the three departments will lead to quite different overhead allocations.

Assume that product A requires 2 hours in Dept 1, 5 hours in Dept 2 and 3 hours in Dept 3. The overhead allocation would be £303.77. If product B requires 5, 1 and 4 hours respectively in each department, the overhead allocation would be £231.25, as Table 13.4 shows.

Table 13.4   Overhead allocation to products based on cost centre budget overhead rate.

	Total cost	Dept 1	Dept 2	Dept 3
Hourly rate	£25.00	£23.18	£40.21	£18.78
Product A: direct labour hours		2	5	3
Overhead allocation	£303.77	£46.36	£201.07	£56.34
Product B: direct labour hours		5	1	4
Overhead allocation	£231.25	£115.91	£40.21	£75.13

The total cost of a product comprises the prime cost (the total of direct costs) and the overhead allocation. Whether a business-wide or cost centre overhead allocation rate is used, the prime cost is unchanged. Assuming that the direct costs per unit for our two example products are:

	Product A	Product B
Direct materials	110	150
Direct labour	75	90
Prime cost	185	240

The allocation of overhead based on cost centre rates (rounded to the nearest £) would be:

Prime cost (from above)	185	240
Overhead allocation	304	231
Full (or absorbed) cost	489	471

By contrast, the overhead allocation to both products (each of which requires 10 hours of production time) using a business-wide rate would be £250 (10 @ £25). The allocation of overhead based on the business-wide rate would be:

	Product A	Product B
Prime cost (from above)	185	240
Overhead allocation	250	250
Full (or absorbed) cost	435	490

As can be seen in the above example, the overhead allocation as a percentage of total cost can be very high relative to direct costs. This is not unusual in business, particularly in those organizations that have invested heavily in technology or in service businesses, where direct costs are a small proportion of total business costs. What is important here is that, just by varying the assumptions in the method of overhead allocation between using a cost centre rate or a business-wide rate, the result can be quite different product costs.

The cost centre rate is more accurate than the business-wide rate because it does attempt to differentiate between the different cost structures of cost centres. However, the absorption method of allocating overhead costs to products/services has received substantial criticism because of the arbitrary way in which overheads are allocated. Most businesses use allocation bases such as direct labour hours, machine hours or production units, because that data is readily available. The implicit assumption of absorption costing is that the allocation base chosen is a reflection of why business overheads are incurred. For example, if the allocation base is direct labour or machine hours, the assumption of absorption costing is that overhead costs are incurred in proportion to direct labour or machine hours. This is unlikely to be the case in most businesses as many overheads are caused by the range and complexity of products/services.

Over- or under-recovery of overhead

The overhead rate per hour is based on budgeted costs and the budgeted level of activity. However, both actual costs and actual activity levels are likely to differ from budget. The result is an under- or over-recovery of overhead.

For example, assume we budgeted for costs of £100,000 and 4,000 direct labour hours, resulting in an overhead rate of £25 per hour. Some alternative outcomes are:

- If actual costs are £105,000 but we still work 4,000 hours, we will charge £100,000 to production (4,000 × £25) and under-recover £5,000 (spending £105,000 less recovered £100,000).
- If actual costs are £102,000 and we work only 3,850 hours, we will charge £96,250 to production (3,850 × £25) and under-recover £5,750 (spending £102,000 less recovered £96,250).
- If actual costs are £98,000 and we work 4,100 hours, we will charge £102,500 to production (4,100 × £25) and over-recover £4,500 (spending £98,000 but recovering £102,500).

The under- or over-recovered overhead amount is most commonly charged to cost of sales but it may be allocated between cost of goods sold and any unsold inventory.

If budget costs and activity levels are not achieved, decisions about pricing or product profitability may be incorrect and the information used for business decisions may not be sound. Therefore it is important for spending to be controlled in line with budget (we discuss this further in Chapter 17) and for unused capacity to be reduced (we discussed the cost of spare capacity in Chapter 11).

As a result of the criticism of absorption costing, Kaplan and Cooper (1998) developed an alternative approach to overhead allocation: activity-based costing.

Activity-based costing

Activity-based costing (or ABC) is an attempt to identify a more accurate method of allocating overheads to products/services. ABC uses *cost pools* to accumulate the cost of significant business activities and then assigns the costs from the cost pools to products based on *cost drivers*, which measure each product's demand for activities.

Cost pools accumulate the cost of business processes, irrespective of the organizational structure of the business. The costs that correspond to the formal organization structure may still be accumulated for financial reporting purposes through a number of cost centres, but this will not be the method used for product costing. For example, the purchasing process can take place in many different departments. A stores-person or computer operator may identify the need to restock a product. This will often lead to a purchase requisition, which must be approved by a manager before being passed to the purchasing department. Purchasing staff will have negotiated with suppliers in relation to quality, price and delivery and will generally have approved suppliers and terms. A purchase order will be raised. The supplier will deliver the goods against the purchase order and the goods will be received into the store. The paperwork (a delivery note from the supplier and a goods received note) will be passed to the accounting department to be matched to the supplier invoice and payment will be made to the supplier. This business process cuts across several departments. Chapter 9 (and Figure 9.1 in particular) explained the business process approach in more detail.

ABC collects the costs for the purchasing *process* in a cost pool, irrespective of the cost centre or department which incurred the cost. The next step is to identify a cost driver.

The cost driver is the most significant cause of the activity for each cost pool. In the purchasing example, the causes of costs are often recognized as the number of suppliers and/or the number of purchase orders. Cost drivers enable the cost of activities to be assigned from cost pools to cost objects (products/services). Rates are calculated for each cost driver and overhead costs are applied to products/services on the basis of the cost driver rates. There are no rules about what cost pools and cost drivers should be used, as this will be contingent on the circumstances of each business and the choices made by its accountants. Examples of cost pools and drivers are:

Cost pool	Cost driver
Purchasing	No. of purchase orders
Sales order entry	No. of sales orders
Material handling	No. of set-ups (i.e. batches)
Scheduling	No. of production orders
Machining	Machine hours (i.e. not labour hours)

For example, a rate will be calculated for each cost driver (e.g. purchase order, set-up) and assigned to each product based on how many purchase orders and set-ups the product has consumed. The more purchase orders and set-ups a product requires, the higher the overhead cost applied to it will be. ABC does not mean that direct labour hours or machine hours or the number of units produced are ignored. Where these are the significant cause of activities for particular cost pools, they are used as the cost drivers for those cost pools.

Using the same example as for absorption costing, assume for our two products that there are two cost pools: purchasing and scheduling. The driver for purchasing is the number of purchase orders and the driver for scheduling is the number of production orders. Costs are collected by an activity-based accounting system (which uses a coding structure to identify the cost pool as well as the cost centre) into cost pools and the measurement of cost drivers takes place, identifying how many activities are required for each product. The cost per unit of activity is the cost pool divided by the cost drivers, as shown in Table 13.5.

Table 13.5 Overhead accumulated in cost pools and allocated by cost drivers.

Cost pool and driver	Total cost	Product A	Product B
Purchasing	£40,000		
– no. of purchase orders	4,000	3,000	1,000
	(£10 each)	£30,000	£10,000
Scheduling	£60,000		
– no. of production orders	100	75	25
	(£600 each)	£45,000	£15,000
Total overhead	£100,000	£75,000	£25,000

We can then calculate the overhead cost per product/service by dividing the total cost pool by the quantity of products/services produced. This is different to the absorption method which calculates the overhead costs per unit of product/service directly. Under the ABC method, overheads are identified with the total volume of a product/service produced and need to be divided by the volume of production to give the overhead per unit of product/service. This is shown in Table 13.6.

Table 13.6 Overhead per product based on ABC.

	Product A	Product B
Total overhead	£75,000	£25,000
Quantity produced	150	250
Per product (total overhead/quantity)	£500	£100

The prime cost (the total of direct costs) is not affected by the method of overhead allocation. The total cost of each product using ABC for overhead allocation is shown in Table 13.7. Table 13.8 compares the cost of each product calculated using both methods of absorption costing with that using ABC.

Although this is an extreme example, significant differences can result in practice from the adoption of an activity-based approach to overhead allocation. In this example, overheads allocated using direct labour hours under absorption costing do not reflect the actual causes for overheads being incurred. Product A not

Table 13.7   Product costing under ABC.

	Direct materials	Direct labour	Manufacturing overhead	Total cost per table
Product A	£110	£75	£500	£685
Product B	£150	£90	£100	£340

Table 13.8   Comparison of product costs under absorption costing and activity-based costing.

	Product A	Product B
Cost using absorption costing – business-wide rate	£435	£490
Total cost using absorption costing – cost centre rate	£489	£471
Total cost using activity-based costing	£685	£340

only uses more purchasing and production order activity (the drivers of overheads), but also has a lower volume of production. Reflecting the cause of overheads in overhead allocations more fairly represents the cost of each product. Under absorption costing, Product B was subsidizing Product A when compared with ABC. Cross-subsidization can be hidden where a business sells a mixture of high-volume and low-volume products/services, where there is a wide product/service variety, and where product/service complexity varies resulting in different demands on resources.

Differences between absorption and activity-based costing

First, it is important to remember that under both methods, direct labour and material costs are the same. Also under both methods, the total overhead incurred by the company is the same. The difference between the two methods is because of different assumptions underlying the method of allocation of overhead costs over multiple products/services.

Under absorption costing, overheads are allocated in proportion to an arbitrary allocation base, typically direct labour hours. This means that the more labour hours allocated to a product/service, the more overhead will be allocated to it. While in some businesses this may be realistic (e.g. professional services), this is not necessarily the case. Under activity-based costing, overheads are traced through their drivers (the causes of activity) to the products/services that consume those activities, i.e. the more overheads a product/service causes to be incurred, the more overheads will be allocated to it.

However, one significant difference that the example in this chapter has not shown is in the distinction between production overhead and non-production overhead. While we have been concerned with allocating production overheads to products/services, to calculate the total cost of a product where a cost-plus approach to pricing is in place (see Chapter 10) there is a need to allocate non-production overheads to products/services. This is more difficult as, by definition, these overheads are applicable more to the accounting period than to products.

Under ABC, the distinction between fixed and variable costs and between production overhead and non-production overhead that applies to absorption costing is less important and can help with the allocation of a wider definition of overhead (production and non-production) to products/services. Rather than focus on the simplistic fixed/variable distinction we introduced in Chapter 10, under an ABC approach costs are identified as follows:

- *Unit-level activities*: these are performed each time a unit is produced, e.g. direct labour, direct materials and variable manufacturing costs such as electricity. These activities consume resources in proportion to the number of units produced. If we are printing books, then the cost of paper, ink and binding, and the labour of printers, are unit-level activities. If we produce twice as many books, unit-level activities will be doubled.
- *Batch-related activities*: these are performed each time a batch of goods is produced, e.g. a machine set-up. The cost of these activities varies with the number of batches, but is fixed irrespective of the number of units produced within the batch. Using our book example, the cost of set-up, or making the printing machines ready for printing, e.g. washing up, changing the ink, changing the paper, is fixed irrespective of how many books are printed in that batch, but variable on the number of batches that are printed.
- *Product-sustaining activities*: these enable the production and sale of multiple products/services, e.g. maintaining product specifications, after-sales support, product design and development. The cost of these activities increases with the number of products, irrespective of the number of batches or the number of units produced. For each differently titled book published, there is a cost incurred in dealing with the author, obtaining copyright approval, typesetting the text and so on. However many batches of the book are printed, these costs are fixed. Nevertheless, the cost is variable depending on the number of books that are published. Similarly, *customer-sustaining activities* support individual customers or groups of customers, e.g. different costs may apply to supporting retail – that is, end-user – customers compared with resellers. In the book example, particular costs are associated with promoting a textbook to academics in universities in the hope that it will be set as required reading. Fiction books will be promoted through advertising and in-store displays.
- *Facility-sustaining activities*: these support the whole business and are common to all products/services. Examples of these costs include senior management and administrative staff, and premises costs. Under ABC these costs are fixed and unavoidable and irrelevant for most business decisions, being unrelated to the number of products, customers, batches or units produced.

While unit-level activities are purely variable and facility-sustaining activities purely fixed, the ability to differentiate batch and product sustaining activities provides more flexibility in understanding the drivers (i.e. causes) of overheads and enables a more accurate allocation of overheads to be carried out.

Because costs are assigned under ABC to cost pools rather than cost centres, and as business processes cross through many cost centres, the distinction between production and non-production overheads also breaks down under ABC. While the distinction is still important for stock valuation (as IAS2 requires the inclusion of production overheads), this distinction is not necessary for management decision making. The more (production and non-production) overheads that are able to be allocated accurately to products/services, the more accurate will be the information for decision making about relevant costs, pricing and product/service profitability.

The ABC method is generally preferred because the allocation of costs is based on *cause-and-effect* relationships, while the absorption costing system is based on an *arbitrary* allocation of overhead costs. However, ABC can be costly to implement because of the need to analyse business processes in detail; requiring an accounting system that collects costs for both cost centres and cost pools; and the need to identify cost drivers and measure the extent to which individual products/services consume resources. Organizations often carry out a pilot study in one business unit to determine whether ABC provides more meaningful management data before it is more widely introduced.

However, although conceptually attractive, surveys of practice show that ABC has not been considered by the majority of organizations, and that it has been abandoned by many organizations which adopted it in the 1990s (Gosselin, 2007).

Why, then, do different organizations adopt different methods of management accounting? One explanation is provided by contingency theory.

Contingency theory

The central argument of contingency theory is that there is no control system (which, as described in Chapter 4, includes accounting systems) that is appropriate to all organizations. Fisher (1995) contrasts contingency with situation-specific and universalist models. The situation-specific approach argues that each control system is developed as a result of the unique characteristics of each organization. The universalist approach is that there is an optimal control system design that applies at least to some extent across different circumstances and organizations. The contingency approach is situated between these two extremes, in which the appropriateness of the control system depends on the particular circumstances faced by the business. However, generalizations in control systems design can be made for different classes of business circumstances.

Fisher (1995) reviewed various contingency studies and found that the following variables have been considered in research studies as affecting control systems design:

- *External environment*: whether uncertain or certain, static or dynamic, simple or complex.
- *Competitive strategy*: whether low cost or differentiated (e.g. Porter, see Chapter 10) and the stage of the product lifecycle (see Chapter 18).
- *Technology*: the type of production technology (see Chapter 11).
- *Industry and business variables*: size, diversification and structure (see Chapter 15).
- *Knowledge and observability of outcomes and behaviour*: the transformation process between inputs and outputs (see Chapter 4).

Otley (1980) argued that a simple linear explanation which assumed that contingent variables affected organizational design, which in turn determined the type of accounting/control system in use and in turn led to organizational effectiveness, was an inadequate explanation. Otley emphasized the importance of other controls outside accounting, the number of factors other than control system design influencing organizational performance and that organizational effectiveness is itself difficult to measure. He argued that the contingent variables were outside the control of the organization, and those that could be influenced were part of a package of organizational controls including personnel selection, promotion and reward systems. Otley also argued that there were other factors that, together with the contingent variables, influenced organizational effectiveness. He believed that an organization 'adapts to the contingencies it faces by arranging the factors it can control into an appropriate configuration that it hopes will lead to effective performance' (p. 421).

The choice of an absorption or activity-based approach to the overhead allocation problem is one example of how a control system will be influenced by contingent factors: the environment, competition, technology, business and observability factors. The comment by Clark (1923), mentioned previously in this book, that there were 'different costs for different purposes' can be seen as an early understanding of the application of the contingency approach. Clark further commented that 'there is no one correct usage, usage being governed by the varying needs of varying business situations and problems'. Most important is the need to use cost information in different ways depending on the business circumstances, which has been the focus of Chapters 10 to 12.

However, we should not assume that the techniques in the Chapters 10–13 are universally applicable. In many cases they are Western constructions, linked to the particular Anglo-centric capitalist system that is most evident in the UK, USA, Canada and Australia. It is therefore worthwhile highlighting some key international differences.

International comparisons

Alexander and Nobes (2001) described various approaches to categorizing international differences in accounting, including:

- different legal systems;
- whether accounting was commercially driven, government-driven or governed by professional regulation;
- the relative strength of equity markets.

Alexander and Nobes argued that legal systems, tax systems and the strength of the accountancy profession all influence the development of accounting, but the main explanation for the most important international differences in financial reporting is the financing system (such as the size and spread of corporate share-holding). For example, the growth of institutional investors (such as pension/superannuation funds, insurance companies) has reduced the size of individual shareholdings in companies. In Germany, it is common for banks to own shares in the companies they lend to, but this is unheard of in the UK.

Financial reporting is largely harmonized within the European Union and elsewhere, using IFRS as the global accounting standards (see Chapter 6). This is likely to be a continuing trend given the globalization of capital markets which is likely to encompass the USA over the next few years. Whether there will be any effect of harmonization on management accounting practices is as yet unknown. In understanding management accounting, practising managers and students of accounting receive little exposure to management accounting practices outside the Anglo-centric economies. It is important to contrast this approach with other practices, particularly those in Japan. These practices are different because they are predicated on different assumptions, particularly the different emphases on long-term strategies for growth versus short-term strategies for profit. There are historical, cultural, political, legal and economic influences underlying the development of different management accounting techniques in that country, to take a single example.

Management accounting in Japan

Japan has a strong history of *keiretsu*, the interlocking shareholdings of industrial conglomerates and banks, with overlapping board memberships. This has, at least in part, influenced long-term strategy because of the absence of strong stock market pressures for short-term performance, as is the case in Anglo-centric countries.

Demirag (1995) studied three Japanese multinationals with manufacturing subsidiaries in the UK, two in consumer electronics and one in motor vehicles. The companies had strongly decentralized divisional profit responsibilities with autonomous plants focused on target results. A complex matrix structure resulted in reporting to general management in the UK as well as to functional and product management in Japan. The company's basic philosophy was that the design team was responsible for profit while continuous processes were in place to monitor and reduce production costs.

According to Demirag (1995), Japanese companies exhibited a strategic planning style of management control rather than an emphasis on financial control. The strategic planning systems were bureaucratic, although business units gave top management the information necessary to formulate and implement plans. As Japanese managers move frequently between plants and divisions, they have a better understanding of communication and coordination than their British counterparts. Japanese managers also put the interest of the organization above their own divisions. There is less attention to accounting and management control in Japan than to smooth production and quality products. Performance targets were set in the context of strategy but results were expected in the longer term.

In the Japanese companies, manufacturing and sales were independent of each other, each having its own profit responsibility, the underlying principle being that each side of the business drives the other to be more effective and efficient. Although traditionally manufacturing had the greatest negotiating power, this did lead to a failure of market information reaching top decision-makers in Japan. There was a top-down approach to capital investment decisions, with managers taking a strategic and company-wide perspective that reduced the importance of financial decisions, with ROI not being seen as a particularly useful measure.

Pressures to meet short-term financial targets were not allowed to detract from long-term progress. In performance measurement, much more emphasis was placed on design, production and marketing than on financial control. Japanese management accounting does not stress optimizing within existing constraints, but encourages employees to make continual improvements. The main emphasis was on market-driven product costing, i.e. target costing (this is explained in Chapter 18), aimed at increasing market share over time by accepting lower short-term profits. A market-driven target costing approach 'emphasizes doing what it takes to achieve a desired performance level under market conditions . . . how efficiently it must be able to build it for maximum marketplace success' (Hiromoto, 1991, p. 70).

Overhead allocation was not important, but there was a focus on how the allocation techniques used encouraged employees to reduce costs. Hiromoto (1991) described Japanese management accounting practices and the central principle that accounting policies should be subservient to corporate strategy, not independent of it. Japanese companies use accounting systems more to motivate employees to act in accordance with long-term manufacturing strategies. Hiromoto describes the example of Hitachi, which used direct labour hours as the overhead allocation base, as this 'creates the desired strong pro-automation incentives throughout the organization' (p. 68). By contrast, another Hitachi factory uses the number of parts as the allocation base in order to influence product engineering to drive reductions in the number of parts. Standard costs are not used in Japan as they are in the West.

Overall, Japanese accounting policies are subservient to strategy, where production engineering knowledge has an equal or higher status to accounting knowledge, with the result that, for example in Toyota, the 'visible benefits' of lower inventory in the financial statements is outweighed by the invisible production benefits, 'especially the ability to run mixed model lines in a small batch factory' (Williams *et al.*, 1995, p. 233). Currie (1995) undertook a comparative study of costing and investment appraisal for the evaluation of advanced manufacturing technology (AMT). Research identified that Japanese managers were uninterested in new management accounting techniques such as activity-based costing, since knowledge that some products were more expensive to produce than others was not important to product strategy decisions. On the contrary, expensive products were likely to have strategic value to the company.

Williams *et al.* (1995) reported similar findings to Demirag and, taking a critical perspective, asserted:

> In Japanese firms financial calculations are integrated into productive and market calculations; the result is a three-dimensional view which denies the universal representational privilege of financial numbers. Furthermore the integration of different kinds of calculation broadens out the definition of performance and identifies new points of intervention in a way which undermines the privilege of financial guidance techniques; in Japanese firms the main practical emphasis is on productive and market intervention rather than orthodox financial control (p. 228).

These Japanese examples, although dated, show that management accounting can be used in many different ways, but should be relevant to the business strategy. The final section of this chapter addresses some behavioural issues associated with management accounting.

Behavioural implications of management accounting

Hopper *et al.* (2001) traced the rise of behavioural and organizational accounting research in management accounting. In the UK, a paradigm shift occurred that did not happen in the USA (where agency theory – see Chapter 6 – has been the dominant research approach). In the UK, contingency theory and neo-human relations approaches were abandoned for more sociological and political approaches that drew from European social theory and were influenced by Scandinavian case-based research.

Burchell *et al.* (1980) argued:

> What is accounted for can shape organizational participants' views of what is important, with the categories of dominant economic discourse and organizational functioning that are implicit within the accounting framework helping to create a particular conception of organizational reality (p. 5).

Reality in the economics and agency-based discourse is about shareholder value, while more sociological and political perspectives (see Chapter 5) see reality as socially constructed or the result of domination by one group over another. Along the same lines, Miller (1994) argued that accounting was a social and institutional practice. Accounting is not a neutral device that merely reports 'facts' but a set of practices that affects the type of world in which we live, the way in which we understand the choices able to be made by individuals and organizations and the way in which we manage activities. Miller argued that 'to calculate and record the costs of an activity is to alter the way in which it can be thought about and acted upon' (p. 2).

We have seen through the examples in Chapters 10–13 how accounting can change the way we see things. Choices about contribution margin or gross profit, avoidable or unavoidable costs, historic cost or relevant cost, cash costs or opportunity costs, and the choice of absorption or activity-based costing approaches all change our understanding of the cost and profitability of a product/service, a business unit, a market segment, and therefore the decisions we take with that understanding.

Cooper *et al.* (1981) reflected that accounting systems are a significant component of power in organizations:

> Internal accounting systems by what they measure, how they measure and who they report to can effectively delimit the kind of issues addressed and the ways in which they are addressed (p. 182).

Various published research studies have adopted an interpretive or critical perspective in understanding the link between accounting systems, organizational change and the behaviour of people in organizations as a result of culture and power (see Chapter 5 for the theoretical framework of these subjects). The interpretive perspective has provided a number of interesting studies. The study of an area of the National Coal Board by Berry *et al.* (1985) emphasized a dominant operational culture and the extent to which accounting reports were 'ignored, trivialised and/or misunderstood' (p. 16). The accounting system was:

> consistent with the values of the dominant managerial culture, and being malleable and ambiguous it reflected and helped coping with the uncertainties inherent with the physical task of coal extraction and its socioeconomic environment (p. 22).

Dent (1991) carried out a longitudinal field study of accounting change in EuroRail (which is one of the readings in this book), in which organizations were portrayed as cultures, i.e. systems of knowledge, belief and values. Prior to the study the dominant culture was engineering and production, in which accounting was incidental. This was displaced by economic and accounting concerns that constructed the railway as a profit-seeking enterprise:

Accounting actively shaped the dominant meanings given to organizational life . . . [in which a] new set of symbols, rituals and language emerged (p. 708).

Dent described how accounting played a role 'in constructing specific knowledges' (p. 727) by tracing the introduction of a revised corporate planning system, the amendment of capital expenditure approval procedures and the revision of budgeting systems, each of which shifted power from railway to business managers.

Roberts (1990) studied the acquisition and subsequent management of ELB Ltd by Conglom Inc. Following acquisition, 'the dominance of a production culture was instantly supplanted by the dominance of a purely financial logic' and the sale of the European operations to a competitor 'signalled the dominance of corporate financial concerns over long-term market concerns' (p. 123), although this was reinforced by share options, bonuses and managers' fear of exclusion. Accounting information was:

able to present an external image of 'success' . . . and hence conceals the possibility of the damaging strategic consequences for individual business units of Conglom's exclusive preoccupation with financial returns (p. 124).

In adopting a critical perspective, Miller and O'Leary (1987) described the construction of theories of standard costing in the period 1900–30, which they viewed as 'an important calculative practice which is part of a much wider modern apparatus of power' aimed at 'the construction of the individual person as a more manageable and efficient entity' (p. 235). The contribution of standard costing was to show how 'the life of the person comes to be viewed in relation to standards and norms of behaviour' (p. 262).

Laughlin (1996) played on 'principal and agent' theory to question the legitimacy of the principal's economic right to define the activities of the agent. He coined the term 'higher principals' to refer to the values held, particularly in the caring professions (education, health and social services), which could, he argued, overrule the rights of economic principals. These higher principals could be derived from religion, professional bodies or personal conscience.

Broadbent and Laughlin (1998) studied schools and GP (medical) practices and identified financial reforms as 'an unwelcome intrusion into the definition of professional activities' (p. 404), which led to resistance in the creation of 'informal and formal "absorption" processes to counteract and "mute" the changes' (p. 405).

Similarly, Covaleski et al. (1998) studied the (then) 'Big Six' professional accounting firms, where management by objectives and mentoring were used as techniques of control, revealing that the 'discourse of professional autonomy' fuelled resistance to these changes.

It is important in making choices about accounting methods to understand that these choices have behavioural consequences, some intended, some unintended, particularly where existing power structures are threatened, or where changes made are inconsistent with the norms and values, or culture, within the organization. In each case, management may face considerable resistance.

In Chapters 4 and 5, we considered rational-economic, interpretive and critical perspectives that help to provide multiple views about the world in which we live. Chapters 10 through 13 have introduced many aspects of costs and how management accounting techniques are used in planning, decision making and control in relation to marketing, operations, human resource and accounting.

Implicit in most of what is contained in these four chapters is an acceptance of the rational-economic paradigm described in Chapter 4. The notion of shareholder value and the importance of profit have dictated acceptable approaches to calculating costs, at least for financial reporting purposes to shareholders. In financial reporting, regulation and audit generally prevents (except in creative accounting or earnings management) any but a single interpretation, the rational-economic one. However, as we have seen through the examples in these chapters, different interpretations of cost are possible, and all are defensible depending on the assumptions used.

The interpretive perspective applied to management accounting accepts that different understandings exist. So, there are alternative approaches to pricing (Chapter 10) in which different solutions are possible, yet all are correct if based on specific assumptions. Different methods of judging the best use of capacity are also possible (Chapter 11). Relevant costs are an entirely different approach to traditional historical costing (Chapters 11 and 12) while variable, absorption and activity-based costing are very different interpretations about the treatment of overhead costs (this chapter). The critical paradigm privileges one or other treatment in each of these examples as a result, not necessarily of rational choice, but of the power of the dominant management group (including the role of accountants in that group) which can influence the particular techniques adopted.

We conclude this chapter on overhead allocation with two case studies illustrating the overhead allocation problem.

Case study 13.1: Tektronix Portables division

Using a case study of the Portables division of Tektronix (a real company) that was facing considerable Japanese competition, Turney and Anderson (1989) argued that 'the accounting function has failed to adapt to a new competitive environment that requires continuous improvement in the design, manufacturing, and marketing of a product' (p. 37). In their research, Turney and Anderson found that many of the accounting systems in use were obsolete, reporting information that was no longer used. The traditional focus for cost collection was labour, material and overhead for a work order. Overhead was 'bloated' due to 'the enormous complexity of the production process' and 'long production runs tended to produce large inventories of the wrong product' (p. 44). The 'additional cost of unique components was not fully reflected in the standard cost of the product' (p. 44) and 'the low-volume and tailored products consumed significantly more support services per unit than did the high-volume, mainline products' (p. 45).

Tektronix introduced new measures of continuous improvement and the role of accounting changed 'from being a watchdog to being a change facilitator' (p. 41). The focus on costs changed to the output of a production line based on standard costs. This shifted attention from improving individual worker performance to improving overall process effectiveness. Production was stopped when a defect was found, something that in Western companies had been unimaginable given the focus on maximizing production volume. A new method of overhead allocation which 'shifts product cost from products with high-volume common parts to those with low-volume unique parts' (p. 46) was introduced, which 'has influenced product design decisions, encouraging a simpler product that is less costly and easier to manufacture' (p. 47).

Source: Turney, P. B. B. and Anderson B. (1989). Accounting for continuous improvement. *Sloan Management Review*, Winter, 37–47.

Case study 13.2: Quality Bank — the overhead allocation problem

Quality Bank has three branches and a head office. Table 13.9 shows how the accounting system, based on absorption costing, has calculated the costs for each branch. Direct costs of €104,000 are traceable based on staff working in each location. Overhead costs of €400,000 for the bank have been allocated as a percentage of the direct labour cost.

Table 13.9 Quality Bank — direct costs and allocated overheads by branch.

	Total	Branch A	Branch B	Branch C	Total branch	HO	Total
Direct labour cost		14,000	11,000	9,000	34,000	70,000	104,000
Overheads	€400,000						
Allocated as % of direct labour	384.6%	53,846	42,308	34,615	130,769	269,231	400,000
Total costs		€67,846	€53,308	€43,615	€164,769	€339,231	€504,000

The bank used its internal staff to study the effects of introducing an activity-based costing system. Table 13.10 shows the cost pools and cost drivers that were identified.

Table 13.10 Quality Bank — cost pools and drivers.

Cost pools	€	Cost driver
Branch costs	120,000	No. of branch transactions
Computer system costs	180,000	No. of total transactions
Telecommunications costs	60,000	No. of customers
Credit checking costs	40,000	No. of new accounts
	€400,000	

The bank calculated costs for each cost driver as shown in Table 13.11. It then analysed the transaction volume for each of its branches and head office. These figures are shown in Table 13.12.

Table 13.11   Quality Bank — costs per driver.

	Branch costs	Computer system	Telecomms	Credit checking	Total
Overheads (€)	120,000	180,000	60,000	40,000	400,000
No. transactions	16,000	38,000	10,000	1,500	
Overhead per transaction	€7.50	€4.74	€6.00	€26.67	
Per	Branch trans.	Total trans.	Customer	New account	

Table 13.12   Quality Bank — transaction volumes by branch.

	Branch A	Branch B	Branch C	Total branch	HO	Total
No. of new accounts	350	100	50	500		500
No. of new loan accounts	600	300	100	1,000		1,000
Total no. new accounts	950	400	150	1,500	0	1,500
No. transactions − cashiers	3,000	1,500	500	5,000		5,000
No. transactions − loans	1,500	2,000	500	4,000		4,000
No. transactions − ATM	3,000	3,000	1,000	7,000		7,000
No. transactions − HO					22,000	22,000
Total no. transactions	7,500	6,500	2,000	16,000	22,000	38,000
No. customers					10,000	10,000

The bank was then able to apply the cost per cost driver against the actual transaction volume for each branch and head office. This resulted in the cost analysis shown in Table 13.13. A comparison of the costs allocated to each branch under absorption and activity-based costing is shown in Table 13.14.

Table 13.13   Quality Bank — cost analysis using ABC.

		Branch A	Branch B	Branch C	Total branch	HO	Total
New accounts	€26.67	25,333	10,667	4,000	40,000	0	40,000
Branch transactions	€7.50	56,250	48,750	15,000	120,000		120,000
Total transactions	€4.74	35,526	30,789	9,474	75,789	104,211	180,000
No. of customers	€6.00					60,000	60,000
Overhead allocation		117,110	90,206	28,474	235,789	164,211	400,000
Direct labour		14,000	11,000	9,000	34,000	70,000	104,000
Total (ABC)		€131,110	€101,206	€37,474	€269,789	€234,211	€504,000

Table 13.14   Quality Bank — comparison of costs under absorption and activity-based costing.

	Branch A	Branch B	Branch C	Total branch	HO	Total
Absorption costing	€67,846	€53,308	€43,615	€164,769	€339,231	€504,000
Activity-based costing	€131,110	€101,206	€37,474	€269,789	€234,211	€504,000

The ABC approach revealed that many of the costs charged to head office under absorption costing should be charged to branches based on transaction volumes. This had a significant impact on the measurement of branch profitability and the profitability of different business segments (e.g. new accounts, lending, ATM transactions).

Conclusion

In Chapters 10, 11 and 12, various accounting techniques were identified that can be used by non-financial managers as part of the decision-making process. With the shift in most Western economies to service and knowledge-based industries and high-technology manufacture, overheads have increased as a proportion of total business costs. This chapter has shown the importance to decision making of the assumptions and methods used by accountants to allocate overheads to products/services. Understanding the methods used, and their limitations, is essential if informed decisions are to be made by accountants and non-financial managers.

This chapter has also shown that we need to consider the underlying assumptions behind the management accounting techniques that are in use. Other countries adopt different approaches and we have something to learn from the success or failure of those practices. We also need to consider the behavioural consequences of the choices made in relation to accounting systems.

The reader is encouraged to read and think about Reading A, which is an early but still relevant critique of traditional cost allocation processes. This critique ultimately led its authors to develop activity-based costing. Reading D is a classic case study of the introduction of accounting to a public enterprise. It reflects the interpretive approach and shows the importance of culture and power in changing accounting systems. As such, it is a useful illustration of the behavioural implications of accounting. The Readings are in Part IV of this book.

References

Alexander, D. and Nobes, C. (2001). *Financial Accounting: An International Introduction*. Harlow: Financial Times/ Prentice Hall.

Berry, A. J., Capps, T., Cooper, D., Ferguson, P., Hopper, T. and Lowe, E. A. (1985). Management control in an area of the NCB: rationales of accounting practices in a public enterprise. *Accounting, Organizations and Society*, *10*(1), 3–28.

Broadbent, J. and Laughlin, R. (1998). Resisting the 'new public management': absorption and absorbing groups in schools and GP practices in the UK. *Accounting, Auditing and Accountability Journal, 11*(4), 403–35.

Burchell, S., Clubb, C., Hopwood, A. and Hughes, J. (1980). The roles of accounting in organizations and society. *Accounting, Organizations and Society, 5*(1), 5–27.

Clark, J. M. (1923). *Studies in the Economics of Overhead Costs*. Chicago: University of Chicago Press.

Cooper, D. J., Hayes, D. and Wolf, F. (1981). Accounting in organized anarchies: understanding and designing accounting systems in ambiguous situations. *Accounting, Organizations and Society, 6*(3), 175–91.

Covaleski, M. A., Dirsmith, M. W., Heian, J. B. and Samuel, S. (1998). The calculated and the avowed: techniques of discipline and struggles over identity in Big Six public accounting firms. *Administrative Science Quarterly, 43*, 293–327.

Currie, W. (1995). *A comparative analysis of management accounting in Japan, USA/UK and West Germany*. In D. Ashton, T. Hopper and R. W. Scapens (Eds), *Issues in Management Accounting* (2nd edn). London: Prentice Hall.

Demirag, I. S. (1995). *Management control systems of Japanese companies operating in the United Kingdom*. In A. J. Berry, J. Broadbent and D. Otley (Eds), *Management Control: Theories, Issues and Practices*. Basingstoke: Macmillan.

Dent, J. F. (1991). Accounting and organizational cultures: a field study of the emergence of a new organizational reality. *Accounting, Organizations and Society, 16*(8), 705–32.

Fisher, J. (1995). Contingency-based research on management control systems: categorization by level of complexity. *Journal of Accounting Literature, 14*, 24–53.

Gosselin, M. (2007). A review of activity-based costing: technique, implementation, and consequences. In C. S. Chapman, A. G. Hopwood and M. D. Shields (Eds), *Handbook of Management Accounting Research* (Vol. 2, pp. 641–71). Oxford: Elsevier.

Hiromoto, T. (1991). Another hidden edge – Japanese management accounting. *Getting Numbers You Can Trust: The New Accounting*. Boston, MA: Harvard Business Review Paperback.

Hopper, T., Otley, D. and Scapens, B. (2001). British management accounting research: whence and whither: opinions and recollections. *British Accounting Review, 33*, 263–91.

Johnson, H. T. and Kaplan, R. S. (1987). *Relevance Lost: The Rise and Fall of Management Accounting*. Boston, MA: Harvard Business School Press.

Kaplan, R. S. and Cooper, R. (1998). *Cost and Effect: Using Integrated Cost Systems to Drive Profitability and Performance*. Boston, MA: Harvard Business School Press.

Laughlin, R. (1996). Principals and higher principals: accounting for accountability in the caring professions. In R. Munro and J. Mouritsen (Eds), *Accountability: Power, Ethos and the Technologies of Managing*. London: International Thomson Business Press.

Miller, P. (1994). Accounting as social and institutional practice: an introduction. In A. G. Hopwood and P. Miller (Eds), *Accounting as Social and Institutional Practice*. Cambridge: Cambridge University Press.

Miller, P. and O'Leary, T. (1987). Accounting and the construction of the governable person. *Accounting, Organizations and Society, 12*(3), 235–65.

Otley, D. (1980). The contingency theory of management accounting: achievement and prognosis. *Accounting, Organizations and Society, 5*(4), 413–28.

Roberts, J. (1990). Strategy and accounting in a UK conglomerate. *Accounting, Organizations and Society, 15*(1/2), 107–26.

Turney, P. B. B. and Anderson B. (1989). Accounting for continuous improvement. *Sloan Management Review*, Winter, 37–47.

Williams, K., Haslam, C., Williams, J., Abe, M., Aida, T. and Mitsui, I. (1995). Management accounting: the Western problematic against the Japanese application. In A. J. Berry, J. Broadbent and D. Otley (Eds), *Management Control: Theories, Issues and Practices*. Basingstoke: Macmillan.

Questions

13.1   Intelco, a professional services firm, has overheads of $500,000. It operates three divisions and an accountant's estimate of the overhead allocation per division is 50% for Division 1, 30% for Division 2 and 20% for Division 3. The divisions respectively bill 4,000, 2,000 and 3,000 hours. Calculate the:

- blanket (organization-wide) overhead recovery rate; and the
- cost centre overhead recovery rate for each division.

13.2   BCF Ltd manufactures a product known as a Grunge. Direct material and labour costs for each Grunge are €300 and €150 respectively. To produce a Grunge requires 20 hours, comprising 10 hours in machining, 7 hours in assembly and 3 hours in finishing. Information for each department is:

	Machining	Assembly	Finishing
Overhead costs (€)	120,000	80,000	30,000
Labour hours	20,000	10,000	10,000

Calculate the cost of producing a Grunge using a departmental overhead recovery rate.

13.3   Engineering Products plc produces Product GH1, which incurs costs of £150 for direct materials and £75 for direct labour. The company has estimated its production overhead and direct labour hours for a period as:

	Dept A	Dept B	Dept C
Overheads £	150,000	200,000	125,000
Direct labour hours	5,000	10,000	5,000

Product GH1 is produced using 10 hours in Dept A, 12 hours in Dept B and 5 hours in Dept C.

Calculate the total cost of each GH1 using:

- a plant-wide overhead recovery rate; and
- cost centre overhead recovery rates.

13.4   Haridan Co. uses activity-based costing. The company has two products, A and B. The annual production and sales of Product A are 8,000 units and of product B 6,000 units. There are three activity cost pools, with estimated total cost and expected activity as follows:

			Expected activity	
Activity cost pool	Estimated cost	Product A	Product B	Total
Activity 1	$20,000	100	400	500
Activity 2	$37,000	800	200	1,000
Activity 3	$91,200	800	3,000	3,800

Calculate the cost per unit of Product A and Product B under activity-based costing.

13.5   Cooper's Components uses an activity-based costing system for its product costing. For the last quarter, the following data relates to costs, output volume and cost drivers:

Overhead costs	€
Machinery	172,000
Set-ups	66,000
Materials handling	45,000
Total	€283,000

Product	A	B	C
Production and sales	4,000 units	3,000 units	2,000 units
Number of production runs	12	5	8
Number of stores orders	12	6	4
	per unit	per unit	per unit
Direct costs	€25	€35	€15
Machine hours	5	2	3
Direct labour hours	4	2	4

a.   If set-up costs are driven by the number of production runs, what is the set-up cost per unit traced to product A?

b.   If materials handling costs are driven by the number of stores orders, what is the materials handling cost per unit traced to product B?

13.6   Elandem PLC produces 20,000 units of Product L and 20,000 units of Product M. Under activity-based costing, £120,000 of costs are purchasing related. If 240 purchase orders are produced each period, and the number of orders used by each product is:

	Product L	Product M
No. of orders	80	160

- Calculate the per-unit activity-based cost of purchasing for Products L and M.
- Calculate the overhead recovery for purchasing costs if those costs were recovered over the number of units of the product produced.

13.7   Heated Tools Ltd uses activity-based costing. It has identified three cost pools and their drivers as follows:

	Purchasing	*Quality control*	*Despatch*
Cost pool	$60,000	$40,000	$30,000
Driver	12,000	4,000	2,000
	Purchase orders	Stores issues	Deliveries

Product Hekla uses $100 of direct materials and $75 of direct labour. In addition, each Hekla has been identified as using five purchase orders, eight stores issues and two deliveries.

Calculate the total cost of each Hekla.

13.8   Samuelson uses activity-based costing. The company manufactures two products, X and Y. The annual production and sales of Product X are 3,000 units and of Product Y 2,000 units. There are three activity cost pools, with estimated total cost and expected activity as follows:

			Expected activity	
Cost pool	*Estimated cost*	*X*	*Y*	*Total*
Activity 1	€12,000	300	500	800
Activity 2	€15,000	100	400	500
Activity 3	€32,000	400	1200	1600
Total costs	€59,000			

a.   Calculate the overhead cost per unit of Product X and Y under activity-based costing.

b.   Samuelson wishes to contrast its overhead allocation with that under the traditional costing method it previously used. Samuelson charged its overheads of €59,000 to products in proportion to machine hours. Each unit of X and Y consumed five machine hours in production. Calculate the overhead cost per unit of Product X and Y under the traditional method of overhead allocation.

13.9   Brixton Industries plc makes three products: Widgets, Gadgets and Helios. The following budget information relates to Brixton for next year (Table 13.15).

Table 13.15   Brixton Industries budget information.

	Widgets	**Gadgets**	**Helios**
Sales and production (units)	50,000	40,000	30,000
Selling price (£ per unit)	£45	£95	£73
Direct labour and materials (£ per unit)	£32	£84	£65
Machine hours per unit in machining dept	2	5	4
Direct labour hours per unit in assembly dept	7	3	2

Overheads allocated and apportioned to production departments (including service cost centres) were to be recovered in product costs as follows:

Machining department at £1.20 per machine hour.
Assembly department at £0.825 per direct labour hour.

However, you have determined that the overheads could be re-analysed into cost pools as in Table 13.16.

Table 13.16   Brixton Industries activity cost pools and drivers.

Cost pool	£ Cost	Cost driver	Quantity
Machining services	£357,000	Machine hours	420,000
Assembly services	£318,000	Direct labour hours	530,000
Set-up costs	£26,000	Set-ups	520
Order processing	£156,000	Customer orders	32,000
Purchasing	£84,000	Supplier orders	11,200

You have also been provided with the following estimates for the period which are in Table 13.17.

Table 13.17   Brixton Industries estimates.

	Widgets	Gadgets	Helios
Number of set-ups	120	200	200
Customer orders	8,000	8,000	16,000
Supplier orders	3,000	4,000	4,200

- Prepare and present a profit calculation showing the profitability of each product using traditional absorption costing.
- Prepare and present a profit calculation showing the profitability of each product using activity-based costing.
- Explain the differences between the product profitability using absorption and activity-based costing.

13.10   Klingon Holdings has prepared a marketing study that shows the following demand and average price for each of its services for the following period:

	A	*B*	*C*
Volume	150,000	200,000	350,000
Estimated selling price per unit	$50	$35	$25
The variable costs for each are	$20	$17	$14

Fixed expenses have been budgeted as $6,900,000.

Using the above information:

- Calculate the contribution per unit of volume (and in total) for each service. Which is the preferred service? Why? What should the business strategy be?
- Determine the absorption (full) cost per unit for the three services using three different methods of allocating overheads.
- How do the results of these different methods compare?
- Assuming a constant mix of the services sold, calculate the breakeven point for the business.

CHAPTER 14

Strategic Investment Decisions

We introduced strategy in Chapter 2 to explain its link with achieving shareholder value. One of the most important elements of strategy implementation is capital investment decision making, because investment decisions provide the physical infrastructure through which businesses produce and sell goods and services. This is the topic of this chapter. In evaluating capital expenditure decisions, we compare three techniques: accounting rate of return; payback; and discounted cash flow techniques to see how investment decisions are evaluated.

Strategy

The traditional approach to strategy formation was described by Ansoff (1988). This approach reflected the cybernetic approach to management control introduced in Chapter 4. For Ansoff, strategy formulation involved setting objectives and goals; and carrying out an internal appraisal of strengths and weaknesses and an external appraisal of opportunities and threats. This led to strategic decisions such as diversification and the development of competitive strategy. A contrasting approach was developed by Quinn (1980), which he called *logical incrementalism*. Quinn argued against formal planning systems, which he believed had become 'costly paper-shuffling exercises', observing that 'most major strategic decisions seemed to be made outside the formal planning structure' (p. 2). Quinn further argued that:

> the real strategy tends to evolve as internal decisions and external events flow together to create a new, widely shared consensus for action among key members of the top management team (p. 15).

Logical incrementalism is similar to work by Mintzberg and Waters (1985), which defined strategy as a pattern in a stream of decisions. Mintzberg and Waters contrasted *intended* and *realized* strategy, arguing that *deliberate* strategies provided only a partial explanation, as some intended strategies were unable to be realized while other strategies *emerged* over time.

Nevertheless, strategy can be crucial in enabling a business to be proactive in increasingly competitive and turbulent business conditions. The absence of strategy can lead to reactivity and a steady erosion of market share. But strategy formulation is only one part of the problem, actually implementing strategy is more difficult because the problem for businesses in the twenty-first century is that they must continually adapt to technological and market change, which may not have been foreseen during the strategy formulation cycle.

Strategy implementation involves ensuring that resource allocations follow strategy. Maritan (2001) used a case study to illustrate how a manufacturing firm invests in production equipment, arguing that the formulation of strategy is linked to capital investment by framing capital plans and budgets in terms of organizational capabilities. Maritan found that the financial evaluation of capital investment decisions took place in the context of a complex organizational decision process in which multiple processes were used simultaneously to make capital investments that were associated with capabilities. This may be investing in new capacity or the capability to achieve lower costs, becoming more flexible or producing a new product, such that embedded in the investment decision for a physical asset is the investment in an organizational capability.

Capital expenditure evaluation

Capital investment or capital expenditure (often abbreviated as 'cap ex') means spending money now in the hope of getting it back later through future cash flows. The process of evaluating or appraising potential investments is to:

- generate ideas based on opportunities or identifying solutions to problems;
- research all relevant information;
- consider possible alternatives;
- evaluate the financial consequences of each alternative;
- assess non-financial aspects of each alternative;
- decide to proceed;
- determine an implementation plan and implement the proposal;
- control implementation by monitoring actual results compared to plan.

There are three main types of investment: new facilities for new product/services; expanding capacity to meet demand; or replacing assets in order to reduce production costs or improve quality or service. Most capital expenditure evaluations consider decisions such as: whether or not to invest; whether to invest in one project or one piece of equipment rather than another; and whether to invest now or at a later time. Capital expenditure evaluations are also used for business mergers and acquisitions.

There are three main methods of evaluating investments:

1. accounting rate of return;
2. payback;
3. discounted cash flow.

While the first is concerned with accounting profits, the second and third are concerned with cash flows from a project. For any project, capital expenditure evaluation requires an estimation of future incremental cash flows, i.e. the additional cash flow (income less expenses and income taxes, and adjusting for increases in working capital) that will result from the investment, compared with the cash outflow for the initial investment. Depreciation is, of course, an expense in arriving at profit that does not involve any cash flow (see Chapter 6). Cash flow is usually considered to be more important than accounting profit in capital expenditure evaluation because it is cash flow that drives shareholder value (see Chapter 2).

It is important to note the following:

- The financing decision is treated separately to the investment decision. Hence, even though there may be no initial cash outflow for the investment (because it may be wholly financed), all capital expenditure evaluation techniques assume an initial cash outflow. If a decision is made to proceed, then the organization is faced with a separate decision about how best to finance the investment. This is more a matter for corporate finance.
- The outflows are not just additional operating costs, as any new investment that generates sales growth is also likely to have an impact on working capital, since inventory, receivables and payables are likely to increase along with sales growth (see Chapter 7).
- Income tax is treated as a cash outflow as it is a consequence of the cash inflows from the new investment.

The detailed work in arriving at these profit and cash flow forecasts is not shown here, but will be the result of estimating an increase in sales volume, pricing, cost of sales, additional expenses and working capital, income taxes and so on. This will typically be developed using a spreadsheet that non-financial managers will have to develop, often with assistance from accountants in the business. Many assumptions will be made in developing these forecasts, which need to be made explicit in order that the forecasts can be understood. Most cap ex proposals need to be approved at board level and hence must be presented in terms that can be understood and interpreted.

As we consider each of the three methods of capital expenditure evaluation, we will assume three alternative investments. Table 14.1 shows the estimated cash flows for each alternative, which are assumed to be the result of the more comprehensive spreadsheet.

In this example five years is used as the planning horizon, but this is only an example. The planning horizon used by each company will be different, contingent on the industry, the rate of technological change, anticipated competition and so on. In practice it is how far ahead a company is reasonably comfortable in predicting. The planning horizon will commonly be equal to the period over which the investment is depreciated, but this does not have to be the case. A mining company like BHP Billiton making a major investment may plan 20–50 years in advance. A rapidly changing technology company like Apple may have a time horizon of only a year or two. Capital expenditure evaluations are also used for business acquisitions.

Table 14.1   Cash flows for investment alternatives.

Year	Project 1	Project 2	Project 3
0 initial investment	−100,000	−125,000	−200,000
1 inflows	25,000	35,000	60,000
2 inflows	25,000	35,000	60,000
3 inflows	25,000	35,000	80,000
4 inflows	25,000	35,000	30,000
5 inflows	25,000	35,000	30,000

As one component of the purchase price of another business is goodwill then the planning horizon will usually be the period over which goodwill is amortized (accounting for goodwill is covered in Chapter 6).

For simplicity, in capital expenditure evaluation we assume that each of the cash flows occurs at the end of each year. Year 0 represents the beginning of the project when the initial funds are paid out. If we add up the cash flows in the above example, Project 1 returns £125,000 (5 @ £25,000), Project 2 returns £175,000 (5 @ £35,000) and Project 3 returns £260,000 (2 @ £60,000 + £80,000 + 2 @ £30,000), although the initial investment in each is different.

Accounting rate of return

The accounting rate of return (ARR) is the profit after tax generated as a percentage of the initial investment. This is equivalent to the return on investment (ROI) that was introduced in Chapter 7. ARR is used here rather than ROI because ROI is based on the ratio of net profit after tax to shareholders' funds, but capital expenditure evaluation does not differentiate the source of funds to finance the investment, i.e. whether the investment is financed through debt or equity. The investment value for ARR is the depreciated value each year. The depreciated value each year, assuming a life of five years with no residual value at the end of that time, is shown in Table 14.2. The accounting rate of return varies annually, as Table 14.3 shows for Project 1.

It is quite common that ARR in early years is lower than in later years, as cash flows often grow and then decline over the lifecycle of an investment. In the final year, when the asset is fully depreciated, the return is infinite, because the ARR is based on an investment of zero. Different businesses use different ways of calculating the annual ARR − based on opening written-down value (the difference between historic cost and

Table 14.2   Depreciated value of alternative investments.

End of year	Project 1	Project 2	Project 3
1	80,000	100,000	160,000
2	60,000	75,000	120,000
3	40,000	50,000	80,000
4	20,000	25,000	40,000
5	0	0	0

Table 14.3   ARR for Project 1.

Year	Cash flow	Depreciation	Profit	Investment	ARR
1	25,000	20,000	5,000	80,000	6.25%
2	25,000	20,000	5,000	60,000	8.3%
3	25,000	20,000	5,000	40,000	12.5%
4	25,000	20,000	5,000	20,000	25%
5	25,000	20,000	5,000	0	

the accumulated depreciation), based on closing written-down value (as in the example in this chapter), or based on the average of opening and closing written-down value each year.

For the whole investment period, the accounting rate of return is the average annual return divided by the average investment. The average annual return is the total profit for the forecast period divided by the number of years. As we assume that depreciation is spread equally throughout the life of the asset, the average investment is half the value of the initial investment.

$$\frac{\text{total profits}/\text{no. of years}}{\textbf{initial investment}/\textbf{2}}$$

The average ARR for Project 1 is:

$$\frac{25,000/5}{100,000/2} = \frac{5,000}{50,000} = 10\%$$

The accounting rate of return for Project 2 is shown in Table 14.4.

Table 14.4   ARR for Project 2.

Year	Cash flow	Depreciation	Profit	Investment	ARR
1	35,000	25,000	10,000	100,000	10%
2	35,000	25,000	10,000	75,000	13.3%
3	35,000	25,000	10,000	50,000	20%
4	35,000	25,000	10,000	25,000	40%
5	35,000	25,000	10,000	0	

The average ARR for Project 2 is:

$$\frac{50,000/5}{125,000/2} = \frac{10,000}{62,500} = 16\%$$

The accounting rate of return for Project 3 is shown in Table 14.5.

Table 14.5   ARR for Project 3.

Year	Cash flow	Depreciation	Profit	Investment	ARR
1	60,000	40,000	20,000	160,000	13%
2	60,000	40,000	20,000	120,000	17%
3	80,000	40,000	40,000	80,000	50%
4	30,000	40,000	−10,000	40,000	−25%
5	30,000	40,000	−10,000	0	

The average ARR for Project 3 is:

$$\frac{60,000/5}{200,000/2} = \frac{12,000}{100,000} = 12\%$$

Project 3 in particular has substantial fluctuations in ARR from year to year. Using this method, Project 2 shows the highest return. However, it does not take into account either the scale of the investment required or the timing of the cash flows. Given that throughout this book we have emphasized that cash flow is more important than profit, it makes sense for capital expenditure evaluation to look not only at profits but also at cash flow. However, we must not forget that if a company has a target ROI (or ROCE, see Chapter 7), then every individual investment must contribute to achieving that ratio. Hence companies will typically have an ARR hurdle rate that reflects the overall company ROI and ROCE ratios it is aiming for.

Payback

This second method calculates how many years it will take — in cash terms — to recover the initial investment, on the assumption that the shorter the payback period, the better the investment, because the risk of technological or market change is less in the short term. Based on the cash flows for each project:

- Project 1 takes four years to recover its £100,000 investment (4 @ £25,000).
- Project 2 has recovered £105,000 by the end of the third year (3 @ £35,000) and will take less than seven months (20/35 = .57 of 12 months) to recover its £125,000 investment. The payback is therefore 3.57 years.
- Project 3 recovers its investment of £200,000 by the end of the third year (£60,000 + £60,000 + £80,000).

Based on the payback method, Project 3 is preferred (followed by Projects 2 and 1) as it has the fastest payback. However, the payback method ignores the size of the investment and any cash flows that take place after the investment has been recovered. This is a particular weakness of the payback method.

Discounted cash flow

Neither the accounting rate of return nor the payback method considers the *time value of money*, i.e. that £100 is worth more now than in a year's time, because it can be invested now at a rate of interest that will increase its value. For example, £100 invested today at 10% interest is equivalent to £110 in a year's time. Conversely, receiving £100 in a year's time is not worth £100 today. Assuming the same rate of interest it is worth only £91, because the £91, invested at 10%, will be equivalent to £100 in a year's time.

The time value of money needs to be recognized in capital expenditure evaluations in order to compare investment alternatives with different initial cash outflows, and different cash flows over different time periods. The third method of capital expenditure evaluation therefore involves discounted cash flow (DCF) techniques. DCF discounts future cash flows to their present values using a discount rate (or interest rate) that is usually the firm's weighted average cost of capital (the risk-adjusted cost of borrowing for the investment, see Chapter 2). The cost of capital may be risk adjusted, i.e. a higher hurdle may be set where an investment is perceived as being more risky.

There are two discounted cash flow techniques: net present value and internal rate of return.

Net present value

The net present value (NPV) method discounts future cash flows to their present value (PV) and compares the *present value of future cash flows* to the initial capital investment. The net present value (NPV) is the difference between the present value of future cash flows and the initial investment outflow.

> **present value (PV) of cash flows = cash flow × discount factor (based on number of years in**
>
> **the future and the cost of capital)**
>
> **net present value (NPV) = present value of future cash flows − initial capital investment**

An investment makes sense financially if the NPV is positive, i.e. that the present value of cash flows exceeds the cost of capital. In this case, the investment is creating shareholder value. If an investment results in a negative NPV, the cost of capital exceeds the present value of cash flows and the investment proposal should be rejected.

The present value of a future cash flow can be derived in four ways:

- using tables (the method used in this chapter);
- using a financial calculator;
- using an Excel spreadsheet (also shown in this chapter); and
- by formula (briefly shown below).

The formula method is $P = F_n (1/(1+r)^n)$, where:

P is the present value;

F_n is the future cash flow in n years;

r is the cost of capital used as the discount factor; and

n is the number of years.

So for example, £133.10 received in three years using a 10% cost of capital would be calculated as:

$$P = 133.10\left(1/(1+.10)^3\right) = 133.10(1/1.331) = 133.10 \times 0.7513 = £100$$

Using the same example, the NPV for Project 1 is shown in Table 14.6. The discount rate can be obtained from the net present value table in the Appendix to this chapter. It can also be obtained using the @NPV function in an Excel spreadsheet. As the net present value is negative, Project 1 should not be accepted since the present value of future cash flows does not cover the initial investment.

Table 14.6   NPV for Project 1.

Year	Project 1 cash flows	Discount factor (10%)	Present value of cash flows
1	25,000	.909	22,725
2	25,000	.826	20,650
3	25,000	.751	18,775
4	25,000	.683	17,075
5	25,000	.621	15,525
Present value of cash flows			94,750
Less: Initial investment			100,000
Net present value			−5,250

The NPV for Project 2 is shown in Table 14.7. Project 2 can be accepted because it has a positive net present value. However, we need to compare this with Project 3 to see if that alternative yields a higher net present value. The NPV for Project 3 is shown in Table 14.8.

Table 14.7   NPV for Project 2.

Year	Project 2 cash flows	Discount factor (10%)	Present value of cash flows
1	35,000	.909	31,815
2	35,000	.826	28,910
3	35,000	.751	26,285
4	35,000	.683	23,905
5	35,000	.621	21,735
Present value of cash flows			132,650
Less: Initial investment			125,000
Net present value			7,650

Table 14.8   NPV for Project 3.

Year	Project 3 cash flows	Discount factor (10%)	Present value of cash flows
1	60,000	.909	54,540
2	60,000	.826	49,560
3	80,000	.751	60,080
4	30,000	.683	20,490
5	30,000	.621	18,630
Present value of cash flows			203,300
Less: Initial investment			200,000
Net present value			3,300

Despite the faster payback for Project 3, the application of the net present value technique to the timing of the cash flows reveals that the net present value of Project 3 is lower than that for Project 2, and therefore Project 2 – which also showed the highest accounting rate of return – is the recommended investment. However, using the NPV method it is difficult to determine how much better Project 2 (with an NPV of £7,650) is than Project 3 (with an NPV of £3,300) because each has a different initial investment.

One way of ranking projects with different NPVs is cash value added (CVA) or profitability index, which is a ratio of the NPV to the initial capital investment:

$$\text{cash value added} = \frac{\text{NPV}}{\text{Initial capital investment}}$$

In the above example, Project 2 returns a CVA of 6.12% (£7,650/£125,000) while Project 3 returns a CVA of 1.65% (£3,300/£200,000). Companies may have a target CVA, such that, for example, to be approved a project must have a CVA of 10% (i.e. the NPV is at least 10% of the initial capital investment). The lower the CVA, the more risk there is of the NPV falling below zero.

The second DCF technique is the internal rate of return.

Internal rate of return

The internal rate of return (IRR) method determines the discount rate that produces a net present value of zero. This involves repeated trial-and-error calculations using the discount tables applying different discount rates until an NPV of 0 is reached. The discount rate may need to be interpolated between whole percentages in the tables. However, it is much easier to use spreadsheet software like Excel which contains an IRR function. The IRR for each project, using the spreadsheet function, is:

Project 1	7.9%
Project 2	12.4%
Project 3	10.7%

This is a more informative presentation of the comparison because it presents the cash flows as an effective interest rate. This interest rate is compared to the risk-adjusted cost of capital. The project with the highest internal rate of return would be preferred, provided that the rate exceeds the cost of capital.

Comparison of techniques

In the above example, each technique provides management with an incomplete picture, but taken together, all the methods help to determine the most appropriate decision to invest limited funds. Table 14.9 shows the rankings for each investment using each technique.

Table 14.9   Comparison of techniques.

Project	ARR	Payback	NPV	CVA	IRR
Project 1	10%	4 years	−$5250		7.9%
Ranking	3	3	x		x
Project 2	16%	3.57 years	$7650	6.12%	12.4%
Ranking	1	2	1	1	1
Project 3	12%	3 years	$3300	1.65%	10.7%
Ranking	2	1	2	2	2

Project 1 should not be accepted because it has a negative NPV and is ranked third on ARR and payback measures. Project 2 has the highest ranking on all techniques other than payback. Project 3 has the fastest payback but is otherwise behind Project 2 on all other measures. In this case it would appear that Project 2 is the preferred alternative investment. However, a business would normally set hurdle rates for its ARR, payback and DCF such that a proposal would need to exceed each hurdle to be accepted. In this case, the board may well send Project 2 back to the managers who submitted it, with a request that cash flows be reviewed to see if they can be brought forward.

The methods themselves inform management and the board about different aspects of the capital expenditure evaluation. While the accounting rate of return method provides an average after tax return on the capital investment and a business may select the highest return, commensurate with its ROI and ROCE targets in its financial statements, the method ignores the timing of cash flows. Sometimes where there are high short-term ARRs, managers may prefer those investments even though the longer term impact is detrimental to the organization. This is because managers may be evaluated and rewarded on their short-term performance (see Chapter 15). On the other hand, projects with a longer term ARR may be rejected by managers as they may not gain the benefit of those investment returns. Payback measures the number of years it will take to recover the capital investment and while this takes timing into account, it ignores cash flows after the payback period. Both ARR and payback methods ignore the time value of money.

Discounted cash flow techniques take account of the time value of money and discount future cash flows to their present value using a risk-adjusted weighted average cost of capital. This is generally seen to be a more reliable method of capital expenditure evaluation. Discounted cash flow is similar to the method of calculating shareholder value proposed by Rappaport (1998) and described in Chapter 2.

However, for investment evaluation, while all projects with a positive net present value are beneficial, a business will usually select the project with the highest net present value, or in other words the highest internal rate of return, sometimes using the initial cash investment (CVA) or the cost of capital (IRR) as a benchmark for the return.

Boards of directors typically set quite high 'hurdle' rates for investing in new assets. These are commonly in terms of payback periods of two to four years or ARR rates of 25–50%. Because of increasing market competition, rapid technological change and increased demands for short-term shareholder value, the use of discounted cash flow techniques has declined in some businesses. Shank (1996) used a case study to show how the conventional NPV approach was limited in high-technology situations as it did not capture the 'richness' of the investment evaluation problem. Shank saw NPV more as a constraint than a decision tool because it was driven by how the investment proposal was framed. However, for larger investments where returns are expected over many years, discounted cash flow techniques are still important. Business mergers and acquisitions, investments in buildings, major items of plant, mining exploration and so on commonly use NPV and IRR as methods of capital expenditure evaluation.

The following case study provides an example of capital expenditure evaluation.

Case study 14.1: Goliath Co. – investment evaluation

Goliath Co. is considering investing in a project involving an initial cash outlay for an asset of €200,000. The asset is depreciated over five years at 20% p.a. Goliath's cost of capital is 10%. The cash flows from the project are expected to be as follows:

Year	Inflow	Outflow
1	75,000	30,000
2	90,000	40,000
3	100,000	45,000
4	100,000	50,000
5	75,000	40,000

The company wishes to consider the accounting rate of return (each year and average), payback and net present value as methods of evaluating the proposal. The depreciation expense is €40,000 per year. Net cash flows and profits are as follows:

Year	Inflow	Outflow	Net cash flow	Depreciation	Profit
1	75,000	30,000	45,000	40,000	5,000
2	90,000	40,000	50,000	40,000	10,000
3	100,000	45,000	55,000	40,000	15,000
4	100,000	50,000	50,000	40,000	10,000
5	75,000	40,000	35,000	40,000	−5,000

Accounting rate of return:

	1	2	3	4	5
Investment (€)	160,000	120,000	80,000	40,000	0
Profit (€)	5,000	10,000	15,000	10,000	−5,000
ARR	3.125%	8.33%	18.75%	25%	−

Over the five years:

Profit 35,000/5,000 = 7000   Investment 200,000/2,000 = 100,000

ARR 7,000/100,000 = 7%

Cumulative cash flows are:

Year	Cash flow	Cumulative
1	45	45
2	50	95
3	55	150
4	50	200

The payback period is the end of year 4 when €200,000 of cash flows has been recovered.
Net present value of the cash flows:

Year	Cash flow	Factor	Present value
1	45,000	.9091	40,910
2	50,000	.8264	41,320
3	55,000	.7513	41,321
4	50,000	.6830	34,150
5	35,000	.6209	21,731
Present value of cash flows			179,432
Initial investment			−200,000
Net present value			−20,568

Using the spreadsheet NPV function, the answer is calculated in Table 14.10 (the difference is due to rounding).

Although the ARR is 7% and the payback is four years, the discounted cash flow shows that the net present value is negative. Therefore the project should be rejected, as the returns are insufficient to recover the company's cost of capital.

Table 14.10   NPV for Goliath Co.

A	B Year 0	C Year 1	D Year 2	E Year 3	F Year 4	G Year 5
Cash flows		45,000	50,000	55,000	50,000	35,000
Present value	179,437					
	↖ =+NPV (10%, C36:G36)					
Initial investment	−200,000					
NPV	−20,563					

Conclusion

In this chapter we have explained the importance of capital expenditure evaluation and its relationship with strategy. In particular, we have described the main techniques for capital expenditure evaluation: accounting rate of return, payback and discounted cash flow.

Often, however, decisions are made subjectively and then justified after the event by the application of financial techniques. This is particularly so for emergent strategy, described earlier in this chapter. Despite the usefulness of these techniques, the assumption has been that future cash flows can be predicted with some accuracy. This is, however, one of the main difficulties in accounting, as we will see in Chapter 16.

References

Ansoff, H. I. (1988). *The New Corporate Strategy*. New York: John Wiley & Sons.

Maritan, C. A. (2001). Capital investment as investing in organizational capabilities: an empirically grounded process model. *Academy of Management Journal*, 44(3), 513–31.

Mintzberg, H. and Waters, J. A. (1985). Of strategies, deliberate and emergent. *Strategic Management Journal*, 6, 257–72.

Quinn, J. B. (1980). *Strategies for Change: Logical Incrementalism*. Homewood, IL: Irwin.

Rappaport, A. (1998). *Creating Shareholder Value: A Guide for Managers and Investors*. New York: Free Press.

Shank, J. K. (1996). Analysing technology investments – from NPV to strategic cost management (SCM). *Management Accounting Research*, 7, 185–97.

Appendix: Present value factors

Table 14.11 gives the present value of a single payment received *n* years in the future discounted at an interest rate of *x*% per annum. For example, with a discount rate of 6% a single payment of £100 in five years' time has a present value of £74.73 (£100 × .7473).

Table 14.11 Present value factors.

Years	1%	2%	3%	4%	5%	6%	7%	8%	9%	10%	11%	12%	13%	14%	15%	16%	17%	18%	19%	20%
1	0.9901	0.9804	0.9709	0.9615	0.9524	0.9434	0.9346	0.9259	0.9174	0.9091	0.9009	0.8929	0.8850	0.8772	0.8696	0.8621	0.8547	0.8475	0.8403	0.8333
2	0.9803	0.9612	0.9426	0.9246	0.9070	0.8900	0.8734	0.8573	0.8417	0.8264	0.8116	0.7972	0.7831	0.7695	0.7561	0.7432	0.7305	0.7182	0.7062	0.6944
3	0.9706	0.9423	0.9151	0.8890	0.8638	0.8396	0.8163	0.7938	0.7722	0.7513	0.7312	0.7118	0.6931	0.6750	0.6575	0.6407	0.6244	0.6086	0.5934	0.5787
4	0.9610	0.9238	0.8885	0.8548	0.8227	0.7921	0.7629	0.7350	0.7084	0.6830	0.6587	0.6355	0.6133	0.5921	0.5718	0.5523	0.5337	0.5158	0.4987	0.4823
5	0.9515	0.9057	0.8626	0.8219	0.7835	0.7473	0.7130	0.6806	0.6499	0.6209	0.5935	0.5674	0.5428	0.5194	0.4972	0.4761	0.4561	0.4371	0.4190	0.4019
6	0.9420	0.8880	0.8375	0.7903	0.7462	0.7050	0.6663	0.6302	0.5963	0.5645	0.5346	0.5066	0.4803	0.4556	0.4323	0.4104	0.3898	0.3704	0.3521	0.3349
7	0.9327	0.8706	0.8131	0.7599	0.7107	0.6651	0.6227	0.5835	0.5470	0.5132	0.4817	0.4523	0.4251	0.3996	0.3759	0.3538	0.3332	0.3139	0.2959	0.2791
8	0.9235	0.8535	0.7894	0.7307	0.6768	0.6274	0.5820	0.5403	0.5019	0.4665	0.4339	0.4039	0.3762	0.3506	0.3269	0.3050	0.2848	0.2660	0.2487	0.2326
9	0.9143	0.8368	0.7664	0.7026	0.6446	0.5919	0.5439	0.5002	0.4604	0.4241	0.3909	0.3606	0.3329	0.3075	0.2843	0.2630	0.2434	0.2255	0.2090	0.1938
10	0.9053	0.8203	0.7441	0.6756	0.6139	0.5584	0.5083	0.4632	0.4224	0.3855	0.3522	0.3220	0.2946	0.2697	0.2472	0.2267	0.2080	0.1911	0.1756	0.1615
11	0.8963	0.8043	0.7224	0.6496	0.5847	0.5268	0.4751	0.4289	0.3875	0.3505	0.3173	0.2875	0.2607	0.2366	0.2149	0.1954	0.1778	0.1619	0.1476	0.1346
12	0.8874	0.7885	0.7014	0.6246	0.5568	0.4970	0.4440	0.3971	0.3555	0.3186	0.2858	0.2567	0.2307	0.2076	0.1869	0.1685	0.1520	0.1372	0.1240	0.1122
13	0.8787	0.7730	0.6810	0.6006	0.5303	0.4688	0.4150	0.3677	0.3262	0.2897	0.2575	0.2292	0.2042	0.1821	0.1625	0.1452	0.1299	0.1163	0.1042	0.0935
14	0.8700	0.7579	0.6611	0.5775	0.5051	0.4423	0.3878	0.3405	0.2992	0.2633	0.2320	0.2046	0.1807	0.1597	0.1413	0.1252	0.1110	0.0985	0.0876	0.0779
15	0.8613	0.7430	0.6419	0.5553	0.4810	0.4173	0.3624	0.3152	0.2745	0.2394	0.2090	0.1827	0.1599	0.1401	0.1229	0.1079	0.0949	0.0835	0.0736	0.0649
16	0.8528	0.7284	0.6232	0.5339	0.4581	0.3936	0.3387	0.2919	0.2519	0.2176	0.1883	0.1631	0.1415	0.1229	0.1069	0.0930	0.0811	0.0708	0.0618	0.0541
17	0.8444	0.7142	0.6050	0.5134	0.4363	0.3714	0.3166	0.2703	0.2311	0.1978	0.1696	0.1456	0.1252	0.1078	0.0929	0.0802	0.0693	0.0600	0.0520	0.0451
18	0.8360	0.7002	0.5874	0.4936	0.4155	0.3503	0.2959	0.2502	0.2120	0.1799	0.1528	0.1300	0.1108	0.0946	0.0808	0.0691	0.0592	0.0508	0.0437	0.0376
19	0.8277	0.6864	0.5703	0.4746	0.3957	0.3305	0.2765	0.2317	0.1945	0.1635	0.1377	0.1161	0.0981	0.0829	0.0703	0.0596	0.0506	0.0431	0.0367	0.0313
20	0.8195	0.6730	0.5537	0.4564	0.3769	0.3118	0.2584	0.2145	0.1784	0.1486	0.1240	0.1037	0.0868	0.0728	0.0611	0.0514	0.0433	0.0365	0.0308	0.0261
21	0.8114	0.6598	0.5375	0.4388	0.3589	0.2942	0.2415	0.1987	0.1637	0.1351	0.1117	0.0926	0.0768	0.0638	0.0531	0.0443	0.0370	0.0309	0.0259	0.0217
22	0.8034	0.6468	0.5219	0.4220	0.3418	0.2775	0.2257	0.1839	0.1502	0.1228	0.1007	0.0826	0.0680	0.0560	0.0462	0.0382	0.0316	0.0262	0.0218	0.0181
23	0.7954	0.6342	0.5067	0.4057	0.3256	0.2618	0.2109	0.1703	0.1378	0.1117	0.0907	0.0738	0.0601	0.0491	0.0402	0.0329	0.0270	0.0222	0.0183	0.0151
24	0.7876	0.6217	0.4919	0.3901	0.3101	0.2470	0.1971	0.1577	0.1264	0.1015	0.0817	0.0659	0.0532	0.0431	0.0349	0.0284	0.0231	0.0188	0.0154	0.0126
25	0.7798	0.6095	0.4776	0.3751	0.2953	0.2330	0.1842	0.1460	0.1160	0.0923	0.0736	0.0588	0.0471	0.0378	0.0304	0.0245	0.0197	0.0160	0.0129	0.0105
26	0.7720	0.5976	0.4637	0.3607	0.2812	0.2198	0.1722	0.1352	0.1064	0.0839	0.0663	0.0525	0.0417	0.0331	0.0264	0.0211	0.0169	0.0135	0.0109	0.0087
27	0.7644	0.5859	0.4502	0.3468	0.2678	0.2074	0.1609	0.1252	0.0976	0.0763	0.0597	0.0469	0.0369	0.0291	0.0230	0.0182	0.0144	0.0115	0.0091	0.0073
28	0.7568	0.5744	0.4371	0.3335	0.2551	0.1956	0.1504	0.1159	0.0895	0.0693	0.0538	0.0419	0.0326	0.0255	0.0200	0.0157	0.0123	0.0097	0.0077	0.0061
29	0.7493	0.5631	0.4243	0.3207	0.2429	0.1846	0.1406	0.1073	0.0822	0.0630	0.0485	0.0374	0.0289	0.0224	0.0174	0.0135	0.0105	0.0082	0.0064	0.0051
30	0.7419	0.5521	0.4120	0.3083	0.2314	0.1741	0.1314	0.0994	0.0754	0.0573	0.0437	0.0334	0.0256	0.0196	0.0151	0.0116	0.0090	0.0070	0.0054	0.0042
35	0.7059	0.5000	0.3554	0.2534	0.1813	0.1301	0.0937	0.0676	0.0490	0.0356	0.0259	0.0189	0.0139	0.0102	0.0075	0.0055	0.0041	0.0030	0.0023	0.0017
40	0.6717	0.4529	0.3066	0.2083	0.1420	0.0972	0.0668	0.0460	0.0318	0.0221	0.0154	0.0107	0.0075	0.0053	0.0037	0.0026	0.0019	0.0013	0.0010	0.0007
45	0.6391	0.4102	0.2644	0.1712	0.1113	0.0727	0.0476	0.0313	0.0207	0.0137	0.0091	0.0061	0.0041	0.0027	0.0019	0.0013	0.0009	0.0006	0.0004	0.0003
50	0.6080	0.3715	0.2281	0.1407	0.0872	0.0543	0.0339	0.0213	0.0134	0.0085	0.0054	0.0035	0.0022	0.0014	0.0009	0.0006	0.0004	0.0003	0.0002	0.0001

Questions

14.1   The Whitton Co. has an opportunity to buy a computer now for €18,000 that will yield annual net cash inflows of €10,000 for the next three years, after which its resale value would be zero. Whitton's cost of capital is 16%.

Calculate the net present value of the cash flows for the computer using spreadsheet formula. What is the IRR?

14.2   SmallCo is considering the following project, whose cost of capital is 12% per annum:

Year	0	1	2	3
	£	£	£	£
Cash flows of project	(2,000)	1,000	800	700

Calculate the NPV of the project.

14.3   Goliath Hotel projects the cash flows for three alternative investment projects (in $'000) as:

Project	Year 0	1	2	3	4	5
A	−350	100	200	100	100	140
B	−350	40	100	210	260	160
C	−350	200	150	240	40	0

Depreciation is $70,000 per annum. For each project, calculate the:

- payback period;
- accounting rate of return (average);
- net present value (assuming a cost of capital of 9%); and
- comment on which (if any) project should be accepted.

14.4   Freddie plc has £5 million to invest this year. Three projects are available and all are divisible, i.e. part of a project may be accepted and the cash flow returns will be pro rata. Details of the projects are:

Project	1	2	3
Cash outlay (£M)	3.0	2.0	1.5
NPV (£M)	1.7	1.1	1.0

What is the ranking of the projects that should be accepted?

14.5 Tropic Investments is considering a project involving an initial cash outlay for an asset of €200,000. The asset is depreciated over five years at 20% p.a. (based on the value of the investment at the beginning of each year). The cash flows from the project are expected to be:

	Inflow	Outflow
Year 1	75,000	30,000
Year 2	90,000	40,000
Year 3	100,000	45,000
Year 4	100,000	50,000
Year 5	75,000	40,000

What is the payback period?

What is the accounting rate of return (each year and average)?

Assuming a cost of capital of 10% and ignoring inflation, what is the net present value of the cash flows? (Use the tables rather than a spreadsheet to answer this question.)

Should the project be accepted?

14.6 Creative Tooling wishes to make a capital investment of $750,000 and the management team has produced an analysis (see Table 14.12) for your consideration. Make a recommendation to the board of Creative Tooling as to whether the capital investment should be made, and give reasons to support your answer. Identify the questions that a board of directors may ask the management team in relation to this proposal.

Table 14.12   Capital investment evaluation for Creative Tooling Company.

Capital investment	$ 750,000					
Cost of capital	12%					
Year	**0**	**1**	**2**	**3**	**4**	**5**
Projected profitability						
Anticipated additional revenue		400,000	450,000	550,000	500,000	400,000
Less anticipated additional costs	60,000	67,500	82,500	75,000	60,000	
Less depreciation expense		150,000	150,000	150,000	150,000	150,000
Profit before tax		190,000	232,500	317,500	275,000	190,000
Less income tax expense		66,500	81,375	111,125	96,250	66,500
Profit after tax		123,500	151,125	206,375	178,750	123,500
Projected cash flow						
Profit after tax		123,500	151,125	206,375	178,750	123,500
Add back depreciation		150,000	150,000	150,000	150,000	150,000
Less income tax paid			−66,500	−81,375	−111,125	−96,250
Change in working capital			−60,000	−60,000	−20,000	0
Net cash flow		273,500	174,625	215,000	197,625	177,250

Table 14.12 Continued

<u>Accounting rate of return</u>

	Total					
Asset cost in Balance Sheet		750,000	750,000	750,000	750,000	750,000
Less provision for depreciation		−150,000	−300,000	−450,000	−600,000	−750,000
Net asset value		600,000	450,000	300,000	150,000	0
Profit after tax	783,250	123,500	151,125	206,375	178,750	123,500
ARR		16.5%	25.2%	45.9%	59.6%	82.3%

Average profits ($783,250/5)	156,650
Average investment ($750,000/2)	375,000
<u>Average ARR</u>	41.8%

<u>Payback</u>

Net cash flow		273,500	174,625	215,000	197,625	177,250
Cumulative cash flow		273,500	448,125	663,125	860,750	1,038,000
<u>Payback period</u>					3.5 years (approx.)	

<u>Discounted cash flow (NPV at 12%)</u>

Initial investment	−750,000					
Projected cash flows		273,500	174,625	215,000	197,625	177,250
Total cash flows	−750,000	273,500	174,625	215,000	197,625	177,250
Present value of cash flows	762,610					
Net present value	12,610					

<u>Discounted cash flow (IRR)</u>	12.7%

CHAPTER 15

Performance Evaluation of Business Units

The shift towards a decentralized, multidivisional business structure and the measurement and management of divisional (i.e. business unit) performance has influenced the development of management accounting. This chapter introduces the structure of business organizations, with emphasis on the divisionalized structure and decentralized profit responsibility. This chapter describes the two main methods by which the performance of divisions and their managers is evaluated: return on investment and residual income. We also consider the issue of controllability and the transfer pricing problem and introduce the theory of transaction cost economics. This chapter suggests that some management accounting techniques may provide an appearance rather than the reality of 'rational' decision making.

Structure of business organizations

Emmanuel *et al.* (1990) described organizational structure as:

> a potent form of control because, by arranging people in a hierarchy with defined patterns of authority and responsibility, a great deal of their behaviour can be influenced or even pre-determined (p. 39).

Child (1972) defined organization structure as 'the formal allocation of work roles and the administrative mechanisms to control and integrate work activities' (p. 2), emphasizing that structure depends on the decision-makers' evaluation of environmental impacts, the standard of required performance and the level of performance actually achieved. This stresses the role of decision-makers, defined as the 'power-holding group' (p. 13).

Galbraith and Nathanson (1976) suggested that the choice of organizational form was the result of choices about five design variables: task; people; structure; reward systems; and information and decision processes. These choices should be consistent with the firm's product–market strategy, i.e. there should be 'fit' or 'congruence'. Galbraith and Nathanson applied Chandler's (1962) four growth strategies – expansion of volume, geographic dispersion, vertical integration and product diversification – to see how each affects the form of organizational structure, based on Chandler's thesis that structure follows strategy. They argued that:

> Variation in strategy should be matched with variation in processes and systems as well as in structure, in order for organizations to implement strategies successfully (p. 10).

Galbraith and Nathanson further built on Chandler's research, adding that diversification leads to multidivisional forms, with internal competition as an important variable.

Businesses produce products/services through a variety of organizational forms, but predominantly through either a functional structure or a divisionalized structure. The *functional structure* locates decision making at the top of the corporate hierarchy, with functional responsibilities for marketing, operations, human resources, finance and so on allocated to *departments*, as shown in the typical functional organization chart in Figure 15.1.

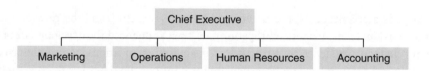

Figure 15.1   Functional organization chart.

In the functional structure, accounting provides a *staff* function to the *line* functions, simplified here as marketing, operations and human resources. Accounting knowledge tends to be centralized in the accounting department, which collects, produces, reports and analyses accounting information on behalf of its (internal) customer departments.

The functional structure may be suitable for smaller organizations or those with a narrow geographic spread or a limited product/service range, but it is not generally suitable for larger organizations.

The *divisional structure* is based on a relatively small head office with corporate specialists supporting the chief executive, with business units established for major elements of the business. The advantage of the divisional structure is that while planning is centrally coordinated, the implementation of plans, decision making and control is devolved to local management who should have a better understanding of their local operations. The divisions are often referred to as business units to describe their devolved responsibility for a segment of the business. These business units may be based on geographic territories or different products/ services, and each division will typically have responsibility for all the functional areas: marketing, operations, human resources and accounting. A typical divisional structure showing three divisions (or business units) is shown in Figure 15.2.

Figure 15.2   Divisional organization chart.

Management within divisions will carry out a significant function in analysing and interpreting financial information as part of their local management responsibilities, typically supported by locally based accounting staff. The role of accounting is quite different in a divisionalized structure as it is more focused on providing advice and information to local management to support planning, decision making and control, rather than carrying out the monitoring role accounting usually undertakes at the corporate head office. At the local level, accounting will typically be associated with more of the management accounting techniques described in this book than with financial reporting, which will more commonly be a head office role. Accounting therefore influences and is influenced by the organizational structure adopted and the extent of delegated managerial responsibility for business unit performance.

Business units are, in accounting, termed responsibility centres. Responsibility centres are business units which, through their managers, are held responsible for achieving certain standards of performance. There are three types of responsibility centres for divisionalized businesses:

- *Cost centres* – where managers are responsible for controlling costs within budget limits. Managers are evaluated on their performance compared to budget in keeping costs within budget constraints.
- *Profit centres* – where managers are responsible for sales performance, achieving gross margins and controlling expenses, i.e. for the 'bottom-line' profit performance of the business unit. Managers are evaluated on their performance compared to budget in achieving or exceeding their profit target. They have more flexibility than cost centres because they are usually able to exceed their cost budget provided they meet or exceed their profit targets.
- *Investment centres* – where managers have profit responsibility but also influence the amount of capital invested in their business units. Managers are evaluated based on a measure of the return on investment made by the investment centre. These managers have even more flexibility because they are able to influence their return on investment not only by increasing profits but by reducing the level of investment in their business units.

The decentralized organization and divisional performance measurement

While the evaluation of new capital expenditure proposals is a key element in allocating resources across the whole organization (see Chapter 14), a further aspect of strategy implementation is improving and maintaining divisional performance. *Decentralization* implies the devolution of authority to make decisions while *divisionalization* adds to decentralization the concept of delegated profit responsibility (Solomons, 1965). Solomons is recognized for having written the earliest and what remains the definitive text on divisional performance evaluation.

Divisionalization makes it easier for a company to diversify, while retaining overall strategic direction and control from a corporate head office. Performance improvement is encouraged by assigning individual responsibility for divisional performance to managers, typically linked to executive remuneration (e.g. bonuses, profit sharing, share options). Since shareholder value is the criterion for overall business success, so divisional performance is the criterion for divisional success. However, divisional performance measurement has also moved beyond purely financial measures to incorporate the drivers of financial results, i.e. non-financial performance measures (see Chapter 4).

Solomons (1965) highlighted three purposes for financial reporting at a divisional level:

1. To guide divisional managers in making decisions.
2. To guide top management in making decisions.
3. To enable top management to appraise the performance of divisional management.

The decentralization of businesses has removed the centrality of the head office in larger organizations with its functional structure and many support functions are now devolved to business units, which may be called subsidiaries (if they are legally distinct entities), divisions or departments. For simplicity, we will use the term divisionalization although the same principle applies to any business unit. Divisionalization allows managers to have autonomy over operational aspects of the business, but those managers are then accountable for the performance of their business units. While budgets and evaluating performance against budget are the subjects of Chapters 16 and 17, evaluating divisional performance is the subject of this chapter.

There are three methods by which divisional performance can be evaluated:

- absolute profit;
- return on investment;
- residual income.

In each case, we are trying to evaluate the performance of the business unit, and the performance of its management team.

Absolute profit

Under this method, the total profit (usually compared with budget) is the method by which divisional performance is evaluated. Although it is easy to use, being based on standard financial reports, absolute profit is not a good measure because it does not consider the investment in the business or how long-term profits can be affected by short-term decisions such as reducing research, maintenance and advertising expenditure. These decisions will improve reported profits in the current year, but will usually have a detrimental long-term impact.

Return on investment

The relative success of managers can be judged by the return on investment (or ROI, which was introduced in Chapter 7). This is the rate of return achieved on the capital employed and was a method developed by the DuPont Powder Company early in the twentieth century. Using ROI, managerial and divisional success is judged according to the rate of return on the investment. As we saw with capital expenditure evaluation in Chapter 14, if a business as a whole desires to achieve a particular ROI, then each investment must contribute to that ROI. Equally, with a divisionalized business, each division must contribute to overall business ROI, hence one way in which divisional ROI can be evaluated is by comparison to the ROI that is calculated from the company's financial statements.

However, a problem with this approach is whether a high rate of return on a small capital investment is better or worse than a lower return on a larger capital. For example:

	Division A	Division B
Capital invested	€1,000,000	€2,000,000
Operating profit	€200,000	€300,000
Return on investment	20%	15%

Division B makes a higher absolute profit but a lower return on the capital invested in the business. While there will always be pressure to improve operating profits, measuring ROI also emphasizes the elimination of under-utilized assets (in Chapter 7 we said that the only reason a business invests in assets is to generate sales and profits).

Solomons (1965) argued that a decision cannot be made about relative performance unless we know the cost of capital, something which we introduced in Chapter 14.

Residual income

A different approach to evaluating performance is residual income, which takes into account the cost of capital. Residual income (or RI) is the profit remaining after deducting the notional risk-adjusted cost of capital from the investment in the division. The RI approach was developed by the General Electric Company and more recently has been compared with Economic Value Added (EVA, see Chapter 2), as both methods deduct a notional cost of capital from the reported profit. Using the above example:

	Division A	Division B
Capital invested	€1,000,000	€2,000,000
Operating profit	€200,000	€300,000
Less cost of capital at 17.5%	€175,000	€350,000
Residual income	€25,000	−€50,000

As the cost of capital is 17.5% in the above example, Division A makes a satisfactory return but Division B does not. Division B is eroding shareholder value while Division A is creating it.

The aim of managers should be to maximize the residual income from the capital investments in their divisions. However, Solomons (1965) emphasizes that the RI approach assumes that managers have the power to influence the amount of capital investment. Solomons argued that an RI target is preferred to a maximization objective because it takes into account the differential investments in divisions, i.e. that a larger division will almost certainly produce – or should produce – a higher residual income. Johnson and Kaplan (1987) believe that the residual income approach:

> overcame one of the dysfunctional aspects of the ROI measure in which managers could increase their reported ROI by rejecting investments that yielded returns in excess of their firm's (or division's) cost of capital, but that were below their current average ROI (p. 165).

One of the problems with both the ROI and RI measures of divisional performance is the calculation of the capital investment in the division: should it be total (i.e. capital employed) or net assets (i.e. equity)? Should it include only non-current assets, or both non-current and current assets? Should non-current assets be valued at cost or written-down value (i.e. net of depreciation?) Should the book value be at the beginning or end of the period? Solomons (1965) argued that it was the amount of capital put into the business, rather than what could be taken out, that was relevant. The investment value, according to Solomons, should be total assets less controllable liabilities, with non-current assets valued at cost using the value at the beginning of the period. ROI calculations therefore relate controllable operating profit as a percentage of controllable investment. An RI approach would measure net residual income plus actual interest expense (because the notional cost of capital has already been deducted in calculating RI) against the total investment in the division.

One of the main problems in evaluating divisional performance is the extent to which managers can exercise control over investments and costs charged to their responsibility centres. Hence controllability is an important element in the performance evaluation of business units.

Controllability

The principle of controllability, according to Merchant (1987, p. 316), is that 'individuals should be held accountable only for results they can control' (p. 336). One of the limitations of operating profit as a measure of divisional performance is the inclusion of some costs over which the divisional manager may have no control. The need for the company as a whole to make a profit often results in corporate costs being allocated to divisions so that these costs can be recovered in the prices charged. The problem arises when a division's profit is not sufficient to cover the head office charge. Solomons (1965) argued that so long as corporate expenses are independent of divisional activity, allocating corporate costs is irrelevant because a positive contribution by divisions will cover at least some of those costs (we introduced this concept in relation to market segmentation in Chapter 10).

Solomons separated the controllable from non-controllable components in the divisional profit report, a simplified example of which is shown below:

Sales		£1,000,000
Less variable cost of goods sold	£200,000	
Other variable expenses	£100,000	£300,000
Contribution margin		£700,000
Less controllable divisional overhead		£250,000
Controllable profit for division		£450,000
Less non-controllable overhead		£175,000
Operating profit for division		£275,000

The controllable profit is the profit after deducting expenses that can be controlled by the divisional manager, but ignoring those expenses that are outside the divisional manager's control. What is controllable or non-controllable will depend on the circumstances of each organization. While the business as a whole may consider the operating profit to be the most important figure for the *business unit*, performance evaluation of the *manager* should only be carried out based on the controllable profit. Solomons (1965) argued that the most suitable figure for appraising divisional managers was the *controllable residual income before taxes*. Using this method, the controllable profit is reduced by the corporate cost of capital. For decisions in relation to a division's performance, the relevant figure is the *net residual income after taxes*.

The following case study provides an example of divisional performance measurement using ROI and RI techniques.

Case Study 15.1: Majestic Services – divisional performance measurement

Majestic Services has two divisions, both of which have bid for $1 million for projects that will generate significant cost savings. Majestic has a cost of capital of 15% and can only invest in one of the projects.

The current performance of each division is as follows:

	Division A	Division B
Current investment	$4 million	$20 million
Profit	$1 million	$2 million

Each division has estimated the additional controllable profit that will be generated from the $1 million investment. A estimates $200,000 and B estimates $130,000.

Each division also has an asset which they would like to dispose of. A's asset currently makes an ROI of 19%, while B's asset makes an ROI of 12%. The business wishes to use ROI and residual income techniques to determine in which of the $1 million projects Majestic should invest, and whether either of the division's identified assets should be disposed of.

Using ROI, the two divisions are compared in Table 15.1. While Division B is the larger division and generates a higher profit in absolute terms, Division A achieves a higher return on investment.

Table 15.1   ROI on original investment.

	A	B
Current investment	$4 million	$20 million
Current profit	$1 million	$2 million
ROI	25%	10%

Again using ROI, the impact of the additional investment can be seen in Table 15.2. Using ROI, Division A may not want its project to be approved as the ROI of 20% is less than the current ROI of 25%. The impact of the new investment would be to reduce the divisional ROI to 24% ($1.2million/ $5 million). However, Division B would want its project to be approved as the ROI of 13% is higher than the current ROI of 10%. The effect would be to increase Division B's ROI slightly to 10.14% ($2.13 million/$21 million). However, the divisional preference for B's investment over A, because of the rewards attached to increasing ROI, are dysfunctional to Majestic. The corporate view of Majestic would be to invest $1 million in Division A's project because the ROI to the business as a whole would be 20% rather than 13%.

Table 15.2   ROI on additional investment.

	A	B
Additional investment	$1 million	$1million
Additional contribution	$200,000	$130,000
ROI on additional investment	20%	13%

The disposal of the asset can be considered even without knowing its value. If Division A currently obtains a 25% ROI, disposing of an asset with a return of only 19% will increase its average ROI. Division B would wish to retain its asset because it generates an ROI of 12% and disposal would reduce its average ROI to below the current 10%. Given a choice of retaining only one asset, Majestic would prefer to retain Division A's asset as it has a higher ROI.

The difficulty with ROI as a measure of performance is that it ignores both the difference in size between the two divisions and Majestic's cost of capital. These issues are addressed by the residual income method.

Using residual income (RI), the divisional performance is compared in Table 15.3. In this case, we can see that Division A is contributing to shareholder value as it generates a positive RI, while Division B is eroding its shareholder value because the profit it generates is less than the cost of capital on the investment.

Table 15.3 RI on original investment.

	A	B
Current investment	$4 million	$20 million
Current profit	$1,000,000	$2,000,000
Cost of capital @ 15%	$600,000	$3,000,000
Residual income (profit − cost of capital)	$400,000	-$1,000,000

Using RI, the impact of the additional investment is shown in Table 15.4. Under the residual income approach, Division A's project would be accepted (positive RI) while Division B's would be rejected (negative RI).

Table 15.4 RI on additional investment.

	A	B
Additional investment	$1 million	$1 million
Additional contribution	$200,000	$130,000
Less cost of capital @ 15%	$150,000	$150,000
Residual income	$50,000	-$20,000

Similarly for the asset disposal, Division A's asset would be retained (ROI of 19% exceeds cost of capital of 15%), while Division B's asset would be disposed of (ROI of 12% is less than cost of capital of 15%).

The main problem facing Majestic is that the larger of the two divisions (both in terms of investment and profits) is generating a negative residual income and consequently eroding shareholder value.

A further problem associated with measuring divisional performance is that of transfer pricing, which was briefly mentioned as a method of pricing in Chapter 10.

Transfer pricing

When decentralized business units conduct business with each other, an important question is what price to charge for within-company transactions, as this affects the profitability of each business unit. Transfer prices may be based on:

- *Market price*: where products/services can be sold on the outside market, the market price is used, including a normal profit margin. This is the easiest way to ensure that divisional decisions are compatible with corporate profit maximization. However, if there is no external market, particularly for an intermediate product – i.e. one that requires additional processing before it can be sold – this method cannot be used.
- *Full cost or cost-plus*: this method would recover both fixed and variable costs, with or without a profit margin included. This method has the same overhead allocation problem as identified in Chapter 13.
- *Marginal cost*: the transfer price is the incremental (or variable) cost incurred, with or without a profit margin included.
- *Negotiated prices*: this may take into account market conditions, marginal costs and the need to motivate managers in each division. It tends to be the most practical solution to align the interests of divisions with the whole organization and to share the profits equitably between each division. In using this method, care must be taken to consider differential capital investments between divisions, so that both are treated equitably in terms of ROI or RI criteria.

In an increasingly globalized marketplace, manufacturing, assembly and selling operations may take place in different countries. In these cases, transfer prices are often set with a goal of ensuring that reported profits are earned in countries where lower corporation tax is payable to maximize the after-tax earnings (and hence shareholder value) of the multinational corporation. These arrangements are consequently scrutinized by taxation authorities. In practice, many organizations negotiate transfer prices with taxation authorities and then adopt negotiated prices between divisions in order to avoid the demotivating effects of the other methods on different business units. However, in some Japanese companies (see Chapter 13 for a discussion of some Japanese management accounting practices) it is common to leave the profit with the manufacturing division, placing the onus on the marketing division to achieve better market prices.

However, transfer prices that are suitable for evaluating divisional performance may lead to divisions acting contrary to the corporate interest (Solomons, 1965). Therefore, an important issue in establishing a transfer price is the motivational effect that this may have on managers of both the buying and selling business units, who may prefer to buy and sell on the open market in order to maximize their divisional profits, ROI or RI, even if that results in detriment to the business as a whole.

For example, consider a company with two divisions. Division A can produce 10,000 units for a total cost of £100,000, but additional production costs are £5 per unit. Division A sells its output to Division B at £13 per unit in order to show a satisfactory profit. Division B carries out further processing on the product. It can convert 10,000 units for a total cost of £300,000, but additional production costs are £15 per unit. The prices B can charge to customers will depend on the quantity it wants to sell. Market estimates of selling prices at different volumes (net of variable selling costs) are:

Volume	Price
10,000 units	£50 per unit
12,000 units	£46 per unit
15,000 units	£39 per unit

The financial results for each division at each level of activity are shown in Table 15.5. Division A sees an increase in profit as volume increases and will want to increase production volume to 15,000 units. However, Division B sees a steady erosion of divisional profitability as volume increases and will seek to keep production limited to 10,000 units, at which point its maximum profit is £70,000. The company's overall profitability increases between 10,000 and 12,000 units, but then falls when volume increases to 15,000 units. From a whole-company perspective, therefore, volume should be maintained at 12,000 units to maximize profits at £112,000. However, neither division will be satisfied with this result, as both will see it as disadvantaging them in terms of divisional profits, against which divisional managers are evaluated.

Table 15.5   Divisional financial results.

Activity level	10,000	12,000	15,000
Division A			
10,000 units	100,000	100,000	100,000
2,000 units @ £5		10,000	
5,000 units @ £5			25,000
Total cost	100,000	110,000	125,000
Transfer price @ £13	130,000	156,000	195,000
Division profit	£30,000	£46,000	£70,000
Division B			
Transfer from Division A	130,000	156,000	195,000
Conversion cost			
10,000 units	300,000	300,000	300,000
2,000 units @ £15		30,000	
5,000 units @ £15			75,000
Total cost	430,000	486,000	570,000
Selling price	@ £50	@ £46	@ £39
Sales revenue	500,000	552,000	585,000
Division profit	£70,000	£66,000	£15,000
Company			
Sales revenue	500,000	552,000	585,000
Division A cost	−100,000	−110,000	−125,000
Division B cost	−300,000	−330,000	−375,000
Company profit	£100,000	£112,000	£85,000

For Division A, variable costs over 10,000 units are £5, but its transfer price is £13, so additional units contribute £8 each to divisional profitability. A's average costs reduce as volume increases, as Table 15.6 shows.

Table 15.6   Division A costs.

	10,000	12,000	15,000
Division A total costs	£100,000	£110,000	£125,000
Average cost per unit	£10.00	£9.17	£8.33

However, for Division B, its variable costs over 10,000 units are £28 (transfer price of £13 plus conversion costs of £15). The reduction in average costs of £2.50 per unit is more than offset by the fall in selling price (net of variable selling costs), as Table 15.7 shows.

Table 15.7   Division B costs.

	10,000	12,000	15,000
Division B total costs	£430,000	£486,000	£570,000
Average cost per unit	£43.00	£40.50	£38.00
Reduction in average cost per unit		£2.50	£2.50
Reduction in selling price		£4.00	£7.00

Transaction cost economics

A useful theoretical framework for understanding divisionalization and the transfer pricing problem is the transactions cost (also called the markets and hierarchies) approach of Oliver Williamson (1975), a winner of the Nobel prize for economics, who was concerned with the study of the economics of internal organization. Transaction cost economics seeks to explain why some separate activities that require coordination occur within the organization's hierarchy (i.e. within the corporate multi-divisional structure), while others take place through exchanges outside the organization in the wider market (i.e. between arm's-length buyers and sellers).

The markets and hierarchies perspective considers the vertical integration of production and the decision about whether organizations should make or buy. Both bounded rationality (the assumption that decision-makers have limited information and limited ability to process that information in an uncertain and complex environment – see Chapter 4); and opportunistic behaviour (see Chapter 6 for a discussion of this in relation to agency theory) are assumed in this perspective. Transaction costs are affected by asset specificity, i.e. when an investment is made for a specific rather than a general purpose. They are also affected by uncertainty and the frequency with which transactions take place.

The work of business historians such as Chandler (1962) reflects a transaction cost approach in explanations of the growth of huge corporations such as General Motors (GM) in the first half of the twentieth century, in which hierarchies were developed as alternatives to market transactions. Recent trends, not only in the automotive industry, have reversed this with the strategy being to outsource as much production as possible to the lowest cost producer – automotive companies like GM, Ford and Toyota now only assemble vehicles, the components for which are manufactured by several tiers of suppliers.

Transactions are more than exchanges of goods, services and money. They incur costs over and above the price for the commodity bought or sold, such as costs associated with negotiation, monitoring, administration and insurance. They also involve time commitments and obligations, and are associated with legal, moral and power conditions. Understanding these costs may reveal that it is more economic to carry out an activity in-house than to accept a market price that appears less costly but may incur 'transaction' costs that are hidden in overhead costs. However, the high costs of market-related transactions can be avoided by specifying the rules for cooperative behaviour within the organization.

For managers using accounting information, attention is focused on the transaction costs associated with different resource-allocation decisions and whether markets or hierarchies are more cost effective. Under transaction cost economics, attention focuses on the transaction costs involved in allocating resources within the organization, and determining when the costs associated with one mode of organizing transactions (e.g. markets) would be reduced by shifting those transactions to an alternative arrangement (e.g. the internal structure of an organization).

Williamson (1975) argued that the desire to minimize transaction costs leads to transactions being kept within the organization, favouring the organizational hierarchy over markets. Markets are favoured where there are a large number of trading partners, which minimizes the risk of opportunistic behaviour. Recurring, complex and uncertain exchanges that involve substantial investment may be more efficiently undertaken when internal organization replaces market transactions. The efficiency of a transaction that takes place within the organization depends on how the behaviour of managers is governed or constrained, how economic activities are subdivided and how the management accounting system is structured. However, decision-makers may themselves indulge in opportunistic behaviour that causes the benefits of internal transactions to be reduced. Therefore, the management accounting system can be used to ensure that these internal transactions are conducted efficiently.

Rather than reflecting a concern with utility maximization (the assumption of agency theory), the transaction cost framework is more concerned with bounded rationality. While an agency perspective ignores the power of owners and also that of employees who can withdraw their labour, transaction cost theory gives recognition to power in the hierarchy that is used to coordinate production.

Conclusion: a critical perspective

In this chapter we have described the divisionalized organization and how divisional performance can be evaluated using return on investment (ROI) and residual income (RI) techniques. The divisional form is a preferred organizational structure because it allows devolved responsibility while linking divisional performance to organizational goals through measures such as ROI and RI that are meaningful at different organizational levels, particularly when these support shareholder value methods such as the link between RI and EVA. In this chapter we have also discussed the controllability principle and the transfer pricing problem and how these can lead to managers making decisions that benefit their divisions but may not be optimal for the organization as a whole.

However, a critical stance can be applied to the divisionalized form of organization. Roberts and Scapens (1985) argued that in a divisionalized company there is distance between the division and the head office, such that 'the context within which accounting information is gathered will typically be quite different from the context in which it is interpreted' (p. 452). Like the social construction perspective in Chapter 5, divisional managers and the corporate head office may see the same financial information in very different ways. This may result in manipulating the appearance of accounting reports. Roberts and Scapens concluded:

> The image of an organization which is given through Accounts will be from a particular point of view, at a particular point in time and will be selective in its focus. Events, actions, etc. which are significant for the organization may be out of focus, or not in the picture at all ... the image conveyed by the Accounts may misrepresent the actual flow of events and practices that it is intended to record (p. 454).

Managers are often critical that the corporate head office fails to distinguish adequately between controllable and non-controllable overhead. Research by Merchant (1987) identified that the controllability principle was not found in practice and that managers should be evaluated 'using all information that gives insight into their action choices'.

Relationships between business units frequently cause friction, particularly in some organizations where the number of business units has been increased to a level that is difficult to manage. Transaction cost economics, a rational markets and hierarchies approach like agency theory (Chapter 6), provides a useful though limited perspective as it does not address the power relations between divisions and between divisions and the corporate head office. The political process inherent in transfer pricing between divisions is also evidenced in many multinational corporations, where transfer pricing has become more concerned with how to shift profits between countries so as to minimize income taxes on profits and maximize after-tax profits to increase shareholder value. While this is undoubtedly in the interests of individual companies and does need the approval of taxation authorities, it raises issues of the ethics of transfer pricing when multinationals minimize their profits and taxation in relatively high-tax countries such as the UK from which they enjoy many benefits.

References

Chandler, A. D. J. (1962). *Strategy and Structure: Chapters in the History of the American Industrial Enterprise.* Cambridge, MA: Harvard University Press.

Child, J. (1972). Organizational structure, environment and performance: the role of strategic choice. *Sociology*, 6, 1–22.

Emmanuel, C., Otley, D. and Merchant, K. (1990). *Accounting for Management Control* (2nd edn). London: Chapman & Hall.

Galbraith, J. R. and Nathanson, D. A. (1976). *Strategy Implementation: The Role of Structure and Process.* St Paul, MN: West Publishing Company.

Johnson, H. T. and Kaplan, R. S. (1987). *Relevance Lost: The Rise and Fall of Management Accounting.* Boston, MA: Harvard Business School Press.

Merchant, K. A. (1987). How and why firms disregard the controllability principle. In W. J. Bruns and R. S. Kaplan (Eds), *Accounting and Management: Field Study Perspectives*. Boston, MA: Harvard Business School Press.

Roberts, J. and Scapens, R. (1985). Accounting systems and systems of accountability – understanding accounting practices in their organizational contexts. *Accounting, Organizations and Society*, 10(4), 443–56.

Solomons, D. (1965). *Divisional Performance: Measurement and Control*. Homewood, IL: Richard D. Irwin.

Williamson, O. E. (1975). *Markets and Hierarchies: Analysis and Antitrust Implications. A Study in the Economics of Internal Organization*. New York: Free Press.

Questions

15.1 Jakobs Ladder has capital employed of £10 million and currently earns an ROI of 15% per annum. It can make an additional investment of £2 million for a five-year life. The average net profit from this investment would be 14% of the original investment. The division's cost of capital is 12%.

Calculate the residual income before and after the investment.

15.2 China Group has a division with capital employed of €10 million that currently earns an ROI of 15% per annum. It can make an additional investment of €2 million for a five-year life with no scrap value. The average net profit from this investment would be €280,000 per annum after depreciation. The division's cost of capital is 9%.

Calculate the ROI and residual income for the:

• original investment;
• additional investment; and
• total new level of investment.

15.3 Brummy Co. consists of several investment centres. Green Division has a controllable investment of $750,000 and profits are expected to be $150,000 this year. An investment opportunity is offered to Green that will yield a profit of $15,000 from an additional investment of $100,000. Brummy accepts projects if the ROI exceeds the cost of capital, which is 12%.

• Calculate Green's ROI currently, for the additional investment and after the investment.
• How will Green and Brummy Co. view this investment opportunity?
• Calculate the effect of the new investment opportunity on Green's residual income.

15.4 Anston Industries is the manufacturing division of a large multinational. The divisional general manager is about to purchase new equipment for the manufacture of a new product. He can buy either the Compax or the Newpax equipment, each of which has the same capacity and an expected life of four years. Each type of equipment has different capital costs and expected cash flows, as follows:

	Compax	Newpax
Initial capital investment	£6,400,000	£5,200,000
Net cash inflows (before tax)		
Year 1	£2,400,000	£2,600,000
Year 2	£2,400,000	£2,200,000
Year 3	£2,400,000	£1,500,000
Year 4	£2,400,000	£1,000,000
Net present value (@ 16% p.a.)	£315,634	£189,615

The equipment will be installed and paid for at the end of the current year (Year 0) and the cash flows accrue at the end of each year. There is no scrap value for either piece of equipment. In calculating divisional returns, divisional assets are valued at net book value at the beginning of each year.

The multinational expects each division to achieve a minimum return before tax of 16%. Anston is just managing to achieve that target. Anything less than a 16% return would make the divisional general manager ineligible for his profit-sharing bonus.

- Prepare accounting rate of return (ARR) and residual income (RI) calculations for the Compax and the Newpax for each year.
- Suggest which equipment is preferred under each method.
- Compare this with the NPV calculation.

15.5   Magna Products has three divisions, A, B and C. The current investments in and net profits earned by each division are as follows:

Division A	
Investment	€1,000,000
Net profit	€75,000
Division B	
Investment	€1,500,000
Net profit	€90,000
Division C	
Investment	€2,000,000
Net profit	€150,000

Each division has put forward to the parent board a capital expenditure proposal for €500,000. Each division expects to produce net profits of €40,000 from that investment. Magna's cost of capital is 7% p.a.

Use ROI and RI calculations to evaluate:

- the current performance of each division; and
- which proposal the board should approve if finance limits the decision to a single proposal.

Case study question: Serendipity Ltd

Serendipity is an Internet Service Provider that has a major investment in computer and telecoms equipment, which needs replacement on a regular basis. The company has recently evaluated a $5 million equipment-replacement programme, which has an expected life of five years. The proposal is supported by the data in Table 15.8.

Table 15.8   Serendipity — capital investment evaluation.

In $'000	Year 0	1	2	3	4	5	6
Capital investment	5,000						
Depreciation 20% p.a.		1,000	1,000	1,000	1,000	1,000	
Asset value end of year		4,000	3,000	2,000	1,000	0	
Profit							
Additional income		1,500	2,000	2,500	2,500	2,500	
Additional expenses		−150	−350	−500	−500	−500	
Depreciation		−1,000	−1,000	−1,000	−1,000	−1,000	
Profit		350	650	1,000	1,000	1,000	
Tax @ 35%		−105	−195	−300	−300	−300	
Profit after tax		245	455	700	700	700	
ROI		6.1%	15.2%	35.0%	70.0%	n/a	
Cash flow							
Capital investment	−5,000						
Cash receipts		1,500	2,000	2,500	2,500	2,500	
Additional expenses		−150	−350	−500	−500	−500	
Tax @ 35%			−105	−195	−300	−300	−300
Net cash flow	−5,000	1,350	1,545	1,805	1,700	1,700	−300
Discount rate	8%						
Net present value	$1,225						

As the ROI and NPV look healthy, the investment proposal will be submitted to the board for approval. Prior to the above figures being submitted, you have been asked for your comments.

CHAPTER 16

Budgeting

This chapter explains the budgeting process. It begins with an overview of what budgeting is and the budgeting process, and then uses four case studies to illustrate both profit budgets and cash forecasts for service, retail and manufacturing businesses. The case studies show how sales, cost of sales and expense predictions are converted using inventory requirements into purchase budgets, and how the cash flow forecast links back to the Statement of Cash Flows that was described in Chapter 6. The chapter concludes with a behavioural perspective on budgeting, and a critique of budgeting.

What is budgeting?

Anthony and Govindarajan (2000) described budgets as 'an important tool for effective short-term planning and control' (p. 360). They saw strategic planning (see Chapter 14) as being focused on several years, contrasted with budgeting that focuses on a single year. Strategic planning:

> precedes budgeting and provides the framework within which the annual budget is developed. A budget is, in a sense, a one-year slice of the organization's strategic plan (p. 361).

Anthony and Govindarajan also differentiated the strategic plan from the budget, on the basis that strategy is concerned with product lines while budgets are concerned with responsibility centres. This is an important distinction, as although there is no reason that budgets for products/services cannot be produced (they tend to stop at the contribution margin level, perhaps because of the overhead allocation problem described in

Chapter 13), traditional budgetary reports are produced for responsibility centres and used for divisional performance evaluation, as described in Chapter 15.

A budget is a plan expressed in monetary terms covering a future time period (typically a year broken down into months). Budgets are based on a defined level of activity, either expected sales revenue (if market demand is the limiting factor) or capacity (if that is the limiting factor). While budgets are typically produced annually, rolling budgets add additional months to the end of the period so that there is always a 12-month budget for the business. Alternatively, budgets may be re-forecast part way through a year, e.g. quarterly or six-monthly, to take into account changes since the last budget cycle (hence the common distinction made by organizations between budget and forecast; a forecast usually refers to a revised estimate, or a budgetary update, part-way through the budget period).

Budgeting provides the ability to:

- implement strategy by allocating resources in line with strategic goals;
- coordinate activities and assist in communication between different parts of the organization;
- motivate managers to achieve targets;
- provide a means to control activities; and
- evaluate managerial performance.

The budgeting process

There are four main methods of budgeting: incremental, priority based, zero based and activity based. Each is described below.

Incremental budgets take the previous year's budget as a base and add (or subtract) a percentage to give this year's budget. The assumption is that the historical budget allocation reflected organizational priorities and was rooted in some meaningful justification developed in the past.

Priority-based budgets allocate funds in line with strategy. If priorities change in line with the organization's strategic focus, then budget allocations would follow those priorities, irrespective of the historical allocation. A public-sector version of the priority-based budget is the planning, programming and budgeting system (PPBS) that was developed for the US space programme. Under PPBS, budgets are allocated to projects or programmes rather than to responsibility centres. Priority-based budgets may be responsibility centre based, but will typically be associated with particular projects or programmes. The intention of PPBS and priority-based budgeting systems is to compare costs more readily with benefits by identifying the resources used to obtain desired outcomes.

An amalgam of incremental and priority-based budgets is *priority-based incremental budgeting*. Here, the budget-holder is asked what incremental (or decremental) activities or results would follow if budgets increased (or decreased). This method has the advantage of comparing changes in resources with the resulting costs and benefits.

Zero-based budgeting identifies the costs that are necessary to implement agreed strategies and achieve goals, as if the budget-holder were beginning with a new organizational unit, without any prior history. This method has the advantage of regularly reviewing all the activities that are carried out to see if they are still required, but has the disadvantage of the cost and time needed for such reviews. It is also very difficult to develop a 'greenfields' budget while ignoring 'brownfields' resource allocations.

Activity-based budgeting is associated with activity-based costing (ABC, see Chapter 13). ABC identifies *activities* that consume resources and uses the concept of *cost drivers* (essentially the cause of costs) to allocate costs to products or services according to how much of the resources of the firm they consume. Activity-based budgeting (ABB) follows the same process to develop budgets based on the expected activities and cost drivers to meet sales (or capacity) projections.

Whichever method of budgeting is used, there are two approaches that can be applied. Budgets may be top down or bottom up. *Top-down budgets* begin with the sales forecast and, using the volume of sales, predict inventory levels, staffing and production times within capacity limitations. These are based on bills of materials, labour routings and standard costs (see Chapter 11). For services, the top-down budget is based largely on capacity utilization and staffing levels needed to meet expected demand. In both cases, senior management establishes spending limits within which departments allocate costs to specific line items (salaries, travel, office expenses etc.). Senior managers set the revenue targets and spending limits that they believe are necessary to achieve profits that will satisfy shareholders. *Bottom-up budgets* are developed by the managers of each department based on current spending and agreed plans, which are then aggregated to the corporate total.

Top-down budgets can ignore the problems experienced by operational managers. However, boards of directors often have a clear idea of the sales growth and profit requirement that will satisfy stock market expectations. By contrast, the bottom-up budget may be inadequate in terms of 'bottom-line' profitability or unachievable as a result of either capacity limitations elsewhere in the business or market demand. Therefore, the underlying factors may need to be modified. Consequently, most budgets are the result of a combination of top-down and bottom-up processes. By adopting both methods, budget-holders are given the opportunity to bid for resources (in competition with other budget-holders) within the constraints of the shareholder value focus of the business.

Budgets are based on standard costs (see Chapter 11) for a defined level of sales demand or production activity. The budget cycle – the period each year over which budgets are prepared – may last several months, with budget preparation commencing some months before the commencement of each financial year. The typical budget cycle will follow a common sequence:

1. Identify business objectives.
2. Forecast economic and industry conditions, including competition.
3. Develop detailed sales budgets by market sectors, geographical territories, major customers and product groups.
4. Prepare production budgets (materials, labour and overhead) by responsibility centre managers in order to produce the goods or services needed to satisfy the sales forecast and maintain agreed levels of inventory.
5. Prepare non-production budgets by cost centre.
6. Prepare capital expenditure budgets.
7. Prepare cash forecasts and identify financing requirements.
8. Prepare master budget (profit, financial position and cash flow).
9. Obtain board approval of profitability and financing targets.

Budgeting will take place at the responsibility centre level (see Chapter 15), where good practice involves looking at the opportunities for earning income, the causes of costs and the business processes in use. Bidding for funds for capital expenditure to fund new initiatives or projects is an important part of budgeting because of the need for growth and continual improvement. The process of budgeting is largely based on making informed judgements about:

- how business-wide strategies will affect the responsibility centre;
- the level of demand placed on the business unit and the expected level of activity to satisfy (internal or external) customers;
- the technology and processes used in the business unit to achieve desired productivity levels, based on past experience and anticipated improvements;
- any new initiatives or projects that are planned and require resources;
- the headcount and historic spending by the business unit.

In preparing a budget it is important to carry out a thorough investigation of current performance, i.e. to get behind the numbers. For example, as many costs (particularly in service industries) follow headcount (as we saw in Chapter 12), it is essential that salary and related costs are accurately estimated, and the impact of recruitment, resignation and training is taken into account in cost and productivity calculations.

The complexity of the budget will depend on a number of factors, such as:

- knowledge of past performance;
- understanding of customer demand trends, seasonal factors, competition etc.;
- whether the business is a price leader or price follower (see Chapter 10);
- understanding the drivers of business costs (see Chapter 13);
- the control that managers are able to exercise over expenses.

How well these factors can be understood and modelled using a spreadsheet will depend on the knowledge, skills and time available to the business. Typically, budgets either at the corporate or responsibility centre level will contain a number of subjective judgements of likely future events, customer demand and a number of simplifying assumptions about product/service mix, average prices, cost inflation etc.

Once the budget is agreed in total, the budget needs to be allocated over each month. This should not be simply dividing the budget into 12 equal monthly amounts. The process of profiling or time-phasing the budget is commonly based on the number of working days each month and takes into account seasonal fluctuations etc. Profiling is important because the process of budgetary control (see Chapter 17) relies on an accurate estimation of when revenue will be earned and when costs will be incurred.

The profit budget

The sales, cost of sales and expense budget looks very much like an Income Statement, with substantially more detail for management than would be provided in the financial statements included in the Annual

Report to shareholders. The budgeted profit would be profiled or time-phased over each accounting period (normally 12 monthly budgets) and would be supported by statistical data from which the income, cost of sales and expense projections were made. The case study of Superior Hotel illustrates the profit budget and how the figures in that budget are derived from the supporting statistical data.

Case study 16.1: Superior Hotel — service budget example

Table 16.1 is an example of a budget for a small hotel. It shows some statistics that the Superior Hotel has used for its budget for next year. Both last year's and the current year's figures are shown. For ease of presentation, the budget year has been divided into four quarters and some simplifying assumptions have been made. The hotel capacity is limited to the number of rooms, but in common with the industry rarely achieves full occupancy, although there are substantial variations both during the week and at peak times. The main income driver is the number of rooms occupied, the price able to be charged (which can vary significantly depending on the number of vacant rooms) and the average spend per head on dining, the bar and business services.

Table 16.1   Service budget example: Superior Hotel — budget statistics.

Superior Hotel	Explanation	Last year	Current year	Qtr 1 Jan–Mar	Qtr 2 Apr–June	Qtr 3 Jul–Sep	Qtr 4 Oct–Dec	Next year
Number of bedrooms		80	80	80	80	80	80	
Days per year (per quarter)		365	365	90	91	92	92	365
Rooms available – 365 days/year	No. days × no. rooms	29,200	29,200	7,200	7,280	7,360	7,360	29,200
Average occupancy rate (7-day basis)	Historical	50%	50%	40%	45%	55%	60%	
Average no. rooms occupied	No. rooms × occup. rate	14,600	14,600	2,880	3,276	4,048	4,416	14,620
Average room rate	Historical/planned	$65.00	$70.00	$70.00	$72.00	$75.00	$75.00	
Average spend on dining per room	Historical/planned	$25.00	$25.00	$25.00	$25.00	$25.00	$25.00	
Average spend on bar per room	Historical/planned	$5.00	$5.00	$5.00	$5.00	$5.00	$5.00	
Average spend on business services per room	Historical/planned	$2.00	$2.00	$2.00	$2.00	$2.00	$2.00	

The statistical information, together with estimations of direct costs (food and drink) and expenses, is based on historical experience and expected cost increases. The budget for the year for the Superior Hotel, based on these assumptions, is shown in Table 16.2.

Table 16.2 Service budget example: Superior Hotel budget.

	Explanation	Last year	Current year	Qtr 1 Jan–Mar	Qtr 2 Apr–June	Qtr 3 Jul–Sep	Qtr 4 Oct–Dec	Next year
INCOME								
Rooms	No. of rooms × average spend	949,000	1,022,000	201,600	235,872	303,600	331,200	1,072,272
Dining	No. of rooms × average spend	365,000	365,000	72,000	81,900	101,200	110,400	365,500
Bar	No. of rooms × average spend	73,000	73,000	14,400	16,380	20,240	22,080	73,100
Business services	No. of rooms × average spend	29,200	29,200	5,760	6,552	8,096	8,832	29,240
Total Income		$1,416,200	$1,489,200	$293,760	$340,704	$433,136	$472,512	$1,540,112
EXPENDITURE								
Direct costs								
Food cost of sales	35% of dining income	127,750	127,750	25,200	28,665	35,420	38,640	127,925
Liquor cost of sales	40% of bar income	29,200	29,200	5,760	6,552	8,096	8,832	29,240
Total cost of sales		156,950	156,950	30,960	35,217	43,516	47,472	157,165
Salaries and wages:								
Hotel staff	increases 3% p.a.	212,000	218,360	56,228	56,228	56,228	56,228	224,911
Dining staff	increases 3% p.a.	75,000	77,250	19,892	19,892	19,892	19,892	79,568
Office staff	increases 4% p.a.	35,000	36,400	9,464	9,464	9,464	9,464	37,856
Management	increases 5% p.a.	50,000	52,500	13,781	13,781	13,781	13,781	55,125
Fuel, light and water	Historical/estimate	12,000	14,000	4,000	4,000	4,000	4,000	16,000
Laundry	Historical/estimate	8,000	9,000	2,500	2,500	2,500	2,500	10,000
Cleaning	Historical/estimate	6,000	7,000	2,000	2,000	2,000	2,000	8,000
Repairs and maintenance	Historical/estimate	12,000	20,000	4,000	4,000	4,000	4,000	16,000
Advertising and promotion	Historical/estimate	10,000	12,000	3,000	3,000	3,000	3,000	12,000
Telephones	Historical/estimate	4,000	5,000	1,500	1,500	1,500	1,500	6,000
Consumables	Historical/estimate	5,000	5,000	1,500	1,500	1,500	1,500	6,000
Other expenses	Historical/estimate	6,000	7,000	2,000	2,000	2,000	2,000	8,000
Total expenditure		591,950	620,460	150,825	155,082	163,381	167,337	636,624
Profit before interest and taxes		824,250	868,740	142,935	185,622	269,755	305,175	903,488

A budget for a retailer will require an estimation, separate from the sales forecast, of the level of inventory to be held. This results in a purchasing budget. Similarly, a budget for a manufacturing business will involve developing a production budget (materials, labour and overhead) by cost centre in order to produce the goods or services needed to satisfy the sales forecast and maintain agreed levels of inventory.

The first problem to consider is inventory, which is shown in Case study 16.2.

Case study 16.2: Sports Stores Co-operative Ltd — retail budget example

Sports Stores Co-operative (SSC) is a large retail store selling a range of sportswear. Its anticipated sales levels and expenses for each of the next six months are shown in Table 16.3. In this example, sales and expenses are budgeted for each of the six months. Although there are several hundred different items of inventory and the product mix does fluctuate due to seasonal factors, SSC is only able to budget based on an average sales mix and applies an average cost of sales of 40%.

Table 16.3   Sports stores co-operative sales and expenses estimate.

	Jan	Feb	Mar	Apr	May	Jun	Total
Sales (in £'000)	75	80	85	70	65	90	465
Average cost of sales 40%	30	32	34	28	26	36	186
Gross profit	45	48	51	42	39	54	279
Less expenses:							
Salaries	10	10	10	8	7	10	55
Rent	15	15	15	15	15	15	90
Insurance	1	1	1	1	1	1	6
Depreciation on shop fittings	2	2	2	2	2	2	12
Advertising and promotion	8	8	8	9	9	8	50
Electricity, telephone etc.	5	5	5	5	5	5	30
Total expenses	41	41	41	40	39	41	243
Net profit	4	7	10	2	0	13	36

SSC carries six weeks' inventory, i.e. sufficient inventory to cover six weeks of sales (at cost price). At the end of each month, therefore, the inventory held by SSC will equal all of next month's cost of sales, plus half of the following month's cost of sales. This is shown in Table 16.4.

Table 16.4   Sports Stores Co-operative inventory calculation.

In £'000	Jan	Feb	Mar	Apr	May	Jun
Inventory required at end of month	49	48	41	44	54	53
Inventory at beginning of month	45	49	48	41	44	54
Increase/-decrease in inventory	4	−1	−7	3	10	−1
Sales during month (at cost)	30	32	34	28	26	36
Total purchases	34	31	27	31	36	35

In Table 16.4, for example, the inventory required at the end of February (£48,000) is the cost of sales for March (£34,000) plus half the cost of sales for April (£14,000). In order to budget for the inventory for May and June, SSC needs to estimate its sales for July and August. As this is the peak selling time, the sales are estimated at £90,000 and £85,000, respectively. The cost of sales (based on 40%) is therefore £36,000 for July and £34,000 for August. Using these figures, the inventory required at the end of June (£53,000) is equal to the cost of sales for July (£36,000) and half the cost of sales for August (£17,000).

SSC also needs to know its inventory on 1 January, which is £45,000.

Purchases can then be calculated as:

inventory required at end of month − inventory at beginning of month
= increase (or decrease) in inventory
plus the cost of sales for the current month (which need to be replaced)

Table 16.4 shows the calculation of total purchases. However, it can also be shown in the more usual format introduced in previous chapters. This format is shown in Table 16.5.

Table 16.5   Sports Stores Co-operative closing inventory.

	Jan	Feb	Mar	Apr	May	Jun
Opening inventory	45	49	48	41	44	54
Plus purchases	34	31	27	31	36	35
Less cost of sales	−30	−32	−34	−28	−26	−36
Closing inventory	49	48	41	44	54	53

If we move from the example of a retailer to a manufacturer, the budget becomes more complex as budgeting must account for the conversion process of raw materials into finished goods. The third case study is the production budget for a manufacturing business.

Case study 16.3: Telcon Manufacturing — manufacturing budget example

Telcon is a manufacturer. Its budget is shown in Table 16.6.

Telcon estimates its sales for July and August as 1,400 units per month. Its production budget is based on needing to maintain one month's inventory of finished goods, i.e. the cost of sales for the following month. Its finished goods inventory at the beginning of January is 1,000 units. Table 16.7

Table 16.6   Telcon Manufacturing budget.

In £'000	Jan	Feb	Mar	Apr	May	Jun	Total
Sales units	1,000	1,100	1,200	1,200	1,300	1,300	7,100
Expected selling price	£10	£10	£10	£10	£10	£11	
Revenue	10,000	11,000	12,000	12,000	13,000	14,300	72,300
Cost of sales							
Direct materials @ £4 (2 kg @ £2)	4,000	4,400	4,800	4,800	5,200	5,200	28,400
Direct labour @ £2.50	2,500	2,750	3,000	3,000	3,250	3,250	17,750
Variable overhead @ £1	1,000	1,100	1,200	1,200	1,300	1,300	7,100
Variable costs	7,500	8,250	9,000	9,000	9,750	9,750	53,250
Contribution margin	2,500	2,750	3,000	3,000	3,250	4,550	19,050
Fixed costs (in total)	1,500	1,500	1,500	1,500	1,500	1,500	9,000
Net profit	1,000	1,250	1,500	1,500	1,750	3,050	10,050

Table 16.7   Telcon Manufacturing Production budget.

	Jan	Feb	Mar	Apr	May	Jun	Total
Variable costs per unit	£7.50	£7.50	£7.50	£7.50	£7.50	£7.50	£7.50
Inventory units at end of month	1,100	1,200	1,200	1,300	1,300	1,400	
Inventory units at beginning of month	1,000	1,100	1,200	1,200	1,300	1,300	
Increase in inventory	100	100	0	100	0	100	
Production required							
Units sold	1,000	1,100	1,200	1,200	1,300	1,300	
Increase in inventory	100	100	0	100	0	100	
Total units to be produced	1,100	1,200	1,200	1,300	1,300	1,400	
Production units @ variable cost	8,250	9,000	9,000	9,750	9,750	10,500	56,250
Of which:							
Materials @ £4	4,400	4,800	4,800	5,200	5,200	5,600	30,000
Labour @ £2.50	2,750	3,000	3,000	3,250	3,250	3,500	18,750
Variable overhead @ £1	1,100	1,200	1,200	1,300	1,300	1,400	7,500

shows that the production required of £56,250 is greater than the cost of sales of £53,250 because of the need to produce an additional 400 units at a variable cost of £7.50, i.e. an increase in inventory of £3,000.

However, in order to produce the finished goods, Telcon must also ensure that it has purchased sufficient raw materials. Once again, it wishes to have one month's inventory of raw materials (2 kg of the materials are required for each unit of finished goods). There are 2,000 units of raw materials at the beginning of January. Table 16.8 shows the materials purchases budget.

Table 16.8 Telcon Manufacturing Materials budget.

	Jan	Feb	Mar	Apr	May	Jun	Total
Total units to be produced	1,100	1,200	1,200	1,300	1,300	1,400	
Total kg of materials (units × 2 kg)	2,200	2,400	2,400	2,600	2,600	2,800	
Inventory units at end of month	2,400	2,400	2,600	2,600	2,800	2,800	
Inventory units at beginning of month	2,000	2,400	2,400	2,600	2,600	2,800	
Increase in inventory	400	0	200	0	200	0	
Materials required							
Kg used in production	2,200	2,400	2,400	2,600	2,600	2,800	
Increase in inventory	400	0	200	0	200	0	
Total kg to be purchased	2,600	2,400	2,600	2,600	2,800	2,800	
Purchase cost @ £2/kg	5,200	4,800	5,200	5,200	5,600	5,600	31,600

The purchases budget of £31,600 is more than the materials usage of £30,000 from the production budget because an additional 800 kg of materials is bought at £2 per kg (i.e. £1,600), due to the need to increase raw materials inventory.

Cash forecasting

Once a profit budget has been constructed, it is important to understand the impact on cash flow. The purpose of the cash forecast is to ensure that sufficient cash is available to meet the level of activity planned by the sales and production budgets and to meet all the other cash inflows and outflows of the business. Cash surpluses and deficiencies need to be identified in advance to ensure effective business financing decisions, e.g. raising short-term finance or investing short-term surplus funds.

There is a substantial difference between profits and cash flow (for a detailed explanation see Chapter 6) because of:

- the timing difference between when income is earned and when it is received (i.e. receivables);
- increases or decreases in inventory for both raw materials and finished goods;
- the timing difference between when expenses are incurred and when they are paid (i.e. payables);
- non-cash expenses (e.g. depreciation);

- capital expenditure;
- income tax;
- dividends;
- new borrowings and repayments; and
- proceeds from new share issues and repurchases of shares.

Case study 16.4 provides a cash forecasting example for a retail business.

Case study 16.4: Retail News Group – cash forecasting example

Retail News is a store selling newspapers, magazines, books, confectionery etc. Its budget for six months has been prepared and is shown in Table 16.9.

Table 16.9   Retail News Group budget.

	Jan	Feb	Mar	Apr	May	Jun	Total
Sales	10,000	12,000	15,000	12,000	11,000	9,000	69,000
Cost of sales (40%)	4,000	4,800	6,000	4,800	4,400	3,600	27,600
Gross profit	6,000	7,200	9,000	7,200	6,600	5,400	41,400
Less expenses							
Salaries and wages	2,000	2,000	2,000	2,200	2,200	2,200	12,600
Selling and distribution expenses (7.5%)	750	900	1,125	900	825	675	5,175
Rent	1,000	1,000	1,000	1,000	1,000	1,000	6,000
Electricity, telephone etc.	500	500	500	500	500	500	3,000
Insurance	500	500	500	500	500	500	3,000
Depreciation	500	500	500	500	500	500	3,000
Total expenses	5,250	5,400	5,625	5,600	5,525	5,375	32,775
Net profit	750	1,800	3,375	1,600	1,075	25	8,625

Retail News makes half of its sales in cash and half on credit to business customers, who typically pay their account in the month following that in which the sale is made. Credit sales in December to customers who will pay during January amount to £3,500. Retail News' sales receipts budget is shown in Table 16.10.

Retail News' receivables have increased by £1,000 from £3,500 to £4,500, since 50% of the sales in June (£9,000) will not be received until July.

Table 16.10   Retail News Group sales receipts budget.

	Jan	Feb	Mar	Apr	May	Jun	Total
50% of sales received in cash	5,000	6,000	7,500	6,000	5,500	4,500	34,500
50% of sales on credit – 30-day terms	3,500	5,000	6,000	7,500	6,000	5,500	33,500
Total receipts	8,500	11,000	13,500	13,500	11,500	10,000	68,000

As in the previous case studies we also need to determine the purchases budget for Retail News, which needs inventory equal to one month's sales (at cost price) at the end of each month. The inventory at the beginning of January is £4,500. The sales and cost of sales estimated for July are £12,000 and £4,800, respectively. The purchases budget is shown in Table 16.11.

Table 16.11   Retail News Group purchase budget.

	Jan	Feb	Mar	Apr	May	Jun	Total
Inventory at end of month	4,800	6,000	4,800	4,400	3,600	4,800	4,800
Inventory at beginning of month	4,500	4,800	6,000	4,800	4,400	3,600	4,500
Increase/-decrease in inventory	300	1,200	−1,200	−400	−800	1,200	300
Sales during month (at cost)	4,000	4,800	6,000	4,800	4,400	3,600	27,600
Total purchases	4,300	6,000	4,800	4,400	3,600	4,800	27,900

Purchases are £27,900 compared with a cost of sales of £27,600, because inventory has increased by £300 (from £4,500 to £4,800). However, purchases are on credit and Retail News has arranged with its suppliers to pay on 60-day terms. Therefore, for example, purchases in January will be paid for in March. Retail News will pay for its November purchases in January (£3,800) and its December purchases in February (£3,500). The creditor payments budget is shown in Table 16.12.

Table 16.12   Retail News Group supplier payments budget.

	Jan	Feb	Mar	Apr	May	Jun	Total
Payment on 60-day terms	3,800	3,500	4,300	6,000	4,800	4,400	26,800

Retail News payables have increased by £1,100 from £7,300 (£3,800 for November and £3,500 for December) to £8,400 (£3,600 for May and £4,800 for June).

We can now construct the cash forecast for Retail News using the sales receipts budget and creditor payments budget. We also need to identify the timing of cash flows for all expenses. In this case, we determine that salaries and wages, selling and distribution costs and rent are all paid monthly, as those expenses are incurred. Electricity and telephone are paid quarterly in arrears in March and June. The annual insurance premium of £6,000 is paid in January. Income tax of £5,000 is due in April. As we know, depreciation is an expense that does not involve any cash flow.

However, the business also has a number of other cash payments that do not affect profit. These non-operating payments are:

- capital expenditure of £2,500 committed in March;
- £3,000 of dividends due to be paid in June;
- a loan repayment of £1,000 due in February.

The opening bank balance of Retail News is £2,500. The cash forecast in Table 16.13 shows the total cash position.

Table 16.13   Retail News Group cash forecast.

	Jan	Feb	Mar	Apr	May	Jun	Total
Receipts from sales	8,500	11,000	13,500	13,500	11,500	10,000	68,000
Payments to suppliers	3,800	3,500	4,300	6,000	4,800	4,400	26,800
Salaries and wages	2,000	2,000	2,000	2,200	2,200	2,200	12,600
Selling and distribution expenses	750	900	1,125	900	825	675	5,175
Rent	1,000	1,000	1,000	1,000	1,000	1,000	6,000
Electricity, telephone etc.			1,500			1,500	3,000
Insurance	6000						6,000
Total payments	13,550	7,400	9,925	10,100	8,825	9,775	59,575
Operating cash flow	−5,050	3,600	3,575	3,400	2,675	225	8,425
Income tax paid				5,000			5,000
Capital expenditure			2,500				2,500
Dividends paid						3,000	3,000
Loan repayments		1,000					1,000
							0
Net cash flow	−5,050	2,600	1,075	−1,600	2,675	−2,775	−3,075
Opening bank balance	2,500	−2,550	50	1,125	−475	2,200	
Closing bank balance	−2,550	50	1,125	−475	2,200	−575	

In summary, the bank balance has reduced from an asset of £2,500 to a liability (bank overdraft) of £575 due to a net cash outflow of £3,075. The main issue here is that, in anticipation of the overdrawn position of the bank account in January, April and June, Retail News needs to make arrangements with its bankers to extend its facility.

One last thing remains, which is for Retail News to produce a cash flow forecast. This is shown in Table 16.14.

Table 16.14   Retail News Group Statement of Cash Flows (cash forecast).

Operating profit		**£8,625**
Plus non-cash expense		
Depreciation		3,000
		11,625
Less income tax paid		5,000
Less increase in working capital –		
Receivables	1,000	
Inventory	300	
Insurance prepayment	3,000	
	4,300	
Less increase in payables	1,100	
Net increase in working capital		3,200
Cash flow from operations		3,425
Cash flow from investing activities		
Capital expenditure		2,500
Cash flow from financing activities		
Dividend	3,000	
Loan repayment	1,000	4,000
Decrease in cash		£3,075

Note that Table 16.14 follows the same format as for the Statement of Cash Flows in Chapter 6. The budgeting process will normally produce a forecast Income Statement, Statement of Financial Position, and Statement of Cash Flows for a company as part of the budget process. Ratio analysis (Chapter 7) may even be performed on the forecast financial statements to understand the likely impact of future performance on ratio targets, trends and benchmark comparisons.

A behavioural perspective on budgeting

Although the tools of budgeting and cash forecasting are well developed and made easier by the wide use of spreadsheet software, the difficulty of budgeting is in predicting the volume of sales for the business, especially the sales mix between different products or services and the timing of income and expenses. This is because there is uncertainty in terms of economic conditions, customer demand and competitor strategies.

As budget targets are often linked to managerial rewards (promotion, bonuses, share options, etc.) budgets result in behavioural consequences that are unintended, and often dysfunctional. Buckley and McKenna (1972) emphasized the importance of participation in the budget process; frequent communications and information flow throughout the organization; inclusion of the budget in decisions about salary, bonuses and career promotion; and clear communication by accountants to non-accountants as elements of 'good budgeting practice.' However, Buckley and McKenna also recognized the impact of setting difficult budget targets and the introduction of bias.

Lowe and Shaw (1968) carried out research into sales budgeting in a retail chain, in which annual budgeting was an 'internal market by which resources are allocated' (p. 304) in which managers had to cooperate and compete. Lowe and Shaw identified three sources of forecasting error: unpredicted changes in the environment; inaccurate assessment of the effects of predicted changes; and forecasting bias. Lowe and Shaw examined the sources of bias: the reward system; the influence of recent practice and norms; and the insecurity of managers, arguing that bias may be a common phenomenon as in 'the desire to please superiors in a competitive managerial hierarchy' (p. 312). They also explained counter bias as 'the attempt by other managers to eliminate that part of a forecast which stems from the personal interest of the forecaster' (p. 312).

Other behavioural problems have been recognized in relation to the budget process. One is with the aggregation of divisional budgets into a corporate budget. Operational managers often prepare their budgets with a degree of deliberate bias, e.g. understating sales projections and overstating expense projections in the hope that either: (i) if head office adjusts these budgets they will fall into line with what the manager wanted as a target in the first place; and/or (ii) managerial performance is perceived to be much better if the budget target is exceeded, hence the tendency by managers to set more easily achievable targets than might be set by head office. Berry and Otley (1975) explored the estimation of budget figures made by individuals at one hierarchical level in an organization, and the coupling of these estimates to those made at a higher level to show the resulting bias in estimating that takes place. Otley and Berry (1979) argued that quite mild deviations from 'expectation budgets' at the unit level can produce severe distortions when budgets are aggregated to the organizational level.

Reflecting interpretive or critical perspectives, budgets are one of the main sources of power in organizations, as a result of the influence of accountants over budgetary allocations. Czarniawska-Joerges and Jacobsson (1989) depicted budgets as:

> a ritual of reason; budgets are presented according to and conforming with prevailing norms of rationality. Budgeting is also a language of consensus; there are several mechanisms in budgetary processes for reducing the level and amount of conflict (pp. 29–30).

Covaleski and Dirsmith (1988) argued that budgeting systems help to represent vested interests in political processes and maintain existing power relationships. In their case study of the introduction of diagnostic-related costing in hospitals, Covaleski *et al.* (1993) found that case-mix accounting systems 'appear also to determine power by redistributing that power from physician to administrator' (p. 73). Czarniawska-Joerges and Jacobsson (1989) depicted budgets as: 'a symbolic performance rather than a decision-making process' (p. 29).

A final word in relation to budgeting concerns risk. Collier and Berry (2002) identified risk as being managed in four different domains: financial, operational, political and personal. These were the result of the unique circumstances, history and technology in different organizations that had led to different ideas about risk. These domains of risk revealed how participants in the budgeting process influenced the content of the budget through their unique perspectives. Collier and Berry distinguished the content of budgets from the process of budgeting and contrasted three types of budget. In the risk-modelled process, there was an explicit use of formal probability models to assess the effect of different consequences over a range of different assumptions. In the risk-considered process, informal sensitivity (or what-if) analysis is used to produce (for example) high, medium and low consequences of different assumptions. The risk-excluded budget manages risk outside the budget process, and the budget relies on a single expectation of performance. Collier and Berry found that little risk modelling was used in practice, and that although risk was considered during the budgeting process, the content of the budget documents largely excluded risk.

A critical perspective: beyond budgeting?

Budgeting has been criticized in recent years because it can disempower the workforce, discourage information sharing and slow the response to market developments. Hope and Fraser (2003) suggested that budgets should be replaced with a combination of financial and non-financial measures, with performance being judged against world-class benchmarks. Business units could also measure their performance against comparable units in the same organization. This, it is argued, shifts the focus from short-term profits to improving competitive position over time.

The Beyond Budgeting Round Table (www.bbrt.co.uk; www.bbrt.org) was established over 10 years ago to find steering mechanisms that could replace budgeting and help to make organizations more adaptive to change. The membership includes (at the time of writing) American Express, John Lewis Partnership, Sydney Water, Telekom Malaysia and Toyota. BBRT has identified 10 reasons why budgets cause problems. They:

- are time consuming and expensive;
- provide poor value to users;
- fail to focus on shareholder value;
- are too rigid and prevent fast response;
- protect rather than reduce costs;
- stifle product and strategy innovation;
- focus on sales targets rather than customer satisfaction;
- are divorced from strategy;
- reinforce a dependency culture;
- can lead to unethical behaviour.

Compared with the traditional management model, 'beyond budgeting' is a more adaptive way of managing. In place of fixed annual plans and budgets that tie managers to predetermined actions, targets are reviewed regularly and based on stretch goals linked to performance against world-class benchmarks and prior periods. Instead of a traditional hierarchical and centralised leadership, 'beyond budgeting' enables decision making and performance accountability to be devolved to line managers and fosters a culture of personal responsibility. This, it is argued, leads to increased motivation, higher productivity and better customer service.

A strong view of the need for change has been presented by the Beyond Budgeting Round Table:

> Budgeting, as most corporations practice it, should be abolished. That may sound like a radical proposition, but it is merely the final (and decisive) action in a long running battle to change organizations from centralized hierarchies to devolved networks. Most of the other building blocks are in place. Firms have invested huge sums in quality programs, IT networks, process reengineering, and a range of management tools including EVA, balanced scorecards, and activity accounting. But they are unable to establish the new order because the budget, and the command and control culture it supports, remains predominant (www.bbrt.org).

The origin of the Beyond Budgeting movement was a case study by Jan Wallander of Swedish bank Handelsbanken. Case study 16.5 providers a summary of Wallender's paper.

Case study 16.5: Svenska Handelsbanken — is budgeting necessary?

Jan Wallander was an executive director of Handelsbanken. He was appointed to the role when the bank, the largest commercial bank in Sweden, faced a crisis. Handelsbanken's goal was to be the most profitable bank in Sweden and its strategy was to be radically decentralized with nearly all lending authority independent of Head Office. Although at the time Swedish banks did not use budgets, Handelsbanken had started to install a sophisticated budgeting system. Wallander (1999) was very critical of budgeting. He argued:

> You can make forecasts very complicated by putting a lot of variables into them and using sophisticated techniques for evaluating the time series you have observed and used in your work. However, if you see through all this technical paraphernalia you will find that there are a few basic assumptions which determine the outcome of the forecast (p. 408).

The accuracy of the budget therefore depended on how accurate the assumptions were. Wallander argued that there were two reasons to abandon budgeting:

1. If there is economic stability and the business will continue as usual, we use previous experience in order to budget. Wallander argued that we do not need an intricate budgeting system in this case, because people will continue working as they presently are. Even when conditions are not normal, the expectation is that they will return to normal.
2. If events arise that challenge economic stability then budgets will not reflect this, because, Wallander says, 'we have no ability to foresee something of which we have no previous experience' (p. 411).

Wallander concluded that traditional budgeting is 'an outmoded way of controlling and steering a company. It is a cumbersome way of reaching conclusions which are either commonplace or wrong' (p. 419).

Wallander did not reject planning but differentiated the need to plan from the need to prepare budgets. He argued that it is important to have an 'economic model' that establishes the basic relationships in the company, such as the ability to plan production. Wallander used the analogy of making and selling cars: 'If they want to be able to produce X cars a year from now, they have to figure out when they have to place their orders with their subcontractors. In the course of that planning activity they have to make a lot of medium-term forecasts about demand, prices etc. Their natural ambition in this context is to place their orders as late as possible and thus not bind their hands more than necessary and keep their inventories as low as possible. This type of planning is something that is going on all the year round and has nothing to do with the annual budget' (Wallander, 1999, p. 416).

To support this business model, Handelsbanken had an information system that was focused on the information needed to influence actual behaviour. It incorporated both financial and 'Balanced Scorecard' measures at the profit centre level, and performance was benchmarked both externally and internally. Because actual performance could not be compared with budget, the real target was not in absolute monetary terms but a relative one, a return on capital better than what other businesses were achieving, not just in the banking industry but in other industries as well. Handelsbanken thus adopted a true shareholder value model.

The bank rewarded its staff through a profit-sharing scheme, with the profit share dependent on the profitability of the bank relative to the other Swedish banks. Interestingly, the share of the employees in the profits of the bank was only paid to them when they retired, which encouraged them to remain with the bank and to continually improve performance.

Despite its abandonment of budgeting, Handelsbanken remained a very successful bank. Wallander concluded, 'abandoning budgeting, which was an essential part of the changes, had no adverse effect on the performance of the bank compared to other banks, which all installed budgeting systems during the period' (p. 407).

Source: Wallander, J. (1999). Budgeting – an unnecessary evil. *Scandinavian Journal of Management*, *15*, 405–21.

Conclusion

In this chapter we have seen budgeting as an extension of the strategy process. We described various approaches to budgeting and the mechanics of the budgeting cycle. Through a series of four case studies we explored budgeting for a service, retail and manufacturing organization and introduced cash forecasting. The chapter concluded with a behavioural perspective on budgeting, and by drawing on the example of the 'Beyond Budgeting' movement and the case of Handelsbanken we questioned whether budgets are necessary at all. The assumptions behind the production of budgets are important for planning purposes, but crucial when managers are held accountable for achieving budget targets. This is the process of budgetary control, which is the subject of Chapter 17.

References

Anthony, R. N. and Govindarajan, V. (2000). *Management Control Systems* (10th edn). New York: McGraw-Hill Irwin.

Berry, A. and Otley, D. (1975). The aggregation of estimates in hierarchical organizations. *Journal of Management Studies*, May, 175–93.

Buckley, A. and McKenna, E. (1972). Budgetary control and business behaviour. *Accounting and Business Research*, Spring, 137–50.

Collier, P. M. and Berry, A.J. (2002). Risk in the process of budgeting. *Management Accounting Research*, 13, 273–97.

Covaleski, M. A. and Dirsmith, M. W. (1988). The use of budgetary symbols in the political arena: an historically informed field study. *Accounting, Organizations and Society*, 13(1), 1–24.

Covaleski, M. A., Dirsmith, M. W. and Michelman, J.E. (1993). An institutional theory perspective on the DRG framework, case-mix accounting systems and health-care organizations. *Accounting, Organizations and Society*, 18(1), 65–80.

Czarniawska-Joerges, B. and Jacobsson, B. (1989). Budget in a cold climate. *Accounting, Organizations and Society*, 14(1/2), 29–39.

Hope, J. and Fraser, R. (2003). *Beyond Budgeting: How Managers Can Break Free from the Annual Performance Trap*. Boston, MA: Harvard Business School Press.

Lowe, E. A. and Shaw, R. W. (1968). An analysis of managerial biasing: evidence from a company's budgeting process. *Journal of Management Studies*, October, 304–15.

Otley, D. and Berry, A. (1979). Risk distribution in the budgetary process. *Accounting and Business Research*, 9(36), 325–7.

Wallander, J. (1999). Budgeting – an unnecessary evil. *Scandinavian Journal of Management*, 15, 405–21.

Questions

16.1   April Co. receives payment from customers for credit sales as follows:

30% in the month of sale.
60% in the month following sale.
8% in the second month following the sale.
2% become bad debts and are never collected.

The following sales are expected:

January	£100,000
February	£120,000
March	£110,000

- Calculate how much will be received in March.
- What is the value of receivables at the end of March?

16.2   Creassos Co. was formed in July 2010 with €20,000 of capital. €7,500 of this was used to purchase equipment. The owner budgeted for the following:

	Sales	Receipts from customers	Purchases	Payments to suppliers	Wages	Other expenses
July	20,000	—	8,000	5,000	3,000	2,000
Aug	30,000	20,000	15,000	10,000	4,000	2,000
Sept	40,000	30,000	20,000	20,000	5,000	3,000

Wages and other expenses are paid in cash. In addition to the above, depreciation is €2,400 per annum. No inventory is held by the company.

- Calculate the profit for each of the three months from July to September and in total.
- Calculate the cash balance at the end of each month.
- Prepare a Statement of Financial Position at the end of September.

16.3   Highjinks Corporation's sales department has estimated revenue of $2,250,000 for East Division. 60% of this will be achieved in the first half year and 40% in the remaining half year. Variable operating costs are typically 30% of revenue and fixed operating costs are expected to be $35,000 per month for the first six months and £40,000 per month thereafter.

The selling expense recharged from the sales department to East Division is $15,000 per month for the first half year, thereafter $12,000. Salaries are $25,000 per month, depreciation is $5,000 per month and council rates $8,000 per month. Light, heat and power are expected to cost $3,000 per month for the first half year, falling to $2,000 thereafter.

- Construct a budget for East Division for the year based on the above figures.
- What can you say about the rate of gross profit?

16.4   Griffin Metals Co. has provided the following data.

Anticipated volumes (assume production equals sales each quarter):

Quarter 1	100,000 tonnes
Quarter 2	110,000 tonnes
Quarter 3	105,000 tonnes
Quarter 4	120,000 tonnes

The selling price is expected to be £300 per tonne for the first six months and £310 per tonne thereafter. Variable costs per tonne are predicted as £120 in the first quarter, £125 in the second and third quarters, and £130 in the fourth quarter.

Fixed costs (in £'000 per quarter) are estimated as follows:

Salaries and wages	£3,000 for the first half year, increasing by 10% for the second half year
Maintenance	£1,500
Council rates	£400
Insurance	£120
Electricity	£1,000
Depreciation	£5,400
Other costs	£2,500 in the first and fourth quarters, £1,800 in the second and third quarters
Interest	£600
Capital expenditure	£6,500 in the first quarter, £2,000 in the second quarter, £1,000 in the third quarter and £9,000 in the fourth quarter
Dividend payment	£10,000 in the third quarter
Debt repayments	£1,000 in the first quarter, £5,000 in the second quarter, £4,000 in the third quarter and £3,000 in the fourth quarter

Griffin has asked you to produce a profit budget and a cash forecast for the year (in four quarters) using the above data.

16.5 Mega Stores is a chain of 125 retail outlets selling clothing under the strong Mega brand. Its sales have increased from €185 million to €586 million over the last five years. The company's gross profit is currently 83% of sales, giving it a little more than 20% mark-up on the cost of goods and retail store running costs. Corporate overhead is €19 million and the operating profit is €81 million.

Mega Stores' finance director has produced a budget, which has been approved by the Board of directors, to increase sales by 35% next year and to improve operating profit margin to 15% of sales. Corporate overheads will be contained at €22 million.

The strategy determined by the marketing director is to continue expanding sales by winning market share from competitors and by increasing the volume of sales to existing customers. It aims to increase use of social marketing to customers, and its television advertising. The company also intends to open new stores to extend its geographic coverage.

Mega Stores also plans to improve its cost effectiveness by continuing its investments in major regional warehouses and distribution facilities servicing its national network of stores, together with upgrading its information systems to reduce inventory and delivery lead times to its retail network.

You have been asked to produce a report for the senior management team identifying the financial information that is required to support the business strategy. You are also asked to identify any non-financial issues arising from the strategy.

16.6 Placibo Ltd has estimated the sales units and selling prices for its products for each of the next four months. This information is shown in Table 16.15.

Placibo's average cost of sales is 30% of revenue. It incurs overhead costs of $55,000 per month, of which $25,000 per month is depreciation. Placibo receives payment from its customers in

Table 16.15 Placibo Ltd.

	June	July	August	September
Forecast sales units	20,000	20,000	22,000	25,000
Selling price per unit	$4.25	$4.50	$4.50	$4.75

the month following the month of sale, and it pays its suppliers in the month following the recognition of the cost of sales in the Income Statement. Overheads are paid in the same month in which they are incurred.

a. Prepare a budgeted Income Statement for each of the three months July–September.
b. Prepare a cash forecast for each of the three months July–September.

Case study question: Carsons Stores Ltd

Carsons is a retail store that has given the task of preparing its budget for next year to a trainee accountant. The budget is prepared in quarters. Table 16.16 is the profit budget report produced by the trainee.

Table 16.16 Carsons Stores Ltd.

In £'000	Quarter 1	Quarter 2	Quarter 3	Quarter 4	Year total
Sales	100	110	110	120	440
Cost of sales	40	44	44	48	176
Gross profit	60	66	66	72	264
Expenses:					
Salaries	10	10	10	10	40
Rent	20	20	20	20	80
Depreciation	5	5	5	5	20
Promotional expenses	10	11	11	12	44
Administration expenses	5	5	5	5	20
Total expenses	50	51	51	52	204
Net profit	10	15	15	20	60

A cash forecast has also been prepared (see Table 16.17).

Table 16.17 Carsons Stores Ltd.

In £'000	Quarter 1	Quarter 2	Quarter 3	Quarter 4	Year total
Cash inflow from sales	100	110	110	120	440
Purchases		40	44	44	128
Expenses	50	51	51	52	204
Capital expenditure		20			20
Income tax			20		20
Dividends		15	20	25	60
Cash outflow	50	126	135	121	432
Net cash flow	50	−16	−25	−1	8
Cumulative cash flow	50	34	9	8	

What are the questions you would want to ask the trainee accountant in order to satisfy yourself that the budget was realistic and achievable? Can you identify any errors that have been made in the budget or cash forecast? If so, make any corrections that you think are necessary and comment on any problems you have identified.

CHAPTER 17

Budgetary Control

Following from budgeting in Chapter 16, in this chapter we describe the process of budgetary control that takes place in organizations to manage performance in line with targets. We demonstrate variance analysis by using flexible budgets. An extended case study is used to show how variances can be identified for sales and costs, separately identifying price and efficiency variances for costs that need to be investigated by operational managers as part of the feedback process. This chapter also contains a critique of variance analysis in the modern business environment although effective management of cost remains a focus for all managers. The chapter concludes with the application of different perspectives to the management accounting techniques covered in Chapters 14 to 17.

What is budgetary control?

Budgetary control is concerned with ensuring that actual financial results are in line with targets. An important part of this *feedback process* (see Chapter 4) is investigating variations between actual results and budgeted results and taking appropriate corrective action.

Budgetary control provides a yardstick for comparison and isolates problems by focusing on variances, which provide an early warning to managers. Buckley and McKenna (1972) argued:

> The sinews of the budgeting process . . . are the influencing of management behaviour by setting agreed performance standards, the evaluation of results and feedback to management in anticipation of corrective action where necessary (p. 137).

Budgetary control is typically exercised at the level of each responsibility centre. Management reports show, for each line item, the budget expenditure, usually for both the current accounting period and the year to date. The report will also show the actual income and expenditure and a variance.

A typical actual versus budget financial report is shown in Table 17.1.

Table 17.1   Actual v. budget financial report.

	Budget for this period	**Actual for this period**	**Budget for the year to date**	**Actual for the year to date**	**Variance**
Materials	40,000	45,000	100,000	96,000	4,000 Fav
Labour	21,000	19,000	30,000	32,000	2,000 Adv
Energy	9,000	7,000	40,000	38,000	2,000 Fav
Other costs	10,000	2,500	50,000	55,000	5,000 Adv
Total	€80,000	€73,500	€220,000	€221,000	€1,000 Adv

There are two types of variance:

- A favourable variance occurs where income exceeds budget and/or expenses are lower than budget.
- An adverse variance occurs where income is less than budget and/or expenses are greater than budget.

It is important to look both at the current period, which in Table 17.1 shows a total underspend of €6,500 (budget of £80,000 less actual spending of €73,500), and the year to date, which shows an overspend of €1,000.

If we look more closely at a simple example of a variance report for one cost item, we see what is reported as a favourable variance:

Budget	Actual	Variance
$80,000	$73,500	$6,500 Favourable

The weakness of traditional management reports for budgetary control is that the business may not be comparing like with like. For example, if the business volume is lower than budgeted, then it follows that any variable costs should (in total) be lower than budgeted. Conversely, if business volume is higher than budget, variable costs should (in total) be higher than budget. In many management reports, the distinction between variable and fixed costs (see Chapter 10) is not made and it becomes very difficult to compare costs incurred at one level of activity with budgeted costs at a different level of activity and to make meaningful judgements about managerial performance.

Flexible budgeting

Flexible budgets provide a better basis for investigating variances than the original budget, because the volume of production may differ from that planned. If the actual activity level is different to that budgeted, comparing revenue and/or costs at different (actual and budget) levels of activity will produce meaningless figures. A flexible budget is a budget that is *flexed*, that is standard costs per unit are applied to the actual level of business activity. A comparison is then made, and a variance calculated, between the actual costs at the actual level of activity, and the budgeted (i.e. standard) costs that should apply at the actual level of activity.

Flexible budgets take into account variations in the volume of activity. Using the same example, additional information shows that costs are budgeted at $2 per unit for 40,000 units but actual costs are $2.10 for 35,000 units. We can show the standard actual versus budget report more clearly as:

Budget	Actual	Variance
$80,000	$73,500	$6,500 Favourable
40,000 @ $2	35,000 @ $2.10	

However, the favourable variance in this example disguises the fact that fewer units were produced. A flexible budget adjusts the original budget to the actual level of activity. The variance under a flexed budget would then show:

Original budget	Flexed budget	Actual	Variance
$80,000	$70,000	$73,500	$3,500 Adverse
40,000 @ $2	35,000 @ $2	35,000 @ $2.10	

This is a more meaningful comparison, because the manager responsible for cost control has spent more per unit and should not have this responsibility negated by the effect of a reduced volume, which may have been outside that manager's control. Separately, the adverse effect of the volume variance – the difference between the original and flexed budgets – is shown as 5,000 units @ $2 or $10,000. This may be controllable by a different manager. As can be seen by comparing the two styles of presentation, there is still a $6,500 favourable variance, but the flexed budget identifies the two separate components of this variance:

- $10,000 favourable variance (in terms of cost) because of the reduction in volume from 40,000 to 35,000 units at $2 each. This is offset by
- $3,500 adverse variance because the 35,000 units produced each cost 10p more than the standard cost.

Variance analysis

An important part of the feedback process (see Chapter 4) is variance analysis. Variance analysis involves comparing actual performance against plan, investigating the causes of the variance and taking corrective action to ensure that targets are achieved. Variance analysis needs to be carried out for each responsibility centre, product/service and for each line item.

The steps involved in variance analysis are:

1. Ascertain the budget and phasing (see Chapter 16) for each period.
2. Report the actual spending.
3. Determine the variance between budget and actual (and determine whether it is either favourable or adverse).
4. Investigate why the variance occurred.
5. Take corrective action.

Not only adverse variances need to be investigated. Favourable variances provide a learning opportunity so that good practice can be repeated. The questions that need to be asked as part of variance analysis are:

- Is the variance significant?
- Is it early or late in the year?
- Is it likely to be repeated?
- Can it be explained (and understood)?
- Is it controllable?

Only significant variations need to be investigated. However, what is significant can be interpreted differently by different people. Which is more significant, for example, a 5% variation on £10,000 (£500) or a 25% variation on £1,000 (£250)? The significance of the variation may be either an absolute amount or a percentage. A variance later in the year will be more difficult to correct, so variances should be detected for corrective action as soon as they occur. Similarly, a one-off variance requires a single corrective action, but a variance that will continue requires more drastic action. A variance that can be understood can be corrected, but if the causes of the variance are not understood or are outside the manager's control, it may be difficult to correct and control in the future.

Explanations need to be sought in relation to different types of variance:

- sales variances: price and quantity of products/services sold;
- material variances: price and quantity of raw materials used;
- labour variances: wage rate and efficiency/productivity;
- overhead variances: spending and efficiency.

The following case study provides an example of variance analysis.

Case study 17.1: Wood's Furniture Co. — variance analysis example

Wood's Furniture has produced a budget versus actual report, which is shown in Table 17.2. The difference between budget and actual is an adverse variance of £16,200. However, the firm's accountant has produced a flexed budget to assist in carrying out a more meaningful variance analysis. This is shown in Table 17.3.

Table 17.2 Budget v. actual report.

	Budget	Actual	Variance
Sales units	10,000	9,000	
Selling price	£170	£175	
Revenue	£1,700,000	£1,575,000	£125,000
Variable costs			
Materials:			
Plastic	30,000	26,600	3,400
Metal	20,000	21,000	1,000
Wood	30,000	26,600	3,400
Labour:			
Skilled	900,000	838,750	61,250
Semi-skilled	225,000	195,000	30,000
Variable overhead	300,000	283,250	16,750
Total variable costs	1,505,000	1,391,200	113,800
Contribution	195,000	183,800	11,200
Fixed costs	125,000	130,000	−5,000
Net profit	£70,000	£53,800	£16,200

Table 17.3 Flexible budget.

	Original budget	Flexed budget	Actual	Variance
Sales units	10,000	9,000	9,000	
Selling price				
Revenue	1,700,000	1,530,000	1,575,000	45,000
Variable costs				
Materials:				
Plastic	30,000	27,000	26,600	400
Metal	20,000	18,000	21,000	−3,000
Wood	30,000	27,000	26,600	400
Labour:				
Skilled	900,000	810,000	838,750	−28,750
Semi-skilled	225,000	202,500	195,000	7,500
Variable overhead	300,000	270,000	283,250	−13,250
Total variable costs	1,505,000	1,354,500	1,391,200	−36,700
Contribution	195,000	175,500	183,800	8,300
Fixed costs	125,000	125,000	130,000	−5,000
Net profit	£70,000	£50,500	£53,800	£3,300

The flexed budget shows a favourable variance of £3,300 compared to the variance on the budget v. actual report. In order to undertake a detailed variance analysis, we need some additional information, which the accountant has produced in Table 17.4.

Table 17.4   Variance report.

	Std cost per unit	Original budget	Std cost per unit	Flexed budget	Usage qty	Act. cost per unit	Actual	Variance
Sales units		10,000		9,000			9,000	
Selling price	£170		£170			£175		
Revenue		£1,700,000		£1,530,000			£1,575,000	£45,000
Variable costs								
Materials:								
Plastic	2 @ £1.50	30,000	2 @ £1.50	27,000	19,000	£1.40	26,600	400
Metal	1 @ £2	20,000	1 @ £2	18,000	10,000	£2.10	21,000	−3,000
Wood	4 @ £0.75	30,000	4 @ £0.75	27,000	38,000	£0.70	26,600	400
Labour:								
Skilled	6 @ £15	900,000	6 @ £15	810,000	55,000	£15.25	838,750	−28,750
Semi-skilled	3 @ £7.50	225,000	3 @ £7.50	202,500	26,000	£7.50	195,000	7,500
Variable overhead	6 @ £5	300,000	6 @ £5	270,000	55,000	£5.15	283,250	−13,250
Total variable costs	£150.50	1,505,000	£150.50	1,354,500		£154.58	1,391,200	−36,700
Contribution	£19.50	195,000	£19.50	175,500		£20.42	183,800	8,300
Fixed costs		125,000		125,000			130,000	−5,000
Net profit		£70,000		£50,500			£53,800	3,300

Sales variance

The sales variance is used to evaluate the performance of the sales team. There are two sales variances for which the sales department is responsible:

- The sales price variance is the difference between the actual price and the standard price for the actual quantity sold.
- The sales quantity variance is the difference between the budget and actual quantity at the standard margin (i.e. the difference between the budget price and the standard variable costs), because it would be inappropriate to hold sales managers accountable for production efficiencies and inefficiencies.

The sales price variance is the difference between the flexed budget and the actual sales revenue, i.e. £45,000. This is calculated in Table 17.5. The variance is favourable because the business has sold 9,000 units at an additional £5 each.

Table 17.5 Sales price variance.

Actual quantity	9,000	
@ actual price	£175	£1,575,000
Actual quantity	9,000	
@ standard price	£170	£1,530,000
Favourable price variance		£45,000

The sales quantity variance is the difference between the original budget profit of £70,000 and the flexed budget profit of £50,500 – an unfavourable variance of £19,500. This is calculated in Table 17.6. The variance is unfavourable because 1,000 units budgeted have not been sold and the standard margin for each of those units was £19.50 (selling price of £170 less variable costs of £150.50), resulting in a lost contribution of £19,500.

Table 17.6 Sales quantity variance.

Budget quantity	10,000	
−Actual quantity	9,000	1,000
@ standard margin	£19.50	
Unfavourable quantity variance		£19,500

It is important to note that the sales mix can affect the quantity and price variances significantly. Therefore, a sales variance analysis should reflect the budget and actual sales mix.

We have now accounted for the variance between the original budget and the flexed budget (i.e. due to volume of units sold) and between the revenue in the flexed budget and the actual (i.e. due to the difference in selling price). We now have to look at the variances between the costs in the flexed budget and the actual costs incurred.

Cost variances

Each cost variance – for materials, labour and overhead – can be split into two types, a price variance and a usage or efficiency variance. This is because each type of variance may be the responsibility of a different manager. Price variances occur because the cost per unit of resources (labour, material, etc.) is higher or lower than the standard cost. Usage variances occur because the actual quantity of labour or materials used is higher or lower than the standard cost contained in the labour routing or bill of materials (these concepts were covered in Chapter 11). The relationship between price and usage variances is shown in Figure 17.1.

The variances for material, labour or overheads are calculated as follows:

- The usage variance is the difference between the standard and actual quantity, while holding the standard price constant, i.e. it tells us, at the standard or expected price, the excess material, labour or variable overhead consumed in producing the actual quantity of finished goods.
- The price variance is the difference between the standard price and the actual price, while holding the actual quantity of material or labour used constant, i.e. it tells us, given the actual quantity of resource used, the additional price or rate paid in producing the actual quantity of finished goods.

In using Figure 17.1, it is important to note that the 'standard quantity' refers to the standard quantity of materials or labour multiplied by the *actual quantity of finished goods*, i.e. it is based on the flexible budget.

Figure 17.1   Price and usage variances.

Materials variance

By using a flexed budget, we can see that the total materials variance is £2,200 unfavourable, as shown in Table 17.7. However, we need to consider the price and usage variances for *each type* of material, because the reasons for the variance and the corrective action may be different for each.

Table 17.7   Materials variance.

	Std cost per unit	Original budget	Std cost per unit	Flexed budget	Usage qty	Act. cost per unit	Actual	Variance
Plastic		2 @ £1.50		2 @ £1.50			£1.40	
		30,000		27,000	19,000		26,600	400
Metal	1 @ £2		1 @ £2			£2.10		
		20,000		18,000	10,000		21,000	−3,000
Wood		4 @ £0.75		4 @ £0.75			£0.70	
		30,000		27,000	38,000		26,600	400
		£80,000		£72,000			£74,200	£−2,200

Materials usage variance

Using the formula in Figure 17.1 we can calculate the usage variance for each of the three materials. This is shown in Table 17.8. In each case, while holding the (standard) price constant, there has been a higher than expected usage of materials. This is an efficiency variance, which may be the result of:

- poor productivity;
- out-of-date bill of materials;
- poor quality materials.

Table 17.8 Materials usage variance.

	Plastic	
Standard quantity	9,000 × 2	
Standard price	@ £1.50	27,000
Actual quantity	19,000	
Standard price	@ £1.50	28,500
Adverse variance		−1,500
	Metal	
Standard quantity	9,000 × 1	
Standard price	@ £2.00	18,000
Actual quantity	10,000	
Standard price	@ £2.00	20,000
Adverse variance		−2,000
	Wood	
Standard quantity	9,000 × 4	
Standard price	@ £0.75	27,000
Actual quantity	38,000	
Standard price	@ £0.75	28,500
Adverse variance		−1,500
Total usage variance − adverse		£−5,000

Materials price variance

Using the formula in Figure 17.1, the price variance for each of the three materials is calculated in Table 17.9. While holding the (actual) quantity constant, we can see the effect of price fluctuations. Both plastic and wood have been bought below the standard price, while metal has cost more than standard. These variances may be the result of:

- changes in supplier prices not yet reflected in the bill of materials;
- poor purchasing.

Table 17.9 Materials price variance.

	Plastic	
Actual quantity	19,000	
Standard price	@ £1.50	28,500
Actual quantity	19,000	
Actual price	@ £1.40	26,600
Favourable variance		1,900
	Metal	
Actual quantity	10,000	
Standard price	@ £2.00	20,000
Actual quantity	10,000	

Table 17.9.   Continued

Actual price	@ £2.10	21,000
Adverse variance		−1,000
	Wood	
Actual quantity	38,000	
Standard price	@ £0.75	28,500
Actual quantity	38,000	
Actual price	@ £0.70	26,600
Favourable variance		1,900
Total price variance − favourable		£2,800

In total, the materials variance is £2,200. We can see that of the three materials, metal contributes the greatest variance − an adverse £3,000 (£2,000 usage and £1,000 price), which needs to be investigated as a matter of priority − while there may be a trade-off between the price and usage variances for plastic and wood, as sometimes quality and price can conflict with each other. The total materials variance is shown in Table 17.10.

Table 17.10   Total materials variance.

Usage − adverse	−5,000
Price − favourable	2,800
Total − adverse	£−2,200
Plastic	400
Metal	−3,000
Wood	400
	£−2,200

Through variance analysis we can separate the variance by usage and price for each of the three materials. Similarly, we need to analyse the usage and price variances for both skilled and semi-skilled labour.

Labour variance

Again by using a flexed budget, we see that the total labour variance is an unfavourable £21,250, as shown in Table 17.11.

Table 17.11   Labour variance.

	Std cost per unit	Original budget	Std cost per unit	Flexed budget	Usage qty	Act. cost per unit	Actual	Variance
Skilled	6 @ £15	900,000	6 @ £15	810,000	55,000	£15.25	838,750	−28,750
Semi-skilled	3 @ £7.50	225,000	3 @ £7.50	202,500	26,000	£7.50	195,000	7,500
		£1,125,000		£1,012,500			£1,033,750	£−21,250

As for materials, we need to look at the usage variance (which is a productivity or efficiency measure) and the price variance (which is a wage rate variance) for each of the two types of labour.

Labour efficiency variance

Using the same formula contained in Figure 17.1, the efficiency variance for labour is shown in Table 17.12. The adverse variance is a result of 1,000 additional hours being worked for skilled labour and 1,000 hours less being worked by unskilled labour. This may have been the result of:

- poor-quality material that required greater skill to work;
- the lack of unskilled labour that was replaced by skilled labour;
- poor production planning.

Table 17.12   Labour efficiency variance.

	Skilled	
Standard quantity	9,000 × 6	
Standard price	@ £15.00	810,000
Actual quantity	55,000	
Standard price	@ £15.00	825,000
Adverse variance		−15,000
	Unskilled	
Standard quantity	9,000 × 3	
Standard price	@ £7.50	202,500
Actual quantity	26,000	
Standard price	@ £7.50	195,000
Favourable variance		7,500
Total efficiency variance − adverse		£−7,500

Labour rate variance

The labour rate variance is shown in Table 17.13. Skilled labour costs an additional 25p for each hour worked, while unskilled labour was paid the standard rate. This may be the result of:

- unplanned overtime payments;
- a negotiated wage increase that has not been included in the labour routing.

The total labour variance is an unfavourable £21,250. This is a combination of efficiency and rate variances, and is shown in Table 17.14.

Table 17.13   Labour rate variance.

	Skilled	
Actual quantity	55,000	
Standard price	@ £15.00	825,000
Actual quantity	55,000	
Actual price	@ £15.25	838,750
Adverse variance		−13,750
	Unskilled	
Actual quantity	26,000	
Standard price	@ £7.50	195,000
Actual quantity	26,000	
Actual price	@ £7.50	195,000
Favourable variance		0
Total rate variance − adverse		£−13,750

Table 17.14   Total labour variance.

Efficiency − adverse	−7,500
Rate − adverse	−13,750
Total − adverse	£−21,250
Skilled	−28,750
Unskilled	7,500
	£−21,250

Through variance analysis we can separate the variance by efficiency and wage rate for each type of labour. Fixed and variable production costs also need to be analysed.

Overhead variances

Variable overhead variance

Once again using a flexed budget, the overhead variance is an adverse variation of £13,250, as shown in Table 17.15.

Table 17.15   Variable overhead variance.

	Std cost per unit	Original budget	Std cost per unit	Flexed budget	Usage qty	Act. cost per unit	Actual	Variance
Variable overhead	6 @ £5	300,000	6 @ £5	270,000	55,000	5.15	283,250	−13,250

There are two types of overhead variance, the efficiency variance and the spending variance. The overhead efficiency variance is £5,000 adverse, as shown in Table 17.16. The variance has occurred because an extra

1,000 labour hours have been worked. The efficiency variance is typically related to production hours and often follows from variances in labour (see Chapter 13). The reason may be that as more hours have been worked this has consumed more variable costs, e.g. the more labour used, the more consumables may be used, or the more machines running, the more electricity may be consumed.

Table 17.16   Overhead efficiency variance.

Standard quantity	9,000 × 6	
Standard price	@ £5.00	270,000
Actual quantity	55,000	
Standard price	@ £5.00	275,000
Adverse efficiency variance		£−5,000

The overhead spending variance is £8,250 adverse. This is shown in Table 17.17. This variance is due to extra spending for each hour worked. The reason for this variance may be a higher cost per hour, e.g. the rate per kilowatt used paid to the utility provider may have increased.

Table 17.17   Overhead spending variance.

Actual quantity	55,000	
Standard price	@ £5	275,000
Actual quantity	55,000	
Actual price	@ £5.15	283,250
Adverse spending variance		£−8,250

The total variable overhead variance is an adverse £13,250, which is a combination of both efficiency and rate variances. The total variable overhead variance is shown in Table 17.18.

Table 17.18   Total variable overhead variance.

Efficiency − adverse	−5,000
Spending − adverse	−8,250
Total − adverse	£−13,250

Fixed cost variance

The fixed cost variance is straightforward. Changes in quantity cannot influence fixed costs (which by definition are constant over different levels of production), so any variance must be the result of a spending variance.

In this case the variance is an adverse £5,000, because costs of £130,000 exceed the budget cost of £125,000.

Reconciling the variances

The difference between the original budget profit of £70,000 and the actual result of £53,800 can now be reconciled, and this has been done in Table 17.19.

Table 17.19   Reconciliation.

Original budgeted net profit			70,000
Sales variances			
Favourable price variance		45,000	
Unfavourable quantity variance	(See note below)	−19,500	25,500
Materials variances			
Total usage variance – adverse		−5,000	
Total price variance – favourable		2,800	−2,200
Labour variances			
Total efficiency variance – adverse		−7,500	
Total rate variance – adverse		−13,750	−21,250
Overhead variances			
Adverse efficiency variance		−5,000	
Adverse spending variance		−8,250	−13,250
Fixed cost spending variance			−5,000
Total variances			−16,200
Actual net profit			£53,800

Note: the difference between the original budget and the flexed budget is £19,500 adverse (the quantity variance). The difference between the flexed budget and the actual is £3,300 favourable. Together, the adverse variance is £16,200. However, it is important to remember that the individual variances for each type of material and labour need to be investigated and corrected as the total material, labour and overhead variances of £41,700 adverse are 'disguised' by the favourable price variance of £45,000.

While the example used here is a manufacturing example, variance analysis is equally applicable to service businesses, although there will, of course, be no need for a materials price variance. In a service business, differences in the volume of activity, sales variances, labour variances and overhead variances will constitute the difference between actual and budgeted profit.

Criticism of variance analysis

In his landmark study, Anthony Hopwood (1973) differentiated three styles of evaluation of budget information. The budget-constrained manager is evaluated based on the ability to meet the budget continually on a short-term basis. The profit-conscious manager is evaluated on the basis of the ability to increase the general effectiveness of operations to meet long-term objectives. In the non-accounting style, accounting information plays little part in the evaluation of a manager's performance. A manager who adopts a budget-constrained style takes budget information at face value and has a short time horizon, considering each month's variances in isolation rather than the trend or the long-term implications. An unfavourable budget variance is an indicator of poor management performance, even though the standards used by the accounting system may be faulty. By contrast, managers adopting a profit-conscious style realize that accounting information is not a constraint, and that variances are a meaningful guide to action, even though they may be misleading. The profit-conscious manager is more likely to experiment and innovate even though cost may exceed budget in the short term. Hopwood found that although managers:

made extensive use of the accounting information, they did so in a rigid manner, either attributing too much validity to the information or being unaware of its intended purposes, with the result that again, despite the thought and consideration which went into the design and operation of the system, its final value was questionable (p. 185).

Hence, as for other management accounting techniques described in this book, the behavioural consequences of budgetary control cannot be ignored. Samuelson (1986) argued that 'senior management often articulate one role for the budget but budgetees then perceive that another very different role may be intended' (p. 35). Samuelson contrasted the 'role articulated' by management for budgetary control (planning), which may be different to the 'real role' and the 'role intended' by managers (responsibility).

Standard costing, flexible budgeting and variance analysis can be criticized as tools of management, because these methods emphasize variable costs in a manufacturing environment. While labour costs are typically a low proportion of manufacturing cost, material costs are typically high and variance analysis has a role to play in many organizations that incur high costs for purchased goods (including retailers). However, even in manufacturing the introduction of new management techniques such as just-in-time (JIT, see Chapter 18) is often not reflected in the design of the management accounting system. Variance analysis has less emphasis in a JIT environment because price variations are only one component of total cost and a higher cost may be justifiable in exchange for a lower investment in inventory, more flexible deliveries, superior quality, etc. We have already described approaches to total quality management (TQM) in Chapter 11 and the implications for cost management. It is important to recognize that reducing variances based on standard costs can be an overly restrictive approach in a TQM or continuous improvement environment. This is because there will be a tendency to aim at the more obvious cost reductions (cheaper labour and materials) rather than issues of quality, reliability, on-time delivery, flexibility etc. in purchased goods and services. It will also tend to emphasize following standard work instructions rather than encouraging employees to adopt an innovative approach to re-engineering processes.

In service, knowledge-based and financial services industries, overheads can form the dominant part of the cost of producing a service and so price and usage variance analysis may have a limited role to play. However, organizations can use variance analysis in a number of ways to support their business strategy, most commonly by investigating the reasons for variations between budget and actual costs, even if those costs are independent of volume. These variations may identify poor budgeting practice, lack of effective cost control, poor purchasing practices, or variations in the usage or purchase price of resources that may be outside a manager's control.

Variance analysis is therefore a tool that can be used in certain circumstances, but is not one that should be used without consideration of the wider impact on strategies being implemented by the business. Nevertheless, neither accountants nor non-financial managers should overlook the importance of effectively managing the organization's costs.

Cost control

Cost control is a process of either reducing costs while maintaining the same levels of productivity, or maintaining costs while increasing levels of productivity through economies of scale or efficiencies in producing goods or services. A particular approach, termed cost down in some industries (notably automotive) involves working with suppliers to reduce the cost of purchased materials or components, improve purchasing processes, reduce inventory and eliminate waste. Because cost control implies budgetary cuts rather than seeking efficiencies and reducing waste, a more accurate term may be cost improvement. Cost improvement needs to be exercised by all budget holders in order to ensure that limited resources are effectively utilized and budgets are not overspent. This is best achieved by understanding the causes of costs – the cost drivers.

For example, the cost of purchasing as an activity might be traced to the number of suppliers and the number of purchase orders that are required for different activities. The more suppliers and purchase orders (the cost drivers), the higher will be the cost of purchasing. Cost control over the administration of purchasing can be exercised by reducing the number of suppliers and/or reducing the number of purchase orders. This is an example of the application of activity-based costing, described in Chapter 13.

Cost control can also be exercised by undertaking a review of horizontal business processes, i.e. the processes that cross organizational boundaries (business units or functional departments), rather than within the conventional hierarchical structure displayed on an organization chart. Such a review aims to find out what activities people are carrying out, why they are carrying out those activities, whether they need to be carried out at all, and whether there is a more efficient method of achieving the desired output. This approach is called business process re-engineering (see Chapter 9).

Understanding cost drivers and reviewing business processes can be used as tools to help in controlling costs such as:

- projects: why are they being undertaken?
- salaries and overtime: what tasks are people performing, and why and how are they performing those tasks?
- materials or consumables: how much waste is there, and what are the causes of that waste?
- travel: what causes people to travel to other locations and by what methods? Is video conferencing a better use of time and money?
- IT costs: what data is being processed and why? Is the information being provided still used by managers?

The questions that can be asked in relation to most costs are: What is being done? Why is it being done? When is it being done? Where is it being done? How is it being done? The answers to these questions can lead to continuous improvement.

Applying different perspectives to management accounting

In Chapters 4 and 5, we considered rational-economic, interpretive and critical perspectives that help to provide multiple views about the world in which we live. Chapters 14 through 17 have introduced many aspects of how management accounting techniques are used in planning, decision making and control in relation to investments, business unit evaluation, budgeting and budgetary control.

Implicit in most of what is contained in these four chapters is an acceptance of the rational-economic paradigm described in Chapter 4. Profit-oriented businesses make investment decisions to maximize profits

(Chapter 14), monitor the performance of different business segments (Chapter 15), budget for future profits (Chapter 16) and use variance analysis for control in order to take appropriate corrective action (this chapter). These are rational-economic choices.

However, numbers often reinforce subjective decisions and accounting choices may not be as straightforward as they seem. The interpretive perspective is useful here. For example, different views exist about the choice of investment evaluation method (accounting return, payback and discounted cash flow in Chapter 14), each of which gives different answers and can result in a different interpretation. There are divergent views about whether divisional performance should be assessed on return on investment or residual income criteria (Chapter 15) and again, different interpretations of performance are possible. Budgeting is itself an estimate of future activity (Chapter 16) involving considerable subjective judgements about the unknowable future, and a wide range of different estimates are possible. Variance analysis itself can be challenged on the basis that in many industries it may no longer be relevant to the way in which modern businesses operate (this chapter).

Equally, we have seen in these chapters that the critical perspective can also apply. Power determines particular choices of approach. The discounted cash flow technique for example (Chapter 14) can be biased in practice by inflated forecast cash flows that support the proposer's view that an investment should be approved. Evaluation criteria can be altered by boards of directors to raise or lower hurdle rates. The choice of transfer pricing technique (Chapter 15) will depend on the relative power of buying and selling divisions within an organization and top-management influence over the selection of the transfer price. The power of accounting departments over every segment of the business due to accountants' control of the budget process is evident in most companies. The adoption (or non-adoption) of variance analysis or particular cost control techniques (this chapter) is also a significant source of power, especially where accountants can use variances to hold selling, purchasing and production managers accountable for their decisions and actions.

Conclusion

In this chapter, we have described budgetary control and the use of flexible budgets. An extended manufacturing case study has explored variance analysis in detail. Sales and cost variances can be analysed in detail with the separation of usage (or efficiency) and price (or wage rate) variances for each different type of materials and labour, as well as overheads. We have concluded the chapter with a critique of variance analysis but emphasized the importance of cost control. Finally, we have seen how different perspectives can be applied to the management accounting techniques covered in Chapters 14–17.

References

Buckley, A. and McKenna, E. (1972). Budgetary control and business behaviour. *Accounting and Business Research*, 137–50.

Hopwood, A. G. (1973). *An Accounting System and Managerial Behaviour*. London: Saxon House.

Samuelson, L. A. (1986). Discrepancies between the roles of budgeting. *Accounting, Organizations and Society*, *11*(1), 35–45.

Questions

17.1 Conrad Corporation has a budget to produce 2,000 units at a variable cost of $3 per unit, but actual production is 1,800 units with an actual cost of $3.20 per unit.

Calculate the variance based on a flexible budget and determine whether it is favourable or adverse.

17.2 Calculate the material price variance for Cracker Barrel based on the following information:

	Standard	Actual
Quantity purchased (units)	5,000	5,200
Price per unit	€3.10	€3.05

17.3 Gargantua plc has produced budget and actual information in Table 17.20.

Table 17.20   Gargantua budget and actual.

	Budget	Actual
Sales units	10,000	11,000
Price per unit	£37.10	£36
Direct materials		
Magna – per unit	4 kg @ £1.50/kg	46,500 kg – cost £67,425
Carta – per unit	1 kg @ £5/kg	11,500 kg – cost £58,650
Labour – per unit	2.5 hours @ £7	26,400 hours – cost £187,440
Fixed costs	£75,000	£68,000

a. Prepare a traditional budget versus actual report using the above figures.
b. Prepare a flexible budget for Gargantua.
c. Calculate all sales and cost price and efficiency variances.
d. Reconcile the original budget and actual profit figures by showing the effect of the variance analysis.

17.4 Eggscell Ltd has produced budget and actual information for one of its business units for the previous month. This information is shown in Table 17.21.

Table 17.21   Eggscell Ltd.

	Budget	Actual
Analysis of labour		
Number of hours	10,000	9000
Average rate per hour	$75	$80

a. Show how a traditional budget versus actual variance report would be presented to the manager of this business unit.
b. Use a flexed budget to present an actual versus budget comparison.
c. Explain how the use of a flexed budget provides variance information that is more meaningful to managers.

Case study question: White Cold Equipment plc

White Cold Equipment (WCE) makes refrigeration equipment for the domestic market. It sells all its production wholesale to a large retail chain. WCE's budget versus actual report for a recent month is shown in Table 17.22.

Table 17.22   White Cold Equipment plc — budget v. actual report.

	Actual	Budget	Variance
Sales units	1,000	1,050	−50
Price	£700	£700	
Revenue	£700,000	£735,000	−35,000
Cost of production			
Materials per unit		£250	
Materials consumed			
Materials cost	245,700	262,500	16,800
Labour per unit		£150	
Labour consumed			
Labour cost	152,250	157,500	5,250
Manufacturing overhead per unit		£70	
Manufacturing overhead cost	75,600	73,500	−2,100
Total manufacturing cost	473,550	493,500	19,950
Gross margin	226,450	241,500	−15,050
Selling and admin expense	183,500	190,000	6,500
Net operating profit	£42,950	£51,500	£−8,550

Management was concerned about the significant shortfall in profits of £8,550 and asked the finance director for more information. The finance director produced a revised report (Table 17.23) based on a flexible budget.

Table 17.23   White Cold Equipment plc — flexible budget report.

	Actual	Flex budget	Variance
Sales units	1,000	1,000	0
Price	£700	£700	
Revenue	£700,000	£700,000	0
Cost of production			
Materials per unit	£270	£250	
Materials consumed	910	1,000	
Materials cost	245,700	250,000	4,300
Labour per unit	£145	£150	
Labour consumed	1,050	1,000	
Labour cost	152,250	150,000	−2,250
Manufacturing overhead per unit	£72	£70	
Manufacturing overhead cost	75,600	70,000	−5,600
Total manufacturing cost	473,550	470,000	−3,550
Gross margin	226,450	230,000	−3,550
Selling and admin expense	183,500	190,000	6,500
Net operating profit	£42,950	£40,000	£2,950

The report showed that by adjusting the budget to the actual volume of production/sales, the profit was £2,950 higher than expected. The finance director also produced a variance analysis (Table 17.24).

Table 17.24   White Cold Equipment plc — Variance analysis.

Materials price variance	£20
Actual no. units	910
Adverse variance	18,200
Materials usage variance	90
Standard cost	£250
Favourable variance	22,500
Favourable materials variance	£4,300
Labour rate variance	£5
Actual no. units	1,050
Favourable variance	5,250
Labour usage variance	50

Table 17.24. Continued

Standard cost	£150
Adverse variance	7,500
Adverse labour variance	£−2,250
Overhead rate variance	£2
Actual no. units	1,050
Adverse variance	2,100
Overhead usage variance	50
Standard cost	£70
Adverse variance	3,500
Adverse overhead variance	£−5,600
Total adverse manufacturing expense variance	£−3,550
Favourable selling and admin variance	6,500
Variance based on actual production volume	£2,950

The variance analysis showed that the gross margin was lower than expected for the 1,000 units actually produced by £3,550, but that selling and administration expenses were below budget by £6,500. Therefore, profits were higher than expected for the 1,000 units actually produced.

On receipt of the finance director's report, comments were sought from the operational executives. Provide comments on the information that has been presented by the finance director.

CHAPTER 18

Strategic Management Accounting

In this final chapter we bring together some of the concepts that have been developed in Part III, and look strategically in three ways. First, we show how non-financial performance measurement and a concern with business processes have extended the ambit of accounting beyond purely financial numbers. Second, we look beyond the narrow accounting period to a long-term view of the organization. Third, we look beyond the organizational boundary to see its role in the supply chain.

In this chapter, we look first at what is meant by strategic management accounting. We then look at the specific accounting techniques that can be used within the umbrella of strategic management accounting.

Strategic management accounting

In Chapters 4 and 5 we looked at management control, in which management accounting plays a considerable role. From the strategic management accounting perspective, the definition of management control systems has evolved from a focus on formal, financially quantifiable information and now includes external information relating to markets, customers and competitors; non-financial information about production processes; predictive information; and a broad array of decision support mechanisms and informal personal and social controls (Chenhall, 2003).

In their book *Relevance Lost*, Johnson and Kaplan (1987) argued that management accounting and control systems could not cope with the information demands of the modern manufacturing environment and the increased importance of service industries. Strategic management accounting (SMA) is so named because it links management accounting tools and techniques with business strategy, and by taking a more strategic perspective than a single business in a single financial year, it aims to maintain and increase competitive advantage. The term strategic management accounting was coined by Simmonds in 1981, who defined it as:

> the provision and analysis of management accounting data about a business and its competitors which is of use in the development and monitoring of the strategy of that business (pp. 27–8).

Simmonds argued that accounting should be more outward looking and help the firm evaluate its competitive position by collecting and analysing data on costs, prices, sales volumes, market share and cash flows for its main competitors. Simmonds emphasized the learning curve through early experience with new products that leads to cost reductions and lower prices.

SMA was a development of an earlier concern with *strategic cost management (SCM)*, which is based on value chain analysis (see Chapter 11) and conceives of the business as the linked set of value-creating activities from raw material to the delivery of the product and its ancillary services to the final customer. The aim of SCM is:

> to expand the domain of management accounting horizontally to include critical elements external to the company with a particular emphasis on adding value for customers and suppliers (Macintosh, 1994, pp. 204–5).

SCM also advocated lengthening the time horizon of management accounting reports over the entire lifecycle of a product. Wilson (1995) suggested that SCM was a variation of SMA that 'aims to reduce unit costs continually in real terms over the long run' (p. 163).

Tayles *et al.* (2002) argued that SMA has a role to play in providing the tools to assist a company to increase shareholder value, and proposed that greater attention should be given to intangible assets and intellectual capital as measures which could be used for internal and external benchmarking. Bromwich (1990) argued that SMA is the management accountant's contribution to corporate strategy, and defined SMA as the:

> provision and analysis of financial information on the firm's product markets and competitors' costs and cost structures and the monitoring of the enterprise's strategies and those of its competitors in these markets over a number of periods (p. 28).

Lord (1996) argued that firms place more emphasis on particular accounting techniques depending on their strategic position, and summarized the characteristics of SMA as:

- the collection of competitor information: pricing, costs, volume, market share;
- the exploitation of cost reduction opportunities: a focus on continuous improvement and on non-financial performance measures;
- matching the accounting emphasis with the firm's strategic position.

One of the conclusions of research by Edwards *et al.* (2005) into knowledge management found that the focus of strategic management accounting has been external when it should have been internal. In ten organizations studied, all believed that knowledge acquired was not being effectively shared, retained or utilized. Management accountants have not recognized their role in broader issues of knowledge management, and top management does not appear to appreciate the link between knowledge management as a source of competitive advantage and financial performance.

However, Lord (1996) questioned the role of accountants in strategic management accounting, arguing that firms successfully collect and use competitor information without any input from the management accountant. In a similar vein, Dixon (1998) argued that:

> the costs of capturing, collating, interpreting and analysing the appropriate data outweighs the benefits ... [and] that the collection and use of competitor information for strategic purposes can be achieved without implementing a formal SMA process (p. 278).

There have been recent criticisms of SMA: the term 'strategic management accounting' is not used widely in practice, and it is specific techniques and processes, such as cost management, strategic analysis, product costing and performance measurement, which are the more relevant and recognizable. Some concepts that we classify as SMA have entered the province of 'management' rather than accounting (Langfield-Smith, 2008).

Nevertheless, the tools that often fall under the umbrella of SMA are tools that are available for use by accountants and non-accountants in planning, decision making and control. These tools and techniques are described in this chapter.

Figure 18.1 shows a representation of strategic management accounting in terms of its relationships with suppliers, customers and competitors over time.

In Chapter 4 we showed how accounting had extended its remit to non-financial performance measurement through techniques such as the Balanced Scorecard. Non-financial performance measures provide a more strategic perspective on organizational performance because they provide a broader understanding of trends in performance than financial measures alone and they can be benchmarked between organizations. In Chapter 9, we showed the value of enterprise resource planning (ERP) systems and how a concern with horizontal business processes can be more useful than vertical departmental/business unit structures. ERP systems are being developed in three directions:

- supplier facing to meet the needs of supply chains;
- customer facing with a customer relationship management (CRM) function;
- management facing to support the information and decision-making needs of managers.

Various accounting techniques have been developed to provide more strategic tools for management accounting. We begin with a brief review of some of the strategic tools that have been mentioned in previous chapters.

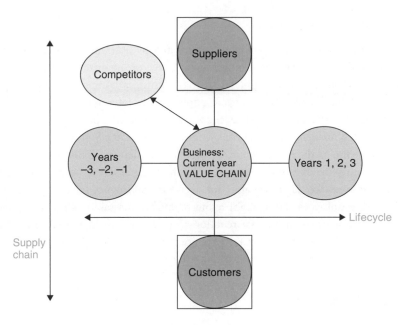

Figure 18.1   Representation of strategic management accounting.

Accounting techniques to support strategic management accounting

Value chain and supply chain management

Chapter 11 showed the value chain and differentiated upstream value-adding activities (e.g. research and development, product design, sourcing) from production and distribution, and downstream activities (such as marketing and after-sales service). Chapter 11 also showed how the value chain could be extended from the focus on a single organization along its supply chain from suppliers through distribution channels to customers.

Strategic management accounting information can be used to understand the costs and profits of suppliers and distributors and determine if excess profits are being earned by some parts of the supply chain. For example, in the automotive industry, the large vehicle assemblers collect vast quantities of information about their suppliers' costs: the cost of labour, the cost of manufacturing equipment and its capacity and the cost of raw materials. This information supports negotiations between the assembler's purchasing department and its suppliers because the assembler knows the costs the supplier is likely to have – or should have if it is efficient – and adds a reasonable profit margin. This is powerful information during the negotiation process and can lead to collaboration to improve efficiencies in the supply chain.

Human resource accounting

In Chapter 12 we introduced the idea that labour is treated by accounting as an expense. However, as the repository of knowledge, employees can be a major source of organizational profits, because it is the knowledge that is held by labour that is crucial to maintaining a competitive advantage and satisfying customers. We hinted in Chapter 12 that a 'lifecycle' approach (see later in this chapter) to labour would also include recruitment and training costs as well as the total remuneration package paid to employees. Whilst for accounting purposes labour is not an asset that would be shown in a Statement of Financial Position, in practical terms labour is one of the most important assets of a business. This is particularly evident when knowledge is lost when employees cannot be retained by the business. A strategic management accounting approach to human resources would be to value (for decision making not reporting) the investment in the knowledge and skills of employees. This might avoid organizations taking short-term decisions to make employees redundant (a not uncommon first reaction to pressures for increased profitability) and take a longer term perspective on the investment and the cost of replacing it. This broader approach was discussed in Chapter 7 in the description of intellectual capital reporting.

Activity-based management

Chapter 13 introduced activity-based costing, which was also mentioned in its role as activity-based budgeting in Chapter 16. Activity-based management is a broader concept which focuses on controlling activities that consume resources, i.e. controlling costs at their source. Kaplan and Cooper (1998) defined activity-based management (ABM) as:

> the entire set of actions that can be taken, on a better informed basis, with activity-based cost information. With ABM, the organization accomplishes its outcomes with fewer demands on organizational resources (p. 137).

Kaplan and Cooper differentiated *operational* and *strategic* ABM. The former is concerned with doing things right: increasing efficiency, lowering costs and enhancing asset utilization. Strategic ABM is about doing the right things, by attempting to alter the demand for activities to increase profitability.

Strategic ABM can be used in relation to product mix and pricing decisions. It works by shifting the mix of activities from unprofitable applications to profitable ones. The demand for activities is a result of decisions about products, services and customers. Costing was the first application of activity-based management. It attempted to remove the distortions caused by traditional methods of overhead allocation based on direct labour.

The process involves moving from managing the vertical hierarchical structure to managing horizontal business processes, which we first saw in Chapter 9.

Figure 18.2 shows the CAM-I model of activity-based cost management. The vertical 'cost assignment view' shows how resources are tracked to cost objects (product/services, processes, customers, etc.) while the horizontal 'process view' reflects the cost drivers of activities and traces these to performance measures. The vertical view is used, as we saw in Chapter 13, for product costing and decisions about pricing, profitability, etc. By comparing activity-based costs with performance measures such as quality, cycle time

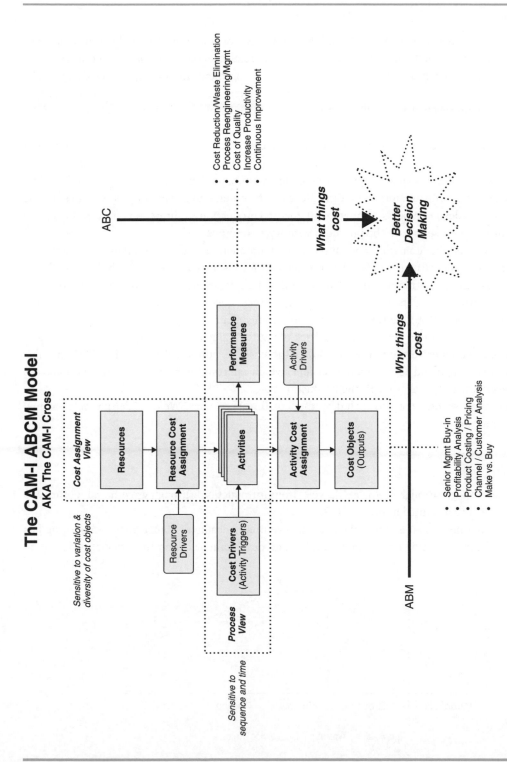

Figure 18.2   CAM-I ABCM model.

(from order to delivery), productivity, etc. it is possible using the horizontal view to make decisions about performance improvement. The horizontal view identifies cost reduction opportunities, including the need for business process re-engineering (see Chapter 9) or quality management improvements (see Chapter 11). The horizontal view, in reflecting the value chain of an organization and its fundamental business processes, takes a more strategic approach than the financially dominated and typically short-term orientation of the vertical focus on cost objects.

In the horizontal perspective, ABC assigned overhead costs to products/services based on the cost drivers of activities and the resources consumed by those activities for individual products (see Chapter 13). Product-related actions can reduce the resources required to produce existing products/services. Pricing and product substitution decisions can shift the mix from difficult-to-produce items to simple-to-produce ones. In the horizontal perspective, redesign, process improvement, focused production facilities and new technology can enable the same products or services to be produced with fewer resources.

Strategic ABM extends the domain of analysis beyond production costs to marketing, selling and administrative expenses, reflecting the belief that the demand for resources arises not only from products/services but from customers, distribution and delivery channels. Cost information can be used to modify a firm's relationships with its customers, transforming unprofitable customers into profitable ones through negotiations on price, product mix, delivery and payment arrangements.

Similarly, strategic ABM can be pushed further back along the value chain to suppliers, designers and developers. Managing supplier relationships can lower the costs of purchased materials. ABM can also inform product/service design and development decisions, which can result in a lowering of production costs for new products/services *before* they reach the production stage.

Strategic management accounting also includes other costing approaches. We consider lifecycle costing, target costing and kaizen.

Lifecycle costing

All products and services go through a typical lifecycle, from introduction, through growth and maturity to decline. The lifecycle is represented in Figure 18.3.

Over time, sales volume increases, then plateaus and eventually declines. Management accounting has traditionally focused on the period after product design and development, when the product/service is in

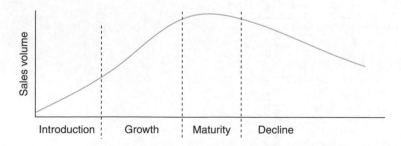

Figure 18.3   Typical product/service life cycle.

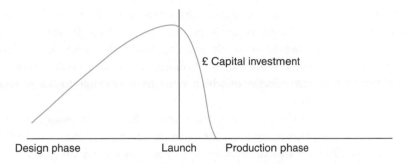

Figure 18.4 Investment decisions.

production for sale to customers. However, the product design phase involves substantial costs that may not be taken into account in product/service costing. These costs may have been capitalized (see Chapters 3 and 6) or treated as an expense in earlier years. Similarly, when products/services are discontinued, the costs of discontinuance are rarely identified as part of the product/service cost.

Lifecycle costing estimates and accumulates the costs of a product/service over its entire lifecycle, from inception to abandonment. This helps to determine whether the profits generated during the production phase cover all the lifecycle costs. This information helps managers make decisions about future product/service development and the need for cost control during the development phase. This kind of costing does not appear in financial statements because it ignores the accounting treatment as to whether a cost was capitalized or expensed, and also ignores the accounting period in which payment was made.

The design and development phase can determine up to 80% of costs in many advanced technology industries. This is because decisions about the production process and the technology investment required to support production are made long before the product/services are actually produced. This is shown in Figure 18.4.

Consequently, efforts to reduce costs during the production phase are unlikely to be successful when the costs are committed or locked in as a result of technology and process decisions made during the design phase.

Target costing

Target costing is concerned with managing whole-of-life costs *during the design phase*. It has four stages:

1. Determining the target price that customers will be prepared to pay for the product/service.
2. Deducting a target profit margin to determine the target cost, which becomes the cost to which the product/service should be engineered.
3. Estimating the actual cost of the product/service based on the current design.
4. Investigating ways of reducing the estimated cost to the target cost.

target price − target profit margin = target cost

The technique was developed in the Japanese automotive industry and is customer oriented. Its aim is to build a product at a cost that can be recovered over the product lifecycle through a price that customers will be willing to pay to obtain the benefits (which in turn drive the product cost). Target costing is equally applicable to a service. For example, the design of an Internet banking service or an online retail system involves substantial upfront investment, the benefits of which must be recoverable in the selling price over the expected lifecycle of the service.

Using a simple example, a new product is expected to achieve a desired volume and market share at a price of £1,000, from which the manufacturer wants a 20% margin, leaving a target cost of £800. Current estimates suggest the cost as £900. An investigation seeks to find which elements of design, manufacture or purchasing contribute to the costs and how those costs can be reduced, or whether features can be eliminated that cannot be justified in the target price. This is an iterative process, often referred to as *value engineering*, a process of improving the ratio of function to cost, in which value can be increased either by improving the function or reducing the cost. Such an investigation is usually a team effort involving designers, purchasing, production/manufacturing, marketing and costing staff. The target cost is rarely achieved from the beginning of the manufacturing phase. Japanese manufacturers tend to take a long-term perspective on business and aim to achieve the target cost during the lifecycle of the product.

This process is essential if the lifecycle costs of the product/service are to be managed and recovered in the (target) selling price. Importantly, this process of estimating costs over the product/service lifecycle and establishing a target selling price takes place *before* decisions are finalized about product/service design and the production process to be used.

Kaizen costing

Kaizen is a Japanese term – literally meaning 'improvement' – for the process of making continuous, incremental improvements to the production process. While target costing is applied during the design phase, kaizen costing is applied during the production phase of the lifecycle when large innovations may not be possible. Target costing focuses on the product/service. Kaizen focuses on the production process, seeking efficiencies in production, purchasing and distribution.

Like target costing, kaizen establishes a desired cost-reduction target and relies on teamwork and employee empowerment to improve processes and reduce costs. This is because employees are assumed to have more expertise in the production process than managers. Frequently, cost-reduction targets are set and producers work collaboratively with suppliers who often have cost-reduction targets passed on to them.

Global competition, the changing demands of the marketplace and advanced manufacturing technologies have led to the need for more sophisticated approaches to management accounting and how cost information is used for planning, decision making and control.

Just-in-time

Just-in-time (JIT) aims to improve productivity and eliminate waste by obtaining manufacturing components in the right quality, at the right time and place to meet the demands of the manufacturing cycle. It requires close cooperation within the supply chain and is generally associated with continuous manufacturing processes with low inventory holdings, a result of eliminating buffer inventories – considered waste – between the different stages of manufacture. Many of these costs are hidden in a traditional cost accounting system. JIT relies on kanban, a Japanese term referring to signals between different points in the production process which provide information on when a raw material or component is required. Rather than relying on comprehensive inventory systems, kanbans can be as simple as visual signals (e.g. the presence or absence of a part in a process) to prompt re-ordering.

The introduction by many manufacturing companies of JIT is intended to bring components from suppliers to the assembly line as they are required for production, rather than for the manufacturer to hold large quantities of raw materials to meet future production requirements. JIT has resulted in a significant reduction in inventories and so inventory valuation becomes less relevant.

The diminished reliance on inventory tracking systems is reflected in an accounting approach known as backflush costing.

Backflush costing

In Chapter 8, we discussed accounting for inventory in detail. Under traditional costing approaches, each raw material issue transaction is recorded separately. Backflush costing aims to eliminate detailed transaction processing. Rather than tracking each movement of materials, the output from the production process determines (based on the *expected* usage and cost of materials) the amount of materials to be transferred from raw materials to finished goods. Importantly, under backflush costing there is no separate accounting for work in progress. The timing of the recording of costs is based on a *trigger point*.

In its simplest version, backflush costing transfers the cost of raw materials from suppliers, and conversion costs, to finished goods inventory when production of finished goods is complete (the trigger point). In a modified version, trigger points occur when raw materials are purchased and when finished goods are completed.

In all of these examples, a holistic consideration of cost, non-financial aspects of supplier performance (quality, on-time delivery, reliability, etc.), inventory holding and the cost of transaction processing leads to an approach that focuses on the *total cost of ownership* rather than the initial purchase price. Variance analysis is impossible under backflush costing as the standard quantity and cost of labour and materials are used, not the actual cost and quantity.

The elimination of what is considered to be wasteful accounting practices has become more evident under lean production, from which has developed lean accounting.

Lean production and lean accounting

Western organizations became aware of lean production methods in the 1990s, with the publication of *The Machine That Changed the World* (Womack *et al.*, 1990), a five-year study of the automotive industry which described the Toyota Production System. Lean production arose as a result of the shift from mass production to more efficient production techniques that were enabled by modern manufacturing, information and communications technologies (Womack and Jones, 2003). Lean production focuses on production processes as a continuous flow, rather than on the hierarchical structures in an organization chart. The adoption of flow production (in which products are manufactured in a continuous process) significantly reduces the cycle time from order to delivery. As cycle time decreases, so does the need for work-in-process inventory. The lean production company can begin to produce to meet demand (demand 'pulls' production), rather than build finished goods inventory (production 'pushes' inventory). Automotive assemblers speak of the concept of the 'five-day car' in which a customer's order for a specific vehicle can be assembled and available for delivery within five days of the order being placed. This goal is only achievable with a lean production system. The benefits of lean production are lower costs, reduced waste, higher product quality and shorter lead times.

The focus of production processes as a continuous flow is called a value stream. A value stream includes everything done to create value for a customer that can reasonably be associated with a product or product group. The value stream matches revenues with the costs of design, marketing and sales activity, production and distribution, as well as costs associated with servicing the customer, purchasing and administration (e.g. invoicing and collection of monies owed). In the lean enterprise, there are typically only a few value streams (perhaps five or six). Value streams usually comprise one or more dedicated production cells, which produce products one at a time, from raw materials to finished product. Both physical assets and people are assigned to a particular value stream. The physical assets are right-sized so that they have enough capacity to support a single value stream, and the work force is multi-skilled, rather than narrow specialists. Because the physical assets and the work force are dedicated, there is no need to assign their costs indirectly (avoiding the overhead allocation problem explained in Chapter 13). Nearly all resource costs are measured directly at the value-stream level, the only major exception being floor space, which can be assigned indirectly based on square footage (Cooper and Maskell, 2008). Each value stream should be managed by a value-stream manager. This manager is responsible for all of the activities that occur within the value stream. Focusing on the entire value stream encourages managers to maximize the performance of that value stream, not just specific functions or departments. So, management accounting reports should follow the value stream.

Lean accounting is a development of lean production. Lean accounting does not rely on, or even require, traditional management accounting tools like standard costing, activity-based costing, variance reporting, cost-plus pricing, transaction reporting systems and financial statements, which are often confusing to non-financial managers. Instead of these traditional approaches, lean accounting relies on value-stream accounting. Value-stream accounting involves assigning employees and assets to a single value stream, rather than costs being allocated to a department or cost centre, or across multiple business processes. Performance measures (financial and non-financial, see Chapter 4) are developed for each value stream and overhead costs are directed to specific value streams, resulting in less arbitrary overhead allocations (see Chapter 13).

Although value-stream accounting has been applied most often in manufacturing companies, it also has been applied widely to service businesses, including hospitals, banks and financial service companies (Cooper and Maskell, 2008).

Value-stream costing measures how much value is added in each step of the process, by costing the various value streams backwards from the customer to their source. Activity-based costing is a tool that helps in these calculations. Value-stream costing produces a simple summarized *direct* costing of each value stream, and in many cases its proponents argue that it is not necessary to calculate product or service costs. This is because *value-based pricing* is based on value to the customer, under which the prices of products/ services are set according to the value created for customers.

Lean accounting includes methods for calculating the amount of value created by a company's products and services, which is used to establish prices. This approach is in contrast to traditional cost-plus pricing methods which can lead to serious errors in pricing because of the assumed (and false) relationship between price and cost. The proponents of value-stream pricing argue that the price of a product is unrelated to the cost of manufacturing and supplying that product. Instead the price of a product or services is entirely determined by the amount of value created by the product in the eyes of the customer. Each value stream has its own financial statements, which provide the information to enable value-stream managers to make decisions to improve the profitability and growth of the value stream. This is because the focus is on more direct costs, permitting the creation of much simpler income statements, which can be read and understood more easily by non-financial managers.

Traditional management accounting techniques are inconsistent with the aims of lean accounting because:

1. As the cost of spare capacity is measured (see Chapter 11), there will be a tendency for managers to fill spare capacity by producing for inventory in order to reduce costs per unit. However, this action over-looks the *total cost of ownership* of inventory, which includes the interest cost, as well as storage, insurance and handling costs, and the risk of damage and obsolescence.
2. The reduction of inventory will, in the short term, result in lower profits. This is because inventory valuation for financial reporting purposes must include a share of fixed and variable production overhead. Lower inventory means that more of the production overhead will be shown as an expense in the Income Statement rather than as part of the inventory valuation in the Statement of Financial Position.

The following case study provides an illustration of one company's approach to strategic management accounting and a lean approach to the accounting function.

Case study 18.1: TNA and strategic management accounting

TNA is a multinational packaging equipment supplier providing equipment to the food industry. It is privately owned and hence does not need to satisfy stock market pressures for short-term performance. About 10% of the company's annual sales revenue has been invested in research and development (R&D) through which TNA developed a computer numerically controlled (CNC) packaging machine that was more efficient than its competitors. Despite the price of TNA's equipment being 2–3 times more than competitive equipment, it operates 50–100% faster than conventional packers and has a much lower reject rate. TNA's machines have worldwide patents, but despite its patent protection, two competitors breached the company's patents and substantial sums were spent to defend TNA's intellectual property. The company has continued to expand geographically and TNA has offices in

Europe, the USA, Australia and the Middle East. The manufacture of the CNC equipment is outsourced to reduce TNA's capital investment and avoid the capacity utilization problem inherent to its competitors.

TNA's major operating costs are salaries, premises, cars, travel, advertising and exhibitions. Most of these costs are driven either by export market development or R&D. In particular, international growth has meant rapidly increasing operating expenses. TNA has had a dual focus on growth and cash flow. However, in developing its business, TNA has not relied on traditional accounting-based financial reports.

TNA did not have profit targets. Short-term profit was not meaningful to the owners as expenditure on R&D, export market development and patent litigation was incurred a year or more in advance of any income generation. The company instead emphasized sales targets as part of a strategy for market development, along with continual expenditure on R&D. Because there was no attempt to allocate R&D or export marketing costs over products, the direct (subcontracted) manufacturing cost was a relatively small proportion of the selling price. Consequently, product costing did not rely on management accounting data.

As TNA became larger, the owners began to focus more on growth in market share. They developed a sophisticated spreadsheet that contained an industry-level top-down analysis of markets and competitors. It calculated the installed packaging machine base by market segment, added a factor for market growth and the anticipated replacement of old machines by customers or potential customers. This was then adjusted by the relative performance of competitors' installed machines to provide a market size at the standard running speed for its own equipment. Using this model, TNA was able to estimate how many machines the company could sell and which of its competitors were likely to lose market share (most had the disadvantage of manufacturing their own equipment and needed to manage an increasingly under-utilized capacity and high fixed cost base). TNA modified its marketing strategy to target the customers of weaker competitors, in order to force those competitors into losses and thereby secure even more market share from their failure. Several of TNA's competitors failed or were taken over by TNA as a result.

TNA's owners developed a network of social contacts from employees and customers to competitors and suppliers by attending industry events such as exhibitions and trade fairs, reading the business press and entertaining. Over time the owners developed a comprehensive market intelligence that they believed was superior to that of any of their competitors. TNA's spreadsheet model was regularly modified in an iterative fashion after market knowledge was gained through these social events. This knowledge became the driver of TNA's continuous investment in both export market development and R&D.

Market share became a key performance measure. The spreadsheet also led to strategic decisions, first to move to a stainless steel construction and second to develop a low-cost machine. Both met emerging market needs and the desire for increased market share. TNA's strategy and its use of the spreadsheet to inform that strategy was an example of strategic management accounting.

The full TNA case study is available from Collier, P.M. (2005). Entrepreneurial cognition and the construction of a relevant accounting. *Management Accounting Research, 16*(3), 321–39.

Conclusion

Strategic management accounting provides the opportunity for management accounting and other performance information to be linked with strategy. In doing so, the scope of management accounting extends beyond the organization and also extends beyond the financial year time horizon. It also moves from a hierarchical view of the organization to one that sees business processes as more important in achieving effectiveness and competitiveness. Various techniques are available under the umbrella of strategic management accounting to help the organization achieve its objectives and compete cost effectively. The introduction of lean accounting principles is also beginning to call into question some of the taken-for-granted approaches described in this book, although the techniques remain in common usage.

This book has attempted to integrate the tools and techniques of accounting as though they were rational, while also introducing alternative ways of seeing accounting through interpretive and critical perspectives. It is hoped that this book may also encourage readers to undertake research into accounting, either in an academic environment or in their own business organizations, in order to challenge conventional wisdom and better understand the context in which accounting is practised and the consequences of the use of accounting information for decision making. In the case studies that have appeared in each chapter we have tried to show the complexity of organizational decision making.

Published financial statements are to a large degree consistent as a result of IFRS, and have the ability to be analysed with common tools. This is a necessity when *representation* is so important for the efficient operation of capital markets. However, the differences in business context and the variety of management accounting techniques that are available, each imbued with their own limitations and assumptions, make more challenging the solving of organizational problems by managers in product markets.

In their introduction to a special issue of *Management Accounting Research* devoted to management accounting change, Burns and Vaivio (2001) noted that many organizations have experienced significant change in their organizational design (structures and processes), competitive environment and information technologies. There is a need for management accounting change, despite the relatively recent (in the last 20 years) introduction of activity-based costing (Chapter 13) and the Balanced Scorecard (Chapter 4). Information technology in particular is driving the routine financial accounting functions into centralized head offices or is being outsourced.

However, management accounting is increasingly decentralized to business units, where it becomes the responsibility of functional and business unit managers, supported by enterprise resource planning systems (Chapter 9). These operating managers are more and more responsible for setting and achieving budget targets. As the role of non-accounting managers is being extended to encompass (management) accounting functions, the role of the professional accountant is also changing to a business consultant, advisory or change management role, often with responsibilities outside the traditional accounting one.

One of the reasons for this changed role for accountants is that they do understand the numbers, both financial and non-financial. The challenge for non-accounting managers is to understand the numbers sufficiently well to be able to contribute to the formulation and implementation of business strategy. Those managers who do not understand, or who do not want to understand, the numbers are likely to be increasingly marginalized in their organizations.

References

Bromwich, M. (1990). The case for strategic management accounting: the role of accounting information for strategy in competitive markets. *Accounting, Organizations and Society*, *15*(1/2), 27–46.

Burns, J. and Vaivio, J. (2001). Management accounting change. *Management Accounting Research*, *12*, 389–402.

Chenhall, R. H. (2003). Management control systems design within its organizational context: findings from contingency-based research and directions for the future. *Accounting, Organizations and Society*, *28*, 127–68.

Collier, P. M. (2005). Entrepreneurial cognition and the construction of a relevant accounting, *Management Accounting Research*, *16*(3), 321–39.

Cooper, R. and Maskell, B. (2008). How to manage through worse-before-better. *Sloan Management Review*, *49*(4), 58–65.

Dixon, R. (1998). Accounting for strategic management: a practical application. *Long Range Planning*, *31*(2), 272–9.

Edwards, J. S., Collier, P. M. and Shaw, D. A. (2005). *Knowledge Management and its Impact on the Management Accountant*. London: CIMA.

Johnson, H. T. and Kaplan, R. S. (1987). *Relevance Lost: The Rise and Fall of Management Accounting*. Boston, MA: Harvard Business School Press.

Kaplan, R. S. and Cooper, R. (1998). *Cost and Effect: Using Integrated Cost Systems to Drive Profitability and Performance*. Boston, MA: Harvard Business School Press.

Langfield-Smith, K. (2008). Strategic management accounting: how far have we come in 25 years? *Accounting, Auditing and Accountability Journal*, *21*(2), 204–28.

Lord, B. R. (1996). Strategic management accounting: the emperor's new clothes? *Management Accounting Research*, *7*, 347–66.

Macintosh, N. B. (1994). *Management Accounting and Control Systems: An Organizational and Behavioral Approach*. Chichester: John Wiley & Sons, Ltd.

Simmonds, K. (1981). Strategic management accounting. *Management Accounting*, *59*(4), 26–9.

Tayles, M., Bramley, A., *et al.* (2002). Dealing with the management of intellectual capital: the potential role of strategic management accounting, Accounting, *Auditing and Accountability Journal*, *15*(2), 251–67.

Wilson, R. M. S. (1995). Strategic management accounting. In D. Ashton, T. Hopper and R.W. Scapens (Eds), *Issues in Management Accounting* (2nd edn). London: Prentice Hall.

Womack, J. P. and Jones, D. T. (2003). *Lean Thinking: Banish Waste and Create Wealth in Your Corporation*. London: Free Press.

Womack, J. P., Jones, D. T. and Roos, D. (1990). *The Machine that Changed the World*. New York: Rawson Associates.

Further Reading

One of the aims of this book has been to encourage readers to access the research-based academic literature of accounting, in particular in relation to the broader social, historical and contextual influences on accounting; the organizational and behavioural consequences of accounting information; and the assumptions and limitations underlying the tools and techniques used by accountants. For those who wish to read further, whether as part of their preparation for academic research at postgraduate level or as part of their personal pursuit of greater knowledge, we identify some recommended additional reading.

Books

Alvesson, M. and Willmott, H. (Eds) (1992). *Critical Management Studies*. London: Sage.

Ashton, D., Hopper, T. and Scapens, R.W. (Eds) (1995). *Issues in Management Accounting* (2nd edn). London: Prentice Hall.

Berry, A. J., Broadbent, J. and Otley, D. (Eds) (2005). *Management Control: Theories, Issues and Performance* (2nd edn). London: Palgrave Macmillan.

Chapman, C. S. (Ed.) (2005). *Controlling Strategy: Management, Accounting, and Performance Measurement*. Oxford: Oxford University Press.

Heliar, C. and Bebbington, J. (Eds) (2004). *Taking Ethics to Heart*. Edinburgh: Institute of Chartered Accountants of Scotland.

Hope, J. and Fraser, R. (2003). *Beyond Budgeting: How Managers Can Break Free from the Annual Performance Trap*. Boston, MA: Harvard Business School Press.

Hopwood, A. G. and Miller, P. (1994). *Accounting as Social and Institutional Practice*. Cambridge: Cambridge University Press.

Johnson, H. T. and Kaplan, R. S. (1987). *Relevance Lost: The Rise and Fall of Management Accounting*. Boston, MA: Harvard Business School Press.

Jones, T. C. (1995). *Accounting and the Enterprise: A Social Analysis*. London: Routledge.

Kaplan, R. S. and Cooper, R. (1998). *Cost and Effect: Using Integrated Cost Systems to Drive Profitability and Performance*. Boston, MA: Harvard Business School Press.

Kaplan, R. S. and Norton, D. P. (2001). *The Strategy-Focused Organization: How Balanced Scorecard Companies Thrive in the New Business Environment*. Boston, MA: Harvard Business School Press.

Macintosh, N. B. (1994). *Management Accounting and Control Systems: An Organizational and Behavioral Approach*. Chichester: John Wiley & Sons, Ltd.

Munro, R. and Mouritsen, J. (Eds) (1996). *Accountability: Power, Ethos and the Technologies of Managing*. London: Thomson.

Puxty, A. G. (1993). *The Social and Organizational Context of Management Accounting*. London: Academic Press.

Ryan, B., Scapens, R. W., *et al.* (2002). *Research Method and Methodology in Finance and Accounting* (2nd edn). London: Thomson.

Scott, W. R. (1998). *Organizations: Rational, Natural, and Open Systems* (4th edn). London: Prentice Hall.

Articles published in the following journals

- *Accounting, Auditing and Accountability Journal*
- *Accounting, Organizations and Society*
- *British Accounting Review*
- *Critical Perspectives in Accounting*
- *Financial Accountability and Management* (public sector)
- *Journal of Management Accounting Research* (US)
- *Management Accounting Research* (UK)

These articles are generally available online for students through university libraries.

Supporting Information

Part IV contains the following supplementary material:

- Introduction to the Readings
- Glossary of Accounting Terms
- Solutions to Questions
- Index

Introduction to the Readings

In Part IV, we reproduce four readings from the academic literature to present four different yet complementary perspectives on accounting in organizations. Each reading has several questions that the reader should think about and try to answer in order to help understand the concepts.

Readings

A Cooper and Kaplan (1988). How cost accounting distorts product costs.

B Otley, Broadbent and Berry (1995). Research in management control: an overview of its development.

C Covaleski, Dirsmith and Samuel (1996). Managerial accounting research: the contributions of organizational and sociological theories.

D Dent (1991). Accounting and organizational cultures: a field study of the emergence of a new organizational reality.

A rationale for this book was to provide a theoretical underpinning to accounting, drawn from accounting research, to assist in interpretation and critical questioning. This underpinning provides a critical perspective on the most common accounting techniques and describes the social and organizational context in which accounting exists. This context influences accounting but is also influenced by accounting, as the way we see the world – even if only our small organizational part of the world – is significantly influenced by the ways in which accounting portrays and represents that world.

The article by Cooper and Kaplan is a classic, explaining clearly how traditional management accounting techniques have distorted management information and the decisions made by managers. The authors criticize the distinction between variable and fixed costs, the limitations of marginal costing and the arbitrary methods by which overhead costs are allocated to products. The activity-based approach recommended by Cooper and Kaplan treats all costs as variable, although only some vary with volume. This paper was the foundation for the development of activity-based costing which was described in Chapter 13.

Covaleski, Dirsmith and Samuel's paper describes a variety of theories from the contribution of contingency theory, to interpretive and critical perspectives using organizational and sociological theories (including institutional theory). The authors call for 'paradigmatic pluralism', not as competing perspectives but as 'alternative ways of understanding the multiple roles played by management accounting in organizations and society' (p. 24). This paper provides a useful comparison of the different approaches introduced in Chapters 4 and 5.

Otley, Berry and Broadbent's paper reviews the development of the management control literature in the context of organization theories and argues for the expansion of management control beyond accounting. The authors use a framework of open/closed systems and rational/natural systems to contrast each of these four perspectives and give examples of research in each. They conclude that management control research needs to recognize the environment in which organizations exist. They argue that while the definition of management control is 'managerialist in focus . . . this should not preclude a critical stance and thus a broader choice of theoretical approaches' (p. S42). Like the Covaleski *et al.* reading, this paper elaborates on the perspectives introduced in Chapter 5.

Dent's case study of EuroRail is a highly regarded field study of accounting change in which organizations are portrayed as cultures, i.e. systems of knowledge, belief and values. Prior to the study, the dominant culture in EuroRail was engineering and production, but this culture was displaced by economic and accounting concerns that constructed the railway as a profit-seeking enterprise. Dent traced the introduction of a revised corporate planning system, the amendment of capital expenditure approval procedures and the revision of budgeting systems, each of which gave power to business managers. Dent describes how accounting played a role 'in constructing specific knowledges' (p. 727). This paper provides an important case study of the role of culture and accounting in organizational change, the topic of Chapter 5.

Taken together, these readings provide a practical critique of traditional costing methods, several theoretical perspectives from which accounting can be viewed, and a field study of how accounting changed the reality in one organization.

Reading A

Cooper, R. and Kaplan, R. S. (1988). How cost accounting distorts product costs. *Management Accounting* (April), 20–27. Reproduced by permission of Copyright Clearance Center, Inc.

Questions

1. What are the criticisms that Cooper and Kaplan make about variable costs and why do they claim that marginal costing has failed?
2. Cooper and Kaplan argue that fixed cost allocations are faulty and that the 'cost of complexity' requires a more comprehensive breakdown of costs. How do they propose that such a breakdown takes place?
3. How can the product cost system proposed by Cooper and Kaplan be strategically valuable to an organization that adopts it?

Further reading

Brignall, S. (1997). A contingent rationale for cost system design in services. *Management Accounting Research*, 8, 325–46.

Kaplan, R. S. (1994). Management accounting (1984–1994): development of new practice and theory. *Management Accounting Research*, 5, 247–60.

Kaplan, R. S. and Cooper, R. (1998). *Cost and Effect: Using Integrated Cost Systems to Drive Profitability and Performance*. Boston, MA: Harvard Business School Press.

Mitchell, F. (1994). A commentary on the applications of activity-based costing. *Management Accounting Research*, 5, 261–77.

Turney, P. B. B. and Anderson, B. (1989). Accounting for continuous improvement. *Sloan Management Review*, Winter, 37–47.

How Cost Accounting Distorts Product Costs

The traditional cost system that defines variable costs as varying in the short-term with production will misclassify these costs as fixed.

by Robin Cooper and Robert S. Kaplan

In order to make sensible decisions concerning the products they market, managers need to know what their products cost. Product design, new product introduction decisions, and the amount of effort expended on trying to market a given product or product line will be influenced by the anticipated cost and profitability of the product. Conversely, if product profitability appears to drop, the question of discontinuance will be raised. Product costs also can play an important role in setting prices, particularly for customized products with low sales volumes and without readily available market prices.

The cumulative effect of decisions on product design, introduction, support, discontinuance, and pricing helps define a firm's strategy. If the product cost information is distorted, the firm can follow an inappropriate and unprofitable strategy. For example, the low-cost producer often achieves competitive advantage by servicing a broad range of customers. This strategy will be successful if the economies of scale exceed the additional costs, the diseconomies of scope, caused by producing and servicing a more diverse product line. If the cost system does not correctly attribute the additional costs to the products that cause them, then the firm might end up competing in segments where the scope-related costs exceed the benefits from larger scale production.

Similarly, a differentiated producer achieves competitive advantage by meeting specialized customers' needs with products whose costs of differentiation are lower than the price premiums charged for special features and services. If the cost system fails to measure differentiation costs properly, then the firm might choose to compete in segments that are actually unprofitable.

Full vs. Variable Cost

Despite the importance of cost information, disagreement still exists about whether product costs should be measured by full or by variable cost. In a full-cost system, fixed production costs are allocated to products so that reported product costs measure total manufacturing costs. In a variable cost system, the fixed costs are not allocated and product costs reflect only the marginal cost of manufacturing.

Academic accountants, supported by economists, have argued strongly that variable costs are the relevant ones for product decisions. They have demonstrated, using increasingly complex models, that setting marginal revenues equal to marginal costs will produce the highest profit. In contrast, accountants in practice continue to report full costs in their cost accounting systems.

The definition of variable cost used by academic accountants assumes that product decisions have a short-time horizon, typically a month or a quarter. Costs are variable only if they vary directly with monthly or quarterly changes in production volume. Such a definition is appropriate if the volume of production of all products can be changed at will and there is no way to change simultaneously the level of fixed costs.

In practice, managers reject this short-term perspective because the decision to offer a product creates a long-term commitment to manufacture, market, and support that product. Given this perspective, short-term variable cost is an inadequate measure of product cost.

While full cost is meant to be a surrogate for long-run manufacturing costs, in nearly all of the companies we visited, management was not convinced that their full-cost systems were adequate for its product-related decisions. In particular, management did not believe their systems accurately reflected the costs of resources consumed to manufacture products. But they were also unwilling to adopt a variable-cost approach.

Of the more than 20 firms we visited and documented, Mayers Tap, Rockford, and Schrader Bellows provided particularly useful insights on how product costs were systematically distorted.[1] These companies had several significant common characteristics.

They all produced a large number of distinct products in a single facility. The products formed several distinct product lines and were sold through diverse marketing channels. The range in demand volume for products within a product line was high, with sales of high-volume products between 100 and 1,000 times greater than sales of low-volume products. As a consequence, products were manufactured and shipped in highly varied lot sizes. While our findings are based upon these three companies, the same effects were observed at several other sites.

In all three companies, product costs played an important role in the decisions that surrounded the introduction, pricing, and discontinuance of products. Reported product costs also appeared to play a significant role in determining how much effort should be assigned to marketing and selling products.

Typically, the individual responsible for introducing new products also was responsible for setting prices. Cost-plus pricing to achieve a desired level of gross margin predominantly was used for the special products, though substantial modifications to the resulting estimated prices occurred when direct competition existed. Such competition was common for high-volume products but rarely occurred for the low-volume items. Frequently, no obvious market prices existed for low-volume products because they had been designed to meet a particular customer's needs.

Accuracy of Product Costs

Managers in all three firms expressed serious concerns about the accuracy of their product-costing systems.

For example, Rockford attempted to obtain much higher margins for its low-volume products to compensate, on an ad hoc basis, for the gross underestimates of costs that it believed the cost system produced for these products. But management was not able to justify its decisions on cutoff points to identify low-volume products or the magnitude of the ad hoc margin increases. Further, Rockford's management believed that its faulty cost system explained the ability of small firms to compete effectively against it for high-volume business. These small firms, with no apparent economic or technological advantage, were winning high-volume business with prices that were at or below Rockford's reported costs. And the small firms seemed to be prospering at these prices.

At Schrader Bellows, production managers believed that certain products were not earning their keep because they were so difficult to produce. But the cost system reported that these products were among the most profitable in the line. The managers also were convinced that they could make certain products as efficiently as anybody else. Yet competitors were consistently pricing comparable products considerably lower. Management suspected that the cost system contributed to this problem.

At Mayers Tap, the financial accounting profits were always much lower than those predicted by the cost system, but no one could explain the discrepancy. Also, the senior managers were concerned by their failure to predict which bids they would win or lose. Mayers Tap often won bids that had been overpriced because it did not really want the business, and lost bids it had deliberately underpriced in order to get the business.

Two-Stage Cost Allocation System

The cost systems of all companies we visited had many common characteristics. Most important was the use of a two-stage cost allocation system: in the first stage, costs were assigned to cost pools (often called cost centers), and in the second stage, costs were allocated from the cost pools to the products.

The companies used many different allocation bases in the first stage to allocate costs from plant overhead accounts to cost centers. Despite the variation in allocation bases in the first stage, however, all companies used direct labor hours in the second stage to allocate overhead from the cost pools to the products. Direct labor hours was used in the second allocation stage even when the production process was highly automated so that burden rates exceeded 1,000%. Figure A.1 illustrates a typical two-stage allocation process.

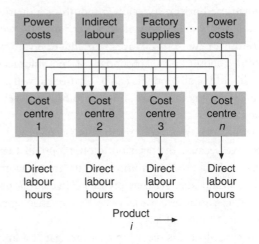

Figure A.1   The two-stage progress.

Of the three companies we examined in detail, only one had a cost accounting system capable of reporting variable product costs. Variable cost was identified at the budgeting stage in one other site, but this information was not subsequently used for product costing. The inability of the cost system to report variable cost was a common feature of many of the systems we observed. Reporting variable product costs was the exception, not the rule.

Firms used only one cost system even though costs were collected and allocated for several purposes, including product costing, operational control, and inventory valuation. The cost systems seemed to be designed primarily to perform the inventory valuation function for financial reporting because they had serious deficiencies for operational control (too delayed and too aggregate) and for product costing (too aggregate).

The Failure of Marginal Costing

The extensive use of fixed-cost allocations in all the companies we investigated contrasts sharply with a 65-year history of academics advocating marginal costing for product decisions. If the marginal-cost concept had been adopted by companies' management, then we would have expected to see product-costing systems that explicitly reported variable-cost information. Instead, we observed cost systems that reported variable as well as full costs in only a small minority of companies.

The traditional academic recommendation for marginal costing may have made sense when variable costs (labor, material, and some overhead) were a relatively high proportion of total manufactured cost and when product diversity was sufficiently small that there was not wide variation in the demands made by different products on the firm's production and marketing resources. But these conditions are no longer typical of many of today's organizations. Increasingly, overhead (most of it considered 'fixed') is becoming a larger share of total manufacturing costs. In addition, the plants we examined are being asked to produce an increasing variety of products that make quite different demands on equipment and support departments. Thus, even if direct or marginal costing were once a useful recommendation to management, direct

costing, even if correctly implemented, is not likely a solution — and may perhaps be a major problem — for product costing in the contemporary manufacturing environment.

The Failure of Fixed-Cost Allocations

While we consistently observed managers avoiding the use of variable or marginal costs for their product-related decisions, we observed also their discomfort with the full-cost allocations produced by their existing cost systems. We believe that we have identified the two major sources for the discomfort.

The first problem arises from the use of direct labor hours in the second allocation stage to assign costs from cost centers to products. This procedure may have been adequate many decades ago when direct labor was the principal value-adding activity in the material conversion process. But as firms introduce more automated machinery, direct labor is increasingly engaged in setup and supervisory functions (rather than actually performing the work on the product) and no longer represents a reasonable surrogate for resource demands by product.

In many of the plants we visited, labor's main tasks are to load the machines and to act as troubleshooters. Labor frequently works on several different products at the same time so that it becomes impossible to assign labor hours intelligently to products. Some of the companies we visited had responded to this situation by beginning experiments using machine hours instead of labor hours to allocate costs from cost pools to products (for the second stage of the allocation process). Other companies, particularly those adopting just-in-time or continuous-flow production processes, were moving to material dollars as the basis for distributing costs from pools to products. Material dollars provide a less expensive method for cost allocation than machine hours because, as with labor hours, material dollars are collected by the existing cost system, A move to a machine-hour basis would require the collection of new data for many of these companies.

Shifting from labor hours to machine hours or material dollars provides some relief from the problem of using unrealistic bases for attributing costs to products. In fact, some companies have been experimenting with using all three allocation bases simultaneously: labor hours for those costs that vary with the number of labor hours worked (e.g., supervision – if the amount of labor in a product is high, the amount of supervision related to that product also is likely to be high), machine hours for those costs that vary with the number of hours the machine is running (e.g., power – the longer the machine is running the more power that is consumed by that product), and material dollars for those costs that vary with the value of material in the product (e.g., material handling – the higher the value of the material in the product, the greater the material-handling costs associated with those products are likely to be).

Using multiple allocation bases allows a finer attribution of costs to the products responsible for the incurrence of those costs. In particular, it allows for product diversity where the direct labor, machine hours, and material dollars consumed in the manufacture of different products are not directly proportional to each other.

For reported product costs to be correct, however, the allocation bases used must be capable of accounting for all aspects of product diversity. Such an accounting is not always possible even using all three volume-related allocation bases we described. As the number of product items manufactured increases, so does the number of direct labor hours, machine hours, and material dollars consumed. The designer of the cost system, in adopting these bases, assumes that all allocated costs have the same behavior; namely that they increase in direct

relationship to the volume of product items manufactured. But there are many costs that vary with the diversity and complexity of products, not by the number of units produced.

The Cost of Complexity

The complexity costs of a full-line producer can be illustrated as follows. Consider two identical plants. One plant produces 1,000,000 units of product A. The second plant produces 100,000 units of product A and 900,000 units of 199 similar products. (The similar products have sales volumes that vary from 100 to 100,000 units.)

The first plant has a simple production environment and requires limited manufacturing-support facilities. Few setups, expediting, and scheduling activities are required.

The other plant presents a much more complex production-management environment. Its 200 products have to be scheduled through the plant, requiring frequent setups, inventory movements, purchases, receipts, and inspections. To handle this complexity, the support departments must be larger and more sophisticated.

The traditional cost accounting system plays an important role in obfuscating the underlying relationship between the range of products produced and the size of the support departments. First, the costs of most support departments are classified as fixed, making it difficult to realize that these costs are systematically varying. Second, the use of volume-related allocation bases makes it difficult to recognize how these support-department costs vary.

Support-department costs must vary with something because they have been among the fastest growing in the overall cost structure of manufactured products. As the example demonstrates, support-department costs vary not with the volume of product items manufactured, rather they vary with the range of items produced (i.e., the complexity of the production process). The traditional definition of variable cost, with its monthly or quarterly perspective, views such costs as fixed because complexity-related costs do not vary significantly in such a short time frame. Across an extended period of time, however, the increasing complexity of the production process places additional demands on support departments, and their costs eventually and inevitably rise.

The output of a support department consists of the activities its personnel perform. These include such activities as setups, inspections, material handling, and scheduling. The output of the departments can be represented by the number of distinct activities that are performed or the number of transactions handled. Because most of the output of these departments consists of human activities, however, output can increase quite significantly before an immediate deterioration in the quality of service is detected. Eventually, the maximum output of the department is reached and additional personnel are requested. The request typically comes some time after the initial increase in diversity and output. Thus, support departments, while varying with the diversity of the demanded output, grow intermittently. The practice of annually budgeting the size of the departments further hides the underlying relationship between the mix and volume of demand and the size of the department. The support departments often are constrained to grow only when budgeted to do so.

Support-department costs are perhaps best described as 'discretionary' because they are budgeted and authorized each year. The questions we must address are: What determines the level of these discretionary fixed costs? Why, if these costs are not affected by the quantity of production, are there eight people in a support department and not one? What generates the work, if not physical quantities of

inputs or outputs, that requires large support-department staffs? We believe the answers to these questions on the origins of discretionary overhead costs (i.e., what drives these costs) can be found by analyzing the activities or transactions demanded when producing a full and diverse line of products.

Transaction Costing

Low-volume products create more transactions per unit manufactured than their high-volume counterparts. The per unit share of these costs should, therefore, be higher for the low-volume products. But when volume-related bases are used exclusively to allocate support-department costs, high-volume and low-volume products receive similar transaction-related costs. When only volume-related bases are used for second-stage allocations, high-volume products receive an excessively high fraction of support-department costs and, therefore, subsidize the low-volume products.

As the range between low-volume and high-volume products increases, the degree of cross-subsidization rises. Support departments expand to cope with the additional complexity of more products, leading to increased overhead charges. The reported product cost of all products consequently increases. The high-volume products appear more expensive to produce than previously, even though they are not responsible for the additional costs. The costs triggered by the introduction of new, low-volume products are systematically shifted to high-volume products that may be placing relatively few demands on the plant's support departments.

Many of the transactions that generate work for production-support departments can be proxied by the number of setups. For example, the movement of material in the plant often occurs at the commencement or completion of a production run. Similarly, the majority of the time spent on parts inspection occurs just after a setup or change-over. Thus, while the support departments are engaged in a broad array of activities, a considerable portion of their costs may be attributed to the number of setups.

Not all of the support-department costs are related (or relatable) to the number of setups. The cost of setup personnel relates more to the quantity of setup hours than to the actual number of setups. The number of inspections of incoming material can be directly related to the number of material receipts, as would be the time spent moving the received material into inventory. The number of outgoing shipments can be used to predict the activity level of the finished-goods and shipping departments. The assignment of all these support costs with a transactions-based approach reinforces the effect of the setup-related costs because the low-sales-volume items tend to trigger more small incoming and outgoing shipments.

Schrader Bellows had recently performed a 'strategic cost analysis' that significantly increased the number of bases used to allocate costs to the products; many second-stage allocations used

transactions costs to assign support-department costs to products. In particular, the number of setups allocated a sizable percentage of support-department costs to products.

The effect of changing these second-stage allocations from a direct labor to a transaction basis was dramatic. While the support-department costs accounted for about 50% of overhead (or about 25% of total costs), the change in the reported product costs ranged from about minus 10% to plus 1,000%. The significant change in the reported product costs for the low-volume items was due to the substantial cost of the support departments and the low batch size over which the transaction cost was spread.

Table A.1 shows the magnitude of the shift in reported product costs for seven representative products. The existing cost system reported gross margins that varied from 26% to 47%, while the strategic analysis showed gross margins that ranged from −258% to +46%. The trends in the two sets of reported product profitabilities were clear: the existing direct-labor-based system had identified the low-volume products as the most profitable, while the strategic cost analysis indicated exactly the reverse.

Table A.1   Comparison of reported product costs at Schrader Bellows.

		Existing cost system		Transaction-based system		Percent of change	
Product	Sales volume	Unit cost[a]	Unit gross margin	Unit cost[a]	Unit gross margin	Unit cost	Unit gross margin
1	43,562	7.85	5.52	7.17	6.19	(8.7)	12.3
2	500	8.74	3.76	15.45	(2.95)	76.8	(178.5)
3	53	12.15	10.89	82.49	(59.45)	578.9	(645.9)
4	2,079	13.63	4.91	24.51	(5.97)	79.8	(221.6)
5	5,670	12.40	7.95	19.99	0.36	61.3	(93.4)
6	11,169	8.04	5.49	7.96	5.57	(1.0)	1.5
7	423	8.47	3.74	6.93	5.28	(18.2)	41.2

[a]The sum of total cost (sales volume × unit cost) for all seven products is different under the two systems because the seven products only represent a small fraction of total production.

There are three important messages in the table and in the company's findings in general.

- Traditional systems that assign costs to products using a single volume-related base seriously distort product costs.
- The distortion is systematic. Low-volume products are under-costed, and high-volume products are over-costed.
- Accurate product costs cannot, in general, be achieved by cost systems that rely only on volume-related bases (even multiple bases such as machine hours and material quantities) for second-stage allocations. A different type of allocation base must be used for overhead costs that vary with the number of transactions performed, as opposed to the volume of product produced.

The shift to transaction-related allocation bases is a more fundamental change to the philosophy of cost-systems design than is at first realized. In a traditional cost system that uses volume-related bases, the costing element is always the product. It is the product that consumes direct labor hours, machine hours, or material dollars. Therefore, it is the product that gets costed.

In a transaction-related system, costs are assigned to the units that caused the transaction to be originated. For example, if the transaction is a setup, then the costing element will be the production lot because each production lot requires a single setup. The same is true for purchasing activities, inspections, scheduling, and material movements. The costing element is no longer the product but those elements the transaction affects.

In the transaction-related costing system, the unit cost of a product is determined by dividing the cost of a transaction by the number of units in the costing element. For example, when the costing element is a production lot, the unit cost of a product is determined by dividing the production lot cost by the number of units in the production lot.

This change in the costing element is not trivial. In the Schrader Bellows strategic cost analysis (see table A.1), product seven appears to violate the strong inverse relationship between profits and production-lot size for the other six products. A more detailed analysis of the seven products, however, showed that product seven was assembled with components also used to produce two high-volume products (numbers one and six) and that it was the production-lot size of the components that was the dominant cost driver, not the assembly-lot size, or the shipping-lot size.

In a traditional cost system, the value of commonality of parts is hidden. Low-volume components appear to cost only slightly more than their high-volume counterparts. There is no incentive to design products with common parts. The shift to transaction-related costing identifies the much lower costs that derive from designing products with common (or fewer) parts and the much higher costs generated when large numbers of unique parts are specified for low-volume products. In recognition of this phenomenon, more companies are experimenting with assigning material-related overhead on the basis of the total number of different parts used, and not on the physical or dollar volume of materials used.

Long-Term Variable Cost

The volume-unrelated support-department costs, unlike traditional variable costs, do not vary with short-term changes in activity levels. Traditional variable costs vary in the short run with production fluctuations because they represent cost elements that require no managerial actions to change the level of expenditure.

In contrast, any amount of decrease in overhead costs associated with reducing diversity and complexity in the factory will take many months to realize and will require specific managerial actions. The number of personnel in support departments will have to be reduced, machines may have to be sold off, and some supervisors will become redundant. Actions to accomplish these overhead cost reductions will lag, by months, the complexity-reducing actions in the product line and in the process technology. But this long-term cost response mirrors the way overhead costs were first builtup in the factory – as more products with specialized designs were added to the product line, the organization simply muddled through with existing personnel. It was only over time that overworked support departments requested and received additional personnel to handle the increased number of transactions that had been thrust upon them.

The personnel in the support departments are often highly skilled and possess a high degree of firm-specific knowledge. Management is loathe to lay them off when changes in market conditions temporarily reduce the level of production complexity. Consequently, when the workload of these departments drops, surplus capacity exists.

The long-term perspective management had adopted toward its products often made it difficult to use the surplus capacity. When it was used, it was not to make products never to be produced again, but rather to produce inventory of products that were known to disrupt production (typically the very low-volume items) or to produce, under short-term contract, products for other companies. We did not observe or hear about a situation in which this capacity was used to introduce a product that had only a short life expectancy. Some companies justified the acceptance of special orders or incremental business because they 'knew' that the income from this business more than covered their variable or incremental costs. They failed to realize that the long-term consequence from accepting such incremental business was a steady rise in the costs of their support departments.

When Product Costs are not Known

The magnitude of the errors in reported product costs and the nature of their bias make it difficult for full-line producers to enact sensible strategies. The existing cost systems clearly identify the low-volume products as the most profitable and the high-volume ones as the least profitable. Focused competitors, on the other hand, will not suffer from the same handicap. Their cost systems, while equally poorly designed, will report more accurate product costs because they are not distorted as much by lot-size diversity.

With access to more accurate product cost data, a focused competitor can sell the high-volume products at a lower price. The full-line producer is then apparently faced with very low margins on these products and is naturally tempted to deemphasize this business and concentrate on apparently higher-profit, low-volume specialty business. This shift from high-volume to low-volume products, however, does not produce the anticipated higher profitability. The firm, believing in its cost system, chases illusory profits.

The firm has been victimized by diseconomies of scope. In trying to obtain the benefits of economy of scale by expanding its product offerings to better utilize its fixed or capacity resources, the firm does not see the high diseconomies it has introduced by creating a far more complex production environment. The cost accounting system fails to reveal this diseconomy of scope.

A Comprehensive Cost System

One message comes through overwhelmingly in our experiences with the three firms, and with the many others we talked and worked with. Almost all product-related decisions – introduction, pricing, and discontinuance – are long-term. Management accounting thinking (and teaching) during the past half-century has concentrated on information for making short-run incremental decisions based on variable, incremental, or relevant costs. It has missed the most important aspect of product decisions. Invariably, the time period for measuring 'variable,' 'incremental,' or 'relevant' costs has been about a month (the time period corresponding to the cycle of the firm's internal financial reporting system). While academics admonish that notions of fixed and variable are meaningful only with respect to a particular time period, they immediately discard this warning and teach from the perspective of one-month decision horizons.

This short-term focus for product costing has led all the companies we visited to view a large and growing proportion of their total manufacturing costs as 'fixed.' In fact, however, what they call 'fixed' costs have been the most variable and rapidly increasing costs. This paradox has seemingly eluded most accounting practitioners and scholars. Two fundamental changes in our thinking about cost behavior must be introduced.

First, the allocation of costs from the cost pools to the products should be achieved using bases that reflect cost drivers. Because many overhead costs are driven by the complexity of production, not the volume of production, nonvolume-related bases are required. Second, many of these overhead costs are somewhat discretionary. While they vary with changes in the complexity of the production process, these changes are intermittent. A traditional cost system that defines variable costs as varying in the short term with production volume will misclassify these costs as fixed.

The misclassification also arises from an inadequate understanding of the actual cost drivers for most overhead costs. Many overhead costs vary with transactions: transactions to order, schedule, receive, inspect, and pay for shipments; to move, track, and count inventory; to schedule production work; to set up machines; to perform quality assurance; to implement engineering change orders; and to expedite and ship orders. The cost of these transactions is largely independent of the size of the order being handled; the cost does not vary with the amount of inputs or outputs. It does vary, however, with the need for the transaction itself. If the firm introduces more products, if it needs to expedite more orders, or if it needs to inspect more components, then it will need larger overhead departments to perform these additional transactions.

Summary

Product costs are almost all variable costs. Some of the sources of variability relate to physical volume of items produced. These costs will vary with units produced, or in a varied, multiproduct environment, with surrogate measures such as labor hours, machine hours, material dollars and quantities, or elapsed time of production. Other costs, however, particularly those arising from overhead support and marketing departments, vary with the diversity and complexity in the product line. The variability of these costs is best explained by the incidence of transactions to initiate the next stage in the production, logistics, or distribution process.

A comprehensive product cost system, incorporating the long-term variable costs of manufacturing and marketing each product or product line, should provide a much better basis for managerial decisions on pricing, introducing, discontinuing, and reengineering product lines. The cost system may even become strategically important for running the business and creating sustainable competitive advantages for the firm.

The Importance of Field Research

The accompanying article, coauthored with Robin Cooper, is excerpted from *Accounting & Management: Field Study Perspectives* (Boston, Mass., Harvard Business School Press, 1987) William J. Bruns, Jr. and Robert S. Kaplan (eds.). The book contains 13 field studies on management accounting innovations presented at a colloquium at the Harvard Business School in June 1986 by leading academic researchers from the U.S. and Western Europe. The colloquium represents the largest single collection of field research studies on management accounting practices in organizations.

The HBS colloquium had two principal objectives. First, the authors were to understand and document the management accounting practices of actual organizations. Some of the organizations would be captured in a process of transition: attempting, and occasionally succeeding to modify their systems to measure, motivate and evaluate operating performance. Other organizations were studied just to understand the system of measurement and control that had evolved in their particular environment.

A second, and even more important, objective of the colloquium was to begin the process by which field research methods in management accounting could be established as a legitimate method of inquiry. Academic researchers in accounting have extensive experience with deductive, model-building,

analytic research with the design and analysis of controlled experiments, usually in a laboratory setting; and with the empirical analysis of large data bases. This experience has yielded research guidance and criteria that, while not always explicit, nevertheless are widely shared and permit research to be conducted and evaluated.

At a time when so many organizations are reexamining the adequacy of their management accounting systems it is especially important that university-based researchers spend more time working directly with innovating organizations. We are pleased that *Management Accounting*, through publication of this article, is helping to publicize the existence of the field studies performed to date.

The experiences described in the accompanying article, as well as in the other papers in the colloquium volume, indicate a very different role for management accounting systems in organizations than is currently taught in most of our business schools and accounting departments. We believe that present and future field research and case writing will lead to major changes in management accounting courses. To facilitate the needed changes in curriculum and research, however, requires extensive cooperation between university faculty and practicing management accountants. As noted by observers at the Harvard colloquium:

> There is a tremendous store of knowledge about management accounting practices and ideas out there in real companies. Academicians as a whole are far too ignorant of that knowledge. When academics begin to see the relevance of this data base, perhaps generations of students will become more aware of its richness. Such awareness must precede any real progress on prescribing good management accounting for any given situation.

To observe is also to discover. The authors have observed interesting phenomena. We do not know how prevalent these phenomena are or under what conditions they exist or do not exist. But the studies suggest possible relationships, causes, effects, and even dynamic process in the sense that Yogi Berra must have had in mind when he said, 'Some times you can observe a lot just by watching.'

With the research support and cooperation of the members of the National Association of Accountants, many university professors are looking forward to watching and also describing the changes now under way so that academics can begin to develop theories, teach, and finally prescribe about the new opportunities for management accounting.

Robert S. Kaplan

Endnotes

1. Mayers Tap (disguised name) is described in Harvard Business School, case series 9-185-111. Schrader-Bellows is described in HBS Case Series 9-186-272.

   Robin Cooper is an associate professor of business administration at the Harvard Business School and a fellow of the Institute of Chartered Accountants in England and Wales. He writes a column, 'Cost Management Principles and Concepts,' in the Journal of Cost Management and has produced research on activity-based costing for the CAM-1 Cost Management System Project. Robert S. Kaplan is the Arthur Lowes Dickinson Professor of Accounting at the Harvard Business School and a professor of industrial administration at Carnegie-Mellon University. Currently, Professor Kaplan serves on the Executive Committee of the CAM-1 Cost Management System Project, the Manufacturing Studies Board of the National Research Council, and the Financial Accounting Standards Advisory Committee.

Reading B

Questions

1. What is the distinction made by Otley *et al.* between management control and financial control?
2. What is the contribution of systems theory to an understanding of management control?
3. How does Scott's distinction between open and closed, rational and natural models help to categorize the accounting literature, and why is any such categorization important?
4. Why does an emphasis on accounting limit an understanding of the broader importance of management control? What contribution can non-financial performance management make to our understanding of management control within organizations?

Further reading

Berry, A. J., Broadbent, J. and Otley, D. (Eds). (1995). *Management Control: Theories, Issues and Practices*. London: Macmillan.

Fitzgerald, L., Johnston, R., Brignall, S., Silvestro, R. and Voss, C. (1991). *Performance Measurement in Service Businesses*. London: Chartered Institute of Management Accountants.

Hopper, T., Otley, D. and Scapens, B. (2001). British management accounting research: whence and whither: opinions and recollections. *British Accounting Review*, 33, 263–91.

Humphrey, C. and Scapens, R. W. (1996). Theories and case studies of organizational and accounting practices: limitation or liberation? *Accounting, Auditing and Accountability Journal*, 9(4), 86–106.

Kaplan, R. S. and Norton, D. P. (2001). *The Strategy-Focused Organization: How Balanced Scorecard Companies Thrive in the New Business Environment*. Boston, MA: Harvard Business School Press.

Macintosh, N. B. (1994). *Management Accounting and Control Systems: An Organizational and Behavioral Approach*. Chichester: John Wiley & Sons.

Otley, D. (1999). Performance management: a framework for management control systems research. *Management Accounting Research*, 10, 363–82.

Otley, D. (2001). Extending the boundaries of management accounting research: developing systems for performance management. *British Accounting Review*, 33, 243–61.

Scott, W. R. (1998). *Organizations: Rational, Natural, and Open Systems* (4th edn). Upper Saddle River, NJ: Prentice Hall International, Inc.

Research in Management Control: An Overview of its Development

David Otley*, Jane Broadbent[†] and Anthony Berry[‡]
*Lancaster University Management School, [†]Department of Accounting and Financial Management, University of Essex, [‡]Manchester Business School

Summary

This paper builds on a series of earlier reviews of the management control literature (Giglioni and Bedeian, 1974; Hofstede, 1968; Merchant and Simons, 1986; Parker, 1986) and considers the development of the management control literature in the context of organizational theories. Early themes which have provided the roots for the development of the subject area are explored as is more recent work which has evolved both as a continuation and a reaction against them, with Scott's (1981) framework being used to organize this literature. It is argued that one of the unintended consequences of the influential work of Robert Anthony (1965) has been a restriction of the subject to an accounting-based framework and that this focus needs to be broadened. The review points to the potential of the subject as an integrating theme for the practice and research of management and some themes for future research are suggested.

Introduction

This paper reviews the development of research in management control, building upon other reviews both to examine the roots of the subject from the turn of the century and to demonstrate the depth and breadth of the subject. Four previous reviews form the foundation for our overview.

Giglioni and Bedeian (1974) review the contribution of the general management and organizational theory literature for the period 1900–1972, drawing out several different strands to conclude that

> even though control theory has not achieved the level of sophistication of some other management functions, it has developed to a point that affords the executive ample opportunity to maintain the operations of his firm under check.

Parker (1986) argues that accounting control developments lagged developments in the management literature, and criticizes accounting models for offering only an imperfect reflection of management models of control. Hofstede (1968) offers an early survey of the behavioural approach to budgetary control. He explores how the role of budgets has been viewed in accounting theory, in motivation theory, and from the perspective of systems theory. Finally, the brief overview of research into control in complex organizations by Merchant and Simons (1986) takes a broad view of what constitutes control, as does the present paper. It differs, however, in also paying attention to agency theory literature and psychological research both omitted from consideration here.[1]

It will be argued that one of the unintended consequences of Anthony's (1965) seminal work is that management control has primarily been developed in an accounting-based framework which has been unnecessarily restrictive. Although radical theorists have studied control processes more extensively, their attention has been focused much more on the exercise of power and its consequences than on the role of control systems as a means of organizational survival. This is an important area, but one which is outside the remit set for this review which is in closer alignment with Mills (1970) who argued for the place of management control as a central management discipline. He suggested that it was a more appropriate integrating discipline for general management courses than the tradition of using business policy or corporate strategy courses. 'Control' is itself a highly ambiguous term as evidenced by the difficulty of translating it into many European languages and the list of '57 varieties' in its connotations given by Rathe (1960). Given this diversity some attention will be paid to matters of definition and the establishment of appropriate boundaries for this review.

Anthony's (1965) classic definition of management control was

the process by which managers assure that resources are obtained and used effectively and efficiently in the accomplishment of the organization's objectives.

He saw management control as being sandwiched between the processes of strategic planning and operational control; these processes being super-imposed upon an organizational hierarchy to indicate the respective managerial levels at which they operate.

Strategic planning is concerned with setting goals and objectives for the whole organization over the long term. By contrast, operational control is concerned with the activity of ensuring that immediate tasks are carried out. Management control is the process that links the two. Global goals are broken down into sub-goals for parts of the organization; statements of future intent are given more substantive content; long-term goals are solidified into shorter term goals. The process of management control is designed to ensure that the day-to-day tasks performed by all participants in the organization come together in a coordinated set of actions which lead to overall goal specification and attainment. This can be seen primarily as the planning and coordination function of management control. The other side of the management control coin is its monitoring and feedback function. Regular observations and reports on actual achievement are used to ensure that planned actions are indeed achieving desired results.

It may be argued that Anthony's approach is too restrictive in that it assumes away important problems (see Lowe and Puxty, 1989 for further discussion of these issues). The first problem is concerned with problems of defining strategies, goals and objectives. Such procedures are typically complex and ill-defined, with strategies being produced as much by accident as by design. It is clear that Anthony was aware of the problems of ambiguity and uncertainty when he located these issues in the domain of strategy, but he then avoided their further consideration. The second problem concerns the methods used to control the production (or service delivery) processes, which are highly dependent upon the specific technology in use and which are widely divergent. Anthony conveniently relegates these issues to the realm of operational control. Finally, his textbooks concentrate upon planning and control through accounting rationales and contain little or no discussion of social-psychological or behavioural issues, despite his highlighting the importance of the latter. Anthony's approach can, thus, be seen as a preliminary ground-clearing exercise, whereby he limits the extent of the problem he sets out to study. In a complex field this was probably a very sensible first step, however, it greatly narrowed the scope of the topic.

A broader view of management control is suggested by Lowe (1971) in a more comprehensive definition:

> A system of organizational information seeking and gathering, accountability and feedback designed to ensure that the enterprise adapts to changes in its substantive environment and that the work behaviour of its employees is measured by reference to a set of operational sub-goals (which conform with overall objectives) so that the discrepancy between the two can be reconciled and corrected for.

This stresses the role of a management control system (MCS) as a broad set of control mechanisms designed to assist organizations to regulate themselves, whereas Anthony's definition is more specific and limited to a narrower sub-set of control activities. Machin (1983) continues this line of thought in his critical review of management control systems as a specialist subject of academic study. He explores each of the terms 'management', 'control' and 'system', defining a research focus:

> Those formal, systematically developed, organization-wide, data-handling systems which are designed to facilitate management control which 'is the process by which managers assure that resources are obtained and used effectively and efficiently in the accomplishment of the organization's objectives.'

Machin notes that such a definition has the merit of leaving scope for academics to disagree violently whilst still perceiving themselves to be studying the same thing! Further, Machin argues that research in MCSs, led, as it was, by qualified accountants, made the research questions

> virtually immune from philosophical analysis,

a critique also reflected in Hofstede's (1978) criticism of the

> poverty of management control philosophy,

– the narrow, accounting focus which had become so prevalent.

Such diverse opinions leave a number of issues to be clarified. First, is the meaning of the term 'control'. In this review we will include within the definition of control both the ideas of informational feedback and the implementation of corrective actions. Equally, we explicitly exclude the exercise of power for its own sake, restricting ourselves to those activities undertaken by managers which have the intention of furthering organizational objectives (at least, insofar as perceived by managers). We are, thus, primarily concerned with the exercise of legitimate authority rather than power. This is no doubt a controversial position, but gives the review a clear managerial focus.

There is also a distinction to be drawn between management control and financial control, which is of some importance given the accounting domination of the subject in recent years. Financial control is clearly concerned with the management of the finance function within organizations. As such it is one business function amongst many, and comprises but one facet of the wider practice of management control. On the other hand, management control can be defined as a general management function concerned with the achievement of overall organizational aims and objectives. Financial information is thus used in practice to serve two interrelated functions. First, it is clearly used in a financial control role, where its function is to monitor financial flows; that is, it is concerned with looking after the money. Second, it is also often used as a surrogate measure for other aspects of organizational performance. That is, management control is concerned with looking after the overall business with money being used as a convenient measure of a variety of other more complex dimensions, not as an end in itself.

Having set some boundaries, the next section of the paper will provide a brief account of the main themes that have formed the starting point for the development of the field. Whilst well known, these roots cannot be ignored as their influence is reflected in work which continues today. There follows a review of the literature that has evolved over the last 20 years both as a continuation of and as a reaction against those roots, using a heuristic map provided by Scott (1981). Finally, we will suggest possible themes for future development.

The Starting Points

The roots of management control issues lie in early managerial thought. The significance of the work of Weber, Durkheim and Pareto upon the development of managerial thought is well rehearsed. Less well known, but providing an excellent example of the classical management theorists, is the contribution of Mary Parker Follett, described by Parker (1986) as providing almost all of the ideas of modern control

theory. Follett saw that the manager controlled not single elements but complex interrelationships and argued that the basis for control lay in self-regulating, self-directing individuals and groups who recognized common interests and objectives. It may be that Follett was an idealist in her search for unity in organizations for she sought a control that was

> 'fact control' not 'man control', and 'correlated control' rather than 'superimposed control'.

Further she saw coordination as the reciprocal relating of all factors in a setting that involved direct contact of all people concerned. The application of these

> fundamental principles of organisation

was the control activity itself, for the whole point of her principles was to ensure predictable performance for the organization.

Scientific management, another important root of management control, is frequently associated with the work of F.W. Taylor (Miller and O'Leary, 1987), although there were earlier contributors to this movement. For example, Babbage (1832) was concerned with improving manufacture and systems and analysed operations, the skills involved, the expense of each process and suggested paths for improvement. In 1874 Fink (*see* Wren, 1994) developed a cost accounting system that used information flows, classification of costs and statistical control devices; innovations which led directly to 20th century processes of management control.

What seems to characterize these theorists is an attention to real problems, a scientific approach which centred upon understanding and conceptual analysis, and a wish to solve problems. Their contribution to management control lay in their attention to authority and accountability, an awareness of the need for analytical and budgetary models for control, forging the link between cost and operational activities, and the separation of cost accounting from financial accounting, with the former being a pre-cursor of management accounting and control. However, these practical theorists may have pursued rationality of economic action and the search for universal solutions too far, although their ideas are still current and form the basis for much work in the field, many being echoed in the work of Robert Anthony. The ideas of the common purpose of social organizations along with a concern for the relationship between effectiveness and efficiency foreshadow the concept of autopoesis (the view that systems can have a 'life of their own') developed by cyberneticians. These will be examined in the next section.

Evolution of the Management Control Literature

As previously noted, Parker (1986) argued that developments in accounting control have followed and lagged developments in management theory. Developments in management control seem to have followed a similar pattern, so we use the schema suggested by Scott (1981) for categorizing developments in organization theory as a framework for organizing this part of our review. We would argue that systems thinking has had an important influence on the development of MCSs and Scott's schema is based on a systems approach, so it is to this we now turn.

Cybernetics and systems theory

Organizational theory in general and management control research in particular have been influenced considerably by cybernetics (the science of communication and control (Weiner, 1948)). These insights have been extended in the holistic standpoint taken by general systems theory and the 'soft systems' approach (Checkland, 1981). Its central contribution has been in the *systemic* approach it adopts, causing attention to be paid to the overall control of the organization, in contrast to the *systematic* approach dominant in accounting control, which has often assumed that the multiplication of 'controls' will lead inexorably to overall 'control', a view roundly routed by Drucker (1964). Cybernetics and systems theory have developed in such an interlinked manner that it is difficult to draw a meaningful dividing line between them (for a fuller survey see Otley, 1983), although a simple distinction would be to suggest that cybernetics is concerned with closed systems, whereas systems theory specifically involves a more open perspective.

The major contribution of cybernetics has been in the study of systems in which complexity is paramount (Ashby, 1956); it attempts to explain the behaviour of complex systems primarily in terms of relatively simple feedback mechanisms (Wisdom, 1956). There have been a number of attempts to apply cybernetic concepts to the issue of management control, but these have all been of a theoretical nature, albeit based on general empirical observation. The process of generating feedback information is fundamental to management accounting on which much management control practice rests, although this is not usually elaborated in any very insightful manner. However, Otley and Berry (1980) developed Tocher's (1970) control model and applied it to organizational control. They maintain that effective control depends upon the existence of an adequate means of predicting the consequences of alternative control actions. In most organizations such predictive models reside in the minds of line managers, rather than in any more formal form, and they argue that improvements in control practice need to focus on improving such models. It is also argued that feed-forward (anticipatory) controls are likely to be of more importance than feedback (reactive) controls. This echoes previous comments by authors such as

Ashby (1956), who points to the biological advantages in controlling not by error but by what gives rise to error, and Amey (1979) who stresses the importance of anticipatory control mechanisms in business enterprises.

Arguably the most insightful use of cybernetic ideas applied to management practice is also one of the earliest. Vickers (1965, 1967) applied many cybernetic ideas to management practice during the 1950s. Although developed in a primarily closed systems context, he also started to explore the issue of regulating institutions from a societal perspective. This is also a major theme of Stafford Beer, most comprehensively in his 1972 book *Brain of the Firm*. Here he uses the human nervous system as an analogy for the control mechanisms that need to be adopted at various levels in the control of an organization. However, Beer's major contribution lies in his attempt to tackle issues of the overall societal and political context within which more detailed organizational forms and controls emerge. This is a theme which is picked up, albeit in a very different form, by the radical theorists of the 1980s and 1990s. The standard concepts of the cybernetic literature do not have such a straightforward application to the issue of organizational control as some presentations of them tend to imply. However, they do provide a language in which any of the central issues of management control may be expressed.

Further progress comes from the use of general systems theory which stresses the importance of *emergent* properties of systems, that is, properties which are characteristic of the level of complexity being studied and which do not have meaning at lower levels; such properties are possessed by the system but not by its parts. Systems thinking is thus primarily a tool for dealing with high levels of complexity, particularly with reference to systems which display adaptive and apparently goal-seeking behaviour (Lilienfeld, 1978). Some useful

conceptual distinctions are drawn by Lowe and McInnes (1971) who attempt to apply a systems approach to the design of MCSs. An important extension to the realm of so-called 'soft' systems (i.e. systems which include human beings, where objectives are vague and ambiguous, decision-making processes ill-defined, and where, at best, only qualitative measures of performance exist) has been made by the Checkland school at Lancaster (Checkland, 1981; Wilson, 1984).

One of the central issues with which the 'soft' systems methodology has to cope is the imputation of objectives to the system. In many ways this methodology reflects the *verstehen* (or insight) tradition of thought in sociology, where great stress is laid upon the accuracy and honesty of observation, the sensitivity and perception of the observer, and on the imaginative interpretations of observations. Although the soft systems approach has had considerable success in producing solutions to real problems, it does not appear to have contributed to the development of the theory of control in the normal academic sense. It is very much an applied problem-solving methodology in its present form rather than a research method designed to yield generalizable explanations, although it undoubtedly has further potential in this area. This raises the issue of the nature and type of theories that can be expected in such a complex area of human and social behaviour.

A framework to map developments in management control research

Scott (1981) analysed the development of organization theory using two dimensions. First, he saw a transition from closed to open systems models of organization, reflecting the influence of systems ideas. Prior to 1960 most theorists tended to assume that organizations could be understood apart from their environments, and that most important processes and events were internal to the organization. After that date it was increasingly recognized that organizations were highly interdependent with their environments, and that boundaries are both permeable and variable. Second, he distinguished between rational and natural systems models. The rational systems model assumes that organizations are purposefully designed for the pursuit of explicit objectives, whereas the natural systems model emphasizes the importance of unplanned and spontaneous processes, with organically emerging informal structures supplementing or subduing rationally designed frameworks. The distinction between rational and natural systems is applicable to both sides of the closed-open system divide, resulting in the definition of the four approaches.

We use these categories to summarize work in MCSs, although we recognize that such categorization is not necessarily 'neat'. Organizations can be viewed as being *both* rational and natural (Thompson, 1967; Boland and Pondy, 1983); they are often intentionally designed to achieve specific purposes, yet also display emergent properties. It can be argued that each successive theoretical development provides an additional perspective which is helpful in understanding organizational processes, and which is likely to be additional and complementary to those which have preceded it. However, it is also recognized that this is a controversial statement that would not be accepted by some of those adopting a post-modernist viewpoint.

The Closed Rational Perspective

This work is characterized by being both universal in orientation and systematic in approach, scientific management being a typical example. In the management control literature we find a continuing emphasis on rational solutions, implicitly assuming a closed systems model of organization, which are universalistic in nature. Indeed, this can also be seen in much of the modern popular management literature, where a universal 'how-to-do-it' approach continues to find a ready market.

From a research point of view, there is much work which has sought to identify the 'one best way' to operate a control system. An excellent example of this approach applied to budgetary control is that conducted by Hofstede (1968). He sought to reconcile the US findings that budgets were extensively used in performance evaluation and control, but were associated with negative feelings on the part of many managers and dysfunctional consequences to the organization, with the European experience that budgets were seen positively but were little used. Multiple perspectives are brought to bear, including systems theory, although this draws primarily on cybernetics. His conclusions list several pages of recommendations as to how budgets could be used effectively without engendering negative consequences, and indicate an implicit universalistic orientation. Similarly, the well known text co-authored by Anthony and a host of collaborators (see for example, Anthony *et al.*, 1984) also clearly falls into the closed rational mode with its heavy emphasis on accounting controls.

The Closed Natural Perspective

The closed natural approach is centred around an increasing interest in the behavioural consequences of control systems operation. This was perhaps first introduced to the control literature by Argyris (1952) in his article entitled 'The Impact of Budgets on People', an emphasis reversed neatly almost 20 years later by Schiff and Lewin (1970) in their article 'The Impact of People on Budgets'. Lowe and Shaw (1968) discussed the tendency of managers to bias budgetary estimates that were subsequently used for control purposes. Buckley and McKenna (1972) were able to publish a review article summarizing current knowledge on the connection between budgetary control and managerial behaviour in the early 1970s. Mintzberg followed his 1973 study of the nature of managerial activity with a 1975 study of the impediments to the use of management information, which dealt with many of the behavioural issues in the operation of control systems. There was thus a growing awareness of the human consequences of control systems use and operation beginning to emerge in the early 1970s, perhaps lagging some 20 years behind the equivalent human relations movement in the organization theory literature.

A behavioural perspective on the theme of managerial performance evaluation also began to emerge at this time. Hopwood (1972, 1974a) identified the different styles that managers could adopt in their use of accounting information and studied their impact on individual behaviour and (implicitly) organizational performance. Rhaman and McCosh (1976) sought to explain why different uses of accounting control information were observed, and concluded that both individual characteristics and organizational climate were significant factors. A study by Otley (1978) yielded almost exactly contrary results to those of Hopwood (1972) because the research site had significant differences; the conflicting findings could be reconciled only by adopting a contingent approach, a task that was more thoroughly undertaken by Hirst (1981).

The idea that systems used to evaluate performance are affected by the information supplied by those being evaluated has led to the concept of information inductance (Prakash and Rappaport, 1977; Dirsmith and Jablonsky, 1979). This generalized the observations of information bias and manipulation reported previously as just one manifestation of a more general phenomenon. Such work was extended by Birnberg et al. (1983) into a unified contingent framework, based on the ideas of Thompson (1967), Perrow (1970) and Ouchi (1979).

Despite the categorization of organizational contingency theorists into the open systems box by Scott (1981), the early contingent work in accounting-based control systems has a clear closed systems flavour. It was only in the late 1970s that the open systems ideas in contingency theory, which followed primarily from the use of environment as a contingent variable, began to be reflected in the management control literature. This parallels developments in Organization Theory (OT), for it is arguable that early contingent work by writers such as Woodward (1958, 1965) concentrated on internal factors such as technology, and did not adopt an open systems approach until later. Thus, texts in the management control area, such as Emmanuel et al. (1985, 1990), Merchant (1985), and Johnson and Gill (1993) which recognized the behavioural aspects of MCSs as well as adopting some tenets of the contingency framework, tend to lie along the boundary of the closed natural category and the open rational approach.

The Open Rational Perspective

As in OT, the emergence of an open systems perspective was accompanied by a return to more rational approaches and a relative neglect of the natural (albeit) closed approaches of the preceding years. The recognition of the external environment, key to the open systems approach, had never been strong in the early MCS literature. However, in the early 1970s there was a movement towards an open systems perspective, if only from a theoretical standpoint, an approach well illustrated by the collection of readings in the monograph New Perspectives in Management Control (Lowe and Machin, 1983). This approach was most cogently led by Lowe (1971) in an article which clearly recognizes the coalition of stakeholders involved in an enterprise (a concept used by Scott (1981) as an exemplar of an open systems approach) and the need for adaptation to the external environment. It is further clarified in Lowe and McInnes'

(1971) article which adds the concept of resolution level. At the same time Beer (1972) was developing his own, somewhat idiosyncratic, approach and moving beyond cybernetics into more general systems analysis drawing heavily on neurophysiological ideas.

More significant, empirically, was the development of the contingency theory of management accounting control systems (summarized by Otley, 1980). Although several contingent variables were shown to be significant (e.g. technology, environment, organizational structure, size, corporate strategy), it was the impact of the external environment in general, and of external uncertainty in particular, that most clearly indicated the adoption of an open systems perspective. It is this distinction that marks the divergence of the study of management accounting systems, which have steadfastly retained their internal orientation (despite valiant attempts by a few proponents of so-called 'strategic management accounting' (Simmonds, 1981; Bromwich, 1990), and the study of the wider area of management control systems. Within management accounting, contingency theory waned in the early 1980s, to be replaced by various critical approaches in Europe, and to continue down a universalistic track in the US with the burgeoning popularity of activity-based costing under the leadership of Kaplan (1983) in particular. The wider study of control systems picked up on the neglected variable of corporate strategy at this point, which led to a small but significant stream of work most notably by Govindarajan and Gupta (1985) and Simons (1987, 1990, 1991, 1995).

The Open Natural Perspective

There are two developments which can be seen to mark a movement into this final perspective, which are illustrated by the collection of papers published in the monograph *Critical Perspectives in Management Control* (Chua *et al.*, 1989). First, there is a recognition that contingent variables are not to be seen as deterministic drivers of control systems design. In particular, the environment is not to be seen only as a factor to be adapted to, but also something which can itself be manipulated and managed. Second, there is the recognition of the political nature of organizational activity. However, although radical theorists have clearly been concerned with the exercise of power in and around organizations, it is not clear that they have contributed greatly to the study of control in its adaptive sense, nevertheless they have clearly indicated the complex political environment within which control systems have to function (see, for example, Ezzamel and Watson, 1993; Hogler and Hunt, 1993). This touches on the theme of legitimacy at various levels of resolution and addresses the question of how legitimacy becomes established and how it works through to different hierarchical levels in organizations. Examples of such work include research examining the reforms of the NHS using a post-modern perspective (Preston, 1992; Preston *et al.*, 1992) and that, taking a critical theory approach, of Laughlin and Broadbent (1993) who examined the impact of attempts to control particular organizations through the medium of the law. In a more general sense the discontinuities of history and the diverse roots of control systems are brought out by Miller and O'Leary (1987). Other work in this field has taken a more interpretive or anthropological approach, examining the role of values or culture in determining the extent to which it is possible to control organizational members. Ansari and Bell (1991) illustrate the effect of national culture; Broadbent (1992) and Dent (1991) focus in different ways on the impact of organizational cultures.

Overview

This retrospective review of the roots of management control provides the opportunity to reflect on its overall nature before moving forward to consider

Table B.1   Representative papers from four perspectives.

Closed system models		Open system models	
Rational models	**Natural models**	**Rational models**	**Natural models**
Classical management theory	*Behavioural approaches*	*Systems and contingent approaches*	*Radical perspectives*
Classical theorists	Argyris (1952)	Ouchi (1979)	Chua *et al*. (1989)
Woodward (1958, 1965, 1970)	Hopwood (1972, 1974a, 1974b)	Beer (1972)	Ansari and Bell (1991)
Burns and Stalker (1961)	Vickers (1965, 1967)	Lowe and Machin (1983)	Dent (1991)
Drucker (1964)	Otley and Berry (1980)	Lowe and McInnes (1971)	Laughlin and Broadbent (1993)
Simon *et al*. (1954)		Otley (1980)	

the prospects for the subject. It is clear that there is a wide range of research into the functioning of MCSs, even when its focus is narrowed to the more managerialist approach which we have adopted. A rough categorization of MCSs research work since 1965 set into this framework is given in Table B.1 and allows some reflection on the basic assumptions which underlie the work that has been undertaken.

As mentioned earlier, whilst the framework developed by Scott provides a means by which to structure this review, it is important to note that every paper reviewed does not fit tidily into such a sequence. Further, it is clear that while practical theorists and scholars have developed ideas in new sectors of the diagram, this has not led to the abandonment of work in earlier sectors. The scientific management tradition is alive and well in areas such as operational research and in the consultancy world (e.g. in business process reengineering). The diversity of research approaches available is illustrated in the contents of the text *Managerial Control, Theories Issues and Practices* (Berry *et al.*, 1995) as well as the special issue of the *British Journal of Management* on MCSs published in 1993 (September, Vol. 4, No. 3). Both these publications (plus the edited collections by Lowe and Machin, 1983 and Chua *et al.*, 1989)

have been spawned by the activities of the Management Control Association, a group of UK academics, which has sought for the past 20 years to promote wide-ranging research in the field. The latest review of nearly 20 research approaches is by Macintosh (1994), which unusually develops the issues through a selection of methodological approaches.

The predominant ontological stance is realist, stemming from the original concentration of the practical theorists on what they saw as real problems in practice. The primary epistemological stance of these control theorists is positivist and functionalist. Functionalist approaches have been severely criticized (e.g. Burrell and Morgan, 1979) as being part of the sociology (and perhaps the economy) of preservation, and thus antithetical to radical change. In the sense that management control is concerned with forms of stability this might be so, but the pursuit of efficiency has led to radical, and often unwelcome, change for many people, and control techniques have been used to promote quite radical social changes. Whilst some of the more radical theorists have examined this issue it, perhaps, remains somewhat under researched. Laughlin and Lowe (1990) using the framework of Burrell and Morgan (1979) along with Scott's framework to review accounting research and demonstrate the diversity of approaches available argued that only the open systems approaches were beginning to move away from the functionalist orientation. Given our argument as to the paucity of open systems research, similar claims can be made for the need to extend the theoretical and methodological boundaries of management control research.[2]

The review shows that accounting still acts as an important element of management control. Whilst there have been developments in control in associated areas (such as Management Information Systems (MIS), human relations, operations research) these disciplines have been less inclined to see themselves as offering themselves as vehicles for integration of the diversity of organizational life than has accounting. Accounting is still seen as a preeminent technology by which to integrate diverse activities from strategy to operations and with which to render accountability. There is a sense in which the reduction of values to accounting measurements can contribute to management control sliding into the merely technical. Such a tendency is reinforced by the very constructs of the management information system and of information management which accounting uses. The ubiquity of computers, data capture, high-speed software, electronic data interchange and open access has changed the speed of data flow without yet having had great impact on either management control research or practice. Yet the topic of management control holds the promise of providing a powerful integrating idea to provide a very practical focus to concepts developed in other disciplines if it is not wholly accounting focused. Mills' (1970) thoughts about the role of management control as an integrative teaching device also appear to apply with some force to its role as an integrative research framework for an important part of management studies. With this in mind we move to the final section.

Themes for Future Development

Here, we suggest some lines of enquiry which we believe it would be fruitful to pursue in developing research in management control. These are our own views, and we acknowledge we come to these issues from our own particular history and perspectives, thus running the risk of being both biased and incomplete. However, we believe they cover a wide-ranging agenda of important issues from both a practical and theoretical perspective. This prospective part of the paper flows from the retrospective review and is in two sub-sections. The first sub-section considers that the nature of the current environment and the needs this engenders are significantly different from those that determined and yet developed the earlier control approaches. The second sub-section considers the possibilities which could be available in the context of a broadening of the theoretical and methodological approaches adopted in research in the area.

The Environment of Control

The development of earlier MCSs theory took place in the context of large, hierarchically structured organizations. It centred upon accounting controls and developed measures of divisional performance, such as return on investment and residual income. It considered the issues raised in utilizing accounting performance measures to control large, diversified companies, in particular the construction of quasi-independent responsibility centres using systems of cost allocation and transfer pricing. The central theme was to produce measures of controllable performance against which managers could be held accountable, yet the empirical evidence (Merchant, 1987; Otley, 1990) suggests that the 'controllability principle' was more often honoured only in its breach. It can also be argued (see Otley, 1994) that changes in the business and social environment have led to the replacement of large integrated organizations by smaller and more focused organizational units, which require appropriate control mechanisms to be developed. Several features of the business environment seem to point towards a change in emphasis. A key trend is in the impact of uncertainty. It is a moot point whether uncertainty has increased, but it is true that the rate of change in both the commercial and governmental environment is rapid, requiring considerable adaptation on the part of organizations. Change appears to be affecting a much broader range of the population, whether it be technological, social or political change. The process of adaptation can no longer be left to a few senior managers who develop organizational strategies to be enacted by others; rather the process of change has become embedded in normal operating practices, and involves a wider range of organizational participants.

One consequence of this rapid rate of change has been encapsulated in ideas of global competition and 'world class' companies. As the rate of change increases, organizations need to devote more of their resources to adaptation and correspondingly less to managing current operations efficiently. One method of adaptation is planning, but this requires the prediction of the consequences of change, which is becoming more difficult; an alternative response is to develop the flexibility to adapt to the consequences of change as they become apparent. The 'management of change' remains an important managerial skill, but it should no longer be seen as a discrete event bounded by periods of stability; rather we are concerned with management in a context of continual change. This requires continual adaptation, a note which is reflected in the current popular terminology of 'continuous improvement'.

A second feature has been a movement towards reducing the size of business units, certainly in terms of the number of people employed. In part, this has been driven by technological change, but there has also often been a strategic choice to encourage units to concentrate on their 'core' business and to avoid being distracted by irrelevant side issues. In turn, this has led to 'non-core' activities being outsourced, a process which can be most reliably undertaken in the context of long-term alliances. Such a trend is emphasized by just-in-time production and the processes of 'market testing' which have been imposed upon the public sector in the UK. The number of middle managers is being reduced and the range of responsibilities of those who remain is being increased. The split between strategic planning, management control and operational control, which was always tendentious has now become untenable, and a much closer integration between those functions has developed.

The boundaries of the organization and the boundaries of the control function are not necessarily co-terminus. Within the organization, ideas of 'business process re-engineering' have reinforced the need to devise control mechanisms that are horizontal (i.e. which follow the product or service through its production process until its delivery to the customer) rather than solely vertical (i.e. which follow the organizational hierarchy within organizational functions). As production processes are increasingly spread across legal boundaries (and often across national boundaries) new processes for the control of such embedded operations are needed (Berry, 1994). That is, control systems need to be devised which coordinate the total production and delivery process regardless of whether these processes are contained within a single (vertically integrated) organization or spread across a considerable number of (quasi-independent) organizations.

Traditional approaches to management control have been valuable in defining an important topic of study, but they have been predicated on a model of organizational functioning which has become increasingly outdated. This has resulted in the study of control systems becoming over narrow by remaining focused primarily upon accounting control mechanisms which are vertical rather than horizontal in their orientation. Contemporary organizations display flexibility, adaptation and continuous learning, both within and across organizational boundaries, but such characteristics are not encouraged by traditional systems. There is considerable anecdotal evidence to suggest that organizational practices are beginning to reflect these needs, so a key task for MCSs researchers is to observe and codify these developments.

In this type of changing environment the logic of systems theory could be argued to be of some importance in emphasizing issues such as the importance of environment and the holism of the organization. Although MCSs theory often makes references to the concepts of cybernetics, and sometimes to those of general systems theory, such approaches rarely inform empirical research work. Perhaps the most important contribution these disciplines can make is to broaden the horizons of management control researchers to include an appreciation of the overall context within which their work is located. The issues of the appropriate level of analysis, the definition of systems boundaries and the nature of systems goals deserve much more thorough attention. Even more importantly, the idea of control in an open system facing a complex and uncertain environment is also central for the design of effective systems to assist organizations to survive.

Current issues

Our suggestions here are seen partly as an attempt to raise important issues which appear under-researched at present and partly to promote the use of broader theoretical and methodological perspectives. Our argument is that the closed and functionalist

perspective which still predominates needs to be extended.

We see the environment of control as changing, we also see it as of central importance and it is this to which we first turn. Although there have been attempts to broaden the scope of what is perceived as part of a control system (notably by Hopwood, 1974b, Merchant, 1985, and Lowe and Machin, 1983), a narrow financially biased perspective still dominates much of the control literature. The management literature has relatively recently emphasized ideas such as the balanced scorecard (predated by many years in France by the 'tableau de bord') where non-financial measures (e.g. customer, operations and innovation perspectives) are placed alongside traditional financial measures (Kaplan and Norton, 1992). The range of what is included as a management control is being extended with studies of performance-related pay, operational and process controls, and the whole issue of the management of corporate culture. However, studies of the overall practice of control, integrating the whole range of such functional controls, within particular organizations are still scarce. It should be clearly recognized that such attempts raise considerable methodological problems, of both a practical and theoretical nature. From a practical point of view, there is the issue of the extent to which a single researcher (or even a small team) can come to grips with such a wide range of practices in a sensible timescale. Such work would seem to be necessarily case study based, which raises issues of generalizability.

More fundamentally, it raises epistemological issues regarding the nature of theory in this field (Otley and Berry, 1994). It may well be that applied problem-solving methodologies are all that can be expected at high levels of resolution such as those necessary when observing practice within single organizations. Nevertheless, it is also our belief that the insight such attempts would provide would form an important basis for subsequent theoretical development. Another potentially fruitful approach is that of 'middle range thinking', as proposed by Laughlin (1995), which is both rooted in the critical tradition and strikes a balance between the notions of reality and subjectivity. This type of theory involves the use of skeletal frameworks which are then 'fleshed out' with empirical details of particular situations.

The recognition of the importance of the environment raises another important issue, the relationships across the boundary of what has traditionally been seen as the firm. Most of the management control literature has concentrated its attention at the level of the firm (or sub-units within it). There has been comparatively little exploration of control from a more macro or societal perspective. Although these issues have been addressed to some extent by the radical theorists, the 'micro' and the 'macro' have been seen as distinct areas. Despite the quite radical changes that have occurred in the UK environment over the past 15 years (not least due to the Thatcher government) the general issue has not been well explored in the control (as distinct from the economic) literature. In particular, the role of competition as a control mechanism is under-researched. Further, such institutional arrangements affect the legitimacy of different methods of control within organizations, such as the appropriate boundaries for managerial action and the role of consultation and participation amongst the work-force and these issues need fuller exploration. This also raises the issue of what have been called embedded organizations. We have already alluded to the fact that control systems increasingly operate across both the legal boundaries of firms and national boundaries. The needs of managing business processes in an extended supply and distribution chain that crosses many organizational boundaries raise challenging control issues. These have been explored to some extent in both the operations management and management information systems literature, and have surfaced in

the popular management literature under the banner of 'business process re-engineering', but have yet to receive proper attention from an overall control framework. The open systems framework appears to be especially appropriate in this area.

We have also found very little research addressing the problems of control in multi-national and international organizations, in either the public or private sector. This is an issue that seems to have been given much more attention in the fields of strategy and marketing, than in control. Undoubtedly a complex field, issues as disparate as the impact of differing legal and institutional structures, financial and exchange control constraints, and the varied impact of national and corporate cultures all seem worthy of attention.

Wider fields also need to be addressed. The advent of environmental management and the attention now paid to 'green' issues has yet to impact on the control literature. However, the developing understanding of both human ecology (including issues of demography, population, ethnicity and religion) and physical ecology suggests that wider considerations need to be brought into the conceptualization of the problems of regulation and control of, and within, organizations. Clearly, these considerations raise new ethical issues for both control theorists and practitioners.

Gender issues in management control have received scant attention, despite an emerging set of questions about the extent to which there are 'feminine' and 'masculine' styles of managing. It may be that the language of management control needs reframing to encompass a wider range of possibilities. There is some support in the popular management literature for styles associated with the feminine gender stereo-type, such as empowerment, group or mutual accountabilities and upward appraisal. The whole concept of the learning organization suggests approaches to management which are more supportive than directive in their orientation. Numbers of women in the workforce continue to increase, although the 'glass ceiling' still exists. The implications of these changes on MCSs remain to be researched.

Conclusions

This paper extends previous reviews of the area of management control and provides some suggestions for further research. Our suggestions stem from the belief that the practice and researching of management control needs to recognize the environment in which organizations exist and to loosen the boundaries around the area of concern. We are also anxious to promote more critical research. Undoubtedly some of the narrowness of the research in the topic which we have highlighted is the result of our choice of definition of management control which remains rather managerialist in its focus. It is clear that the field of management control is of relevance to the practice of management but this should not preclude a critical stance and thus a broader choice of theoretical approaches.

The area is also under-researched, which might be explained by the nature of the methodologies required for its study and their unpopularity over the last 25 years especially in the US. This indicates a significant opportunity for contributions, offering a broader set of methodological stances, to be made in an important and developing field. In conclusion, we hope that this paper might play a small part in defining and developing management control as a coherent field of study within the management disciplines.

References

Amey, L. R. (1979). *Budget Planning and Control Systems*. Pitman, London.

Ansari, S. and J. Bell (1991). 'Symbolism, Collectivism and Rationality in Organizational Control', *Accounting, Auditing and Accountability Journal*, pp. 4–27.

Anthony, R. N. (1965). *Planning and Control Systems: A Framework for Analysis*. Division of Research, Harvard Business School, Boston.

Anthony, R. N., J. Dearden *and N. M. Bedford* (1984). *Management Control Systems*. Irwin, Homewood, IL.

Argyris, C. (1952). *The Impact of Budgets on People*. The Controllership Foundation, Ithaca, NY.

Ashby, W. R. (1956). *An Introduction to Cybernetics*. Chapman and Hall, London.

Babbage, C. (1832). *On the Economy of Machinery and Manufacturers*. Charles Knight, London.

Beer, S. (1972). *Brain of the Firm*. Allen Lane, Harmondsworth, Middlesex.

Berry, A. J. (1994). 'Spanning Traditional Boundaries: Organization and Control of Embedded Operations', *Leadership and Organisational Development Journal*, pp. 4–10.

Berry, A. J., J. Broadbent and D. T. Otley (eds) (1995). *Managerial Control: Theories, Issues and Practices*. Macmillan, London.

Birnberg, J. G., L. Turopolec and S. M. Young (1983). 'The Organizational Context of Accounting', *Accounting, Organizations and Society*, pp. 111–129.

Boland, R. J. Jnr. and L. R. Pondy (1983). 'Accounting in Organizations: A Union of Rational and Natural Perspectives', *Accounting, Organizations and Society*, pp. 223–234.

Broadbent, J. (1992). 'Change in Organisations: A Case Study of the Use of Accounting Information in the NHS', *British Accounting Review*, pp. 343–367.

Bromwich, M. (1990). 'The Case for Strategic Management Accounting: The Role of Accounting Information for Strategy in Competitive Markets', *Accounting, Organizations and Society*, pp. 27–46.

Buckley, A. and E. McKenna (1972). 'Budgetary Control and Business Behaviour', *Accounting and Business Research*, pp. 137–150.

Burns, T. *and G. M. Stalker* (1961). *The Management of Innovation*. Tavistock, London.

Burrell, G. and G. Morgan (1979). *Sociological Paradigms and Organizational Analysis*. Heinemann, London.

Checkland, P. B. (1981). *Systems Thinking, Systems Practice*. Wiley, Chichester.

Chua, W. F., T. Lowe and T. Puxty (1989). *Critical Perspectives in Management Control*. Macmillan, London.

Dent, J. F. (1991). 'Accounting and Organizational Cultures: A Field Study of the Emergence of a New Organizational Reality', *Accounting, Organizations and Society*, pp. 705–732.

Dirsmith, M. W. and S. F. Jablonsky (1979). 'MBO, Political Rationality and Information Inductance', *Accounting, Organizations and Society*, pp. 39–52.

Drucker, P. (1964). *'Control, Controls and Management'*. In: C. P. Bonini, R. K. Jaedieke and H. M. Wagner, *Management Controls: New Directions in Basic Research*, McGraw-Hill, Maidenhead.

Emmanuel, C. R. and D. T. Otley (1985). *Accounting for Management Control*. Van Nostrand Reinhold, Wokingham.

Emmanuel, C. R., D. T. Otley and K. Merchant (1990). *Accounting, for Management Control* (2nd edition). Chapman and Hall, London.

Ezzamel, M. and R. Watson (1993). 'Organizational Form, Ownership Structure and Corporate Performance: A Contextual Empirical Analysis of UK Companies', *British Journal of Management*, pp. 161–176.

Giglioni, G. B. and A. B. Bedeian (1974). 'A Conspectus of Management Control Theory: 1900–1972', *Academy of Management Journal*, pp. 292–305.

Govindarajan, V. and A. K. Gupta (1985). 'Linking Control Systems to Business Unit Strategy: Impact on Performance', *Accounting, Organizations and Society*, pp. 51–66.

Hirst, M. K. (1981). 'Accounting Information and the Evaluation of Subordinate Performance: A Situational Approach', *Accounting Review*, pp. 771–784.

Hofstede, G. H. (1968). *The Game of Budget Control*. Tavistock, London.

Hofstede, G. H. (1978). 'The Poverty of Management Control Philosophy', *Academy of Management Review*, July.

Hogler, R. L. and H. G. Hunt (1993). 'Accounting and Conceptions of Control in the American Corporation', *British Journal of Management*, pp. 177–190.

Hopwood, A. G. (1972). 'An Empirical Study of the Role of Accounting Data in Performance Evaluation', Supplement to Journal of Accounting Research, pp. 156–193.

Hopwood, A. G. (1974a). 'Leadership Climate and the Use of Accounting Data in Performance Appraisal', *Accounting Review*, pp. 485–495.

Hopwood, A. G. (1974b). *Accounting and Human Behaviour*. Prentice-Hall.

Johnson, P. and J. Gill (1993). *Management Control and Organizational Behaviour*. Paul Chapman, London.

Kaplan, R. S. (1983). 'Measuring Manufacturing Performance: A New Challenge for Management Accountants', *Accounting Review, LVIII*, pp. 686–705.

Kaplan, R. S. and D. P. Norton (1992). 'The Balanced Scorecard – Measures that Drive Performance', *Harvard Business Review, Jan/Feb*, pp. 71–79.

Laughlin, R. C. (1995). 'Empirical Research in Accounting: A Case for Middle Range Thinking', *Accounting, Auditing and Accountability*, pp. 63–87.

Laughlin, R. C. and J. Broadbent (1993). 'Accounting and Law: Partners in the Juridification of the Public Sector in the UK?', *Critical Perspectives on Accounting*, pp. 337–368.

Laughlin and Lowe (1990). *'A Critical Analysis of Accounting Thought: Prognosis and Prospects for Understanding and Changing Accounting Systems Design'*. In: D. J. Cooper, and T. M. Hopper (eds), *Critical Accounts*, Macmillan, London, pp. 15–43.

Lilienfeld, R. (1978). *The Rise of Systems Theory: An Ideological Analysis*. Wiley, New York.

Lowe, E. A. (1971). 'On the Idea of a Management Control System: Integrating Accounting and Management Control', *Journal of Management Studies*, pp. 1–12.

Lowe, E. A. and J. L. J. Machin (eds) (1983). New *Perspectives in Management Control*. Macmillan, London.

Lowe, E. A. and J. M. McInnes (1971). 'Control in Socio-Economic Organizations: A Rationale for the Design of Management Control Systems (Section 1)', *Journal of Management Studies*, pp. 213–227.

Lowe, E. A. and R. W. Shaw (1968). 'An Analysis of Managerial Biasing: Evidence from a Company's Budgeting Process', *Journal of Management Studies*, pp. 304–315.

Machin, J. L. J. (1983). *'Management control systems: whence and whither?'* pp. 22–42. In: E. A. Lowe and J. L. J. Machin (eds), New *Perspectives in Management Control*. Macmillan, London.

Macintosh, N. B. (1994). *Management Accounting and Control Systems, An Organizational and Behavioural Approach*. John Wiley and Sons, Chichester.

Merchant, K. A. (1985). *Control in Business Organizations*. Pitman, Boston.

Merchant, K. A. (1987). 'How and Why Firms Disregard the Controllability Principle'. In: W. J. Bruns and R. Kaplan (eds), *Accounting and Management: Field Study Perspectives*. Harvard Business School Press, Boston.

Merchant, K. A. and R. Simons (1986). 'Research and Control in Complex Organizations: An Overview', *Journal of Accounting Literature*, pp. 183–203.

Miller, P. and T. O'Leary (1987). 'Accounting and the Construction of the Governable Person', *Accounting, Organizations and Society*, pp. 235–266.

Mills, A. E. (1970). 'Management Controls and Integration at the Conceptual Level', *Journal of Management Studies*, pp. 364–375.

Mintzberg, H. (1973). *The Nature of Managerial Work*. Harper and Row, London.

Mintzberg, H. (1975). 'The Managers Job: Folklore and Fact', *Harvard Business Review*, pp. 49–61.

Otley, D. T. (1978). 'Budget Use and Managerial Performance', *Journal of Accounting Research*, pp. 122–149.

Otley, D. T. (1980). 'The Contingency Theory of Management Accounting: Achievement and Prognosis', *Accounting, Organizations and Society*, pp. 413–428.

Otley, D. T. (1983). 'Concepts of Control: The Contribution of Cybernetics and Systems Theory to Management Control'. In: E. A. Lowe and J. L. J. Machin (eds), *New Perspectives in Management Control*. Macmillan, London.

Otley, D. T. (1990). 'Issues in Accountability and Control: Some Observations from a Study of Colliery Accountability in the British Coal Corporation', *Management Accounting Research*, pp. 91–165.

Otley, D. T. (1994). 'Management Control in Contemporary Organizations: Towards a Wider Framework', *Management Accounting Research*, pp. 289–299.

Otley, D. T. and A. J. Berry (1980). 'Control, Organization and Accounting', *Accounting, Organizations and Society*, pp. 231–244.

Otley, D. T. and A. J. Berry (1994). 'Case Study Research in Management Accounting and Control', *Management Accounting Research*, pp. 45–65.

Ouchi, W. G. (1979). 'A Conceptual Framework for the Design of Organizational Control Systems', *Management Science*, pp. 833–848.

Parker, L. D. (1986). *Developing Control Concepts in the 20th Century*. Garland, New York.

Perrow, C. (1970). *Organizational Analysis: A Sociological View*. Wadsworth, Belmont, California.

Prakash, P. and A. Rappaport (1977). 'Information Inductance and its Significance for Accounting', *Accounting, Organizations and Society*, pp. 29–38.

Preston, A. M. (1992). 'The Birth of Clinical Accounting: A Study of the Emergence and Transformation of Discourses on Costs and Practices of Accounting in US Hospitals', *Accounting, Organizations and Society*, pp. 63–100.

Preston, A. M., D. J. Cooper and R. W. Coombs (1992). 'Fabricating Budgets: A Study of the Production of Management Budgeting in the NHS', *Accounting, Organizations and Society*, pp. 561–594.

Rathe, A. W. (1960). 'Management Controls in Business'. In: D. G. Malcolm and A. J. Rowe, *Management Control Systems*, Wiley, New York.

Rhaman, M. and A. M. McCosh (1976). 'The Influence of Organizational and Personal Factors on the Use of Accounting Information: An Empirical Study', *Accounting, Organizations and Society*, pp. 339–355.

Scott, W. R. (1981). 'Developments in Organization Theory: 1960–1980', *American Behavioral Scientist*, pp. 407–422.

Simmonds, K. (1981). 'Strategic Management Accounting', *Management Accounting*, 59(4), pp. 26–29.

Simon, H. A., G. Kozmetsky, H. Guetzkow and G. Tyndall (1954). *Centralization vs. Decentralization in the Controller's Department*. Reprinted by Scholar's Book Co., Houston (1978).

Simons, R. (1987). 'Accounting Control Systems and Business Strategy: An Empirical Analysis', *Accounting, Organizations and Society*, pp. 357–374.

Simons, R. (1990). 'The Role of Management Control Systems in Creating Competitive Advantage: New Perspectives', *Accounting, Organizations and Society*, pp. 127–143.

Simons, R. (1991). 'Strategic Orientation and Top Management Attention to Control Systems', *Strategic Management Journal*, pp. 49–62.

Simons, R. (1995). *Levers of Control*. Harvard Business School Press.

Thompson, J. D. (1967). *Organizations in Action*. McGraw-Hill, Maidenhead.

Tocher, K. D. (1970). 'Control', *Operational Research Quarterly*, pp. 159–180.

Vickers, G. (1965). *The Art of Judgement: A Study of Policy-Making*. Chapman and Hall, London.

Vickers, G. (1967). *Towards a Sociology of Management*. Chapman and Hall, London.

Weiner, N. (1948). *Cybernetics*. MIT Press. Cambridge, MA.

Wilson, B. (1984). *Systems: Concepts, Methodologies and Applications*. Wiley, Chichester.

Wisdom, J. O. (1956). 'The Hypothesis of Cybernetics', *Yearbook for the Advancement of General Systems Theory*, Vol. *1*.

Woodward, J. (1958). *Management and Technology*. HMSO, London.

Woodward, J. (1965). *Industrial Organization: Theory and Practice*. Oxford University Press, London.

Woodward, J. and J. Rackham (1970). *Industrial Organization: Behaviour and Control*. Oxford University Press, London.

Wren, P. A. (1994). *The Evolution of Management Thought* (4th edition). Wiley, Chichester.

Endnotes

1. The authors recognize that this provides a narrow focus for the review, but space restraints preclude the possibility of providing a more comprehensive survey. Our choice has been, therefore, to restrict the survey to one which focuses on the literature which sees management control as a practical activity of managers. See pages S32–S33 for a discussion of the boundaries of our survey.

2. Agency theory research, not included in this review, would not be immune from this comment.

Reading C

Covaleski, M. A., Dirsmith, M. W. and Samuel, S. (1996). Managerial accounting research: the contributions of organizational and sociological theories. *Journal of Management Accounting Research*, 8, 1–35. Reproduced by permission of the American Accounting Association.

Questions

1. Contrast contingency theory, interpretive and critical perspectives in terms of how each perspective can inform an understanding of management accounting. What are the strengths and weaknesses of each paradigm?
2. What is the advantage of the 'paradigmatic pluralism' that Covaleski *et al.* promote?
3. In undertaking management accounting research in an organizational setting, how would you determine the methods of enquiry that you would adopt?

Further reading

Boland, J. R. J. and Pondy, L. R. (1983). Accounting in organizations: a union of natural and rational perspectives. *Accounting, Organizations and Society*, 8(2/3), 223–34.

Hopper, T. and Powell, A. (1985). Making sense of research into the organizational and social aspects of management accounting: a review of its underlying assumptions. *Journal of Management Studies*, 22(5), 429–65.

Lowe, T. and Puxty, T. (1989). *The problems of a paradigm: a critique of the prevailing orthodoxy in management control*. In W. F. Chua, T. Lowe and T. Puxty (Eds), *Critical Perspectives in Management Control*. London: Macmillan.

Neimark, M. and Tinker, T. (1986). The social construction of management control systems. *Accounting, Organizations and Society*, 11(4/5), 369–95.

Otley, D. (1989). *A strategy for the development of theories in management control*. In W. F. Chua, T. Lowe and T. Puxty (Eds), *Critical Perspectives in Management Control*. London: Macmillan.

Managerial Accounting Research: The Contributions of Organizational and Sociological Theories

Mark A. Covaleski*, Mark W. Dirsmith† and Sajay Samuel‡
*University of Wisconsin-Madison, †Pennsylvania State University,
‡Bucknell University

Abstract

Organizational and sociological theories explicitly recognize the centrality of issues of social control and coordination in organizations, thus providing intellectual approaches from which to study managerial accounting as important aspects of the manner in which organizations and society function. This paper examines various organizational and sociological perspectives which have provided meaningful contributions to our understanding of managerial accounting. The credibility of both the theoretical and methodological traditions which typically underpin these alternative organizational and sociological perspectives is then discussed. Finally, this paper considers the unique insights which organizational and sociological theories offer in contrast to more traditional managerial accounting research perspectives for understanding the multiple roles of management accounting in contemporary organizations.

We wish to thank Anthony Hopwood (Oxford University), John Meyer (Stanford University), Mike Shields (University of Memphis), and S. Mark Young (University of Southern California) for their many useful suggestions.

Managerial accounting research, which has adapted organizational or sociological theories to examine the development, maintenance and change in managerial accounting practices, explicitly recognizes the centrality of issues of social control and coordination in organizations, thus providing intellectual approaches from which to study managerial accounting as problematic aspects of the organizational and social context. The purpose of our paper is to provide a critique of the organizational and sociological theoretical traditions which have been used in managerial accounting research in order to facilitate understanding, and perhaps influence usage, by accounting scholars adopting more traditional research perspectives. In our effort to provide a sweeping critique of organizational and sociological perspectives, rather than a detailed and nuanced treatment of this stream of management accounting research from these theoretical perspectives, there are points of omission, under-representation, and compression of the multitude of views within these theoretical traditions. And yet, it is precisely through such a broad treatment that we hope to reveal the distinctiveness of these organizational and sociological research traditions which exhibit a cluster of tendencies that distinguish it from the more familiar research traditions which draw on neoclassical economics and contemporary social and organizational psychology[1].

The paper is organized into four sections. The first section addresses the contributions which contingency theory has had in situating managerial accounting in the control processes and structures of organizations. Contingency theory (Thompson 1967; Perrow 1967; Lawrence and Lorsch 1969) represents a rich blend of organizational theory – i.e., it has roots in the organizational decision-making perspectives of the 1950s (Simon 1957; March and Simon 1958) – and sociological functionalist perspectives of organizations – i.e., it has roots in the sociological concerns about organizational structure

of the 1960s (Burns and Stalker 1961; Woodward 1965; Aiken and Hage 1966; Hickson 1966). Contingency theory took the insights on such critical organizational processes as decision-making and control as depicted in the literature on organizational decision-making and combined these with sociological functionalist concerns regarding the impact of such structural factors as environment, size, technology, etc., on organizational behavior. Important to both the decision-making perspective of organizations and the sociological concerns for organizational structure are issues of organizational control and coordination. This explicit concern for issues of coordination and control, in turn, has provided important contributions to managerial accounting research in our understanding of such issues as the design of information and control systems, budgeting and strategic planning.

The second major section of this paper deals with the various organizational and sociological theories which concern themselves with the social construction and spread of rationality and, in turn, the manner in which this rationality impacts the power and politics in organizational functioning (Weber 1947). These organizational and sociological theories – often referred to as interpretive perspectives – also draw from the organizational decision-making perspective (Simon 1957; March and Simon 1958), thus sharing intellectual heritage with contingency theory. We also see, however, the influence of more interpretive sociological traditions beginning with the work of Weber (1947) and his concerns for the 'politics of rationality,' as well as the work of Berger and Luckmann (1967) (see also Garfinkel 1967) and their work on the social construction (the development of cognitive processes) and the manner in which subjective meaning becomes objective facts. Specifically, we examine the relevance of interpretive perspectives by considering a number of organizational and social theories including institutional theory (Meyer and Rowan 1977; DiMaggio and

Powell 1983), resource dependency theories (Pfeffer 1981), political perspectives (Edelman 1977; Wildavsky 1964), and the sociology of professions (Abbott 1988; Freidson 1986).

The third section of this paper examines the critical organizational and sociological perspectives which provide an even more direct explanation of power and politics. Perhaps the most important attribute of critical perspectives is its attention to issues of conflict, domination and power – an attention motivated by a theoretical backdrop of capitalist social relations, and premised upon an irreducible conflict between capital and labor which ensures perpetual antagonistic relations between the classes. Despite theoretical differences within critical perspectives regarding the manner and form in which to conceptualize power, a common attribute is that they eschew a consensus view of society. These critical perspectives argue that functionalist and interpretive views of power stipulate that individual interests mesh into a harmony at the societal level which contrasts with the critical perspectives' focus on presumed perpetual antagonistic relations between the classes. More specifically, whether through general equilibrium in economics (e.g., the functionalist concern for market value) or the public good in politics (the interpretive concerns for the negotiation and bargaining), the social interest is assumed to emerge from the interaction of individual interests. In sharp contrast, critical perspectives deal explicitly with the role that accounting plays in relation to issues of conflict, domination and power as defined by the presumed irreducible conflict between capital and labor (Cooper and Sherer 1984). Here we will confine our attention to two major research strands of the many critical perspectives that have illuminated our understanding of managerial accounting: labor process theory which is concerned with the extraction of surplus from laborers (e.g., Hopper *et al.* 1987; Hopper and Armstrong 1991), and the Foucaultian perspective which is concerned with the methods by which the actions of individuals are made visible and susceptible to discipline and control, thereby rendering the individual to be governed (e.g., Miller and O'Leary 1987; Walsh and Stewart 1993).

The fourth section of the paper offers concluding remarks in which we consider the relationship among the three dominant organizational and sociological perspectives considered in this paper, as well as their relationship to more orthodox, neoclassical, and social and organizational psychology perspectives of managerial accounting with a focus on the issue as to whether these various perspectives can be meaningfully blended, or whether a 'champion' perspective may emerge. This section also addresses issues pertaining to assessing the credibility of the field-based research methods commonly (but not necessarily) utilized in these alternative theoretical traditions[2]. Finally, this section considers the unique contributions that the different organizational and sociological theories may make beyond those offered by more traditional approaches.

Contingency Theory

Contingency theory has provided considerable inspiration to managerial accounting researchers through an elaboration of the basic theme that 'tight' control systems should be used in centralized organizations faced with simple technology and stable task environments; 'loose' control systems should be used in decentralized organizations, presumably faced with dynamic, complex task environments. Furthermore, a given means of control such as embedded in managerial accounting information can only be understood through reference to other control approaches used in organizations as well as their organizational/task environment context. For example, budgets may take on important meaning both for planning and control purposes for work processes or product lines which are more routine, standardized and predictable. However, in situations where the processes or product lines are less routine, less standardized and less predictable, the budgets may be generated but are subject to much revision and are of little use as a control benchmark (Swieringa and Moncur 1975). Contingency theory is essentially a theoretical perspective of organizational behavior that emphasizes how contingent factors such as technology and the task environment affected the design and functioning of organizations. For example, Thompson's (1967) *Organizations in Action* attempted to link task environment and technological contingencies to various organizational arrangements, focusing particularly on the different mechanisms of coordination which were appropriate for more complex, dynamic technologies and task environmental conditions. Perrow's (1967) theory of technology focused on the congruence between different types of technologies and organizational arrangements, emphasizing that more flexible, loosely-structured arrangements were more appropriate for organizations with non-routine technologies, while just the opposite type of organizational arrangements were more likely to fit routine technologies. Lawrence and Lorsch's (1969) *Organizations and Environment* developed, in a related manner the fit between organizational arrangements, including mechanisms of social control and coordination, and environments of organizations.

The sociological tradition embedded in contingency theory developed during the 1960s through various 'structural' approaches to organizational studies (Woodward 1965; Aiken and Hage 1966; Hage and Aiken 1967; Blau 1970, 1973; Hickson 1966; Child 1972; Pugh *et al.* 1968). These studies suggested that organizations' structures are contingent upon contextual factors which have been variously defined to include technology (Woodward 1965), dimensions of task environment (Burns and Stalker 1961), and organizational size (Pugh *et al.*

1969; Blau 1970). These contextual factors are hypothesized to influence dimensions of structure including the degree of formalization, specialization, differentiation and bureaucratization. Discussions of social control and coordination were sometimes elicited to explain some of the observed relationships among structural properties, but, by and large, were not of a central importance.

Not all functionalist theories of organizations developed during this period presented such static images of organizations. Contingency frameworks, for example, drew directly from these sociological functionalist theories of organization structure, while also using March and Simon's (1958) organizational decision-making perspective. March and Simon (1958) developed a complex macro-perspective of organizations that viewed them as flexible, loosely-coupled systems in which human choice and voluntarism, and hence unpredictability, were major characteristics. The very essence of this decision-making perspective held that decision-makers in organizations are unlikely in most circumstances to have the information they need and want, and therefore, that many if not most decisions are made under conditions of uncertainty. In short, the primary concern of the organizational decision-making perspective is for the treatment of the problematic 'boundedly rational' person which, in turn, is the core legacy passed onto contingency theory as it seeks to provide insight as to this boundedly rational decision-maker in relation to the various contingent contextual factors (technology, environment, etc.) as suggested by the sociological structural perspectives.

March and Simon's (1958) depiction of the organizational decision-maker under such conditions of uncertainty was influenced by an earlier organizational theory tradition: the 'human relations' approach to organizational analysis as developed in the work of Mayo (1933) and more concretely articulated by Barnard's (1938) seminal work, *The Functions of the Executive*. Perhaps the fundamental insight of this human relations approach in terms of its contribution to the organizational decision-making of March and Simon (1958), and eventually the contingency theory perspective, was that social and psychological attitudes were significant factors to be considered in the design of production processes and its related control systems. The human relations approach, in turn, extended the early scientific management work of Frederick W. Taylor was concerned with the rationalization of work in order to maximize efficiency and productivity and, hence, profits. Scientific management ushered in the monitoring of the individual worker, but ultimately contributed to the monitoring of work units within organizations as well. The fascinating issue which the human relations perspective brought forth (as compared to earlier scientific management work) and pervades through contingency theory was the depiction of corporations existing in a tentative equilibrium which is inherently fragile, short lived and ever subject to a complex of personal, social, physical and biological destructive forces (Miller and O'Leary 1989). As Miller and O'Leary (1989) argued, it was axiomatic for the human relations perspective that all organizations are founded on self-interest and a contractual principle; this is the core reason that they are so fragile. This characterization of the organizations founded on self-interest and contractual principles becomes a major thrust of the organizational decision-making perspective as articulated in the work of March and Simon (1958) but also in the related work of Simon (1957) and the later work of Cyert and March (1963) and March and Olsen (1976).

In summary, March and Simon (1958) and the organizational decision-making perspective started with an image of human behavior and individual decision-making that was considerably more complex than the human relations perspective that had preceded them, but nonetheless, reflected a common concern for the managing of the organization. In

turn, contingency theory blended the insights on human behavior and individual decision-making as depicted in March and Simon's (1958) organizational decision-making perspective with the sociological functionalist concerns regarding the impact of such structural factors as environment, size, technology, etc., on organizational behavior. Important in this lineage of work were issues of organizational control and coordination which are so germane to managerial accounting research.

Traditional management accounting research which has been based in the contingency literature (as well as its predecessors – organizational decision-making, human relations and scientific management) suggests that managerial accounting information should reflect and promote rationality in decision-making. Accordingly, management accounting information used by managers serve as quantitative expressions of organizational goals and are used to support rational decision-making (Ijiri 1965). The prescriptive character of managerial accounting information espoused by this traditional school of thought is essentially internal and downward and also prescriptive in character (Anthony 1965), thus reflecting the strong scientific management heritage, albeit later becoming more complex when sociological and psychological as well as structural factors are brought in.[3]

Among the earliest managerial accounting research which adopted a contingency perspective was Hofstede's (1967) classic field work which found that economic, technological and sociological considerations have a significant impact on the way budgeting systems function, concluding that managers used budgetary information in difficult economic environments to pressure workers; but in more lucrative environments, the budget was used more in a problem solving mode. Golembiewski (1964) was also among the earliest to explicitly examine various aspects of organizational structure in relationship to the use of budgets. In this tradition, Hayes (1977) investigated the appropriateness of management accounting systems for measuring the effectiveness of different departments in large industrial organizations, finding that contingency factors proved to be the major predictors of effectiveness for production departments. Extending this theme, Hirst (1981, 1983) examined external control factors such as environmental uncertainty and their impact on the reliance on accounting measures of performance. In applying contingency theories to control systems design, some researchers have sought to uncover direct relationships between these contextual factors and organizations' accounting and information systems (Khandwalla 1972). Technology also was specifically introduced as a major explanatory variable of an effective accounting information system by Daft and MacIntosh (1981). Others have articulated more subtle relationships between contextual factors, structural characteristics, and control system design (Gordon and Miller 1976; Waterhouse and Tiessen 1978). For example, Gordon and Miller (1976) hypothesized that accounting information systems could be designed to cope with environmental uncertainty by incorporating more nonfinancial data, increasing reporting frequency, and tailoring systems to local needs (see also MacIntosh 1981; Ansari 1977). Dent's (1987) focus was on the design of formal control systems in complex organizations, being concerned with the question of appropriate contingency principles underlying the design of such systems.

More recently, accounting researchers have sought to extend contingency arguments to embrace relationships between firms' strategies and the design of their control systems (see Govindarajan and Gupta 1985; Merchant 1985; Simons 1987). For example, Kaplan (1983) reasoned that managerial accounting has served business inadequately; it has become overly simplistic, structured and misdirected. He urged a close scrutiny of organizational activity of successful organizations so that the managerial

accounting systems adopted accurately reflect the complex conditions confronting contemporary organizations. Merchant (1981, 1984, 1985) found contingent relationships between corporate context (size, product diversity and extent of decentralization) and the uses of budgeting information. Govindarajan (1984, 1988) found environmental uncertainty to be a major explanatory variable regarding the appropriateness of accounting data in evaluating the performance of business units. Govindarajan and Gupta (1985) extended the concern for contingency relationships between organizational control mechanisms and variables such as technology, environment and size, by exploring the utility of relating these contingency relationships to strategy, where the utility of a particular incentive bonus system is contingent upon the strategy of the focal strategic bonus unit. The work of Shank (1989) and Simons (1987) also are important research efforts which mobilized contingency principles in the examination of the use of managerial accounting systems and information in a strategic manner.

Reflecting concerns for the role of managerial accounting information in contemporary organizations, the work of McNair and Mosconi (1988) and McNair et al. (1989) also reflects an implicit contingency tradition, finding that changes in technologies are accompanied by changes in performance management systems. Furthermore, McNair's group (McNair and Mosconi 1988; McNair et al. 1989) found that actual costs have begun to replace standards in JIT environments because of the ability to trace costs more easily and because of the more simplified manufacturing process. On this point, Foster and Gupta (1990) provided a cross sectional comparison of manufacturing plants in an electronics firm, arguing that contingency variables (size and complexity of cost drivers) affect manufacturing overhead. Patell's (1987) longitudinal study of JIT implementation and changes in cost accounting procedures also highlighted the importance of contingency structural factors in the coordination problems of many new manufacturing operations with regards to information for control and evaluation. The impact of structural factors is also apparent in the work of Banker *et al.* (1991) who found that firms that have implemented JIT or other teamwork programs are more likely to provide manufacturing performance information to shop-floor workers. A contingency theme underlies Young's (1992) work which raises the intriguing issue that power shifting can occur within the organization as a result of the implementation of JIT. Here it is argued that workers are given much more power under JIT than management may realize (i.e., a workers' strike could cripple them) because of the tight coupling that takes place (see Wilkinson and Oliver 1989). Finally, Selto *et al.* (1995) provided a rather comprehensive contingency perspective of the adaptation of JIT manufacturing and a total quality control system (JIT/TQC system) when they considered JIT in relationship to classical contingency theory constructs, organizational structure, context and control to get some sense of the fit of these organizational variables and the JIT system. Drawing from Drazin and Van de Ven's (1985) review of the extensive contingency literature, Selto *et al.* (1995) found contingency theory to have intuitive appeal in understanding broad issues of management controls, but also argued that the extensive interaction of variables as well as continuous changes in organizations would make it difficult to apply contingency theory.

The influence of contingency theory and its precursor theoretical traditions on managerial accounting research, however, have been criticized for presenting a deterministic, ahistorical view of organizations which provides limited insight as to the mediating processes of organizations. Among the earlier critiques of the application of contingency theory in managerial accounting, Otley (1980) observed that reliance tended to be placed on a relatively few number of very general variables, task environment and structure, which, in turn, were used to explain organization structure and design of managerial accounting systems. He argued that these variables tended to be ill-defined and measured, and were not comparable across earlier accounting studies, thus yielding fragmented results. Further, the proposal that the link between accounting systems design and organizational effectiveness was far from proven. Otley (1980) concluded that there remained a need to imbed accounting systems in the overall package of organizational control approaches, to develop more nuanced expressions of organizational effectiveness, and in general to move to a more complex expression of the contingency framework. Also, he observed that many of the issues relating to the development of accounting systems, and the relationships with the organization's differentiated environment, were political as opposed to technical in nature, and urged the application of a field study approach to examine these issues.

Interpretive Perspectives

By focusing on the management of complex relational networks and the exercise of coordination and control, contingency theory has adhered to the strong influence of the classical sociological functionalist perspectives (Durkheim 1938) at the cost of neglecting alternative sociological theories such as expressed in the work of Weber (1947, 1958, 1964) whose primary concern was with the source of formal structure: the legitimacy of rationalized formal structures. In contingency theory, legitimacy is given; assertions about bureaucratization such as the role of managerial accounting practices and information systems rest on the assumptions of norms of rationality. When such norms do play causal roles in theories of bureaucratization, it is because they are thought to be built into modern societies and organizations as very general values, which are thought to facilitate formal organization. But norms of rationality are not simply general values. They exist in much more specific and powerful ways in the rules, understandings and meanings attached to institutionalized social structures. The causal importance of such institutions has been neglected. According to Meyer and Rowan (1977, 343):

> Formal structures are not only the result of their relational network in the social organization . . . [t]he elements of rationalized formal structure are also deeply ingrained in, and reflect, widespread understandings of social reality. . . . Such elements of formal structure are manifestations of powerful institutional rules which function as highly rationalized myths that are binding on particular organizations.

Strands of this Weberian sociological tradition are embedded in March and Simon's (1958) organizational decision-making model which provides a key contribution in its focus on the routine, taken-for-granted aspects of organizational life. Traces of a cognitive orientation in Weber's theory of bureaucracy – his emphasis on the role of calculable rules in reducing uncertainty and rationalizing power relations – are apparent in the richness of March and Simon's (1958) decision-making model where they urged a focus on understanding the initiation and preservation of power relationships on two fronts: (1) the power to set premises and define the norms and standards that shape and channel behavior; and (2) the power to delimit appropriate models of bureaucratic structure and policy that go unquestioned for years. Weber's concern was to understand the dominance of organizations and their forms of rationality upon society's technical, economic and political forms of life. Weber reasoned that rationalization is concerned not only with the long-term process of social structure transformation, but simultaneously and more importantly, the perpetuation of existing power relations concealed in the advancement of rational imperatives. Thus, the critical issue is the politics of rationality itself.

This concern for the power and politics of rationality is inherent in other interpretive sociological work such as Berger and Luckmann's (1967), *The Social Construction of Reality*, in which they reasoned that the central question for sociological theory is: How is it possible that subjective meanings become objective facts? Berger and Luckmann's (1967) argument is that social order is based fundamentally on a shared social reality which, in turn, is a human construction, being created in social interaction. The process by which actions become repeated over time and are assigned similar meanings by self and others is defined as institutionalization. Further, Berger and Luckmann (1967) emphasized the importance of employing an historical approach, arguing that it is impossible to understand an institution adequately without an understanding of the historical processes in which it was produced. The result is the paradox 'that man is capable of producing a world that he then experiences as something other than a human product' (Berger and Luckmann 1967, 61). Similarly, Garfinkel (1967) developed an approach to social investigation, ethnomethodology, which shifted the image of cognition from a rational, discursive, quasiscientific process to one that operates largely beneath the level of consciousness, a routine and conventional practical reason governed by rules that are recognized only when they are breached. To this he added a perspective on interaction that casts doubts on the importance of normative or cognitive consensus. Here Garfinkel (1967) argued that action is largely scripted and justified, after the fact, by reference to a stock of culturally available legitimating accounts. Interpretive perspectives, and their underlying concerns pertaining to the cognitive decision-making issues of the organizational decision-making model, the Weberian concern for the politics of rationality, and the ethno-methodological concerns for the construction of social reality, have perhaps been most forcefully developed within institutional theory. Following Selznick's (1957, 17) definition ' . . . to institutionalize is to infuse with value beyond the technical requirements of the task at hand,' the general theme of the institutional perspective is that an organization's survival requires it to conform to social norms of acceptable behavior as much as to achieve levels of production efficiency. Among the sociologists whose work reflected the Weberian tradition, Selznick (1957) viewed organizational structure as an adaptive vehicle shaped in reaction to the characteristics and commitments of participants as well as to influences and constraints from the external environment. Institutionalization refers to this adaptive process: the processes by which societal expectations of appropriate organizational form and behavior come to take on rule-like status in social thought and action. In particular, institutional theory extends beyond the focus of contingency theory on an organization's task environment, which has received much attention in managerial accounting research, to instead focus on its institutional environment. According to Scott (1987, 507):

> Until the introduction of institutional conceptualizations, organizations were viewed as being shaped largely by their technologies, their transactions, or the power-dependency relations growing out of such interdependencies. Environments were conceived of as task environments . . . While such views are not wrong, they are clearly incomplete. Institutional theorists have directed attention to the importance of symbolic aspects of organizations and their environments. They reflect and advance a growing awareness that no organization is just a technical system and that many organizations are not primarily technical systems. All social systems, hence all organizations, exist in an institutional environment that defines and delimits social reality.

The general theme of the institutional perspective is that an organization's survival requires it to conform to social norms of acceptable behavior as much as to achieve high levels of production efficiency. Thus, many aspects of an organization's formal structure, policies and procedures serve to demonstrate a conformity with institutionalized rules, thereby legitimizing it, to assist in gaining society's continued support (Meyer and Rowan 1977; Scott 1987; DiMaggio and Powell 1983, 1991). Meyer and Rowan (1977) proposed that such externally legitimated, formal assessment criteria as managerial accounting information play a heightened though ritualistic role in a variety of settings as organizations grope to find, conform to, and demonstrate for their internal and external constituents some form of rationality in order to gain legitimacy. Thus, rather than merely representing some notion of an objective reality, managerial accounting may serve as a ceremonial means for symbolically demonstrating an organization's commitment to a rational course of action. Here accountants gain their power by the responsible development and application of generally legitimated categories. Similarly, Zucker (1977) argued that the rationalization in formal control systems is an important part of a network of political and power relations which are built into the fabric of social life, a process of transforming the moral into the merely factual.

Covaleski and Dirsmith (1988a, 1988b) adopted an institutional perspective to examine the manner in which societal expectations of acceptable budgetary practices are articulated, enforced and modified during a period of organizational decline. They examined a large university system's budgeting process both through extensive archival documents and through in-depth interview with budgetary actors (see also Covaleski and Dirsmith 1983, 1986 for work pertaining to health care settings). Covaleski and Dirsmith (1988a, 1988b) followed a university budget category through periods of ascent, transformation and decline, describing the process of how a university challenged and rejected a traditional institutionalized budgetary framework for allocating state funding when this framework became inconsistent with the university's goals and interests. Self-interest is foremost in the minds of the various parties who propose, oppose, co-opt and contest the budget category. Covaleski and Dirsmith (1988a, 1988b) show how conflicting interests get couched in the common and legitimate language of budgeting, thus concluding that the budgetary process is an important manner in which societal expectations are reproduced.

Ansari and Euske (1987) also drew from institutional theory to examine the role of accounting information in the public sector, identifying this role in terms of documenting institutional compliance, i. e., seeking external legitimation or masking underlying sociopolitical reality. Ansari and Euske (1987) examined the manner in which cost information is used in the Department of Defense, finding disparity between the formally stated objective of the system to improve organization efficiency, and the lack of accounting system use for this purpose. The authors drew from an institutional perspective to explain the use of accounting information in the Department of Defense, in the light of this agency having ambiguous missions that foster rationalizing uses of accounting information.

Mezias (1990) examined the financial reporting practices of the Fortune 200 and concluded that the institutional model adds significant explanatory power over and above the models that currently dominate the applied economics literature. Recognizing the institutional work that has been done pertaining to the accounting practices of not-for-profit organizations, Mezias (1990) studied relationships between institutional variables and the financial reporting practices used by for-profit organizations. Mezias and Scarselletta (1994) extended this work by examining the decision process of a public policy task force that plays a role in establishing financial reporting standards to determine the affects of the kinds of decisions made. Drawing upon institutional theory, this study modeled the decision process as an organized anarchy embedded in a larger institutional context of accounting.

In summary, Carruthers (1995) argued that institutionalism views accounting practices as one of a larger set of features that can legitimize organizations through the construction of an appearance of rationality and efficiency. As Carruthers (1995, 326) stated, 'Accounts are the quintessential rationalized myth, and it is surprising that new institutionalists have not devoted more time to studying them.' Perhaps the single most important contribution of institutional theorists to the study of organizations is their reconceptualization of the environments of organizations. Earlier organizational and sociological models had emphasized technical facets. Meyer and Rowan's (1977) work, however, called attention to a neglected facet of environments: institutional beliefs, rules and roles – symbolic elements capable of affecting organizational forms independent of resource flows and technical requirements. They emphasized (drawing from Berger and Luckmann 1967; Garfinkel 1967) that shared cognitive systems, although created in interaction by humans, come to be viewed as objectified and external structures defining social reality. This is an ethnomethodological view of human action as shaped by conventions, built up by participants in the course of interactions to the point that much behavior takes on a taken-for-granted quality. The more institutionalized the cognitive categories and belief systems, the more human actions are defined by a widening sphere of taken-for-granted routines (Weber 1947).

Reflecting a theme similar to institutional theory, resource dependency theorists argue that organizations are limited by a variety of external pressures (Pfeffer and Salancik 1978; Pfeffer 1981), that environments are collectivities and interconnected, and that organizations must be responsive to external demands and expectations in order to survive. Resource dependency theorists also suggest that organizations attempt to obtain stability and legitimacy, and that organizational stability is achieved through the exercise of power or control for purposes of achieving a predictable inflow of vital resources and reducing environmental uncertainty (Oliver 1991). In this tradition, Weick (1976) stated that the chief responsibilities of organizational administrators are to provide a common language from which to reaffirm and solidify ties with outsiders through symbol management, consistent articulation of a common vision, and interpretation of diverse actions in terms of common themes. In like manner, Burns (1986) observed that such 'rule systems' as formal control systems, rather than being neutral or merely technical in nature, constitute power resources that actors use in advocating organizational structural forms which serve their own interests. On this theme, Boland and Pondy's (1983, 1986) accounting studies highlight the ceremonial, seemingly irrational, aspects of resource allocation activities where, for example, they found that in a university case, the budget provided a context for state agencies to exercise their legitimate authority in allocating funds to particular priorities. At the same time the underlying flexibility was such that funds could be diverted from one program to another at will. In short, resource dependency theorists also have placed a strong emphasis on the role of political language, particularly in budgeting processes.

Generally, the resource dependency tradition has recognized that budgeting is closely linked with power, self-interest and political advocacy in contemporary organizations (Pfeffer and Salancik 1974, 1978; Salancik and Pfeffer 1974; Rose 1977; Pfeffer 1981; Schick 1985). More specifically, self-interest and internal power and politics, actively expressed, for example, through budgeting systems, have been found to play heightened roles during periods of organizational decline in terms of resource allocation decisions made within organizations, possibly so that the organization maintains some semblance of subunit harmony (Hackman 1985; Hills and Mahoney 1978; Gray and Ariss 1985). In addition, not only do organizations appear to use budgeting in a political mode to allocate resources internally, but the visibility of these internal budgetary allocations to external constituents also appears to influence the generation of resources (Hackman 1985). This dual role of budgeting in generating and allocating resources suggests an expanded linkage between the values of external constituents and the internal resource needs and uses of an individual organization, most particularly in times of financial stress.

Cyert and March (1963) have defined budgets as both the substance and result of political bargaining processes that are useful for legitimizing and maintaining systems of power and control within organizations. Similarly, Pfeffer (1981) argued that a particularly effective way of influencing resource allocation decisions is to do it as unobtrusively as possible, such as through the apparently objective mechanism of the budgetary process which tends to legitimate subjective and political decision-making processes (see also Pfeffer and Salancik 1974, 1978). Here, according to Hopwood (1974), the trivial, dull, seemingly objective nature of accounting enables it to be used in taking the debatable out of the realm of open debate and into the realm of calculation. Consequently, these theorists considered managerial accounting information such as budgeting as a socially constructed phenomenon rather than a technically rational function driven by and serving the internal operations of organizations. Moreover, these perspectives recognized that once implemented, what a budgeting system accounts for shapes organizational members' views of what is important and, more radically, what constitutes reality. Budgeting, then, has been implicated in the construction of social reality rather than being the passive mirror of a technical reality. On this point, Pfeffer (1981, 184) concluded:

> [t]he task of political language and symbolic activity is to rationalize and justify decisions that are largely a result of power and influence, in order to make these results acceptable and legitimate in the organization.

Regarding the political perspective of budgeting, Wildavsky (1964, 1975, 1979) long argued that budgeting systems achieve many purposes beyond control, that they are at once forms and sources of power, and that they serve both the guardians of scarce resources and the advocates of budgetary units. Wildavsky also reasoned that inherently conflictual organizations may use budgets in establishing and maintaining existing power relations as opposed to serving decision-making and problem solving directly in a technically rational manner. Instead, he argued, decision-making and problem solving are served by the sometimes asymmetrical political confrontation between budgeters and budgetees. Wildavsky concluded that the political nature of budgeting may well be inherent in complex organizational life, and is not an aberrant defect in budgetary practice. Resource allocation, he suggests, is not the consequence of dispassionate analysis, but emerges through a subtle role of advocates and guardians. Building on Wildavsky's analysis, Jonsson (1982) sought to capture some of the implicit political dynamics by following the way in which the budgetary process unfolded over three years in a Swedish municipality in a time of financial stringency.

Edelman's (1977) broader political view and his concern for probing the consent of the governed in American politics also reflects concern for the significance of power and language. He argued that power relationships are seen as being reflected in daily life through the use of language, myths and symbolic displays directed at maintaining the status quo. Viewed as a form of language, quantitative data is selectively deployed by the state not to reflect underlying economic conditions, but to create public values, acquiescence and support. As Edelman (1977, 58) observed:

> Language is always an intrinsic part of some particular social situation; it is never an independent instrument or simply a tool for description. By naively perceiving it as a tool, we mask its profound part in creating social relationships and in evoking the roles and the selves of those involved in the relationships.

Consent of the governed, then, comes about not from the conscious acceptance of rules of procedure, but as acquiescence to and taking for granted an accepted language, thus at once creating and supporting a hierarchical relationship between the governed and the state. Always cloaked in the appearance of objectivity and neutrality, this language is ultimately directed toward establishing and maintaining hierarchies of authority and status (Clegg 1987). This acceptable discourse, such as accounting information, is always an intrinsic part of some particular social situation; it is never an independent instrument or simply a tool to be assessed for such attributes as its representational faithfulness. On this point, Scott (1987, 509) emphasized that:

> Outcomes will . . . be strongly shaped by the agents' differential ability to lay successful

claim to the normative and cognitive facets of the political processes: those identified by such concepts as authority, legitimacy, and sovereignty.

Finally, Abbott's (1988) work on professions can be meaningfully integrated into the concern of interpretive perspectives. Here Abbott has observed both that the professions seek to legitimize themselves to society by attaching their expertise to the widely held values of rationality, efficiency and science, and that a key characteristic lies in the use of power both externally to preserve an abstract system of knowledge and, more importantly, internally in terms of hierarchical stratification and differentiation (see also Sarfatti-Larson 1977). Joining Abbott in recognizing the importance of power, Freidson (1986) alluded to a decoupling between the administrative or formalized and structurally oriented component of professional bureaucracies and the practitioner component comprised of those possessing and using internalized values and norms. Objectivity, having a close association with scientific endeavor, encodes expertise in an organizational structure and away from individuals (Freidson 1986; Abbott 1988). Both authors pointed to the necessity of conducting research at the micro-level of everyday practitioner experience, where self-interest may come into play, in order to understand professional endeavor. Abbott (1988) lamented that insufficient attention has been directed at studying professionals, not as freestanding autonomous agents, but as members of organizations, particularly for professions arising out of a commercial enterprise such as accounting. Abbott's (1988, 226–235) findings suggest that in the early twentieth century, U.S. engineers battled accountants for professional jurisdiction over the growing volume of quantitative work associated with corporations; a battle won by the accountants who won control and established a professional monopoly (Loft 1986; see also Armstrong 1985).

In summary, interpretive perspectives of managerial accounting and organizations take issue with the assumption of an objective reality, arguing that the implementation of such apparently rational, bureaucratic mechanisms as managerial accounting systems is one manner in which the social world flows through organizations and changes them. These theorists have begun to see managerial accounting practices and information as socially constructed phenomena with the full implications of the power and politics of social construction rather than as a technically rational function driven by and serving the internal operations of organizations. Furthermore, these interpretive perspectives recognize that once managerial accounting practices and information are implemented, what it accounts for shapes organizational members' views of what is important and, more radically, what constitutes reality. Managerial accounting, then, is seen as being implicated in the social construction of reality rather than as being passively reflective of the reality as depicted in contingency theory and its predecessors.

Although the thrust of the interpretive perspectives in general and institutional theory in particular have received a growing amount of empirical support, a number of useful criticisms of them have been offered. DiMaggio (1988), for example, suggested that an apparent paradox resides in the two senses in which theorists have used the term 'institutionalization.' Institutionalization as an *outcome* places societal expectations and organizational structures and practices beyond the reach of power and self-interest; expectations of acceptable practice merely exist and are taken for granted (Perrow 1985; Powell 1985). By contrast, institutionalization as a *process* may be profoundly political and reflects the relative power of organized interests (see also Tolbert 1988; DiMaggio and Powell 1991). Within this concern for institutionalization as a process, the major problem in institutionalized settings can be defined in terms of finding some mechanism that can be mobilized by interested actors to change an overly stable social system (DiMaggio 1988), or in terms of finding some process wherein social order is produced in a system where organizations are constantly eroding (Zucker 1988). Regarding power and group interest, DiMaggio (1988) has observed that institutional and interest-based explanations of organizational practices are not necessarily antagonistic to one another, but combined, may yield a more comprehensive theoretical apparatus for gaining insight into the social dynamics of organizations. He concluded that allusions to power and group interests tend to be smuggled into the institutional perspective rather than provide the focus of a sustained theoretical analysis.

Critical Perspectives

Since the early 1980s an increasing number of researchers have begun to adopt diverse critical perspectives to explore and investigate the roles of accounting practices in society. These critical perspectives in accounting research are marked by a great deal of intellectual ferment evident in the different theoretical approaches and methodologies deployed and the wide range of topics and issues addressed. Accordingly, in the light of such heterogeneity and the constraints of space, our intent is to provide a flavor of these alternative accounting research agendas without claiming to be exhaustive.[4]

Classifying these heterogeneous theoretical stances as 'critical perspectives,' in contrast to the functionalist and interpretative traditions explored above, can be justified by their singular attention to the interrelation between accounting and issues of conflict, domination and power. Despite the theoretical differences within the different strands of the critical perspectives regarding the manner and form in which to conceptualize power, they all avoid a consensus view of society that is the hallmark of both the functional and interpretive perspectives.

It may be argued that power, in both the functional and interpretive perspectives, is formulated as if it were a possession belonging to someone which he or she exercises for individual gain and further, that this power is diffused over society in a manner as to preclude the sustained and systematic negation of any individuals' preferences (Alford and Friedland 1985). In sharp contrast, this individualist basis of power and ultimately consensus view of society is eschewed by the critical perspectives which attempt to deal explicitly with conflict, domination and power (Cooper and Sherer 1984). For example, rather than treating various managerial accounting practices as a response to transaction costs considerations as in Johnson and Kaplan (1987) or agency cost considerations as in Christensen (1983), they are treated as modes by which the extraction of labor from laborers is made possible (Hopper and Armstrong 1991) and as methods by which the actions of individuals are made visible and susceptible to greater discipline and control (Hoskins and Macve 1988, Miller and O'Leary 1987). Accordingly, class conflict, the hegemony of elites, and the power of experts and professionals are some of the elements that the critical perspectives systematically foreground (not all such analyses incorporate all of these emphases) in their attempt to understand accounting practices.

Despite the theoretical richness within the critical perspectives, we will confine our attention to two major research strands that have illuminated our understanding of managerial accounting. First, we will consider the labor process perspective which draws from the Marxist tradition and then we will examine the Foucaultian perspective which, as the name suggests, draws from the work of Michel Foucault. While both of these alternatives are critical in orientation, there are significant differences in the kinds of insights they offer and consequently, we will first describe their relevant theoretical infrastructure and then, tease out from extant accounting studies their implications for our understanding of managerial accounting.

The labor process perspective

> It thus becomes essential for the capitalist that control over the labor process pass from the hands of the worker into his own. The transition presents itself in history as the progressive alienation of the process of production from the worker; to the capitalist, it presents itself as the problem of management. (Braverman 1974, 58, emphasis in original)

Harry Braverman, in the much acclaimed *Labor and Monopoly Capitalism: The Degradation of Work in the Twentieth Century*, offered a resounding critique of conventional understandings of work processes in capitalist economic systems. Drawing from the pioneering work of Karl Marx, Braverman asserted the primacy of the social relations of production for any attempt to understand the manner and modes in which goods and services are created in the capitalist economy. Specifically, Braverman (1974, 52) following Marx, suggested that the *differentia specifica* of capitalist economies was 'the purchase and sale of labor power.' Understanding the historical novelty of this feature is crucial, for this defining aspect of modern economies which we take for granted is, as a general phenomenon, unknown to prior epochs of human history. Capitalist economies are accordingly differentiated from prior epochs by the social relation embedded within the employment relation. Employment relations in contrast to, say, self-employment as the general form by which modern people earn their livelihood is an extremely recent phenomenon, and requires that workers sell their labor power to capitalists; for a wage. This historical reduction of persons to hired hands deprive them of

their connectedness to the production process. Treated as a commodity, labor consequently 'has no material interest in doing more than securing the highest wages and best conditions for the minimum of sacrifice' (Hopper *et al.* 1987, 445).[5]

Wage labor, or hired labor, is treated within capitalist economies as a cost of production – as any other input factor of production – which need, *from the capitalist's point of view*, to be both minimized and optimized. The minimization of labor costs is 'rational' since it avoids the dependence on a factor of production that, unlike other factors, can rebel against its own use. Similarly, optimizing the use of labor is 'rational' since, as with any other factor of production, the efficient use of resources is the precondition for profits. Consequently, and built into the capitalist relations of production are the pressures to not only supplant labor by machinery but also to control the labor process – how labor power is deployed, the actual mode of work – in all its aspects, in the interest of capital accumulation. It is this pressure that motivates the capitalist to gain control over the labor process and make the latter 'the responsibility of the capitalist' (Braverman 1974, 57). However, treating human beings as just another factor of production sets the stage for the exploitation and expropriation of labor by capital. Accordingly, there is an irreducible conflict between capital and labor ensuring perpetually antagonistic relations between the classes. It is on this backdrop of capitalist social relations that the labor process perspective on cost and managerial accounting is fleshed out (see also Edwards 1979; Burawoy 1979; Noble 1977; Clawson 1980).

Hopper *et al.* (1987) introduced the labor process perspective to accounting by contrasting this perspective from both functional and interpretative understandings of managerial accounting. Their central argument was that management accounting cannot be properly understood, except in the light of the social relations of production. They argued that to view organizations as united by a common purpose is to fictionalize what is, in fact, a site of irreconcilable conflict. Such organization goals as the maximization of the net present value of future cash flows transform what is the goal of one sectional interest into the overriding goal of all, thus obscuring the class-based distributional conflicts inherent in all capitalist organizations.

Accordingly, labor process theorists deny that management accounting is a neutral tool serving the general interests of efficiency and emphasize its role in legitimizing partisan interests, in contributing to the control and domination of labor, and in reinforcing the dominant mode of production, i.e., capitalist production, albeit in a contested terrain. Moreover, management accounting also is capable of showing up the ambiguous position of managers within capitalist firms. Where on the one hand, they are 'materially privileged' agents of the capitalists' class and must accordingly serve the interests of the latter, they are on the other hand, wage labor and to that extent interested in 'securing their own employment, and in fighting for an improved share of available resources' (Hopper *et al.* 1987, 450–451). Thus, managers are at once 'both agents and victims of control' such that phenomena such as budget games and divisional budgeting slack must not be seen as the consequence of some 'individual pathology' but rather as the 'deep effects of exploitative and oppressive social structures' that are embedded and presupposed in the capitalist system of production.

While Hopper *et al.* (1987) offered a programmatic introduction to the labor process perspective and distinguish it from the more functionalist and interpretive traditions, a later paper by Hopper and Armstrong (1991) presented a historically rooted reflection on the development of management and cost accounting since the middle of the nineteenth century, in part by challenging the very popular reading of the history of cost and managerial accounting given by Johnson and Kaplan (1987) (see also Johnson 1972, 1981, 1983). Deploying a transactions-cost approach, Johnson and Kaplan (1987) argued for understanding the emergence and prevalence of cost accounting as techniques which contributed to increasing operational efficiencies, and for ROI and budgets as techniques which reduced the costs of managing large vertically integrated bureaucracies as opposed to securing market-based coordination. In contrast, Hopper and Armstrong (1991) challenged this interpretation by linking the presence and even subsequent absence of cost and managerial accounting practices to the changing forms of control over the labor process that are in turn linked to different phases of capitalism.

Accordingly, Hopper and Armstrong (1991) suggested that for the early factory organizations of the mid-nineteenth century (they especially consider Lyman Mills which was also the focus for Johnson and Kaplan (1987)), increases in profits were secured primarily from extending the number of hours worked without significantly changing the wages and from applying a closer degree of control over the labor process. Such 'innovations' as the 'stretch-out (an increase in the number of machines supervised by each operator), the speed-up (an increase in the operating speed of machines),' and 'a premium bonus system' for overseers to enforce productivity, were monitored and achieved by accounting records, while such labor practices as firing workers for trade union activity and disciplining dormitory behavior of workers by the 'moral police' ensured a relatively docile labor force which was the precondition for managerial action that is based on cost accounting information (Hopper and Armstrong 1991, 414–415). Hence, they argued that some of the accounting and cost information was not used for making the production process more efficient but rather used to intensify the extraction of labor from the labor force.

Moreover, the decline of internal contracts (outsourcing products and skilled labor) during the late nineteenth century was based on appropriating the profits made by subcontractors, though it involved increased costs for the companies (from replacing contractors with college trained executive who lacked knowledge of production processes). Where previously 'companies kept no records of the hours worked by the contractors' employees, or of how much and on what basis they were paid,' by paying workers directly, companies began to keep a host of new records including 'work records' (Hopper and Armstrong 1991, 416). Consequently, the creation of these new records, which also 'laid the foundation for the later development of standard costing systems' had 'nothing to do with the efficiency of the conversion process . . . but was a means of redistributing [the] profits . . . made by the contractors to the companies' (Hopper and Armstrong 1991, 417). Furthermore, these records not only transferred 'financial knowledge from the worker to the factory owner' but also fostered the 'imposition of an additional system of activity surveillance' (Hopper and Armstrong 1991, 417). Again, they argued that accounting records are hardly neutral but are deeply intertwined with the expropriation of profits, the intensification of the labor process and the surveillance of worker activities.

Regarding the late nineteenth and the early twentieth century, Hopper and Armstrong (1991) said that such developments as standard costing, ROI measures, and budgets cannot be understood except in the context of the correlative destruction of craft labor. Management accounting was one element in the development of a vast paper bureaucracy (measured by the increase in record-keeping and the swelling ranks of white-collar employees) by which the production process should be replicated, monitored and controlled. In the continual attempt to control the labor process, owners, and by now also managers, sought to redesign, fragment and simplify the labor process 'so that skill levels were reduced and the mental aspects of production incorporated

into management' (Hopper and Armstrong 1991, 419).

The labor process perspective has illuminated not only historical issues but also has been successfully applied to contemporary times. For example, Knights and Collinson (1987) found that British workers in one factory were unable to contest management's accounting reports, even when these reports led to worker layoffs. They suggested that accounting has inherent characteristics which make it difficult for workers to challenge these numbers, thus accounting information is not contested by labor on the grounds that its cultural values of 'objectivity' and 'hard facts' mirror the 'masculine values' on the shop floor. Similarly, Oakes and Covaleski (1994) examined organized labor's involvement with accounting-based incentive plans, and the role this involvement played in labor-management relations. This study involved case studies of profit-sharing plans implemented at three firms, Parker Pen, Kaiser Steel, and American Motors, in the 1950s and early 1960s, suggesting that 'accounting takes on characteristics or is constructed in ways that make it more or less likely that it will be contested at certain periods of time' (Oakes and Covaleski 1994, 595). Bougen *et al.* (1990) (see also Bougen 1989) documented the appearance and disappearance of accounting in British coal industry labor debates. Their study showed the partisan nature of the disclosure of financial reports to trade unions, the contested and sometimes self-defeating results of such disclosures, and of the many alternative managerial mechanisms (joint consultations committees and profit-sharing schemes) that attempt to gain cooperation by persuasion and cooperation.

In summary, labor process theory is consistent with the other organizational sociological perspectives such as contingency theory and interpretive work in the sense that it embeds management accounting in a wider context than more orthodox approaches. However, labor-process theory departs from these alternative approaches by focusing on the structural antagonism between classes inherent in capitalist societies. Also consistent with other organizational and sociological perspectives, labor-process theory offers a relatively non-technical understanding of management accounting in that management accounting appears within the context of a class-divided society to aid economic expropriation. Finally, the labor-process perspective moves towards considering accounting as a social practice rather than merely a technique, arguing that political events and ideologies, status, class, trust and technological changes impel people to act in certain ways, all potentially impinging on the roles served by management accounting.

The Foucaultian Perspective

Michel Foucault (1926–1984) was both a philosopher and historian who used history to raise philosophical questions.[6] A central motif that runs through his work and one which has also been productive for accounting scholarship is perhaps best described in his own words: ' . . . the goal of my work during the last twenty years . . . has been to create a history of the different modes by which, in our culture, human beings are made subjects' (Foucault 1983, 208). To begin to unpack this seemingly innocuous statement let us consider the key word here – 'subject' – in both the meanings that it admits: 'subject to someone else by control and dependence, and tied to his own identity by a conscience or self-knowledge. Both meanings suggest a form of power which subjugates and makes subject to' (Foucault 1983, 212). While the first meaning is a relatively familiar one (hierarchical employment relations, prisoner-guard, parent-child etc.), the second hints at the radical and innovative nature of Foucault's thought. What is equally significant regarding the exercise of this power, is the interrelation between power and knowledge which Foucault signifies by the slash in the term 'Power/ Knowledge.' Foucault argued that to properly grasp the conditions for the emergence of the 'human sciences' – all those 'sciences' that are concerned with describing, explaining, understanding, predicting and controlling human behavior – one must understand its complicity with the historically unprecedented presence of a widespread and general control of human beings. Foucault (1979, 191) argued that the 'birth of the sciences of man' probably lies in the various written techniques (of notation, registration, columnar and tabular presentation, of measurement, classification etc.) by which individuals are turned into a 'case.' Transforming a human being into a 'case' (patient, student, prisoner, worker) simultaneously homogenizes (by classifying as one within a series) and individualizes (by measuring the individual differences). Implicit in such classification and measurement is the presence of normalizing judgments wherein the measurement of individual differences are made in regard to deviations from a norm (for example, students' grades, standard cost, time and motion studies, budgets, benchmarks). According to Foucault, it was only by the late eighteenth century that this manner of describing, or more precisely, writing up individuals as cases became widespread and general. It furthermore represented a reversal of historic proportions, as stated by Foucault (1979, 191):

> For a long time ordinary individuality – the everyday individuality of everybody – remained below the threshold of description. To be looked at, observed, described in detail, followed from day to day by an uninterrupted writing was a privilege. . . . The disciplinary methods reversed this relation, lowered the threshold of describable individuality and made of this description a means of control and a method of domination.

Power, in this light, is not negative or repressive but rather positive and productive, because 'it produces reality; it produces domains of objects and rituals of truth. The individual and the knowledge gained of him belongs to this production' (Foucault 1979, 194). Accordingly, for Foucault (1990, 98), power and knowledge are constitutive of, but not identical, to each other, since 'between techniques of knowledge and strategies of power, there is no exteriority, even if they have specific roles and are linked together on the basis of their difference.' The scientific disciplines which generate our knowledge of human beings are thus also complicit in their disciplining, or as Foucault (1979, 222) suggested, 'The "Enlightenment," which discovered the liberties, also invented the disciplines.'

Foucault's work has, as already stated, sparked much attention in the critical accounting tradition. In a recent paper, Walsh and Stewart (1993) explored the history of managerial accounting practices from a rigorously Foucaultian perspective. In comparing 'two assemblages of people making things,' one from the 1700s and the other from the 1800s, they find support for one of Foucault's most provocative theses. By asserting that 'the individual' was the result of disciplinary mechanisms, Foucault also is implying that prior to the late eighteenth century individuals could not be known and therefore controlled since they lay below the threshold of description. Accordingly, what we consider axiomatic in managerial accounting – namely the linking of accounting calculations and measures to the work of individuals and groups – must not have been prevalent prior to the late eighteenth century. Indeed, this is precisely what Walsh and Stewart (1993) find when they compare the New Mills Woolen Manufactory (1681–1703) with the New Lanark Cotton Factory (1800–1812). Some features which characterized the manufactory of the late seventeenth century include: master-servant relationships between the managers and workers; customary rather than market driven rates of profit, calculations of selling prices and wages; use of the pillory and the prison as threats of retribution to workers for pilferage or shortages in piece work; bookkeeping as a 'physical memory of the real proceedings of each day and each week to be certified by the masters' (Walsh and Stewart 1993, 786).

While Walsh and Stewart (1993) focused on the early days of the factory system to provide some solid evidence and support for Foucault's thesis, Miller and O'Leary (1994) studied another time period to examine the rising popularity of standard costing and budgetary practices in the U.S. during the turn of the century. Again, using a Foucaultian perspective, they illuminated dimensions of that much studied period that have hitherto escaped attention. Miller and O'Leary (1994, 99) argued that such accounting practices as standard costing and budgeting should be understood 'as a technology of government,' where the latter is understood as 'the ensemble of rationalities and technologies' by which 'authorities attempt to act on the conduct of others, to shape their beliefs and behavior in directions deemed desirable.' Accordingly, the widespread emergence of standard costing and budgetary techniques by the 1930s in both the U.K. and the U.S. are seen as indicative of a new modality in the governance of economic life. This emergence was linked not only to the scientific management movement associated with Taylor and the spread of industrial psychology but also to the concern with national efficiency in the U.K. and the 'efficiency craze' in the U.S. The term efficiency was deployed in a wide range of contexts from individual performance on the factory floor to articulation of the social responsibilities of the state in correcting the ills of society, and subsumed under itself a host of financial and nonfinancial techniques. Linkages were also forged between the scientific management of industrial enterprises and the rational and orderly planning of society as a whole. A host of such social sciences as public administration, engineering, and sociology as well as a slew of such experts as accountants, urban planners and economists sought to 'normalize and govern populations of individuals' (Miller and O'Leary 1994, 111). It is this new modality of governing economic life that forms a context that is both constitutive of and constituted by the standard costing and budgetary practices of the early twentieth century.

To date, within accounting as well as organizational theory, a majority of work applying what has been termed Foucault's archeological and genealogical perspectives have had an historical perspective. However, the application of Foucault's insights into the functioning of modern societies is not limited to forays into the past. More pertinently, his work proves to be of continuing value as it is being profitably used to illuminate certain aspects of the contemporary uses and redefinitions of accounting. For example, Preston (1992, 64) studied the relative emergence of Diagnostic Related Groups (DRGs) as an 'accounting technology based upon principles of cost control rather than cost reimbursement.' Using a longitudinal study Preston (1992, 97) showed how this practice of reimbursement cannot be exclusively related to 'a logic of economic incentives and rational economic behavior.' Rather, a shifting complex of events, including Medicare and Medicaid, the private structure of American health care, the power of professional associations, changing public attitudes towards health care, is seen as being part of this transformation of accounting practices. Accordingly, Preston, following Foucault, revealed the emergence of DRGs as being implicated in a wider and more general transformation in the 'politics of health' which involves not only economic factors but more decisively, social and cultural ones as well. On this same issue of contemporary application of Foucault's work, Rose (1991) argued for an interrelation between the mode of liberal democratic governance and the technology of quantification,

numeracy and statistics. Rose (1991, 691) stated that 'numbers have an unmistakable power in modern political culture' evident from opinion polls to the federal budget and the national income statistics. The role of accounting in this Foucaultian view, is that accounting, along with other various calculations, form the basis for democratic politics whose singular characteristic is 'arms-length' management from a distance.

Consistent with the underpinnings of critical perspectives, the Foucaultian view situates management accounting in a wider political and social context. Specifically, in the Foucaultian approach, management accounting is considered as part of a larger historical trend through which people at large were subjected to a variety of disciplinary techniques. Whereas in labor-process theory, management accounting appears within the context of a class-divided society to aid economic expropriation, the Foucaultian tradition reveals management accounting as an element of a general historical process by which people are made calculable and governable. The Foucaultian view also considers management accounting as a social practice rather than a technique by examining the intricacies and richness in such social relations that are embedded in social patterns of interaction as language, discipline and intimacy, all cultural norms and forces which potentially impinge on the roles and nature of management accounting.

Closing Discussion

It is important to note our interpretation of the relationship among the alternative managerial and sociological theories considered, as well as their relationship to more traditional perspectives of managerial accounting: can these various perspectives be compared and contrasted or possibly blended, and a 'champion' paradigm isolated? In exploring the structure of more general scientific revolutions,

Kuhn (1970) reasoned that because of fundamentally different philosophical presumptions, it is impossible to employ the tenets of one paradigm to assist those subscribing to a second paradigm to transition to understand the first paradigm. But rather, the 'leap' from one paradigm to another must be based on faith in order to fully appreciate what a particular paradigm may offer for understanding our existence. In this spirit, and more closely concerned with organizational analysis, Morgan (1980) (see also Burrell and Morgan 1979; in accounting see Dirsmith *et al.*1985) theorized that different paradigms both address different sorts of problems and, where paradigms address common problems, portray them in fundamentally different ways and thereby offer differing insights into their nature. Thus, what is called for is not a blending of paradigms nor the isolation of a particular paradigm as champion, but rather paradigmatic pluralism as a way of enhancing our understanding of issues in the social sciences. Consequently, we offer the various paradigms not as competing perspectives but in some sense as alternative ways of understanding the multiple roles played by management accounting in organizations and society.

Extending this theme and drawing upon Churchman's (1971) characterization of influencing systems, Mitroff and Mason (1982) offered a useful way to understand the properties of more orthodox research approaches and one which calls for a plurality of theories used in a dialectic fashion. The argument of Mitroff and Mason (1982) also highlights fundamental differences in the types of problems which may be addressed. Within the traditional approach to management accounting research, one seeks regularity, consistency or consensus by two means. In the first, one seeks patterns in specific sets of empirical data in a purely inductive mode. 'Consensus' of data is in essence a guarantor of faithfully representing a concrete reality. Any lack of regularity or consensus in the data (e.g., low r^2)

serves to question the validity of the pattern isolated or theory used. One seeks improved understanding by refining the model's specification. In the second approach, one seeks internal consistency in a postulational system wherein reality *is* the axiomatic structure. In a deductively driven system, only the lack of internal consistency or conflict in the propositional network can cause one to abandon it in favor of a competing network.

The rational frame of reference importantly assumes that the phenomena under investigation are either well specified and well known, or able to be well known through some preliminary fieldwork (Keating 1995), or further refinement of the model or propositional network, and hence, are eminently structurable. However, because of its reliance on a set of fixed concrete data or variables expressed in a fixed postulational structure, it is limited in its abilities to preserve or reflect anomalies and uniqueness in phenomena and to capture the essence of ill structured problems. Its use is, therefore, relegated to examining well structured though perhaps technically complex problems. Paradoxically, because of their very comprehensiveness, these traditional perspectives tend to suppress conflict, anomaly and uniqueness. By contrast, a more interpretive or critical view emphasizes the use of multiple conceptual views of ill structured, anomalous phenomena on the presumption that reality is too ill structured to be meaningfully represented by any set of data or propositional network, no matter how comprehensive they may appear.

The use of alternative research theories also has resulted in alternative research methods or forms of inquiry. The general literature which describes the use of qualitative, naturalistic methods in field research is growing in volume and stature. From this literature, it is possible to outline various criteria of 'good' research which are provisionally consistent with the knowledge claims advanced by its theoretical perspective discussed in the paper (Morgan

(1983) sounds a useful warning note in such matters). However, we avoid detailed treatment of such philosophical issues as epistemology, or such methodological issues as falsification, or indeed of research methods. These and related matters have been adequately dealt with in both the philosophy of science and accounting literatures.[7]

Denzin and Lincoln (1983) offer a useful discussion regarding criteria to consider for alternative methods of research inquiry. The first criteria is credibility which relates to the believability of the observations and interpretations to both the academic community and participants in the study. This criteria is addressed through such techniques as prolonged engagement at the organizational context studied which provides research scope, and persistent observations which concerns penetration into the context studied to identify relationships, forces, etc., which have salience in understanding the lived experiences of organizational members. Representative adequacy also is important to credibility which entails having sufficient notes, transcripts, audio or video recordings to enable different researchers to examine field observations and form similar though not necessarily identical interpretations.

The second criteria is transferability, or the ability of the interpretations of one organizational context to be transferred to another. Given the primary focus on the context or substantive domain and the lived experience of its members, interpretive and critical field members would typically emphasize the importance of providing thick description in the research text, presenting vibrant, exact interview quotes, archival abstracts, etc., that provide both scope and depth in understanding the context. This thick description, in turn, influences theoretical perspectives being provisionally used to interpret the organizational context. It is this informed theory, not the observations, that may be transferred to begin providing another organizational context.

The third and fourth criteria are dependability and conformability. The former concerns developing reliable interpretations, but interpretations that simultaneously recast the state of the organization studied (i.e., its stability) and the process by which the organization is changing (i.e., its instability); in turn the field worker concedes instrumental unreliability, albeit a constructive unreliability. The latter criterion relates to the field observations themselves, can observations be corroborated by another investigator or another method? On this theme, Van Maanen (1995), has observed that the accounts rendered by field researchers employing qualitative, naturalistic methods may be described as 'impressionist takes,' using the analogy of impressionist art wherein the viewer of a piece of art sees both the subject being painted *and* the artist.

It is also important to note what may be gained by management accounting scholars beyond a more general appreciation of the technical, social and interest-based forces which may flow through and influence management accounting, and how management accounting, by embodying and reproducing these forces, may come to influence its own historical, socio political context. Christenson (1983) argues that what may be derived is not the first-order concern of somehow modifying management accounting as a set of somewhat disembodied practices to somehow more faithfully represent an objective, albeit complex reality and thereby solve the technical problems of running an organization. But rather, what can be gained is a second-order focus of serving the problem solver, i.e., helping them recognize the multiple realities they confront and live, and the multiple meanings attached to and served by management accounting.

One of the principle tendencies exhibited by alternative research theories and related methods which distinguish them from the more familiar approaches is that of embedding management accounting in a wider social context than usual.

Accounting research inspired by contemporary social and organizational psychology and neo-classical economics largely examines the roles and nature of management accounting from the perspective of the individual decision-maker or information processor within the organization. The alternative streams of research discussed here, in contrast, typically approach the study of managerial accounting from an inter-organizational and sociological perspective.

To illustrate the broader orientation, Selto et al.'s (1995) field study of a Fortune 500 firm examines the adaptation of JIT manufacturing and a total quality control system (JIT/TQC system) in relationship to classical contingency theory constructs – organizational structure, context and control – to ascertain the fit of these organizational variables and the JIT system. An interpretive perspective, such as institutional theory, might relate the adaption of the JIT/TQC system to even larger societal values of rationality while perhaps sacrificing on the robustness of insight provided by contingency theory regarding the impact of organizational-level variables. Here the theoretical and empirical focus would be more on probing the firm's broader field of relations, such as mimicking the structure of dominant firms in the industry, or responding to the coercion of the government, or adapting the norms of professional associations, expressed in terms of a more widespread JIT/TQC movement. Finally, critical perspectives would advance their theoretical frame of reference by characterizing the JIT/TQC efforts in this firm as related to the structural antagonism between classes inherent in capitalist societies (labor process perspective), or as part of a larger historical trend through which people at large were subjected to a variety of disciplinary techniques rendering the minute details of their behavior more visible (the Foucaultian approach). With the critical perspective's theoretical and empirical point of departure being at the broadest social and historical level (i.e., parts of larger historical trends of structural antagonism or disciplinary techniques) the more immediate organizational influences (contingency theory) or organizational fields (interpretive perspectives) become more tangential to the research focus. In summary, despite the differences between the theoretical points of departure and related demands for empirical inquiry pertaining to the contingency, interpretive, and critical perspectives, these approaches to management accounting provide multiple understandings of management accounting that are not offered by more narrowly focused analysis which centers around individual preference and cognitive functions.

A second aspect that distinguishes the management accounting research which draws on organizational and sociological traditions is its tendency to offer a relatively non-technical understanding of management accounting. For example, it is usual to suppose that management accounting is an information system that can be designed to influence decisions and to so gain control over behavior. Here, accounting is a tool that not only signals certain states of the world, but also works as an instrument by which certain outcomes are made more probable. This instrumental and consequently asocial, ahistorical and apolitical view of accounting contrasts with that gained from the various alternative research streams. Again, referring to the contributions of Selto et al.'s (1995) contingency perspective-driven field work, such management accounting practices as JIT/TQC systems are seen to be invested with the social aspects of worker empowerment, workgroup performance, and relations within and between workgroups, operators and supervisors. By modifying the system, aided by management accounting, the fit may be enhanced and performance consequently improved. An interpretive perspective of management accounting would particularly probe the issue as to whether JIT/TQC systems are as much a symbol demonstrating efficiency and rationality to be displayed for external consumption as they are an instrument for achieving efficiencies, thus focusing their theoretical and empirical efforts to inform our understanding of the symbolic nature of JIT/TQC. Critical perspectives, in turn, might mobilize their empirical efforts around their respective theoretical motivations to examine JIT/TQC systems within the context of a class-divided society to aid economic expropriation of workers' surplus, or, in the Foucaultian tradition, to examine JIT/TQC systems as artifacts of a general historical mechanism by which people are made calculable and manageable.

Accordingly, alternative streams of research, to varying degrees, move towards considering accounting as a social practice rather than a technique. To treat accounting as a 'practice' instead of a 'technique' is to embed accounting within the web of human actions which are, in turn, constitutive of social relations. The intricacies and richness of social relations that are suffused by such aspects of sociality as symbols, myths, language, status, class, trust and intimacy, comprises the backdrop for the organizationally and sociologically informed studies of accounting. More specifically, management accounting research rooted in the contemporary social and organizational psychology and neoclassical economics usually examines management accounting procedures and techniques with the intent to improve its efficacy. In general, these traditional approaches are problem driven and directed towards improving and refining the instrument that is management accounting to better serve exogenously given organizational goals and thus somewhat narrow in focus. Designing better costing procedures, incentive contracts, information systems to account for processing biases, and so on, are examples of the problem-driven nature of mainstream management accounting research.

In contrast, the research drawing on organizational and sociological theories, to different degrees, situate management accounting practice within the context of social life in general. The problem-driven focus is less apparent since, in part, the very ways in which problems come to be defined as problems needing solutions, or indeed how particular calculative techniques come to be called 'accounting,' comprise the subject for analysis. From this perspective, managerial accounting practices are not techniques that can be abstracted from the general milieu of social life but rather one strand in the complex weave that makes up the social fabric. Political events and ideologies, cultural norms and forces, social patterns of interaction and societal presuppositions, technological changes and subjective meanings that impel people to act in certain ways, all potentially impinge on the roles and nature of management accounting. It is in this manner that a different light is shed on the role and nature of management accounting practices by the research which draws from organizational and sociological theories.

References

Abbott, A. (1988). *The System of Professions*. Chicago: University of Chicago Press.

Aiken, M., and J. Hage (1966). Organizational alienation. *American Sociological Review*, **31**: 497–507.

Alford, R., and R. Friedland (1985). *Powers of Theory*. Cambridge: Cambridge University Press.

Ansari, S. L. (1977). An integrated approach to control systems design. *Accounting, Organizations and Society*, **2**: 101–112.

———, and K. J. Euske (1987). Rational, rationalizing and reifying uses of accounting data in organizations. *Accounting, Organizations and Society*, **12**: 549–570.

Anthony, R. (1965). *Planning and Control Systems: A Framework for Analysis*. Boston, MA: Harvard University Press.

Argyris, C. (1952). *The Impact of Budgets on People*. New York: Controllership Foundation.

Armstrong, P. (1985). Changing management control strategies: the role of competition between accountancy and other organizational professions. *Accounting, Organizations and Society*, **10**: 129–148.

Banker, R. D., S. M. Datar, and L. Kemerer (1991). A model to evaluate variables impacting the productivity of software maintenance. *Management Science*, 1–18.

Barnard, C. (1938). *The Functions of the Executive.* Boston: Harvard University Press.

Becker, S., and D. Green (1962). Budgeting and employee behavior. *Journal of Business (October)*: 392–402.

Berger, P. L., and T. Luckmann (1967). *The Social Construction of Reality.* New York: Doubleday.

Bernstein, R. (1978). *The Restructuring of Social and Political Theory.* Philadelphia: University of Pennsylvania Press.

Blau, P. M. (1970). A formal theory of differentiation in organizations. *American Sociological Review*, **35**: 201–218.

———(1973). *The Organization of Academic Work.* New York: John Wiley.

Boland, R. J., and L. R. Pondy (1983). Accounting in organizations: A union of natural and rational perspectives. *Accounting, Organizations and Society*, **8**: 223–234.

———, and ———(1986). The micro-dynamics of a budget cutting process: Modes, models and structure. *Accounting, Organizations and Society*, **11**: 403–422.

Bougen, P. D. (1989). The emergence, roles and consequences of an accounting-industrial relations interaction. *Accounting, Organizations and Society*, **14**: 203–234.

———, S. G. Ogden, and Q. Outram (1990). The appearance and disappearance of accounting: wage determination in the U.K. Coal industry. *Accounting, Organizations and Society*, **15**: 149–170.

Braverman, H. (1974). *Labor and Monopoly Capital.* New York: Monthly Review Press.

Brownell, P. (1981). Participation in budgeting, locus of control and organizational effectiveness. *The Accounting Review*, **56**: 844–860.

———(1982). The role of accounting data in performance evaluation, budgetary participation, and organizational effectiveness. *Journal of Accounting Research*, 12–27.

Burawoy, M. (1979). *Manufacturing Consent.* Chicago: University of Chicago Press.

Burns, T. R. (1986). *Actors, transactions and social structures.* In: *Sociology: From Crisis to Science?*, edited by V. Hemmelstrand, 8–37. London: Sage.

———, and G. M. Stalker (1961). *The Management of Innovation.* Tavistock.

Burrell, G., and G. Morgan (1979). *Sociological Paradigms and Organizational Analysis.* Heinemann.

Caplan, E. H. (1971). *Management Accounting and Behavioral Science.* Reading, MA: Addison-Wesley.

Carruthers, B. G. (1995). Accounting, ambiguity, and the new institutionalism. *Accounting, Organizations and Society*, **20**: 313–328.

Child, J. (1972). Organization structure and strategies of control: A replication of the Ashton Study. *Administrative Science Quarterly*, **17**: 163–177.

Christensen, J. (1983). The determination of performance standards and participation. *Journal of Accounting Research*, **20**: 589–603.

Christenson, C. (1983). The methodology of positive accounting. *The Accounting Review*, **58** (January): 1–22.

Chua, W. F. (1986). Radical developments in accounting thought. *The Accounting Review*, **61**(4): 601–632.

Churchman, C. W. (1971). *The Design of Inquiry Systems.* New York: Basic Books.

Clawson, D. (1980). *Bureaucracy and the Labor Process: The Transformation of U.S. Industry*, 1860–1920. New York: Monthly Review Press.

Clegg, S. (1987). The language of power and the power of language. *Organization Studies*, **8**: 61–70.

Collins, F. (1978). The interaction of budget characteristics and personality variables with budgetary response attitudes. *The Accounting Review*, **53**: 324–335.

Cooper, D., and T. Hopper (1990). Critical studies in accounting. *Accounting, Organizations and Society*, **12**: 407–414.

———, and M. Sherer (1984). The value of corporate accounting reports: Arguments for a political economy of accounting. *Accounting, Organizations and Society*, **9**: 407–414.

Covaleski, M. A., and M. W. Dirsmith (1983). Budgeting as a means for control and loose coupling. *Accounting, Organizations and Society*, **8**: 323–340.

———, and ——— (1986). The budgetary process of power and politics. *Accounting, Organizations and Society*, **11**: 193–214.

———, and ——— (1988a). The use of budgetary symbols in the political arena: An historically informed field study. *Accounting, Organizations and Society*, **13**: 1–24.

———, and ——— (1988b). An institutional perspective on the rise, social transformation, and fall of a university budget category. *Administrative Science Quarterly*, **33**: 562–587.

Cyert, R. N., and J. G. March (1963). *A Behavioral Theory of the Firm.* Englewood Cliffs, NJ: Prentice Hall.

Daft, R. L., and N. B. MacIntosh (1981). A tentative exploration into the amount and equivocality of information processing in organizational work units. *Administrative Science Quarterly*, **26**: 207–224.

Dent, J. F. (1987). Tensions in the design of formal control systems: A field study in a computer company. In: *Accounting and Management Field Study Perspectives*, edited by W. J. Bruns and R. S. Kaplan, *119–145*. Harvard.

Denzin, N., and Y. Lincoln (1983). *Beyond Method: Strategies for Social Research*. London: Sage.

DiMaggio, P. J. (1988). Interest and agency in institutional theory. In: *Institutional Patterns and Organizations: Culture and Environment*, edited by L. G. Zucker, 3–22. Cambridge, MA: Ballinger Publishing Company.

———, and W. W. Powell (1983). The iron cage revisited: institutional isomorphism and collective rationality in organizational field. *American Sociological Review*, **48**: 147–160.

———, and ——— (1991). Introduction to the new institutionalism in organizational analysis. In: *The New Institutionalism in Organizational Analysis*, edited by W. W. Powell and P. J. DiMaggio, 1–38. Chicago: University of Chicago Press.

Dirsmith, M., M. Covaleski, and J. McAllister (1985). Of paradigms and metaphors in auditing thought. *Contemporary Accounting Research*, **2**: 46–68.

Drazin, R., and A. Van de Ven (1985). Alternative forms of fit in contingency theory. *Administrative Science Quarterly*, **30**: 514–539.

Durkheim, E. (1938). *The Rules of Sociological Method*. Glencoe, IL: Free Press.

Edelman, J. M. (1977). *Political Language: Words that Succeed and Policies that Fail*. New York: Academic Press.

Edwards, R. (1979). *Contested Terrain*. New York: Basic Books.

Foster, G., and M. Gupta (1990). Manufacturing overhead cost driver analysis. *Journal of Accounting and Economics*, 309–337.

Foucault, M. (1979). *Discipline and Punish: The Birth of the Prison*. New York: Vintage Books.

——— (1983). The subject and power. In: *Power/Knowledge: Selected Interviews and Other Writing: 1972–1977*, edited by C. Gordon, 78–108. New York: Pantheon Books.

——— (1990). *The History of Sexuality, Vol. 1: An Introduction*, trans. by R. Hurley. New York: Vintage Books.

Freidson, E. (1986). *Professional Powers: A Study of the Institutionalization of Formal Knowledge*. Chicago: University of Chicago Press.

Garfinkel, H. (1967). *Studies in Methodology*. Prentice Hall.

Golembiewski, R. T. (1964). Accountancy as a function of organization theory. *The Accounting Review*, **39**: 333–341.

Gordon, L. A., and D. Miller (1976). A contingency framework for the design of accounting information systems. *Accounting, Organizations and Society*, **1**: 59–70.

Govindarajan, V. J. (1984). Appropriateness of accounting data in performance evaluation: An empirical examination of environmental uncertainty as an intervening variable. *Accounting, Organizations and Society*, **9**: 125–136.

——— (1988). A contingency approach to strategy implementation at the business level: Integrating administrative mechanisms with strategy. *Academy of Management Journal*, 828–853.

———, and A. K. Gupta (1985). Linking control systems to business unit strategy: Impact on performance. *Accounting, Organizations and Society*, **10**: 51–66.

Gray, B., and S. S. Ariss (1985). Politics and strategic change across organizational life. *Academy of Management Review*, **10**: 707–723.

Hackman, J. D. (1985). Power and centrality in the allocation of resources in colleges and universities. *Administrative Science Quarterly*, **30**: 61–77.

Hage, J., and M. Aiken (1967). Relationship of centralization to other structural properties. *Administrative Science Quarterly*, **12**: 79–92.

Hayes, D. (1977). The contingency theory of management accounting. *The Accounting Review*, **52**: 22–39.

Hickson, D. (1966). A convergence in organization theory. *Administrative Science Quarterly*, **11**: 225–237.

Hills, F. S., and T. Mahoney (1978). University budgets and organizational decision-making. *Administrative Science Quarterly*, **23**: 61–77.

Hirst, M. K. (1981). Accounting information and the evaluation of subordinate performance: A situational approach. *The Accounting Review*, **56**: 771–784.

——— (1983). Reliance on accounting performance measures, task uncertainty, and dysfunctional behavior: some extensions. *Journal of Accounting Research*, **20**: 596–605.

Hofstede, G. (1967). *The Game of Budget Control*. London: Tavistock.

Hopper, T., and P. Armstrong (1991). Cost accounting, controlling labor and the rise of conglomerates. *Accounting, Organizations and Society*, **16**: 408–438.

———, and A. Powell (1985). Making sense of research into the organizational and social aspects of management accounting: A review of its underlying assumptions. *Journal of Management Studies*, **22**: 429–465.

———, J. Storey, and H. Willmott (1987). Accounting for accounting: Towards the development of a dialectical view. *Accounting, Organizations and Society*, **12**: 43 7–456.

Hopwood, A. (1973). *An Accounting System and Managerial Behavior*. Saxon House.

———, (1974). *Accounting and Human Behavior*. London: Haymarket.

———, and P. Miller (1994). *Accounting as a Social and Institutional Practice*. Cambridge: Cambridge University Press.

Hoskins, K., and R. Macve (1988). The genesis of accountability: The West Point connections. *Accounting, Organizations and Society*, **13**: 37–73.

Ijiri, Y. (1965). *Management Goals and Accounting for Control*.New York: North Holland.

Johnson, H. T. (1972). Early cost accounting for internal management control: Lyman Mills in the late 1850s. *Business History Review*: 466–474.

——— (1981). Toward a new understanding of nineteenth century cost accounting. *The Accounting Review*, **56**: 510–518.

——— (1983). The search for gain in markets and firms: A review of the historical emergence of management accounting systems. *Accounting, Organizations and Society*, **8**: 139–146.

———, and R. S. Kaplan (1987). *Relevance Lost: The Rise and Fall of Management Accounting*. Boston: Harvard Business School Press.

Jonsson, S. (1982). Budgetary behavior in local government – A case study over 3 years. *Accounting, Organizations and Society*, **7**: 287–304.

Kaplan, R. S. (1983). Measuring manufacturing performance: A new challenge for managerial accounting research. *The Accounting Review*, **58**: 686–705.

Keating, P. J. (1995). A framework for classifying and evaluating the theoretical contribution of case research in management accounting. *Journal of Management Accounting Research*, **7**: 66–86.

Khandwalla, P. (1972). The effect of different types of competition on the use of management controls. *Journal of Accounting Research*, **9**: 276–295.

Knights, D., and D. Collinson (1987). Disciplining the shopfloor: A comparison of the disciplinary effects of managerial psychology and financial accounting. *Accounting, Organizations and Society*, **12**: 457–477.

Kuhn, T. (1970). *The Structure of Scientific Revolutions*. Chicago: University of Chicago Press.

Lawrence, P. R., and J. W. Lorsch (1969). *Organizations and Environment*. Homewood, IL: Irwin.

Loft, A. (1986). Towards a critical understanding of accounting: A case of cost accounting in the U.K., 1914–1925. *Accounting, Organizations and Society*, **11**: 137–169.

MacIntosh, N. (1981). A contextual model for information systems. *Accounting, Organizations and Society*, **6**: 39–52.

March, J., and J. P. Olsen (1976). *Ambiguity and Choice in Organizations*. Oslo: Universitiete Forlaget.

———, and H. A. Simon (1958). *Organizations*. New York: Wiley.

Mayo, E. (1933). *Human Problems of an Industrial Civilization*. New York: Macmillan.

McMann, P., and A. J. Nanni, Jr. (1996). Means versus ends: A review of the literature on Japanese management accounting. *Journal of Management Accounting Research* (forthcoming).

McNair, C. J. and W. Mosconi (1989). *Beyond the Bottom Line*. New York: Dow Jones-Irwin.

———, ———, and T. Norris (1988). *Meeting the Technology Challenge: Cost Accounting in a JIT Environment*. Montvale, NJ: National Association of Accountants.

Merchant, K. A. (1981). The design of the corporate budgeting system: Influences on managerial behavior and performance. *The Accounting Review*, **56**: 813–829.

——— (1984). Influences on departmental budgeting: An empirical examination of a contingency model. *Accounting, Organizations and Society*, **9**: 291–307.

——— (1985). Organizational controls and discretionary program decision-making: A field study. *Accounting, Organizations and Society*, **10**: 67–86.

Meyer, J. W., and B. Rowan (1977). Institutional organizations: Formal structures as myth and ceremony. *American Journal of Sociology*, **80**: 340–363.

Mezias, S. J. (1990). An institutional model of organizational practice: Financial reporting at the Fortune 200. *Administrative Science Quarterly*, **35**: 431–457.

———, and M. Scarselletta (1994). Resolving financial reporting problems: An institutional analysis of the process. *Administrative Science Quarterly*, **39**: 654–678.

Milani, K. (1975). The relationship of participation in budget setting to industrial supervisor performance and attitudes: A field study. *The Accounting Review*, **50**: 2 74–284.

Miller, P. (1994). Governing the calculable person. In: *Accounting as a Social and Institutional Practice*, edited by A. Hopwood and P. Miller, 98–115. Cambridge: Cambridge University Press.

——, and T. O'Leary (1987). Accounting and the construction of the governable person. *Accounting, Organizations and Society*, *12*: 235–265.

——, and —— (1989). Hierarchies and American ideals, 1900–1940. *Academy of Management Review*, *14*: 250–265.

Mitroff, I., and R. Mason (1982). Business policy and metaphysics: some philosophical considerations. *Academy of Management Review*, 7: 361–371.

Morgan, G. (1980). Paradigms, metaphors and puzzle solving in organizational theory. *Administrative Science Quarterly*, *25*: 605–622.

——(1983). *Beyond Method: Strategies for Social Research*. London: Sage.

Noble, D. (1977). *American by Design*. London: Oxford University Press.

Oakes, L. S., and M. A. Covaleski (1994). A historical examination of the use of accounting-based incentive plans in the structuring of labor-management relations. *Accounting, Organizations and Society*, *19*: 579–599.

Oliver, C. (1991). Strategic responses to institutional processes. *Academy of Management Review*, *16*: 145–179.

Otley, D. (1978). Budget use and managerial behavior. *Journal of Accounting Research*, *15*: 122–149.

—— (1980). The contingency theory of management accounting: Achievement and prognosis. *Accounting, Organizations and Society*, *5*: 413–428.

Patell, J. M. (1987). Cost accounting process controls and product design: A case study of the H-P personal office computer division. *The Accounting Review*, *63*: 808–839.

Perrow, C. (1967). A framework for comparative organizational analysis. *American Sociological Review*, *32*: 194–208.

——(1985). Review essay: Overboard with myths and symbols. *American Journal of Sociology*, *91*:194–208.

Pfeffer, J. (1981). *Power in Organizations*. Marshfield, MA: Pitman.

——, and G. R. Salancik (1974). Organizational decision-making as a political process: The case of a university budget. *Administrative Science Quarterly*, *19*: 135–151.

——, and —— (1978). *The External Control of Organizations: A Resource Dependence Perspective*. New York: Harper & Row.

Powell, W. W. (1985). The institutionalization of rational organizations. *Contemporary Sociology*, *14*: 151–155.

Preston, A. (1992). The birth of clinical accounting: A study of the emergence and transformation of discourse on costs and practices of accounting in U.S. hospitals. *Accounting, Organizations and Society*, *17*: 63–100.

Pugh, D. S., D. J. Hickson, and C. R. Hinnings (1969). The context of organization structures. *Administrative Science Quarterly*, *14*: 91–114.

——, ——, ——, and C. Turner (1968). Dimensions of organization structure. *Administrative Science Quarterly*, *13*: 65–105.

Puxty, A. (1993). *The Social and Organizational Context of Managerial Accounting*. New York: Academic Press.

Rabinow, P. (1984). *The Foucault Reader*. Pantheon Press.

Rose, N. (1991). Governing by the numbers: Figuring out democracy. *Accounting, Organizations and Society*, *16*: 673–692.

Rose, R. (1977). Implementation and cooperation: The record of MBO. *Public Administrative Review*, *64*–71.

Rosenlender, R. (1992). *Sociological Perspective in Modern Accounting*. Englewood Cliffs, NJ: Prentice Hall.

Salancik, G. R., and J. Pfeffer (1974). The base and use of power in organizational decision making: the case of a university. *Administrative Science Quarterly*, *19*: 453–473.

Sarfatti-Larson, M. (1977). *The Rise of Professionalism*. Berkley: University of California Press.

Schick, A. G. (1985). University budgeting: Administrative perspective, budget structure, and budget process. *Academy of Management Review*, *19*: 794–802.

Schiff, M., and A. Y. Lewin (1970). The impact of people on budgets. *The Accounting Review*, *45*: 259–268.

Scott, W. R. (1987). The adolescence of institutional theory. *Administrative Science Quarterly*, *32*: 493–511.

Selto, F. H., C. J. Renner, and S. M. Young (1995). Assessing the organizational fit of a just-in-time manufacturing system: Testing selection, interaction and systems models of contingency theory. *Accounting, Organizations and Society*, *20*: 665–684.

Selznick, P. (1957). Foundations of the theory of organizations. *American Sociological Review*, *12*: 25–35.

Shank, J. K. (1989). Strategic cost management: New wine, or just new bottles. *Journal of Management Accounting Research*, *1*: 47–65.

Simon, H. A. (1957). *Administrative Behavior*. Glencoe, IL: The Free Press.

Simons, R. (1987). Accounting control systems and business strategy. *Accounting, Organizations and Society*, **12**: 357–374.

Stedry, A. (1960). *Budget Control and Cost Behavior*. Englewood Cliffs, NJ: Prentice Hall.

Swieringa, R., and R. Moncur (1975). *Some Effects of Participative Budgeting on Managerial Behavior*. National Association of Accountants.

Thompson, J. D. (1967). *Organizations in Action*. New York: McGraw-Hill.

Tinker, A., B. Merino, and M. Neimark (1982). The normative origins of positive theories: Ideology and accounting thought. *Accounting, Organizations and Society*, 7: 167–200.

Tolbert, P. (1988). Institutional sources of organizational culture in major law firms. In: *Institutional Patterns and Organizations: Culture and Environment*, edited by L. Zucker, 101–113. Cambridge, MA: Ballinger Publishing Company.

Van Maanen, J. (1995). The end of innocence: The ethnography of ethnography. In: *Representation in Ethnography*, edited by J. Van Maanen, 1–35. London: Sage.

Walsh, E., and R. Stewart (1993). Accounting and the construction of institutions: The case of a factory. *Accounting, Organizations and Society*, **18**: 783–800.

Waterhouse, J. H., and P. A. Tiessen (1978). A contingency framework for management accounting systems research. *Accounting, Organizations and Society*, **3**: 65–76.

Weber, M. (1947). *The Theory of Social and Economic Organizations*. Glencoe, IL: Free Press.

——— (1958). *From Max Weber*. Glencoe, IL: Free Press.

——— (1964). *Basic Concepts in Sociology*. New York: Citidal Press.

Weick, K. (1976). Education organizations as loosely coupled systems. *Administrative Science Quarterly*, **24**: 1–19.

Wildavsky, A. B. (1964). *The Politics of the Budgetary Process*. Boston, MA: Little Brown.

——— (1975). *Budgeting: A Comparative Theory of Budgeting Processes*. Boston, MA: Little Brown.

——— (1979). *Speaking Truth to Power: The Art and Craft of Policy Analysis*. Boston, MA: Little Brown.

Wilkinson, B., and N. Oliver (1989). Power, control and the Kanban. *Journal of Management Studies*, **26**: 47–58.

Woodward, J. (1965). *Industrial Organizations: Theory and Practice*. London: Oxford University Press.

Young, S. M. (1992). A framework for research on successful adoption and performance of Japanese manufacturing practices in the United States. *Academy of Management Review*, **17**: 677–700.

———, and F. Selto (1991). New manufacturing practices and cost management: A review of the literature and direction for research. *Journal of Accounting Literature*, **10**: 265–298.

Zucker, L. (1977). The role of institutionalization in cultural persistence. *American Sociological Review*, **42**: 725–743.

———(1988). Where do institutional patterns come from? Organizational actors as social systems. In: *Institutional Patterns and Organizations: Culture and Environment*, edited by L. Zucker, 23–52. Cambridge, MA: Ballinger Publishing Company.

Endnotes

1. Our focus on managerial accounting research motivated by organizational and sociological theories precludes this paper from addressing managerial accounting research generated from other theoretical traditions (economic, psychological, historical); nor does our paper address some excellent descriptive and applied work in managerial accounting. Here our approach complements such recent work as that of Young and Selto (1991) whose primary concern was to review the managerial accounting literature by topic, i.e., strategic cost accounting, product life cycle cost management, flexible manufacturing systems, etc., while embracing a variety of theoretical and non-theoretical work, albeit with less of an explicit focus on critiquing the theoretical traditions. McMann and Nanni (1996) took the same approach as Young and Selto (1991), however with a more specific focus on one topic – Japanese managerial accounting. This explicit focus allowed them to provide more insight on such critical subtopics as continuous improvement, quality, target costing, etc. – with the research once again cutting across theoretical and non-theoretical traditions, as well as across research methods.

2. Our paper is primarily organized along theoretical traditions, thus cutting across methodological approaches including fieldwork, surveys, lab experiments, etc., without a particular intent to critique the use of these

various methods. In this sense, our paper complements the recent work of Keating (1995) who examined management accounting research in terms of methodology – focusing exclusively on case research in managerial accounting with the intent of providing an in-depth review of case research as a methodology – without a particular concern to critique the theoretical traditions which motivate these research studies.

3. Caplan (1971, 13) identifies scientific management as providing the basis for the 'Traditional Management Accounting of the Firm' where the accounting system is assumed to be neutral and rational as it serves as ' . . . a control device which permits management to identify and correct undesirable performance.' In contrast, entitling the human relations tradition as 'The Modern Organizational Theory Model,' Caplan (1971, 43) defined management accounting issues coming from this perspective as being concerned with social and psychological factors as stated in his terms, ' . . . the interaction of the accounting technique of the individual to be controlled.' Both of these functionalist perspectives are precursors to contingency theory and reflect work in managerial accounting research much earlier than contingency theory. For example, the human relations tradition is the intellectual basis for the classic work of Argyris (1952) who found that budgetee participation in the budgetary process tends to foster fuller and more robust control over budgetees. He suggested that genuine participation in the budget process is a remedy to negative budget attitudes at lower levels (also see Hopwood (1973) as to the importance of budgetary participation in the behavioral attitudes of employees). Through this initial work of Argyris (1952) accounting researchers have adapted this human relations approach and have been concerned with modifying and assessing the effects of budgetary participation. This research tradition advocated bringing managers into the budgetary process with the objective of exercising fuller and more robust control over them (Stedry 1960; Becker and Green 1962). Further extensions of this human relations research tradition which eventually led into contingency theory included Schiff and Lewin's (1970) analysis of the budget process, which identified the dysfunctional aspects of participative budgeting in terms of using it to create organizational slack. Swieringa and Moncur's (1975) study found self-

assurance and assertiveness to be the most important predictors of how managers achieve their budget and how influential they are in the budgeting process. Otley (1978) studied the use of financial control systems in a coal mining firm and observed that consideration on the part of the immediate superior may be a moderating factor. Otley's (1978, 143) findings suggested that a non-considerate, non-supportive leadership style combined with high emphasis on budget performance, was primarily 'punitive in its ethos and may have a net result that is counterproductive.' Finally, Brownell (1981, 1982) also examined the influence of personality as a moderating factor in the budgetary participation process. In summary of the human relations tradition, research pertaining to managerial accounting suggests that personality traits, participative budgeting patterns, and other psychological and sociological factors are important issues to consider in the design of information systems (Milani 1975; Collins 1978). This managerial accounting research tradition eventually included consideration of the structural factors espoused in contingency theory.

4. For a more in-depth treatment of alternative research agendas in accounting, consult for example, *Critical Accounts* by David Cooper and Trevor Hopper (1990), *Sociological Perspectives on Modern Accounting* by Robin Rosenlender (1992), *The Social and Organizational Context of Management Accounting* by Anthony Puxty (1993), and *Accounting as a Social and Institutional Practice* by Anthony Hopwood and Peter Miller (1994).

5. According to Braverman (1974, 53) 'In the United States, perhaps four-fifths of the population was self-employed in the early part of the nineteenth century . . . by 1970 only about one-tenth of the population was self-employed.' Laborers in having to sell their labor power as a commodity, are now alienated from the fruits of their labor. This is the significance of the *labor theory of value* which asserts that the value of goods and services originate from and thus belong to those who make them. Moreover, since workers can produce far more per unit time than is necessary to keep them alive, this surplus value created is the source and object of capitalist strategies to make more profits. Accordingly, profits come from extracting as much labor from the purchased labor power, and then expropriating the surplus value so generated.

6. A solid entry into the work and thought of Michel Foucault is the Paul Rabinow, ed. (1984) *Foucault Reader*. The introductory essay is an especially good and clear statement while the selection of readings is representative.

7. Notable in this regard was the paper by Tinker *et al*. (1982). Others addressing the philosophical underpinnings of different accounting research include Christenson (1983), Chua (1986) and Hopper and Powell (1985). For statements by philosophers on the philosophy of science, consult Bernstein (1978), for those by organizational theorists see Burrell and Morgan (1979).

Reading D

Reprinted from *Accounting, Organizations and Society*, Vol 16, No. 8, J. F. Dent, Accounting and organizational cultures: A field study of the emergence of a new organizational reality, pp 705–32. Copyright 1991, with permission from Elsevier Science.

Questions

1. How does Dent define culture in his study of EuroRail?
2. What was the research method used by Dent in this study? Why do you think he chose this particular method?
3. How does the transition from a 'railway' to a 'business' culture take place in Dent's study? What was the role of accounting in this transition? What meaning did accounting have to each of the two cultures?
4. How does accounting help to construct a particular knowledge?

Further reading

Allaire, Y. and Firsirotu, M. E. (1984). Theories of organizational culture. *Organization Studies*, 5(3), 193–226.

Atkinson, A. A. and Shaffir, W. (1998). Standards for field research in management accounting. *Journal of Management Accounting Research*, 10, 41–68.

Deal, T. E. and Kennedy, A. A. (1982). *Corporate Cultures*. Reading, MA: Addison-Wesley.

Humphrey, C. and Scapens, R. W. (1996). Theories and case studies of organizational and accounting practices: limitation or liberation? *Accounting, Auditing and Accountability Journal*, 9(4), 86–106.

Langfield-Smith, K. (1995). Organisational culture and control. In A. J. Berry, J. Broadbent and D. Otley (Eds), *Management Control: Theories, Issues and Practices*. London: Macmillan.

Otley, D. T. and Berry, A. J. (1994). Case study research in management accounting and control. *Management Accounting Research*, 5, 45–65.

Pettigrew, A. M. (1979). On studying organizational cultures. *Administrative Science Quarterly*, 24, 570–81.

Scapens, R. W. (1990). Researching management accounting practice: the role of case study methods. *British Accounting Review*, 22, 259–81.

Smircich, L. (1983). Concepts of culture and organizational analysis. *Administrative Science Quarterly*, 28, 339–58.

Smith, C., Whipp, R. and Willmott, H. (1988). Case-study research in accounting: methodological breakthrough or ideological weapon? *Advances in Public Interest Accounting*, 2, 95–120.

Accounting and Organizational Cultures: A Field Study of the Emergence of a New Organizational Reality*

Jeremy F. Dent
London School of Economics and Political Science

Abstract

Organizations have long been known to have cultural properties. A more recent innovation is the study of organizations as cultures: systems of knowledge, beliefs and values in which action and artifact are vested with expressive qualities. We know little about the way in which accounting is implicated in organizations' cultures. This paper reports a longitudinal field study of organizational change, tracing out the way in which new accounting practices were implicated in an emergent reconstruction of the organization's culture.

The train arrived at Capital City Terminus at 12.10. It was on time despite a delay on the line. Walking up the platform, I saw the train driver leaning out of his cab. He must have driven the train fast to recover the time: the windscreens were spattered with dead insects. He exchanged some words with men dressed in smart overalls. Muttering a few words into 'walkie-talkies', they jumped down onto the track to check the engine. Men driving small electric trucks towing streams of trailers with logos on the side collected parcels and mail bags from the guard's van. Others set about replenishing water and food supplies in the train. At the barrier, a man wearing a smile and a dark

*This research was generously supported by the Chartered Institute of Management Accountants. Earlier versions of the paper were presented at the AAA Annual Convention, New York, 1986, the EAA Annual Congress, London, 1987, and the EIASM Workshop on Strategy, Accounting & Control, Venice, 1990. Ken Euske, Anthony Hopwood, Keith Hoskins, Kenneth Merchant, Peter Miller and two anonymous reviewers provided helpful comments.

uniform with red piping on the seams checked my ticket.

Moving on, the concourse was bright and airy, concealed lighting illuminating the white tiled floor. People were milling about. Soft music was playing on the tannoy. Large electronic screens indicated arrival and departure times. There were colourful boutiques displaying ties, handkerchiefs, socks and bags, and cafés where people were drinking coffee and eating croissants. What a change, I thought, from just a short time ago, when the station was dark and grimy, and a grumpy employee had greeted my question about departure times with a crude response.

At the new executive offices across the street I tangled with the revolving glass and stainless steel door. In the foyer, a manicured receptionist called upstairs to say I'd arrived. The security guard, at least I presumed he was a security guard (his appearance was quite like a ticket inspector, but his commanding presence was more like a policeman), showed me to the lift. He deftly pressed the fourth floor button, removing himself before the doors closed. After a few moments the lift doors opened onto what appeared to be open-plan office space, but in fact comprised zones of compartmentalized activity separated by cleverly positioned shoulderheight cabinets and screens. A person came up to me: 'Mr Charles will be here in a minute', he said; 'he's at a retirement do'. The man looked busy; his tie was loose, the top button of his shirt was undone, he must have left his jacket on his chair. He was courteous: 'his secretary just popped out for a few minutes, but she told me to expect you. Why don't you wait in his office?'

Walking through the office space, I could see over the cabinets. The arrangements were utilitarian. Some people were stabbing at computer keyboards, others were studying documents, others were writing or working out sums on calculators. There were piles of print-out everywhere.

We entered Mr Charles' office through his secretary's room. From the large windows there was a fine view into, and over, the station. I could see trains arriving and leaving. I followed one right into the hills across the city. The office was softly furnished. At one end, there was a large desk, at the other a couple of sofas; opposite the windows there were bookshelves and a cabinet. The lighting was bright but unobtrusive. There wasn't a computer in sight. My guide and I made small talk – incidental conversation about the comforts of the new building and the air conditioning. Conscious that his work was pressing and not wishing to detain him, I told him not to worry about me. Eventually he made to leave. 'Ah! Mr General Manager', I heard him say before he had even left the secretary's office. 'Your visitor has arrived'. 'Thanks John', came the reply. Mr Charles, the General Manager, entered the room. 'Good to see you again, Mr Charles', I said to him as we exchanged greetings.

Settling down in one of the sofas he said to me 'I am glad you could come. I think you will find this afternoon's meeting interesting. We're deeply embroiled in cost allocations. Intercity are holding Freight to ransom'. After my query, he continued: 'At night, we push freight up the main line routes. Intercity don't use them at night. You don't want the speed then; after all you can't expect passengers to get off the train at 2 or 3 in the morning. Sleeper trains make their separate way on roundabout routes. Intercity say the wear and tear caused by freight trains, and they are very heavy, means they need to increase the engineering specification of the track. As it's an Intercity track, they pick up the cost; and they want Freight to pay. They're holding them to ransom. Freight have responded by running their trains slower. This reduces the damage to the track. They don't go very fast anyway, so I mean SLOW. Now Intercity say they can't get back on the track when they want it in the morning. They have threatened not to let Freight use the track unless they pay. Its going to be an interesting meeting. Would you like a drink before we have lunch?'

Going to the cabinet, he poured two glasses of mineral water . . .

Organizations have long been known to have distinct cultural properties (cf. Weber, 1947; Parsons, 1951). They create and sustain particular work customs. They establish norms for proper and improper behaviour and performance. They propagate stories and myths, and are replete with rituals (Van Maanen & Barley, 1984; Martin *et al.*, 1983). Communities in organizations have particular codes of communication: behaviour, language, dress, presentation, design, architecture, ceremony . . . The operation of work technologies in organizations is not a purely technical-rational affair. Rather it is embedded in a cultural system of ideas (beliefs, knowledges) and sentiments (values), in which actions and artifacts are vested with symbolic qualities of meaning. The appreciation of organizational dynamics requires a sensitivity to local frames of significance and interpretation.

Accounting practices are a common feature of most work organizations. Planning and budgeting activities, systems of hierarchical accountability, performance appraisal procedures, budgetary controls and remuneration arrangements, all rely to a greater or lesser extent on accounting practices. Inevitably, therefore, accounting is likely to be implicated in organizations' cultural systems. But how, and in what way? Drawing on the insights of Meyer & Rowan (1977), Pfeffer & Salancik (1978), DiMaggio & Powell (1983), Scott (1987), Zucker (1988) and others, one theme in the literature appeals to accounting's potential significance in the context of wider societal values and beliefs. Put crudely, organizations depend on a flow of resources for survival; society has beliefs in the efficacy of 'rational' management practices; organizations which adopt such practices are more likely to be rewarded. Thus, recent empirically grounded studies (Berry *et al.*, 1985; Ansari & Euske, 1987; Covaleski & Dirsmith, 1988) have cast accounting

as a culturally expressive symbol of rationality, particularly oriented towards powerful external constituencies, moderating environmental control. In this view, following especially Meyer & Rowan's (1977) discussion, accounting is often seen to be neutral in its effects within the organization. It is kept at arm's length, symbolically construed as necessary but irrelevant, and, as it were, not taken seriously. It is purposefully uncoupled from organizations' core technological activities.

All knowledges and practices can be reflexive, however. Accounting can reflect back on those institutions which adopt it. Hopwood (1987), Hines (1988), Miller & O'Leary (1987) and others have argued for its constitutive role in the construction of organizational life. Finely crafted notions of costliness, efficiency, profitability, earnings-per-share and so forth, actively construct particular definitions of reality which privilege the financial and economic sphere. Rather than being kept at arm's length, uncoupled from organizations' core technological activities, these can permeate into organizational settings, leading to the creation of particular agendas (in the sense of objectives and priorities and the means for their achievement), stylized definitions of success and failure, the characterization of heroic performance and the mobilization of particular dynamics of change. This suggests the possibility of a more intimate involvement of accounting in organizational cultures.

In fact, evidence in the field suggests that accounting practices are not uniformly implicated in organizational activities (Goold & Campbell, 1987; Miles & Snow, 1978). In some organizations, accounting is centrally involved in work rituals: financial achievement is celebrated; budgets are massaged, pored over, and matter. In others, accounting is incidental, perhaps existing as a practice, but with no particular significance. Similarly, entrepreneurial risk taking is sometimes valued for its own sake. Dynamic, decisive, action-oriented men and women who innovate are heroes, almost irrespective of the financial consequences. In other organizations, risk taking is valued only if successful in financial terms. Arguably, the multi-faceted interplay of accounting with organizations' cultural and technical systems is under-researched. More empirically grounded research is needed to ascertain the way in which accounting is drawn upon by actors within organizations in the creation and maintenance of cultures.

Responding, with others, to appeals for field studies (e.g. Bruns & Kaplan, 1987) and for the study of accounting in its organizational and social context (e.g. Hopwood, 1978, 1983; Dent, 1986), this paper reports a longitudinal study undertaken in one organization to research this issue. The organization is a railway company. The study focuses on its senior management élite: a group of approximately 120 people including head office executives, senior line management and people in senior staff positions (i.e. finance and engineering). Prior to the study, the dominant culture within this management group was well established, and centred on engineering and production concerns. Accounting was incidental in this culture: it was necessary in the technical-rational sense of ensuring that revenues were accounted for and suppliers were paid, but it was not incorporated into the culture among the senior management élite in any significant way. Rituals, symbols and language celebrated the primacy of the engineering and production orientation. During the course of the study, a new culture emerged. The previously dominant orientation was displaced by a new preoccupation with economic and accounting concerns. New accounts were crafted. Gradually, through action and interaction, they were coupled to organizational activities to reconstitute interpretations of organizational endeavour. Accounting actively shaped the dominant meanings given to organizational life, ultimately obtaining a remarkable significance in the senior management culture.

A new set of symbols, rituals and language emerged to celebrate an economic rationale for organized activity. This paper carefully traces the events and interactions through which accounting was endowed with significance.

The paper is written from a cultural perspective, but in a very real sense the study is also concerned with power and influence in the organization. A new culture can be a major source of power, particularly if it gains ascendancy to become dominant, for it effectively alters the legitimacy of accepted criteria for action.

The next section of the paper outlines the cultural approach adopted in the subsequent analysis. The following section explains the method employed in the study. Two sections then document the study itself. Thereafter, some implications for accounting and culture are drawn out. Finally, there is a concluding comment.

Culture

In recent years, a prolific literature has emerged to offer a wide array of perceptual, symbolic and processual characterizations of organization (e.g. Hedberg et al.,1976; Jonsson & Lundin, 1977; Hedberg & Jonsson, 1978; Pondy, 1978; Weick, 1979; Ranson et al.,1980; Argyris & Schon, 1981; Pfeffer, 1981; Starbuck, 1982; Pondy et al., 1983; Brunsson, 1985; Greenwood & Hinings, 1988). As a result, we are now used to conceptualizing organizations as bodies of thought, variously described as myths, causal schema, theories-of-action, interpretive schemes, ideologies, paradigms and so forth. The concept of culture, drawn from anthropology and ethnography, has entered the organizational literature as a framework for extending this ideational understanding of organizations[1] (Pettigrew, 1979; Smircich, 1983a; Allaire & Firsirotu, 1984; Van Maanen & Barley, 1984; Meek, 1988).

Culture is an elusive concept.[2] Here, drawing on Geertz' (1973, 1983) interpretive anthropology, it is defined to be the broad constellation of interpretive structures through which action and events are rendered meaningful in a community. Balinese cockfights, a sheep raid in Morocco, funeral rites in Java – or nearer home, the graduation ceremony, the distinguished lecture series, the publication of papers in prestigious journals – all have singular meanings in their respective communities (as does all social action). Culture is the 'ordered clusters of significance' (Geertz, 1973, p. 363), the shared 'webs of significance' (p. 5) through which people appreciate the meaningfulness of their experience, and are guided to action. Culture, as an ideational system, is produced and reproduced through action and interaction. But it is not just lodged in people's minds. Culture is public, the product of minds, between minds. Culturally significant events give public expression to the ideational system.

The appreciation of organizations as cultures brings the interpretive, experiential aspects of their activities to the foreground of analysis, emphasizing their expressive qualities[3] (Van Maanen, 1979, 1988; Feldman, 1986). Looking at the railway, for example, the train is not seen as cold technology; the concourse is not just glass and marble; 'Mr General Manager' is not an anybody; cost allocations are not mere calculations: everything is expressive. Local knowledge, beliefs and values vest them with symbolic qualities of meaning. The train may be vested with a sacred quality (or not, as the case may be) quite beyond its technical properties; beliefs about the skills required to operate a railway and appropriate forms of organizing may endow the General Manager with special status and privilege (or not). Cultural analysis attempts to uncover these meanings and to trace the underlying thematic relationships. The objective is interpretation and 'thick description': the production of rich contextually laden accounts conveying the symbolic content of social action.

Meaning systems may differ within organizations, of course. The train, the framing of the routing problem as a cost allocation issue and so on are likely to be interpreted differently by different groups. Within the overarching concept of an organization as a culture, it is sensible to recognize the possibility and likelihood of distinct subcultures existing among managerial teams, occupational groups, members of different social classes and so on; many of which may transcend organizational boundaries (Van Maanen & Barley, 1984). As a limiting case, these subcultures may be isomorphic; more commonly, they may only partially overlap.[4] Also, some may be dominant-cultures and others counter-cultures (Martin & Siehl, 1983), perhaps partially uncoupled from each other (Berry et al., 1985), or co-existing in an 'uneasy symbiosis' (Martin & Siehl, 1983), or in contest with each other for dominance (Gregory, 1983; Riley, 1983; Pettigrew, 1985; Feldman, 1986). Moreover, cultures in organizations are not independent of their social context. They are interpenetrated by wider systems of thought, interacting with other organizations and social institutions, both importing and exporting values, beliefs and knowledge.

Accounting is likely to be differentially implicated in these subcultures in organizations. Accounting systems, and information systems more generally, inevitably offer highly stylized views of the world. Any representation is partial, an interpretation through a particular framing of reality, rendering some aspects of events important and others unimportant; counter-interpretations are possible (Hedberg & Jonsson, 1978). Accounting systems embody particular assumptions about organization, rationality, authority, time and so forth. These may be more or less consonant with local subcultures in organizations (cf. Markus & Pfeffer, 1983). For example, to senior managers in some organizations accounting may symbolize efficiency, calculative rationality, order and so forth: 'the name of the game is profit'. This may motivate the development of sophisticated accounting systems measuring economic performance this way and that. To others (nearer the ground?), accounting may symbolize confusion or irrelevance: 'no one understands the business'; 'when all else fails they resort to the numbers' (see Jones & Lakin, 1978, chapter 11, for a graphic example). Similarly, meanings may differ across occupational groups. Commercial managers may appreciate accounting rather differently to engineers, for example.

It is useful to think of societal cultures as emergent, unfolding through time[5] (Geertz, 1973; Douglas, 1966), and similarly with organizational cultures (Pettigrew, 1985; Feldman, 1986). That is not to say that given cultures do not survive for long periods, or that changes may be proactively managed: organizational cultures probably have inertial tendencies (cf. Miller & Friesen, 1984), perhaps sometimes not even incorporating changes in wider patterns of social thought[6] (cf. Burns & Stalker's, 1961, pathological responses in mechanistic firms). Rather, the implication is that culture is not programmed or static. The processes of cultural change in organizations are poorly understood, however. Perhaps cultural change is a political process: subcultures competing with one another for legitimacy and dominance (Pettigrew, 1985). Perhaps cultural change is akin to the diffusion of organizational forms, whole fields of organizations rapidly adopting knowledge innovations in leading firms (cf. Fligstein, 1990). Perhaps in a Kuhnian sense, cultural change is precipitated by crisis: the adoption of new cultural knowledge only being possible when faith is undermined, for example by the failure of strategies for subsistence. Maybe new cultures are autonomously crafted in organizations (cf. 'groping' towards 'solutions-in-principle' and their subsequent elaboration: Mintzberg, 1978; Jonsson & Lundin, 1977); or perhaps they are already there, 'lying around' in counter-cultures, waiting to be discovered by others (cf. Cohen et al., 1972); alternatively, cultures may

be imported from the environment through new actors (cf. Starbuck & Hedberg, 1977).

Clearly, there are multiple modes and possibilities for cultural change. However, the point of importance for this paper is the conceptualization of cultural change as the uncoupling of organizational action from one culture and its recoupling to another (cf. Greenwood & Hinings, 1988; Hedberg, 1981). It is a process of fundamental reinterpretation of organizational activities. Things cease to be what they were and become what they were not: a new reality, if you will. In the railway, for example, the sacred train could turn into cold steel, or the priest-like general manager could become an anybody. Moreover, this process of uncoupling and recoupling is unlikely to be sudden, but emergent: the gradual disintegration of one coupling and the crystallization of another. This crystallization may be around an idea not fully understood, a kind of ill-articulated new knowledge, perhaps imported from the environment. In the railway, this idea was a new accounting.

Research Method

Arm's length analysis is clearly inappropriate for cultural analysis of the kind described here. Instead, it calls for closer engagement in the research setting and 'interpretive' methodology (Geertz, 1973; Burrell & Morgan, 1979; Denzin, 1983). Necessarily, this precludes the imposition of exteriorized accounts, and radical critique. In part, the goal is 'to grasp the native's point of view, his relation to life, to realise his vision of his world' (Malinowski, 1922, p. 25); in part it is to reflect on the processes through which that vision comes to be and is sustained.[7]

This kind of research is necessarily qualitative. Data consist of descriptions and accounts provided by participants in the research site, together with the *researcher's observations* on activities and interactions and the context in which they take place. Data must be collected over an extended period of time so that processes can be recorded. The researcher, in general, does not seek to test a prior hypothesis. Rather, he or she seeks to theorize through the data in an inductive manner. Analysis of the data is itself an emergent process.

The researcher seeks gradually to develop an empathy with the data, to understand what they tell of participants' realities and the process through which they unfold. The researcher must constantly construct alternative interpretations ('readings': Levi Strauss, quoted in Turner, 1983) until he or she is satisfied that the representation is a faithful account. Interpretations must be grounded in context and consistent with the chronological ordering of events and interactions. Finally, research results must be presented in such a way that the reader can independently judge their credibility, as far as is possible.[8]

The study reported here was conducted over a period of two years, with follow up visits one year and two years later. It involved ongoing iterations between data collection and analysis. Access to the organization was gained through various channels and contacts. The researcher was given freedom to interview anyone he wished. At no point in the data collection process did the researcher express opinions, save where it was necessary to prompt interviewees. Data were collected from staff within the organization in several ways. The first source was a series of unstructured interviews. Approximately 30 managers were interviewed, sometimes twice or more times at the researcher's request. These included head office executives and their advisors or assistants, senior line management and people in senior staff positions (finance and engineering). Interviews averaged one and a half hours in length, and were spread over the period of the research. They were tape-recorded and transcribed. Secondly, access was granted to various internal meetings. Debates were observed and dialogue noted. Activities in these meetings were subsequently written up in abbreviated form. Thirdly, data were collected through casual conversations and by simply 'being around'.

As the project progressed, the data were repeatedly analysed. At first, it seemed that there was a real probability of drowning in the data. Transcripts and notes were accumulating rapidly, and the material appeared to be incoherent. This is apparently a common feature of the initial stages of cultural research (Smircich, 1983b). But different ways of making sense of it all were explored and gradually a pattern began to emerge. At each stage emerging appreciations were checked against the next round of data in an attempt to confirm the researcher's understanding of the situation. This continued until such time as the subsequent data became predictable.

It may be useful to indicate the precise way in which the data were found to give a coherent picture. Ultimately, the analysis hinged on three dimensions: role (function), and level of hierarchy of the subject, and time. Firstly, the data were categorized according to content and underlying values. Opinions, sentiments, interpretations, confusions and so forth in each interview transcript were noted. This was done without reference to the identity of the person who had been interviewed. The data collected at any one time seemed to fall naturally into distinct constellations or clusters (in the sense that groups of people expressed similar views). Attaching identity to the data, it transpired that these constellations corresponded broadly to interviewees' roles and positions in the hierarchy. Among those performing similar roles (functions) at a similar level in the hierarchy, there was a marked similarity of perspective. Perspectives differed, however, across roles and at different levels of the hierarchy. These data were set up on a two-dimensional space with role on one axis and hierarchy on the other.

This exercise was repeated on data collected at different times, and found to give similar results, in the sense that the data again fell into role-hierarchy clusters. The specific content of the data differed over time, however. So, the two-dimensional spaces were set out in chronological order. In effect, a third dimension was added to the space, representing elapsed time. Studying the content of the data as one moved through time, it transpired that the opinions, sentiments and interpretations of each group were in fact evolving in a systematic way. In this three-dimensional space was a story of unfolding meanings in the organization.

This was indicative of the existence of different cultures in the organization, and some systematic underlying trajectory in the emergence of those cultures. In fact, during the data collection process, it became clear that new interviewees' views were predictable, given a knowledge of (a) the role (function) of the participant, (b) his or her position in the hierarchy, and (c) the time of the interview.

At this point, the data were analysed from a different perspective. Specifically, the level of analysis shifted from content to process. The data were re-examined to see if the process through which the new meanings were emerging was observable. Some key turning points were obvious in the data. There was a series of events and interactions through which the emergence of the new meaning structure could be traced. These are documented in following sections. Finally, the findings of the research project were noted and informally discussed with various participants.[9]

The Organization: An Overview

The research was undertaken in a major railway company. The company is referred to here as ER[10] ('Euro Rail'). It is, and has been for some while, in public sector ownership. It is large by any standards, employing approximately 160,000 people. It has a distinguished history.

History and traditions

ER has its origins in the great private-sector railway companies set up in the middle decades of the last century. These each built and operated a main line out of the capital city, i.e. radial routes and associated branch lines.[11] The companies are legendary. They raised capital to fund their projects on an unprecedented scale. Their railways were built by world-famous engineers who pioneered emerging industrial technology, designing magnificent steam locomotives and tracks and bridges which the world admired. The railways were, and are, a visible celebration of Victorian accomplishment.

These companies enjoyed a monopoly in the nation's transport well into this century. They had good relationships with successive governments. They paid consistent dividends and their shares were blue-chip stocks. This monopoly position and government patronage, coupled with a remarkable continuity in the underlying nature of their operations, rendered them highly bureaucratic: rules and procedures were well defined, there were clear chains of command and formalized systems for managing operations.[12] Their managements were conservative, cultivating a belief in the uniqueness of railway management and the wisdom of practices built up over many decades.

Importantly, though, while established as commercial concerns and earning their founders a handsome return,[13] these companies also embraced a spirit of public service, for the railway network provided a transport infrastructure much needed for the pursuit of trade and manufacturing, and for social mobility. This notion of public service was significant in the managements' interpretations of the railways: they took the rough with the smooth. They were run by 'railway men': engineers and operators who took pride in the professional management of the railway and its public service.

The railway companies were nationalized in the late 1940s. In many respects, this was of limited significance. The nationalized railway consolidated the old management structure: it was organized by region, each representing one of the radial routes out of the capital city; and each still managed by a General Manager (the same title as before). An Executive Committee was established to oversee policy decisions and to interface with government. This committee comprised the regional General Managers together with the Chief Executive of ER and various engineering chiefs.[14] Management practices of the former railways survived intact. Furthermore, nationalization reinforced the public service orientation, for this was the era of the Welfare State. Public-sector ownership established the railway as a social service. Its prime purpose was to provide a transport infrastructure. Profitability was secondary.

This interpretation of the railway remained dominant among senior managers for thirty years or more. Post-nationalization governments, faced with deficits and huge investment sums required for modernization, frequently sought to contain the costs of maintaining this infrastructure. Following a fundamental review in the 1960s many branch lines were closed. Later, during the 1970s, the government imposed investment ceilings and set out expectations for the maximum level of its support. But, although now tempered with a concern for thrift and the avoidance of waste, old traditions endured. Financial deficits continued. ER remained a bureaucratic organization with a heritage of railway engineering and public service. The railways were still run for practical purposes by regional General Managers, each one of these standing in a direct line of descent from a founding pioneer. They occupied the same grand offices. There were portraits of previous incumbents on their walls. They were, very consciously, carrying on a tradition of professional railway management.

This was the reality of the dominant 'railway culture'. The railway was a public service. The purpose of the railway was to run trains. In so doing profitability was secondary. The accepted professional concerns were to do with railway engineering and the logistical problems of operating trains. And although the 'golden age' of steam had passed, new electrical and electronic technologies still offered scope for railway people to further their engineering heritage.[15]

The emergence of the economic perspective

In a profound sense, nationalization thirty years before had created a relationship of dependence for the railways, a dependence on government for sustenance. In the early 1980s the implications of this became clear. Government policy became stringent. Social aims ceased to be a legitimate criterion for support. Government sought to impose harsh economic disciplines in all areas of public and private endeavour. Declaring a determination to 'take on' the public services in particular, it orchestrated a campaign challenging the competence of public-sector management. For the railway, government 'expectations' were translated into more specific financial 'objectives'. These were progressively tightened. Investment funds were withheld. Reporting escalating losses, ER found itself in a malign, resource constrained environment.

We need, for a moment, to backtrack. Apparently, in the late 1970s, the Chief Executive of the railway had set up a strategy think-tank to improve long-term planning.[16] Embryonic ideas developed there, and subsequently nurtured by a small group of executives, were now rolled out for more general consideration. Senior managers, by this time fully appreciative of the real hostility of government and the precarious position of the railway, fastened onto the ideas as a solution to the current problems.

The organization, through the Executive Committee, created new management positions. For the first time, 'Business Managers' were appointed. For analytical purposes (only), railway operations were broken down into market sectors: for example, long distance passenger traffic, short distance passenger traffic, freight, parcels and postal traffic. Business Managers were assigned responsibility for developing strategies to enhance financial performance in each sector – in effect to manage the 'bottom line(s)'.

These people were appointed outside the main line-management hierarchy of the railway. They were long-range planning people in staff positions at the Head Office, with no formal control or authority over railway operations. In fact, their initial responsibilities were thought to be confined to the identification of market-related initiatives. The Business Managers reported to the Chief Executive and joined the Executive Committee. But the regional management hierarchies remained intact. Regional General Managers, carrying on the old traditions, continued to run the railway.

The appointment of Business Managers was to have far reaching consequences, however, for it introduced a new 'business' culture, a counter-culture. They brought a different interpretation of reality. For them the railway was a business, its purpose was to make profit. Engineering and logistical operations were essentially a means for extracting revenues from customers. Professional management was about making the railway profitable.

Business Managers were appointed without staff or support at the margins of the organization. But during the course of the study, they gained influence at the expense of the regional General Managers. They persuaded many around them of their idea of a business railway. Gradually, people converted to the 'business culture'. Others left the organization. The nature of dialogue and debate changed. Appeals to the old traditions of railway excellence and public service were repudiated. New kinds of policy decisions emerged, motivated by the business logic. Operational activities out in the regions began to be informed by the new rationale.

Now, the old world view, the preoccupation with engineering and logistics, the belief in the railway as a social service, the railway culture, has been substantially displaced by the business perspective, the belief that railways should be instrumental in making profit and managed to that end. The counter-culture has emerged to become the dominant-culture among the senior management. Traditions established over longer than a century were quickly overthrown.

Tracing the Dynamics of Change

The story is one of evolving interpretations, meanings and perceived possibilities. No one in the organization foresaw the outcome at the start, not even the Business Managers. At first, their 'business culture' was vague and indistinct, a kind of abstract generality. But as events unfolded, it became more specific. Possibilities for coupling their business reality to organizational action were perceived. Gradually, as people elaborated the new logic for organized activity, momentum was created. Capturing the emergent nature of these developments, one senior manager described the experience as 'a voyage of discovery and development'.

This section traces the dynamics of change. Firstly, it considers the context surrounding the appointment of Business Managers. Then it outlines the crafting of new accounting systems. Subsequently, it traces the process through which the new accounting was coupled to organizational activities and endowed with meaning. Finally, it gives an account of the regional General Managers' perspective in these events. The section is interspersed with representative comments from managers in the organization.

People and context

The context of the Business Managers' appointments in ER is important in appreciating the trajectory of events. The railway was under acute threat. The competence of public-sector management was openly under challenge. The railway was charged with being 'old fashioned'. Governmental pressures for profitability were onerous, and sanctions were being applied. These threats were clearly appreciated by senior management. The railway has always prided itself on being modern in its technological activities. The charge of being 'old-fashioned' in its management practice was deeply challenging. Moreover, there was some recognition that the old traditions were not, in themselves, proving sufficient to manage the threats away, and needed to be supplemented in some way. The skills the Business Managers brought, marketing, long-term planning, 'bottom line' management, had an image of modernity, enabling the railway to throw off the charge of being 'old-fashioned', and were thought to be a useful supplementation of the railway traditions. Moreover, they were thought to be unintrusive, a 'grafting- on' to the old traditions. The Business Managers had no operational authority. They were 'back office' planning people. Their roles were defined through a remote accounting construct, the 'bottom line', outside the prevailing mainstream understanding of railway activities. In bringing new knowledge to bear to cope with environmental pressures, they were not expected to disrupt the railway or existing patterns of authority. Senior managers commented:

> Everything has its time. You've got to realize the environment of the (transport) industry. We're now in the most competitive environment the railway has ever faced. And there were clear objectives emerging from the Government. These things made people think differently. . . . It's all in the market place in the end, and how to exploit the market place. The traditional railway wasn't sensitive to the market place (Senior Executive).

> We were weak in marketing and business issues generally. The government targets were stiff. We needed those skills (General Manager).

Equally important are the personalities and backgrounds of the Business Managers. While they had all at some time worked in or with the railway, practically all had also worked outside. Thus, while they understood the railway culture and could talk railway talk, they also appreciated what they saw as wider business practice: 'managing for profit'. Furthermore, these men became evangelists, hungry people with a mission. They developed a zeal to convert the railway from a social service to a business enterprise.

In addition, the nature of their appointments was rather unusual (at least for a mechanistic organization). There were no briefs or manuals. Ultimate intentions were not articulated. Business Managers were just told to see what they could do.

> We introduced it in an evolutionary way. We said: 'Let's appoint Business Managers and then let it evolve. Be patient and let it evolve' (Senior Executive).

> When the Chief Executive introduced the Business Managers he didn't have any idea how to take the concept forward. I think he deliberately chose people who would win the day, and left them to get on with it. It was up to each of us to build our influence. The regional General Managers had great centres of power: buildings and armies of people. They were the Gods on high, the last remnants of the Railway Companies. He wanted to stand back from it all, and see what would happen (Business Manager).

They had, at best, a vague job description, one which they could legitimately expand.

Subsequent events were not independent of changes in the social and political climate during the decade. It was one dominated by economic liberalism: deregulation in many spheres of activity, privatization of state owned enterprises, and a sea change in attitudes towards the public services and the Welfare State. These substantive effects were to come later, but there was already a clear 'idealization' by government of private sector management practices, and a belief that they could be introduced in the public sector. (Industrialists were rationalizing 'old fashioned' work routines in the Civil Service, for example.) There was also a stated political agenda to subject the public services to 'market disciplines' wherever possible.

Evolutionary change and organizational acclimatization

The railway has long traditions and consensually accepted preoccupations. At first, the Business Managers could only see limited opportunities for coupling their concept to day-to-day activities. But as events unfolded, tentative new possibilities were perceived. Stage-by-stage, as if in episodes, their abstract notion of the business railway became more concrete.

The railway is a very formal organization. People in it describe the management process in bureaucratic analogies, talking of 'chains-of-command' and 'good old soldiers falling into line'. In meetings, people are often referred to through their official titles. There is much deference to authority. The Business Managers recognized the significance of this formal management style in their quest to convert the railway. In fact they worked through it. As their ideas evolved, in each episode they sought first to persuade the Chief Executive and his advisors. These people were likely to be the most sympathetic to their economic rhetoric, for they interfaced with government and felt the external pressures most immediately. Carefully negotiating in principle a course of action, often after much private and closed debate, then, sure of their support, the Business Managers set out to convert a wider group.

Each episode involved a fairly small incremental step. None, in isolation, was especially threatening or difficult to accommodate in the old railway culture. Indeed, at first, even those who ultimately stood to lose influence and status appreciated the blending of the business perspective into the railway culture. As the organization became acclimatized to each change, however, as each episode had a chance to 'soak', so new possibilities were perceived. Repeatedly, new episodes were enacted.

Commenting on the way in which they operated, a Business Manager reflected:

> In the early days, there was nothing in writing, except that we had a responsibility for improving the bottom line. There were no organization charts. This made life difficult. It was all about relationships. We had to persuade everyone around us . . . As we did so, our ideas evolved. We became increasingly aware of the potential of the Businesses.

Senior Executives recalled:

> Our ideas were constrained because we were . . . well I was going to say traditional railwaymen. We were coloured by the views of the complexity of running a railway. No one foresaw the present state as a possibility. Our minds were opened.

> It takes time to change an organization like the railways and to change attitudes. There's 150 years' history. You don't overturn that lightly. Nor

would you want to, or the railways would cease to operate . . . The Business Managers recognized that. First, they convinced a small group, then gradually widened that group until everyone was aboard . . .

They operated in stages . . . Incremental changes were easier to sell. It was easier to build commitment and minimize opposition from those who stood to lose . . . They took each stage to the limit.

Creating an alternative account

For the Business Managers the purpose of the railway was to make a profit. The significance of customers was revenues; the significance of operations, that is, trains, infrastructure and staff, was cost. Upon their appointment, however, there was no account of the railway's activities in each market sector consistent with their reality. While profit or loss was measured for the organization as a whole, and was used in dealings with government, no such measures existed for component parts of the railway.[17]

In fact, during the 1970s, primarily for analytical purposes (rather than for responsibility accounting), the railway had moved towards a system of contribution accounting, matching directly traceable costs to revenues for various market segments.[18] Common costs were not allocated to the segments. The railway is a remarkably integrated activity, with common staff, infrastructure and, to some extent, train-related activities, so these unallocated costs were very substantial. Senior accounting executives had long argued, both privately and publicly, that allocation was neither possible nor meaningful. Fundamental to the Business Managers' appointments, however, was not just a profit-contribution responsibility, but a 'bottom line' responsibility, and this called for the allocation of common costs. In

a definite way, this 'bottom line' responsibility had a normative symbolism – private sector managers were concerned with the 'bottom line'. But there was a more practical logic: this was to ensure that one or other of the Business Managers would be responsible for all costs, and motivated, as events unfolded, to ask questions about the necessity and consequences of incurring cost. A Senior Executive commented:

> You appoint a Business Manager and say: 'We believe this is freight'. The first thing he says is: 'What's mine? What are the boundaries of my business?' Then he pursues questions such as: 'How are costs being allocated to me? I want to know more about it. Let me analyse and fillet all the cost you are suggesting is mine' . . . Then he asks: 'How do these costs relate to my revenues'.

An individual within the accounting department was appointed to develop profit or loss measures by business sector. This person was in rather an invidious position. Given senior finance officials' former public repudiation of the possibility of developing these measures, he had to tread carefully. He later recalled:

> At first I was not convinced that it was either sensible or feasible. There's a whole history of avoiding cost allocations in the railway. But if the Business Managers were to take responsibility, they needed different Management Accounting. I was persuaded of this new way to run the railway. I wanted Finance to play a fundamental part in supporting it.
>
> When I was appointed I spent several months bouncing ideas off walls – walls not people – because finance people didn't believe you could or should develop the information they needed.

He became involved in intensive discussions with the Business Managers, and with representatives of the Chief Executive's office. Different ways of apportioning costs were discussed, and a firm of accountants consulted. The guiding principle was 'cost exhaustion' – all costs incurred by the railway had somehow to be attributed to one or more of the businesses.

The precise details of the method of arriving at the profit or loss for each business are unimportant here. It suffices to say that it was founded on principles reflecting the primacy of use of resources, and that the development of computer systems to operationalize the principle in full took some while. The significant point is that these measures were introduced, manually at first, and that they were fundamental to the emergence of the new culture.

Business Managers were appointed without any operational authority. Their positions were an abstract economic construct. They were made meaningful through the new accounting constructs. Moreover, the accounting measures provided a means through which they could later couple debate on operational and physical concerns to an economic calculus. Reflecting on the penetration of the new account of organizational activities, one Business Manager observed:

> It's my impression that the engineers, and after all we are an engineering company, had no real understanding of what they were doing in terms of the 'bottom line' . . . Now the engineers know what a 'bottom line' specification really is and they can respond to it.

One regional General Manager commented:

> I always behaved with the 'bottom line' in mind. But the Business Managers took it further. They challenge to a much greater extent. Making the railway profitable is the real meaning of the Business.

And another:

> I didn't realize the extent to which budgets would be challenged, and challenged so vehemently.

Coupling railway activities to the new account

At the head of the railway is the office of Chief Executive. Attached to this are various staff functions – Finance, Engineering Directorates and so forth. Reporting to the Chief Executive in a line-management relationship are the General Managers of the regions. Underneath these are the railway operations. Overlaid on this management structure are formal planning and decision-making systems of various kinds.

The Business Managers were appointed in staff positions outside the formal line-management structure of the railway organization. They wished to explore their reality with others. But, there was, at first, no formal context for them to interact with others. Neither did they have the formal status they perceived necessary to influence others. In a sequence of moves, they sought, first, to institutionalize their status, and then to secure bases for participating in an increasing range of dialogue and debate.

Securing status. First they lobbied the Chief Executive and his advisors for a change in reporting relationships. If he was serious about the idea of marketing and business planning in the railway, they argued, then they had to have comparable status to the regional General Managers. After some considerable debate, a new management structure was introduced. The Chief Executive appointed two Joint Managing Directors, one taking a responsibility for the regions – the operations side of the railway, the regional General Managers; the other taking a responsibility for planning and marketing – in effect, the Business Managers. In a symbolic sense, although not at first in practice, this gave the Business Managers parity with the regional General Managers. It also stood for the Chief Executive's acknowledgement of the legitimacy of the 'business' reality, the reality of the railways being managed for profit. Commenting on the significance of this, one Business Manager observed:

> The General Managers used to report directly to the Chief Executive. The joint Managing Directors gave us parity.

Creating contexts for interaction. Later, in subsequent episodes, they lobbied for successive changes in the formal planning and decision-making systems. Changes, they argued at each juncture, were necessary to provide a balance to the overbearing influence of the regional General Managers and engineers. Over the period of the study, three changes were forthcoming. Each change secured opened up possibilities for perceiving the potential of the next. Firstly, the corporate planning system was revised. This dealt with longer-term matters. Formerly, regional General Managers prepared plans and presented them to the Executive Committee for ratification. The change gave Business Managers a formal input into the preparation of plans. In fact, the planning process became 'business-led', with these managers setting financial and other objectives for the regions, the regions being required to identify actions to achieve those objectives. Next, capital expenditure approval procedures were amended. Formerly, regional General Managers and engineering chiefs had significant autonomy in the approval of capital expenditures. The new system required expenditure proposals to be underwritten by one or more Business Managers, and effectively gave them a right to veto if they thought the proposals were uneconomic. Finally, budgeting systems were revised. Budgets emanating from each region were

analysed by market sector. Business Managers became involved in their review.

The significance of these changes is that, in the context of ER's formal management style, formal systems and procedures imply rights to participate in and influence decisions and actions. The Business Managers' participation in the operation of these systems gave them a context to interact with others and question the rationale underlying railway decisions. In meetings, they could be seen translating operational and engineering concerns into the new profit calculus, feeding their financial vocabulary back into the stream of discourse. Appealing to the 'ideal' of the profit-conscious customer-oriented private sector manager, they challenged and sometimes ridiculed beliefs.

Thus, participation in the planning procedures enabled them to reinterpret longer-run engineering and operational initiatives in business terms: what does it mean for the customer? Will it improve journey times and punctuality? What implications does it raise in terms of costs and revenues? Their sponsorship of capital investments enabled them to ask: will it improve train reliability, eliminating the need for back up resources? Can the businesses afford it? What are the investment options? The redesign of the budgeting system gave them opportunities to challenge the cost effectiveness and profit implications of operational issues like train routing, train scheduling and the programming of maintenance.

Moving from the remote concerns of long-term planning, through capital investments, to immediate issues of train scheduling and maintenance programming, they recast management debate into a language of the 'bottom line'. Others began to take up their vocabulary. Railway matters gradually came to be discussed as financial matters. Furthermore, planning and budgeting activities began to assume a new significance. Formerly, they were introverted acts of cost containment. Now they came to symbolize the search for profit-maximizing opportunities.

Commenting on the importance of these changes in formal systems, a Business Manager observed:

> We had responsibility for improving the profitability of the railway. But it wasn't clear who was in control — I think there was some diffidence in spelling that out with the utmost clarity. We lobbied to get control of the planning process. Clarity has emerged, now that we have taken responsibility for planning and budgeting. That's become our power base.

Over time, these changes cumulatively extended the opportunity for Business Managers to interact with engineers and operators far beyond their original remit. Through this interaction, their ideas became more specific. But they were still located in the Head Office. Accordingly, in a later episode, they set about extending their influence into the regional organizations. They appealed to the Chief Executive for the appointment of individuals to represent their interests within the regions. These Regional Business Managers, once appointed, carried the economic perspective deep into the regional organizations, carving underneath the regional General Managers and giving Business Managers a direct line of influence to operational activities. One commented:

> People in the regions are used to doing things without asking. They find themselves subject to our scrutiny. I can take things up in a big way, if necessary, and howl for their blood.

And commenting on their influence, an operations manager in the regions observed:

> Five years ago it would have been revolutionary to challenge what an engineer wanted to spend money on. Now it happens frequently.

Consolidating the emerging reality through symbolic events. Through interaction in meetings and elsewhere, many in the organization began to understand the Business Managers' emerging reality. Most also found it appealing. The continual attacks on the competence of public sector managers had worn morale down. To be business-like was 'good', it gave them pride, and made the railway modern. Increasingly people came to share the normative symbolism of the 'bottom line'. But to a large extent this was uncoupled from their concrete day-to-day activities. Meaningful symbols relating to everyday tasks, events and recollections through which people could connect the business reality to their ongoing decisions and actions, were absent.

As the situation unfolded, this changed, however. In parallel with the formal changes, a sequence of important events was enacted. The Business Managers staged 'contests' with the regional General Managers, forcing collisions between the railway culture and the business culture. As before, they worked through the bureaucratic structure of the railway. Focusing, in each episode, on a specific issue demonstrative of their concerns, they sought first to persuade the Chief Executive and his advisors. Once sure of this group's support they set out to convert a wider group. Finally, they forced the issue for resolution. Again, each issue resolved opened up the possibility of the next. Three events stand out. They are reported in sequence.

The first concerned the disposition of locomotives and rolling stock. Over a period of time, one regional General Manager had been successful in acquiring resources to invest in high speed trains for passenger transport. These he zealously guarded against suggestions from other regional General Managers that they should be more widely dispersed on the railway network. The relevant Business Manager's analysis suggested that this situation was uneconomic. Profit could be improved by relocating some of these train sets to other regions. This Business

Manager lobbied the Chief Executive and his advisors to have the location decision determined by economic criteria. This was supported and the trains were moved. Commenting on this event, the relevant Business Manager observed:

> Regional prejudices had stopped the movement of high speed trains to the areas where they could earn the most money. The General Managers were barons. You just didn't go into their territory. It was a sort of unwritten law. I got those trains moved early on, it was one of the first things I did.

A second event concerned capital investments. In this case, a major track was being upgraded to take faster trains. According to engineering precedent, it was usual to renew signalling equipment at the same time. The Business Manager's analysis indicated that this was neither necessary nor economic. Again, the Chief Executive was lobbied. The signalling was not renewed. As the Business Manager observed:

> The main line was being electrified at significant expense. When wires are being strung over the track, it is customary to renew signalling equipment at the same time.
>
> We can't afford it. Anyway, the existing signalling will last another 15 years. All we needed to do was immunize the signals for electrification. The General Manager and his engineers were horrified. 'This isn't the way to run a railway', they said. 'It's a cash flow decision'.

A third decision concerned the scheduling of trains. Note that this is getting down to operational and logistical detail, by any standards the province of professional railway operators. Traditionally, train schedules had been set to maximize operational convenience. For the sake of passenger convenience,

a Business Manager wanted to alter the schedule on a route. This intervention was bitterly resented by the regional General Managers. Even in this case, the Business Manager's judgement was supported by the Chief Executive.

> Traditionally, timetables have been set for operational convenience. I was dissatisfied and wanted to change the frequency of trains on the route.
>
> The General Manager was determined not to have it. I took it to the Chief Executive. I said to the General Manager half an hour before the meeting: 'I've got to win, and will win, the writing's on the wall whether you like or not. I like you, why are you putting your head in a noose? Why don't you back off?'. But he didn't (Business Manager).

All these events came to have a significance way beyond the decisions themselves. Each stood for a whole class of decisions, signifying the primacy of the business reality in relation to those kinds of decisions. The high speed train issue redefined all decisions concerning the location of locomotives and rolling stock as economic decisions. The signalling decision redefined all investment decisions as economic decisions. The scheduling decision established the economic nature of detailed operational issues.

These events coupled the business culture to concrete railway activities. They were widely celebrated in the organization, both in public documents and in internal discussions, and are recalled in explanations of the emergence of the business rationale for railway management. Cumulatively, they embrace almost all aspects of the railway. People used them to attribute a new meaning to their everyday activities.

Not all decisions went in the Business Managers' favour, though. Secure in their conversion of the majority of the senior management élite, the Business Managers sought to explore their new reality with those within the organization. As already noted, representatives were appointed in regional offices: Regional Business Managers. At first, these individuals reported formally to the regional General Managers, and were on their payroll. The Business Managers wanted to pay their salaries from their own budgets to avoid them having divided loyalties. Regional General Managers found this unacceptable.

Apparently the Business Managers acted too soon; they lost. But the momentum they had already established was too great and they came back to win support some weeks later. A Business Manager explained:

> There was a famous breakfast meeting where I soundly lost. The organization was not ready. But of course, one rises again. Later, we were on firmer ground. I raised the matter again, and I won the votes of everyone.

In the regions, a similar process of change seems to be being enacted. These individuals appear to be following a similar strategy, gaining contexts for interaction, persuading others of their views, and staging contests. The 'bottom line' for each business is now decomposed into subsidiary 'bottom line' accounts. In regional meetings, these managers reinterpret dialogue and debate through the subsidiary accounts. A sequence of new symbolic events is being enacted in each region. Commenting on his experiences, one Regional Business Manager observed:

> At first we had to stand out there in front battling on our own. But now it's like a tide coming in. Nobody can actually fight the tide. I'm coming in on a surfboard really.

The picture then, is one of sequencing, momentum and cumulation. The Business Managers started on their mission with a vague concept of a business railway. They secured increasing contexts for interaction. Their ideas gradually became more concrete and they persuaded others around them. In an episodic manner, moving from the general to the particular, they secured changes to reporting relationships and systems. Each episode was punctuated by a key event. These events became symbols of the business culture, endowing railway activities with a new meaning, and provided a basis for continual and cumulative reinterpretations of railway operations.

Of course, there was tension. These decisions challenged the status of the regional General Managers and others who still subscribed to old beliefs. There was resentment and hostility. But the Business Managers let each step 'soak' so the organization could acclimatize, before embarking on the next episode, and a majority of the senior management gradually converted to the 'business culture'. Appealing to another metaphor, a Senior Executive commented:

> We've lit a bonfire and it's burning like mad.

The Regional General Managers' perspective

Regional General Managers were steeped in tradition. They were the descendants of the railway pioneers, the bastions of the railway culture. The business culture struck at their values and beliefs. When asked why and how they had let these things happen, they responded:

> It wasn't obvious at the time. The Business Managers were planners. We didn't expect the railway operations to change (General Manager).

One quoted from a memo he had written to his staff immediately after the Executive Committee meeting which had approved the principle of the Business Managers' appointment:

> The respective roles of Headquarters and the Regions will not change . . . Policies, as now will evolve from discussions. The Regions will participate . . .

In fact, from the General Managers' perspective, the story is one of initial seduction, followed by surprise and ambivalence, defection and resignation. They were aware of external pressures for financial performance. Some thought it was a whim, and would pass. But most perceived a need for a business perspective, and supported the creation of the Business Managers' positions in the Executive Committee. When the Business Managers were appointed, most welcomed their influence. At an early stage, one General Manager commented:

> This is good for us. I'm quite pleased at the way the culture is changing. You talk around now and nobody is in any doubt that the railway is business-led.

And another, commenting on the decision to relocate the high speed trains:

> Why do we have fancy train sets? It's not for General Managers to play trains. It's to make the businesses more profitable.[19]

One joined the Senior Executives, representing the Business Managers. According to his critics, he is reputed to have seen 'which way the wind was blowing', but he himself described it thus:

> Initially I was opposed. But I saw the logic of the changes. I was converted.

Thus, most found the abstract normative symbolism of the 'bottom line' appealing. They thought it 'good' to be more business-like. They aspired to 'private sector practice'. Few perceived the underlying momentum of events or their potential significance. Acting out the new rationale, they thought they need have no fear for the railway traditions. In fact, sitting in their grand offices with portraits and plaques around their walls and other symbols of former grandeur, it was inconceivable to them that the railway traditions could be undermined by anything.

As the significance of the economic reality emerged through subsequent events, however, the situation became less congenial for them. It threatened their pride as professional railway operators. Commenting on the resignalling decision noted earlier, a General Manager said:

> We'll have to do it all again in 15 years' time. It's not a sensible long-term decision.

Furthermore, the appointment of Regional Business Managers within their own organizations undermined their authority.

At this point, they protested vigorously. This prompted a report from the centre discussing the relationship between Businesses and the Regions. The report placated them with the soothing idea of Business Managers and regional General Managers as equals in a team-based organization. Nevertheless, the business perspective continued to impinge on operational matters.

Many General Managers became unhappy. They thought the emerging decisions unprofessional, and feared for the quality of the railway. By this time, however, their appeals fell on deaf ears. Most others among the senior management élite had converted to the business culture. The General Managers were characterized as reactionary, protective and old-fashioned.

Towards the end of the study, most of them left the organization or took 'early retirement'. One stayed in office a while longer. Shortly before his retirement he had this to say:

With the benefit of hindsight, I think the Chief Executive was right in allowing it through . . . But it's gone too far . . .

While I've been in office, through good engineering management, I've just about managed to get rid of all the speed restrictions on the main line. Business Managers are taking a maintenance holiday [i.e. neglecting maintenance]. In five years someone will be faced with exactly the situation I inherited.

Former regional General Managers have been replaced with sympathetic men. They repudiate the old traditions. They are proud to subscribe to the business culture. A newly appointed General Manager had this to say:

I personally feel that this new approach is right. I support the businesses. I see it as my job to influence my current staff to accept the business managers.

Far from being equals in a team, the regional General Managers are seen to be subservient to Business Managers. 'Business managers set policy and standards; regions implement'. Career patterns have changed. To become a regional General Manager was the ultimate aspiration for a railway-man; by the end of the field research it was to become a Business Manager. There was open discussion of removing the regional General Managers from the Railway Executive.

Accounting and Culture

Initially, there was a dominant 'railway' culture. The Business Managers brought a counter 'business' culture. This cascaded across the senior management élite to become dominant. The Business

Managers had an abstract idea of a business railway. New accounts were crafted representing the railway as a series of businesses. The Business Managers gained contexts to interact with others. In these contexts, they recast dialogue and debate from a railway language of operations and engineering to their business language of markets and profit. Gradually the idea of a business railway became more specific. Moving from remote concerns to immediate issues, they persuaded others of their interpretations. There were contests over the definition of specific activities. The outcomes became symbols through which people attributed new meaning to railway operations. Momentum built up behind the business culture. People converted, others left. For senior managers, the abstract idea became a tangible, energizing reality, a source of pride. Now the railway culture is repudiated.

A broad range of theories can be brought to bear to interpret the pattern of these events. Fundamental to this account is the notion of culture as a system of ideas: beliefs, knowledges and values in which action and artifacts are vested with expressive qualities (Geertz, 1973, 1983); and the idea that organizations have distinctive cultures (Pettigrew, 1979). This is exemplified in the contrasting 'railway' and 'business' cultures described. Associated with this is the conceptualization of organizational change as a process of uncoupling and recoupling (cf. Greenwood & Hinings, 1988): exemplified in the railway by the uncoupling of activities from the railway culture and their recoupling to the business culture.[20] We can also see a theory of inertia in operation, change being precipitated by crisis (cf. Starbuck & Hedberg, 1977; Jonsson & Lundin, 1977; Mintzberg, 1978; Miller & Friesen, 1984). The railway culture was remarkably resilient over many previous decades, despite several attacks; real threats only being perceived when the severity of the current onslaught on the public services became apparent. There are also traces of the 'garbage can' (Cohen *et al.*, 1972;

March & Olsen, 1976): the Business Management idea was developed independently of the crisis, only subsequently coupled to the threats facing the organization.

Continuing, change was emergent (March & Olsen, 1976; Pettigrew, 1985). This was not a controlled process, relying on plans and rational analyses engineered by those standing outside, untainted as it were; the whole management group was bound up in the creation of the business culture. The process unfolded through tentative initiatives, buffeted by the timing of events, the ambition and (relative) political skills of the 'champions' (Kanter, 1983) and other actors involved, and their failures and successes. Nor were the vagaries of chance unimportant[21] (Pettigrew, 1985). Moreover, we see changes in systems (planning, capital investment, budgeting) interpenetrating the emergence and elaboration of the business culture.

It also is possible to appeal to the insights of institutional theory (Meyer & Rowan, 1977; DiMaggio & Powell, 1983; Scott, 1987; Zucker, 1988). Government, the railway's key environmental constituency, was intolerant of (what it saw as) managerial incompetence. The Business Management initiative could be interpreted as a symbol of the railway becoming more modern and businesslike: the 'bottom line' idea standing for the railway adopting private sector practices. Such solutions may have real and unintended internal consequences, however. One was the Business Managers amassing power and influence at the expense of the General Managers. Although a theoretically impoverished theory in this context, there is some link here with the strategic contingencies' perspective of intraorganizational power (Hickson et al.,1971; Hinings et al.,1974). Subsequent to the appointment of the Business Managers, the railway managed to persuade government to make funds available, on a one-off basis, for a major electrification project (giving rise to the signalling controversy discussed earlier). Apparently, approval was forthcoming as a result of the 'rigorous business case' orchestrated by the relevant Business Manager.

The purpose here is not to discuss these theories further, however. It is to develop a cultural appreciation of accounting. The study shows that accounting was implicated differently in the two cultures described. At this point, it is appropriate to explicate its linkages to underlying knowledge, values and beliefs.

A cultural system incorporates, among other things, knowledge about environments, and strategies for extracting subsistence from them. This knowledge is quite different in the two cultures. In the railway culture it revolved around the public service idea, later coupled to notions of thrift. Essentially, the knowledge was this: if the organization provided the nation with a transport infrastructure (without undue waste), then sustenance would be forthcoming from government. This knowledge is not unique to the railway culture. The expectation that low-cost, generally available services will be rewarded by the state is common to many public service organizations in Europe, for example the health and education services. Given this knowledge, accounting was incidental in the railway culture: it was necessary to ensure that revenues were accounted for and suppliers paid, and perhaps to contain waste, but that was the limit of its significance in the structures of meaning. The purpose of the railway was to run trains; operating the railway would be rewarded by government. In this knowledge, the train, therefore, was endowed with a special significance.

The business culture, revolving around the 'bottom line', incorporates a quite different knowledge. Rather obviously, in view of events in ER, the bottom line constructs the notion of the railway as a profit-seeking enterprise. This is not just a matter of 'cost efficiency', however, although that is important. More importantly, in ER it constructs the idea of looking to product markets, rather than to government, for sustenance. There is nothing somehow uniquely 'public service' about the railway network in this construction. Rail transport is a product (or service), to be bought and sold like any other; in fact it is a series of products: intercity travel, freight, suburban commuting, etc. Revenues from these products, rather than government support, must cover costs; and, critically, revenues are earned in the market place. Survival depends on extracting resources from these markets, perhaps in competition with other firms. Hence the new-found concern for competition with other means of transport (road, air, buses), expressed by railway managers early in the account above, a concern which in the railway culture would have been probably inconsequential.[22] Given this knowledge, accounting activities become hugely significant. The search for profit opportunities, and the elimination of non-profit-making activities, is a quest for survival. It is now the customer, not the train, which has special importance.

No culture is completely coherent, of course. Each has ambiguities and contradictions. In ER, residues of the past create tensions. One is the partial incompatibility of the business culture with the restrictions placed on it by state ownership. ER is not allowed to borrow in financial markets to fund investment, for example, and as government funds are tight, this means investments necessary for competitive purposes cannot always be made. It also has statutory obligations to keep certain branch lines open, even if they are unprofitable. Here it still looks to government for support (although a government conceptualized as a customer). Nevertheless, the underlying knowledge systems are quite different, and constitute different realities.

This shift in knowledge which accounting helps to construct, the shift from looking to the state for subsistence to looking to markets, is fundamental, and it interpenetrates the operation and management of ER's core technology with pervasive effects. For a start, it changes the appropriate form of organization. In the old knowledge, the prime task was the operation of trains. The meaningful management structure was one which facilitated operations. The physical facilities of the railway are geographically laid out along the radial routes of the old prenationalization companies. Thus the appropriate management organization was around these routes, i.e. the regional management structures. The regional General Managers and engineers, because of their acknowledged expertise in operating trains, were afforded substantial status and influence.

Now, in the new knowledge, this is 'mere' production, subservient to markets. The prime task is serving markets. The meaningful form of management organization is one which reflects and confronts markets. Since the long distance intercity travel market is not confined to one main line, for example, or the freight market confined to one region, the regional and business forms of organization do not map perfectly onto one another. Hence the reorientation of management structures and systems around the Business Managers, and their subsequent elaboration through the Business Manager's subordinates located in the regions. Of course, there is still an operational task to be performed: trains, tracks, maintenance and so forth. But in this new knowledge it is Business Managers, with supposed expertise in markets and extracting resources from them, who attract status and influence.

The changing knowledge also redefines the appropriate form of action. In the old knowledge, that of the celebration of the train, there were norms that made things intrinsically necessary. 'Of course' professional railwaymen renewed signalling equipment when they electrified the track, for example; it was inconceivable not to do so. The train needs to be taken care of and nurtured. The interest in thrift, the avoidance of waste, also meant the elimination of activities not strictly necessary for the operation of trains: training staff to smile at customers, for example. In the new knowledge, activities are neither intrinsically necessary, nor intrinsically wasteful. Rather they are judged for their consequences in the market. Through the 'bottom line', activities become desirable to the extent that they add more 'value' than they cost. This is not simply cost minimization: the avoidance of unnecessary gold-plating. The 'bottom line engineering specification', mentioned earlier, means designing for the market, as it were: adding comfort, reliability, speed, customer service where its returns outweigh its cost. Attractive concourse design is not wasteful extravagance, it is reinterpreted as a 'good' thing which brings in custom.

Action is also judged against a different concept of time. In the old knowledge, time was practically infinite. The railways were built to last for decades, for centuries. The nation would always need a transport infrastructure. Professional standards were oriented towards doing a long-lasting thorough job. Government would reward the railway for maintaining the viability of the network into the future. In the new knowledge, the concept of time is much shorter. Survival is a day-to-day affair. Markets are ephemeral. Don't spend money now on activities that you can put off until the future. Take 'maintenance holidays' where you can: deterioration of the infrastructure can be remedied later.

The point being made here is that accounting can play a significant role in constructing specific knowledges. Accounting systems embody particular assumptions about rationality, organization, authority, time and so forth. If these permeate into underlying values, knowledges and beliefs they can have very real consequences. Above we see accounting coming into the organization to construct a new theory of subsistence, which in turn implies particular modes of organizing, patterns of influence and authority, criteria for action and a new concept of time.

The cultural knowledge described here was not discovered completely formed. Nor was it coupled to the railway's management structures (or to action) in an instant. Rather the meaning of the bottom line gradually crystallized around the initial accounts, and the coupling had to be actively crafted. The business culture unfolded in episodes: bursts of exhausting creativity, each building on what had previously been accomplished, and punctuated by a concluding event; followed by a pause for consolidation, recovery and imagination before the next. Successive episodes moved from the abstract realm to the particular; from long-term issues to immediate issues. In each, senior management struggled to reconceptualize a class of activities; then it was uncoupled, or perhaps one should say wrenched, from the railway culture and recoupled to the business culture. Again and again these episodes continued, until cumulatively practically all classes of railway activity were redefined. Later, in the regions, a similar process of episodic uncoupling and recoupling was enacted. In the process, linkages to the railway culture were only bit-by-bit ruptured.

The general point arising is that organizations have different classes of activity. Cultural change is not simply uncoupling and recoupling, or even reconceptualization. Each class of activity may need to be separately uncoupled and recoupled. During the process, different classes of activity may be informed by different rationales and knowledge. In ER, this led to a strange schizophrenia in the organization (and difficulties in making sense of the data), in which some activities were railway-culture issues, and some business-culture issues. It also led to strange disjunctures between the interpretive schemes brought to bear in the head office and in the regions. Only towards the end of the research did this schizophrenia begin to be resolved.

This process, however, needs to be enveloped in an awareness of the conditions for its possibility, conditions for the emergence of the particular culture described. In some ways, perhaps, the business culture in ER may be seen to be inevitable. Today, the belief in markets (as an optimal form of organization) seems to be firmly entrenched in Anglo-American political cultures, and in those of some continental-European states. Governmental pressures, inevitably, in this view, led to investment in financial calculation and the construction of the railway as a business enterprise. Support for this 'theory of inevitability' might be sought by retrospective application of the present political determination to privatize ER, or at least some of its businesses.

As Fligstein (1990) notes, in a rather different critique, such an interpretation relies on understandings of the present to construct appreciations of the past: interpreting the past through the present, rather than the present through the past. ER had a remarkably strong heritage which survived previous attacks. In the early 1980s, its privatization was not just undiscussed, it was inconceivable. Arguably, the business culture in ER, the reconstruction of the railway through the 'bottom line(s)' as a series of businesses, actually created preconditions for the discussion of privatization, not vice versa.

For sure, the early 1980s witnessed the beginnings of the sea change in attitudes towards the public services that swept across the political culture later in the decade. Through influential right-wing think-tanks the idea of subjecting public services to an entrepreneurial principle was then emerging, later to be manifested in the 'rolling back' of the public sector through the privatization of many public utilities and attempts to introduce market mechanisms in others. Associated with this was the emerging idea of the 'dependence' culture, and its repudiation; to be replaced by an 'enterprise' culture. Individuals, and organizations, were expected to take a responsibility for their own destiny.

However, the initiative for business management in ER, conceived in the late 1970s, preceded these political developments, and appears to have been a substantially autonomous development in a separate arena: as one of the initiators in the senior management group explained, it was 'the product of

thinking railwaymen'. Explicating this claim would require careful analysis of historical materials beyond the scope of this paper. But such evidence as is available supports the view that the initiative was developed largely independently of political ideas, its private sector leanings probably owing more to the advice of a few business consultants than to any political agenda. Certainly it was not government-inspired; indeed government was initially sceptical, only later endorsing the ideas (and applying them to its own ends).

That said, the initiative was congruent with the ideas emerging outside, and its subsequent elaboration into the business culture undoubtedly owes much to their development. Even here, though, due importance must be attached to the specific circumstances within the organization. Public sector management was under challenge, morale was low. Many in the senior management group were receptive to the new ideas. Business Management was seen as a home-grown solution to governmental attack. It expressed some kind of empowerment, a potential freedom from the yoke of government restriction, and an opportunity for managers to show their entrepreneurial capabilities.

Concluding Comment

The purpose of this paper is to articulate a cultural analysis of accounting in organizations. The appreciation of organizations as cultures provides a rich insight into organizational life, drawing out the expressive qualities of action and artifact. Cultural knowledge in organizations vests organizational activities with symbolic meanings; so also it vests accounting with symbolic meaning. A cultural analysis of accounting seeks to uncover these particular meanings, and to locate them in underlying local knowledges, values and beliefs.

The paper has sought to apply this cultural perspective in an empirical setting. Through a field study of organizational change, it showed how accounting can be vested with different meanings in local cultures. And it showed how accounting can enter into organizational settings to constitute cultural knowledge in particular ways, creating particular rationalities for organizational action; and in turn how this can lead to new patterns of organization, of authority and influence, new concepts of time and legitimate action. The study also traced the emergent, episodic process through which cultural knowledge was constituted in this organization, and coupled to organizational activities.

The study certainly fleshes out the constitutive potential of accounting proposed by Hopwood (1987), Hines (1988) and others. However, the specific findings of the field study – the reorientation of a strategy for subsistence from government to markets, and its subsequent elaboration; and the process through which this realization was accomplished – are not offered as a general proposition on the cultural significance of accounting. Accounting systems are implicated in organizational cultures in different, possibly unique ways. The cultural knowledge constructed in this organization is but one possibility; there are many others. In this, as in other fields, 'the road to the grand abstractions of science winds through a thicket of singular facts' (Geertz, 1973, p. 145).

Rather, the purpose of the field study is to explicate a mode of theorizing linkages between accounting and culture. The mode of theorizing is interpretive, getting underneath surface descriptions to understand the significance of accounting in local settings; and it is reflective, in the sense that the theorist reflects on that significance in the context of the underlying ideational system. Applying this mode of analysis in different settings would contribute hugely to our emergent appreciation of the way in which accounting is used in organizations, usefully supplementing the more quantitative approaches to research pursued by contingency theorists, for example. It may be particularly valuable also in the development of comparative theories of the use of accounting in different social contexts. We know, for example, that accounting systems within organizations in different countries are often not that dissimilar to Anglo-American designs; it seems, however, that they may be used quite differently. The mode of theorizing advanced here would enable us to address this issue in a productive way.

Finally, while the paper has deliberately refrained from casting judgements on the developments described in the organization studied, it is probably worth acknowledging that there is widespread criticism of 'bottom line' orientations such as those described here, particularly for their construction of time. Far from creating an underlying competitiveness in organizations, the preoccupation with the 'bottom line' is seen to discourage technological innovation and investments in operational capability (e.g. Hayes & Abernathy, 1980; Johnson & Kaplan, 1987). ER, it seems, has adopted this vocabulary just as those organizations that have it are being exhorted to move towards longer-term, more strategic appreciations of time. In the railway, assets have long lives and the lead-time on capital investment is also long. To some extent the maintenance of the infrastructure is inevitably compromised by its new culture. Quite possibly with innovations in transport, the railway network will be an irrelevance in 50 years' time; on the other hand, it may not be. The green lobby, in particular, might argue that it is sensible to keep options open in a way that at present may not be possible.

Postscript

The process of change in ER continues. The regional management structure is today being dissolved.

The operational side of the railway is currently being reorganized and assimilated into the Businesses. The crafted accounts representing the railway as a series of businesses have now permeated through management structures and systems to operations on the ground. The railway quite literally has become its businesses. There are no longer any regional General Managers, no vestiges of the railway culture . . . or are there? High up on a building above one of the main-line termini, out of sight except to observant motorists on a nearby flyover, there is a residue of the past: a large illuminated logo – the logo of a pre-nationalization railway.

Bibliography

Aldrich, H. E., *Organizations & Environments* (Englewood Cliffs, NJ: Prentice Hall, 1979).

Allaire, Y. & Firsirotu, M. E., Theories of Organizational Culture, *Organizational Studies* (1984) pp. 51–64.

Ansari, S. & Euske, K. J., Rational, Rationalizing and Reifying Uses of Accounting Data in Organizations, *Accounting, Organizations and Society* (1987) pp. 549–570.

Argyris, C. & Schon, D. A., *Organizational Learning* (Reading, MA: Addison-Wesley, 1981).

Barley, S. R., Meyer, G. W. & Gash, D. C., Cultures of Culture: Academics, Practitioners and the Pragmatics of Normative Control, *Administrative Science Quarterly* (March 1988) pp. 24–60.

Berry, A., Capps, T., Cooper, D., Fergusson, P., Hopper, T. & Lowe, A., Management Control in an Area of the National Coal Board, *Accounting, Organizations and Society* (1985) pp. 3–28.

Blau, P. M., *The Dynamics of Bureaucracy: A Study of Interpersonal Relationships in Two Government Agencies* (Chicago, IL: University of Chicago Press, 1955).

Bruns, W. & Kaplan, R. S. (eds), *Accounting and Management: A Field Study Perspective* (Cambridge, MA: Harvard Business School Press, 1987).

Brunsson, N., *The Irrational Organization* (New York: Wiley, 1985).

Bryer, R. A., Accounting for the Railway Mania of 1845 – A Great Railway Swindle?, *Accounting, Organizations and Society* (1991) pp. 439–486.

Burns, T. & Stalker, G. M., *The Management of Innovation* (London: Tavistock Press, 1961).

Buroway, M., *Manufacturing Consent* (Chicago, IL: University of Chicago Press, 1979).

Burrell, G. & Morgan, G., *Sociological Paradigms and Organizational Analysis* (London: Heineman, 1979).

Chandler, A. D., *The Railroads* (New York: Harcourt, Brace & World, 1965).

Clifford, J. & Marcus, G. E. (eds), *Writing Culture* (Berkeley, CA: University of California Press, 1986).

Cohen, M. D., March, J. G. & Olsen, J. P., A Garbage Can Model of Organizational Choice, *Administrative Science Quarterly* (March 1972) pp. 1–25.

Covaleski, M. & Dirsmith, M., The Use of Budgetary Symbols in the Political Arena: An Historically Informed Field Study, *Accounting, Organizations and Society* (1988) pp. 1–24.

Crapanzano, V., Hermes Dilemma: The Masking of Subversion in Ethnographic Description, in Clifford, J. & Marcus, G. E. (eds), *Writing Culture* (Berkeley, CA: University of California Press, 1986) pp. 51–76.

Crozier, M., *The Bureaucratic Phenomenon* (London: Tavistock, 1964).

Dalton, M., *Men Who Manage* (New York: Wiley, 1959).

Deal, T. E. & Kennedy, A. A., *Corporate Culture: The Rites and Rituals of Corporate Life* (Reading, MA: Addison-Wesley, 1982).

Dent, J. F., Organizational Research in Accounting: Perspectives, Issues and a Commentary, in Hopwood, A. G. & Bromwich, M., *Research and Current Issues in Management Accounting* (London: Pitman, 1986).

Denzin, N. K., *Interpretive Interactionism*, in Morgan, G. (ed), *Beyond Method* (Beverly Hills, CA: Sage, 1983) pp. 129–146.

DiMaggio, P. J. & Powell, W. W., The Iron Cage Revisited: Institutional Isomorphism and Collective Rationality in Organizational Fields, *American Sociological Review* (April 1983) pp. 147–160.

Douglas, M., *Purity and Danger: An Analysis of Concepts of Pollution and Taboo* (London: Routledge & KeganPaul, 1966).

Evans Pritchard, E. E., *Witchcraft, Oracles and Magic among the Azande* (Oxford: Oxford University Press, 1937).

Evans Pritchard, E. E., *The Nuer* (Oxford: Oxford University Press, 1940).

Feldman, S. P., Management in Context: An Essay on the Relevance of Culture to the Understanding of

Organizational Change, *Journal of Management Studies* (November 1986) pp. 587–607.

Fligstein, N., *The Transformation of Corporate Control* (Cambridge, MA: Harvard University Press, 1990).

Geertz, C., *The Interpretation of Cultures* (New York: Basic Books, 1973).

Geertz, C., *Local Knowledge* (New York: Basic Books, 1983).

Geertz, C., *Works and Lives: The Anthropologist as Author* (Cambridge: Polity Press, 1988).

Goffman, E., *The Presentation of Self in Everyday Life* (New York: Doubleday, 1959).

Goodenough, W. H., *Culture, Language and Society* (Reading, MA: Addison-Wesley, 1971).

Goold, M. & Campbell, A., *Strategies and Styles* (Oxford: Blackwell, 1987).

Gouldner, A. W., *Patterns of Industrial Bureaucracy* (New York: Free Press, 1954).

Gourvish, T. R., *British Railways 1948–73: A Business History* (Cambridge University Press, 1986).

Gourvish, T. R., *British Rail's 'Business Led' Organization, 1977–90: Government–Industry Relations in Britain's Public Sector, Business History Review* (1990) pp. 109–149.

Greenwood, R. & Hinings, C. R., Organization Design Types, Tracks and the Dynamics of Strategic Change, *Organization Studies* (1988) pp. 293–316.

Gregory, K. L., Native-View Paradigms: Multiple Cultures & Culture Conflicts in Organizations, *Administrative Science Quarterly* (September 1983) pp. 359–377.

Harris, M., *Cultural Materialism: the Struggle for a Science of Culture* (New York: Random House, 1979).

Hayes, R. & Abernathy, S. J., Managing Our Way to Economic Decline, *Harvard Business Review* (July–August 1980) pp. 67–77.

Hedberg, B. L. T., How Organizations Learn and Unlearn, in Nystrom, P. C. & Starbuck, W. H. (eds), *Handbook of Organization Design: Volume 1* (Oxford: Oxford University Press, 1981).

Hedberg, G. & Jonsson, S., Designing Semi-confusing Information Systems for Organizations in Changing Environments, *Accounting, Organizations and Society* (1978) pp. 47–65.

Hedberg, B., Nystrom, P. C. & Starbuck, W. H., Camping on See Saws: Prescriptions for a Self-Designing Organization, *Administrative Science Quarterly* (March 1976) pp. 41–65.

Hickson, D. J., Hinings, C. R., Lee, C. A., Schneck, R. E. & Pennings, J. M., A Strategic Contingencies' Theory of Intra Organizational Power, *Administrative Science Quarterly* (June 1971) pp. 216–229.

Hines, R., Financial Accounting: In Communicating Reality, We Construct Reality, *Accounting, Organizations and Society* (1988) pp. 251–261.

Hinings, C. R., Hickson, D. J., Pennings, J. M. & Schneck, R. E., Structural Conditions of Intra Organizational Power, *Administrative Science Quarterly* (March 1974) pp. 22–44.

Hopwood, A. G., Towards an Organizational Perspective for the Study of Accounting and Information Systems, *Accounting, Organizations and Society* (1978) pp. 3–13.

Hopwood, A. G., On Trying to Study Accounting in the Contexts in which it Operates, *Accounting, Organizations and Society* (1983) pp. 287–305.

Hopwood, A. G., The Archaeology of Accounting Systems, *Accounting, Organizations and Society* (1987) pp. 207–234.

Hughes, E. C., *Men and their Work* (Glencoe, IL: Free Press, 1958).

Johnson, H. T. & Kaplan, R. S., *Relevance Lost: The Rise and Fall of Management Accounting* (Cambridge, MA: Harvard, 1987).

Jones, P. R. & Lakin, C., *The Carpet Makers* (Maidenhead: McGraw-Hill, 1978).

Jonsson, S. & Lundin, R. A., Myths and Wishful Thinking as Management Tools, in Nystrom, P. C. & Starbuck, W. H. (eds), *Prescriptive Models of Organization*, pp. 157–170 (Amsterdam: North-Holland, 1977).

Kanter, R., *The Change Masters: Corporate Entrepreneurs at Work* (New York: Simon & Schuster, 1983).

Kilmann, R. H., Saxton, M. J. & Serpa, R. (eds), *Gaining Control of the Corporate Culture* (San Francisco: Jossey Bass, 1985).

Lawrence, P. R. & Lorsch, J. W., *Organization and Environment:Managing Differentiation and Integration* (IL: Irwin, [1967] 1969).

Levi Strauss, C., *Structural Anthropology* (New York: Basic Books, 1963).

Levi Strauss, C., *The Savage Mind* (Chicago, IL: University of Chicago Press, [1962] 1966).

Malinowski, B., *Argonauts of the Western Pacific* (London: Routledge & Kegan Paul, 1922).

March, J. G. & Olsen, J. P., *Ambiguity and Choice in Organizations* (Oslo: Universitetforlaget, 1976).

Solutions to Questions

One of the problems that most students of accounting face is being able to tackle calculation problems. The 'fear of numbers' is quite common with postgraduate students and practising managers. Students often look back to find a similar 'model question' and then try to repeat the calculation, simply replacing the numbers. This is not good practice as it does not help the student to think about the concepts involved. Each problem is different, and this mirrors day-to-day business decisions. Solving these problems is about applying the underlying concepts.

The questions in each chapter require the reader to perform calculations. In attempting to solve these problems, you need to think about

- what the business problem is;
- the information that is provided to solve the problem;
- the most appropriate technique to apply to the problem; and
- how to apply the technique to solve the problem.

Solutions for Chapter 1

1.1

Accounting is a collection of systems and processes used to record, report and interpret business transactions. An account is an explanation or report in financial terms about those transactions. Accountability arises from the stewardship function under which managers have to provide an account to other stakeholders in the business.

1.2

i. The main activities of financial accountants involve collecting financial transaction data in the company's accounting system; classifying those transactions in terms of their effect on income, expenses, assets, liabilities and equity; and producing regular financial reports (e.g. Income Statement, Statement of Financial Position) for publication to interested parties (e.g. shareholders, banks, financiers).

ii. The main activities of management accountants include participation in planning, primarily through budgets; generating, analysing, presenting and interpreting information to support decision making; and monitoring and controlling performance. Management accountants will use financial accounting data but will produce it more frequently and in greater detail for the external users.

Solutions for Chapter 2

2.1

Value-based management uses a variety of techniques to measure increases in shareholder value, which is assumed to be the primary goal of all business organizations. Shareholder value refers to the economic value of an investment by discounting future cash flows to their present value using the cost of capital for the business. To achieve shareholder value, a business must generate profits in its markets for goods and services (product markets) that exceed the cost of capital (the weighted average cost of equity and borrowings) in the capital market.

2.2

The responsibilities of the board include setting the company's strategic goals, providing leadership to senior management, monitoring business performance and reporting to shareholders. The last two of these explicitly relate to accounting, and the first two implicitly do so. In the UK the Combined Code, in Australia the Corporations Act, and in the USA the Sarbanes–Oxley Act include important responsibilities of the board in relation to financial statements and performance management. The role of a board is to provide leadership of the company within a framework of prudent and effective controls which enables risk to be assessed and managed. These controls include many accounting controls such as budgets and capital expenditure evaluations. The financial reports of a company are the responsibility of the board which must ensure that the company keeps proper accounting records that disclose with reasonable accuracy the financial position of the company at any time and that financial reports comply with the relevant legislation. The board is also responsible for safeguarding the company's assets and for taking reasonable steps to prevent and detect fraud.

Solutions for Chapter 3

3.1

Answer c.

3.2

Answer d. Note there also is an associated entry for the cost of sales: increase cost of sales and reduce inventory.

3.3

Answer b.

Profit		
	Sales	100,000
	Cost of sales	−35,000
	Salaries	−15,000
	Rent	−4,000
	Advertising	−8,000
		£38,000

Cash		
	Equity	£25,000
	Sales	100,000
	Salaries	−15,000
	Rent	−4,000
	Advertising	−8,000
	Inventory	−40,000
		£58,000

Equity		
	Initial	£25,000
	Plus profit	38,000
		£63,000

Assets

Cash 58,000 + Equipment 20,000 + Inventory 5,000 = 83,000

Liabilities

Creditors (Equipment) 20,000 + Equity 63,000 = 83,000

3.4

Answer b.

Capital = Assets − Liabilities = 240,000 − 125,000 = 115,000

3.5

Answer c.

3.6

Transaction	Profit = Income − Expenses	Cash flow	Assets (excluding cash)	Liabilities
Issues shares to public		Increases		Increases (equity)
Borrows money over 5 years		Increases		Increases (long-term debt)
Pays cash for equipment		Decreases	Increases (non-current asset)	
Buys inventory on credit			Increases (current asset: inventory)	Increases (current liability: payables)
Sells goods on credit	Increases (selling price less cost price)		1. Increases (current asset: receivables at selling price) 2. Decreases (current asset: inventory at cost price)	
Pays cash for salaries, rent, etc.	Decreases (expenses)	Decreases		
Pays cash to suppliers		Decreases		Decreases (current liability: payables)
Receives cash from customers		Increases	Decreases (current asset: receivables)	

3.7

a. Profit is £35,000 (income £135,000 less expenses of advertising £15,000, rent £10,000 and salaries £75,000).

b. Equity at end of year is £106,000 (£71,000 plus profit for year of £35,000).

The Statement of Financial Position would show assets of £117,000 (non-current assets £100,000, bank £5,000 and receivables £12,000) less liabilities (payables £11,000) therefore net assets of £106,000 (equal to equity).

Solutions for Chapter 6

6.1

Kazam Services' accounting records are shown in Table S6.1.

Table S6.1

	Non-current assets	Receivables	Bank	Payables	Long-term loan	Equity	Income	Expenses
Opening balance	+500,000	+125,000	−35,000	+90,000	+300,000	+200,000		
Takes out loan for new building	+150,000				+150,000			
Money from Receivables		−45,000	+45,000					
Reduction of Payables			−30,000	−30,000				
Invoice for services performed		+70,000					+70,000	
Pay salaries			−15,000					+15,000
Pay office expenses			−5,000					+5,000
Depreciation	−20,000							+20,000
	630,000	150,000	−40,000	60,000	450,000	200,000	70,000	40,000
Profit transferred						+30,000	30,000	
						230,000		

Notes:

+ indicates the account increases.

− indicates the account decreases.

The bank account is a liability (withdrawals exceed deposits) and is shown here as a minus to distinguish it from an asset.

Kazam Services
Income Statement

Income	70,000
Less expenses	40,000
Operating profit	30,000

Statement of Financial Position
Assets

Non-current assets	650,000	
Less depreciation	20,000	630,000

Current assets

Receivables	150,000
Total assets	780,000

Liabilities
Non-current liabilities

Long-term loan	450,000

Current liabilities

Bank overdraft	40,000
Payables	60,000
	100,000

Total liabilities		550,000
Net assets		230,000
Equity		
Share capital		200,000
Retained earnings		30,000
Total Equity		230,000

6.2

See Table S6.2.

Table S6.2

Non-current assets		250,000
Current assets	125,000	
Payables	−75,000	
Working capital		50,000
Capital employed		300,000
Long-term debt		−125,000
Shareholders' capital (equity)		175,000

6.3

Answer e: although the operating profit has increased (from €137,000 to €139,000), the operating margin has decreased (from 11.6% to 11.1%) as a result of a reduction in the gross margin (from 39% to 37%) and higher expenses (from €323,000 to €324,000), despite sales growth (of 6.4%). See Table S6.3.

Table S6.3

	2011	2010
Sales	1,250,000	1,175,000
Sales growth	6.4%	
Cost of sales	787,000	715,000
Gross profit	463,000	460,000
Gross margin	37%	39%
Selling and admin expenses	324,000	323,000
Operating profit	139,000	137,000
Operating margin	11.1%	11.6%

6.4

a. Prepayment

The annual payment is $24 \times \$400 = \$9,600$ (this is \$800/month). The prepayment at 31 March is 9/12 (Apr–Dec) @ \$800 = \$7,200.

Profit is reduced by $2,400 (expense: 3 months @ $800).

Asset in the Statement of Financial Position is increased by $7,200 (prepayment is an asset: 9 months @ $800).

Cash flow is reduced by $9,600 (payment 31 December).

NB: the effect of the prepayment of $7,200 is to carry forward the expense to the next financial year.

b. Accrual

The simple solution is to divide $6,000 by 12 months and charge $500/month to profit. However, this ignores seasonal fluctuations and cash flow differences from quarter to quarter.

The quarterly bills have been paid during the year, but the last quarterly bill was in November. Therefore the business is missing one month's expense (i.e. December). To determine the amount we need to calculate the seasonal charges:

$6,000 × 70% = $4,200 for September–February/6 = $700/month

$6,000 × 30% = $1,800 for March–August/6 = $300/month

Accrue for one month (December) = $700

Profit reduced by $700 (expense). This is the profit adjustment. In total, expenses are $6,000 for the year.

Statement of Financial Position reduced by $700 (accrual is a creditor).

Cash flow has no impact (no money yet paid).

NB: the effect of the accrual is to reduce by $700 the expense impact of the expected bill for three months of $2,100, which will be received in February. This leaves $1,400 as the expense ($700 for each of January and February).

c. Depreciation

Depreciation is 20% of $12,000 = $2,400 p.a. or $200/month. As depreciation is charged from the next month, it needs to be provided for the period July–March. For that period, depreciation is $200 × 9 = $1,800.

Profit reduced by $1,800 (depreciation expense).

Statement of Financial Position increased by $12,000 (new asset) and reduced by $1,800 (depreciation), leaving a net value of $10,200.

Cash flow reduced by $12,000 (payment for new system).

NB: the Statement of Financial Position value of the asset will be reduced by $2,400 p.a. until the asset is written down to a nil value, or sold or disposed of.

6.5

Net assets are

| Plant & Equipment | £7,000,000 |
| Receivables | £1,500,000 |

Inventory	£2,300,000
	£10,800,000
Payables	£ 500,000
	£10,300,000
Purchase price	£12,000,00
Goodwill	£1,700,000

Amortization over 10 years:
£170,000 per annum	£170,000
Net goodwill in Statement of Financial Position at end of first year	£1,530,000

6.6

Depreciation and interest

Payments made to the lessor are apportioned between the interest cost which is treated as an expense in the Income Statement and a reduction of the liability in the Statement of Financial Position. The asset is depreciated in the Income Statement and reduces the Statement of Financial Position asset value as though it was owned.

6.7

As a loss (not expense, see below).

6.8

As a gain (not revenue, see below).

Note re 6.7 and 6.8:

Revenue arises in the ordinary course of business (e.g. sales, fees, interest, dividends, royalties and rent). Gains represent other items such as income from the disposal of non-current assets or revaluations of investments.

Expenses arise in the ordinary course of business (e.g. salaries, advertising). Losses represent other items such as those resulting from disasters such as fire and flood and following the disposal of non-current assets or losses following from changes in foreign exchange rates.

6.9

Gross sales are $5,875,000. Sales tax is 17.5%, therefore net sales are $5,875,000/1.175 giving net sales in the Income Statement of $5,000,000.

6.10

Income statement

Depreciation	30,000
Advertising	5,000
Loss	− 35,000

Statement of Cash Flows

Loss	− 35,000
Depreciation added back	30,000
Cash flow from operations	− 5,000
Asset purchase	− 150,000
Cash flow from investing	− 150,000
Borrowing	200,000
Cash flow from financing	200,000
Change in cash	45,000

Statement of Financial Position

Non current assets	120,000
Current asset: Bank	45,000
Total assets	165,000
Non-current liability	− 200,000
Net assets	− 35,000
Equity (Loss)	− 35,000

Workings: this question can be answered by using the double entry format introduced in Chapter 3 and illustrated in Tables 6.7 and 6.8 of Chapter 6.

	Asset	Loan	Bank	Depreciation	Advertising
Loan		200,000	200,000		
Asset purchase	150,000		−150,000		
20% depreciation	−30,000			30,000	
Advertising			−5,000		−5,000
	120,000	200,000	45,000	30,000	5,000

Solutions for Chapter 7

7.1

	2010	2009
Return on (shareholders') investment (ROI)		
$\dfrac{\text{net profit after tax}}{\text{shareholder's funds}}$	$\dfrac{13.8}{131.5} = 10.5\%$	$\dfrac{16.3}{126.6} = 12.9\%$

Return on capital employed (ROCE)

$$\frac{\text{profit before interest and tax}}{\text{shareholders' funds + long-term debt}} \quad \frac{27.2}{131.5 + 96.7} = 11.9\% \qquad \frac{29.5}{126.6 + 146.1} = 10.8\%$$
$$= 228.2 \qquad\qquad = 272.7$$

Operating profit/sales

$$\frac{\text{profit before interest and tax}}{\text{sales}} \quad \frac{27.2}{141.1} = 19.3\% \qquad \frac{29.5}{138.4} = 21.3\%$$

Sales growth

$$\frac{\text{sales year 2 - sales year 1}}{\text{sales year 1}} \quad \frac{141.1 - 138.4}{138.4} = 2.7 \qquad = +1.95\%$$

Expense growth

$$\frac{\text{expenses year 2 - expenses year 1}}{\text{expenses year 1}} \quad \frac{113.9 - 108.9}{108.9} = 5 \qquad = +4.6\%$$

Gearing ratio

$$\frac{\text{long-term debt}}{\text{shareholders' funds + long-term debt}} \quad \frac{96.7}{131.5 + 96.7} = 42.3\% \qquad \frac{146.1}{126.6 + 146.1} = 53.5\%$$
$$= 228.2 \qquad\qquad = 272.7$$

Asset turnover

$$\frac{\text{sales}}{\text{total assets}} \quad \frac{141.1}{266.7 + 28.3} = 47.8\% \qquad \frac{138.4}{265.3 + 35} = 46.1\%$$
$$= 295 \qquad\qquad = 300.3$$

ROI has reduced but ROCE has increased. This is because shareholders' funds have increased but total assets have declined relative to the small change in profits. There has been a very small sales growth (less than 2%, but remember the effect of inflation) but expenses have increased by 4.6%. Consequently, operating profit has fallen, as has profit as a percentage of sales. The fall in profits and the increase in shareholders' funds and capital employed have resulted in the decline in ROI. Gearing has also fallen as a result of a large reduction in long-term debt. Asset turnover has improved marginally. The reduced total assets and lower gearing has resulted in a higher ROCE. Although two years is too short a period to draw any meaningful trends, we can say that Drayton needs to increase its sales and/or contain its expenses.

7.2

Conclusions include:

- Profit has declined on each of the measures.
- Liquidity: working capital has deteriorated and customers are taking longer to pay their accounts.

- Gearing: long-term debt has increased in proportion to shareholders' funds and there is less profit to pay a higher amount of interest.
- Assets are being used less efficiently to generate sales.

Overall, Jupiter's performance on all four criteria has been worse in the current year.

7.3

Receivables/average daily sales

$$\frac{200,000}{1,200,000/250} = \frac{200,000}{4,800} = 41.7 \text{ days' sales outstanding}$$

Inventory turnover
Cost of sales/inventory

$$\frac{450,000}{200,000} = 2.25 \text{ times p.a.}$$

or every 100 days (250/2.5).
Payables/average daily purchases

$$\frac{100,000}{450,000/250} = \frac{100,000}{1,800} = 55.5 \text{ days' purchases outstanding}$$

7.4

Sales (in €m)	2010	2009	2008	2007	2006
	155	144	132	130	120
Sales growth	$\frac{155-144}{144}$	$\frac{144-132}{132}$	$\frac{132-130}{130}$	$\frac{130-120}{120}$	
	7.6%	9.1%	1.5%	8.3%	

7.5

Overheads are €65 million. Sales are €155 million. The overhead/sales ratio is 65/155 or 41.9%.

Solution to case study question: Paramount Services plc

It is important to remember that ratio analysis is really only useful to identify trends and comparisons. Trends require more than two years' data, while comparisons require either budget data or industry/competitor results that can be used as a performance benchmark.

Nevertheless, although the two years' data is limited, some conclusions can be drawn from the ratios.

Sales growth is high (17.2%) but overhead growth is greater (26.9%), suggesting the need to control expenses. Consequently, profit growth (9.4%) has not been maintained at the same level as sales growth. Interest cost has increased due to higher long-term borrowings and consequently the interest cover has fallen, a slightly more risky situation for lenders.

All profitability measures (PBIT/Sales, ROCE and ROI) have fallen, as a result of the above-mentioned reasons. However, dividend payout has increased in total (and consequently per share for a constant number of shares) while the yield has increased, predominantly a result of the fall in the share price. For the same reason (a reduced share price) the price/earnings ratio has fallen.

Asset efficiency is constant at 1.2, although Paramount does appear to have a very high level of investment in non-current assets in relation to its income from services. Days' sales outstanding have increased significantly from 60 days to 76 days, a reflection of a credit control problem. Although payables have also increased, the working capital ratio has increased and is adequate at 1.7. Gearing has increased, but the level of long-term debt is quite low in comparison to the investment in non-current assets, an indication that a substantial part of the capital and reserves has been invested in non-current assets, possibly real estate.

Perhaps the major area of concern is whether the large non-current asset investment can be justified in terms of the business services that the company carries out.

Solution to case study question: General Machinery Ltd

After a decline, the company's profitability (ROI, ROCE, operating margin) has improved recently. However, the gross margin has dropped for five consecutive years, suggesting that selling prices are not being increased to pass on purchase (or production) cost increases. This deteriorating gross margin is a significant risk for the company as profits have only been increased by the large reduction in overhead as a percentage of sales in 2010. If gross margins continue to erode and if overheads as a percentage of sales cannot be continually cut, profits may be at serious risk. The company needs to continue to increase sales growth, fix its gross margins and continue to manage overheads.

One of the impacts on the depressed margins may be the company's inability to negotiate cost of sales reductions with suppliers due to the late payment of suppliers. Days' purchases outstanding (DPO) are 78, representing over 2.5 months. This is likely to give the company a poor credit rating and may impact its ability to maintain continuity of supply. Although the DPO has reduced over the five years, it is still taking too long to pay suppliers.

Working capital has been at extremely high levels but has fallen to close to 2:1, an improvement, but with an acid test greater than 1, is probably still too high. This is demonstrated by the relatively high days' sales outstanding (60- against 30-day terms), which even though it has improved is still too high. Inventory represents the biggest concern to working capital as at 3.3 it represents an average stockholding of 110 days (365/3.3). The company needs to manage its ordering to a just-in-time basis. Reduction of outstanding receivables and inventory would assist the company to pay its suppliers more quickly and potentially achieve savings in cost of sales, thereby improving the gross margin.

The Statement of Cash Flows shows that most cash has been used in 2010, hence working capital is strained by a lack of cash and slow receivables collections and inventory turnover. The Statement of Cash Flows reveals that net cash from operating activities, after deducting dividend payments, is very low. The major cash flow impacts are capital expenditure of €300,000 over the last three years and borrowings of €150,000. The balance of €150,000 has been funded from operating activities and has been the cause of the reduction in the closing bank balance to €20,000. This in turn has affected the working capital ratio (cash at bank is the only other item in working capital not measured by the three efficiency ratios for receivables, inventory and payables).

Asset turnover has steadily increased, a trend which needs to continue. It is likely that there is a time lag between the high capital expenditure in the most recent year so it might be expected that sales (and asset turnover) should increase in subsequent years.

The company has spent money on capital expenditure that has worsened its ability to pay suppliers more quickly. An alternative would have been to use the available cash to pay suppliers more quickly and to borrow the balance of €150,000. The question 'should the company have borrowed more?' is interesting because on the surface it needs to do so to replenish the bank balance. This is because it is less risky for non-current assets to be financed by non-current liabilities. However, further borrowings would be disguising poor credit control and inventory practices. It would be better for the company to fix its inventory problems and collect its debts on time, pay its overdue creditors and then look to see how much additional borrowing was required.

Gearing at 42% has increased slightly over five years but is at acceptable levels (anything in the range 40–60% being very common). However, interest cover has fallen significantly and is less than 2:1, with banks and financiers likely to consider this as risky in terms of the company's long-term ability to make interest payments. Hence any further borrowing would need to be offset by increases in profit to improve the interest cover.

Shareholder ratios are somewhat erratic with a lack of consistency in dividend per share likely to make some investors nervous. Dividend payout remains at about a 50% level, consistent with common practice, although it is noticeable that depressed profits seem to have led to a reduction in the dividend per share in 2008 and 2009 made worse by the dividend payment being a higher proportion of after-tax profits. The dividend yield is very low compared to risk-free government securities or bank interest rates. The P/E ratio of 16 (years) is an improvement and probably reflects market optimism about the company's future sustainable cash flows as a result of recent capital expenditure.

So the company faces three major issues it needs to address. (i) Fix the declining gross margin to maintain profitability. (ii) Fix the inventory and receivables problem to improve cash flow. (iii) Reduce its payables by paying its suppliers on time and try to use faster payments to negotiate lower cost of sales with suppliers. Profitability needs to be increased and if gross margins cannot be increased, there will be further pressure to reduce overheads, perhaps to unrealistic levels. Whether or not the company needs to borrow further will only be clear after the effects of these improvements are seen.

Solutions for Chapter 8

8.1

Answer c.

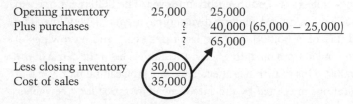

Opening inventory	25,000	25,000
Plus purchases	?	40,000 (65,000 − 25,000)
	?	65,000
Less closing inventory	30,000	
Cost of sales	35,000	

8.2

Answer b.

8.3

Answer c.

The lower of cost or net realizable value is the discounted selling price of £1,350 less transport cost of £100 = £1,250. The even lower scrap value of £1,100 − £100 = £1,000 is irrelevant as the higher net realizable value is £1,250.

8.4

a. Weighted average:

6,000 @ $2	$12,000
3,000 @ $2.20	6,600
2,000 @ $2.30	4,600
11,000	$23,200

$23,200/11,000 = $2.11

Cost of sales 8,000 @ $2.11	$16,873
Inventory 3,000 @ $2.11	$ 6,327
	$23,200

b. FIFO:

Purchased	Cost of sales	Inventory
6,000 @ $2	6000@ $2 = $12,000	0
3,000 @ $2.20	2000@$2.20 = $4,400	1,000@$2.20 = $2,200
2,000 @ $2.30	0	2,000@$2.30 = $4,600
Total	8000 = $16,400	3,000 = $6,800
	$23,200	

8.5

	Units
Opening WIP	20,000
Units commenced	60,000
	80,000
Closing WIP	15,000
Completed	65,000

Cost per unit:

	Opening WIP £	Cost for month £	Total £	Completed units	WIP Equivalent units	Total equivalent units	Cost per equivalent unit £
Material	62,000	192,000	254,000	65,000	15,000	80,000	£3.175
Conversion	25,000	85,150	110,150	65,000	4,500	69,500	£1.585
					15,000 @ 30%		
Total	£87,000	277,150	£364,150				£4.76

Work in progress:

Materials 15,000 @ £3.175	£47,625
Conversion 4,500 @ £1.585	£7,132
	£54,757

Finished goods:

65,000 units @ £4.76	£309,400
Total costs	£364,157 (difference due to rounding)

8.6

	Raw materials	Job A101 Qty: 40	Job B202 Qty: 60
Materials purchased:			
400 sqm timber @ £14.50 =	£5800		
80 l glue @ £6 =	480		
Materials issued:			
200 sqm timber @ £14.50			
150 @ £14.50	(5075)	2,900	2,175
20 l glue @ £6	(240)	120	120
Direct labour			
200 hours @ £30		6,000	
100 hours @ £30			3,000

Overhead		
200 DLH @ £25	5,000	
100 DLH @ £25		2,500
Total job cost	£14,020	**£7,795**
	Completed	**WIP**
	£14,020/40 =	**Inventory**
	£350.50 each	

Raw materials inventory	£965	
Transferred to finished goods		£14,020
Less 30 sold @ cost of £350.50		10,515
Finished goods inventory		**£3,505**
Sales		£15,000
Cost of sales		10,515
Gross profit		**£4,485**

8.7

Costs incurred to date	€850,000
Estimated costs to complete	€2,650,000
	€3,500,000
Estimated profit	500,000
Contract price	€4,000,000

Percentage completed is €850,000/€3,500,000 = 24.3%

24.3% of estimated profit of €500,000 = €121,500 (ignore any rounding differences).

8.8

Manufacturing statement

	$	$
Direct material:		
Raw material at beginning of period	100,000	
Purchases of raw materials	250,000	
Raw material available for use	350,000	
Less raw material at end of period	150,000	
Raw material usage in production		200,000
Direct labour		450,000
Manufacturing overhead:		
Factory rental	75,000	
Depreciation of plant & equipment	50,000	

Light & power	25,000	
Salaries & wages of factory labour	100,000	250,000
Total manufacturing costs		900,000
Add work in progress at beginning of period		300,000
		1,200,000
Less work in progress at end of period		400,000
Cost of goods manufactured		800,000

Cost of goods sold statement

Finished goods at beginning of period	150,000
Cost of goods manufactured	800,000
Goods available for sale	950,000
Less finished goods at end of period	250,000
Cost of goods sold	700,000

Income statement

Sales	900,000
Less cost of goods sold	700,000
Gross profit	200,000
Less selling and administrative expenses	75,000
Net profit	125,000

The inventory valuation in the Balance
Sheet totals $800,000 and comprises:

Inventory raw materials	150,000
Inventory work in progress	400,000
Inventory finished goods	250,000

Solutions for Chapter 10

10.1

See Table S10.1.

Table S10.1

Sales		1,100,000
Less cost of sales		
Opening inventory	150,000	
Purchases	650,000	
	800,000	
− Closing inventory	200,000	
Cost of sales		600,000
Gross profit		500,000
− Expenses		275,000
Operating profit		225,000

10.2

See Table S10.2.

Table S10.2

Units	Fixed	Variable @ €7	Total	Average
100,000	645,000	700,000	1,345,000	€13.45
150,000	645,000	1,050,000	1,695,000	€11.30
200,000	645,000	1,400,000	2,045,000	€10.22

10.3

Volume	Variable	Fixed	Total	Standard	Actual	Marginal
150,000	1,050	300	1,350	9.00		7.00
140,000	980	300	1,280		9.14	

The standard cost per unit is $9.00 at the budgeted level of activity.

The actual cost per unit is $9.14 – this is the actual average production cost per unit.

The marginal cost per unit is $7.00 – this is the variable cost per unit.

10.4

Volume	Variable	Fixed	Total	Avg cost/unit
10,000	70,000	100,000	170,000	£17
20,000	140,000	100,000	240,000	£12

The average cost reduces by £5 from £17 to £12. This is because the fixed costs of £100,000 are spread over 20,000 documents (£5 per document) rather than 10,000 documents (£10 per document).

The marginal cost is £7, i.e. the variable cost. It does not change per unit irrespective of volume within the relevant range.

The costs per unit at each activity level are:

	10,000	20,000
Variable costs	£7	£7
Fixed costs	£10	£5
Average cost	£17	£12

10.5

Current position:

	Eastern €	Western €	Total €
Sales	550,000	500,000	1,050,000
Variable costs	275,000	200,000	475,000
Divisional fixed costs	180,000	150,000	330,000
Contribution to corporate costs	95,000	150,000	245,000
Allocated corporate costs	170,000	135,000	305,000
Operating profit	(75,000)	15,000	(60,000)

After closure of Eastern division:

	Eastern €	Western €	Total €
Sales	–	500,000	1,050,000
Variable costs	–	200,000	200,000
Divisional fixed costs	–	150,000	150,000
Allocated corporate costs	–	305,000	305,000
Operating profit	–	(155,000)	(155,000)

The Eastern division should not be closed. It currently contributes €95,000 towards corporate costs. If the division were closed, the corporate costs would remain unchanged and the current loss of €60,000 would increase to €155,000.

10.6

	Last year		Current year
Sales price	80		
Variable cost	55		
Contribution margin	25	+20% (£5)	30
Units	5,000		5,000
Contribution	125,000		150,000
−Fixed costs	25,000	−10% (£2,500)	22,500
Operating profit	100,000		127,500

Contribution margin is £25 (£80 − £55) + 20% = increase of £5 × 5,000 units =   +£25,000
Fixed costs £25,000 Reduction of 10% =   +£2,500
Increase in profit is   £27,500

10.7

Variable costs are $750,000/300,000 batons = $2.50/baton.
  As the selling price is $5/baton, the normal contribution/baton = $2.50 ($5 − $2.50).

If 240,000 batons are sold at the normal price:

Contribution = 240,000 @ $2.50 $600,000
−Fixed costs   450,000
Operating profit $150,000

If 60,000 batons are sold at a 40% discount:
Sales = 60% of $5 = $3/baton, and contribution is 50p ($3 − variable costs $2.50)

Contribution = 60,000 @ 50p/baton $30,000
Total operating profit $180,000

10.8

Profit = selling price per unit × no. units − (VC/unit × no. units + fixed costs) therefore, £40,000 = SP × 20,000 − ((£8 × 20,000) + £100,000)

$$\text{Selling price} = \frac{£40,000 + £160,000 + £100,000}{20,000 \text{ units}}$$

$$= £300,000/20,000 \text{ units} = £15$$

10.9

Breakeven is:

$$\frac{(10,000 \times 35) + 450,000 + 0}{10,000} = \frac{800,000}{10,000} = 80$$

Or:

Profit = price × no. units − (fixed costs + variable costs × no. units)
0 = 10,000P − (450,000 + 35 × 10,000)
0 = 10,000P − (450,000 + 350,000)
0 = 10,000P − 800,000
800,000 = 10,000P
P = 800,000/10,000 = 80
Proof
10,000 × (80 − 35) = 10,000 × 45 = 450,000 − 450,000 = 0

10.10

Contribution per unit is $75 - 30 = 45$
Fixed costs are $1,000 \times 12 = 12,000$

$$\text{Breakeven} = \frac{12,000 + 10,000}{45} = 489 \text{ p.a.}$$

10.11

$$\frac{200,000 \times 12\%}{18,000 \text{ units}} = \frac{£24,000}{18,000} = £1.33 \text{ per unit}$$

10.12

Selling price		20
Direct materials	8	
Direct labour	5	13
Contribution margin		7

$$\text{Breakeven} = \frac{7,000 + 5,000}{7} = \frac{12,000}{7} = 1,714$$

10.13

See Table S10.13.

Table S10.13

Price	VC	Contribution p.u.	Quantity	Total contribution
26	15	11	1,075	11,825
27	15	12	1,000	12,000
28	15	13	925	12,025
29	15	14	850	11,900
30	15	15	775	11,625

The maximum contribution is at a selling price of £28. Note that this is not necessarily the highest sales revenue. The highest contribution will also be the highest profit because the same amount of fixed costs is deducted from each level of activity (within the relevant range).

10.14

Direct labour costs	25.00
Variable costs	4.00
Fixed costs $250,000/20,000	12.50
Target return (750,000*25%)/20,000	9.38
Price	50.88

10.15

See Table S10.15.

Table S10.15

Number of rooms sold	Price per room per night	Revenue	Variable costs @ £25	Contribution
120	90	10,800	3,000	£7,800
100	105	10,500	2,500	£8,000
80	135	10,800	2,000	£8,800
60	155	9,300	1,500	£7,800
50	175	8,750	1,250	£7,500

Contribution maximized at £135 (80 rooms). This is an occupancy rate of 67% (80/120).

Solutions for Chapter 11

11.1

Variable costs are £2 per unit (£10,000/5,000), for December 10,000 @ £2 = £20,000.

Fixed costs do not change with activity, for December £30,000.
As total costs are £75,000, semi-variable costs for December are £25,000 (£75,000 − £20,000 − £30,000).

11.2

	Product R	Product S
Selling price	12	20
Direct materials	4	11
Throughput contribution	€8	€9
Machine hours	4	3
Return per machine hour	€2	€3
Ranking	2	1

Product S generates more throughput contribution per machine hour (the limiting factor). Labour hours are irrelevant.

11.3

	Hours	Cost $
	15,000	345,000
	7,000	185,000
Increase	8,000	160,000

The increase in hours sold of 8,000 has generated a higher cost of $160,000. This cost must be a variable cost as, by definition, fixed costs do not vary with the volume of activity. Therefore variable costs are $160,000/8,000 or $20 per hour.

At the 15,000 level of activity, 15,000 @ $20 = $300,000. Therefore fixed costs are $45,000 ($345,000 − $300,000).

At the 7,000 level of activity, 7,000 @ $20 = $140,000. Therefore fixed costs are $45,000 ($185,000 − $140,000).

However, this only applies in the relevant range, as outside the relevant range the cost structure of fixed and variable costs may alter.

11.4

Direct materials	40 @ 2.50		100
Direct labour	7 @ £12	84	
	4 @ £7	28	112
	11		212
Variable overhead	11 @ £5 =		55
Variable production cost			267
Fixed production overhead			
£1,000,000/12,500			80
Total production cost			347

11.5

Production will be 8,000 units special order plus 12,000 units regular sales to give a maximum production capacity of 20,000 units.

Variable costs are €49 per unit (€588,000/12,000 units).

Fixed costs are €345,000 (€245, 000 + €100,000).

Sales 12,000 units at €100	€1,200,000
Sales 8,000 @ €95	760,000
Total	€1,960,000
Variable costs 20,000 @ €49	980,000
Contribution margin	980,000
Fixed costs	345,000
Operating profit	€635,000

11.6

As the material is in regular use and has to be replaced, it is irrelevant that some is already in stock as the relevant cost – the future, incremental cash flow (in this case the replacement cost) – is 150 kg @ $12.50, a total of $1,875. The scrap value is not relevant.

11.7

	Macro	Mezzo	Micro
Contribution per unit	£6	£9	£14
Machine hours	2	2	2
Contribution per hour	£3	£4.50	£7
Ranking	3	2	1

Therefore the ranking should be to maximize production of Micro, followed by Mezzo, and finally Macro.

11.8

	Cost to produce in-house	Outsourcing cost
	€	€
Raw materials	15,000	
Production labour	10,000	
Fixed manufacturing costs	7,000	3,000
Outsourcing cost	0	27,000
Total costs	32,000	30,000
Production units	4,000	4,000
Cost per Widget	€8	€7.50

On a purely financial basis Europa should outsource production, although there may be many non-financial reasons that compensate for the cost saving.

11.9

See Table S11.9.

Table S11.9

Sales		$850,000
Less cost of production		
Materials	450,000	
Labour	175,000	
Variable manufacturing expense	30,000	
Cost of production	655,000	
Opening inventory	120,000	
	775,000	
– Closing inventory	95,000	
Cost of sales		680,000
Contribution margin		170,000
– Fixed non-manufacturing expenses		65,000
– Selling and administrative expenses		40,000
Operating profit		$65,000

Solution to case study question: Swift Airlines

By separating the controllable and non-controllable costs for the route, which the route manager has not done, we can see the true position (Table S11cs).

Table S11cs   Swift Airlines.

	Outbound	Inbound	Total
Revenue	14,195	15,500	29,695
Costs per passenger	87 @ £25	120 @ £25	
	2,175	3,000	5,175
Costs per flight	7,500	7,500	15,000
Costs per route	2,000	2,000	4,000
Controllable costs	11,675	12,500	24,175
Contribution to head office overhead	2,520	3,000	5,520
Head office costs	3,000	3,000	6,000
Profit/–loss	–480	0	–480

Contrary to the route manager's belief, the loss is £480, not £1,305. This is because she did not take into account the per passenger variable cost of £25. This reduces the costs by £825 per flight ($120 - 87 = 33$ @ £25).

While the additional revenue of £600 would help, the route manager has also overlooked the additional per passenger variable cost of £25. Each passenger would therefore contribute £15 to profits (£40 − £25), a total of £225, although this is only half the loss.

It is important to identify the relevant costs. On a per passenger basis, the relevant cost is £25 as that is the only extra cost to cover the additional fuel, insurance, baggage handling etc. The relevant costs for the Nice destination are the flight costs of £7,500 (£15,000 for the outbound and inbound legs) and £4,000 for the costs that support each route. If the route were discontinued, Swift would save £11,500, particularly as it could reassign the aircraft and crew costs to another route. The £3,000 allocation of business overhead (£6,000 for the return flight) is not a relevant cost as this cost would not be saved, but would have to be reallocated to other routes.

Importantly, the route still makes a positive contribution to the recovery of head office overheads, which are allocated over each route. The route manager still needs to address the capacity utilization problem and the average price needed to generate a profit on each flight. The average price based on Swift Airlines' model is £175 (£21,000/120). The average price being achieved on the outbound route is £163.16 (£14,195/87). There is a likely trade-off between price and volume (of passengers).

The breakeven per flight can be calculated based on fixed costs of £12,500 (£7,500 + £2,000 + £3,000) and variable costs of £25 per passenger. A range of breakeven prices can be calculated.

The breakeven price for 120 passengers is:

$$\frac{12{,}500}{120(P-25)}$$
$$P = £129.17$$

The breakeven price for 100 passengers is:

$$\frac{12{,}500}{100(P-25)}$$
$$P = £150$$

Using Swift's business model average price of £175, the breakeven number of passengers is:

$$\frac{12{,}500}{(175-25)n}$$
$$n = 83.3 \text{ or } 84 \text{ passengers}$$

Using a range of volume/price scenarios, the route manager should be able to present a report to head office asking for additional time to reduce the losses, emphasizing the small size of the loss, the positive contribution to head office costs being made, and how flexibility in pricing and capacity utilization could overcome the current problem.

Solutions for Chapter 12

12.1

	£
Salary	40,000
National Insurance 11%	4,400
Pension 6%	2,400
Total employment cost	46,800
Working weeks per person	
52 − 4 − 2 = 46	
Cost per week 46,800/46	£1,017
Chargeable hours per week	25
Hourly rate (£1,017/25)	£40.68 or £41 to the nearest hour

12.2

	Volume	Cost
	1,200,000	€850,000
	1,000,000	€750,000
Increase	200,000	€100,000

Variable costs = €100,000/200,000 = €0.50

1,200,000 @ .50 = €600,000. Therefore fixed costs are €250,000 (€850,000 − €600,000)

12.3

Raw materials and variable costs are relevant costs as they are only incurred if manufacture takes place. Production labour is avoidable, i.e. it will only be incurred if Cardinal makes the part. As 60% of the fixed costs will continue regardless of the decision, only 40% of the fixed cost is relevant for the decision. Therefore, relevant costs of in-house manufacture:

Raw materials	$4
Production labour	16
Variable costs	8
Fixed costs (40% of $10)	4
Total	$32

$32 × 20,000 units = $640,000

Relevant costs of outsourcing to Oriole are:

Purchase cost $36 × 20,000 units = $720,000

Consequently, based on relevant costs, it is cheaper to manufacture the part in-house.

Note: the fixed manufacturing overhead of $10 per unit is an arithmetic calculation of total fixed costs divided by the number of units produced. This does *not* mean that the cost is a variable cost, just because it is expressed as a cost per unit.

12.4

The manufactured cost is £235 (120 + 60 + 30 + 25). The relevant costs are raw materials £120 and variable overhead £30, a total of £150. Production labour and fixed costs are not relevant. Production labour cannot be avoided as the business has spare capacity and wishes to retain its skilled employees. As the cost of purchasing the component is £140, on a relevant cost basis Cirrus should buy the component rather than make it.

12.5

Partners' cost	€200,000
Total hours 800 =	€250 per hour
Juniors' cost	€450,000
Total hours 5,000 =	€90 per hour

See Table S12.5.

Table S12.5

	Accounting	Audit	Tax	Total
Partner hours	150	250	400	800
@ €250	37,500	62,500	100,000	200,000
Junior hours	1200	2800	1000	5,000
@ €90	108,000	252,000	90,000	450,000
Total	€145,500	€314,500	€190,000	€650,000

Audit services cost €314,500.

12.6

The comparison of costs under each alternative is shown in Table S12.6a.

Table S12.6a

	Manufacture 100	Purchase 100
Production labour 100 @ $200	20,000	20,000
Raw material 100 @ $600	60,000	
Variable overhead 100 @ $100	10,000	
Fixed overheads 100 @ $300	30,000	30,000
Supplier price 100 @ $1,000	0	100,000
Total	$120,000	$150,000

Production labour and fixed overheads are irrelevant in making a choice between alternatives.Raw materials and variable overheads will not be incurred if the components are purchased, and are therefore relevant costs. Relevant costs are as in Table S12.6b.

Table S12.6b

	Manufacture 100	Purchase 100
Raw material	60,000	
Variable overhead	10,000	
Supplier price		100,000
Total	$70,000	$100,000

If employees were on a temporary contract, labour cost would be avoidable and therefore the comparison of costs would be as in Table S12.6c.

Table S12.6c

	Manufacture 100	Purchase 100
Production labour 100 @ $200	20,000	
Raw material 100 @ $600	60,000	
Variable overhead 100 @ $100	10,000	
Fixed overheads 100 @ $300	30,000	30,000
Supplier price 100 @ $1,000		100,000
Total	$120,000	$130,000

Fixed overheads are irrelevant in making a choice between alternatives. Production labour, raw materials and variable overheads will not be incurred if the components are purchased, and are therefore relevant costs.

Relevant costs are as in Table S12.6d.

Table S12.6d

	Manufacture 100	Purchase 100
Production labour	20,000	
Raw material	60,000	
Variable overhead	10,000	
Supplier price		100,000
Total	$90,000	$100,000

Costs based on stock valuation are not relevant as they are sunk costs, as we are concerned with future incremental cash flows only.

12.7

An alternative format for these figures is as in Table S12.7.

Table S12.7

	Franklin Industries	Engineering Partners	Zeta	Other customers	Total (average)
Sales	1,000,000	1,500,000	2,000,000	1,500,000	6,000,000
Cost of materials	250,000	600,000	750,000	750,000	2,350,000
Contribution	750,000	900,000	1,250,000	750,000	3,650,000
% contribution	75%	60%	62.5%	50%	(60.8%)
Cost of labour	300,000	200,000	300,000	75,000	875,000
Gross profit	450,000	700,000	950,000	675,000	2,775,000
% Gross profit	45%	46.7%	47.5%	45%	(46.25%)
No. of hours (labour/£100)	3,000	2,000	3,000	750	8,750
Contribution per labour hour	£250	£450	£417	£1,000	(£417)

This format shows that at 75% the contribution margin as a percentage of sales (i.e. after deducting material) is in fact highest for Franklin. However, calculating the contribution per labour hour (we can divide the cost of labour for each customer by the cost per labour hour of £100 to give the number of hours required) verifies the lower contribution by Franklin per unit of the limiting factor, i.e. labour capacity. This is reflected in the rate of gross profit being the lowest of the three main customers.

The issues that arise from these figures are:

1. Labour is in effect a fixed cost given the circumstances of the business and its allocation to different products is questionable, other than in terms of determining the most profitable utilization of the limited capacity.

2. Can the high labour cost for Franklin be reduced by automation given that Franklin contributes almost 17% of total sales (£1,000,000/£6,000,000) with the highest contribution margin of 75%?
3. While Engineering Partners and Zeta are the most profitable customers in the accountant's report, the revised format shows the highest contribution per labour hour from the 'other' customer segment. Zeta, which on the accountant's figures, appears more profitable than Engineering Partners, is using the revised format, less profitable per labour hour.
4. Do the corporate overheads, presently allocated arbitrarily in proportion to sales volume (overheads are 30% of sales), accurately reflect the different cost structure of each segment of the business in terms of space utilization (rent), capital investment in production processes (depreciation), non-production salaries, selling and administration expenses? A more meaningful allocation of costs may lead to a different decision as to the profitability of different business segments.

12.8

Total costs	Cost to make	Cost to buy
Materials	$1.25	
Labour	$0.70	
Variable overheads	$0.20	
Total variable cost	$2.15	
Cost for 100,000 eggs	$215,000	
Cost to buy from int'l company @ $2.50 per egg	_____	$250,000
Transport cost 100,000 @ $0.25		$25,000
Fixed costs	$150,000	$100,000
Total cost for each alternative	$365,000	$375,000

Relevant costs	Cost to make	Cost to buy
Variable production/purchase cost for 100,000 eggs	$215,000	$250,000
Plus transport		$25,000
Fixed costs	$50,000	
Relevant costs	$265,000	$275,000

Both approaches show that it is more cost effective by $10,000 to make in-house rather than to buy from the international company. The maximum price that could be paid by Seaford which would result in the same cost as currently incurred to produce in-house is $2.40 ($265,000 − $25,000 = $240,000/100,000).

Solution to case study question: Call Centre Services plc

The staffing level in the call centre provides a capacity of 60,000 calls (10 staff @ 6,000), but 70,000 calls have been taken. The telemarketing division has subsidized the operations of the call centre. In the short term, all costs in CCS are fixed costs. The standard cost of a call is €250,000/60,000 calls = €4.17. The standard cost for 70,000 calls is €291,900. It could therefore be argued that a more accurate presentation of the divisional performance is as in Table S12csa.

Table S12csa   Call Centre Services.

	Call centre	Telemarketing	Total
Number of calls	70,000	25,000	
Revenue	350,000	250,000	600,000
@ standard cost (€4.17)	291,900	148,100	440,000
Operating profit	€58,100	€101,900	€160,000

Note: telemarketing expenses have been calculated as total expenses (€440,000) less standard cost for 70,000 calls in the call centre (€291,900).

This shows quite a different picture. However, the telemarketing manager is likely to point out that his staff are paid considerably more than call centre staff (€22,000 compared to €15,000) and that the standard cost is based on a salary of €15,000.

The appropriate staffing for the call centre to handle 70,000 calls is 12 staff (70,000/6,000 = 11.7). Given the recruitment freeze, two of the telemarketing staff costs should be transferred to the call centre. Rental costs are adjusted accordingly. It is arguable as to whether the lease costs should be allocated 50/50, but in the absence of more information this is left unchanged. The revised profitability is as in Table S12csb.

Table S12csb   Call Centre Services.

	Call centre	Telemarketing	Total
Number of calls	70,000	25,000	
Fee per call	€5	€10	
Revenue	€350,000	€250,000	€600,000
Less expenses			
Staff costs			
10 @ €15,000 p.a.	150,000		
2 @ €22,000 p.a.	44,000		
3 @ €22,000 p.a.		66,000	260,000
Lease costs on telecoms and IT equipment (shared 50/50)	20,000	20,000	40,000
Rent (shared in proportion to staffing: 4/5, 2/5	96,000	24,000	120,000
Telephone call charges		20,000	20,000
Total expenses	310,000	130,000	440,000
Operating profit	€40,000	€120,000	€160,000

Whether based on standard costs or a reallocation of expenses between the divisions, the originally reported profit of €100,000 to the call centre and €60,000 to telemarketing is distorted. As the standard cost and reallocation calculations demonstrate, the call centre is making a much smaller profit and telemarketing a much larger profit than originally reported.

Solutions for Chapter 13

13.1

See Table S13.1.

Table S13.1

Division	1	2	3	Total
Overheads	50%	30%	20%	
	250,000	150,000	100,000	500,000
Hours	4,000	2,000	3,000	9,000
Hourly rate	$62.50	$75	$33.33	$55.55

13.2

	Machining	Assembly	Finishing	Total
Overhead costs	€120,000	€80,000	€30,000	€230,000
Labour hours	20,000	10,000	10,000	40,000
Hourly rate	€6	€8	€3	€5.75
Costing:				
Material			€300	
Labour			€150	
Overhead	10 @ €6	60		
	7 @ €8	56		
	3 @ €3	9	125	
Total			€575	

13.3

	Dept A	Dept B	Dept C	Total
Overheads	£150,000	£200,000	£125,000	£475,000
Direct labour hours	5,000	10,000	5,000	20,000
Overhead per hour	£30	£20	£25	£23.75
Hours for GH1	10	12	5	27
Overhead per product	£300	£240	£125	£641.25

Using plant-wide rate:	
Direct materials	£150
Direct labour	£75
Overhead	£641
Total	£866

Using cost centre rate:

Direct materials	£150
Direct labour	£75
Overhead (£300 + £240 + £125)	£665
Total	£890

13.4

Cost pool	Estimated cost	Product A	Expected activity Product B	Total	Rate $/activity
Activity 1	$20,000	100	400	500	40.00
Activity 2	$37,000	800	200	1,000	37.00
Activity 3	$91,200	800	3,000	3,800	24.00

Product A:

		Total	per unit (/8,000)
Activity 1:	$40.00 × 100	$4,000	$0.50
Activity 2:	$37.00 × 800	$29,600	$3.70
Activity 3:	$24.00 × 800	$19,200	$2.40
			$6.60

Product B:

		Total	per unit (/6,000)
Activity 1:	$40.00 × 400	$16,000	$2.67
Activity 2:	$37.00 × 200	$7,400	$1.23
Activity 3:	$24.00 × 3,000	$72,000	$12.00
			$15.90

13.5

a. Set-up costs €66,000

Production runs $12 + 5 + 8 = 25$
Cost per set-up €66,000/25 = €2,640
Product A has 12 runs @ €2,640 = €31,680
And 4,000 units are produced
Cost per set-up per unit is €31,680/4,000 = €7.92

b. Materials handling costs €45,000

Stores orders $12 + 6 + 4 = 22$
Cost per store order €45,000/22 = €2,045
Product B has 6 stores orders @ €2,045 = €12,270
And 3,000 units are produced
Cost per stores order per unit is €12,270/3,000 = €4.09

13.6

Purchasing cost	£120,000
No. purchase orders	240
Cost per purchase order	£500
L uses 80 @ £500	£40,000
For 20,000 units =	£2 per unit
M uses 160 @ £500	£80,000
For 20,000 units =	£4 per unit

If £120,000 of costs were recovered over the number of units produced (20,000 + 20,000 = 40,000), the purchasing cost per unit would be £3 (£120,000/40,000 units) for both L and M.

13.7

	Purchasing	Quality control	Dispatch
Total cost	$60,000	$40,000	$30,000
Driver	12,000	4,000	2,000
Cost/driver	$5	$10	$15
Hekla uses	5	8	2
Overhead	$25	$80	$30
Total overhead $25 + 80 + 30 =	$135		
Direct materials	$100		
Direct labour	$75		
Total cost	$310		

13.8

a.

Cost pool	Estimated cost	Expected activity X	Y	Total	Cost/activity
Activity 1	€12,000	300	500	800	12,000/800 = €15
Activity 2	€15,000	100	400	500	15,000/500 = €30
Activity 3	€32,000	400	1,200	1,600	32,000/1,600 = €20

X		Y	
	300 @ €15 = 4,500		500 @ €15 = 7,500
	100 @ €30 = 3,000		400 @ €30 = 12,000
	400 @ €20 = 8,000		1,200 @ €20 = 24,000
	Total €15,500		Total €43,500
	Units 3,000		2,000
	Overhead cost per unit €5.17		Overhead cost per unit €21.75

b.

	X	Y	
Units	3,000	2,000	
Machine hours	5	5	
Total machine hours	15,000	10,000	25,000

Hourly rate €59,000/25,000 =
€2.36 per hour

	X	Y
Overhead cost	5 @ €2.36	5 @ €2.36
Overhead cost per unit	€11.80	€11.80

13.9

Traditional absorption costing
Machining overheads:

Widgets	50,000 × 2 @ £1.20	120,000
Gadgets	40,000 × 5 × £1.20	240,000
Helios	30,000 × 4 @ £1.20	144,000

Assembly overheads:

Widgets	50,000 × 7 @ £0.825	288,750
Gadgets	40,000 × 3 × £0.825	99,000
Helios	30,000 × 2 @ £0.825	49,500

See Table S13.9a.

Table S13.9a

	Widgets	Gadgets	Helios
Sales volume	50,000	40,000	30,000
Selling price	45	95	73
Direct labour and materials	32	84	65
Contribution per unit	13	11	8
Total contribution	650,000	440,000	240,000
Less machining overheads	120,000	240,000	144,000
Less assembly overheads	288,750	99,000	49,500
Profit	£241,250	£101,000	£46,500

Total profit £388,750.

Activity-based costing
See Tables S13.9b and S13.9c.

Table S13.9b

	Machining	Assembly	Set-ups	Order processing	Purchasing
Cost pool	£357,000	£318,000	£26,000	£156,000	£84,000
Cost drivers	420,000	530,000	520	32,000	11,200
Rate	£0.85 Per machine hour	£0.60 Per direct labour hr	£50 Per set-up	£4.875 Per customer order	£7.50 Per supplier order

Table S13.9c

	Widgets	Gadgets	Helios
Sales volume	50,000	40,000	30,000
Total contribution	£650,000	£440,000	£240,000
Machining @ £0.85	85,000	170,000	102,000
Assembly @ £0.60	210,000	72,000	36,000
Set-up @ £50	6,000	10,000	10,000
Order processing @ £4.875	39,000	39,000	78,000
Purchasing @ £7.50	22,500	30,000	31,500
Profit/(loss)	£287,500	£119,000	£ (17,500)

Total £389,000.

The total overhead and therefore the total profit is the same under both methods of overhead allocation (the difference is due to rounding). Each method has simply allocated the total overheads in different ways. The activity-based approach charges overheads to products based on the activities that are carried out in producing each product. This demonstrates, for example, that the Helios is actually making a loss as its high overheads compared with its low volume are not being recovered in the selling price. Under traditional absorption costing, the Helios is being subsidized by the other two products.

13.10

See Table S13.10a.

Table S13.10a

	A	B	C	Total
No. units	150,000	200,000	350,000	
Selling price	$50	$35	$25	
Variable costs	$20	$17	$14	
Contribution per unit	$30	$18	$11	
Sales revenue	7,500,000	7,000,000	8,750,000	23,250,000
Variable costs	3,000,000	3,400,000	4,900,000	11,300,000
Contribution (total)	4,500,000	3,600,000	3,850,000	11,950,000
Fixed expenses				6,900,000
Operating profit				$5,050,000

Preferred services

Based on volume of production (Production Dept preference?):

C, B, A

Based on sales revenue (Sales Dept preference?):

C, A, B

Based on contribution per unit of volume

A, B, C

Based on total contribution (Accounting Dept preference?):

A, C, B

Strategy should be to shift sales mix as far as possible to Product A (highest contribution per unit).

Absorption of overhead

See Table S13.10b.

Table S13.10b

	A	B	C	Total
Absorption costs	7,500,000	7,000,000	8,750,000	23,250,000
based on sales value	32.2%	30.1%	37.7%	
Variable costs	3,000,000	3,400,000	4,900,000	11,300,000
Fixed expenses	2,221,800	2,076,900	2,601,300	6,900,000
Total costs	$5,221,800	$5,476,900	$7,501,300	$18,200,000
Cost per unit of volume	$34.81	$27.38	$21.43	
Absorption costs	150,000	200,000	350,000	700,000
based on volume	21.4%	28.6%	50%	
Variable costs	3,000,000	3,400,000	4,900,000	11,300,000
Fixed expenses	1,476,600	1,973,400	3,450,000	6,900,000
Total costs	$4,476,600	$5,373,400	$8,350,000	$18,200,000
Cost per unit of volume	$29.84	$26.87	$23.86	
Absorption costs based on equal allocation				
Variable costs	3,000,000	3,400,000	4,900,000	11,300,000
Fixed expenses	2,300,000	2,300,000	2,300,000	6,900,000
Total costs	5,300,000	5,700,000	7,200,000	18,200,000
Cost per unit of volume	$35.33	$28.50	$20.57	

While there is not much difference between using sales value and equal allocations for overhead, the volume method leads to lower costs for Products A and B and higher costs for Product C. The important point here is that different methods of overhead allocation (of the same value of overhead) can lead to different costs for products and services.

Breakeven

See Table S13.10c.

	A	B	C	Total
No. units	150,000	200,000	350,000	700,000
Sales revenue	7,500,000	7,000,000	8,750,000	23,250,000
Variable costs	3,000,000	3,400,000	4,900,000	11,300,000
Contribution (total)	4,500,000	3,600,000	3,850,000	11,950,000
Average contribution per unit of volume				$17.07

Fixed costs	$6,900,000	404,218 units of volume
Contribution per unit	$17.07	

Maintaining the same sales mix, the breakeven sales units of each product are:

86,619 of A
115,490 of B
202,109 of C

Solutions for Chapter 14

14.1

Formula for present value = +NPV (16%, C3:E3). The cash flows are entered in columns C (Year 1) to E (Year 3). See Table S14.1.

Table S14.1

Col A	Col B Year 0	Col C Year 1	Col D Year 2	Col E Year 3
Cash flows		10,000	10,000	10,000
Present value	22,459			
Initial investment	−18,000			
NPV	€4,459			

To calculate IRR using the spreadsheet function, a negative figure (the initial cash investment) must be part of the range of values.

Formula for IRR = +IRR (B3:E3).

	Year 0	Year 1	Year 2	Year 3
Cash flows	−18,000	10,000	10,000	10,000
IRR	31%			

14.2

See Table S14.2.

Table S14.2

	Year 0	Year 1	Year 2	Year 3
Cash flows		1,000	800	700
Present value	2,029			
Initial investment	−2,000			
NPV	£29			

14.3

Payback

Project A	2.5 years	$(100 + 200 + 1/2 \times 50)$
Project B	3 years	$(40 + 100 + 210)$
Project C	2 years	$(200 + 150)$

Accounting rate of return

	Total cash flow	Depreciation	Profit	Average profit	ARR
Project A	640	350	290	58	33.1%
Project B	770	350	420	84	48%
Project C	630	350	280	56	32%

Average investment $350,000/2 = \$175,000$

$$\text{ARR is } \frac{\text{average profit (profit/5 years)}}{\text{Average investment}}$$

NPV

See Table S14.3.

Table S14.3

	Year 0	Year 1	Year 2	Year 3	Year 4	Year 5
Project A						
Cash flows		100	200	100	100	140
Present value	499					
Initial investment	−350					
NPV	$149					

Table S14.3. Continued

	Year 0	Year 1	Year 2	Year 3	Year 4	Year 5
Project B						
Cash flows		40	100	210	260	160
Present value	571					
Initial investment	−350					
NPV	$221					
Project C						
Cash flows		200	150	240	40	0
Present value	523					
Initial investment	−350					
NPV	$173					
IRR						
Project A	24%					
Project B	26%					
Project C	33%					

The ranking is different depending on the technique:

On a payback basis, the ranking of projects (with preference to the quickest payback) is C, then A then B.

The accounting rate of return method favours B, then A then C.

The NPV method ranks B followed by C then A.

The IRR suggests that Project C has the highest return (as the cash flows are returned more quickly).

No absolute preference is clear, although Project A is slightly less attractive. As the accounting profits are likely to be important in terms of satisfying shareholders, this may be the optimum solution.

14.4

Project	1	2	3
NPV	1.7	1.1	1.0
Outlay	3.0	2.0	1.5
PI	.57	.55	.67
	57%	55%	67%
Ranking	2	3	1
Select	All	Part	All
Ranking 1:	Project 3 requires	£1.5 million	
Ranking 2:	Project 1 requires	£3 million	
Ranking 3:	Project 2	£0.5 million available	
		(25% of project)	
Total investment		£5 million	

14.5

Payback period

End of year 4, i.e. €200,000.

ARR

Year	1	2	3	4	5
Investment	200	160	120	80	40
Cash flows	45	50	55	50	35
− Depreciation 20%	40	40	40	40	40
Profit	5	10	15	10	−5
ARR	2.5%	6.25%	12.5%	12.5%	−12.5%

Over the 5 years:

Profit €35,000/5 000 = €7,000 Investment €200,000/2 = €100,000

ARR 7,000/100,000 = 7%

NPV

	Inflow	Outflow	Net	Factor	PV
Year 1	75,000	30,000	45,000	.9091	40,910
Year 2	90,000	40,000	50,000	.8264	41,320
Year 3	100,000	45,000	55,000	.7513	41,321
Year 4	100,000	50,000	50,000	.6830	34,150
Year 5	75,000	40,000	35,000	.6209	21,731
PV of cash flows					179,432
Cash outflow					−200,000
NPV					−20,568

Although the project has a payback of four years and an ARR of 7%, it should not be accepted as the NPV is negative, i.e. the cash flows do not cover the cost of capital.

14.6

The average accounting rate of return is an average of 41.8%, although the annual ARR increases from 16.5% to 82.3% as a result of the reducing asset value after depreciation. This is a very high ARR.

The payback of about 3.5 years suggests some risk, in that market or technology changes could impact on the company's ability to generate the forecast profits and cash flow. A shorter payback period would usually be preferred.

The NPV is positive, but the small amount of $12,610 represents a cash value added of only 1.68% of the initial investment. The ARR is only 0.7% above the cost of capital. While these DCF techniques do support a positive return, the return is very small and even a small reduction or delay in forecast profits and cash flows would likely result in a longer payback period and a negative NPV.

Despite the high ARR, the payback and DCF techniques suggest that while this is potentially a positive investment for shareholders, it is a marginal one at best, given the risks associated with the profit and cash flow projections.

The very high ARR should be challenged by the board. The questions that should be asked of the management team include: What are the assumptions behind the additional sales revenue that has been forecast and the relatively low additional costs? Are these figures realistic? Do they take into account the impact of competition? Does the asset have a life of five years, and if so, how much risk is associated with the profit and cash flow projections in years 3–5?

In addition, the board would be advised to set hurdle rates for each of the ARR, payback period and IRR. The board should also validate the 12% cost of capital as being correct and reflecting the risks involved.

On balance therefore, until such time as the management team is able to answer these questions satisfactorily, and in the absence of any known hurdle rates, it is recommended that the proposal be rejected given the low return based on DCF measures, and the fairly long payback period, despite the high ARR.

Note for students: while your actual answer may vary from the above (it is not incorrect to support the project), it is important that reasons are given to support the recommendation. In giving reasons, you must be critical of the figures presented, and not accept them on face value.

Solutions for Chapter 15

15.1

	Original	Additional	New
Investment (in	£10,000,000	£2,000,000	£12,000,000
ROI	15%	14%	14.8%
Profit	£1,500,000	£280,000	£1,780,000
Cost of capital 12%	1,200,000	240,000	1,440,000
RI	£300,000	£40,000	£340,000

15.2

	Original	Additional	New
Investment	€10,000,000	€2,000,000	€12,000,000
ROI	15%	14% (280/2000)	14.8% (1,780/12,000)
Profit	€1,500,000	€280,000	€1,780,000
Cost of capital 9%	900,000	180,000	1,080,000
RI	€600,000	€100,000	€700,000

15.3

	Current	Additional	After
Controllable investment	$750,000	$100,000	$850,000
Profit	$150,000	$15,000	$165,000
ROI	20%	15%	19.4%

Green may not want to accept the investment as it decreases the divisional ROI, but for Brummy Co. the project is better than the cost of capital (15% compared to 12%) and will increase shareholder value.

	Current	Additional	After
Controllable investment	750,000	100,000	850,000
Profit	150,000	15,000	165,000
Cost of capital 12%	90,000	12,000	102,000
RI	$60,000	$3,000	$63,000

Using residual income, both Green and Brummy Co. see an increase and will support the investment.

15.4

Compax

Figures in £m	1	2	3	4	Total
Cash flow	2.4	2.4	2.4	2.4	9.6
Depreciation	1.6	1.6	1.6	1.6	
Profit	0.8	0.8	0.8	0.8	3.2
Asset value					
Opening	6.4	4.8	3.2	1.6	
Closing	4.8	3.2	1.6	0	
Cost of capital 16% of opening asset value	1.02	.77	.51	.26	
RI	−.22	0.03	0.29	0.54	0.64
ARR	12.5%	16.67%	25%	50%	

Average ARR

Average profit 3.2/4 = 0.8
Average investment = 6.4/2 = 3.2
Average ARR = 0.8/3.2 = 25%

Newpax

Figures in £m	1	2	3	4	Total
Cash flow	2.6	2.2	1.5	1.0	7.3
Depreciation	1.3	1.3	1.3	1.3	
Profit	1.3	0.9	0.2	-0.3	2.1
Asset value					
Opening	5.2	3.9	2.6	1.3	
Closing	3.9	2.6	1.3	0	

Cost of capital 16% of opening asset value	0.83	.62	.42	.21	
RI	.47	.28	−.22	−.51	.02
ARR	25%	23%	7.7%	−23%	

Average ARR

Average profit 2.1/4 = 0.525
Average investment = 5.2/2 = 2.6
Average ARR = 0.525/2.6 = 20.2%

The NPV calculations show that Compax has a higher NPV at £315,634, giving a cash value added of 4.9% (315,634/6,400,000). Newpax has an NPV of £189,615 and a cash value added of 3.6% (189,615/5,200,000).

Overall, Compax has a higher ROI (the ARR calculation above is the same as the ROI), a higher RI and a higher cash value added based on the NPV. This is the preferred investment. However, it is important to realize that the returns for Compax are in the third and fourth years. Newpax looks more appealing in the first two years, when both its ARR/ROI and RI are higher. This may make Newpax more attractive from a divisional perspective or if Anston has a short-term focus.

15.5

See Table S15.5.

Table S15.5

	Division A €	Division B €	Division C €
Original investment	1,000,000	1,500,000	2,000,000
Original net profit	75,000	90,000	150,000
Original ARR	7.5%	6.0%	7.5%
Cost of capital 7%	70,000	105,000	140,000
Original RI	€5,000	€−15,000	€10,000
Additional investment	500,000	500,000	500,000
Additional profit	40,000	40,000	40,000
Additional ARR	8.0%	8.0%	8.0%
Cost of capital at 7%	35,000	35,000	35,000
Additional RI	€5,000	€5,000	€5,000
New investment	1,500,000	2,000,000	2,500,000
New profit	115,000	130,000	190,000
New ARR	7.7%	6.5%	7.6%
New cost of capital	105,000	140,000	175,000
New RI	€10,000	€−10,000	€15,000

Before the new investment, Divisions A and C have the highest ROI and Division C has the highest residual income. The additional investment achieves the same ROI and RI for each division. After the new investment, Division A has the highest ROI and Division C the highest RI. Division B has a negative RI before and after the new investment because the current ROI of 6% is less than the cost of capital of 7%. The additional investment improves that position, but Division B still erodes shareholder value.

Solution to case study: Serendipity PLC

The first comment to be made is in relation to the accuracy of the expected additional cash inflows and outflows, which are notoriously difficult to assess. The proposer of the capital investment will need to have some information to support the revenue growth projections and expected cost increases.

The ROI calculations are important, although as is common with 'cap ex' proposals, the higher ROIs are achieved in later years. A fuller picture may be seen by looking at the average ROI over the life of the investment. Average profits are $560,000 (total profits/5) and average investment is $2.5 million ($5 million/2). The average ROI is therefore 22.4% (560/2,500).

Given a cost of capital of 8% used in the NPV calculation (which needs to be verified as the weighted average cost of capital for Serendipity), a residual income approach may also present a fuller picture (Table S15csa).

Table S15csa   Serendipity.

Year		1	2	3	4	5
Residual income						
Profit after tax		245	455	700	700	700
Cost of capital on asset value	8%					
Cost of capital on asset value		320	240	160	80	0
Residual income		−75	215	540	620	700

The total RI over the project is $2 million.

The NPV produces a positive $1.225 million at a cost of capital of 8%. Again, to present a fuller picture, an internal rate of return calculation shows the discount rate that equates to a nil NPV. The IRR is 16.8%, which is double the cost of capital, a more meaningful figure than the NPV residual value.

Finally, a payback calculation shows that on a cash flow basis the investment is paid back after three years and two months (Table S15csb).

Table S15csb Serendipity.

Year	0	1	2	3	4	5	6
Payback							
Net cash flow	−5,000	1,350	1,545	1,805	1,700	1,700	−300
Cumulative	−5,000	−3,650	−2,105	−300	1,400	3,100	2,800

Payback is 3 years and 2.1 months $(300/1{,}700 = 176 \times 12 = 2.1 \text{ months})$

Provided that payback, ROI, RI, NPV and IRR meet any board criteria, the investment proposal appears to be sound, but inclusion of the additional information should assist in obtaining board approval.

Solutions for Chapter 16

16.1

Cash received (in £'000)		Jan	Feb	Mar	later	never
Sales made in Jan	100	30	60	8	–	2.0
Sales made in Feb	120		36	72	9.6	2.4
Sales made in Mar	110			33	74.8	2.2
	330	30	96	113	84.4	6.6

Cash received in March £113,000
Receivables at end of March $84.4 + 6.6 = £91{,}000$

16.2
Profit

See Table S16.2a.

Table S16.2a

	July	August	September	Total
Sales	20,000	30,000	40,000	90,000
Purchases	8,000	15,000	20,000	43,000
Gross profit	12,000	15,000	20,000	47,000
Wages	3,000	4,000	5,000	12,000
Other expenses	2,000	2,000	3,000	7,000
Depreciation	200	200	200	600
Operating profit	€6,800	€8,800	€11,800	€27,400

Note: Depreciation is €2,400 p.a. or €200 per month.

Cash

See Table S16.2b.

	July	August	September	Total
Receipts		20,000	30,000	50,000
Payments to creditors	−5,000	−10,000	−20,000	−35,000
Wages	−3,000	−4,000	−5,000	−12,000
Other expenses	−2,000	−2,000	−3,000	−7,000
Net cash flow	−10,000	4,000	2,000	−4,000
Opening balance	12,500	2,500	6,500	12,500
Closing bank balance	€2,500	€6,500	€8,500	€8,500

Note: Depreciation does not involve any cash flow. The opening bank balance is the capital of €20,000 less the equipment purchased of €7,500.

Statement of Financial Position

Non current assets	7,500	
Less depreciation	600	6,900
Current assets:		
Receivables		40,000
Bank		8,500
		48,500
Total assets		55,400
Liabilities:		
Payables		8,000
Net assets		47,400
Equity:		
Share capital		20,000
Retained earnings		27,400
		€47,400

Note: Receivables €90,000 − 50,000 = €40,000
Payables €43,000 − 35,000 = €-8,000

16.3

See Table S16.3.

Table S16.3

Budget (in $'000)	Apr	May	Jun	Jul	Aug	Sep	Oct	Nov	Dec	Jan	Feb	Mar	Total
Revenue	225	225	225	225	225	225	150	150	150	150	150	150	2,250
Variable operating costs	68	68	68	68	68	68	45	45	45	45	45	45	675
Fixed operating costs	35	35	35	35	35	35	40	40	40	40	40	40	450
Total operating costs	103	103	103	103	103	103	85	85	85	85	85	85	1,125
Gross profit	123	123	123	123	123	123	65	65	65	65	65	65	1,125
Overheads:													
Sales charge	15	15	15	15	15	15	12	12	12	12	12	12	162
Salaries	25	25	25	25	25	25	25	25	25	25	25	25	300
Depreciation	5	5	5	5	5	5	5	5	5	5	5	5	60
Council rates	8	8	8	8	8	8	8	8	8	8	8	8	96
Heat, light and power	3	3	3	3	3	3	2	2	2	2	2	2	30
Total overheads	56	56	56	56	56	56	52	52	52	52	52	52	648
Operating profit	$67	$67	$67	$67	$67	$67	$13	$13	$13	$13	$13	$13	$477

The gross profit is 55% in the first half year and 43% in the second half year, because an increased fixed cost is spread over a lower volume of sales.

16.4

See Table S16.4.

Table S16.4

Budget	Qtr 1	Qtr 2	Qtr 3	Qtr 4	Total
Volume (tonne)	100,000	110,000	105,000	120,000	
Selling price (per tonne)	300	300	310	310	
Variable costs (per tonne)	120	125	125	130	
Budget in £'000					
Sales and production	30,000	33,000	32,550	37,200	132,750
Variable costs (raw materials)	12,000	13,750	13,125	15,600	54,475
Contribution	18,000	19,250	19,425	21,600	78,275
Fixed costs:					
Salaries and wages	3,000	3,000	3,300	3,300	12,600
Maintenance	1,500	1,500	1,500	1,500	6,000
Council rates	400	400	400	400	1,600
Insurance	120	120	120	120	480
Electricity	1,000	1,000	1,000	1,000	4,000

Table S16.4. Continued

Budget	Qtr 1	Qtr 2	Qtr 3	Qtr 4	Total
Depreciation	5,400	5,400	5,400	5,400	21,600
Other costs	2,500	1,800	1,800	2,500	8,600
Total fixed costs	13,920	13,220	13,520	14,220	54,880
Operating profit	4,080	6,030	5,905	7,380	23,395
Interest expense	600	600	600	600	2,400
Profit after interest	3,480	5,430	5,305	6,780	20,995
Cash forecast					
Profit after interest	3,480	5,430	5,305	6,780	20,995
Add back depreciation	5,400	5,400	5,400	5,400	21,600
	8,880	10,830	10,705	12,180	42,595
Less capital expenditure	6,500	2,000	1,000	9,000	18,500
Less dividend			10,000		10,000
Less debt repayments	1,000	5,000	4,000	3,000	13,000
Net cash flow	1,380	3,830	−4,295	180	1,095
Cumulative cash flow	1,380	5,210	915	1,095	

16.5

The known information is:

	Current year € mill	Next year € mill
Sales	586	+ 35% = 791
Cost of sales	486	
Gross profit	17% 100	
Overheads	−19	−22
Operating profit	13.8% 81	15% 119

Therefore, gross profit can be calculated as 141 or 17.8% of sales.

Sales	586	+ 35% = 791
Cost of sales	486	(791 - 41) = 650
Gross profit	17% 100	17.8% (119 + 22) = 141
Overheads	−19	−22
Operating profit	13.8% 81	15% 119

The company plans to increase sales substantially and improve margins through better purchasing and/or higher prices, and will incur significant costs in store openings, warehousing and IT systems while maintaining only a 15% increase in corporate overheads.

A detailed budget projection would need to support these broad figures. The budget should identify, as a minimum:

- The sales mix by whatever categories are relevant (products, geographic sales, type of customer etc.).
- The margins on different categories of sales.
- The cost of materials, retail store salaries and property costs that are deducted to arrive at gross profit.
- The warehousing and distribution costs.
- Central overhead costs.

In terms of marketing, there are three distinct market strategies in existence:

- Increasing sales to existing customers through social marketing.
- Winning market share through television advertising.
- Increasing sales in new geographic areas through opening new stores.

The information needed to support these strategies is the expected contribution from each strategy, drawing from past experience. Questions to be asked include:

- How effective is social marketing likely to be, given this is a relatively new domain?
- What is the cost of TV advertising and what additional sales and margins does it contribute?
- What is the cost of new store openings and what is the impact on capital expenditure (and therefore on cash flow) and the effect on running costs (especially salaries and property costs, including non-cash depreciation)?

The cost effectiveness of operations may improve by investing in warehousing and distribution facilities and IT systems, but the cost/benefit of this needs to be demonstrated. Questions include:

- What is the current level of inventory and delivery lead time and how much is this expected to improve through new warehousing and IT systems?
- How does this saving compare with the additional capital expenditure?
- What is the impact of additional capital expenditure on operating costs?

This information needs to be modelled to determine whether the strategies will in fact lead to the desired profit target. The impact on capital expenditure, cash flow and financing also has to be determined.

Non-financial issues include whether the existing staff in stores, distribution and head office will be able to cope with the extra volume of business that is expected while retaining at least current standards of customer satisfaction, delivery lead time and product quality.

16.6

Table S16.6a   Income Statement.

	June	July	August	September	3 mth total
Forecast sales units	20,000	20,000	22,000	25,000	
Selling price per unit	$4.25	$4.50	$4.50	$4.75	
Forecast revenue	$85,000	$90,000	$99,000	$118,750	$307,750
Cost of sales 30%	$25,500	$27,000	$29,700	$35,625	$92,325
Gross profit	$59,500	$63,000	$69,300	$83,125	
Overheads	$30,000	$30,000	$30,000	$30,000	
Depreciation	$25,000	$25,000	$25,000	$25,000	
Operating profit	$4,500	$8,000	$14,300	$28,125	

Table S16.6b   Cash forecast.

	June	July	August	September	3 mth total
Receipts - 30 day terms		$85,000	$90,000	$99,000	$274,000
Payables - 30 days terms		−$25,500	−$27,000	−$29,700	$82,200
Overheads - current month	−$30,000	−$30,000	−$30,000	−$30,000	
Operating cash flow		$29,500	$33,000	$39,300	

Table S16.6b provides a sufficient answer, but it can also be shown in the format of a Statement of Cash Flows, as shown in Table S16.6c.

Table S16.6c   Cash forecast (detailed version).

	June	July	August	September	3 mth total
Operating profit		$8,000	$14,300	$28,125	
Add Depreciation		$25,000	$25,000	$25,000	
		$33,000	$39,300	$53,125	
Change in working capital					
Increase in receivables		−$5,000	−$9,000	−$19,750	$33,750
Decrease in payables		$1,500	$2,700	$5,925	$10,125
Operating cash flow		$29,500	$33,000	$39,300	

Note in Table S16.6c that the increase in receivables is calculated by subtracting the receipts from sales from the forecast revenue in the Income Statement. The decrease in payables is calculated by subtracting the payments to suppliers from the cost of sales.

Case study solution: Carsons Stores Ltd

The first set of questions to be asked is how the level of sales was arrived at. In particular, have the sales been analysed by department/product? Have managers been consulted to see if the budget sales figures are achievable? Is the seasonal increase over the four quarters consistent with past trends, consumer spending patterns and market share? Does it reflect changing prices and competitive trends?

The second set of questions is in relation to the rate of gross profit ($264/440 = 60\%$). In particular, is this broken down by product or supplier? Is the cost of sales consistent with previous trading? Does it reflect current negotiations with suppliers? Does it reflect changing prices?

The third set of questions is in relation to expenses. Is the salary budget consistent with the headcount and approved salary levels for each grade of staff? Has an allowance for across-the-board (i.e. inflation-adjusted) salaries been built in? Have all the oncosts been included? Is the rental figure consistent with the property lease? How has depreciation been calculated (e.g. what is the asset value and expected life)? Promotional expenses appear to be 10% of sales – is this consistent with past experience and/or with marketing strategy? Are administration expenses consistent with past experience and any changes that have been introduced in the administration department?

The fourth set of questions is in relation to the cash flow. Are all sales for cash (because there is no assumption about delayed receipts for sales on credit)? Cost of sales appear to be on 30-day terms, but there is no payment showing for Quarter 1 – the payments for purchases made in Quarter 4 of the previous year have not been included. It also appears from the pattern of payments for purchases that there is no increase or decrease in inventory – is this correct given the trend of increasing sales over the year? All expenses have been treated as cash expenses, i.e. no allowance has been made for payment to suppliers for credit purchases – is this correct? The inclusion of depreciation expense in the cash flow is incorrect. Have the assumptions as to the timing and amount of capital expenditure, income tax and dividends been checked with the appropriate departments?

An adjusted cash forecast, taking into account the missing purchases figure (assume £40,000) and removing depreciation as a cash outflow, is shown in Table S16cs.

Table S16cs   Carsons Stores.

In £'000	Quarter 1	Quarter 2	Quarter 3	Quarter 4	Year total
Cash receipts from sales	100	110	110	120	440
Purchases	40	40	44	44	168
Expenses	45	46	46	47	184
Capital expenditure		20			20
Income tax			20		20
Dividends		15	20	25	60
Cash outflow	85	121	130	116	452
Net cash flow	15	−11	−20	4	−12
Cumulative cash flow	15	4	−16	−12	

The previous cash flow of £8,000 has been increased by the non-cash depreciation expense of £20,000 and reduced by the omission of the estimated Quarter 1 purchases of £40,000. This results in a negative cash flow of £12,000. Importantly, this raises the question as to whether Carsons has an adequate overdraft facility to cover the negative cash flows in the third and fourth quarters. Due to the errors, this was not disclosed by the trainee accountant's cash forecast.

Note: there are many possible answers to this case study. The indicative answer provided above is intended to demonstrate the wide-ranging questions that need to be asked in relation to any budget projections and the assumptions behind budget figures.

Solutions for Chapter 17

17.1

	Budget	Flex	Actual
Units	2,000	1,800	1,800
@	$3	$3	$3.20
Cost	$6,000	$5,400	$5,760
Variance			$360 − adverse

17.2

(Standard price − actual price) × quantity purchased
(€3.10 − €3.05) × 5200 = €260 favourable

17.3

a. See Table S17.3a.

Table S17.3a

	Budget	**Actual**
Sales units	10,000	11,000
Price per unit	£37.10	£36
Sales revenue	£371,000	£396,000
Direct materials		
Magna − per unit	40,000 kg @ £1.50/kg	46,500 kg @ £1.45
− total	60,000	67,425
Carta − per unit	10,000 kg @ £5/kg	11,500 @ £5.10
− total	50,000	58,650
Labour − per unit	25,000 hours @ £7	26,400 hrs @ £7.10
− total	175,000	187,440
Total direct costs	285,000	313,515

Table S17.3a. Continued

	Budget	Actual
Contribution margin	86,000	82,485
Fixed costs	75,000	68,000
Profit	£11,000	£14,485

Note: an additional column could be included showing the variance between budget and actual.

b. See Table S17.3b.

Table S17.3b

	Budget	Flexible budget	Actual
Sales units	10,000	11,000	11,000
Price per unit	£37.10	£37.10	£36
Sales revenue	371,000	408,100	396,000
Direct materials			
Magna – per unit	60,000	11,000 × 4 = 44,000	67,425
– total		@ £1.50 = 66,000	
Carta – per unit	50,000	11,000 × 1 = 11,000	58,650
– total		@ £5 = 55,000	
Labour – per unit	175,000	11,000 × 2.5 = 27,500	187,440
– total		@ £7 = 192,500	
Total direct costs	285,000	313,500	313,515
Contribution margin	86,000	94,600	82,485
Fixed costs	75,000	75,000	68,000
Profit	11,000	19,600	14,485

Note: an additional column could be included showing the variance between the flexed budget and actual.

c. See Table S17.3c.

Table S17.3c

Cost variances:	Standard Quantity × Standard Price	Actual Quantity × Standard Price	Actual Quantity × Actual Price
Magna	11,000 × 4 = 44,000 kg @ £1.50 66,000	46,500 kg @ £1.50 69,750	46,500 kg @ £1.45 67,425
Variances	*Quantity 3,750 A*		*Price 2,325 F*
Carta	11,000 × 1 = 11,000 kg @ £5 55,000	11,500 @ £5 57,500	11,500 @ £5.10 58,650
Variances	*Quantity 2,500 A*		*Price 1,150 A*
Labour	11,000 × 2.5 = 27,500 hrs @ £7 192,500	26,400 @ £7 184,800	26,400 @ £7.10 187,440
Variances	*Quantity 7,700 F*		*Price 2,640 A*
Fixed costs	75,000	75,000	68,000
Variance			*7,000 F*

Sales price variance

(Actual price – standard price) × actual quantity
(£36 – £37.10) × 11,000   12,100 Adverse

Sales quantity variance

(Budget quantity – actual quantity) × standard margin
(10,000 – 11,000) × £8.60   8,600 Favourable
(Standard margin: selling price £37.10 – variable costs £28.50)

d.

Budget		11,000
Variances		
Sales price	12,100 A	
Sales quantity	8,600 F	
Magna price	2,325 F	
Magna quantity	3,750 A	
Carta price	1,150 A	
Carta quantity	2,500 A	
Labour price	2,640 A	
Labour quantity	7,700 F	
Fixed costs	7,000 F	
	3,485 F	
Actual	£14,485	

17.4

a. See Table S17.4a.

Table S17.4a

	Budget	Actual	Budget-Act Variance
Analysis of labour			
Number of hours	10,000	9000	
Average rate per hour	$75	$80	
Value of labour	$750,000	$720,000	$30,000

b. See Table S17.4b.

Table S17.4b

	Budget	Flex budget	Actual	Flex-Actual Variance
Analysis of labour				
Number of hours	10,000	9000	9000	
Average rate per hour	$75	$75	$80	
Value of labour	$750,000	$675,000	$720,000	−$45,000

c. In the traditional budget report, the variance cannot be interpreted properly because we are comparing the value of labour when the number of hours in the budget and actual data is not the same. The variance using the flexed budget equates the actual number of hours and compares the cost difference based on the same number of units. In this second example we can see that the variance is more sensible at $45,000, being 9,000 hours @ $5 ($80 − $75). This overspending on the average rate per hour cannot be determined from the traditional budget report.

Case study solution: White Cold Equipment plc

While the flexible budget provides a better tool for evaluating manufacturing performance, the business cannot ignore the difference between the budgeted level of sales (1,050 units) and the actual level of sales (1,000 units). The loss of margin is shown in Table S17csa.

Table S17csa   White Cold Equipment.

Loss of gross margin	
Shortfall no. of units	50
Gross margin per unit	£230
Loss of gross margin	£11,500

The full variance reconciliation is as in Table S17csb. This comes back to the variance in the original actual versus budget report for the month.

Table S17csb   White Cold Equipment.

Total adverse manufacturing expense variance	−3,550
Favourable selling and admin variance	6,500
Variance based on actual production volume	2,950
Loss of margin on units not produced	−11,500
Total variance	£−8,550

In explaining the variances, it must be remembered that WCE can sell all its output and that it has failed to produce (and therefore sell) 50 units. This may be the result of a productivity or a quality problem.

Although 9% fewer materials have been used (90/1,000), this has been at an additional 8% cost (£20/£250). The overall favourable materials variance may be a result of less wastage or a greater productivity of materials used in the manufacture of the final product. However, the adverse labour and overhead variances cannot be ignored.

Labour cost 3.3% less (£5/£150), which may be the result of lower paid employees or less overtime. However, 5% more labour units than expected have been used (50/1,000). This may be linked to the lower materials usage, which may have caused quality problems. The overhead rate is 2.85% higher (£2/£70) and, as usage follows labour usage, this is also 5% higher (50/1,000).

Consequently, if the change in materials has caused excess labour to be worked, then the favourable materials variance of £4,300 may be more than offset by the adverse labour usage (£7,500) and adverse overhead usage (£3,500), resulting in an overall adverse variance of £6,700. This is offset by the favourable rate variance on labour (£5,250) less the adverse rate variance on overhead (£2,100). The danger is that the adverse usage variances persist while the rate variances are eliminated. These issues are particularly important if the effect of the variances has been to reduce the actual production volume from 1,050 to 1,000 units! The most important questions are therefore what usage and rates will persist in the future? And is there a quality problem caused by materials that is influencing labour productivity?

Of course, the actual production situation may be something different to what has been described here. In a real business situation, managers would undertake an investigation into the causes of the material, labour and overhead rate and usage variances. In the absence of such an investigation, the above comments may be reasonable conclusions to draw from the variance analysis.

Index